SAMS Teach Yourself

XML

THIRD EDITION

Michael Morrison

SAMS 800 East 96th Street, Indianapolis, Indiana, 46240 USA

Sams Teach Yourself XML in 24 Hours, Third Edition

International Standard Book Number: 0-672-32797-X

Library of Congress Catalog Card Number: 2005933163

Printed in the United States of America

First Printing: November 2005

12 11 10 09 08   10 9 8 7 6 5

Trademarks

All terms mentioned in this book that are known to be trademarks or service marks have been appropriately capitalized. Sams Publishing cannot attest to the accuracy of this information. Use of a term in this book should not be regarded as affecting the validity of any trademark or service mark.

Warning and Disclaimer

Every effort has been made to make this book as complete and as accurate as possible, but no warranty or fitness is implied. The information provided is on an "as is" basis. The author(s) and the publisher shall have neither liability nor responsibility to any person or entity with respect to any loss or damages arising from the information contained in this book.

Bulk Sales

Sams Publishing offers excellent discounts on this book when ordered in quantity for bulk purchases or special sales. For more information, please contact

U.S. Corporate and Government Sales
1-800-382-3419
corpsales@pearsontechgroup.com

For sales outside of the U.S., please contact

International Sales
international@pearsoned.com

Publisher
Paul Boger

Acquisitions Editor
Loretta Yates

Development Editor
Mark Renfrow

Managing Editor
Charlotte Clapp

Senior Project Editor
Matthew Purcell

Copy Editor
Kate Givens

Indexer
Chris Barrick

Proofreader
Susan Eldridge

Technical Editor
Alan Moffet

Publishing Coordinator
Cindy Teeters

Designer
Gary Adair

Contents at a Glance

Part V: XML's Impact on HTML

Part VI: Appendix

Table of Contents

Part III. Formatting and Displaying XML Documents

About the Author

Michael Morrison is a writer, developer, toy inventor, and author of a variety of technology books, including *BlackBerry In a Snap, Beginning Mobile Phone Game Programming*, and *Teach Yourself HTML and CSS in 24 Hours*. In addition to his primary profession as a writer and freelance nerd for hire, Michael is the creative lead at Stalefish Labs, an entertainment company he co-founded with his wife, Masheed. The first web-based project for Stalefish Labs is an online music game called Guess That Groove (http://www.guessthatgroove.com/). When not glued to his computer, playing hockey, skateboarding, or watching movies with his wife, Michael enjoys hanging out by his koi pond. You can visit Michael on the web and discuss this book at http://www.michaelmorrison.com/.

Dedication

To my wife, Masheed, the love of my life.

Acknowledgments

Thanks to Loretta Yates, Mark Renfrow, Charlotte Clapp, Matt Purcell, and the rest of the gang at Sams Publishing for giving me yet another writing opportunity, and for being such a pleasure to work with, as always.

A big thanks also goes to my buddy Stephen Tallent, who graciously offered up his considerable XML knowledge in the wee hours of the night as I peppered him with email questions.

And finally, the biggest thanks of all goes to my wonderful family and friends.

We Want to Hear from You!

As the reader of this book, *you* are our most important critic and commentator. We value your opinion and want to know what we're doing right, what we could do better, what areas you'd like to see us publish in, and any other words of wisdom you're willing to pass our way.

As publisher for Sams Publishing, I welcome your comments. You can email or write me directly to let me know what you did or didn't like about this book—as well as what we can do to make our books better.

Please note that I cannot help you with technical problems related to the topic of this book. We do have a User Services group, however, where I will forward specific technical questions related to the book.

When you write, please be sure to include this book's title and author as well as your name, email address, and phone number. I will carefully review your comments and share them with the author and editors who worked on the book.

Email: feedback@samspublishing.com

Mail: Paul Boger
Publisher
Sams Publishing
800 East 96th Street
Indianapolis, IN 46240 USA

For more information about this book or another Sams Publishing title, visit our website at www.samspublishing.com. Type the ISBN (excluding hyphens) or the title of a book in the Search field to find the page you're looking for.

We Want to Hear from You!

Introduction

Of all the software technologies that have come and gone in the relatively short time since we all plugged in to the Web, few have been as far-reaching yet misunderstood as XML. Even with its catchy name that conjures up images of extreme sports, the true nature of XML continues to elude many technical people. The reason has to do with the fact that XML is very much a behind-the-scenes technology that helps to ensure that data is structured in an orderly fashion. There are very few situations where an end-user can see XML at work in a practical application. In this way, XML is a lot like residential building codes. When a house is built, thousands of building codes are used to guide contractors so that the house goes up safe and sound. As a homeowner, it's difficult to look at a finished house and grasp how all these building codes impacted the wood, shingles, and brick that you can see and feel. The building codes are abstract in a sense that you can't touch them, but they play a critical role in the construction process all the same. XML plays a similar role in software, including web sites, operating systems, and distributed applications.

I often hear people describe XML as "the new HTML," which sounds good but is not very accurate. XML, unlike HTML, is an extremely broad data-structuring standard that has implications far beyond web pages. For example, consider this question: HTML is to web pages as XML is to what? This is a difficult question to answer because XML isn't really geared toward any one solution. Instead, XML provides the framework for creating customized solutions to a wide range of problems. This is made possible through XML-based markup languages, which are custom markup languages that you create using XML. If you want to chart the statistics of your child's baseball team, you could create your own Little League Markup Language, or LLML, which includes custom tags and attributes for keeping up with important stats such as hits, runs, errors, and parental outbursts. The high degree of structure in your Little League data would allow it to be easily sorted, manipulated, and displayed according to your needs; the data would have the mathematical flexibility of a spreadsheet along with the visual accessibility of a web page. XML makes all this possible.

Maybe you have bigger plans for your XML knowledge than just tracking stats for a Little League team. If so, you'll be glad to know that XML is the enabling technology behind all kinds of interesting software applications. Practically all of the big Internet players have invested heavily in XML. As an example, Amazon.com uses XML to expose its product data so that developers can build custom shopping applications. Another interesting application of XML that has caused quite a stir recently is Google Maps, which is Google's innovative online mapping application. Google Maps relies on XML for map data. In fact, in Hour 15 of this book, "Using XML to Hack Google Maps," you learn how to "hack" Google Maps to use your own XML-based maps. One last example of how XML may have sneakily entered your life already is iTunes, Apple's incredibly popular online music store. iTunes uses XML to store information about your music library locally on your computer. With a little bit of effort, you can access your iTunes music library via XML and view or manipulate it any way you choose. This task is covered in Hour 13, "Access Your iTunes Music Library via XML."

XML is worth learning because it is an excellent back-end technology for storing and sharing data in a highly structured manner. Another reason for learning XML has to do much more directly with the web: XML is very much shaping the future of HTML. As you may know, HTML is somewhat unstructured in the sense that web developers take great liberties with how they use HTML code. Although this isn't entirely HTML's fault, HTML shares a considerable amount of the blame because it doesn't have the structured set of rules that are part of XML. In an attempt to add structure and consistency to the Web, a reformulated version of HTML known as XHTML was created that adds the structure of XML to HTML. It may still be quite a while before XHTML fully unseats HTML, but web developers are busy making the move to a more structured Web thanks to XHTML.

This book, in many ways, is a testament to the fact that XML is a technology for both the present and the future. The majority of the book focuses on XML in the present and how it can be used to do interesting things today. My goal was to strike a careful balance between giving you practical knowledge for the present along with some foreshadowing of what might lie ahead for XML.

How This Book Is Structured

As the title suggests, this book is organized into 24 lessons that are intended to take about an hour each to digest. Don't worry, there are no penalties if you take more than an hour to finish a given lesson, and there are no special prizes if you speed through them faster! The hours themselves are grouped together into five parts, each of which tackles a different facet of XML:

- Part I, "XML Essentials"—In this part, you get to know the XML language and what it has to offer in terms of structuring data. You also learn how to create XML documents.
- Part II, "Defining XML Data"—In this part, you will find out how to define the structure of XML documents using schemas. You learn about the two major types of schemas (DTDs and XSDs), as well as how to use namespaces and how to validate XML documents. You even learn about a real XML language, SVG, along with how to use it to create vector graphics for the web.

- Part III, "Formatting and Displaying XML Documents"—In this part, you will learn how to format XML content with style sheets so that it can be displayed. XML formatting is explored using several different style sheet technologies—CSS, XSLT, and XSL-FO. This part of the book also guides you through some interesting practical applications, including how to access your iTunes music library using XML and how to create your own XML-based maps for Google Maps.
- Part IV, "Processing and Managing XML Data"—In this part, you will find out how to process XML documents and manipulate their contents using the Document Object Model (DOM), which provides access to the inner workings of XML documents. You will also learn about SAX, which is a popular programming interface used to access XML documents. Databases are also tackled, including how to access data from a database via XML. And finally, this part of the book shows you how to use XML to mine Google for information.
- Part V, "XML's Impact on HTML"—In this part, you will explore XML's relationship to HTML and the Web. You will learn about XHTML, which is the merger of XML and HTML, along with advanced XML linking technologies. You will also learn how XML is being used to provide a means of creating web pages for wireless devices via a language called WML, as well as how to syndicate the web using RSS news feeds.

What You'll Need

This book assumes you have some familiarity with a markup language, such as HTML. You don't have to be an HTML guru by any means, but it definitely helps if you understand the difference between a tag and an attribute. Even if you don't, you should be able to tackle XML without too much trouble. It will also help if you have experience using a web browser. Even though there are aspects of XML that reach beyond the web, this book focuses a great deal on using web browsers to view and test XML code. For this reason, I encourage you to download and install the latest release of a major web browser such as Internet Explorer, Mozilla Firefox, Opera, or Safari.

In addition to web browsers, there are a few other tools mentioned throughout the book that you may consider downloading or purchasing based upon your individual needs. At the very least, you'll need a good text editor to edit XML documents. Windows Notepad is sufficient if you're working in a Windows environment, and I'm sure you can find a suitable equivalent for other environments. If you want to check into a more full-featured XML editor, it certainly won't hurt you. I mention several editors to consider in Hour 2 of the book, "Creating XML Documents." That's really all you need; a web browser and a trusty editor will carry you a long way toward becoming proficient in XML.

How to Use This Book

In code listings, line numbers have been added for reference purposes. These line numbers aren't part of the code. The code used in this book is also on this book's web site at `http://www.samspublishing.com`.

This book uses different typefaces to differentiate between code and regular English. Text that you type and text that appears on your screen is presented in `monospace` type.

`It will look like this to mimic the way text looks on your screen.`

Placeholders for variables and expressions appear in *`monospace italic`* font. You should replace the placeholder with the specific value it represents.

In addition, the following elements appear throughout the book:

Notes provide you with comments and asides about the topic at hand.

PART I

XML Essentials

HOUR 1

Getting to Know XML

> World domination isn't my thing, but if it was, I'd be using XML.
> —Norman Walsh

As you undoubtedly know, the World Wide Web has grown in leaps and bounds in the past several years, both in magnitude and in technologies. The fact that people who, only a few short years ago had no interest in computers are now "net junkies", is a testament to how quickly the Web has infiltrated modern culture. Just as the usefulness and appeal of the Web have grown rapidly, so have the technologies that make the Web possible. It all pretty much started with HTML (HyperText Markup Language), but a long list of acronyms, buzzwords, pipedreams, and even a few killer technologies have since followed. XML (eXtensible Markup Language) is one of the rare technologies that actually progressed from bleeding edge hype to misunderstood buzzword to standard building block. XML has officially arrived, and is used behind the scenes in countless applications and web services. Even so, I'll leave it to you to decide whether it is truly a killer technology as you progress through this book.

XML's usage is continuing to grow quickly as both individuals and companies realize its potential. However, in many ways XML is still a relatively new technology, and many people, possibly you, are just now learning what it can do for them. Unlike some other software technologies such as HTML or even Java, XML is a little fuzzier in terms of how it is applied in different scenarios. Just as it's difficult to look at a person and grasp how their DNA makes them who they are, it can also be challenging to look at an application and get a grasp for how XML fits into the equation. This hour introduces you to XML and gives you some insight as to why it was created and what it can do.

In this hour, you'll learn

- Exactly what XML is
- The relationship between XML and HTML
- How XML fits into web browsers
- How XML is impacting the real world

The What and Why of XML

With the universe expanding, human population increasing at an alarming rate across the globe, and a new boy band created every week, was it really necessary to introduce yet another web technology with yet another cryptic acronym? In the case of XML, the answer is yes. Next to HTML itself, XML is positioned to have the most widespread and long-term ramifications of any web technology to date. The interesting thing about XML is that its impact has gone and will continue to go largely unnoticed by most web users. Unlike HTML, which reveals itself in flashy text and graphics, XML is more of an under-the-hood kind of technology. If HTML is the fire engine red paint and supple leather interior of a sports car, XML is the turbocharged engine and sport suspension. Okay, maybe the sports car analogy is a bit much, but you get the idea that XML's impact on the Web is hard to see with the naked eye. However, the benefits are directly realized in all kinds of different ways. More specifically, if you've ever shopped on Amazon.com, purchased music from Apple iTunes, or read a syndicated news feed via RSS (Really Simple Syndication), you've used XML without realizing it.

By the Way

> By the way, you might as well get used to seeing loads of acronyms. Virtually every technology associated with XML has its own acronym, so it's impossible to learn about XML without getting to know a few dozen acronyms. Don't worry, I'll break them to you gently!

A Quick History of HTML

To understand the need for XML, at least as it applies to the Web, you have to first consider the role of HTML. In the early days of the Internet, some European physicists created HTML by simplifying another markup language known as SGML (Standard Generalized Markup Language). I won't get into the details of SGML, but let's just say it was overly complicated, at least for the purpose of sharing scientific documents on the Internet. So, pioneering physicists created a simplified version of SGML called HTML that could be used to create what we now know as web pages. The creation of HTML represented the birth of the World Wide Web—a layer of visual documents that resides on the global network known as the Internet.

HTML was great in its early days because it allowed scientists to share information over the Internet in an efficient and relatively structured manner. It wasn't until later that HTML started to become an all-encompassing formatting and display language for web pages. It didn't take long before web browsers caught on and HTML started being used to code more than scientific papers. HTML quickly went from a tidy little markup language for researchers to a full-blown online publishing language. And once it was established that HTML could be jazzed up simply by adding new tags, the creators of web browsers pretty much went crazy by adding lots of nifty features to the language. Although these new features were neat at first, they compromised the simplicity of HTML and introduced lots of inconsistencies when it came to how browsers rendered web pages. HTML had started to resemble a bad remodeling job on a house that really should've been left alone.

As with most revolutions, the birth of the Web was very chaotic, and the modifications to HTML reflected that chaos. More recently, a significant effort has been made to reel in the inconsistencies of HTML and to attempt to restore some order to the language. The problem with disorder in HTML is that web browsers have to guess at how a page is to be displayed, which is not a good thing. Ideally, a web page designer should be able to define exactly how a page is to look and have it look the same regardless of what kind of browser or operating system someone is using. This utopia is still off in the future somewhere, but XML is playing a significant role in leading us toward it, and significant progress has been made.

Getting Multilingual with XML

XML is a *meta-language*, which is a fancy way of saying that it is a language used to create other markup languages. I know this sounds a little strange, but it really just means that XML provides a basic structure and set of rules to which any markup language must adhere. Using XML, you can create a unique markup language to model just about any kind of information, including web page content. Knowing that XML is a language for creating other markup languages, you could create your own version of HTML using XML. You could also create a markup language called VPML (Virtual Pet Markup Language), for example, which you could use to create and manage virtual pets. The point is that XML lays the ground rules for organizing information in a consistent manner, and that information can be anything from web pages to virtual pets.

By the Way

> Throughout this book you will learn about several of the more intriguing markup languages that are based on XML. For example, you will find out about SVG and RSS, which allow you to create vector graphics and syndicate news feeds from web sites, respectively.

You might be thinking that virtual pets don't necessarily have anything to do with the Web, so why mention them? The reason is because XML is not entirely about web pages. In fact, XML in the purest sense really has nothing to do with the Web, and can be used to represent any kind of information on any kind of computer. If you can visualize all the information whizzing around the globe between computers, mobile phones, televisions, and radios, you can start to understand why XML has much broader ramifications than just cleaning up web pages. However, one of the first applications of XML is to restore some order to the Web, which is why I've provided an explanation of XML with the Web in mind. Besides, one of the main benefits of XML is the ability to develop XML documents once and then have them viewable on a range of devices, such as desktop computers, handheld computers, mobile phones, and Internet appliances.

One of the really awesome things about XML is that it looks very familiar to anyone who has used HTML to create web pages. Going back to our virtual pet example, check out the following XML code, which reveals what a hypothetical VPML document might look like:

```
<pets>
  <pet name="Maximillian" type="pot bellied pig" age="3">
    <friend name="Augustus"/>
    <friend name="Nigel"/>
  </pet>
  <pet name="Augustus" type="goat" age="2">
    <friend name="Maximillian"/>
  </pet>
  <pet name="Nigel" type="chipmunk" age="2">
    <friend name="Maximillian"/>
  </pet>
</pets>
```

This XML (VPML) code includes three virtual pets: Maximillian the pot-bellied pig, Augustus the goat, and Nigel the chipmunk. If you study the code, you'll notice that tags are used to describe the virtual pets much as tags are used in HTML code to describe web pages. However, in this example the tags are unique to the VPML language. It's not too hard to understand the meaning of the code, thanks to the descriptive tags. In fact, an important design parameter of XML was for XML content to always be human-readable. By studying the VPML code for a few seconds, it becomes apparent that Maximillian is friends with both Augustus and Nigel, but Augustus and Nigel aren't friends with each other. Maybe it's because they are the same age, or maybe it's just that Maximillian is a particularly friendly pig. Either way, the code describes several pets along with the relationships between them. This is a good example of the flexibility of the XML language. Keep in mind that you could create a virtual pet application that used VPML to share information with other virtual pet owners.

Unlike HTML, which consists of a predefined set of tags such as <head>, <body>, and <p>, XML allows you to create custom markup languages with tags that are unique to a certain type of data, such as virtual pets.

The virtual pet example demonstrates how flexible XML is in solving data structuring problems. Unlike a traditional database, XML data is pure text, which means it can be processed and manipulated very easily, in addition to being readable by people. For example, you can open up any XML document in a text editor such as Windows Notepad (or TextEdit on Macintosh computers) and view or edit the code. The fact that XML is pure text also makes it very easy for applications to transfer data between one another, across networks, and also across different computing platforms such as Windows, Macintosh, and Linux. XML essentially establishes a platform-neutral means of structuring data, which is ideal for networked applications, including web-based applications.

XML isn't just for web-based applications, however. As an example, the entire Microsoft Office line of products use XML under the hood to store and share document data.

The Convergence of HTML and XML

Just as some Americans are apprehensive about the proliferation of spoken languages other than English, some web developers initially feared XML's role in the future of the Web. Although I'm sure a few HTML purists still exist, is it valid to view XML as posing a risk to the future of HTML? And if you're currently an HTML expert and have yet to explore XML, will you have to throw all you know out the window and start anew with XML? The answer to both of these questions is a resounding no! In fact, once you fully come to terms with the relationship between XML and HTML, you'll realize that XML actually complements HTML as a web technology. Perhaps more interesting is the fact that XML is in many ways a parent to HTML, as opposed to a rival sibling—more on this relationship in a moment.

Earlier in the hour I mentioned that the main problem with HTML is that it got somewhat messy and unstructured, resulting in a lot of confusion surrounding the manner in which web browsers render web pages. To better understand XML and its relationship to HTML, you need to know why HTML has gotten messy. HTML was originally designed as a means of sharing written ideas among scientific researchers. I say "written ideas" because there were no graphics or images in the early versions of HTML. So, in its inception, HTML was never intended to support fancy graphics, formatting, or page-layout features. Instead, HTML was intended to focus on the meaning of information, or the content of information. It wasn't until web browser vendors got excited that HTML was expanded to address the presentation of information. In fact, HTML was in many ways changed to focus entirely on how information appears, which is what ultimately prompted the creation of XML.

You'll learn throughout this book that one of the main goals of XML is to separate the meaning of information from the presentation of it. There are a variety of reasons why this is a good idea, and they all have to do with improving the organization and structure of information. Although presentation plays an important role in any web site, modern web applications have evolved to become driven by data of very specific types, such as financial transactions. HTML is a very poor markup language for representing such data. With its support for custom markup languages, XML makes it possible to carefully describe data and the relationships between pieces of data. By focusing on content, XML allows you to describe the information in web documents. More importantly, XML makes it possible to precisely describe information that is shuttled across the Net between applications. For example, Amazon.com uses XML to describe products on its site and allow developers to create applications that intelligently analyze and extract information about those products.

By the Way

You might have noticed that I've often used the word "document" instead of "page" when referring to XML data. You can no longer think of the web as a bunch of linked pages. Instead, you should think of it as linked documents. Although this may seem like a picky distinction, it reveals a lot about the perception of web content. A *page* is an inherently visual thing, whereas a *document* can be anything ranging from a stock quote to a virtual pet to a music CD on Amazon.com.

If XML describes data better than HTML, does it mean that XML is set to upstage HTML as the markup language of choice for the Web? Not exactly. XML is not a replacement for HTML, or even a competitor of HTML. XML's impact on HTML has to do more with cleaning up HTML than it does with dramatically altering HTML. The best way to compare XML and HTML is to remember that XML establishes a set of strict rules that any markup language must follow. HTML is a relatively unstructured markup language that could benefit from the rules of XML. The natural merger of the two technologies is to make HTML adhere to the rules and structure of XML. To accomplish this merger, a new version of HTML has been formulated that adheres to the stricter rules of XML. The new XML-compliant version of HTML is known as XHTML. You learn a great deal more about XHTML in Hour 21, "Adding Structure to the Web with XHTML." For now, just understand that one long-term impact XML will have on the Web has to do with cleaning up HTML.

By the Way

Most standardized web technologies, such as HTML and XML, are overseen by the W3C, or the World Wide Web Consortium, which is an organizational body that helps to set standards for the Web. You can learn more about the W3C by visiting its web site at http://www.w3.org/.

XML's relationship with HTML doesn't end with XHTML, however. Although XHTML is a great idea that is already making web pages cleaner and more consistent for web browsers to display, we're a ways off from seeing a Web that consists of cleanly structured XHTML documents (pages). It's currently still too convenient to take advantage of the freewheeling flexibility of the HTML language. Where XML is making a significant immediate impact on the Web is in web-based applications that must shuttle data across the Internet. XML is an excellent medium for representing data that is transferred back and forth across the Internet as part of a complete web-based application. In this way, XML is used as a behind-the-scenes data transport language, whereas HTML is still used to display traditional web pages to the user. This is evidence that XML and HTML can coexist happily both now and into the future.

XML and Web Browsers

One of the stumbling blocks to learning XML is figuring out exactly how to use it. You now understand how XML complements HTML, but you still probably don't have a good grasp on how XML data is used in a practical scenario. More specifically, you're probably curious about how to view XML data. Because XML is all about describing the content of information, as opposed to the appearance of information, there is no such thing as a generic XML viewer, at least not in the sense that a web browser is an HTML viewer. In this sense, an "XML viewer" is simply an application that lets you view XML code, which can be a simple text editor or a visual editor that shows how XML data is structured. To view XML code according to its actual meaning, you must use an application that is specially designed to work with a specific XML language. If you think of HTML as an XML language, then a web browser is an application designed specifically to interpret the HTML language and display the results. This is, in fact, exactly what happens when you view an XHTML web page in a browser.

Another way to view XML documents is with style sheets using either *XSL* (*eXtensible Stylesheet Language*) or *CSS* (*Cascading Style Sheets*). Style sheets have finally reached the mainstream and are established as a better approach to formatting web pages than many of the outdated HTML presentation tags. Style sheets work in conjunction with HTML code to describe in more detail how HTML data is to be displayed in a web browser. Style sheets play a similar role when used with XML. Most modern web browsers (Internet Explorer, Firefox, Opera, Safari, and so on) support CSS, as well as providing some level of support for XSL. You learn a great deal more about style sheets in Part III, "Formatting and Displaying XML Documents."

By the Way

In addition to popular commercial web browsers, the W3C offers its own open source web browser that can be used to browse XML documents. The Amaya web browser supports the editing of web documents and also serves as a decent browser. However, Amaya is intended more as a means of testing XML documents than as a commercially viable web browser. You can download Amaya for free from the W3C web site at http://www.w3c.org/Amaya/.

In addition to style sheets, there is another important XML-related technology that is supported in major web browsers. I'm referring to the *DOM* (*Document Object Model*), which allows you to use a scripting language such as JavaScript to programmatically access the data in an XML document. The DOM makes it possible to create web pages that intelligently access and display XML data based upon scripting code. You learn how to access XML documents using JavaScript and the DOM in Hour 16, "Parsing XML with DOM."

One last point to make in regard to viewing XML with web browsers is that some browsers allow you to view XML code directly. This is a neat feature because it automatically highlights the code so that the tags and data are easy to see and understand. Additionally, an XML document is usually displayed as a hierarchical tree that allows you to expand and collapse sections of the data just as you expand and collapse folders in a file manager such as Windows Explorer. This hierarchical user interface reveals the tree-like structure of XML documents. Figure 1.1 shows the virtual pets XML document as viewed in Internet Explorer.

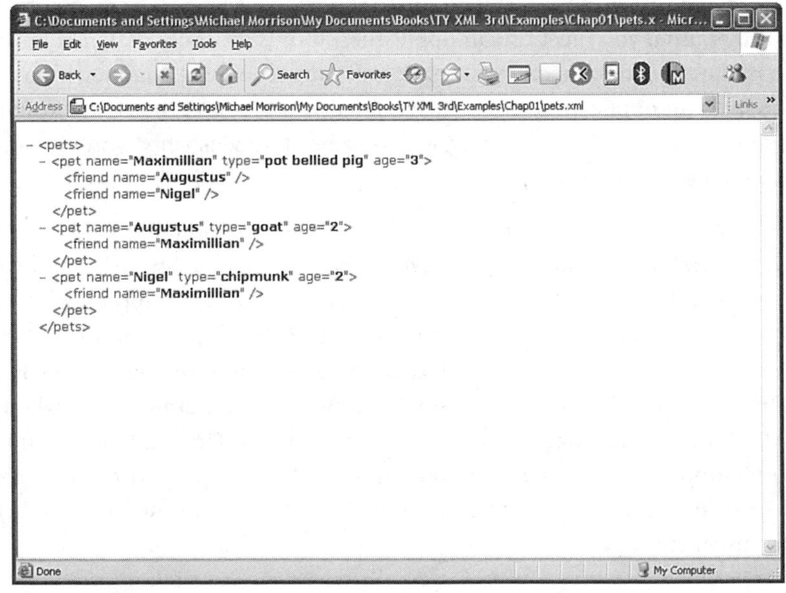

FIGURE 1.1 You can view the code for an XML document by opening the document in a web browser that supports XML, such as Internet Explorer.

Although this black and white figure doesn't reveal it, Internet Explorer actually uses color to help distinguish the different pieces of information in the document. To expand or collapse a section in the document, just click anywhere on the tag. Figure 1.2 shows the document with the first pet element (Maximillion) collapsed; notice that the minus sign changes to a plus sign (+) to indicate that the element can be expanded.

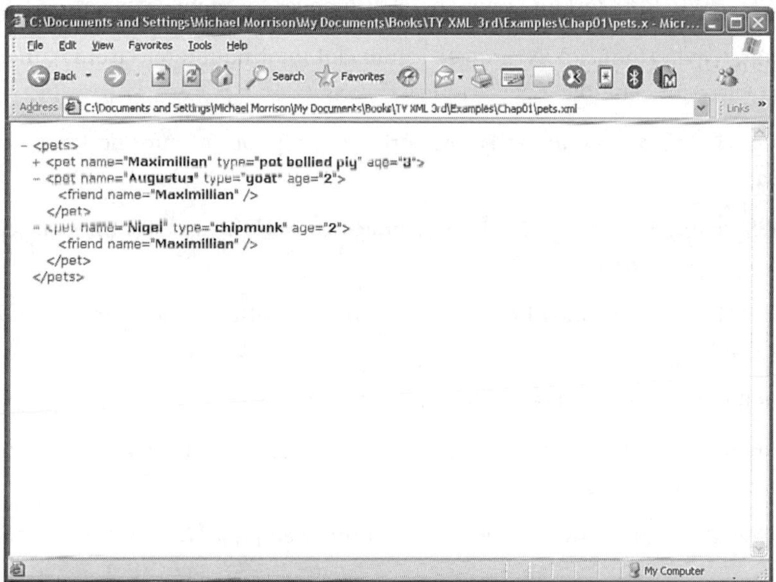

FIGURE 1.2 In addition to highlighting XML code for easier viewing, XML-supported web browsers make it possible to expand and collapse sections of a document.

Keep in mind that the web browser in this case is only showing the XML document as a tree of data because it doesn't know anything else about how to render it. You can provide a style sheet that lays out the specifics of how the data is to be formatted and displayed, and the browser will carefully format the data instead of displaying it as a tree. You will tackle this topic in Part III. This approach is commonly used to style XML data for viewing on the Web. Even so, it can be handy opening an XML document in a browser without any styling applied (as shown in Figures 1.1 and 1.2) and studying it as a tree of data. Although browsers provide a neat approach to viewing XML code in a tree-like structure, you'll probably rely on an XML editor to view most of the XML code that you develop. Or you can use a simple text editor such as Windows Notepad. You learn about XML editors in the next hour, "Creating XML Documents."

Real-World XML

Hopefully by now you understand some of the reasons XML came into being, as well as how it will likely fit in with HTML as the future of the web unfolds. What I haven't explained yet is how XML is impacting the real world with new markup languages. Fortunately, a lot of work has been done to make XML a technology that you can put to work immediately, and there are numerous XML-related technologies that are being introduced as I write this. Following is a list of some of the major XML-based languages that are supported either on the web or in major XML-based applications, along with the kinds of information they represent:

- WML (Wireless Markup Language)—Web pages for mobile devices
- OFX (Open Financial Exchange)—Financial information (electronic funds transfer, for example)
- RDF (Resource Description Framework)—Descriptions of information in web pages
- RSS (Really Simple Syndication)—Syndicated web site updates (news feeds and blog entries, for example)
- MathML (Mathematical Markup Language)—Mathematical symbols and formulas
- OeB (Open eBook)—Electronic books
- OpenDocument—Open file format for office applications (word processing, spreadsheet, and so on)
- OWL (Web Ontology Language)—Semantic web pages (an extension of RDF)
- P3P (Platform for Privacy Preferences)—Web privacy policies
- SOAP (originally Simple Object Access Protocol)—Distributed application communication
- SVG (Scalable Vector Graphics)—Vector graphics
- SMIL (Synchronized Multimedia Integration Language)—Multimedia presentations
- UDDI (Universal Description, Discovery, and Integration)—Business registries
- WSDL (Web Services Description Language)—Web services
- XAML (eXtensible Application Markup Language)—Graphical user interfaces (used by Microsoft in the new version of Windows, codenamed Longhorn)
- XBRL (eXtensible Business Reporting Language)—Business and financial data

I told you earlier that XML people love acronyms! And as the brief descriptions of each language suggest, these XML languages are as varied as their acronyms. A few of these languages are supported in the latest web browsers, and the remaining languages have special applications that can be used to create and share data in each respective format. To give you an idea regarding how these languages are impacting the real world, consider the fact that the next major release of the Windows operating system, codenamed Longhorn, is using XAML (pronounced "zammel") throughout to describe its user interfaces in XML. Additionally, Microsoft and Intuit have invested heavily in OFX (Open Financial eXchange) as the future of electronic financial transactions. OFX is already supported by more than 2,000 banks and brokerages, in addition to payroll-processing companies. In other words, your paycheck may already depend on XML!

By the Way

Another interesting usage of an XML language is SVG, which is used to code plats for real estate. A plat is an overhead map that shows how property is divided. Plats play an important role in determining divisions of land for ownership (and taxation) purposes and comprise the tax maps that are managed by the property tax assessor's office in each county in the U.S. SVG is actually much more broad than just real estate plats and allows you to create virtually any vector graphics in XML. You learn more about SVG in Hour 6, "Using SVG to Draw Scalable Graphics."

I could go on and on about how different XML languages are infiltrating the real world, but I think you get the idea. You'll get to know several of the languages listed throughout the remainder of the book. More specifically, Hour 23, "Going Wireless with WML and XHTML Mobile," shows you how to code web pages for mobile devices, while Hour 24, "Syndicating the Web with News Feeds via RSS," shows you how to use the RSS language to efficiently stay up to date with your favorite web sites.

As more evidence of the importance that major technology players have placed on XML, consider the fact that Microsoft's .NET development platform is based entirely upon XML.

Summary

Although it doesn't solve all of the world's problems, XML has a lot to offer the web community and the computing world as a whole. Not only does XML represent a path toward a cleaner and more structured HTML, it also serves as an excellent means of transporting data in a consistent format that is readily accessible across networks and different computing platforms. A variety of different XML-based languages are available for storing different kinds of information, ranging from financial transactions to mathematical equations to multimedia presentations.

This hour introduced you to XML and helped to explain how it came to be as well as how it fits into the future of the Web. You also learned that XML has considerable value beyond its impact on HTML. This hour, although admittedly not very hands on, has given you enough knowledge of XML to allow you to hit the ground running and begin creating your own XML documents in the next hour.

Q&A

Q. ***Why isn't it possible to create custom tags in HTML, as you can in XML?***

A. HTML is a markup language that consists of a predefined set of tags that each has a special meaning to web browsers. If you were able to create custom tags in HTML, web browsers wouldn't know what to do with them. XML, on the other hand, isn't necessarily tied to web browsers, and therefore has no notion of a predefined set of tags. When you do tie an XML document to a web browser, you typically couple it with a style sheet that styles or transforms the XML data into a format more easily displayed in the browser.

Q. ***Is it necessary to create a new XML-based markup language for any kind of custom data that I'd like to store?***

A. No. Although you may find that your custom data is unique enough to warrant a new markup language, you'll find that a variety of different XML-based languages are already available. In fact, most major industries have developed or are working on standardized markup languages to handle the representation of industry-specific data. OFX (Open Financial eXchange) is a good example of an industry-specific markup language that is already being used widely by the financial industry. Additionally, you may find that your XML needs are so simple that you can format data in XML without the formality of creating your own full-blown XML language.

Workshop

The Workshop is designed to help you anticipate possible questions, review what you've learned, and begin learning how to put your knowledge into practice.

Quiz

1. What is meant by the description of XML as a meta-language?
2. What is XHTML?

3. What organizational body oversees standardized web technologies such as HTML and XML?

Quiz Answers

1. When XML is referred to as a meta-language, it means that XML is a language used to create other markup languages. Similar to a meta-language is metadata, which is data that is used to describe other data. XML relies heavily on metadata to add meaning to the content in XML documents. RDF and OWL are examples of XML vocabularies that expand on the concept of metadata by attempting to add meaning to web pages.

2. XHTML is the XML-compliant version of HTML, which you will learn about in Hour 21.

3. Most standardized web technologies, such as HTML and XML, are overseen by the World Wide Web Consortium, or W3C, which is an organizational body that helps to set standards for the Web.

Exercises

1. Consider how you might construct a custom markup language for data of your own. Do you have a collection of movie posters you'd like to store in XML, or how about your Wiffle ball team's stats? What kind of custom tags would you use to code this data?

2. Visit the W3C Web site at http://www.w3.org/ and browse around to get a feel for the different web technologies overseen by the W3C.

HOUR 2

Creating XML Documents

> Plain Old Text still reigns supreme, despite the many predictions of its demise.
>
> —Bob Foster

Similar to HTML, XML is a technology that is best understood by working with it. I could go on and on for pages about the philosophical ramifications of XML, but in the end I'm sure you just want to know what you can do with it. Most of your XML work will consist of developing XML documents, which are sort of like HTML web pages, at least in terms of how the code is generally structured. Keep in mind, however, that XML documents can be used to store any kind of information. After you've created an XML document, you will no doubt want to see how it appears in a web browser or how it is used in a functioning application. Because there is no standard approach to viewing an XML document according to its meaning, you must either find or develop a custom application for viewing the document or use a style sheet to view the document in a web browser. This hour uses the latter approach to provide a simple view of an XML document that you create.

In this hour, you'll learn

- The basics of XML
- How to select an XML editor
- How to create XML documents
- How to view XML documents

A Quick XML Primer

You learned in the previous hour that XML is a markup language used to create other markup languages. Because HTML is a markup language, it stands to reason that XML documents should in some way resemble HTML documents. In fact, you saw in the previous hour how an XML document looks a lot like an HTML document, with the obvious difference that XML documents can use custom tags. So, instead of seeing `<head>` and `<body>` you saw `<pet>` and `<friend>`. Nonetheless, if you have some experience with coding web pages in HTML, XML will be very familiar. You will find that XML isn't nearly as lenient as HTML, so you may have to unlearn some bad habits carried over from HTML.

Of course, if you don't have any experience with HTML you probably won't even realize that XML is a somewhat rigid language.

XML Building Blocks

Like some other markup languages, XML relies heavily on three fundamental building blocks: elements, attributes, and values. An *element* is used to describe or contain a piece of information; elements form the basis of all XML documents. Elements consist of two tags: an opening tag and a closing tag. Opening tags appear as words contained within angle brackets (<>), such as `<pet>` or `<friend>`. Closing tags also appear within angle brackets, but they have a forward-slash (/) just before the tag name. Examples of closing tags are `</pet>` and `</friend>`. Elements always appear as an opening tag, followed by optional data, followed by a closing tag:

```
<pet>
</pet>
```

In this example, there is no data appearing between the opening and closing tags, which illustrates that the data is indeed optional. XML doesn't care too much about how whitespace appears between tags, so it's perfectly acceptable to place tags together on the same line:

```
<pet></pet>
```

Keep in mind that the purpose of tags is to denote pieces of information in an XML document, so it is rare to see a pair of tags with nothing between them, as the previous two examples show. Instead, tags typically contain text content or additional tags. Following is an example of how the `pet` element can contain additional content, which in this case is a couple of friend elements:

```
<pet>
  <friend />
  <friend />
</pet>
```

It's important to note that an element is a logical unit of information in an XML document, whereas a tag is a specific piece of XML code that comprises an element. That's why I always refer to an element by its name, such as pet, whereas tags are always referenced just as they appear in code, such as `<pet>` or `</pet>`.

You're probably wondering why this code broke the rule requiring that every element has to consist of both an opening and a closing tag. In other words, why do the `friend` elements appear to involve only a single tag? The answer to this question is that XML allows you to abbreviate empty elements. An empty element is an element that doesn't contain any content within its opening and closing tags. The earlier pet examples you saw are empty elements. Because empty elements don't contain any content between their opening and closing tags, you can abbreviate them by using a single tag known as an empty tag. Similar to other tags, an empty tag is enclosed by angle brackets (<>), but it also includes a forward slash (/) just before the closing angle bracket. So, the empty friend element, which would normally be coded as `<friend></friend>` can be abbreviated as `<friend />`. The space before the `/>` isn't necessary but is a standard style practice among XML developers.

By the Way

> Any discussion of opening and closing tags wouldn't be complete without pointing out a glaring flaw that appears in most HTML documents. I'm referring to the <p> tag, which is used to enclose a paragraph of text, and is often found in HTML documents with an opening tag but no closing tag. The p element in HTML is not an empty element, and therefore should always have a </p> closing tag, but most HTML developers make the mistake of leaving it out. This kind of freewheeling coding will get you in trouble quickly with XML!

All this talk of empty elements brings to mind the question of why you'd want to use an element that has no content. The reason for this is because you can still attach attributes to empty elements. *Attributes* are small pieces of information that appear within an element's opening tag. An attribute consists of an attribute name and a corresponding attribute value, which are separated by an equal symbol (=). The *value* of an attribute appears to the right of the equal symbol and must appear within quotes. Following is an example of an attribute named name that is associated with the friend element:

```
<friend name="Augustus" />
```

By the Way

> Attributes represent another area where HTML code is often in error, at least from the perspective of XML. HTML attributes are regularly used without quotes, which is a clear violation of XML syntax. Always quoting attribute values is another habit you'll need to learn if you're making the progression from free-spirited HTML designer to ruthlessly efficient XML coder.

In this example, the `name` attribute is used to identify the name of a friend. Attributes aren't limited to empty elements—they are just as useful with nonempty elements. Additionally, you can use several different attributes with a single element. Following is an example of how several attributes are used to describe a pet in detail:

```
<pet name="Maximillian" type="pot bellied pig" age="3">
```

As you can see, attributes are a great way to tie small pieces of descriptive information to an element without actually affecting the element's content.

Inside an Element

A *nonempty* element is an element that contains content within its opening and closing tags. Earlier I mentioned that this content could be either text or additional elements. When elements are contained within other elements, they are known as nested elements. To understand how nested elements work, consider an apartment building. Individual apartments are contained within the building, whereas individual rooms are contained within each apartment. Within each room there may be pieces of furniture that in turn are used to store belongings. In XML terms, the belongings are nested in the furniture, which is nested in the rooms, which are nested in the apartments, which are nested in the apartment building. Listing 2.1 shows how the apartment building might be coded in XML.

LISTING 2.1 An Apartment Building XML Example

```
 1: <apartmentbldg>
 2:   <apartment>
 3:     <room type="bedroom">
 4:       <furniture type="armoire">
 5:         <belonging type="t-shirt" color="navy" size="xl" />
 6:         <belonging type="sock" color="white" />
 7:         <belonging type="watch" />
 8:       </furniture>
 9:     </room>
10:   </apartment>
11: </apartmentbldg>
```

If you study the code, you'll notice that the different elements are nested according to their physical locations within the building. It's important to recognize in this example that the belonging elements are empty elements (lines 5–7), which is evident by the fact that they use the abbreviated empty tag ending in />. These elements are empty because they aren't required to house (no pun intended!) any additional information. In other words, it is sufficient to describe the belonging elements solely through attributes.

It's important to realize that nonempty elements aren't just used for nesting purposes. Nonempty elements often contain text content, which appears between the opening and closing tags. Following is an example of how you might decide to expand the belonging element so that it isn't empty:

```
<furniture type="desk">
  <belonging type="letter">
    Dear Michael,
    I am pleased to announce that you may have won our sweepstakes. You are
    one of the lucky finalists in your area, and if you would just purchase
    five or more magazine subscriptions then you may eventually win some
    money. Or not.
  </belonging>
</furniture>
```

In this example, my ticket to an early retirement appears as text within the belonging element. You can include just about any text you want in an element, with the exception of a few special symbols, which you learn about a little later in the hour.

XML's Five Commandments

Now that you have a feel for the XML language, it's time to move on and learn about the specific rules that govern its usage. I've mentioned already that XML is a more rigid language than HTML, which basically means that you have to pay attention when coding XML documents. In reality, the exacting nature of the XML language is actually a huge benefit to XML developers—you'll quickly get in the habit of writing much cleaner code than you might have been accustomed to writing in HTML, which will result in more accurate and reliable code. The key to XML's accuracy lies in a few simple rules, which I'm calling XML's five commandments:

1. Tag names are case sensitive.
2. Every opening tag must have a corresponding closing tag (unless it is abbreviated as an empty tag).
3. A nested tag pair cannot overlap another tag.
4. Attribute values must appear within quotes.
5. Every document must have a root element.

Admittedly, the last rule is one that I haven't prepared you for, but the others should make sense to you. First off, rule number one states that XML is a case-sensitive language, which means that `<pet>`, `<Pet>`, and `<PET>` are all different tags. If you're coming from the world of HTML, this is a very critical difference between XML and HTML. It's not uncommon to see HTML code that alternates back and forth between tags such as `<b>` and `<B>` for bold text. In XML, this mixing of case is a clear no-no. Generally speaking, XML standards encourage developers to use either lowercase tags or mixed case tags, as opposed to the uppercase tags commonly found in HTML web pages. The same rule applies to attributes. If you're writing XML code in a specific XML-based markup language, the language itself will dictate what case you should use for tags and attributes.

The second rule reinforces what you've already learned by stating that every opening tag (`<pet>`) must have a corresponding closing tag (`</pet>`). In other words, tags must always appear in pairs (`<pet></pet>`). Of course, the exception to this rule is the empty tag, which serves as an abbreviated form of a tag pair (`<pet />`). Rule three continues to nail down the relationship between tags by stating that tag pairs cannot overlap each other. This really means that a tag pair must be completely nested within another tag pair. Perhaps an example will better clarify this point:

```
<pets>
  <pet name="Maximillian" type="pot bellied pig" age="3">
  </pet>
  <pet name="Augustus" type="goat" age="2">
</pets>
  </pet>
```

Do you see the problem with this code? The problem is that the second pet element isn't properly nested within the pets element. The code indentation helps to make the problem more apparent but this isn't always the case. For example, consider the following version of the same code:

```
<pets>
  <pet name="Maximillian" type="pot bellied pig" age="3">
  </pet>
  <pet name="Augustus" type="goat" age="2">
  </pets>
</pet>
```

Remembering that whitespace doesn't normally affect the structure of XML code, this listing is functionally no different than the previous listing but the nesting problem is much more hidden. In other words, the second pet element is still split out across the pets element, which is wrong. This code is wrong because it is no longer clear whether the second pet element is intended to be nested within the pets element or not—the relationship between the elements is ambiguous. And XML despises ambiguity! To resolve the problem you must either move the closing </pet> tag so that it is enclosed within the pets element, or move the opening <pet> tag so that it is outside of the pets element.

Getting back to the XML commandments, rule number four reiterates the earlier point regarding quoted attribute values. It simply means that all attribute values must appear in quotes. So, the following code breaks this rule because the name attribute value Maximillian doesn't appear in quotes:

```
<friend name=Maximillian />
```

As I mentioned earlier, if you have used HTML this is one rule in particular that you will need to remember as you begin working with XML. Most web page designers are very inconsistent in their usage of quotes with attribute values. In fact, the tendency is to not use them. XML requires quotes around all attribute values, no questions asked!

The last XML commandment is the only one that I haven't really prepared you for because it deals with an entirely new concept: the root element. The *root element* is the single element in an XML document that contains all other elements in the document. Every XML document must contain a root element, which means that exactly one element must be at the top level of any given XML document. In the "pets" example that you've seen throughout this hour and the previous hour, the `pets` element is the root element because it contains all the other elements in the document (the `pet` and `friend` elements). To make a quick comparison to HTML, the `html` element in a web page is the root element, so HTML adheres to XML rules in this regard. However, technically HTML will let you get away with having more than one root element, whereas XML will not.

Watch Out!

> Because the root element in an XML document must contain other elements, it cannot be an empty element. This means that the root element must always consist of a pair of opening and closing tags, and can never be shortened to an empty tag a la />.

Special XML Symbols

There are a few special symbols in XML that must be entered differently than other text characters when appearing as content within an XML document. The reason for entering these symbols differently is because they are considered part of XML syntax by identifying parts of an XML document such as tags and attributes. The symbols to which I'm referring are the less than symbol (<), greater than symbol (>), quote symbol ("), apostrophe symbol ('), and ampersand symbol (&). These symbols all have special meaning within the XML language, which is why you must enter them using a symbol instead of just using each character directly. So, as an example, the following code isn't allowed in XML because the apostrophe (') character is used directly in the name attribute value:

```
<movie name="All the King's Men" />
```

The trick to referencing these characters is to use special predefined symbols known as entities. An *entity* is a symbol that identifies a resource, such as a text character or even a file. There are five predefined entities in XML that correspond to each of the special characters you just learned about. Entities in XML begin with an ampersand (&) and end with a semicolon (;), with the entity name sandwiched between. Following are the predefined entities for the special characters:

- Less than symbol (<) — <
- Greater than symbol (>) — >

- Quote symbol (“) — "
- Apostrophe symbol (‘) — '
- Ampersand symbol (&) — &

To fix the movie example code, just replace the ampersand and apostrophe characters in the attribute value with the appropriate entities:

```
<movie name="All the King&apos;s Men" />
```

Here’s another movie example, just to clarify how another of the entities is used:

```
<movie name="Pride &amp; Prejudice" />
```

In this example, the & entity is used to help code the movie title, “Pride & Prejudice.” Admittedly, these entities make the attribute values a little tougher to read, but there is no question regarding the usage of the characters. This is a good example of how XML is willing to make a trade-off between ease of use on the developer’s part and technical clarity. Fortunately, there are only five predefined entities to deal with, so it’s pretty easy to remember them.

The XML Declaration

One final important topic to cover in this quick tour of XML is the XML declaration, which is not strictly required of all XML documents but is a good idea nonetheless. The *XML declaration* is a line of code at the beginning of an XML document that identifies the version of XML used by the document. Currently there are two versions of XML: 1.0 and 1.1. XML 1.1 primarily differs from XML 1.0 in how it supports characters in element and attribute names. XML 1.1’s broader character support is primarily of use for mainframe programmers, which likely explains why XML 1.1 isn’t very widely supported. Given this scenario, you should only worry about supporting XML 1.0 in your documents, at least for the foreseeable future.

> There have been some rumblings in the XML community about a possible XML 2.0 but nothing concrete has materialized as of yet.

Getting back to the XML declaration, it notifies an application or web browser of the XML version that an XML document is using, which can be very helpful in processing the document. Following is the standard XML declaration for XML 1.0:

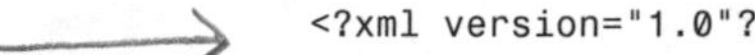

```
<?xml version="1.0"?>
```

This code looks somewhat similar to an opening tag for an element named `xml` with an attribute named version. However, the code isn't actually a tag at all. Instead, this code is known as a *processing instruction*, which is a special line of XML code that passes information to the application that is processing the document. In this case, the processing instruction is notifying the application that the document uses XML 1.0. Processing instructions are easily identified by the <? and ?> symbols that sandwich each instruction.

> **Watch Out!** As of XML 1.1, all XML documents are required to include an XML declaration.

Selecting an XML Editor

To create and edit your own XML documents, you must have an application to serve as an XML editor. Because XML documents are raw text documents, a simple text editor can serve as an XML editor. For example, if you are a Windows user you can just use the standard Windows Notepad or WordPad applications to edit XML documents. Or on a Macintosh computer you can use TextEdit. If you want XML-specific features such as the ability to edit elements and attributes visually, you'll want to go beyond a simple text editor and use a full-blown XML editor. Before introducing you to some popular XML editors, it's worth taking a quick step back and explaining how XML editors differ in their fundamental approaches.

There are three basic types of XML editors: WYSIWYG, WYSIWYM, and plain text. If you have any experience with web development or desktop publishing, you're probably familiar with the term WYSIWYG, which stands for What You See Is What You Get. The idea behind WYSIWYG tools is that you edit content exactly as you want it to appear. Microsoft Word and Macromedia Dreamweaver are examples of WYSIWYG tools in that they allow you to edit word processing documents and web pages just as they will appear when printed or viewed on the Web. WYSIWYG XML editors take a similar approach by focusing on the final appearance of an XML document for display purposes, as opposed to the meaning of the XML content itself.

If you want to focus more on the meaning of XML content, you should consider using a WYSIWYM XML editor. Any guesses as to what the acronym stands for? You get two points if you said What You See Is What You Mean! A WYSIWYM XML editor focuses on the meaning of XML code as opposed to how the code is rendered for viewing. WYSIWYM editors often take into consideration specific XML languages, and offer you context-sensitive help in using tags and attributes. Most WYSIWYM editors display XML code as a tree-like structure roughly similar to the default browser view of XML that you saw in the previous chapter (Figures 1.1 and 1.2).

By the Way

WYSIWYM XML editors are also sometimes referred to as semantic editors because they focus on the semantics (meaning) of XML code, as opposed to the resulting appearance of the code.

The third type of XML editor is the plain text editor, which simply allows you to edit an XML document as plain text. The plain text approach is neither WYSIWYG or WYSIWYM because there is no clue provide regarding the eventual appearance of the code or the context of its meaning. You're pretty much on your own if you go the plain text route, which is not entirely a bad thing, at least in terms of learning the ropes and understanding every single character of an XML document.

There are several commercial XML editors available at virtually every price range and supporting both major approaches to XML editing (WYSIWYG and WYSIWYM). Although a commercial XML editor might prove beneficial at some point, I recommend spending at least a little time with a plain text editor because it allows you to work directly at the XML code level with no frills. Figure 2.1 shows the "talltales" example XML document open in Windows Notepad.

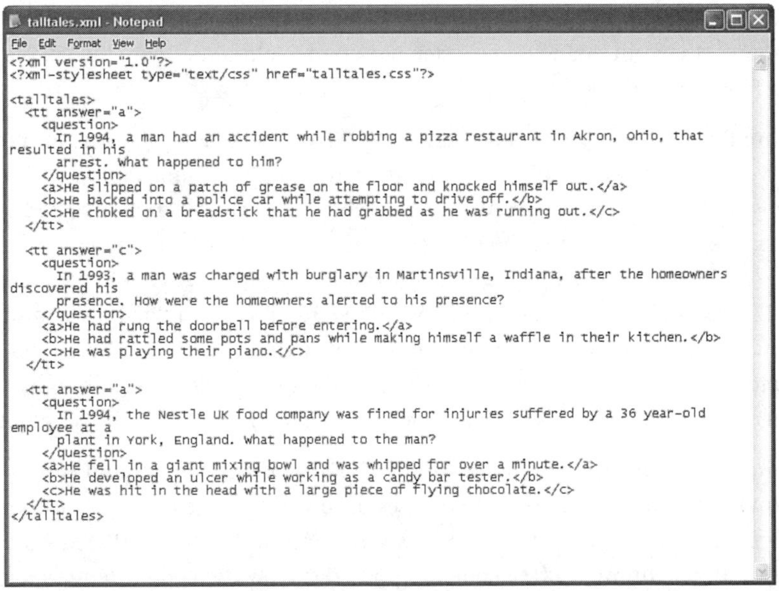

```
talltales.xml - Notepad
File Edit Format View Help
<?xml version="1.0"?>
<?xml-stylesheet type="text/css" href="talltales.css"?>

<talltales>
  <tt answer="a">
    <question>
      In 1994, a man had an accident while robbing a pizza restaurant in Akron, Ohio, that
resulted in his
      arrest. What happened to him?
    </question>
    <a>He slipped on a patch of grease on the floor and knocked himself out.</a>
    <b>He backed into a police car while attempting to drive off.</b>
    <c>He choked on a breadstick that he had grabbed as he was running out.</c>
  </tt>

  <tt answer="c">
    <question>
      In 1993, a man was charged with burglary in Martinsville, Indiana, after the homeowners
discovered his
      presence. How were the homeowners alerted to his presence?
    </question>
    <a>He had rung the doorbell before entering.</a>
    <b>He had rattled some pots and pans while making himself a waffle in their kitchen.</b>
    <c>He was playing their piano.</c>
  </tt>

  <tt answer="a">
    <question>
      In 1994, the Nestle UK food company was fined for injuries suffered by a 36 year-old
employee at a
      plant in York, England. What happened to the man?
    </question>
    <a>He fell in a giant mixing bowl and was whipped for over a minute.</a>
    <b>He developed an ulcer while working as a candy bar tester.</b>
    <c>He was hit in the head with a large piece of flying chocolate.</c>
  </tt>
</talltales>
```

FIGURE 2.1 Simple text editors such as Windows Notepad allow you to edit XML documents as plain text.

By the Way

If you use Windows WordPad or some other text editor that supports file formats in addition to standard text, you'll want to make sure to save XML documents as plain text. This means you will need to use the Save As command instead of Save, and choose Text Only (`.txt`) as the file type.

As far as WYSIWYG XML editors go, one of the better editors I've seen is called Vex, and it is freely available for download at http://vex.sourceforge.net/. Vex presents a visual user interface generally similar to a word processor such as Microsoft Word. More importantly, Vex earns the WYSIWYG label because it hides XML tags from you, allowing you to focus solely on the appearance of your code. Vex uses CSS (Cascading Style Sheets) to render the appearance of XML code. You learn how to use CSS to style XML code in Hour 10, "Styling XML Content with CSS." Unfortunately, Vex is a little tricky to get the hang of in terms of creating and managing XML projects, so I'd recommend sticking with a WYSIWYM or plain text for the creation of XML documents until you have more experience. Keep in mind that you can always use a web browser for a WYSIWYG view of an XML document that you create in a WYSIWYM or plain text XML editor.

Many XML documents aren't about appearance at all, in which case you'll want to look into using an editor that focuses on meaning as opposed to appearance. One of my favorite WYSIWYM XML editors is Butterfly XML, which is available for free download at http://www.butterflyxml.org/. Unlike Vex, Butterfly XML is geared toward editing XML content with a focus on what the content means, not what it will look like. Butterfly XML displays an XML document as both a hierarchical tree of data and context-highlighted text. In other words, you get to see both the tree-like structure of an XML document as well as how each portion of the tree is associated with plain text in the document. However, instead of entering raw text in the document, you are presented with editing aids such as a pop-up list of available tags. Figure 2.2 shows an example of how Butterfly XML allows you to edit an XML document with a focus on the meaning of the content.

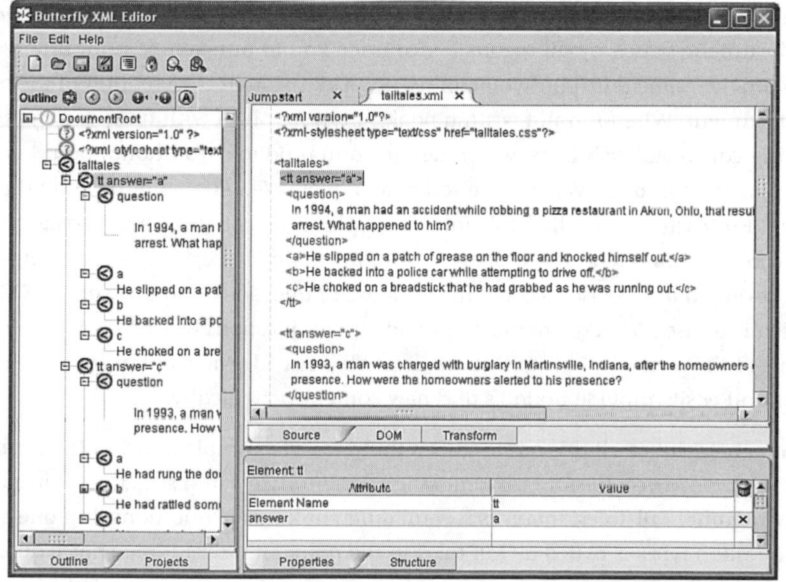

FIGURE 2.2
The Butterfly XML WYSIWYM XML editor gives you an opportunity to focus on the meaning of XML documents as you edit them.

I've actually done a bit of foreshadowing here by showing you the `talltales.xml` document in Figure 2.2. You create this document as your first XML document in the next section of this hour.

In case you're concerned that I'm being too cheap by only showing you free XML editors, there are plenty of commercial editors you can buy if you want to go that route. Many of the commercial editors allow you to edit XML documents using a combination of WYSIWYG and WYSIWYM approaches, which gives you lots of flexibility. One of the more powerful commercial XML editors I've run across is <oXygen/> XML Editor, which is available for Windows, Macintosh, Linux, and Eclipse. <oXygen/> isn't free but it could very well pay for itself with its advanced XML features. To learn more about <oXygen/>, visit it on the Web at http://www.oxygenxml.com/.

Another solid XML editor is XML Spy, which is available for Windows computers. XML Spy has been around a while, and is packed with support for a wide range of XML technologies. Perhaps of more interest to you at this stage of the game, XML Spy is available for free in a special Home Edition. There is also an Enterprise Edition and a Professional Edition, both of which are not free but pack in a lot more features. You can download and try out XML Spy Home Edition at http://www.altova.com/download_spy_home.html.

Constructing Your First XML Document

You now have the basic knowledge necessary to create an XML document of your own. You may already have in mind some data that you'd like to format into an XML document, which by all means I encourage you to pursue. For now, however, I'd like to provide some data that you can use to work through the creation of a simple XML document. When I'm not writing books, I am involved with a toy and game company called Stalefish Labs, which designs and produces traditional board games, social games, toys, and even mobile software games. We released a traditional print version of a trivia game called Tall Tales a couple of years ago (http://www.talltalesgame.com/), and we're in the process of putting together a software version of the game. It only makes sense to code the database of questions and answers in XML. The idea is to use XML documents to provide trivia questions to web and mobile versions of the game. By using XML, we'll be able to code the content in a consistent format and easily provide updates and new content periodically.

Anyway, the point of all this game stuff is that a good example of an XML document is one that allows you to store trivia questions and answers in a structured format. My trivia game, Tall Tales, involves several different kinds of questions, but one of the main question types is called a "tall tale" in the game. It's a multiple-choice question consisting of three possible answers. Knowing this, it stands to reason that the XML document will need a means of representing each question plus three different answers. Keep in mind, however, that in order for the answers to have any meaning, you must also provide a means of specifying the correct answer. A good place to do this is in the main element for each question/answer group.

Don't forget that earlier in this hour you learned that every XML document must have a root element. In this case, the root element is named `talltales` to match the name of the game. Within the `talltales` element you know that there will be several questions, each of which has three possible answers. Let's code each question with an element named `question` and each of the three answers with the three letters `a`, `b`, and `c`. It's important to group each question with its respective answers, so you'll need an additional element for this. Let's call this element `tt` to indicate that the question type is a tall tale. The only remaining piece of information is the correct answer, which can be conveniently identified as an attribute of the `tt` element. Let's call this attribute `answer`. Just in case I went a little too fast with this description of the Tall Tales document, let's recap the explanation with the following list of elements that are used to describe pieces of information within the document:

- `talltales`—The root element of the document
- `tt`—A tall tale question and its associated answers
- `question`—A question
- `a`—The first possible answer to a question
- `b`—The second possible answer to a question
- `c`—The third possible answer to a question

In addition to these elements, an attribute named `answer` is used with the `tt` element to indicate which of the three answers (`a`, `b`, or `c`) is correct. Also, don't forget that the document must begin with an XML declaration. With this information in mind, take a look at the following code for a complete `tt` element:

```
<tt answer="a">
  <question>
    In 1994, a man had an accident while robbing a pizza restaurant in Akron,
    Ohio, that resulted in his arrest. What happened to him?
  </question>
  <a>He slipped on a patch of grease on the floor and knocked himself out.</a>
  <b>He backed into a police car while attempting to drive off.</b>
  <c>He choked on a breadstick that he had grabbed as he was running out.</c>
</tt>
```

This code reveals how a question and its related answers are grouped within a `tt` element. The answer attribute indicates that the first answer (a) is the correct one.

All of the elements in this example are nonempty, which is evident by the fact that they all either contain text content or additional elements. Notice also how every opening tag has a matching closing tag and how the elements are all nested properly within each other. Now that you understand the code for a single question, check out Listing 2.2, a complete XML document that includes three trivia questions.

LISTING 2.2 The Tall Tales Sample XML Document

```
<?xml version="1.0"?>

<talltales>
  <tt answer="a">
    <question>
      In 1994, a man had an accident while robbing a pizza restaurant in
      Akron, Ohio, that resulted in his arrest. What happened to him?
    </question>
    <a>He slipped on a patch of grease on the floor and knocked himself out.</a>
    <b>He backed into a police car while attempting to drive off.</b>
    <c>He choked on a breadstick that he had grabbed as he was running out.</c>
  </tt>

  <tt answer="c">
    <question>
      In 1993, a man was charged with burglary in Martinsville, Indiana,
      after the homeowners discovered his presence. How were the homeowners
      alerted to his presence?
    </question>
    <a>He had rung the doorbell before entering.</a>
    <b>He had rattled some pots and pans while making himself a waffle in
    their kitchen.</b>
    <c>He was playing their piano.</c>
  </tt>

  <tt answer="a">
    <question>
      In 1994, the Nestle UK food company was fined for injuries suffered
      by a 36 year-old employee at a plant in York, England. What happened
      to the man?
    </question>
    <a>He fell in a giant mixing bowl and was whipped for over a minute.</a>
    <b>He developed an ulcer while working as a candy bar tester.</b>
    <c>He was hit in the head with a large piece of flying chocolate.</c>
  </tt>
</talltales>
```

Although this may appear to be a lot of code at first, upon closer inspection you'll notice that most of the code is simply the content of the trivia questions and answers. The XML tags should all make sense to you given the earlier explanation of the Tall Tales trivia data. You now have your first complete XML document that has some pretty interesting content ready to be processed and served up for viewing. Be sure to take a look back at Figure 2.2 to see how this exact same code appears within the Butterfly XML WYSIWYM XML editor.

Viewing Your XML Document

Short of developing a custom application from scratch, the best way to view XML documents is to use a *style sheet*, which is a series of formatting descriptions that determine how elements are displayed on a web page. In its most basic usage, a style sheet allows you to carefully control what the content in a web page looks like in a web browser. In the case of XML, style sheets allow you to determine exactly how to display data in an XML document. Although style sheets can improve the appearance of HTML web pages, they are especially important for XML because web browsers typically don't understand what the custom tags mean in an XML document.

You learn a great deal about style sheets in Part III, "Formatting and Displaying XML Documents," but for now I just want to show you a style sheet that is capable of displaying the Tall Tales trivia document that you created in the previous section. Keep in mind that the purpose of a style sheet is typically to determine the appearance of XML content. This means that you can use styles in a style sheet to control the font and color of text, for example. You can also control the positioning of content, such as where an image or paragraph of text appears on the page. Styles are always applied to specific elements. So, in the case of the trivia document, the style sheet should include styles for each of the important elements that you want displayed: `tt`, `question`, `a`, `b`, and `c`.

Later in the book, in Hour 16, "Parsing XML with DOM," you learn how to incorporate interactivity to the Tall Tales example using scripting code, but right now all I want to focus on is displaying the XML data in a web browser using a style sheet. The idea is to format the data so that each question is displayed followed by each of the answers in a smaller font and different color. The code in Listing 2.3 is the `talltales.css` style sheet for the Tall Tales trivia XML document.

LISTING 2.3 A CSS Style Sheet for Displaying the Tall Tales XML Document

```
tt {
  display: block;
  width: 750px;
  padding: 10px;
  margin-bottom: 10px;
  border: 4px double black;
  background-color: silver;
}

question {
  display: block;
  color: black;
  font-family: Times, serif;
  font-size: 16pt;
  text-align: left;
```

LISTING 2.3 Continued

```
16: }
17:
18: a, b, c {
19:   display: block;
20:   color: brown;
21:   font-family: Times, serif;
22:   font-size: 12pt;
23:   text-indent: 15px;
24:   text-align: left;
25: }
```

Don't worry if the style sheet doesn't make too much sense. The point right now is just to notice that the different elements of the XML document are addressed in the style sheet. Even without any knowledge of CSS, if you study the code closely you should be able to figure out what many of the styles are doing. For example, the code `color: black;` (line 12) states that the text contained within a `question` element is to be displayed in black. If you create this style sheet and include it with the `talltales.xml` document, the document as viewed in the Mozilla Firefox browser appears as shown in Figure 2.3.

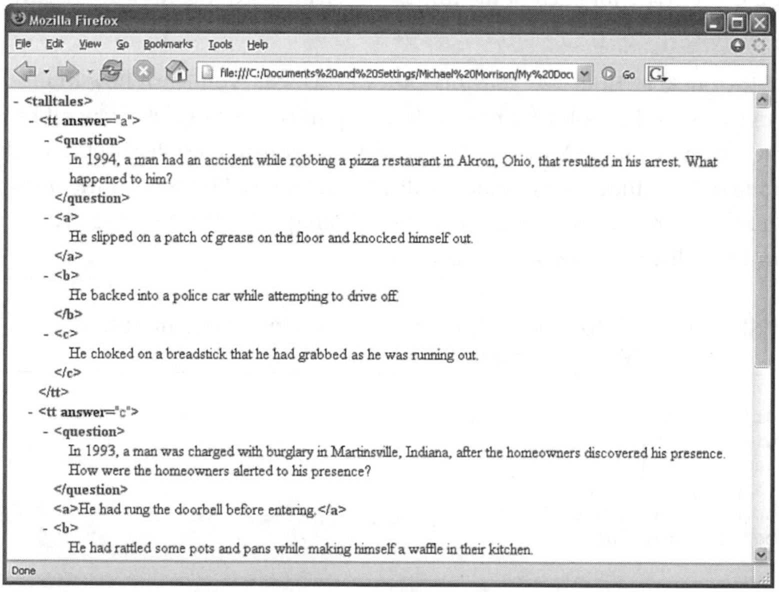

FIGURE 2.3 The `talltales.xml` document is displayed as XML code because the style sheet hasn't been attached to it.

The page shown in the figure probably doesn't look like you thought it should. In fact, the style sheet isn't even impacting this figure because it hasn't been associated with the XML document yet. So, in the absence of a style sheet, Firefox just displays the XML code as a hierarchical tree of XML data. To attach the style sheet to the document, add the following line of code just after the XML declaration for the document.

```
<?xml-stylesheet type="text/css" href="talltales.css"?>
```

So, the start of the `talltales.xml` document should now look like this:

```
<?xml version="1.0"?>
<?xml-stylesheet type="text/css" href="talltales.css"?>

<talltales>
  <tt answer="a">
    ...
```

If you've been following along closely, you'll recognize the new line of code as a processor instruction, which is evident by the <? and ?> symbols. This processor instruction notifies the application processing the document (the web browser) that the document is to be displayed using the style sheet `talltales.css`. After adding this line of code to the document, it is displayed in Firefox in a format that is much easier to read (see Figure 2.4).

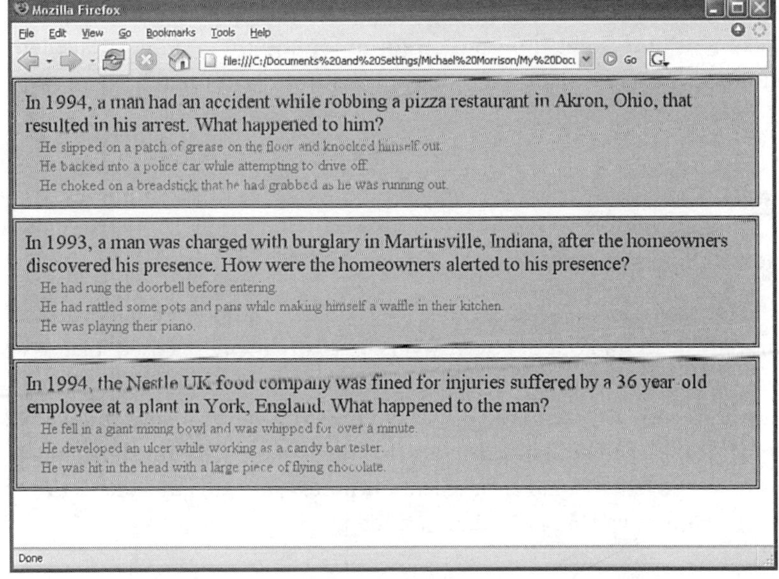

FIGURE 2.4 A simple style sheet provides a means of formatting the data in an XML document for convenient viewing in a web browser.

That's a little more like it! As you can see, the style sheet does wonders for making the XML document viewable in a web browser. You've now successfully created your first XML document, along with a style sheet to view it in a web browser.

If you're concerned that I glossed over the details of style sheets in this section, please don't be. I readily admit to glossing them over, but I just wanted to quickly show you how to view a web page in a web browser. Besides, you'll get a heavy dose of style sheets in Part III of the book, so hang in there.

Summary

As you learned in this hour, the basic rules of XML aren't too complicated. Although XML is admittedly more rigid than HTML, once you learn the fundamental structure of the XML language, it isn't too difficult to create XML documents. It's this consistency in structure that makes XML such a useful technology in representing diverse data. Just as XML itself is relatively simple, the tools required to develop XML documents can be quite simple—all you really need is a text editor such as Windows Notepad. Even so, more powerful tools can ultimately come in handy as you progress onward and develop more complex XML documents.

This hour began by teaching you the basics of XML, after which you learned how XML documents are created and edited using XML editors. After covering the fundamentals of XML, you were then guided through the creation of a complete XML document that stores information for an online trivia game. You then learned how a style sheet is used to format the XML document for viewing in a web browser.

Q&A

Q. ***How do I know what the latest version of XML is?***

A. The latest version of XML to date is version 1.1, although it isn't widely supported. To find out about new versions as they are released, please visit the World Wide Web Consortium (W3C) web site at http://www.w3c.org/. Keep in mind, however, that XML is a relatively stable technology, and isn't likely to undergo version changes nearly as rapidly as more dynamic technologies such as Java or even HTML. For practical purposes, you can still consider XML 1.0 as the current version of XML in use today.

Q. ***What happens if an XML document breaks one or more of the XML commandments?***

A. Well, of course, your computer will crash immediately and erupt in a ball of flames! No, actually nothing tragic will happen unless you attempt to process the document via an automated XML tool or application. Even then, you will likely get an error message instead of any kind of fatal result. XML-based applications expect documents to follow the rules, so they will likely notify you of the errors whenever they are encountered. Fortunately, even web browsers are pretty good at reporting errors in XML documents, which is in sharp contrast to how loosely they interpret HTML web pages.

Q. ***Are there any other approaches to using style sheets with XML documents?***

A. Yes. The Tall Tales trivia example in this hour makes use of CSS (Cascading Style Sheets), which is used primarily to format HTML and XML data for display. Another style sheet technology known as XSL (eXtensible Style Language) allows you to filter, transform, and otherwise finely control exactly what information is displayed from an XML document. You learn about both style sheet technologies in Part III, "Formatting and Displaying XML Documents."

Workshop

The Workshop is designed to help you anticipate possible questions, review what you've learned, and begin learning how to put your knowledge into practice. The answers to the quiz can be found following the quiz.

Quiz

1. What is an empty element?
2. What is the significance of the root element of a document?
3. What is the XML declaration, and where must it appear?
4. How would you code an empty element named `movie` with an attribute named `format` that is set to `dvd`?

Quiz Answers

1. An empty element is an element that doesn't contain any content within its opening and closing tags. Empty elements can be coded as a pair of tags (`<friend></friend>`) or the more concise empty element tag (`<friend />`).
2. The root element of a document contains all of the other elements in the document; every document must have exactly one root element.
3. The XML declaration is a line of code at the beginning of an XML document that identifies the version of XML used by the document.
4. `<movie format="dvd" />`

Exercises

1. Add another trivia question to the `talltales.xml` document, complete with three possible answers, including which answer is the correct answer. Then view the document in a web browser using the `talltales.css` style sheet to see the new question.

2. Modify the `talltales.css` style sheet so that the questions and answers are displayed in different colors. Hint: You can edit a style sheet in a text editor just as you edit an XML document.

PART II

Defining XML Data

HOUR 3

Defining Data with DTD Schemas

> Computers are not intelligent. They only think they are.
>
> —Unknown

One thing XML aims to solve is human error. Because of XML's structure and rigidity as a language, there isn't much room for error on the part of XML developers. If you've ever encountered an error at the bank (in their favor!), you can no doubt appreciate the significance of errors in critical computer systems. XML is rapidly being integrated into all kinds of computer systems, including financial systems used by banks. The rigidity of XML as a markup language will no doubt make these systems more robust. The facet of XML that allows errors to be detected is the schema, which is a construct that allows XML developers to define the format and structure of XML data.

This hour introduces you to schemas, including the two major types that are used to define data for XML documents. The first of these schema types, DTDs, is examined in detail in this hour, while the latter is saved for a later lesson. This hour explores the inner workings of DTDs and shows you how to create DTDs from scratch.

In this hour, you'll learn

- How XML allows you to create custom markup languages
- The role of schemas in XML data modeling
- The difference between the types of XML schemas
- What constitutes valid and well-formed documents
- How to declare elements and attributes in a DTD
- How to create and use a DTD for a custom markup language

Creating Your Own Markup Languages

Before you get too far into this hour, I have to make a little confession. When you create an XML document, you aren't really using XML to code the document. Instead, you are using a markup language that was created in XML. In other words, XML is used to create markup languages that are then used to create XML documents. The term "XML document" is even a little misleading because the type of the document is really determined by the specific markup language used. So, as an example, if I were to create my very own markup language called MML (Michael's Markup Language), then the documents I create would be considered MML documents, and I would use MML to code those documents. Generally speaking, the documents are still XML documents because MML is an XML-based markup language, but you would refer to the documents as MML documents.

The point of this discussion is not to split hairs regarding the terminology used to describe XML documents. It is intended to help clarify the point that XML is a technology that enables the creation of custom markup languages. If you're coming from the world of HTML, you probably think in terms of there being only one markup language—HTML. In the XML world, there are thousands of different markup languages, with each of them applicable to a different type of data. As an XML developer, you have the option of using an existing markup language that someone else created using XML, or you can create your own. An XML-based markup language can be as formal as XHTML, the version of HTML that adheres to the rules of XML, or as informal as my simple Tall Tales trivia language.

When you create your own markup language, you are basically establishing which elements (tags) and attributes are used to create documents in that language. Not only is it important to fully describe the different elements and attributes, but you must also describe how they relate to one another. For example, if you are creating a markup language to keep track of sports information so that you can chart your local softball league, you might use tags such as `<schedule>`, `<game>`, `<team>`, `<player>`, and so on. Examples of attributes for the `player` element might include `name`, `hits`, `rbis`, and so on.

By the Way

> Just in case you're thinking of creating your own sports markup language, I might be able to save you some time by directing you to SportsML (Sports Markup Language). This markup language has elements and attributes similar to the ones I described for your hypothetical softball markup language, except SportsML is much broader and covers many different sports. For more information regarding SportsML, please visit the SportsML web site at http://www.sportsml.org/.

The question you might now be asking yourself is how exactly do you create a markup language? In other words, how do you specify the set of elements and attributes for a markup language, along with how they relate to each other? Although you could certainly create sports XML documents using your own elements and attributes, there really needs to be a set of rules somewhere that establishes the format and structure of documents created in the language. This set of rules is known as the *schema* for a markup language. A schema describes the exact elements and attributes that are available within a given markup language, along with which attributes are associated with which elements and the relationships between the elements. You can think of a schema as a legal contract between the person who created the markup language and the person who will create documents using that language.

By the Way

> Although I describe a schema as a "legal contract," in reality there is nothing legal about schemas. The point is that schemas are very exacting and thorough, and leave nothing to chance in terms of describing the makeup of XML documents—this degree of exacting thoroughness is what we all look for in an ideal legal contract.

Schemas and XML Data Modeling

The process of creating a schema for an XML document is known as *data modeling* because it involves resolving a class of data into elements and attributes that can be used to describe the data in an XML document. Once a data model (schema) is in place for a particular class of data, you can create structured XML documents that adhere to the model. The real importance of schemas is that they allow XML documents to be validated for accuracy. This simply means that a schema allows an XML developer (or an application) to process a document and see if it adheres to the set of constraints laid out in the schema. If not, you know the document could prove to be problematic. A valid XML document is kind of like a stamp of approval that declares the document suitable for use in an XML application. You learn how to validate your own XML documents in Hour 8, "Validating XML Documents."

To help clarify the role schemas play in XML, let's consider a practical real-world analogy. Pretend you just met a friend whom you haven't seen in years and she gives you her email address so that you can get in touch with her later. However, she lists her email address as `lucy*stalefishlabs.com`. You know that all email addresses consist of a name followed by an "at" symbol (`@`), followed by a domain name, which means that something is wrong with her email address. The `name@domainname` format of email addresses is actually a simple schema—you used this schema to "validate" your friend's email address and determine that it is in error. The obvious fix is to replace the asterisk (`*`) in her email address with an "at" symbol (`@`).

You now understand in the simplest of terms how schemas are used to determine the validity of XML documents, but you don't entirely know why. The main reason schemas are used in XML is to allow machine validation of document structure. In the invalid email example, you were easily able to see a problem because you knew that email addresses can't have asterisks in them. But how would an email application be able to make this determination? The developer of the application would have to write specific code to make sure that email addresses are structured to follow a given syntax, such as the name and domain name being separated by an "at" symbol. Whereas an email application developer writes code to check the validity of an email address, an XML document creator uses a schema. This schema can then be used by XML applications to ensure that documents are valid; schemas provide a mechanism to facilitate the process of validating XML documents.

When it comes to creating schemas, there are two primary approaches you can take:

- Document Type Definitions (DTDs)
- XML Schemas (XSDs)

These two schema approaches represent different technologies that make it possible to describe the data model of an XML-based markup language. The next two sections explain each approach in more detail.

Document Type Definitions (DTDs)

Warning, I'm about to roll out a new acronym! The new acronym I want to introduce you to now is *DTD*, which stands for *Document Type Definition*. DTDs represent the original approach of creating a schema for XML documents. I say "original approach" because DTDs did not originate with XML; DTDs originated with XML's predecessor, SGML (Standard General Markup Language). DTDs made their way into XML because it eased the transition from SGML to XML—many SGML tools existed that could be used for XML. Things have changed since the early days of XML, however, and now there is a more powerful approach to establishing schemas than DTDs. Even so, DTDs are still in use so it's important for you to understand how they work.

By the Way

> You learn about the more powerful XML Schema approach in the next section, "XML Schema."

The main drawback to DTDs is that they are based upon a somewhat cryptic language. XML provides a highly structured approach to formatting data, so why should you have to learn an entirely new language to describe XML schemas? I don't have a good answer to this question except to say that DTDs are a carryover from XML's beginnings and they still play a role in some XML applications, so you should learn how to use them. The good news is that DTDs are actually quite simple for describing most XML-based markup languages. This is due to the fact that the DTD language is extremely compact, which is why it has a cryptic appearance. Rather than continue to describe DTDs in words, let's just look at an example in Listing 3.1.

LISTING 3.1 A Simple DTD for the Tall Tales XML Document

```
 1: <!ELEMENT talltales (tt)+>
 2:
 3: <!ELEMENT tt (question, a, b, c)>
 4: <!ATTLIST tt
 5:   answer (a | b | c) #REQUIRED>
 6:
 7: <!ELEMENT question (#PCDATA)>
 8:
 9: <!ELEMENT a (#PCDATA)>
10:
11: <!ELEMENT b (#PCDATA)>
12:
13: <!ELEMENT c (#PCDATA)>
```

I warned you it was kind of cryptic. However, if you take a moment to read through the DTD code you can actually start to make some sense of it. You might even recognize that this DTD is for the Tall Tales trivia document that you saw in the previous hour. By studying the code, you can see that the word `ELEMENT` precedes each element that can be used in a TTML (Tall Tales Markup Language) document. Also the attributes for the `tt` element are listed after the word `ATTLIST` (line 4); in this case there is only one attribute, `answer` (line 5). Also notice that the three possible values of the answer attribute (`a`, `b`, and `c`) are listed out beside the attribute (line 5). Although there are a few strange looking pieces of information in this DTD, such as the `<!` at the beginning of each line and `(#PCDATA)` following each element, it's pretty apparent that DTDs aren't overly complex.

You learn a great deal more about DTDs later in this hour, so I won't go into more detail just yet. Instead, we'll move on and learn about the other approach to data modeling that uses a syntax that should be very familiar to you.

XML Schema (XSDs)

XML Schema replaces DTDs with a more powerful and intuitive approach to creating schemas for XML-based markup languages. Schemas created using XML Schema are coded in the XSD (XML Schema Definition) language, and are therefore referred to as XSDs. XML Schema and the XSD language were created by the W3C (World Wide Web Consortium), and represent a considerably more powerful and flexible approach to schemas than DTDs. The idea behind XML Schema is to use XML as the basis for creating schemas. So, instead of using the special DTD language to create a schema, you can use familiar XML elements and attributes that are defined in the XSD language.

An XSD is very similar in purpose to a DTD in that it is used to establish the schema of a class of XML documents. Similar to DTDs, XSDs describe elements and their content models so that documents can be validated. However, XSDs go several steps beyond DTDs by allowing you to associate data types with elements. In a DTD, element content is pretty much limited to text. An XSD is more flexible in that it can set the data type of elements to specific types, such as integer numbers and dates.

Of course, the most compelling aspect of XSDs is the fact that they are based upon an XML vocabulary (XSD). This means that you create an XSD as an XML document. So, the familiar tag/attribute approach to encoding XML documents is all you need to know to code an XSD document. You still have to learn the specific elements and attributes that comprise the XSD language, but it isn't too terribly difficult to learn. To give you an example, the code in Listing 3.2 is for an XSD that describes the familiar Tall Tales document.

LISTING 3.2 An XSD Document That Serves as a Schema for the Tall Tales XML Document

```
<?xml version="1.0"?>

<xsd:schema xmlns:xsd="http://www.w3.org/2000/10/XMLSchema">

<xsd:element name="talltales" minOccurs="1" maxOccurs="1">
  <xsd:complexType>
    <xsd:element name="tt">
      <xsd:complexType>
        <xsd:sequence>
          <xsd:element name="question" type="xsd:string" maxOccurs="1" />
          <xsd:element name="a" type="xsd:string" maxOccurs="1" />
          <xsd:element name="b" type="xsd:string" maxOccurs="1" />
          <xsd:element name="c" type="xsd:string" maxOccurs="1" />
        </xsd:sequence>
        <xsd:attribute name="answer" type="answerType" use="required" />
        <xsd:simpleType name="answerType">
          <xsd:restriction base="xsd:NMTOKEN">
            <xsd:enumeration value="a" />
            <xsd:enumeration value="b" />
            <xsd:enumeration value="c" />
          </xsd:restriction>
        </xsd:simpleType>
      </xsd:complexType>
    </xsd:element>
  </xsd:complexType>
</xsd:element>

</xsd:schema>
```

As you can see, XSDs aren't nearly as compact as DTDs, and can be more difficult to understand initially. The reason for this is because XSDs are considerably more powerful and flexible than DTDs, and with advanced features comes complexity. You learn all about creating XSDs in Hour 7, "Using XML Schema XSDs," after which this code will make complete sense to you. For now, the main thing to understand is that XML Schema allows you to use XML code to model data in a more detailed manner than DTDs. For example, in an XSD you can specify exactly the number of times an element is allowed to appear when nested.

By the Way

> Another schema technology exists that helps to simplify the complexities associated with XSDs. I'm referring to RELAX NG, which many people consider to be more powerful, more concise, and easier to use than XML Schema. RELAX NG doesn't yet enjoy the widespread support of DTDs and XSDs but that scenario is likely to change. You learn more about RELAX NG and how it compares to XML Schema in Hour 7, "Using XML Schema."

Comparing Schema Technologies

Although you haven't really learned much about the inner workings of DTDs and XSDs, you do understand that they represent two of the fundamental approaches to modeling XML document data. I alluded earlier that DTDs aren't as powerful as XSDs but there are advantages to DTDs when you consider that they have a long history and also are easier to create. On the other hand, XSDs offer considerable technical advantages over DTDs when you consider how much control they give you when nailing down the specifics of an XML data model. I'd like to take a moment to cover the specific differences between DTDs and XSDs so that you can better understand when to use each. Following is a list of the major differences between DTDs and XSDs:

- DTDs are coded using a special language, whereas XSDs are coded in XML.
- XSDs can be processed just like any other XML documents.
- XSDs support a variety of data types (integer numbers, floating point numbers, Booleans [true/false], dates, and so on), whereas DTDs treat all data as strings or lists of strings.

- XSDs present an open-ended data model, which allows you to extend custom markup languages and establish complex relationships between elements without invalidating documents. DTDs employ a closed data model that doesn't allow for much in the way of extensibility.

This list of differences obviously tips the scales in favor of XSDs. This is not just a matter of me being enamored with XML Schema. Keep in mind that XML Schema was created long after DTDs, so it stands to reason that it would address many of the weaknesses found in DTDs. Knowing this, you might think that it's a no-brainer choosing XSDs over DTDs to describe the data model for all of your XML documents. Although XSDs represent a more modern approach to XML data modeling, DTDs aren't quite dead yet.

The one thing DTDs have going for them is the fact that they've been around for so long and are so widely accepted. If you think an inferior technology has never been able to survive solely on its longevity and widespread acceptance, think again. Look no further than your VCR to see such a technology in action; Betamax was known to be a more powerful technology but somehow the VHS standard stuck and the better technology lost. Even so, DTDs are being supplanted by XML Schema and other schema standards such as the newer RELAX NG schema technology.

One compelling argument for understanding DTDs is that many XML-based markup languages are still expressed as DTDs. So, if you plan on using any existing XML languages, you may need to be familiar with DTDs in order to understand how they work. The other point to keep in mind is that DTDs are actually very good at describing the structure of XML documents. The fact that XSDs do a better job is not enough to discount DTDs entirely.

The Importance of Document Validation

Before digging deeper into DTDs, I'd like to address a topic that has been already been touched on a few times: document validation. I've already mentioned that the primary purpose of schemas is to provide a means of validating XML documents. What I didn't point out is that an XML document doesn't necessarily have to be valid in order to be useful. So, there is a little more to the document validation story than I've let on.

In addition to document validity, XML establishes the concept of a well-formed document, which is a document that meets all of the general language rules of XML. A well-formed document follows the five XML commandments you learned about in the previous hour, but it doesn't necessarily qualify as being a valid document. The reason is because a well-formed document doesn't have to be associated with a schema. Looking at XML documents in this light, it becomes apparent that there are two different degrees of "correctness" with respect to XML documents. The first degree is met by well-formed documents, which must meet the strict language requirements of XML. Taking things a step further leads us to valid documents, which are well-formed documents that also adhere to a schema of some sort (DTD or XSD, for example).

By the Way

> A valid document is always a well-formed document, but the reverse is not always true.

The terms *valid* and *well-formed* are extremely important to XML and are used throughout the remainder of the book. Whether or not a document needs to be valid is up to the particular application in which it is being used. However, all XML documents must be well-formed or you will undoubtedly encounter errors when the document is processed. To help keep valid and well-formed documents clear, remember that well-formed documents must adhere to the general XML rules, whereas valid documents must also adhere to a schema. You learn how to use DTDs and XSDs to validate XML documents in Hour 8.

DTD Construction Basics

You already know that DTDs represent the original schema technique supported by XML, and are tightly integrated with the documents they describe. Therefore, to understand how DTDs are constructed, you must first understand how they relate to XML documents. In order to use a DTD with a document, you must somehow associate the DTD with the document. This association is carried out through the *document type declaration*, which must be placed at the beginning of an XML document just after the XML declaration:

```
<?xml version="1.0"?>
<!DOCTYPE talltales SYSTEM "talltales.dtd">
```

The second line in this code is the document type declaration for the Tall Tales document you saw earlier. The main thing to note about this code is how the Tall Tales DTD is specified.

The terminology surrounding DTDs and document type declarations is admittedly confusing, so allow me to clarify that DTD stands for document type *definition* and contains the actual description of a markup language. A document type *declaration* is a line of code in a document that identifies the DTD. So, the big distinction here is that the definition (DTD) describes your markup language, whereas the declaration associates it with a document. Got it? Let's move on!

A DTD describes vital information about the structure of a document using *markup declarations*, which are lines of code that describe elements, attributes, and the relationship between them. The following types of markup declarations may be used within a DTD:

- The elements allowed in the document
- The attributes that may be assigned to each element
- Entities that are allowed in the document
- Notations that are allowed for use with external entities

Elements and attributes you know about, but the last two markup declarations relate to entirely new territory. Don't worry because you learn more about entities and notations in the next hour, "Digging Deeper into XML Documents." For now, it's important to understand that the markup declarations within a DTD serve a vital role in allowing documents to be validated against the DTD.

When associating a DTD with a document, there are two approaches the document type declaration can take:

- It can directly include markup declarations in the document that form the *internal* DTD.
- It can reference external markup declarations that form the *external* DTD.

These two approaches to declaring a DTD reveal that there are two parts to a DTD: an internal part and an external part. When you refer to the DTD for a document, you are actually referring to the internal and external DTDs taken together. The reason for breaking the DTD into two parts has to do with flexibility. The external DTD typically describes the general structure for a class of documents, whereas the internal DTD is specific to a given document. XML gives preference to the internal DTD, which means you can use it to override declarations in the external DTD.

By the Way

> If you have any experience with CSS (Cascading Style Sheets) in web design, you may recognize a similar structure in DTDs where the internal DTD overrides the external DTD. In CSS style sheets, local styles override any external style sheets.

Breaking Down a DTD

The following code shows the general syntax of a document type declaration:

```
<!DOCTYPE RootElem SYSTEM ExternalDTDRef [InternalDTDDecl]>
```

By the Way

> You could argue that it isn't necessary to understand the inner workings of DTDs in order to use XML, and to some extent that is true. In fact, you don't necessarily have to know anything about schemas to do interesting things with XML. However, it's impossible to truly understand the XML technology without having a firm grasp on what constitutes an XML-based markup language. And, of course, XML-based markup languages are described using DTDs and other types of schemas.

The external DTD is referenced by ExternalDTDRef, which is the URI (Uniform Resource Identifier) of a file containing the external DTD. The internal DTD corresponds to InternalDTDDecl and is declared between square brackets ([]). In addition to the internal and external DTDs, another very important piece of information is mentioned in the document type declaration: the root element. `RootElem` identifies the root element of the document class in the document type declaration syntax. The word `SYSTEM` indicates that the DTD is located in an external file. Following is an example of a document type declaration that uses both an internal and external DTD:

```
<!DOCTYPE talltales SYSTEM "TallTales.dtd"> [
<!ELEMENT question (#PCDATA)> ]>
```

By the Way

A URI (Uniform Resource Identifier) is a more general form of a URL (Uniform Resource Locator) that allows you to identify network resources other than files. URLs should be familiar to you as they are used to represent the addresses of web pages.

This code shows how you might create a document type declaration for the Tall Tales trivia sample document. The root element of the document is `talltales`, which means that all documents of this type must have their content housed within the `talltales` element. The document type declaration references an external DTD stored in the file `TallTales.dtd`. Additionally, an element named `question` is declared as part of the internal DTD. Remember that internal markup declarations always override external declarations of the same name if such declarations exist. It isn't always necessary to use an internal DTD if the external DTD sufficiently describes a language, which is often the case.

By the Way

The document type declaration must appear after the XML declaration but before the first element (tag) in a document.

In the previous hour you learned about the XML declaration, which must appear at the beginning of a document and indicates what version of XML is being used. The XML declaration can also contain additional pieces of information that relate to DTDs. I'm referring to the standalone status and character encoding of a document. The *standalone status* of a document determines whether or not a document relies on any external information sources, such as an external DTD. You can explicitly set the standalone status of a document using the standalone document declaration, which looks like an attribute of the XML declaration:

```
<?xml version="1.0" standalone="no"?>
```

By the Way

You learn about the character encoding of a document in the next hour, "Digging Deeper into XML Documents."

A value of yes for `standalone` indicates that a document is standalone and therefore doesn't rely on external information sources. A value of no indicates that a document is not standalone and therefore may rely on external information sources. Documents that rely on an external DTD for validation can't be considered standalone, and must have `standalone` set to `no`. For this reason, `no` is the default value for `standalone`.

Pondering Elements and Attributes

The primary components described in a DTD are elements and attributes. Elements and attributes are very important because they establish the logical structure of XML documents. You can think of an element as a logical unit of information, whereas an attribute is a characteristic of that information. This is an important distinction because there is often confusion over when to model information using an element versus using an attribute.

A useful approach to take when assessing the best way to model information is to consider the type of the information and how it will be used. Attributes provide tighter constraints on information, which can be very helpful. More specifically, attributes can be constrained against a predefined list of possible values and can also have default values. Element content is very unconstrained and is better suited for storing long strings of text and other child elements. Consider the following list of advantages that attributes offer over elements:

- Attributes can be constrained against a predefined list of enumerated values.
- Attributes can have default values.
- Attributes have data types, although admittedly somewhat limited.
- Attributes are very concise.

Attributes don't solve every problem, however. In fact, they are limited in several key respects. Following are the major disadvantages associated with attributes:

- Attributes can't store long strings of text.
- Attributes can't contain nested information.
- Whitespace can't be ignored in an attribute value.

Given that attributes are simpler and more concise than elements, it's reasonable that you should use attributes over child elements whenever possible. Fortunately, the decision to use child elements is made fairly straightforward by the limitations of attributes: if a piece of information is a long string of text, requires nested information within it, or requires whitespace to be ignored, you'll want to place it in an element. Otherwise, an attribute is probably your best choice. Of course, regardless of how well your document data maps to attributes, it must have at least a root element.

Digging Deeper into Elements

To declare an element in a DTD, you must use an *element declaration*, which takes the following form:

```
<!ELEMENT ElementName Type>
```

The name of the element determines the name of the tag(s) used to mark up the element in a document and corresponds to `ElementName` in the element declaration. This name must be unique within the context of a DTD. The type of the element is specified in `Type`; XML supports four different types of elements, which are determined by the content contained within the element:

- Empty—The element doesn't contain any content (it can still contain attributes).
- Element-only—The element only contains child elements.
- Mixed—The element contains a combination of child elements and character data.
- Any—The element contains any content allowed by the DTD.

> **Watch Out!**
> The name of an element must not contain the ampersand character (&) or begin with the sequence of letters `X`, `M`, and `L` in any case combination (`XML`, `xml`, `XmL`, and so on).

The next few sections explore the different element types in more detail.

Peeking Inside Empty Elements

An *empty element* is an element that doesn't contain any element content. An empty element can still contain information, but it must do so using attributes. Empty elements are declared using the following form:

```
<!ELEMENT ElementName EMPTY>
```

Following is an example of declaring an empty element using this form:

```
<!ELEMENT clothing EMPTY>
```

After an empty element is defined in a DTD, you can use it in a document in one of two ways:

- With a start tag/end tag pair
- With an empty tag

Following is an example of an empty element defined using a start tag/end tag pair:

```
<clothing></clothing>
```

Notice that no content appears between the tags; if any content did appear, even a single space, the document would be invalid. A more concise approach to defining empty elements is to use an empty tag. Following is an example of using an empty tag to define an empty element:

```
<clothing />
```

As you can see, an empty tag is somewhat of a combination of a start tag and end tag. In addition to being more concise, empty tags help to make it clear in a document that an element is empty and therefore can't contain content. Remember that empty elements can still contain information in attributes. Following is an example of how you might use a few attributes with an empty element:

```
<clothing type="t-shirt" color="navy" size="xl" />
```

Housing Children with Element-Only Elements

An *element-only* element contains nothing but child elements. In other words, no text content is stored within an element-only element. An element is declared element-only by simply listing the child elements that can appear within the element, which is known as the element's *content model*. Following is the form expected for declaring an element's content model:

```
<!ELEMENT ElementName ContentModel>
```

The content model is specified using a combination of special element declaration symbols and child element names. The symbols describe the relationship between child elements and the container element. Within the content model, child elements are grouped into sequences or choice groups using parentheses (()). A sequence of child elements indicates the order of the elements, whereas a choice group indicates alternate possibilities for how the elements are used. Child elements within a sequence are separated by commas (,), whereas elements in a choice group are separated by pipes (¦). Following are the different element declaration symbols used to establish the content model of elements:

- Parentheses (())—Encloses a sequence or choice group of child elements
- Comma (,)—Separates the items in a sequence, which establishes the order in which they must appear
- Pipe (¦)—Separates the items in a choice group of alternatives

- No symbol—Indicates that a child element must appear exactly once
- Question mark (?)—Indicates that a child element must appear exactly once or not at all
- Plus sign (+)—Indicates that a child element must appear at least once
- Asterisk (*)—Indicates that a child element can appear any number of times

Although I could use several paragraphs to try and explain these element declaration symbols, I think an example is much more explanatory. Following is the declaration for an element named `resume` that might be used in a resume markup language:

```
<!ELEMENT resume (intro, (education | experience+)+, hobbies?, references*)>
```

The `resume` element is pretty interesting because it demonstrates the usage of every element declaration symbol. The `resume` element is element-only, which is evident by the fact that it contains only child elements. The first child element is `intro`, which must appear exactly once within the `resume` element; this is because no symbols are used with it. The `education` or `experience` elements must then appear at least once, which is indicated by the plus sign just outside of the parentheses. Within the parentheses, the `education` element must appear exactly once, whereas the `experience` element must appear at least once but can also appear multiple times. The idea is to allow you to list part of your education followed by any relevant work experience; you may have worked multiple jobs following a single block of education. The `hobby` element can appear exactly once or not at all; all of your hobbies must be listed within a single `hobby` element. Finally, the `references` element can appear any number of times.

To get a practical feel for how element-only elements affect XML documents in the real world, take a look at the following line of code from the DTD for the RSS language:

```
<!ELEMENT item (title | link | description)*>
```

RSS is an XML-based language that is used to syndicate web sites so that applications and other web sites can obtain brief descriptions of new articles and other content. For example, Sports Illustrated (http://sportsillustrated.cnn.com/) offers RSS news feeds for all major sports. Other web sites can tap into these feeds or you can use an RSS aggregator application such as FeedDemon(http://www.feeddemon.com/), which allows you to view news feeds much like you view email in an email client.

Anyway, getting back to the RSS DTD, the previous line of code reveals that the `item` element can contain any combination of `title`, `link`, or `description` elements as long as there is no more than one of each. To see how this DTD translates into real XML code, check out the following excerpt from a real Sports Illustrated NFL news feed:

```
<item>
  <title>Titans' trio of young WRs showing promise</title>
  <link>http://sportsillustrated.cnn.com/rssclick/2005/football/nfl/06/22/
  bc.fbn.titans.receivers.ap/index.html?section=si_nfl</link>
  <description>Read full story for latest details.</description>
</item>
```

By the Way

> To view the XML code for a Sports Illustrated news feed for yourself, visit the main Sports Illustrated page, scroll down to the bottom, and click the small XML logo. A list of news feeds appears—click any of them to open the RSS document containing the feed data.

As this code reveals, the `item` element contains exactly one each of `title`, `link`, and `description` elements. To see how this code affects a real web page, check out the syndicated NFL news feed on my web site in Figure 3.1.

FIGURE 3.1 The example syndicated NFL news feed is visible on my web site.

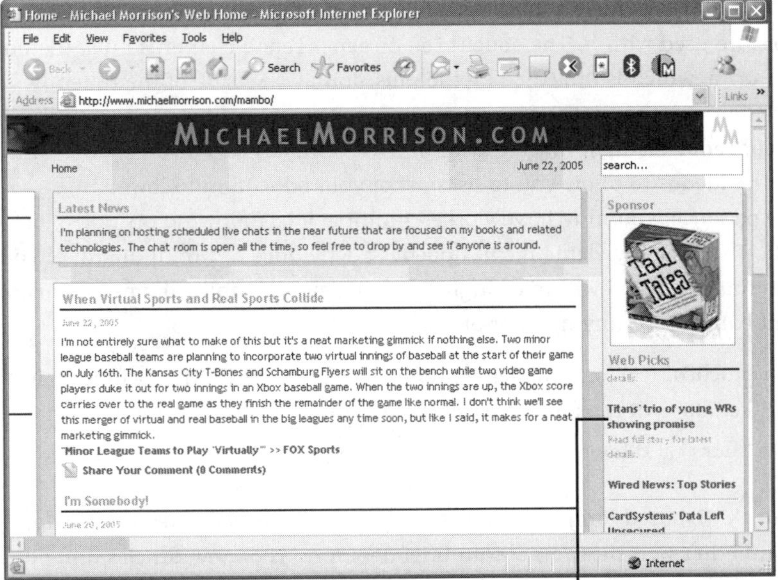

The figure reveals how the Tennessee Titans news story shown in the previous RSS code is syndicated and visible as an RSS news feed on my web site.

In the next section you see how the individual RSS elements mentioned here are defined in the RSS DTD. You also find out more details about how to syndicate news feeds and create your own in Hour 24, "Syndicating the Web with RSS News Feeds."

Combining Content and Children with Mixed Elements

Mixed elements are elements that contain both character data (text) and child elements. The simplest mixed element is also known as a *text-only element* because it contains only character data. Text-only elements are declared using the following form:

```
<!ELEMENT ElementName (#PCDATA)>
```

The content model for text-only elements consists solely of the symbol `#PCDATA` contained within parentheses, which indicates that an element contains Parsed Character DATA. Following is an example of a simple text-only element declaration:

```
<!ELEMENT hobbies (#PCDATA)>
```

By the Way

> The word "parsed" in Parsed Character DATA (PCDATA) refers to the fact that PCDATA within a document is processed (parsed) by an XML application. Most of the text content in an XML document is considered PCDATA, including character entities for example. The parsing process involves stripping out extraneous whitespace and, in the case of character entities, replacing entities with the appropriate text. The alternative to PCDATA is CDATA (Character DATA), which is text that isn't processed by an XML application. Later in the book you learn when it is useful to include CDATA in a document.

This element might be used to mark up a list of hobbies in an XML document that helps to describe you to other people. Following is an example of how you might define the `hobbies` element in a document:

```
<hobbies>juggling, unicycling, tight-rope walking</hobbies>
```

Speaking of examples, the following code shows the `title`, `link`, and `description` elements from the RSS DTD that you learned about in the previous section:

```
<!ELEMENT title (#PCDATA)>
<!ELEMENT link (#PCDATA)>
<!ELEMENT description (#PCDATA)>
```

As you can see, these elements are all defined as text-only elements, which makes sense given the sample RSS data you saw in the previous section.

In reality, a text-only element is just a mixed element that doesn't contain any child elements. Mixed elements that contain both text data and child elements are declared very much like element-only elements, with the addition of a few subtle requirements. More specifically, the content model for a mixed element must contain a repeating choice list of the following form:

```
<!ELEMENT ElementName (#PCDATA | ElementList)*>
```

If this looks a little confusing at first, don't worry. Let's break it down. The symbol #PCDATA at the start of the choice list indicates that the mixed element can contain character data. The remainder of the choice list contains child elements, and resembles a regular element-only content model. Additional #PCDATA symbols may be interspersed throughout the content model to indicate that character data appears throughout the child elements. An asterisk (*) must appear at the end of the content model's choice list to indicate that the entire choice group is optional—this is a requirement of mixed elements. Also, although a mixed element declaration constrains the type of child elements allowed, it doesn't constrain the order of the elements or the number of times they may appear.

By the Way

> In the content model for a mixed element, the character data (#PCDATA) must always be specified first in the choice group, and the choice group itself must be declared as repeating by following it with an asterisk (*).

Although mixed elements provide a considerable amount of flexibility, they lack the structure of element-only elements. So, with the exception of text-only elements, you're better off using element-only elements instead of mixed elements whenever possible; you can often get the equivalent of a mixed element by declaring attributes on a text-only element.

Keeping Your Options Open with Any Elements

The *any* element is the most flexible element of all because it has virtually no structure. The any element is declared using the symbol ANY, and earns its name by being able to contain any declared element types, character data, or a mixture of both. You can think of the any element as a mixed element with a wide-open content model. Following is the form used to declare an any element:

```
<!ELEMENT ElementName ANY>
```

Not surprisingly, the lack of structure associated with the any element makes it something you should avoid at all costs in a production DTD. I mention a production (completed) DTD because the any element is typically used only during the development of a DTD for testing purposes.

Putting Attributes to Work

Attributes go hand in hand with elements and are incredibly important to the construction of DTDs. Attributes are used to specify additional information about an element. More specifically, attributes are used to form a name/value pair that somehow describes a particular property of an element. Attributes are declared in a DTD using attribute list declarations, which take the following form:

```
<!ATTLIST ElementName AttrName AttrType Default>
```

This form reveals that an attribute has a name (`AttrName`) and a type (`AttrType`), as well as a default value (`Default`). The default value for an attribute refers to either a value or a symbol that indicates the use of the attribute. There are four different types of default values you can specify for an attribute in `Default`:

- `#REQUIRED`—The attribute is required.
- `#IMPLIED`—The attribute is optional.
- `#FIXED` value—The attribute has a fixed value.
- `default`—The default value of the attribute.

The `#REQUIRED` value identifies a required attribute, which means the attribute must be set if you use the element. The `#IMPLIED` value identifies an optional attribute, which means the attribute is optional when using the element. The `#FIXED` attribute is used to assign a fixed value to an attribute, effectively making the attribute a constant piece of information; you must provide the fixed attribute value after the `#FIXED` symbol when declaring the attribute. The last option for declaring attribute defaults is to simply list the default value for an attribute; an attribute will assume its default value if it isn't explicitly set in the element. Following is an example of an attribute list for an element that specifies the units for a duration of time:

```
<!ELEMENT distance (#PCDATA)>
<!ATTLIST distance units (miles | kilometers | laps) "miles">
```

In this example, the element is named `distance` and its only attribute is named `units`. The `units` attribute can only be set to one of three possible values: `miles`, `kilometers`, or `laps`. The default value of the `units` attribute is `miles`, which means that if you don't explicitly set the attribute it will automatically take on a value of `miles`.

By the Way

> Although attribute lists don't have to be declared in a particular place within a DTD, it is common practice to place them immediately below the declaration for the element to which they belong.

In addition to the default value of an attribute value, you must also specify the type of the attribute in the attribute list declaration. There are 10 different attribute types, which follow:

- CDATA—Unparsed character data
- Enumerated—A series of string values
- NOTATION—A notation declared somewhere else in the DTD
- ENTITY—An external binary entity
- ENTITIES—Multiple external binary entities separated by whitespace
- ID—A unique identifier
- IDREF—A reference to an ID declared somewhere else in the DTD
- IDREFS—Multiple references to IDs declared somewhere else in the document
- NMTOKEN—A name consisting of XML token characters (letters, numbers, periods, dashes, colons, and underscores)
- NMTOKENS—Multiple names consisting of XML token characters

To help in understanding these attribute types, it's possible to classify them into three groups: string, enumerated, and tokenized.

String attributes are the most commonly used attributes and are represented by the CDATA type. The CDATA type indicates that an attribute contains a simple string of text. Following is an example of declaring a simple CDATA attribute that must be defined in the education element:

```
<!ATTLIST education school CDATA #REQUIRED>
```

In this example, the school a person attended is a required character data attribute of the education element. If you wanted to make the school attribute optional, you could use the #IMPLIED symbol:

```
<!ATTLIST education school CDATA #IMPLIED>
```

Enumerated attributes are constrained to a list of predefined strings of text. The enumerated type is similar to the CDATA type except the acceptable attribute values must come from a list that is provided in the attribute list declaration. Following is an example of how you might provide an enumerated attribute for specifying the type of degree earned as part of the education element:

```
<!ATTLIST education degree (associate | bachelors | masters | doctorate)
  "bachelors">
```

When using the degree attribute in a document, you are required to select a value from the enumerated list. If you don't use the attribute at all, it will assume the default value of bachelors.

Tokenized attributes are processed as tokens by an XML application, which means the application converts all contiguous whitespace to a single space character and eliminates all leading and trailing whitespace. In addition to eliminating the majority of whitespace in a tokenized attribute value, the XML application also validates the value of a tokenized attribute based upon the declared attribute type: ENTITY, ENTITIES, ID, IDREF, IDREFS, NMTOKEN, or NMTOKENS.

By the Way

A *token* is the smallest piece of information capable of being processed by an XML application. A tokenized attribute is simply an attribute that is processed into tokens by an XML application, which has the effect of eliminating extraneous whitespace (space characters, newline characters, and so on). Contrast this with a string attribute, which goes unprocessed, and therefore retains all of its whitespace.

The ENTITY and ENTITIES types are used to reference entities, which you learn about in the next hour. As an example, images are typically referenced as binary entities, in which case you use an ENTITY attribute value to associate an image with an element type:

```
<!ATTLIST photo image ENTITY #IMPLIED>
```

The ENTITIES type is similar to ENTITY but it allows you to specify multiple entities. The ID, IDREF, and IDREFS attribute types all relate to unique identifiers. The ID type is a unique identifier that can be used to uniquely identify an element within a document:

```
<!ATTLIST part id ID #REQUIRED>
```

Only one attribute of type ID may be assigned to a given element type. The NMTOKEN and NMTOKENS attribute types are used to specify attributes containing name token values. A *name token value* consists of a single name, which means that it can't contain whitespace. More specifically, a name token value can consist of alphanumeric characters in addition to the following characters: ., -, _, and :.

Working with Multiple Attributes

I've only shown you example of individual attributes thus far, but you'll likely create elements that rely on several attributes. You can list all of the attributes for an element in a single attribute list by listing the attributes one after the next within the attribute list declaration. Following is an example of declaring multiple attributes within a single attribute list:

```
<!ELEMENT photo (image, format)>
<!ATTLIST photo
  image ENTITY #IMPLIED
  photo format NOTATION (gif ¦ jpeg) #REQUIRED
>
```

This example shows how the two attributes of the `photo` element, `image` and `photo`, are declared in a single attribute list declaration.

A Complete DTD Example

Admittedly, this hour has thrown a great deal of information at you, most of which is quite technical. But there's a method to the madness, and now it's time to see some of the payoff. To help you get some perspective on how elements and attributes fit into a DTD for a new custom markup language, let's work through the design of a DTD for a sports training markup language. This markup language, which we'll call ETML (Endurance Training Markup Language), might come in handy if you even decide to compete in a marathon or triathlon—it models training data related to endurance sports such as running, swimming, and cycling. The following are the major pieces of information that are associated with each individual training session:

- Date—The date and time of the training session
- Type—The type of training session (running, swimming, cycling, and so on)
- Heart rate—The average heart rate sustained during the training session
- Duration—The duration of the training session
- Distance—The distance covered in the training session (measured in miles or kilometers)
- Location—The location of the training session
- Comments—General comments about the training session

Knowing that all of this information must be accounted for within a training session element, can you determine which ones would be better suited as child elements and which would be better suited as attributes? There really is no correct answer but there are a few logical reasons you might separate some of the information into elements and some into attributes. The following is how I would organize this information:

- Attributes—Date, Type, Heart rate
- Child elements—Duration, Distance, Location, Comments

The date, type, and heart rate for a training session are particularly well suited for attributes because they all involve short, simple values. The type attribute goes a step further because you can use an enumerated list of predefined values (running, cycling, and so on). The duration and distance of a session could really go either way in terms of being modeled by an element or an attribute. However, by modeling them as elements you leave room for each of them to have attributes that allow you to specify additional information such as the exact units of measure. The location and comments potentially contain descriptive text, and therefore are also better suited as child elements.

By the Way

> A golden rule of XML design is that the more constraints you can impose on a document, the more structured its content will be. In other words, try to create schemas that leave little to chance in terms of how elements and attributes are intended to be used.

With the conceptual design of the DTD in place, you're ready to dive into the code. Listing 3.3 contains the code for the ETML DTD, which is stored in the file `etml.dtd`.

LISTING 3.3 The `etml.dtd` DTD That Is Used to Validate ETML Documents

```
 1: <!ELEMENT trainlog (session)+>
 2:
 3: <!ELEMENT session (duration, distance, location, comments)>
 4: <!ATTLIST session
 5:   date CDATA #IMPLIED
 6:   type (running | swimming | cycling) "running"
 7:   heartrate CDATA #IMPLIED
 8: >
 9:
10: <!ELEMENT duration (#PCDATA)>
11: <!ATTLIST duration
12:   units (seconds | minutes | hours) "minutes"
13: >
14:
15: <!ELEMENT distance (#PCDATA)>
16: <!ATTLIST distance
17:   units (miles | kilometers | laps) "miles"
18: >
19:
20: <!ELEMENT location (#PCDATA)>
21:
22: <!ELEMENT comments (#PCDATA)>
```

You should be able to apply what you've learned throughout this hour to understanding the ETML DTD. All of the elements and attributes in the DTD flow from the conceptual design that you just completed. The `trainlog` element (line 1) is the root element for ETML documents and contains `session` elements for each training session. Each `session` element consists of `duration`, `distance`, `location`, and `comments` child elements (line 3) and `date`, `type`, and `heartrate` attributes (lines 4–7). Notice that the `type` attribute of the `session` element (line 6) and the `units` attributes of the `duration` and `distance` elements (lines 12 and 17) are constrained to lists of enumerated values.

Of course, no DTD is really complete without an XML document to demonstrate its usefulness. Listing 3.4 shows a sample document that is coded in ETML.

LISTING 3.4 The Training Log Sample ETML Document

```
 1: <?xml version="1.0"?>
 2: <!DOCTYPE trainlog SYSTEM "etml.dtd">
 3:
 4: <trainlog>
 5:   <session date="11/19/05" type="running" heartrate="158">
 6:     <duration units="minutes">50</duration>
 7:     <distance units="miles">5.5</distance>
 8:     <location>Warner Park</location>
 9:     <comments>Mid-morning run, a little winded throughout.</comments>
10:   </session>
11:
12:   <session date="11/21/05" type="cycling" heartrate="153">
13:     <duration units="hours">1.5</duration>
14:     <distance units="miles">26.4</distance>
15:     <location>Natchez Trace Parkway</location>
16:     <comments>Hilly ride, felt strong as an ox.</comments>
17:   </session>
18:
19:   <session date="11/24/05" type="running" heartrate="156">
20:     <duration units="hours">2.5</duration>
21:     <distance units="miles">16.8</distance>
22:     <location>Warner Park</location>
23:     <comments>Afternoon run, felt reasonably strong.</comments>
24:   </session>
25: </trainlog>
```

As you can see, this document strictly adheres to the ETML DTD both in terms of the elements it defines as well as the nesting of the elements. The DTD is specified in the document type declaration, which clearly references the file `etml.dtd` (line 2). Another couple of aspects of the document to pay attention to are the `type` and `units` attributes (lines 5, 12, and 19), which adhere to the lists of available choices defined in the DTD. Keep in mind that even though only three training sessions are included in the document, the DTD allows you to include as many as you want. So if you're feeling energetic, go sign up for a marathon and start logging away training sessions in your new markup language!

Hour 8 shows you how to validate an XML document against a DTD.

Summary

XML is a markup language that allows you to create other markup languages. The process of establishing the structure of XML-based markup languages is known as data modeling. The resulting data model for a custom markup language is defined in a construct known as a schema. Two primary approaches exist for creating schemas for XML languages: DTDs and XSDs. There are advantages and disadvantages to each approach, but they are both suitable for most XML applications.

In this hour you gained some important insight into document validation and found out what it means for a document to be well formed. You also explored the details of the DTD approach to defining XML schemas, and found out how DTDs are responsible for describing the structure and format of a class of XML documents. You saw that a DTD consists of markup declarations that determine the rules for a custom markup language. In addition to providing a formal set of rules for a markup language, DTDs form a critical part of XML in that they provide a means of validating documents for accuracy. The hour culminated with the creation of a complete DTD for the Endurance Training Markup Language (ETML). You also saw a sample XML document created in ETML.

Q&A

Q. ***I don't plan on creating any of my own custom markup languages. Do I still need to know the details of DTDs and XSDs?***

A. Yes. In many cases, markup languages aren't documented too well, which means the DTD or XSD for a language may be all you have to go by when it comes to figuring out the format of documents.

Q. ***Would I ever want to create both a DTD and an XSD for a custom markup language?***

A. Probably not. The only reason you might do this is if you create a DTD initially for convenience, and later replace it with an XSD as your needs change and as you migrate to tools that demand support for XML Schema (XSDs).

Q. ***Why would you ever want to use an internal DTD?***

A. Because an internal DTD is declared directly in an XML document and not in an external file, it applies only to that particular document. Therefore, you should only use an internal DTD for markup declarations that apply to a specific document. Otherwise, all markup declarations should be placed in an external DTD so that they can be reused with other documents.

Q. ***Why would you use an attribute over an element when designing a DTD?***

A. Attributes provide tighter constraints on data, can be constrained against a predefined list of possible values, and can have default values. Element content is much less constrained, and is better suited for housing long strings of text and other child elements. A golden rule of XML design is that the more constraints you can impose on a document, the more structured its content will be. Knowing this, you should attempt to fit data into attributes whenever possible.

Workshop

The Workshop is designed to help you anticipate possible questions, review what you've learned, and begin learning how to put your knowledge into practice.

Quiz

1. What is the purpose of a schema?
2. If you wanted to create a schema for a markup language with specific data types, such as integer numbers and dates, which schema technology would you need to use?
3. What is the difference between valid and well-formed documents?

Quiz Answers

1. A schema describes the exact elements and attributes that are available within a given markup language, along with which attributes are associated with which elements and the relationships between the elements.
2. XML Schema is the schema technology of choice for schemas that require specific data types such as integer numbers and dates.
3. Well-formed documents must adhere to the general XML rules, whereas valid documents must also adhere to a schema.

Exercises

1. Modify the ETML DTD so that it includes a new attribute of the `session` element that stores a rating for the training session—the rating indicates how well you felt during the session on a scale of 1 to 10. Design the new `rating` attribute so that it is constrained to a list of numeric values between 1 and 10.

2. Modify the `trainlog.xml` document so that it takes advantage of the new `rating` attribute.

HOUR 4

Digging Deeper into XML Documents

> Promoting XML is kinda like selling illegal drugs, where the first acronym is always free.
>
> —Jeff Lowery

Unfortunately, the steady stream of XML acronyms will only continue to flow by as you progress through this book. This hour introduces you to a few more acronyms, and along the way takes a closer look at the inner workings of XML documents. You will find out that in addition to the logical structure of documents that is dictated by elements, there is also a physical structure that is very important. This physical structure of documents is determined by *entities*, which are units of storage that house content within documents. Closely related to entities are *notations*, which make it possible for XML applications to handle certain types of entities that aren't capable of being processed. This hour tackles entities and notations along with a few other important topics related to the inner workings of XML documents. Oh, and don't forget about those new acronyms you get to add to your rapidly growing XML vocabulary!

In this hour, you'll learn

- How to document your XML code with comments
- How characters of text are encoded in XML
- All about entities and how they are used
- Why notations make it possible to use certain kinds of entities

Leaving a Trail with Comments

It shouldn't come as a surprise that any self-respecting XML developer would want to write clean XML code that is as easy to understand as possible. Part of the process of writing clean XML code is documenting the code whenever necessary. *Comments* are used in XML to add descriptions to code and include information that isn't part of a document's content. Comments aren't considered part of a document's content because XML processors ignore them.

Technically speaking, it's possible for an XML processor to actually pay attention to comments and not ignore them, which might make sense in an XML development tool such as a WYSIWYM editor. Such a tool might allow you to enter and modify comments through a graphical user interface, in which case it would need to process comments to some degree. Even so, the comments wouldn't be interpreted as document content.

Comments are specified in a document between the `<!--` and `-->` symbols. The only limitation on comments is that you can't include double-hyphens (`--`) in the body of a comment because they conflict with XML's comment syntax. Following is an example of how you could use a comment to add information to a Tall Tales question in the Tall Tales sample document that you've worked with in previous hours:

```
<!-- This question still needs to be verified. -->
<tt answer="a">
  <question>
    In 1994, the Nestle UK food company was fined for injuries suffered by a
    36 year-old employee at a plant in York, England. What happened to the man?
  </question>
  <a>He fell in a giant mixing bowl and was whipped for over a minute.</a>
  <b>He developed an ulcer while working as a candy bar tester.</b>
  <c>He was hit in the head with a large piece of flying chocolate.</c>
</tt>
```

The information contained within the comment isn't considered part of the document data. The usefulness of comments will naturally vary with the type of XML documents you are creating. Some documents tend to be relatively self-explanatory, whereas others benefit from comments that make them more understandable. In this example, the comment is used to flag a question that still needs to be verified before being incorporated into the final game. In reality, an attribute might provide a better approach for flagging unverified questions but the comment still works as a simpler approach.

Characters of Text in XML

As you know, XML documents are made of text. More specifically, an XML document consists of characters of text that have meaning based upon XML syntax. The characters of text within an XML document can be encoded in a number of different ways to suit different human languages. All of the character-encoding schemes supported by XML are based on the Unicode text standard, which specifies the set of characters available for use in text documents. The character-encoding scheme for an XML document is determined within the XML declaration in a piece of code known as the *character encoding declaration*. The character encoding declaration looks like an attribute of the XML declaration, as the following code shows:

```
<?xml version="1.0" encoding="UTF-8"?>
```

The UTF-8 value assigned in the character encoding declaration specifies that the document is to use the Unicode UTF-8 character-encoding scheme, which is the default scheme for XML. All XML applications are required to support the UTF-8 and UTF-16 character encoding schemes; the difference between the two schemes is the number of bits used to represent each character of text (8 or 16). If you don't expect your documents to be used in a scenario with multiple human languages, you can probably stick to UTF-8. Otherwise, you'll need to go with UTF-16, which requires more memory but allows for multiple languages.

There are other character encoding standards in addition to UTF-8 and UTF-16, such as ISO-8859-1, which is used in Western Europe. You'll want to look into other character encoding options if you plan on developing XML documents that target languages other than English.

Regardless of the scheme you use to encode characters within an XML document, you need to know how to specify characters numerically. All characters in an encoding scheme have a numerical value associated with them that can be used as a character reference. Character references come in very handy when you're trying to enter a character that can't be typed on a keyboard. For example, the copyright symbol (©) is an example of a character that can only be specified using a character reference. There are two types of numeric character references:

- Decimal reference (base 10)
- Hexadecimal reference (base 16)

A *decimal character reference* relies on a decimal number (base 10) to specify a character's numeric value. Decimal references are specified using an ampersand followed by a pound sign (&#), the character number, and a semicolon (;). So, a complete decimal character reference has the following form:

```
&#Num;
```

The decimal number in this form is represented by Num. Following is an example of a decimal character reference:

```
&#169;
```

This character reference identifies the character associated with the decimal number 169, which just so happens to be the copyright symbol. Following is the copyright symbol character reference used within the context of other character data:

```
&#169;2005 Michael Morrison
```

Even though the code looks a little messy with the character reference, you're using a symbol (the copyright symbol) that would otherwise be difficult to enter in a normal text editor since there is no copyright key on your keyboard.

> The actual decimal number associated with the copyright symbol is determined by a standard that applies to both XML and HTML. To learn more about special characters that can be encoded using character references, please refer to the following web page: http://www.w3.org/TR/REC-html40/sgml/entities.html.

Table 4.1 lists some common character references you may find useful when developing XML documents of your own:

TABLE 4.1 Common Character References

Symbol	Character Reference
¢ (cent)	`¢`
£ (pound)	`£`
© (copyright)	`©`
® (registered)	`®`
° (degree)	`°`
[1/4] (one-fourth)	`¼`
[1/2] (one-half)	`½`
[3/4] (three-fourths)	`¾`

There are many more character references that you can use to code obscure or otherwise difficult-to-enter characters. This list should give you a good start on using some of the more popular character references.

Thus far you've focused on the first approach to specifying characters numerically in XML, which involves using decimal character references. If you're coming from a programming background, you may opt for the second approach to specifying numeric characters: hexadecimal references. A *hexadecimal reference* uses a hexadecimal number (base 16) to specify a character's numeric value. Hexadecimal references are specified similarly to decimal references, except that an x immediately precedes the number:

```
&#xNum;
```

Using this form, the copyright character with the decimal value of 169 is referenced in hexadecimal as the following:

```
&#xA9;
```

Because decimal and hexadecimal references represent two equivalent solutions to the same problem (referencing characters), there is no technical reason to choose one over the other. However, most of us are much more comfortable working with decimal numbers because it's the number system used in everyday life. It ultimately has to do with your degree of comfort with each number system; the decimal system is probably much more familiar to you.

Quick Hexadecimal Primer

If you aren't naturally a binary thinker (few of us are), you might find hexadecimal numbers to be somewhat confusing. Hexadecimal numbers are strange looking because they use the letters A–F to represent the numbers 10–15. As an example, the decimal number 60 is 3C in hexadecimal; the C represents decimal 12, whereas the 3 represents decimal 48 (3 × 16); 12 plus 48 is 60. Most programming languages denote hexadecimal numbers by preceding them with an x, which was no doubt an influence on the XML representation of hexadecimal character references.

The Wonderful World of Entities

Just as bricks serve as the building blocks of many houses, *entities* are special units of storage that serve as the building blocks of XML documents. Entities are typically identified with a unique name and are used to contain content within a document. To help understand the role of entities, it helps to think of elements as describing the logical structure of a document, whereas entities describe the physical structure. Entities often correspond with files that are stored on a file system, such as the file that holds an XML document. However, entities don't have to be associated with files in any way; an entity can be associated with a database record or even a piece of memory. The significance is that entities represent a unit of storage in an XML document.

Although most entities have names, a few notable ones do not. The *document entity*, which is the top-level entity for a document, does not have a name. The document entity is important because it serves as a storage container for the entire document. This entity is then broken down into subentities, which are often broken down further. The breakdown of entities ends when you arrive at nothing but pure content. The other entity that goes unnamed is the external DTD (Document Type Definition), if one exists. You learned in the previous hour that a DTD is used to describe the format and structure of documents created in a specific XML-based language. For example, the DTD for HTML would specify exactly how the `<img>` tag is used to mark up images.

Getting back to entities, the `TallTales.dtd` external DTD you saw in the previous hour is an entity, as is the root document element `talltales` in the `talltales.xml` document. Following is an excerpt from the `talltales.xml` document that illustrates the relationship between the external DTD and the root document element:

```
<?xml version="1.0"?>
<!DOCTYPE talltales SYSTEM "TallTales.dtd">

<talltales>
  <!-- Document markup -->
</talltales>
```

In this code, the `talltales` root element and the `TallTales.dtd` external DTD are referenced in the document type declaration. To clarify how entities are storage constructs, consider the fact that the contents of the external DTD could be directly inserted in the document type declaration, in which case it would no longer be considered an entity. What makes the DTD an entity is the fact that its storage is external. A good analogy to this concept is a JPEG image on an HTML web page. The image itself is stored externally in a JPEG file, and then referenced from the web page via an `<img>` tag. Because the storage of the image is external to the HTML document, the image is considered an entity. The `talltales.dtd` schema in the previous example works in a similar way because it is referenced externally from `talltales.xml`.

The XML document entity is a unique entity in that it is declared in the document type declaration. Most other entities are declared in an entity declaration, which must appear before the entities can be used in the document. An entity declaration consists of a unique entity name and a piece of data that is associated with the name. Following are some examples of data that you might reference as entities:

- A string of text (a boilerplate copyright notice, for example)
- A section of the DTD
- An external file containing text data (a list of email addresses, for example)
- An external file containing binary data (a GIF or JPEG image, for example)

This list reveals that entities are extremely flexible when it comes to the types of data that can be stored in them. Although the specific data within an entity can certainly vary widely, there are two basic types of entities that are used in XML documents: parsed entities and unparsed entities. *Parsed entities* store data that is parsed (processed) by an XML application, which means that parsed entities can contain only text. *Unparsed entities* aren't parsed and therefore can be either text or binary data. As an example, a text name would be a parsed entity whereas a JPEG image would be an unparsed entity.

Parsed entities end up being merged with the contents of a document when they are processed. In other words, parsed entities are directly inserted into documents as if they were directly part of the document to begin with. Unparsed entities cannot be handled in this manner because XML applications are unable to parse them. Going back to the JPEG image example, consider the difficulty of combining a binary JPEG image with the text content of an HTML document. Because binary data and text data don't mix well, unparsed entities are never merged directly with a document.

If an XML application can't process and merge an unparsed entity with the rest of a document, how does it use the entity as document data? The answer to this question lies in *notations*, which are XML constructs used to identify the entity type to an XML processor. In addition to identifying the type of an unparsed entity, a notation also specifies a helper application that can be used to process the entity. A good example of a helper application for an unparsed entity is an image viewer, which would be associated with a GIF or JPEG image entity or maybe a lesser-used image format such as TIFF. The point is that a notation tells an XML application how to handle an unparsed entity using a helper application.

By the Way

> If you've ever had your web browser prompt you for a plug-in to view a special content type such as an Adobe Acrobat file (.PDF document), you understand how important helper applications can be.

Parsed Entities

You learned that parsed entities are entities containing XML data that is processed by an XML application. There are two fundamental types of parsed entities:

- General entities
- Parameter entities

The next couple of sections explore these types of entities in more detail.

General Entities

General entities are parsed entities that are designed for use in document content. If you have a string of text that you'd like to isolate as a piece of reusable document data, a general entity is exactly what you need. A good example of such a reusable piece of text is the copyright notice for a web site, which appears the same across all pages. Before you can reference a general entity in a document, you must declare it using a general entity declaration, which takes the following form:

```
<!ENTITY EntityName EntityDef>
```

The unique name of the entity is specified in `EntityName`, whereas its associated text is specified in `EntityDef`. All entity declarations must be placed in the DTD, although you can decide whether they go in the internal or external DTD. If an entity is used only in a single document, you can place the declaration in the internal DTD; otherwise you'll want to place it in the external DTD so it can be shared. Of course, if you're using an existing XML language you may be forced to include your entity declarations in the internal DTD. Following is an example of a general entity declaration:

```
<!ENTITY copyright "Copyright &#169;2005 Michael Morrison.">
```

> Just in case you've already forgotten from earlier in the hour, the `©` character reference in the code is the copyright symbol.

You are now free to use the entity anywhere in the content of a document. General entities are referenced in document content using the entity name sandwiched between an ampersand (&) and a semicolon (;), as the following form shows:

```
&EntityName;
```

Following is an example of referencing the `copyright` entity:

```
My Life Story.
&copyright;
My name is Michael and this is my story.
```

In this example, the contents of the `copyright` entity are replaced in the text where the reference occurs, in between the title and the sentence. The `copyright` entity is an example of a general entity that you declare yourself. This is how most entities are used in XML. However, there are a handful of predefined entities in XML that you can use without declaring. I'm referring to the five predefined entities that correspond to special characters, which you learned about back in Hour 2, "Creating XML Documents." Table 4.2 lists some of the entities just in case you don't quite remember them.

TABLE 4.2 Common Entities

Character	Entity
Less-than symbol (<)	`<`
Greater-than symbol (>)	`>`
Quote symbol (")	`"`
Apostrophe symbol (')	`'`
Ampersand symbol (&)	`&`

These predefined entities serve as an exception to the rule of having to declare all entities before using them; beyond these five entities, all entities must be declared before being used in a document.

Parameter Entities

The other type of parsed entity supported in XML is the *parameter entity*, which is a general entity that is used only within a DTD. Parameter entities are used to help modularize the structure of DTDs by allowing you to store commonly used pieces of declarations. For example, you might use a parameter entity to store a list of commonly used attributes that are shared among multiple elements. As with general entities, you must declare a parameter entity before using it in a DTD. Parameter entity declarations have the following form:

```
<!ENTITY % EntityName EntityDef>
```

Parameter entity declarations are very similar to general entity declarations, with the only difference being the presence of the percent sign (%) and the space on either side of it. The unique name of the parameter entity is specified in `EntityName`, whereas the entity content is specified in `EntityDef`. Following is an example of a parameter entity declaration:

```
<!ENTITY % autoelems "year, make, model">
```

This parameter entity describes a portion of a content model that can be referenced within elements in a DTD. Keep in mind that parameter entities apply only to DTDs. Parameter entities are referenced using the entity name sandwiched between a percent sign (%) and a semicolon (;), as the following form shows:

```
%EntityName;
```

Following is an example of referencing the `autoelems` parameter entity in a hypothetical automotive DTD:

```
<!ELEMENT car (%autoelems;)>
<!ELEMENT truck (%autoelems;)>
<!ELEMENT suv (%autoelems;)>
```

This code is equivalent to the following:

```
<!ELEMENT car (year, make, model)>
<!ELEMENT truck (year, make, model)>
<!ELEMENT suv (year, make, model)>
```

It's important to note that parameter entities really come into play only when you have a large DTD with repeating declarations. Even then you should be careful how you modularize a DTD with parameter entities because it's possible to create unnecessary complexity if you layer too many parameter entities within each other.

Unparsed Entities

Unparsed entities aren't processed by XML applications and are capable of storing text or binary data. Because it isn't possible to embed the content of binary entities directly in a document as text, binary entities are always referenced from an external location, such as a file. Unlike parsed entities, which can be referenced from just about anywhere in the content of a document, unparsed entities must be referenced using an attribute of type `ENTITY` or `ENTITIES`. Following is an example of an unparsed entity declaration using the `ENTITY` attribute:

```
<!ELEMENT player EMPTY>
<!ATTLIST player
  name CDATA #REQUIRED
  position CDATA #REQUIRED
  photo ENTITY #IMPLIED>
```

In this code, `photo` is specified as an attribute of type `ENTITY`, which means that you can assign an unparsed entity to the attribute. Following is an example of how this is carried out in document content:

```
<player name="Rolly Fingers" position="pitcher" photo="rfpic" />
```

In this code, the binary entity `rfpic` is assigned to the `photo` attribute. Even though the binary entity has been properly declared and assigned, an XML application won't know how to handle it without a notation declaration, which you find out about a little later in the hour.

Internal Versus External Entities

The physical location of entities is very important in determining how entities are referenced in XML documents. Thus far I've made the distinction between parsed and unparsed entities. Another important way to look at entities is to consider how they are stored. *Internal entities* are stored within the document that references them and are parsed entities out of necessity. *External entities* are stored outside of the document that references them and can be either parsed or unparsed.

> By definition, any entity that is not internal must be external. This means that an external entity is stored outside of the document where the entity is declared. A good example of an external entity is a binary image; images are always stored in separate files from the documents that reference them.

Unparsed external entities are often binary files such as images, which obviously cannot be parsed by an XML processor. Unparsed external entities are identified using the NDATA keyword in their entity declaration; NDATA (Not DATA) simply indicates that the entity's content is not XML data.

External entity declarations are different than internal entity declarations because they must reference an external storage location. Files associated with external entities can be specified in one of two ways, depending on whether the file is located on the local file system or is publicly available on a network:

- SYSTEM—The file is located on the local file system or on a network
- PUBLIC—The file is a public-domain file located in a publicly accessible place

Watch Out!

> When specifying the location of external entities, you must always use the SYSTEM keyword to identify a file on a local system or network; the PUBLIC keyword is optional and is used in addition to the SYSTEM keyword.

The file for an external entity is specified as a URI, which is very similar to the more familiar URL. You can specify files using a relative URI, which makes it a little easier than listing a full path to a file. XML expects relative URIs to be specified relative to the document within which an entity is declared. Following is an example of declaring a JPEG image entity using a relative URI:

```
<!ENTITY skate SYSTEM "pond.jpg" NDATA JPEG>
```

In this example, the pond.jpg file must be located on the local file system in the same directory as the file (document) containing the entity declaration. The NDATA keyword is used to indicate that the entity does not contain XML data. Also, the type of the external entity is specified as JPEG. Unfortunately, XML doesn't support any built-in binary entity types such as JPEG, even though JPEG is a widely known image format. You must use notations to establish entity types for unparsed entities.

The Significance of Notations

Unparsed entities are unable to be processed by XML applications, which means that applications have no way of knowing what to do with them unless you specify helper information that allows an application to rely on a helper application to process the entity. The helper application could be a browser plug-in or a standalone application that has been installed on a user's computer. Either way, the idea is that a notation directs an XML application to a helper application so that unparsed entities can be handled in a meaningful manner. The most obvious example of this type of handling is an external binary image entity, which could be processed and displayed by an image viewer (the helper application).

Notations are used to specify helper information for an unparsed entity and are required of all unparsed entities. Following is an example of a notation that describes the JPEG image type:

```
<!NOTATION JPEG SYSTEM "image/jpeg">
```

In this example, the name of the notation is JPEG, and the helper information is `image/jpeg`, which is a universal type that identifies the JPEG image format. It is expected that an XML application could somehow use this helper information to query the system for the JPEG type in order to figure out how to view JPEG images. So, this information would come into play when an XML application encounters the following image entity:

```
<!ENTITY pond SYSTEM "pond.jpg" NDATA JPEG>
```

If you didn't want to trust the XML application to figure out how to view the image on its own, you can get more specific with notations and specify an application, as follows:

```
<!NOTATION JPEG SYSTEM "Picasa2.exe">
```

This code associates Google's popular Picasa image editing application (`Picasa2.exe`) with JPEG images so that an XML application can use it to view JPEG images. Following is an example of what a complete XML document looks like that contains a single image as an unparsed entity:

```
<?xml version="1.0" standalone="no"?>

<!DOCTYPE image [
<!NOTATION JPEG SYSTEM "Picasa2.exe ">
<!ENTITY pond SYSTEM "pond.jpg" NDATA JPEG>

<!ELEMENT image EMPTY>
<!ATTLIST image source ENTITY #REQUIRED>
]>

<image source="skate" />
```

Although this code does all the right things in terms of providing the information necessary to process and display a JPEG image, it still doesn't work in major web browsers because none of them support unparsed entities. In truth, web browsers know that the entities are unparsed; they just don't know what to do with them. Hopefully this will be remedied at some point in the future. Keep in mind, however, that although web browsers may not support unparsed entities, plenty of other XML applications and tools do support them.

Working with CDATA

Just as an XML processor doesn't process unparsed entities, you can deliberately mark content within an XML document so that it isn't processed. This type of content is known as unparsed character data, or CDATA. CDATA in a document must be specially marked so that it is treated differently than the rest of an XML document. For this reason, the part of a document containing CDATA is known as a CDATA section. You define a section of CDATA code by enclosing it within the symbols <![CDATA[and]]>. Following is an example of a CDATA section, which should make the usage of these symbols a little clearer:

```
This is my self-portrait:
<![CDATA[
   *****
  * @ @ *
  *  )  *
  * ~~~ *
   *****
]]>
```

In this example, the crude drawing of a face is kept intact because it isn't processed as XML data. If it wasn't enclosed in a CDATA section, the white space within it would be processed down to a few spaces, and the drawing would be ruined. CDATA sections are very useful any time you want to preserve the exact appearance of text. You can also place legitimate XML code in a CDATA section to temporarily disable it and keep it from being processed.

Using XML to Create an Online Radio

I realize that this discussion of the internals of XML documents has been mind-numbingly technical and that you haven't really done anything practical to justify the effort. Unfortunately, this is a necessary part of your XML education. However, I want to close this hour with a practical and fun example that demonstrates the use of comments and entities in the context of an online radio. By online radio, I mean a music player you can embed in a web page that is entirely driven by XML data. The radio itself is a Flash animation called Catalist Radio that was developed by Grant Hinkson of the design studio Catalist Creative (http://www.catalistcreative.com/). Grant was kind enough to allow me to use Catalist Radio as a demonstration of how to feed XML data into a practical online application.

If the idea of manipulating music data via XML appeals to you, you'll be glad to know that Hour 13, "Access Your iTunes Music Library via XML," shows you how to access and manipulate an iTunes music library with XML.

Catalist radio consists of a Flash animation that is stored in a file with a `.swf` extension, along with an HTML web page that contains the embedded Flash Player. The web page is set up to use the file `radio.xml` as the XML data source for the radio. This is the file that is of primary interest to you.

You can download the complete code for the Catalist Radio example, along with all of the code for this book, from my web site at http://www.michaelmorrison.com/.

The idea behind Catalist Radio is that you can specify multiple radio channels along with multiple songs in each channel. You can think of each channel as a playlist very much like playlists that you might already use in media players such as Windows Media Player or iTunes. When you launch the XML Radio application by opening the `radio.html` page in a browser, the first channel opens and begins playing the first song in the list. You can navigate forward and back through songs in a given channel, as well as change channels. The songs themselves must be stored as MP3 files in the same folder as the other files: `radio.html`, `radio.xml`, and `GH_radiov2.swf`.

The `radio.xml` file is where the interesting stuff takes place in the Catalist Radio application. Rather than try to lay the groundwork of how this file is structured up front, I'd rather just let you dive right into it. Listing 4.1 shows the complete XML code for the Catalist Radio example, which includes several different channels of music.

LISTING 4.1 The XML Data File for the Catalist Radio Example

```
<?xml version="1.0" encoding="UTF-8"?>

<radio>
  <station name="Rock">
    <song>
      <title>Ol&apos; 55</title>
      <composer>Tom Waits</composer>
      <file>tomwaits_ol55.mp3</file>
    </song>
    <song>
      <title>King Contrary Man</title>
      <composer>The Cult</composer>
      <file>thecult_kingcontraryman.mp3</file>
    </song>
    <song>
```

```
16:       <title>Drunken Chorus</title>
17:       <composer>The Trashcan Sinatras</composer>
18:       <file>trashcansinatras_drunkenchorus.mp3</file>
19:     </song>
20:   </station>
21:   <station name="Rap">
22:     <song>
23:       <title>Follow the Leader</title>
24:       <composer>Eric B. &amp; Rakim</composer>
25:       <file>ericbrakim_followtheleader.mp3</file>
26:     </song>
27:     <song>
28:       <title>My Philosophy</title>
29:       <composer>Boogie Down Productions</composer>
30:       <file>bdp myphilosophy.mp3</file>
31:     </song>
32:     <song>
33:       <title>I Pioneered This</title>
34:       <composer>M.C. Shan</composer>
35:       <file>mcshan_ipioneeredthis.mp3</file>
36:     </song>
37:   </station>
38: <!-- DISABLE COUNTRY
39:   <station name="Country">
40:     <song>
41:       <title>Mama Tried</title>
42:       <composer>Merle Haggard</composer>
43:       <file>merlehaggard_mamatried.mp3</file>
44:     </song>
45:     <song>
46:       <title>A Boy Named Sue</title>
47:       <composer>Johnny Cash</composer>
48:       <file>johnnycash_aboynamedsue.mp3</file>
49:     </song>
50:     <song>
51:       <title>Big Iron</title>
52:       <composer>Marty Robbins</composer>
53:       <file>martyrobbins_bigiron.mp3</file>
54:     </song>
55:   </station>
56: -->
57: </radio>
```

This code isn't quite as tricky as you might initially think given its size. What you're seeing is three different channels that are specified via the `<station>` tag (lines 4, 21, and 39). Notice that the name of each station is identified using the `name` attribute. Within each station, songs are coded using the `<song>` tag. And finally, within each song element you provide the song specifics via the `title`, `composer`, and `file` elements.

Of particular interest in this code is how comments are used. Notice that a comment appears about two-thirds of the way down the document (line 38), and doesn't close until near the end of the document (line 56). The effect is that the country music station is completely ignored by the Catalist Radio application, and therefore is disabled. This is a perfect example of how you can use comments in XML code to temporarily remove a section of code.

Entities are also used in the `radio.xml` document to handle characters in the names of song titles and song composers. For example, the apostrophe in the Tom Waits song "Ol' 55" is specified using the `'` entity (line 6). Similarly, the ampersand in the rap artist name "Eric B. & Rakim" is specified using the `&` entity (line 24).

You're no doubt itching to see what this code actually does in the context of the Catalist Radio application. Figure 4.1 shows the Tom Waits song "Ol' 55" playing using the Catalist Radio application.

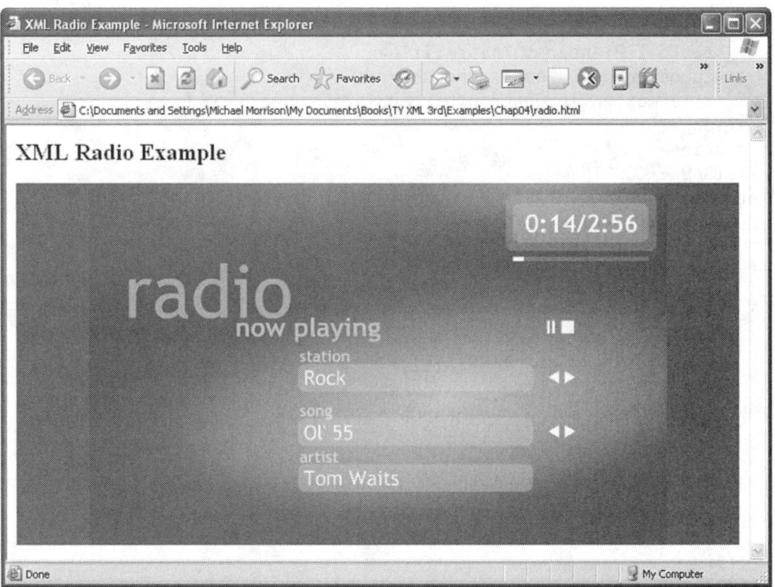

FIGURE 4.1 Catalist Radio provides a way to organize and play MP3 music online via an XML data feed.

Keep in mind that all you have to do create your own Catalist Radio online music player is to change the `radio.xml` file to reference your songs and then publish the application files and MP3 songs to the Web.

By the Way

> If you download the sample code for Catalist Radio and open radio.html in a web browser, you won't hear any music because I haven't provided the actual MP3 files. You'll have to modify radio.xml to use your own MP3 music. The last thing I need is the Recording Industry Association of America breathing down my neck for illegally distributing copyrighted music!

Summary

Although the code for many XML documents is somewhat self-explanatory, there are situations where it can be beneficial to provide additional information about XML code using comments or even temporarily disable XML code with comments. This hour showed you how to use comments, which allow you to make your code easier to understand. In addition to comments, you also learned how characters of text are encoded in an XML document. Although you might never change the character encoding scheme of your documents from the default setting, it is nonetheless important to understand why there are different encoding options.

After learning about comments and character encoding schemes, you spent the bulk of this hour getting acquainted with entities. You found out about parsed entities and unparsed entities, as well as the difference between internal and external entities. From there you learned the significance of notations and how they affect unparsed entities. Finally, the hour concluded with a practical XML application that allowed you to create an online radio driven by an XML document.

Q&A

Q. ***How exactly are parsed entities merged with document content?***

A. You can think of the merger of parsed entities with document content as a search-and-replace operation. For example, if you had a certain word in a word processor document that you wanted to replace with a phrase, you would perform a search-and-replace, which replaces each occurrence of the word with the phrase. Parsed entities work in a very similar manner, except that the word is the entity reference and the phrase is the entity data; an XML processor carries out the search-and-replace process.

Q. ***Why is it necessary to use notations for familiar binary data types such as GIF and JPEG images?***

A. GIF and JPEG images are "familiar" only within the context of a web browser, which is inherently associated with HTML. XML is a much broader technology that doesn't necessarily have a direct tie with a web browser. Therefore, no partiality is given to web data types over any other data types. XML's approach is to require notations for all binary entities.

Q. ***Why would I ever want to place text in an external entity?***

A. Although any text could be included directly in an XML document as an internal entity, any large pieces of text that are shared among several documents would benefit greatly from being placed in external files. The storage of these entities would then be isolated in one place, and they could simply be referenced by each document.

Workshop

The Workshop is designed to help you anticipate possible questions, review what you've learned, and begin learning how to put your knowledge into practice.

Quiz

1. How do you identify a comment in an XML document?
2. What is the significance of the document entity?
3. If you needed to reference a binary image file in an XML document, what kind of entity would you use?
4. What is the difference between internal and external entities?

Quiz Answers

1. Comments are specified in a document between the `<!--` and `-->` symbols.
2. The document entity is the top-level entity for a document and contains all other entities in the document.
3. In order to reference binary data in an external file, you must use an unparsed entity.
4. Internal entities are stored within the document that references them and are always parsed entities. External entities are stored outside of the document that references them and can be either parsed or unparsed entities.

Exercises

1. Change the comments in the `radio.xml` example document so that the Rap station is disabled and the Country station is enabled.
2. Modify the `trainlog.xml` example document so that it uses general entities for each of the training locations: Warner Park and Natchez Trace Parkway. These entities eliminate the need to repeatedly enter the locations as additional training sessions are entered.

HOUR 5

Putting Namespaces to Use

> Namespaces and whitespace; anything that ends with "space" in XML is a pain in the butt.
>
> —Jason Hunter

Although it's true that namespaces have caused their fair share of confusion in the XML community, they nonetheless represent a reasonable solution to a tricky problem that is inherent in XML. As you know, XML allows you to create custom markup languages, which are languages that contain elements and attributes of your own creation. XML is incredibly flexible in this regard, but there is nothing stopping two people from creating markup languages with very similar, if not identical, elements and attributes. What happens if you need to use both of these markup languages in a single document? There would obviously be a clash between identically named elements and attributes in the languages. Fortunately, as you will learn in this hour, namespaces provide an elegant solution to this problem.

In this hour, you'll learn

- Why namespaces are important to XML
- How namespace names are guaranteed to be unique
- How to declare and reference namespaces in XML documents
- How to use namespaces to merge schemas

Understanding Namespaces

As a young kid I was often confused by the fact that two people could have the same name yet not be related. It just didn't register with me that it's possible for two families to exist independently of one another with the same last name. Of course, now I understand why it's possible, but I'm still kind of bummed by the fact that I'm not the only Michael Morrison walking around. In fact, I'm not even close to being the most famous Michael Morrison—the real name of John Wayne, the famous actor, was actually Marlon Michael Morrison. But I digress.

The reason I bring up the issue of people having the same names yet not being related is because it parallels the problem in XML when different markup languages have elements and attributes that are named the same. The XML problem is much more severe, however, because XML applications aren't smart enough to judge the difference between the context of elements from different markup languages that share the same name. For example, a tag named `<goal>` would have a very different meaning in a sports markup language than the same tag in a markup language for a daily planner. If you ever used these two markup languages within the same application, it would be very important for the application to know when you're talking about a goal in hockey and when you're talking about a personal goal. The responsibility falls on the XML developer to ensure that uniqueness abounds when it comes to the elements and attributes used in documents. Fortunately, namespaces make it possible to enforce such uniqueness without too much of a hassle.

A *namespace* is a collection of element and attribute names that can be used in an XML document. To draw a comparison between an XML namespace and the real world, if you considered the first names of all the people in your immediate family, they would belong to a namespace that encompasses your last name. When I call my brother by his first name, Steve, it is implied that his last name is Morrison because he is within the Morrison namespace. XML namespaces are similar because they represent groups of names for related elements and attributes. Most of the time an individual namespace corresponds directly to a custom markup language, but that doesn't necessarily have to be the case. You also know that namespaces aren't a strict requirement of XML documents, as you haven't really used them throughout the book thus far.

The purpose of namespaces is to eliminate name conflicts between elements and attributes. To better understand how this type of name clash might occur in your own XML documents, consider an XML document that contains information about a video and music collection. You might use a custom markup language unique to each type of information (video and music), which means that each language would have its own elements and attributes. However, you are using both languages within the context of a single XML document, which is where the potential for problems arises. If both markup languages include an element named `title` that represents the title of a video or music compilation, there is no way for an XML application to know which language you intended to use for the element. The solution to this problem is to assign a namespace to each of the markup languages, which will then provide a clear distinction between the elements and attributes of each language when they are used.

In order to fully understand namespaces, you need a solid grasp on the concept of scope in XML documents. The scope of an element or attribute in a document refers to the relative location of the element or attribute within the document. If you visualize the elements in a document as an upside-down tree that begins at the top with the root element, child elements of the root element appear just below the root element as branches (see Figure 5.1). Each element in a "document tree" is known as a *node*. Nodes are very important when it comes to processing XML documents because they determine the relationship between parent and child elements. The *scope* of an element refers to its location within this hierarchical tree of elements. So, when I refer to the scope of an element or attribute, I'm talking about the node in which the element or attribute is stored.

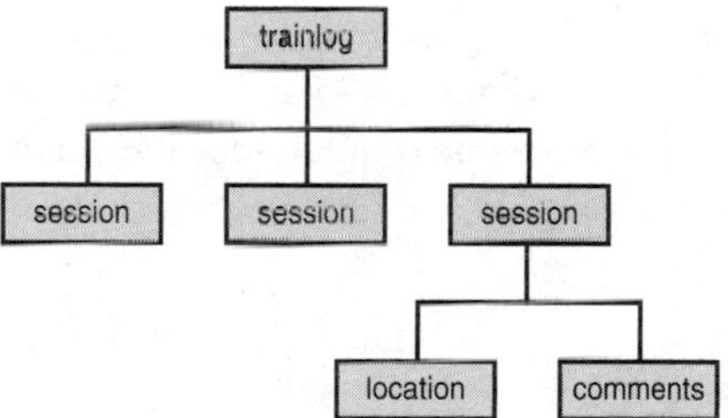

FIGURE 5.1
An XML document coded in ETML can be visualized as a hierarchical tree of elements, where each leaf in the tree is known as a node.

In this figure, the hypothetical ETML example markup language first mentioned in Hour 3, "Defining Data with DTD Schemas," is used to demonstrate how an XML document consists of a hierarchical tree of elements. Each node in the tree of an XML document has its own scope, and can therefore have its own namespace.

Scope is important to namespaces because it's possible to use a namespace within a given scope, which means it affects only elements and attributes beneath a particular node. Contrast this with a namespace that has global scope, which means the namespace applies to the entire document. Any guess as to how you might establish a global namespace? It's easy—you just associate it with the root element, which by definition houses the remainder of the document. You learn much more about scope as it applies to namespaces throughout the remainder of this hour. Before you get to that, however, it's time to learn where namespace names come from.

Naming Namespaces

The whole point of namespaces is that they provide a means of establishing unique identifiers for elements and attributes. It is therefore imperative that each and every namespace have a unique name. Obviously, there would be no way to enforce this rule if everyone was allowed to make up their own names out of thin air, so a clever naming scheme was established that tied namespaces to URIs (Uniform Resource

Identifiers). URIs usually reference physical resources on the Internet and are guaranteed to be unique. So, a namespace is essentially the name of a URI. For example, my web site is located at http://www.michaelmorrison.com. To help guarantee name uniqueness in any XML documents that I create, I could associate the documents with my namespace:

```
<mediacollection xmlns:mov="http://www.michaelmorrison.com/ns/movies">
```

The ns in the namespace name http://www.michaelmorrison.com/ns/movies stands for "namespace" and is often used in URL namespace names. It isn't a necessity but it's not a bad idea in terms of being able to quickly identify namespaces. If you don't want to use a URI as the basis for a namespace name, you could also use the URN (Universal Resource Name) of a web resource to guarantee uniqueness. URNs are slightly different from URLs and define a unique location-independent name for a resource that maps to one or more URLs. Following is an example of using a URN to specify a namespace for my web site:

```
<mediacollection xmlns:mov="urn:michaelmorrison.com:ns:movies">
```

Making Sense of URLs, URNs, and URIs

There is often confusion among XML developers regarding the relationship between URLs, URNs, and URIs. Perhaps the most important distinction to make is that URIs encompass both URLs and URNs. URNs differ from URLs in that URLs describe the physical location of a particular resource, whereas URNs define a unique location-independent name for a resource that maps to one or more URLs. An easy way to distinguish between URLs and URNs is to examine their names: URLs all begin with an Internet service prefix such as `ftp:`, `http:`, and so on, whereas URNs typically begin with the `urn:` prefix.

Keep in mind that a namespace doesn't actually point to a physical resource, even if its URI does. In other words, the only reason namespaces are named after URIs is because URIs are guaranteed to be unique—they could just as easily be named after social security numbers. This means that within a domain name you can create URIs that don't actually reference physical resources. So, although there may not be a directory named `pets` on my web server, I can still use a URI named http://www.michaelmorrison.com/ns/pets to name a namespace. The significance is that the michaelmorrison.com domain name is mine and is therefore guaranteed to be unique. This is important because it allows you to organize XML documents based upon their respective namespaces while guaranteeing uniqueness among the namespace names.

Declaring and Using Namespaces

Namespaces are associated with documents by way of elements, which means that you declare a namespace for a particular element with the scope you want for the namespace. More specifically, you use a *namespace declaration*, which looks a lot like an attribute of the element. In many cases you want a namespace to apply to an entire document, which means you'll use the namespace declaration with the root element. A namespace declaration takes the following form:

```
xmlns:Prefix="NameSpace"
```

The `xmlns` attribute is what notifies an XML processor that a namespace is being declared. The `NameSpace` portion of the namespace declaration is where the namespace itself is identified. This portion of the declaration identifies a URI that guarantees uniqueness for elements and attributes used within the scope of the namespace declaration.

The `Prefix` part of the namespace declaration allows you to set a prefix that will serve as a shorthand reference for the namespace throughout the scope of the element in which the namespace is declared. The prefix of a namespace is optional and ultimately depends on whether you want to use qualified or unqualified element and attribute names throughout a document. A qualified name includes the `Prefix` portion of the namespace declaration and consists of two parts: the prefix and the local portion of the name. Examples of qualified names include `mov:title`, `mov:director`, and `mov:rating`. To use qualified names, you must provide `Prefix` in the namespace declaration. Following is a simple example of a qualified name:

```
<mov:title>Raising Arizona</mov:title>
```

> Declaring a namespace in an XML document is a little like declaring a variable in a programming language—the declared namespace is available for use but doesn't actually enter the picture until you specify an element with a qualified name.

In this example, the prefix is `mov` and the local portion of the name is `title`. Unqualified names don't include a prefix and are either associated with a default namespace or no namespace at all. The prefix of the namespace declaration isn't required when declaring a default namespace. Examples of unqualified names are `title`, `director`, and `rating`. Unqualified names in a document look no different than if you weren't using namespaces at all. The following code shows how the movie example would be coded using unqualified names:

```
<title>Raising Arizona</title>
```

Notice that in this example the <title> and </title> tags are used so that you would never know a namespace was involved. In this case, you are either assuming a default namespace is in use or that there is no namespace at all.

It's important to clarify why you would use qualified or unqualified names because the decision to use one or the other determines the manner in which you declare a namespace. There are two different approaches to declaring namespaces:

- Default declaration—The namespace is declared without a prefix; all element and attribute names within its scope are referenced using unqualified names and are assumed to be in the namespace.
- Explicit declaration—The namespace is declared with a prefix; all element and attribute names associated with the namespace must use the prefix as part of their qualified names or else they are not considered part of the namespace.

The next sections dig a little deeper into these namespace declarations.

Default Namespaces

Default namespaces represent the simpler of the two approaches to namespace declaration. A *default namespace declaration* is useful when you want to apply a namespace to an entire document or section of a document. When declaring a default namespace, you don't use a prefix with the xmlns attribute. Instead, elements are specified with unqualified names and are therefore assumed to be part of the default namespace. In other words, a default namespace declaration applies to all unqualified elements within the scope in which the namespace is declared. Following is an example of a default namespace declaration for a movie collection document:

```
<mediacollection xmlns="http://www.michaelmorrison.com/ns/movies">
  <movie type="comedy" rating="PG-13" review="5" year="1987">
    <title>Raising Arizona</title>
    <comments>A classic one-of-a-kind screwball love story.</comments>
  </movie>

  <movie type="comedy" rating="R" review="5" year="1988">
    <title>Midnight Run</title>
    <comments>The quintessential road comedy.</comments>
  </movie>
</mediacollection>
```

In this example, the http://www.michaelmorrison.com/ns/movies namespace is declared as the default namespace for the movie document. This means that all the unqualified elements in the document (mediacollection, movie, title, and so on) are assumed to be part of the namespace. A default namespace can also be set for any other element in a document, in which case it applies only to that element and its children. For example, you could set a namespace for one of the `title` elements, which would override the default namespace that is set in the `mediacollection` element. Following is an example of how this is done:

```
<mediacollection xmlns="http://www.michaelmorrison.com/ns/movies">
  <movie type="comedy" rating="PG-13" review="5" year="1987">
    <title>Raising Arizona</title>
    <comments>A classic one-of-a-kind screwball love story.</comments>
  </movie>

  <movie type="comedy" rating="R" review="5" year="1988">
    <title xmlns="http://www.michaelmorrison.com/ns/title">Midnight Run</title>
    <comments>The quintessential road comedy.</comments>
  </movie>
</mediacollection>
```

Notice in the `title` element for the second `movie` element that a different namespace is specified. This namespace applies only to the `title` element and overrides the namespace declared in the `mediacollection` element. Although this admittedly simple example doesn't necessarily make a good argument for why you would override a namespace, it can be a bigger issue in documents where you mix different XML languages.

By the Way

> Generally speaking, default namespaces work better when you're dealing with a single namespace. When you start incorporating multiple namespaces, it is better to explicitly refer to each namespace using a prefix.

Explicit Namespaces

An explicit namespace is useful whenever you want exacting control over the elements and attributes that are associated with a namespace. This is often necessary in documents that rely on multiple schemas because there is a chance of having a name clash between elements and attributes defined in the two schemas. *Explicit namespace declarations* require a prefix that is used to distinguish elements and attributes that belong to the namespace being declared. The prefix in an explicit declaration is used as a shorthand notation for the namespace throughout the scope in which the namespace is declared. More specifically, the prefix is paired with the local element or attribute name to form a qualified name of the form `Prefix:Local`. Following is the movie example with qualified element and attribute names:

```
<mediacollection xmlns:mov="http://www.michaelmorrison.com/ns/movies">
  <mov:movie mov:type="comedy" mov:rating="PG-13" mov:review="5" mov:year="1987">
    <mov:title>Raising Arizona</mov:title>
    <mov:comments>A classic one-of-a-kind screwball love story.</mov:comments>
  </mov:movie>
```

```
  <mov:movie mov:type="comedy" mov:rating="R" mov:review="5" mov:year="1988">
    <mov:title>Midnight Run</mov:title>
    <mov:comments>The quintessential road comedy.</mov:comments>
  </mov:movie>
</mediacollection>
```

The namespace in this code is explicitly declared by the shorthand name `mov` in the namespace declaration; this is evident in the fact that the name `mov` is specified after the `xmlns` keyword. Once the namespace is declared, you can use it with any element and attribute names that belong in the namespace, which in this case is all of them.

I mentioned earlier that one of the primary reasons for using explicit namespaces is when multiple schemas are being used in a document. In this situation, you will likely declare both namespaces explicitly and then use them appropriately to identify elements and attributes throughout the document. Listing 5.1 is an example of a media collection document that combines both movies and music information into a single format.

LISTING 5.1 The Media Collection Example Document

```
<?xml version="1.0"?>

<mediacollection xmlns:mov="http://www.michaelmorrison.com/ns/movies"
  xmlns:mus="http://www.michaelmorrison.com/ns/music">
  <mov:movie mov:type="comedy" mov:rating="PG-13" mov:review="5"
    mov:year="1987">
    <mov:title>Raising Arizona</mov:title>
    <mov:comments>A classic one-of-a-kind screwball love story.
    </mov:comments>
  </mov:movie>

  <mov:movie mov:type="comedy" mov:rating="R" mov:review="5" mov:year="1988">
    <mov:title>Midnight Run</mov:title>
    <mov:comments>The quintessential road comedy.</mov:comments>
  </mov:movie>

  <mus:music mus:type="indy" mus:review="5" mus:year="1990">
    <mus:title>Cake</mus:title>
    <mus:artist>The Trash Can Sinatras</mus:artist>
    <mus:label>Polygram Records</mus:label>
    <mus:comments>Excellent acoustical instruments and extremely witty
      lyrics.</mus:comments>
  </mus:music>

  <mus:music mus:type="rock" mus:review="5" mus:year="1991">
    <mus:title>Travelers and Thieves</mus:title>
    <mus:artist>Blues Traveler</mus:artist>
    <mus:label>A&amp;M Records</mus:label>
    <mus:comments>The best Blues Traveler recording, period.</mus:comments>
  </mus:music>
</mediacollection>
```

By the Way

> Just because attributes are considered parts of elements, they don't have to be fully qualified with a namespace prefix. As the media collection example reveals, attributes require a namespace prefix in order to be referenced as part of a namespace.

In this code, the mov and mus namespaces (lines 3 and 4) are explicitly declared in order to correctly identify the elements and attributes for each type of media. Notice that without these explicit namespaces it would be difficult for an XML processor to tell the difference between the title and comments elements because they are used in both movie and music entries.

> When you actually start using XML languages that aren't of your own creation, you'll specify a namespace that doesn't involve your own URI. For example, the namespace for the SVG (Scalable Vector Graphics) markup language that you learn about in the next hour is http://www.w3.org/2000/svg.

Just to help hammer home the distinction between default and explicit namespace declarations, let's take a look at one more example. This time the media collection declares the movie namespace as the default namespace and then explicitly declares the music namespace using the mus prefix. The end result is that the movie elements and attributes don't require a prefix when referenced, whereas the music elements and attributes do. Check out the code in Listing 5.2 to see what I mean.

LISTING 5.2 A Different Version of the Media Collection Example Document That Declares the Movie Namespace as a Default Namespace

```
<?xml version="1.0"?>

<mediacollection xmlns="http://www.michaelmorrison.com/ns/movies"
  xmlns:mus="http://www.michaelmorrison.com/ns/music">
  <movie type="comedy" rating="PG-13" review="5" year="1987">
    <title>Raising Arizona</title>
    <comments>A classic one-of-a-kind screwball love story.</comments>
  </movie>

  <movie type="comedy" rating="R" review="5" year="1988">
    <title>Midnight Run</title>
    <comments>The quintessential road comedy.</comments>
  </movie>

  <mus:music mus:type="indy" mus:review="5" mus:year="1990">
    <mus:title>Cake</mus:title>
    <mus:artist>The Trash Can Sinatras</mus:artist>
    <mus:label>Polygram Records</mus:label>
    <mus:comments>Excellent acoustical instruments and extremely witty
      lyrics.</mus:comments>
  </mus:music>
```

LISTING 5.2 Continued

```
22:
23:   <mus:music mus:type="rock" mus:review="5" mus:year="1991">
24:     <mus:title>Travelers and Thieves</mus:title>
25:     <mus:artist>Blues Traveler</mus:artist>
26:     <mus:label>A&amp;M Records</mus:label>
27:     <mus:comments>The best Blues Traveler recording, period.</mus:comments>
28:   </mus:music>
29: </mediacollection>
```

The key to this code is the default namespace declaration, which is identified by the lone xmlns attribute (line 3); the xmlns:mus attribute explicitly declares the music namespace (line 4). When the xmlns attribute is used by itself with no associated prefix, it is declaring a default namespace, which in this case is the music namespace.

Summary

If you're familiar with the old sitcom *Newhart*, you no doubt remember the two brothers who were both named Darrel. Although brothers with the same first name make for good comedy, similar names in XML documents can be problematic. I'm referring to name clashes that can occur when elements and attributes are named the same across multiple custom markup languages. This problem can be easily avoided by using namespaces, which allow you to associate elements and attributes with a unique name. Namespaces are an important part of XML because they solve the problem of name clashing among XML documents.

This hour introduced you to namespaces and also gave you some practical insight regarding how they are used in XML documents. You began the hour by learning the basics of namespaces and their significance to XML. From there you learned how namespaces are named. You then found out how to declare and use namespaces in documents. And finally, the hour concluded by revisiting XSD schemas and uncovering a few interesting tricks involving schemas and namespaces.

Q&A

Q. ***When a name clash occurs in an XML document, why can't an XML processor resolve it by looking at the scope of the elements and attributes, as opposed to requiring namespaces?***

A. Although it is technically possible for an XML processor to resolve an element or attribute based solely on its scope, it isn't a good idea to put that much faith in the processor. Besides, there are some situations where this simply isn't possible. For example, what if the element causing the name clash is the root element in a document? Because it has a global scope, there is no way to determine the schema to which it belongs.

Q. *Do I have to use a namespace to uniquely identify the elements and attributes in my custom markup language?*

A. No. In fact, if you plan on using your XML documents internally and never sharing them with others, there really is no pressing need to declare a unique namespace. However, if you choose to incorporate multiple XML-based markup languages within a single document or application, you'll need to use namespaces to keep things straight and not confuse the XML processor.

Workshop

The Workshop is designed to help you anticipate possible questions, review what you've learned, and begin learning how to put your knowledge into practice.

Quiz

1. Why are namespaces named after URIs?
2. What is the general form of a namespace declaration?
3. What is the difference between default and explicit namespace declaration?

Quiz Answers

1. Namespaces are named after URIs because URIs are guaranteed to be unique.
2. The general form of a namespace declaration is `xmlns:Prefix="NameSpace"`.
3. A default namespace declaration is useful when you want to apply a namespace to an entire document or section of a document, whereas an explicit namespace is useful whenever you want exacting control over the elements and attributes that are associated with a namespace.

Exercises

1. Using a domain name that you or your company owns, determine a unique namespace name that you could use with the Tall Tales document from previous hours.
2. Modify the Tall Tales document so that the elements and attributes defined in its schema are associated with the namespace you just created.

HOUR 6

Using SVG to Draw Scalable Graphics

> One picture is worth 1,000 words.
>
> —Unknown

Ever since the early days of the Web, HTML has supported images on web pages. However, we've had to limit ourselves to primitive, static bitmap files. As you may or may not know, bitmap files are somewhat inefficient because they describe images using thousands of little rectangles called pixels. Although bitmaps are necessary for photo-realistic images, a type of graphic approach known as *vector graphics* is actually much more efficient for many kinds of web graphics. If you've ever watched a Macromedia Flash animation or visited a web site built in Flash, you already have some idea of what vector graphics can do. There are a few vector graphics file formats supported on the web, including Flash, but XML makes it possible to construct vector graphic images directly on web pages using straight XML code. Using a plug-in such as Adobe's SVG Viewer, web browsers are able to process SVG (*Scalable Vector Graphics*) images just as they do bitmap images such as GIF, JPEG, and PNG images.

As with any promising new web medium, SVG defines new spaces for development and creativity. Unlike other static image formats, an SVG-format image is scriptable; it can be referenced and manipulated with JavaScript and other scripting languages. You could, for example, customize the text in an SVG graphic so that it is displayed in whatever language the browser specifies. You could also process a database of map information from a web page and construct a graphical map as an SVG image. And talk about graphics capabilities! Photoshop and Illustrator enthusiasts will be impressed at the range of features SVG offers. Besides the basic shapes, colors, and strokes, you can take advantage of animation, clipping, masking, and gradient capabilities—all in a text file!

Needless to say, I could fill a book with everything you can do with SVG. But for the next hour, you'll explore the rudiments and just a couple of the more advanced features. This includes the following:

- Why to use SVG
- How to configure your browser to handle the SVG format

- The basics of shapes, lines, and colors
- Placing text on a path
- Rotating a shape

Those who have worked with drawing programs will have a good frame of reference for the material that follows, but readers new to computer graphics will also find this an easy entry point.

What Is SVG?

SVG is an XML application designed for the creation of vector graphics. It was created by the World Wide Web Consortium with the collaboration of industry players like Adobe. For a thorough treatment of SVG, its specifications, supporting documents, and related products, please see the W3C and Adobe Web sites:

- http://www.w3.org/Graphics/SVG/
- http://www.adobe.com/svg/

The current SVG specification is version 1.1, although version 1.2 is in the works. The current version of Adobe's browser plug-in is 3.0. The SVG Viewer browser plug-in is a free download that you can get from Adobe's web site (mentioned above).

Bitmap Versus Vector Graphics

Before getting into the details of SVG, it's worth asking the question "what are vector graphics?" First of all, keep in mind that the idea behind all graphics technologies is to describe the appearance of a graphical object using some kind of inherently non-graphical scheme. The specifics of each scheme used to represent a graphical object are ultimately what determine the differences between graphics formats. Though not necessarily superior to bitmap, or raster, graphics, vector graphics have several characteristics that make them just the right tool for the job in many circumstances.

A bitmap image file is a list of instructions on how the monitor or printer should render each rectangular dot, or pixel, that comprises an image. If an image measures 64 × 64 pixels, that means a total of 4,096 separate instructions, each with its own recipe of red, green, and blue components. And this is a tiny icon-sized graphic! Although it is very accurate at representing complex images, such as photographs, bitmap technology results in very large image files—slow to transmit, tedious to edit, and very difficult to interact with dynamically. On the other hand, they remain the tool of choice for photographs and other images where subtle gradations of tone are critical.

Vector graphics are the result of mathematical equations instead of thousands of pixels. SVG stands for Scalable Vector Graphics—a somewhat redundant term because vector graphics are scalable by definition. They are composed of a series of mathematical equations that describe graphics objects. So, for instance, if you wanted to draw a red circle, you would simply specify the center point, the radius, and the color, and SVG takes care of the details of rendering the red circle on the screen. The actual pixels that go into drawing the circle are irrelevant to SVG. To modify your drawing, you'd simply go in and change the parameters of the graphical objects being drawn. To modify the same picture with bitmap technology, by contrast, you would have to change the instructions for every pixel affected, up to thousands or millions. Because vector graphics are represented by mathematical equations, as opposed to pixels, they can be easily transformed and scaled while retaining a high level of quality. If you zoom in or blow up a vector graphic image, it will look much, much better than a zoomed or blown up bitmap equivalent.

In the desktop and print world, Adobe Photoshop, which produces mainly bitmap graphics, and Adobe Illustrator, which handles vector formats, typify the two different graphics approaches. They are also referred to as painting and drawing applications, respectively. It is worthwhile to note that, although you can create SVG files in any text editor (like any other XML file), many current graphics programs offer the capability of exporting an image to SVG without the need to get involved with the code. Please see the section "Creating an SVG Drawing" later in this hour for further discussion.

SVG and Related Technologies

Revolutionary as SVG is, it is not alone in its class of web-based vector graphics applications. Microsoft's short-lived VML (Vector Markup Language) is another XML-based solution, and Flash is a very successful proprietary format with capabilities comparable to SVG. Although Flash has enormous support across the Web, SVG is the vector graphics format being touted by the W3C, which means that it stands a good chance of eventually becoming the web standard for vector graphics. Two other developments that assist SVG in becoming a more widely supported standard are SVG Tiny (SVGT) and SVG Basic (SVGB), which are aimed at bringing SVG support to devices with more limited processing, memory, and display capabilities, such as handheld computers and mobile phones.

Microsoft's Answer to Vector Graphics

Ever loyal to its longstanding tradition of "my way or the highway," Microsoft developed its own XML application for creating graphics: VML, or Vector Markup Language. Its main advantage—at least, for existing Microsoft customers—was that it is well-integrated with Microsoft Office 2000 products. Hence, you could use the drawing tools in Word, Excel, or PowerPoint without having to leave your current workspace. Unfortunately for VML, it was never latched onto by users and ultimately gave way to SVG as the desire to have a standardized, open vector graphics format proved to be more appealing than a solution tied to Microsoft.

Macromedia Flash

Macromedia Flash provides a WYSIWYG environment for the creation and editing of vector graphics in the proprietary SWF format, with a sophisticated specialty in motion graphics. Web sites featuring Flash graphics—stunning but at times bandwidth hungry—have become quite popular and in many ways put the Web on par with television as a venue for complex and compelling animations. If nothing else, Flash has served as an excellent vehicle for delivering slick, interactive banner ads; like them or not, banner ads owe a great deal to Flash for their pizzazz. Although Flash covers the full range of SVG capabilities, its main focus is animation, and it might be considered overkill for simpler purposes. The other big distinction between Flash and SVG is that Flash relies on a proprietary binary file format, which means you can't just open up a Flash movie as a text file and view or modify it. It also means you can't generate Flash movies dynamically with script code as you can with SVG. Of course, SVG doesn't ship as a sophisticated development tool that allows you to put together complex animations with relative ease, which is Flash's forte.

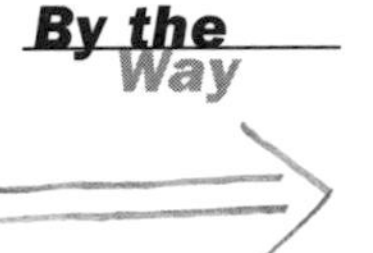

It is technically possible, albeit not entirely straightforward, to convert a Flash animation in the SWF format to an SVG document. Check out Steve Probets' Flash to SVG Converter at the following web site to learn more about how this is done: http://www.eprg.org/~sgp/swf2svg.html.

SVG for Mobile Devices

Seeing as how mobile devices are increasingly becoming the focus of online development efforts, it really should come as no surprise that SVG has been repurposed for such devices. In fact, there are two different flavors of SVG available for mobile devices: SVGT and SVGB. SVGT (SVG Tiny) is a dramatically scaled down version of SVG that targets extremely constrained mobile devices such as mobile phones. SVGB (SVG Basic) isn't as limited as SVGT, and is designed to support more powerful mobile devices such as handheld computers and PDA (Personal Digital Assistants).

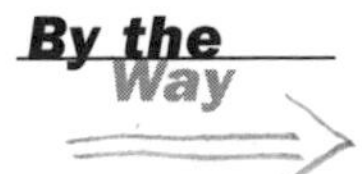

Macromedia offers a mobile version of its Flash technology that is called Flash Lite. Interestingly enough, Flash Lite supports SVGT.

Inside the SVG Language

As is the case with most XML-based languages, there are some housekeeping issues associated with SVG that you must know about before diving into the creation of SVG documents. Following are some key pieces of information related to SVG that are helpful to know as you begin learning more about the SVG language:

- SVG has four different DTDs (Document Type Definition), which are declared as follows:

```
<!DOCTYPE svg PUBLIC "-//W3C//DTD SVG 1.0//EN"
  "http://www.w3.org/TR/2001/REC-SVG-20010904/DTD/svg10.dtd">
<!DOCTYPE svg PUBLIC "-//W3C//DTD SVG 1.1//EN"
  "http://www.w3.org/Graphics/SVG/1.1/DTD/svg11.dtd">
<!DOCTYPE svg PUBLIC "-//W3C//DTD SVG 1.1 Basic//EN"
  "http://www.w3.org/Graphics/SVG/1.1/DTD/svg11-basic.dtd">
<!DOCTYPE svg PUBLIC "-//W3C//DTD SVG 1.1 Tiny//EN"
  "http://www.w3.org/Graphics/SVG/1.1/DTD/svg11-tiny.dtd">
```

- The SVG namespace is http://www.w3.org/2000/svg.
- For server considerations, the MIME type for SVG is `image/svg+xml`.

The SVG DTDs are important for SVG document validation. The first DTD is for the original version of SVG, 1.0, while the latter three DTDs refer to different variations of SVG 1.1. More specifically, the latter three DTDs refer to the full version of SVG 1.1, the basic version of SVG 1.1 (SVGB), and the tiny version of SVG 1.1 (SVGT), respectively. Although the DTDs are all important for SVG document validation, the SVG namespace is necessary for using elements and attributes within the SVG language. The SVG MIME type isn't quite as critical and really enters the picture only from a web-server perspective when SVG documents are being served to web browsers.

The Bare Bones of SVG

As with all XML documents, SVG documents are required to have a root element, which in the case of SVG is the `svg` element. Beneath the SVG element is where you place specific SVG content consisting of additional SVG elements and attributes. There are three fundamental types of graphical objects that can be used within SVG drawings:

- Primitive vector shapes (squares, circles, and so on)
- Vector text
- External bitmap images

Vector shapes are what you might typically think of as traditional vector graphics objects, with examples including lines, squares, circles, and so on. Additionally, you can include vector text, which is basically any text rendered in a mathematical font, such as a TrueType font. To style vector text, SVG makes use of CSS (Cascading Style Sheet) attributes. Please see Hour 9, "XML Formatting Strategies," and Hour 10, "Styling XML Content with CSS," for more information about using CSS to create style sheets and the section in this hour, "Drawing Shapes with SVG Child Elements," for specifics of style rule names and functions that have been adapted for use in SVG.

By the Way

> In the wider scheme of things, you can also use XSL transformations and XSL formatting objects to broaden the reach of SVG or to broaden another application's access to SVG. See Hours 11, 12, and 14 for an in-depth discussion of XSL technologies.

SVG Coordinate Systems

To render graphics on a page or monitor, a graphics application must refer to a system of coordinates that determines the size and units of measurement associated with the drawing surface. SVG supports a few different systems, depending on your specific needs. By default, SVG measures its drawing surface in arbitrary "non-dimensional local units." Whereas some shapes can be defined by pixels (px), points (pt), inches (in), or centimeters (cm), other elements can be described only in abstract units, which the browser maps to pixels on the screen. When you don't specify real-world units of measurement—for instance, when you say `r="50"` to indicate the radius of a circle—SVG uses these non-dimensional local units to determine how an object is drawn to the screen. Additionally, some graphical elements, like `path` and `polygon`, support only such units. If you need to work with real-world measurements, you must redefine the coordinate system, as discussed in the following section.

By default, the opening "canvas" of an SVG drawing is infinite, which means it has no width or height. It's generally a good idea to set the size of the canvas using the `width` and `height` attributes of the root `svg` element. You learn how this is accomplished in the next section when you start assembling your first SVG drawing. In fact, let's get started now.

Creating an SVG Drawing

As you now know, SVG is an XML-based markup language, which means that you create SVG documents in a text editor (or XML editor) using markup tags. The astute observer may well ask, "Isn't it much easier for a user to create an image in a graphics application than in a text editor?" The answer, of course, is "yes." The latest versions of all of the major drawing programs do allow you to create SVG files, and even SVGZ, the compressed variety of the format. Moreover, Adobe Illustrator offers an SVG Interactivity Palette that enables you to wire various JavaScript actions to selected parts of your image. What more could you want?

Before you put away this book and go the graphical route, let me clarify that there are reasons it might be worth your while to learn the SVG language:

- You may not want to invest in an expensive drawing application, or may not have one handy.
- WYSIWYG tools are great, but there's nothing like getting down and dirty with the code for ultimate control. You can always create a graphic in a drawing application and edit as needed in the raw SVG file.

- For collaborative projects, an image's SVG file will be more readily accessible from the web site than the original, say, Illustrator file.
- You may need to generate SVG code on the fly or import SVG code into an application, which means you need to understand how the SVG language works.

Another popular drawing application that supports SVG is CorelDraw from Corel, which is available in a Windows version. Batik, from the makers of Apache, is a dedicated Java-based SVG editor and viewer, available at http://xml.apache.org/batik. Microsoft has even jumped on the SVG bandwagon by supporting SVG in Visio, which allows you to import and export flowcharts using SVG. And finally, OpenOffice, the open source office application suite, supports SVG in its vector-based Draw application. To learn more about OpenOffice, visit it online at http://www.openoffice.org/

Before getting started creating SVG documents, it's a good idea to have a browser or viewer set up to check your work as you go. There are essentially three ways to view an SVG document:

- Web browser with native support
- Web browser with a plug-in
- Dedicated SVG viewer

Opera was the first major browser to offer built-in support for SVG, as it added support for SVGT in version 8 (http://www.opera.com/). Support for SVG is also slated for inclusion in the next major Firefox web browser, version 1.1. There is still no word on which direction Microsoft will go in supporting SVG in future releases of Internet Explorer. Fortunately, you can use Adobe's SVG Viewer plug-in if your browser of choice doesn't yet support SVG natively. There is one other

SVG-compatible browser that I haven't mentioned. I'm referring to the Amaya browser and editor, which is a "reference" browser offered by the W3C that provides native support for viewing SVG documents. You can download Amaya from http://www.w3c.org/amaya.

Adobe's SVG Viewer plug-in is available for free download at http://www.adobe.com/svg/. Until SVG is more widely accepted natively in popular browsers, I encourage you to download and use the latest version of Adobe's SVG viewer.

The Root Element

Every SVG document begins with the root element, which is svg. The svg element has many attributes and children, the most fundamental of which are described throughout this section.

The width and height elements describe the size of the drawing canvas. If no width and height elements are specified, the canvas is assumed to stretch infinitely in both dimensions. You can define these dimensions in a number of real-world units, including inches (in), centimeters (cm), points (pt), or pixels (px). Or, you can specify a percentage of the display window. If you don't indicate a unit of measurement, SVG defaults to non-dimensional local units, an arbitrary designation that it maps as it sees fit to your monitor's pixels, and displays the image at 100% of the available window space.

SVG borrows the title element from HTML to provide a means of assigning a title to SVG documents. Listing 6.1 shows a basic SVG document with a circle element that uses the attributes r, cx, and cy to define the circle, which you learn about shortly.

LISTING 6.1 A Basic SVG Document That Creates a Circle

```
<?xml version="1.0" encoding="UTF-8"?>
<!DOCTYPE svg PUBLIC "-//W3C//DTD SVG 1.1//EN"
  "http://www.w3.org/Graphics/SVG/1.1/DTD/svg11.dtd">

<svg xmlns="http://www.w3.org/2000/svg">
  <title>Circle 1</title>
  <circle r="100px" cx="200px" cy="200px"/>
</svg>
```

Figure 6.1 shows this document as viewed in the Opera web browser. Because no width or height is specified for the canvas, the canvas is assumed to extend infinitely, and therefore no bounds are placed on the drawing surface.

The width and height attributes define the space available to place your graphic. By setting the width and height attributes, you control the available drawing surface (see Listing 6.2).

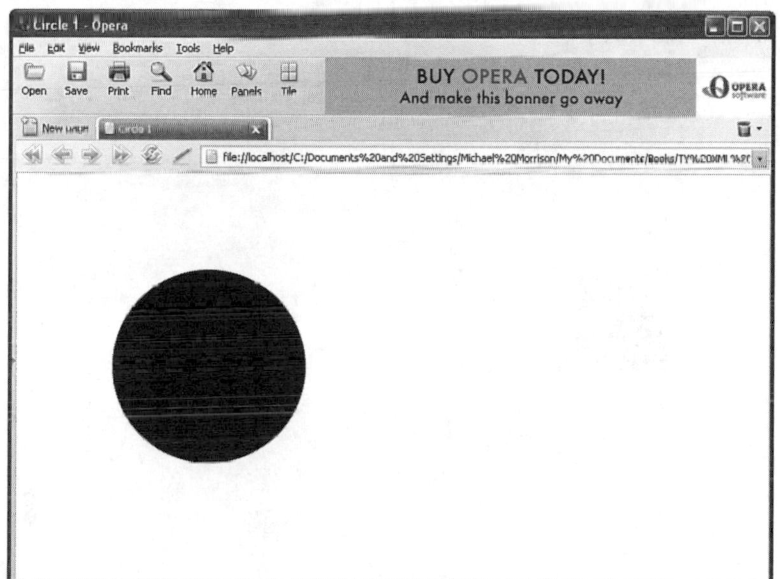

FIGURE 6.1
A simple circle is drawn with no width or height specified in the svg element.

LISTING 6.2 An SVG Document with the Width and Height Set

```
<?xml version="1.0" encoding="UTF-8"?>
<!DOCTYPE svg PUBLIC "-//W3C//DTD SVG 1.1//EN"
  "http://www.w3.org/Graphics/SVG/1.1/DTD/svg11.dtd">

<svg xmlns="http://www.w3.org/2000/svg" width="200" height="200">
  <title>Circle 2</title>
  <circle r="100px" cx="200px" cy="200px"/>
</svg>
```

Figure 6.2 shows how the width and height of the canvas in this document aren't sufficient to allow the entire circle to fit. On the other hand, if you wanted to draw only a quarter circle, this is one way to do it.

Drawing Shapes with SVG Child Elements

As you just learned, the `circle` element is used to create circles in SVG, which are one of many graphical shapes supported in SVG. These primitive graphical shapes are associated with elements in the SVG language that appear as child elements within the root svg element. Examples of such shapes include circles and rectangles, user-defined shapes like polygons, and text. The next few sections introduce you to the elements and attributes that make it possible to create graphical shapes in SVG.

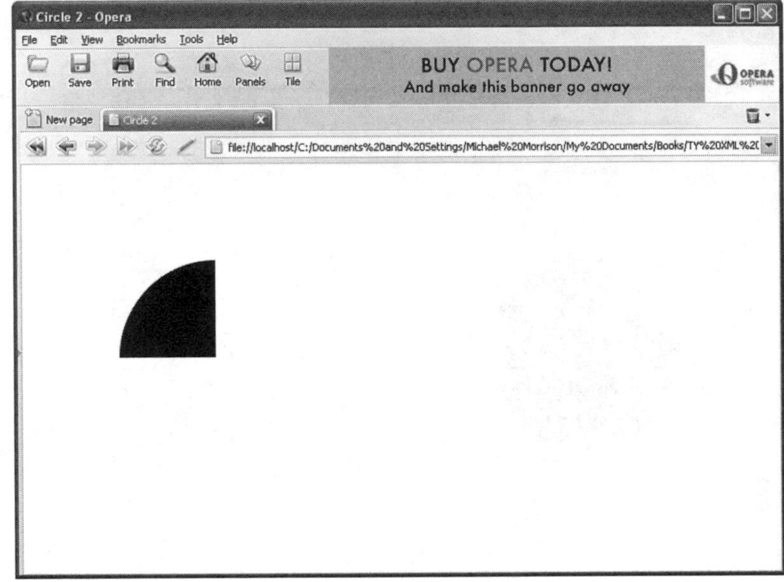

FIGURE 6.2 A circle is truncated by inadequate `width` and `height` attributes.

Rectangles

The `rect` element is used to create rectangles, and is described with four attributes:

- `x`—The horizontal coordinate, measured from an origin point of the upper-left corner of the display space
- `y`—The vertical coordinate, measured from an origin point of the upper-left corner of the display space
- `width`—The horizontal dimension of the rectangle, parallel to the x axis
- `height`—The vertical dimension of the rectangle, parallel to the y axis

Listing 6.3 contains an example of a `rect` element, which illustrates the usage of the `x`, `y`, `width`, and `height` attributes.

LISTING 6.3 A Simple SVG Rectangle

```
<?xml version="1.0" encoding="UTF-8"?>
<!DOCTYPE svg PUBLIC "-//W3C//DTD SVG 1.1//EN"
  "http://www.w3.org/Graphics/SVG/1.1/DTD/svg11.dtd">

<svg xmlns="http://www.w3.org/2000/svg">
  <title>Rectangle 1</title>
  <rect x="350" y="350" width="450" height="70"/>
</svg>
```

This code results in the shape shown in Figure 6.3.

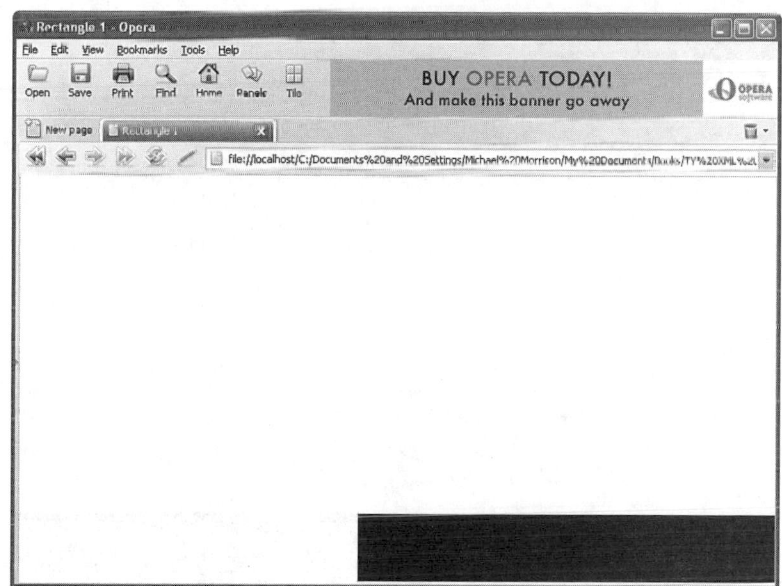

FIGURE 6.3
A simple rectangle is created using the `rect` element.

Keep in mind that you can use CSS styles in conjunction with the `style` attribute to jazz up shapes in SVG. Listing 6.4 shows the same rectangle with a different fill color and outline stroke.

> You'll learn more about fills, strokes, and stroke-widths in "Styling Shapes with CSS Style Properties" later in the hour.

LISTING 6.4 A Rectangle That Uses CSS for a Little More Style

```
<?xml version="1.0" encoding="UTF-8"?>
<!DOCTYPE svg PUBLIC "-//W3C//DTD SVG 1.1//EN"
  "http://www.w3.org/Graphics/SVG/1.1/DTD/svg11.dtd">

<svg xmlns="http://www.w3.org/2000/svg">
  <title>Rectangle 2</title>
  <rect x="350" y="350" width="450" height="70"
    style="fill:red; stroke:blue; stroke-width:10"/>
</svg>
```

Figure 6.4 shows the new and improved colored rectangle.

Should you need a rectangle oriented at an oblique angle, you have a choice of creating one with the `polygon` element, described in a moment, or of performing a transformation on the basic `rect` element.

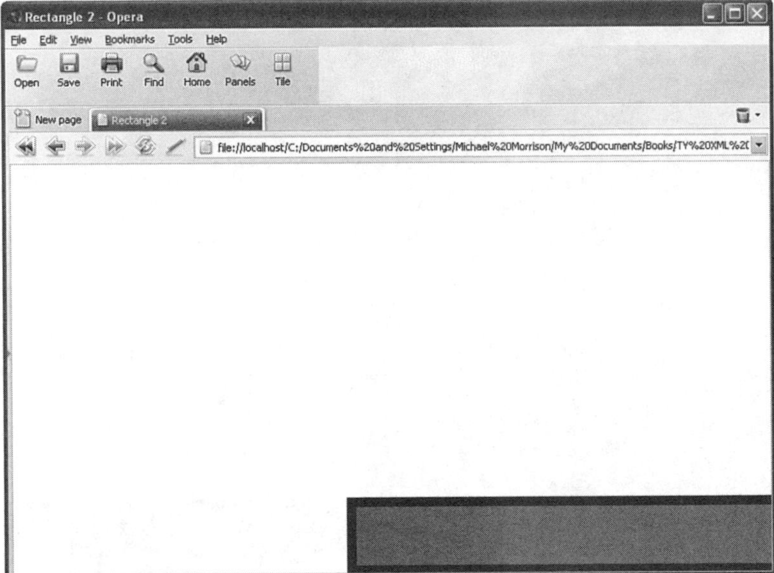

FIGURE 6.4 You can use CSS styles to add color and other effects to SVG elements.

Circles

You've already learned about the `circle` element, which has three required attributes:

- `cx`—The x coordinate of the centerpoint of the circle
- `cy`—The y coordinate of the centerpoint of the circle
- `r`—The radius of the circle in real-world units of measurement or in non-dimensional local units

Remember that the x and y coordinates are measured from the upper-left corner of the display space. Thus, for circles and ellipses, it's important to place the center point far enough into the display space to avoid truncating it, as shown earlier in Figure 6.2.

Ellipses

An ellipse is a circular shape whose width and height aren't equal, which gives it the appearance of a stretched circle. The `ellipse` element has four required attributes:

- `cx`—Horizontal coordinate of the centerpoint of the ellipse
- `cy`—Vertical coordinate of the centerpoint of the ellipse

- `rx`—The radius of the x-axis
- `ry`—The radius of the y-axis

The two radii (`rx` and `ry`) for the `ellipse` element should give you a clue as to how an ellipse differs from a circle. Listing 6.5 shows an example of how to create an ellipse using the `ellipse` element.

By the Way

> You can create a circle using the `ellipse` element by setting the `rx` and `ry` attributes to the same value. Of course, you could also use the `circle` element because that's what it's there for!

LISTING 6.5 A Simple SVG Ellipse

```
<?xml version="1.0" encoding="UTF-8"?>
<!DOCTYPE svg PUBLIC "-//W3C//DTD SVG 1.1//EN"
  "http://www.w3.org/Graphics/SVG/1.1/DTD/svg11.dtd">

<svg xmlns="http://www.w3.org/2000/svg">
  <title>Ellipse</title>
  <ellipse cx="380" cy="180" rx="190" ry="40"
    style="fill:red; stroke:blue; stroke-width:10"/>
</svg>
```

Figure 6.5 shows the ellipse as viewed in Internet Explorer with the help of the SVG Viewer plug-in.

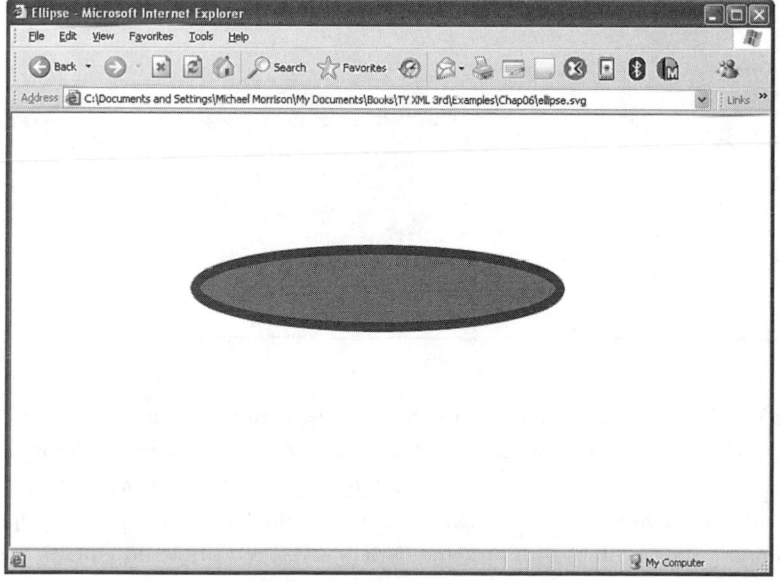

FIGURE 6.5 The `ellipse` element allows you to create ellipses.

Lines

The `line` element speaks for itself in that it allows you to create lines; a line is defined by two connected endpoints. To define a line using the line `element`, you simply specify the coordinates of the two endpoints: (x1, y1) and (x2, y2). Listing 6.6 shows an example of how to create a line.

LISTING 6.6 A Simple SVG Line

```
<?xml version="1.0" encoding="UTF-8"?>
<!DOCTYPE svg PUBLIC "-//W3C//DTD SVG 1.1//EN"
  "http://www.w3.org/Graphics/SVG/1.1/DTD/svg11.dtd">

<svg xmlns="http://www.w3.org/2000/svg">
  <title>Line</title>
  <line x1="40" y1="40" x2="240" y2="120"
    style="stroke:green; stroke-width:5"/>
</svg>
```

Figure 6.6 shows the results of this code as viewed in Internet Explorer.

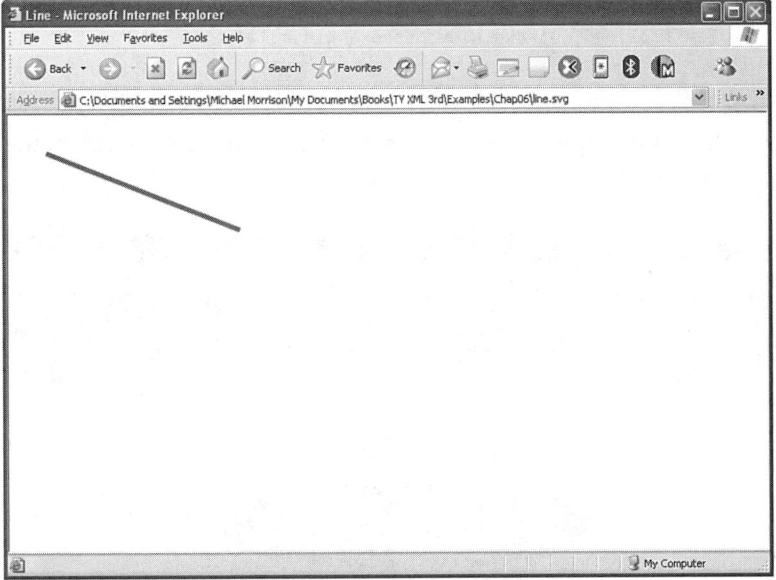

FIGURE 6.6 A simple line is drawn using the `line` element.

It's worth pointing out that you can use the `line` element to describe a polygon (a shape with multiple straight sides), but it is usually more economical to use the `polygon` element discussed in the next section or the `path` element, which is discussed a little later in the hour. The `path` element is interesting because it offers the capability of combining straight lines with arcs and Bezier curves in a single statement.

By the Way

Incidentally, a Bezier curve is a curved line defined mathematically using special equations. The curve is named after the French engineer Pierre Bezier, who used the curve for the body design of the Renault automobile.

Compound Shapes

In addition to the simple graphical objects, such as circles, rectangles, and lines, there are also some additional shapes you can draw in SVG that are more flexible. I'm referring to shapes known as *compound shapes*, two of which are supported in SVG:

- `polygon`—A closed figure consisting of an unlimited number of sides
- `polyline`—An open figure consisting of an unlimited number of sides

Polygons

A polygon is considered a compound shape because it combines an unlimited number of straight lines to create a closed figure. A polygon may be convex or concave, typified by the star and pentagon in Figure 6.7. If you're creating shapes by hand as complex as those in the figure, it's a good idea to block them out on graph paper before hacking out the SVG code.

The polygon, no matter how elaborate, is described by sequential sets of x,y coordinates in its required `points` attribute. Listing 6.7 shows the code required to draw the star and pentagon shown in Figure 6.7.

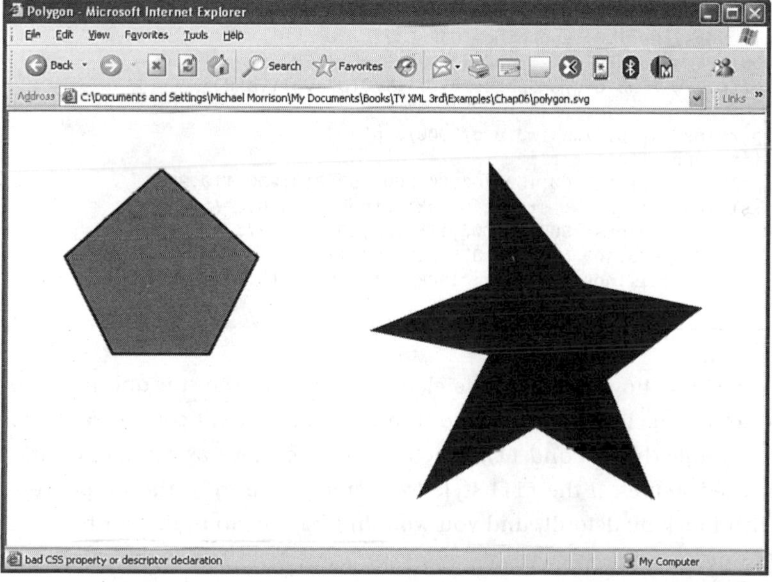

FIGURE 6.7 Polygons drawn with the `polygon` element may be concave or convex.

LISTING 6.7 A Star and Pentagon Drawn Using polygon Elements

```
 1: <?xml version="1.0" encoding="UTF-8"?>
 2: <!DOCTYPE svg PUBLIC "-//W3C//DTD SVG 1.1//EN"
 3:   "http://www.w3.org/Graphics/SVG/1.1/DTD/svg11.dtd">
 4:
 5: <svg xmlns="http://www.w3.org/2000/svg">
 6:   <title>Polygon</title>
 7:   <polygon points="60,150 160,60 260,150 210,250 110,250"
 8:     style="fill:red; stroke:black; stroke-width:3"/>
 9:   <polygon points="500,50 600,175 725,200 625,275 675,400
10:     550,325 425,400 500,250 375,225 500,175"
11:     style="fill:red stroke:black; stroke-width:3"/>
12: </svg>
```

Notice in the code that a series of points are used to describe each polygon. For example, the pentagon is described by a series of 5 points (line 7), whereas the star is described by a series of 10 points (lines 9 and 10).

Polylines

The polyline element is very similar to polygon, except there is no line drawn to close the shape. The reason for this is because polyline is used to create unclosed regions, which are shapes that don't automatically close with a final line connecting the first and last points. The best way to understand how the polyline element works is to look at how the same coordinates from the polygon example appear when used in polyline elements (see Listing 6.8).

LISTING 6.8 The polyline Element Results in the Star and Pentagon Shapes Not Quite Materializing

```
 1: <?xml version="1.0" encoding="UTF-8"?>
 2: <!DOCTYPE svg PUBLIC "-//W3C//DTD SVG 1.1//EN"
 3:   "http://www.w3.org/Graphics/SVG/1.1/DTD/svg11.dtd">
 4:
 5: <svg xmlns="http://www.w3.org/2000/svg">
 6:   <title>Polyline</title>
 7:   <polyline points="60,150 160,60 260,150 210,250 110,250"
 8:     style="fill:none; stroke:black; stroke-width:3"/>
 9:   <polyline points="500,50 600,175 725,200 625,275 675,400
10:     550,325 425,400 500,250 375,225 500,175"
11:     style="fill:none; stroke:black; stroke-width:3"/>
12: </svg>
```

Figure 6.8 shows how the polyline element results in the star and pentagon shapes not being closed. It's important to note that the fill color is set to none in this example (lines 8 and 11), which makes it easier to see the lines and the unclosed shapes. If the fill style was removed entirely, the shape would be filled with black by default, and you wouldn't be able to make out the missing line.

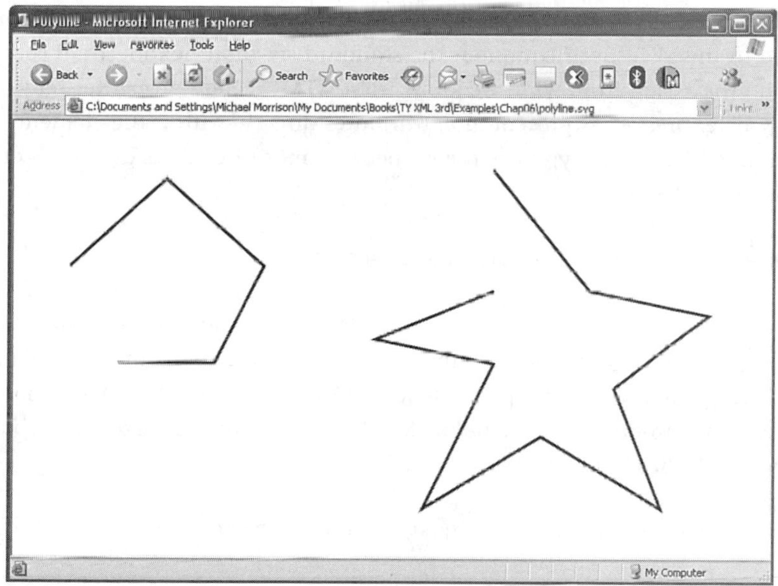

FIGURE 6.8 The `polyline` element allows you to draw connected lines that form unclosed shapes.

Styling Shapes with CSS Style Properties

As you've seen throughout the hour thus far, each child shape has its own unique attributes, which are required to describe its dimensions and other parameters. Additionally, they share CSS formatting properties, such as `stroke`, `fill`, and `stroke-width`, which are specified in the familiar CSS style attribute. These formatting properties make it possible to inject color into SVG drawings, as well as control the width of the lines used to draw different shapes. The common CSS properties used with SVG include the following:

- `stroke`—The color of the outline of the shape, or in the case of a line, the substance of the line itself.
- `fill`—The interior color of the shape. Even the `polyline` element can take a `fill` property; the viewer or browser draws an imaginary (invisible) line between the start and end points.
- `stroke-width`—The thickness of the stroke, often given in points.

There are many, many more CSS formatting properties you can use with SVG. Please consult the CSS specification at http://www.w3.org/TR/REC-CSS2 for a full treatment.

The value of the stroke and fill properties is a color, either its text string name, as listed in the SVG specification, or the standard six-digit hexadecimal code following the # sign from what we know from HTML. These properties may actually be expressed as presentation attributes directly within the element definition, which means you use the property names directly as attributes of SVG elements, like this:

```
<circle ...
  stroke="black" fill="white" stroke-width="2"/>
```

In this example, ... denotes content and other optional tags. This is a little different approach than what you've seen throughout the hour where the style attribute is used to group the CSS style properties together. Following is an example of how this latter approach works, which should be familiar to you from the examples you've already seen in this hour:

```
<circle ...
  style="stroke: black; fill: white; stroke-width: 2pt"/>
```

There is one other approach you can use if you want to associate a set of common formatting properties with multiple SVG elements. I'm referring to the class attribute, which is used to associate a CSS style rule with an element. Assuming there is a style rule named goldenorb in a style sheet accessible by the SVG document, the following code shows how to apply the goldenorb style rule to a circle:

```
<circle ...
  class="goldenorb"/>
```

Filling with Gradients

Lest you think SVG isn't capable of fancy graphical effects, let me share with you how to create radial and linear gradients, which is where a range of colors are used to fill graphical objects. Radial and linear gradients constitute a special case of a fill. radialGradient and linearGradient are two separate elements, but they function similarly. These elements define patterns rather than specific objects, and the patterns may be referenced to fill any shape anywhere in the document, or indeed, anywhere on the Web, as the reference is a URI. The SVG server refers to them—and other painting-type capabilities—as "paint servers," or you can think of them as being like color swatches in a paint application.

The stop child element defines the transition point between one color and the next. For a linear gradient, the color changes proceed from left to right; with a radial gradient, it emanates from the center to the periphery of an imaginary circle. There is no limit to how many stops you can have. The following attributes are used to further describe a gradient stop:

- `offset`—Property measures the distance—typically as a percentage of the available space—from the origin of the gradient to its outer limit.
- `stop-color`—Defines the color that begins at the transition point.
- `fx` and `fy`—Coordinates of the focal point of a radial gradient, identical to `cx` and `cy` by default.

The following code shows how to create a radial gradient that makes use of two stops to define the manner in which colors emanate from the center of an object:

```
<radialGradient id="gradient01" cx="300" cy="150" r="200" fx="250" fy="125">
  <stop offset="0%" stop-color="red"/>
  <stop offset="75%" stop-color="black"/>
</radialGradient>
```

One problem with this code is that it must be housed within another special element in order to be used by graphical objects in an SVG drawing. I'm referring to the `defs` element, which is the means by which you define "building blocks" to be used throughout a drawing. Following is how you place the gradient code within the `defs` element to make it accessible to elements in an SVG drawing:

```
<defs>
  <radialGradient id="gradient01" cx="300" cy="150" r="200" fx="250" fy="125">
    <stop offset="0%" stop-color="red"/>
    <stop offset="75%" stop-color="black"/>
  </radialGradient>
</defs>
```

Having defined this gradient within the `defs` element, you can reference it from other graphical objects to apply gradient fills by specifying the ID of the gradient in the CSS `fill` property, like this:

```
<ellipse cx="380" cy="180" rx="190" ry="40"
  style="fill:url(#gradient01); stroke:black; stroke-width:10"/>
```

Drawing a Path

Those who are familiar with path technology in Adobe Photoshop and Illustrator will be well ahead of the game when learning paths in SVG. A path is nothing but a connected set of points, straight or curved, that can be stroked, filled, transformed (see next section), edited point-by-point, transformed wholesale, or used as the baseline for a string of text.

The one required attribute of the path element is the d (data) attribute, which in turn contains values specifying the type of equation needed to establish the desired component of the path. This really does require the higher math it sounds like it needs, which is beyond the scope of this lesson. In real life, you would probably not attempt such a task with a mere text-editing tool but would rely on a graphics application. The concepts and their mapping, however, are quite simple, and worth becoming familiar with.

The following letters are mnemonics for the tasks they perform. The uppercase letter indicates an absolute positioning of coordinates on the grid, whereas its lowercase counterpart designates coordinates relative to the insertion point. Every path statement starts with an M/m to position the insertion point and a Z/z to announce the end of the task.

- M/m: Establish these x, y coordinates as the starting point of the path
- L/l: Draw a line from the current position to a specified point
- H/h: Draw a horizontal line to the specified x coordinate, keeping the y coordinate the same
- V/v: Draw a vertical line to the specified y coordinate, keeping the x coordinate the same
- A/a: Draw an elliptical or circular arc from the current position to the specified point
- C/c: Draw a cubic Bezier curve from the current position to the specified point
- S/s: Draw a smooth cubic Bezier curve from the current position to the specified point
- Q/q: Draw a quadratic Bezier curve from the current position to the specified point
- T/t: Draw a smooth quadratic Bezier curve from the current position to the specified point
- Z/z: Close the path—draw a straight line back to the first point

If you are not already a mathematician, you will probably not find it worth your while to learn (or re-learn, for those of us who learned and forgot it in high school) trigonometry and other forms of higher math just to create vector graphics. However, you may at some point find it useful to do a quick edit and tweak a value here or there, in which case it's helpful to have some understanding of what's before you.

Figure 6.9 shows a path created in Adobe Illustrator, and Listing 6.9 contains the SVG code underlying it. The arcane-looking notations for the d values are the fruits of differential calculus—very, very far beyond the scope of this lesson.

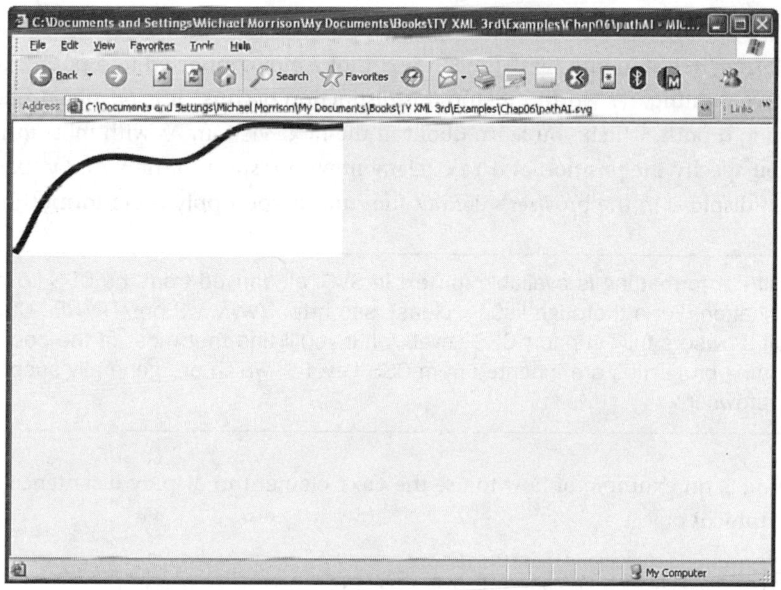

FIGURE 6.9
A path exported to SVG from Adobe Illustrator.

LISTING 6.9 Code for an SVG Path That Was Exported from Adobe Illustrator

```
<?xml version="1.0" encoding="iso-8859-1"?>

<!-- Generator: Adobe Illustrator 9.0.1, SVG Export Plug-In  -->
<!DOCTYPE svg PUBLIC "-//W3C//DTD SVG 20000303 Stylable//EN"
  "http://www.w3.org/TR/2000/03/WD-SVG-20000303/DTD/svg-20000303-
  stylable.dtd" [
<!ENTITY st0 "fill:none;stroke-width:5.04;">
<!ENTITY st1 "fill-rule:nonzero;clip-rule:nonzero;stroke:#000000;
  stroke-miterlimit:4;">]>

<svg width="254.989pt" height="104.255pt" viewBox="0 0 254.989 104.255"
  xml:space="preserve">
  <g id="Layer_x0020_1" style="&st1;">
    <path style="&st0;" d="M2.815,100.415c-0.147,0.822-0.159,1.598-0.354,
      2.401c9.705-13.879,14.356-30.552,24.381-44.408c9.544-13.191,
      22.468-24.158,38.313-28.809c21.493-6.308,43.011,4.355,64.516,
      1.717c15.429-1.893,28.255-17.305,41.55-24.599c8.506-4.667,
      17.982-4.18,27.42-4.185c18.782-0.011,37.527,1.272,56.301,1.606"/>
  </g>
</svg>
```

Text in SVG

Text in SVG enjoys the benefits of both vector graphics and word-processed text. As a graphic, it can be filled, stroked, transformed, and more. As text, it can be modified by CSS's standard text-formatting properties such as `font-family`, `font-weight`, as well as traditional properties such as bolding or underlining.

Free-Standing Text

When I say "free-standing text" I mean text that is not connected to a path; I don't mean free-floating. It's worth making this distinction because it is possible to flow text along a path, which you learn about in the next section. As with most attributes, you specify the position of a text element with respect to the x and y axes. The text displays in the browser's default font unless you apply other formatting.

By the Way

> A wealth of formatting is available for text in SVG, all derived from the CSS Level 2 specification. For a thorough listing, please see http://www.w3.org/TR/REC-CSS2. Not all browsers fully support CSS Level 2, but you'll find that most of the popular formatting properties are inherited from CSS Level 1, which are generally supported by all browsers.

Following is an example of how to use the text element to display a sentence as a graphical object:

```
<?xml version="1.0" encoding="UTF-8"?>
<!DOCTYPE svg PUBLIC "-//W3C//DTD SVG 1.1//EN"
  "http://www.w3.org/Graphics/SVG/1.1/DTD/svg11.dtd">

<svg xmlns="http://www.w3.org/2000/svg">
  <title>Just Text</title>

  <text x="40" y="100" font-family="palatino" font-size="36pt">
    The quick brown fox jumped over the lazy dog.
  </text>
</svg>
```

Figure 6.10 shows this code as viewed in Internet Explorer.

Although the SVG coordinate system starts at the top left, the starting point of the text string is the *bottom* left. This means if you start at 0, 0—or n, 0, for that matter—most of the text will be above the top boundary of the window, except for the descenders.

Text Along a Path

SVG also provides for text associated with a path, in which case the text is drawn along the path. The text and the path are created separately—that is, each in its own element statement—and joined together by an xlink:href attribute. To accomplish this, you give the path an id attribute, and reference it from the textPath element, which is a child of the text element.

Also, the xlink prefix needs to be mapped to the w3.org namespace. This can be done either on a containing element or on the textPath element itself. Listing 6.10 declares the xmlns attribute directly on the textPath element and references the path id as "path-demo" to associate the text with it. The stroke of the path disappears when you add text to the path in Illustrator, but we're going to leave that issue alone for the moment. We give the path element the id "newPath," and reference it from the textPath element that encloses the content.

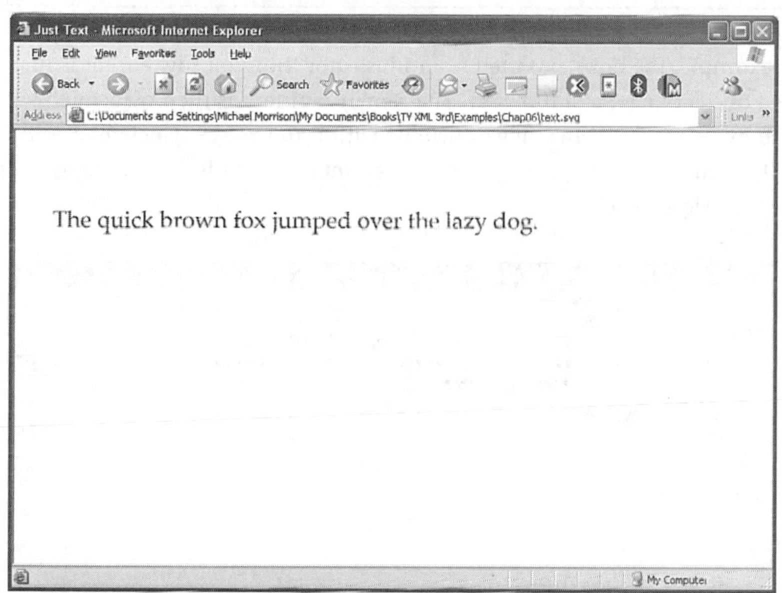

FIGURE 6.10
A sentence is drawn using the text element in SVG.

LISTING 6.10 Text That Is Associated with a Path

```
<?xml version="1.0" encoding="iso-8859-1"?>

<!-- Generator: Adobe Illustrator 9.0.1, SVG Export Plug-In  -->
<!DOCTYPE svg PUBLIC "-//W3C//DTD SVG 20000303 Stylable//EN"
"http://www.w3.org/TR/2000/03/WD-SVG-20000303/DTD/svg-20000303-
  stylable.dtd" [
<!ENTITY st0 "fill:none;stroke-width:5.04;">
<!ENTITY st1 "fill-rule:nonzero;clip-rule:nonzero;stroke:#000000;
  stroke-miterlimit:4;">]>

<svg width="254.989pt" height="104.255pt" viewBox="0 0 254.989 104.255"
  xml:space="preserve">
  <g id="Layer_x0020_1" style="&st1;">
    <path id="newPath" style="&st0;" d="M2.815,100.415c-0.147,0.822-0.159,
      1.598-0.354,2.401c9.705-13.879,14.356-30.552,
      24.381-44.408c9.544-13.191,22.468-24.158,38.313-28.809c21.493-6.308,
      43.011,4.355,64.516,1.717c15.429-1.893,28.255-17.305,
      41.55-24.599c8.506-4.667,17.982-1.18,27.42-4.185c18.782-0.011,37.527,
      1.272,56.301,1.606"/>
    <text x="40" y="100" font-family="palatino" font-size="18pt">
      <textPath xlink:href="#newPath"
        xmlns:xlink="http://www.w3.org/1999/xlink">
```

LISTING 6.10 Continued

```
23:       The quick brown fox jumped over the lazy dog.
24:     </textPath>
25:   </text>
26:  </g>
27: </svg>
```

In this example, the path exported from Illustrator that you saw earlier is first assigned an ID of `newPath` (line 14). The sentence of text is then associated with the path by using the `xlink:href` attribute within the `textPath` element (line 22), where the path ID is referenced. Once this is done, the text is drawn along the path, as shown in Figure 6.11.

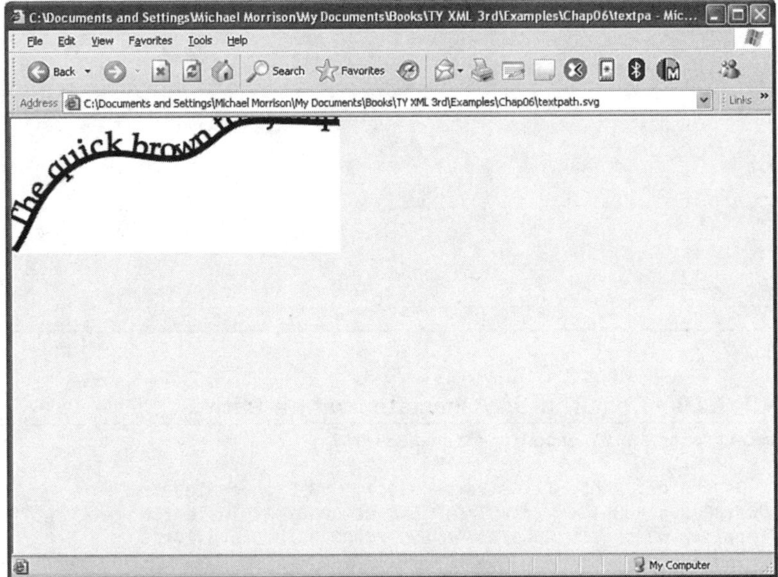

FIGURE 6.11 By linking text to a path, you can draw text along a path in SVG.

Embedding an SVG Drawing in a Web Page

Although you can view SVG documents directly in browsers that have the appropriate plug-in installed, you might prefer referencing an SVG drawing as part of a larger web page. To do so, you must embed a reference to the SVG document in an HTML document, where it is displayed in the context of the web page (see Listing 6.11).

LISTING 6.11 An SVG Document Embedded in an HTML Web Page

```
<html>
<head>
  <title>A Great Shape</title>
</head>

<body>
  <h1>A Great Shape</h1>
    <embed width="600" height="600" src="Ellipse.svg" align="left"
      pluginspage="http://www.adobe.com/svg/viewer/install/">
</body>
</html>
```

This code describes a web page that includes an SVG graphic much as you might include a bitmap image using the HTML <img> tag. Don't forget that it will work only if the browser includes built-in support for SVG or if a suitable SVG viewer plug-in is installed in the browser. Let's hope that this issue diminishes in significance as the major browsers begin adopting native support for SVG. Until then, you may want to encourage end users to download an SVG plug-in if you plan on serving web pages with SVG graphics.

By the Way

> If this example seems a bit novel, allow me to point out that in Hour 17, "SAX: The Simple API for XML," you learn how to translate raw XML data from any document into meaningful SVG graphics.

Summary

In this hour, you developed a good foundation in the basic shapes and components that constitute the SVG markup language. Although you explored only the most basic of SVG's abilities, you've been introduced to the rudiments that will enable you to expand into advanced capabilities, such as transformations, links (like image mapping), clipping, and masking. This can serve two audiences: those with modest aspirations, who will be happy for the ability to create simple graphics with a text file, and those who want a glimpse at SVG's underpinnings before embarking on outputting SVG files from a commercial drawing application. Regardless of which camp you fall into, you're hopefully leaving this hour with a newfound appreciation for how XML is impacting the look and feel of the Web, not to mention your own web pages.

Q&A

Q. ***Can I use SVG to create an image on a Web page instead of using a GIF or PNG image file?***

A. Yes, but keep in mind that the benefit to using SVG in this case is the ability to generate an image dynamically. If you are just displaying a static image on a Web page, then a GIF or PNG image will probably work better. However, if you do need to dynamically generate a vector image, then SVG is certainly your answer.

Q. ***Is it possible to validate SVG documents?***

A. Absolutely. Just make sure you've referenced the appropriate SVG DTD in your document, and then feed it to the W3C Markup Validation Service at http://validator.w3.org/. The online validator will use the DTD as the basis for validating the document against the requirements of the SVG language.

Workshop

The Workshop is designed to help you anticipate possible questions, review what you've learned, and begin learning how to put your knowledge into practice.

Quiz

1. What is the essential difference between bitmap and vector graphics?
2. Which element and attribute are used to enable the viewing of an SVG file in existing (that is, non–SVG-dedicated) browsers?
3. When using the `d` attribute of the path element, what is the significance of uppercase versus lowercase letters indicating the tool and its value?
4. With which elements or attributes can you control the overall size of an SVG document?

Quiz Answers

1. A bitmap graphic is described as a pixel-by-pixel list of instructions, whereas a vector graphic is described as a mathematical equation.
2. Use the embed element with the `pluginspage` attribute pointing to the URL where the plug-in can be found.

3. An uppercase letter is used to reference an absolute set of x, y coordinates; a lowercase letter designates coordinates relative to the insertion point.

4. You can do any or all of the following:

    - Set the `width` and `height` attributes of the `svg` element.
    - Use the `viewBox` attribute of the `svg` element with `width` and `height` values.
    - Specify `width` and `height` attributes in the `img` element when presenting the graphic in an HTML document.

Exercises

1. Create an SVG document named `olympics.svg` that uses circle elements to recreate the familiar Olympics symbol, which consists of five interlocking colored circles.

2. Create an HTML document that embeds the `olympics.svg` document as a vector graphic.

HOUR 7
Using XML Schema

Any good strategy will seem ridiculous by the time it is implemented.

—Scott Adams (cartoonist, creator of Dilbert)

Back in Hour 3, "Defining Data with DTD Schemas," you learned how to describe a custom markup language using a DTD. Although DTDs can certainly get the job done, a more modern alternative is available for describing XML-based markup languages. This alternative is called *XML Schema,* and schemas developed using XML Schema are known as XSDs. Getting back to the Scott Adams quote, some XML developers have argued that maybe there is a shred of Dilbert ridiculousness to XML Schema given the complexity of the resulting code involved in creating an XSD. The W3C (World Wide Web Consortium) initially set out to improve upon DTDs by developing a schema technology that was based on XML. The end result is known as the *XML Schema Definition Language*, or *XSD*, which is now an official W3C standard. XSD schemas are used similarly to DTDs in that they provide a means of defining a custom markup language and validating XML documents. However, XSDs are considerably more powerful than DTDs and give you much finer control over the design of markup languages. As with many technologies, power and flexibility adds complexity, so you'll find that XSD schemas are generally a bit larger and more complex than DTDs. This hour introduces you to XML Schema and shows you how to create XSD schemas that can be used to validate your own documents.

In this hour, you'll learn

- The basics of XML Schema
- How to use elements and attributes in XSD schemas
- How to work with simple and complex data types
- How to build a complete XSD schema and use it to validate a document

XML Schema Construction Basics

In a DTD you lay out the elements and attributes that can be used to describe a particular type of data. Similar to a DTD, XML Schema allows you to create markup languages by carefully describing the elements and attributes that can be used to code information. Unlike DTDs, schemas created with XML Schema are coded in XML, which makes them more consistent in terms of keeping everything in the XML domain; if you recall, DTDs use their own cryptic language. The language used to describe markup languages in XML Schema is *XSD*. Schemas created in this language are often referred to simply as XSDs.

The XSD language is an XML-based language, which means you use XML elements and attributes to describe the structure of your own custom markup languages. This means that XSD itself was created in XML. Although this might seem confusing at first, keep in mind that it is necessary for there to be a means of validating XSD documents, which means the XSD language must be spelled out in terms of XML. More specifically, the elements and attributes in the XSD language are described in none other than a DTD. This is because it isn't exactly possible to use XSD to describe the XSD schema. Admittedly, this is a "chicken and egg" kind of problem because we're talking about creating a schema for a schema language that is in turn used to create schemas. Which one comes first? To be honest, it really doesn't matter. Rather than confuse you further, I'd rather push on and learn how an XSD document comes together. The main point here is that XSD is an XML-based markup language, similar in many ways to any other custom markup language you might create.

Because XSD schema documents are really just XML documents, you must include the familiar XML declaration at the start of them:

```
<?xml version="1.0"?>
```

After entering the XML declaration, you're ready to start coding the XSD document. All of the elements and attributes in XSD are part of what is known as a namespace, which if you recall from Hour 5, "Putting Namespaces to Use," is essentially a grouping of elements and attributes that guarantees uniqueness in their names. You typically assign a namespace a prefix that is used throughout a document to reference elements and attributes within the namespace. In order to reference XSD elements and attributes, you must first declare the XSD namespace in the root element of the XSD document. The prefix of the XSD namespace is typically set to `xsd`, which means that all XSD elements and attributes are preceded by the prefix `xsd` and a colon (`:`). The root element of XSD documents is named `xsd:schema`. Following is an example of how you declare the XSD namespace in the `xsd:schema` element:

```
<xsd:schema xmlns:xsd="http://www.w3.org/2001/XMLSchema">
```

In this code, the `xmlns:xsd` attribute is used to set the XSD namespace, which is a standard URI made available by the W3C. This means that you must precede each element and attribute name with `xsd:`. So, to recap, the general structure of an XSD schema document has the following form:

```
<?xml version="1.0"?>

<xsd:schema xmlns:xsd="http://www.w3.org/2001/XMLSchema">
</xsd:schema>
```

Of course, this code has no content within the root element, so it isn't doing much. However, it lays the groundwork for the basis of all XSD schema documents.

XSD Data Types

The XSD language is defined by the elements and attributes that can be used within it, as well as their relationship to one another. At the heart of XSD are data types, which determine the type of data that can be represented by a particular piece of markup code. For example, numeric data in XSD is coded differently than text data and therefore has an associated data type that is used when creating a schema with XSD. There are two different general types of data used in XSDs: simple data and complex data. *Simple data* corresponds to basic pieces of information such as numbers, strings of text, dates, times, lists, and so on. *Complex data*, on the other hand, represents more involved information such as mixed elements and sequences of elements. Generally speaking, complex data types are built upon simple data types.

Simple data types can be used with both elements and attributes and provide a means of describing the exact nature of a piece of information. The `xsd:element` element is used to create elements of a simple type, whereas the `xsd:attribute` element is used to create attributes. Following are a few examples of each:

```
<xsd:element name="name" type="xsd:string"/>
<xsd:element name="title" type="xsd:string"/>
<xsd:element name="occupation" type="xsd:string"/>
<xsd:attribute name="birthdate" type="xsd:date"/>
<xsd:attribute name="weight" type="xsd:integer"/>
```

Although these examples show how simple data types enter the picture with elements and attributes, they don't reveal the relationship between elements and attributes, which is critical in any XSD document. These relationships are established by complex data types, which are capable of detailing the content models of elements. Following is an example of how simple data types can be used within a complex type to describe the content model of an element named `person`:

```
<xsd:element name="person">
  <xsd:complexType>
    <xsd:sequence>
      <xsd:element name="name" type="xsd:string"/>
      <xsd:element name="title" type="xsd:string"/>
      <xsd:element name="occupation" type="xsd:string"/>
    </xsd:sequence>

    <xsd:attribute name="birthdate" type="xsd:date"/>
    <xsd:attribute name="weight" type="xsd:integer"/>
  </xsd:complexType>
</xsd:element>
```

Keep in mind that this XSD code describes a custom markup language that is used to create XML documents. In order to fully understand how the schema code works, it's a good idea to take a look at what XML code might look like that adheres to the schema. Following is an example of some XML document data that follows the data structure laid out in the prior XSD schema code:

```
<person birthdate="1969-10-28" weight="160">
  <name>Milton James</name>
  <title>Mr.</title>
  <occupation>mayor</occupation>
</person>
```

This code should look much more familiar to you as it is basic XML code with custom elements and attributes. It doesn't take too much analysis to see that this code adheres to the XSD schema code you just saw. For example, the `person` element includes two attributes, `birthdate` and `weight`, as well as three child elements: `name`, `title`, and `occupation`. Unlike a DTD, the schema is able to carefully describe the data type of each element and attribute. For example, the `birthdate` attribute is a date (`xsd:date`), not just a string that happens to store a date, and the `weight` attribute is an integer number (`xsd:integer`).

XSD Schemas and XML Documents

You now have a basic knowledge of how a schema is used to establish a markup language that in turn is used to create XML documents. What you don't know is how a schema is actually associated with such documents. If you recall, a DTD is associated with a document by way of a document type declaration. XSDs don't rely on a document type declaration and instead use a special attribute called `noNamespaceSchemaLocation`. To associate a schema with an XML document for validation purposes, you set this attribute of the root element to the location of the schema document. However, in order to use this attribute you must first declare the namespace to which it belongs. Following is how this is accomplished in XML code:

```
<contacts xmlns:xsi="http://www.w3.org/2001/XMLSchema-instance"
  xsi:noNamespaceSchemaLocation="contacts.xsd">
  <person birthdate="1969-10-28" weight="160">
    <name>Milton James</name>
    <title>Mr.</title>
    <occupation>mayor</occupation>
  </person>
</contacts>
```

There is also a `schemaLocation` attribute for referencing a schema that has its own namespace. This is useful if you want to explicitly reference elements using a prefix for the schema. You find out more about this attribute later in the lesson.

This code shows how to declare the appropriate namespace and then set the noNamespaceSchemaLocation attribute for the schema document. Assuming the schema for the contacts document is located in the file named contacts.xsd, this XML document is ready for validation. This brings up an important point regarding schema documents—they are coded in XML but they are stored in files with a .xsd extension. This makes it possible to determine quickly if a file is an XSD schema.

By the Way

Many XML documents are stored in files with extensions other than .xml. Although .xml is certainly a suitable extension for any XML document, it is generally better to use the more specific extension dictated by the markup language, assuming that such an extension exists. As an example, in the previous hour you worked with SVG documents that were stored in files with a .svg extension.

Working with Simple Types

XSD includes several different simple data types, or *simple types*, that make it possible to model a wide range of data in XML documents. These types can be classified according to the kind of data they represent. Following are the major categories of simple data types supported in the XSD language, along with the specific XSD elements associated with each category:

- String types—xsd:string
- Boolean types—xsd:boolean
- Number types—xsd:integer, xsd:decimal, xsd:float, xsd:double
- Date and time types—xsd:time, xsd:timeInstant, xsd:duration, xsd:date, xsd:month, xsd:year, xsd:century, xsd:recurringDate, xsd:recurringDay
- Custom types—xsd:simpleType

These simple types are typically used to create elements and attributes in a schema document. In order to create an element based upon a simple type, you must use the xsd:element element, which has two primary attributes used to describe the element: name and type. The name attribute is used to set the element name, which is the name that appears within angle brackets (<>) when you use the element in XML code. The type attribute determines the type of the element and can be set to a simple or complex type. Following are the element examples you saw a little earlier in the hour that make use of the xsd:string simple type:

```
<xsd:element name="name" type="xsd:string"/>
<xsd:element name="title" type="xsd:string"/>
<xsd:element name="occupation" type="xsd:string"/>
```

Attributes are created in much the same manner as elements and even rely on the same two attributes, `name` and `type`. However, you create an attribute using the `xsd:attribute` element. Following are the attribute examples you saw earlier that use the `xsd:date` and `xsd:integer` simple types:

```
<xsd:attribute name="birthdate" type="xsd:date"/>
<xsd:attribute name="weight" type="xsd:integer"/>
```

Now that you understand how simple types enter the picture with elements and attributes, you're ready to learn more about the types themselves.

The String Type

The string type represents a string of text and is represented in the `type` attribute by the `xsd:string` value. The string type is probably the most commonly used type in XSD. Following is an example of how to use the `xsd:string` value to create a string element:

```
<xsd:element name="name" type="xsd:string"/>
```

In an XML document, this element might be used like this:

```
<name>Milton James</name>
```

The Boolean Type

The Boolean type represents a true/false or yes/no value and is represented in the `type` attribute by the `xsd:boolean` value. When using a Boolean type in an XML document, you can set it to `true` or `false`, or `1` or `0`, respectively. Following is an example of an attribute that is a Boolean type:

```
<xsd:attribute name="retired" type="xsd:boolean"/>
```

In an XML document, this attribute might be used like this:

```
<person retired="false">
  <name>Milton James</name>
</person>
```

Number Types

Number types are used in XSD to describe elements or attributes with numeric values. The following number types are available for use in schemas to represent numeric information:

- `xsd:integer`—Integer numbers (with no fractional part); for example, 3
- `xsd:decimal`—Decimal numbers (with a fractional part); for example, 3.14

- `xsd:float`—Single precision (32-bit) floating point numbers; for example, 6.022E23
- `xsd:double`—Double precision (64-bit) floating point numbers; same as float but for considerably more precise numbers

> If you'd like to exert exacting control over the sign of integer numbers, you might consider using one of these additional numeric types: `xsd:positiveInteger`, `xsd:negativeInteger`, `xsd:nonPositiveInteger`, or `xsd:nonNegativeInteger`. The latter two types are zero-inclusive, whereas the first two don't include zero.

To create an element or attribute for a numeric piece of information, you simply select the appropriate number type in the XSD. Following is an example of a couple of attributes that are number types:

```
<xsd:attribute name="height" type="xsd:decimal"/>
<xsd:attribute name="weight" type="xsd:integer"/>
```

In an XML document, this attribute might be used like this:

```
<person height="5.75" weight="160">
  <name>Milton James</name>
</person>
```

Date and Time Types

XSD includes support for date and time types, which is very useful when it comes to modeling such information. Following are the different date and time types that are supported in XSD:

- `xsd:time`—A time of day; for example, 4:40 p.m.
- `xsd:timeInstant`—An instant in time; for example, 4:40 p.m. on August 24, 1970
- `xsd:duration`—A length of time; for example, 3 hours and 15 minutes
- `xsd:date`—A day in time; for example, August 24, 1970
- `xsd:month`—A month in time; for example, August, 1970
- `xsd:year`—A year in time; for example, 1970
- `xsd:century`—A century; for example, 20th century
- `xsd:recurringDate`—A date without regard for the year; for example, August 24
- `xsd:recurringDay`—A day of the month without regard for the month or year; for example, the 24th of the month

To create an element or attribute for a date or time, you must select the appropriate date or time type in the XSD. Following is an example of an attribute that is a date type:

```
<xsd:attribute name="birthdate" type="xsd:date"/>
```

This attribute is of type `xsd:date`, which means that it can be used in XML documents to store a day in time, such as October 28, 1969. You don't just set the `birthdate` attribute to `October 28, 1969`, however. Dates and times are actually considered highly formatted pieces of information, so you must enter them according to predefined formats set forth by the XSD language. The format for the `xsd:date` type is ccyy–mm–dd, where cc is the century (19), yy is the year (69), mm is the month (10), and dd is the day (28). The following code shows how you would specify this date in the `birthdate` attribute using the CCYY-MM-DD format:

```
<person birthdate="1969-10-28" height="5.75" weight="160">
  <name>Milton James</name>
</person>
```

Other date and time types use similar formats. For example, the `xsd:month` type uses the format ccyy–mm, `xsd:year` uses ccyy, and `xsd:century` uses the succinct format cc. The `xsd:recurringDate` type uses – mm-dd to format recurring dates, whereas the `xsd:recurringDay` type uses---dd. Following is an example of the `xsd:recurringDate` type so that you can see how the dashes fit into things:

```
<person birthday="-10--28" height="5.75" weight="160">
  <name>Milton James</name>
</person>
```

In this example, an attribute named `birthday` is used instead of `birthdate`, with the idea being that a birthday is simply a day and month without a birth year (a birth date implies a specific year). Notice that an extra dash appears at the beginning of the `birthday` attribute value to serve as a placeholder for the intentionally missing year.

The remaining time types are `xsd:duration`, `xsd:time`, and `xsd:timeInstant`. The `xsd:duration` type uses an interesting format to represent a length of time—to specify a value of type `xsd:duration` you must enter the length of time according to the format PyyYmmMddDThhHmmMssS. The `P` in the format indicates the period portion of the value, which consists of the year (yy), month (mm), and day (dd). The `T` in the format begins the optional time portion of the value and consists of hours (hh), minutes (mm), and seconds (ss). You can precede a time duration value with a minus sign (`-`) to indicate that the duration of time goes in the reverse direction (back in time). Following is an example of how you would use this format to code the time duration value 3 years, 4 months, 2 days, 13 hours, 27 minutes, and 11 seconds:

```
<worldrecord duration="P3Y4M2DT13H27M11S">
</worldrecord>
```

The `xsd:time` type adheres to the format hh:mm:ss.sss. In addition to specifying the hours (hh), minutes (mm), and seconds (ss.sss) of the time, you may also enter a plus (+) or minus (-) sign followed by hh:mm to indicate the offset of the time from Universal Time (UTC). As an example, the U.S. Central Standard Time zone is six hours behind UTC time, so you would need to indicate that in an `xsd:time` value that is in Central Standard Time (CST). Following is an example of a CST time:

```
<meeting start="15:30:00-06:00">
</meeting>
```

By the Way

UTC stands for Coordinated Universal Time and is the same as Greenwich Mean Time (GMT). UTC time is set for London, England, and therefore must be adjusted for any other time zones. Other time zones are adjusted by adding or subtracting time from UTC time. For example, U.S. Pacific Standard Time (PST) is UTC – 8, whereas Japan is UTC + 9.

Notice in the code that the hours in the time are entered in 24-hour form, also known as "military time," meaning that there is no a.m. or p.m. involved. The time specified in this example is 3:30 p.m. CST.

The `xsd:timeInstant` type follows the type ccyy–mm–ddThh:mm:ss.sss and is essentially an `xsd:time` type with the year, month, and day tacked on. As an example, the previous `xsd:time` type could be coded as a `xsd:timeInstant` type with the following code:

```
<meeting start="2002-02-23T15:30:00-06:00">
</meeting>
```

Custom Types

One of the neatest things about XSD is how it allows you to cook up your own custom data types. Custom data types allow you to refine simple data types to meet your own needs. For example, you can limit the range of numbers for a number type, or constrain a string type to a list of possible strings. Regardless of how you customize a type, you always begin with the `xsd:simpleType` element, which is used to create custom simple types. Most of the time your custom types will represent a constraint of a simple type, in which case you'll also need to use the `xsd:restriction` element. The restriction element supports a type named `base` that refers to the base type you are customizing. Following is the general structure of a custom simple type:

```
<xsd:simpleType name="onetotenType">
  <xsd:restriction base="xsd:integer">
  </xsd:restriction>
</xsd:simpleType>
```

This code merely sets up the type to be created; the actual restrictions on the custom type are identified using one of several different elements. To constrain the range of values a number may have, you use one of the following elements:

- `xsd:minInclusive`—Minimum number allowed
- `xsd:minExclusive`—One less than the minimum number allowed
- `xsd:maxInclusive`—The maximum number allowed
- `xsd:maxExclusive`—One greater than the maximum number allowed

These types allow you to set lower and upper ranges on numeric values. Following is an example of how you would limit a numeric value to a range of 1 to 10:

```
<xsd:simpleType name="onetotenType">
  <xsd:restriction base="xsd:integer">
    <xsd:minInclusive value="1"/>
    <xsd:maxInclusive value="10"/>
  </xsd:restriction>
</xsd:simpleType>
```

It's important to note that this code only establishes a custom type named `onetotenType`; it doesn't actually create an element or attribute of that type. In order to create an element or attribute of a custom type, you must specify the type name in the `type` attribute of the `xsd:element` or `xsd:attribute` element:

```
<xsd:element name="rating" type="onetotenType">
```

Although this approach works fine, if you plan on using a custom type with only a single element or attribute, you may want to declare the type directly within the element or attribute, like this:

```
<xsd:element name="rating">
  <xsd:simpleType>
    <xsd:restriction base="xsd:integer">
      <xsd:minInclusive value="1"/>
      <xsd:maxInclusive value="10"/>
    </xsd:restriction>
  </xsd:simpleType>
</xsd:element>
```

In addition to controlling the bounds of simple types, it is also possible to control the length of them. For example, you might want to limit the size of a string of text. To do so, you would use one of the following elements:

- `xsd:length`—The exact number of characters
- `xsd:minlength`—The minimum number of characters
- `xsd:maxlength`—The maximum number of characters

Because the `xsd:length` element specifies the exact length, you can't use it with the `xsd:minLength` or `xsd:maxLength` elements. However, you can use the `xsd:minLength` and `xsd:maxLength` elements together to set the bounds of a string's length. Following is an example of how you might control the length of a string type:

```
<xsd:element name="password">
  <xsd:simpleType>
    <xsd:restriction base="xsd:string">
      <xsd:minLength value="8"/>
      <xsd:maxLength value="12"/>
    </xsd:restriction>
  </xsd:simpleType>
</xsd:element>
```

In this example, a `password` element is created that must have at least 8 characters but no more than 12. This shows how to control the length of strings, but it is also possible to control the length of numbers. More specifically, you can use the `xsd:precision` and `xsd:scale` elements to control how many digits appear to the left or right of a decimal point; this is known as the *precision* of a number. The `xsd:precision` element determines how many total digits are allowed in a number, whereas `xsd:scale` determines how many of those digits appear to the right of the decimal point. So, if you wanted to allow monetary values up to $9999.00 with two decimal places, you would use the following code:

```
<xsd:element name="balance">
  <xsd:simpleType>
    <xsd:restriction base="xsd:decimal">
      <xsd:precision value="6"/>
      <xsd:scale value="2"/>
    </xsd:restriction>
  </xsd:simpleType>
</xsd:element>
```

Keep in mind that the `xsd:precision` and `xsd:scale` elements set the maximum allowable number of digits for the total number and to the right of the decimal place, which means that all of the following examples are valid for the `balance` element:

```
<balance>3.14</balance>
<balance>12.95</balance>
<balance>1.1</balance>
<balance>524.78</balance>
```

One other customization I'd like to mention at this point has to do with default and fixed values. In the event that an element or attribute isn't specified in a document, you may want to declare a *default value* that is assumed. You may also want to limit an element or attribute so that it can have only one possible value, which is known as a *fixed value*. Default and fixed values are established with the `default` and `fixed` attributes of the `xsd:element` and `xsd:attribute` elements. Following are a few examples of default and fixed elements and attributes:

```
<xsd:element name="balance" type="xsd:decimal" default="0.0"/>
<xsd:element name="pi" type="xsd:decimal" fixed="3.14"/>
<xsd:attribute name="expired" type="xsd:boolean" default="false"/>
<xsd:attribute name="title" type="xsd:string" fixed="Mr."/>
```

The `balance` element has a default value of `0.0`, which means it will assume this value if it isn't used in a document. The same thing goes for the `expired` attribute, which assumes the default value of `false` if it goes unused. The `pi` element is fixed at the value `3.14`, which means if it is used it must be set to that value. Similarly, the `title` attribute must be set to `Mr.` if it is used. Notice that none of the examples are defined as having both default and fixed values; that's because you aren't allowed to define both a default and a fixed value for any single element or attribute.

In addition to customizing simple types as you've seen thus far, you can also do some other interesting things with custom types. The next few sections explore the following data types, which are considered slightly more advanced custom types:

- Enumerated types
- List types
- Patterned types

Enumerated Types

Enumerated types are used to constrain the set of possible values for a simple type and can be applied to any of the simple types except the Boolean type. To create an enumerated type, you use the `xsd:enumeration` element to identify each of the possible values. These values are listed within an `xsd:restriction` element, which identifies the base type. As an example, consider an element named `team` that represents the name of an NHL hockey team. Following is an example of how you might code this element with the help of enumerated types:

```
<xsd:element name="team">
  <xsd:simpleType>
    <xsd:restriction base="xsd:string">
      <xsd:enumeration value="Nashville Predators"/>
      <xsd:enumeration value="Detroit Red Wings"/>
      <xsd:enumeration value="St. Louis Blues"/>
      <xsd:enumeration value="Chicago Blackhawks"/>
      <xsd:enumeration value="Columbus Blue Jackets"/>
    </xsd:restriction>
  </xsd:simpleType>
</xsd:element>
```

This code obviously doesn't include every NHL team, but you get the idea. The important thing to note is that the schema won't allow an XML developer to use any value for the `team` element other than those listed here. So, if you were creating a fantasy hockey data service that allowed people to access hockey data on a team-by-team basis, they would only be able to choose from your predefined list of teams. Enumerated types therefore provide a very effective means of tightly defining data that is limited to a set of predefined possibilities.

List Types

Whereas enumerated types force an XML developer to use a value from a predefined set of values, list types allow an XML developer to provide multiple values for a given element. The `xsd:list` element is used to create list types, which are useful any time you need to allow for a list of information. As an example, you might want to create an element that stores rainfall totals for each month of the year as part of an XML-based weather application. Following is code that carries out this function:

```
<xsd:element name="rainfall">
  <xsd:simpleType>
    <xsd:list base="xsd:decimal">
      <xsd:length value="12"/>
    </xsd:list>
  </xsd:simpleType>
</xsd:element>
```

This code allows you to list exactly 12 decimal numbers, separated by white space. Following is an example of what the XML code might look like for the `rainfall` element:

```
<rainfall>1.25 2.0 3.0 4.25 3.75 1.5 0.25 0.75 1.25 1.75 2.0 2.25</rainfall>
```

If you wanted to be a little more flexible and not require exactly 12 items in the list, you could use the `xsd:minLength` and `xsd:maxLength` elements to set minimum and maximum bounds on the list. You can also create a completely unbounded list by using the `xsd:list` element by itself, like this:

```
<xsd:element name="cities">
  <xsd:simpleType>
    <xsd:list base="xsd:string"/>
  </xsd:simpleType>
</xsd:element>
```

Patterned Types

Patterned types are undoubtedly the trickiest of all custom types, but they are also the most powerful in many ways. Patterned types allow you to use a regular expression to establish a pattern that tightly controls the format of a simple type. A *regular expression* is a coded pattern using a special language that describes an arrangement of letters, numbers, and symbols. The regular expression language employed by XSD is fairly complex, so I won't attempt a complete examination of it. Instead, I'd like to focus on the basics and allow you to investigate it further on your own if you decide you'd like to become a regular expression guru. Getting back to patterned types, you create a patterned type using the `xsd:pattern` element.

The `xsd:pattern` element requires an attribute named `value` that contains the regular expression for the pattern. Following are the building blocks of a regular expression pattern:

- `.`—Any character
- `\d`—Any digit
- `\D`—Any nondigit
- `\s`—Any white space
- `\S`—Any nonwhite space
- `x?`—One x or none at all
- `x+`—One or more x's
- `x*`—Any number of x's
- `(xy)`—Groups x and y together
- `x|y`—x or y
- `[xyz]`—One of x, y, or z
- `[x-y]`—in the range x to y
- `x{n}`—`n` number of x's in a row
- `x{n,m}`—At least `n` number of x's but no more than `m`

See, I told you regular expressions are kind of tricky. Actually, these regular expression symbols and patterns aren't too difficult to understand when you see them in context, so let's take a look at a few examples. First off, how about a phone number? A standard U.S. phone number including area code is of the form xxx-xxx-xxxx. In terms of patterned types and regular expressions, this results in the following code:

```
<xsd:element name="phonenum">
  <xsd:simpleType>
    <xsd:restriction base="xsd:string">
      <xsd:pattern value="\d\d\d-\d\d\d-\d\d\d\d"/>
    </xsd:restriction>
  </xsd:simpleType>
</xsd:element>
```

As you can see, the phonenum element is described by a pattern that consists of sequences of digits separated by hyphens. Although this pattern works fine, it's important to note that regular expressions are extremely flexible, often offering more than one solution to a given problem. For example, the following xsd:pattern element also works for a phone number:

```
<xsd:pattern value="\d{3}-\d{3}-\d{4}"/>
```

In this example a phone number is described using curly braces to indicate how many decimal numbers can appear at each position in the pattern. The code \d{3} indicates that there should be exactly three decimal numbers, whereas \d{4} indicates exactly four decimal numbers.

Let's now consider a slightly more advanced regular expression pattern such as a pizza order. Our pizza order pattern must have the form s-c-t+t+t+, where s is the size (small, medium or large), c is the crust (thin or deep), and each t is an optional topping (sausage, pepperoni, mushroom, peppers, onions, and anchovies) in addition to cheese, which is assumed. Following is how this pizza order pattern resolves into an XSD regular expression pattern:

```
<xsd:element name="pizza">
  <xsd:simpleType>
    <xsd:restriction base="xsd:string">
      <xsd:pattern value="(small|medium|large)-(thin|deep)-(sausage+)?
        (pepperoni+)?(mushroom+)?(peppers+)?(onions+)?(anchovies+)?"/>
    </xsd:restriction>
  </xsd:simpleType>
</xsd:element>
```

Following is an example of how you might code a pizza element based upon this pattern:

```
<pizza>medium-deep-sausage+mushroom+</pizza>
```

Obviously, there is a great deal more that can be done with regular expression patterns. Hopefully this is enough information to get you going in the right direction with patterned types.

Digging into Complex Types

Complex data types represent a step up from simple types because they allow you to do more interesting things such as define the content model of elements. Complex types effectively build upon simple types, so your knowledge of simple types will come in quite handy as you work with complex types. All complex types are created using the xsd:complexType element. This element includes an attribute named name that is used to name a complex type. You can also declare a complex type directly within an element, in which case it doesn't require a name.

Complex types can be broken down into four major classifications, as follows:

- Empty elements
- Element-only elements
- Mixed elements
- Sequences and choices

The next few sections explore these different complex types in detail.

Empty Elements

Empty elements contain no text content or child elements but are capable of having attributes. In fact, attributes are the only way to associate information with empty elements. You create empty elements using the xsd:complexType element in conjunction with the xsd:complexContent element. Following is an example of how you create an empty element:

```
<xsd:element name="automobile">
  <xsd:complexType>
    <xsd:complexContent>
      <xsd:extension base="xsd:anyType">
        <xsd:attribute name="vin" type="xsd:string"/>
        <xsd:attribute name="year" type="xsd:year"/>
        <xsd:attribute name="make" type="xsd:string"/>
        <xsd:attribute name="model" type="xsd:string"/>
      </xsd:extension>
    </xsd:complexContent>
  </xsd:complexType>
</xsd:element>
```

Although this may seem like a lot of work to simply create an empty element with a few attributes, it is necessary. The xsd:complexType and xsd:complexContent elements are necessary to establish that this is a complex type, whereas the xsd:extension element is used to declare that there is no specific base type (xsd:anyType) for the element. Finally, the attributes for the element are created using the familiar xsd:attribute element. Following is an example of how you would use the automobile element in an XML document:

```
<automobile vin="SALHV1245SA661555" year="1995"
  make="Land Rover" model="Range Rover"/>
```

Element-Only Elements

Element-only elements are elements that contain only child elements with no text content. They can also contain attributes, of course, but no text content is allowed within an element-only element. To create an element-only element, you simply use the `xsd:complexType` element. Following is an example of an element-only element that contains a single child element:

```
<xsd:element name="assets">
  <xsd:complexType>
    <xsd:element name="automobile" type="automobileType"/>
  </xsd:complexType>
</xsd:element>
```

This code presents a new wrinkle because the child element of `assets` is declared as type `automobileType`. This kind of named complex type is created much like the named simple types you saw earlier in the hour. Another approach to creating an element-only element involves coding the element as a named type. Following is an example of how you might code the `automobileType` named complex data type:

```
<xsd:complexType name="automobileType">
  <xsd:complexContent>
    <xsd:extension base="xsd:anyType">
      <xsd:attribute name="vin" type="xsd:string"/>
      <xsd:attribute name="year" type="xsd:year"/>
      <xsd:attribute name="make" type="xsd:string"/>
      <xsd:attribute name="model" type="xsd:string"/>
    </xsd:extension>
  </xsd:complexContent>
</xsd:complexType>
```

This is the same empty complex type you saw in the previous section, except in this case it has been created as a named type with additional attributes. Following is an example of XML code that uses the `assets` element, `automobile` element, and `automobileType` complex type:

```
<assets>
  <automobile vin="SALHV1245SA661555" year="1995"
    make="Land Rover" model="Range Rover"/>
</assets>
```

You might be wondering exactly how useful the `assets` element is because it can contain only a single `automobile` element. In reality, practically all element-only elements are capable of storing multiple child elements, sometimes of different types. However, in order to allow for multiple child elements you must use a special construct known as a sequence. You learn about sequences a little later in this hour in the section titled "Sequences and Choices."

Mixed Elements

Mixed elements contain both text and child elements and are the most flexible of all elements. Text-only elements are considered a type of mixed element and can contain only text with no child elements. You create text-only elements using the xsd:complexType element in conjunction with the xsd:simpleContent element. Following is an example of a text-only element:

```
<xsd:element name="distance">
  <xsd:complexType>
    <xsd:simpleContent>
      <xsd:extension base="xsd:decimal">
        <xsd:attribute name="units" type="xsd:string" use="required"/>
      </xsd:extension>
    </xsd:simpleContent>
  </xsd:complexType>
</xsd:element>
```

The distance element can be used to store a distance traveled and is capable of using different units of measure to give meaning to the numeric content it stores. The actual distance is located in the element's content, whereas the units are determined by the units attribute, which is a string. It's important to notice the extra use attribute, which is set to required. This attribute setting makes the units attribute a requirement of the distance element, which means you must assign a value to the units attribute. Following is an example of how the distance element and units attribute might be used in an XML document:

```
<distance units="miles">12.5</distance>
```

Although text-only elements are certainly useful in their own right, there are some situations where it is necessary to have the utmost freedom in coding element content, and that freedom comes with the mixed element. Mixed elements are created similarly to other complex types but with the addition of the xsd:mixed attribute. Keep in mind that mixed types allow for text and child element content, as well as attributes. Following is an example of a mixed type:

```
<xsd:element name="message">
  <xsd:complexType mixed="true">
    <xsd:sequence>
      <xsd:element name="emph" type="xsd:string"/>
    </xsd:sequence>

    <xsd:attribute name="to" type="xsd:string" use="required"/>
    <xsd:attribute name="from" type="xsd:string" use="required"/>
    <xsd:attribute name="timestamp" type="xsd:timeInstant" use="required"/>
  </xsd:complexType>
</xsd:element>
```

In this example, a mixed element is created that can contain text, an emph element, and three attributes. Admittedly, I skipped ahead a little by placing the emph child element in a sequence, but that will be cleared up in the next section. Following is an example of how the message element might be used in an XML document:

```
<message to="you" from="me" timestamp="2001-03-14T12:45:00">
I hope you return soon. I've <emph>really</emph> missed you!
</message>
```

In this example the emph child element is used to add emphasis to the word "really" in the message.

Sequences and Choices

One powerful aspect of complex types is the ability to organize elements into sequences and choices. A *sequence* is a list of child elements that must appear in a particular order, whereas a *choice* is a list of child elements from which only one must be used. You create a sequence with the xsd:sequence element, which houses the elements that comprise the sequence. Following is an example of creating a sequence:

```
<xsd:element name="quiz">
  <xsd:complexType>
    <xsd:sequence>
      <xsd:element name="question" type="xsd:string">
      <xsd:element name="answer" type="xsd:string">
    </xsd:sequence>
  </xsd:complexType>
</xsd:element>
```

In this example, the quiz element contains two child elements, question and answer, that must appear in the order specified. By default, a sequence can occur only once within an element. However, you can use the xsd:minOccurs and xsd:maxOccurs attributes to allow the sequence to occur multiple times. For example, if you wanted to allow the quiz element to contain up to 20 question/answer pairs, you would code it like this:

```
<xsd:element name="quiz">
  <xsd:complexType>
    <xsd:sequence minOccurs="1" maxOccurs="20">
      <xsd:element name="question" type="xsd:string">
      <xsd:element name="answer" type="xsd:string">
    </xsd:sequence>
  </xsd:complexType>
</xsd:element>
```

> You can set the maxOccurs attribute to unbounded to allow for an unlimited number of sequences. The maxOccurs attribute can also be used with individual elements to control the number of times they can occur.

Following is an example of how you might use the quiz element in an XML document:

```
<quiz>
  <question>What does XML stand for?</question>
  <answer>eXtensible Markup Language</answer>
  <question>Who is responsible for overseeing XML?</question>
  <answer>World Wide Web Consortium (W3C)</answer>
  <question>What is the latest version of XML?</question>
  <answer>1.0</answer>
</quiz>
```

If you want to allow an element to contain one of a series of optional elements, you can use a choice. A choice allows you to list several child elements and/or sequences, with only one of them allowed for use in any given element. Choices are created with the `xsd:choice` element, which contains the list of choice elements. Following is an example of a choice:

```
<xsd:element name="id">
  <xsd:complexType>
    <xsd:choice>
      <xsd:element name="ssnum" type="xsd:string">

      <xsd:sequence>
        <xsd:element name="name" type="xsd:string">
        <xsd:element name="birthdate" type="xsd:date">
      </xsd:sequence>

      <xsd:element name="licensenum" type="xsd:string">
    </xsd:choice>
  </xsd:complexType>
</xsd:element>
```

In this example, an element named `id` is created that allows three different approaches to providing identification: social security number, name and birth date, or driver's license number. The choice is what makes it possible for the element to accept only one of the approaches. Notice that a sequence is used with the name and birth date approach because it involves two child elements. Following is an example of a few `id` elements that use each of the different choice approaches:

```
<id>
  <ssnum>123-89-4567</ssnum>
</id>
<id>
  <name>Milton James</name>
  <birthdate>1969-10-28</birthdate>
</id>
<id>
  <licensenum>12348765</licensenum>
</id>
```

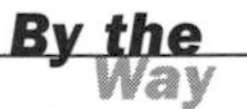

> If you're looking to create content models with little structure, you might consider using the `xsd:all` type, which is used to create complex types that can hold any number of elements in any order. The xsd:all element is used much like a sequence except that the child elements within it can appear any number of times and in any order.

One last topic worth covering before moving on to a complete XSD example has to do with how data types are referenced. With the exception of the root element, which is automatically referenced in an XSD, global document components must be referenced in order to actually appear as part of a document's architecture. You should consider using a global component when you have an element or attribute that appears repeatedly within other elements. In most of the examples you've seen, the components have been declared locally, which means they are automatically referenced within the context that they appear. However, consider an element, such as the following one, which is declared globally:

```
<xsd:element name="password">
  <xsd:simpleType>
    <xsd:restriction base="xsd:string">
      <xsd:minLength value="8"/>
      <xsd:maxLength value="12"/>
    </xsd:restriction>
  </xsd:simpleType>
</xsd:element>
```

Although this element has been declared and is ready for use, it doesn't actually appear within the structure of an XSD until you reference it. You reference elements using the `ref` attribute, which applies to both elements and attributes. Following is an example of how the `password` element might be referenced within another element:

```
<xsd:element name="login" >
  <xsd:complexType>
    <xsd:sequence>
      <xsd:element name="userid" type="xsd:string"/>
      <xsd:element ref="password"/>
    </xsd:sequence>
  </xsd:complexType>
</xsd:element>
```

In this example the `userid` element is created and used locally, whereas the `password` element is referenced from the previous global element declaration. Whether or not you use elements and attributes locally or globally primarily has to do with how valuable they are outside of a specific context; if an element or attribute is used only in a single location then you might as well simplify things and keep it local. Otherwise, you should consider making it a global component and then referencing it wherever it is needed using the `ref` attribute.

By the Way

> The difference between local and global elements has to do with how they are created, which determines how you can use them. An element (`userid` in the previous example) declared within another element is considered local to that element, and can only be used within that element. A global element (`password` in the previous example) is declared by itself and can be referenced from any other element.

Namespaces and XSD Schemas

Although I didn't mention it back in Hour 5, namespaces actually play an extremely important role in XSD schemas. I didn't want to digress too much in that hour and sidetrack you since I hadn't really gotten into the details of XSD schemas just yet. For this reason, it's now worth tackling the topic of namespaces as they relate to XSD schemas to clarify exactly how namespaces impact XSDs.

The `xsd` Prefix

The first thing to understand about namespaces and schemas is that there is nothing magical about the prefix `xsd`. The prefix `xsd` is used with the XSD schema as a means of referencing elements and attributes that are used to construct schemas for your own custom markup languages. For example, following is the namespace declaration for the `etml.xsd` example schema document, which you will learn about in just a moment:

```
<xsd:schema xmlns:xsd="http://www.w3.org/2001/XMLSchema">
```

This code shows how the prefix `xsd` is used to declare the XSD schema explicitly. Now that you understand how prefixes work with explicit namespace declarations, you know that this prefix could be named anything you want. Of course, there is no reason to deviate from `xsd` since it has become somewhat of a standard among XML developers, but I wanted to point out that there is nothing hardwired into XML when it comes to namespace prefixes.

Referencing Schema Documents

In addition to providing a means of referencing the schema of a schema document, namespaces also play an important role in documents that rely on an XSD schema for validation. If this sounds confusing, I think a quick explanation will clear things up. In order to identify the physical schema document for a document, you must use a special attribute and assign the location of the schema document to it. There are two attributes you can use to accomplish this task:

- `schemaLocation`—Locates a schema and its associated namespace
- `noNamespaceSchemaLocation`—Locates a schema with no namespace

These attributes are standard attributes that are located in a namespace named http://www.w3.org/2001/XMLSchema-instance. In order to properly reference either of these attributes, you must first explicitly declare the namespace in which they are located. It is standard to use the xsi prefix for this namespace, as the following attribute assignment shows:

```
xmlns:xsi="http://www.w3.org/2001/XMLSchema-instance"
```

With this namespace declared, you can now use one of the schema location attributes to reference the physical schema document. Following is an example of how this task is carried out for the training log example document, which is based on the etml.xsd schema:

```
<trainlog
  xmlns:xsi="http://www.w3.org/2001/XMLSchema-instance"
  xsi:noNamespaceSchemaLocation="etml.xsd">
```

In this example the noNamespaceSchemaLocation attribute is used because you don't care about associating the ETML schema with a namespace. If, however, you wanted to associate it with a namespace, you would use the schemaLocation attribute instead:

```
<trainlog
  xmlns:xsi="http://www.w3.org/2001/XMLSchema-instance"
  xsi:schemaLocation="http://www.michaelmorrison.com/ns/etml etml.xsd">
```

Notice in the schemaLocation attribute that two pieces of information are provided: the namespace for the schema and the location of the schema document. The schemaLocation attribute is useful whenever you are working with a schema and you want to associate it with a namespace. It's important to understand that this sample code doesn't actually establish a schema prefix for the ETML document. Instead, it simply establishes that the etml.xsd schema document is associated with the ETML namespace. To establish prefix for the ETML tags and attributes, you must declare the ETML namespace, as shown in this code:

```
<trainlog
  xmlns:xsi="http://www.w3.org/2001/XMLSchema-instance"
  xmlns:etml="http://www.michaelmorrison.com/ns/etml"
  xsi:schemaLocation="http://www.michaelmorrison.com/ns/etml etml.xsd">
```

Now the prefix etml can be used to reference tags and attributes as part of the ETML namespace, as in <etml:distance>.

A Complete XML Schema Example

You've covered an awful lot of territory in this hour and hopefully have a pretty good understanding of the XSD language and how it is used to create XSD schemas. To help pull together everything that you've learned, it might be helpful for you to see a complete example. If you recall, in Hour 3 you constructed a DTD for a sports training markup language known as ETML. Listing 7.1 contains the XSD equivalent for this markup language, which puts to use many of the XSD construction techniques you've learned about throughout this hour.

LISTING 7.1 The etml.xsd XSD Schema Used to Validate ETML Documents

```
<?xml version="1.0"?>

<xsd:schema xmlns:xsd="http://www.w3.org/2001/XMLSchema">
  <xsd:element name="trainlog">
    <xsd:complexType>
      <xsd:sequence>
        <xsd:element name="session" type="sessionType" minOccurs="0"
          maxOccurs="unbounded"/>
      </xsd:sequence>
    </xsd:complexType>
  </xsd:element>

  <xsd:complexType name="sessionType">
    <xsd:sequence>
      <xsd:element name="duration" type="xsd:duration"/>
      <xsd:element name="distance" type="distanceType"/>
      <xsd:element name="location" type="xsd:string"/>
      <xsd:element name="comments" type="xsd:string"/>
    </xsd:sequence>

    <xsd:attribute name="date" type="xsd:date" use="required"/>
    <xsd:attribute name="type" type="typeType" use="required"/>
    <xsd:attribute name="heartrate" type="xsd:positiveInteger"/>
  </xsd:complexType>

  <xsd:complexType name="distanceType">
    <xsd:simpleContent>
      <xsd:extension base="xsd:decimal">
        <xsd:attribute name="units" type="unitsType" use="required"/>
      </xsd:extension>
    </xsd:simpleContent>
  </xsd:complexType>

  <xsd:simpleType name="typeType">
    <xsd:restriction base="xsd:string">
      <xsd:enumeration value="running"/>
      <xsd:enumeration value="swimming"/>
      <xsd:enumeration value="cycling"/>
    </xsd:restriction>
  </xsd:simpleType>

  <xsd:simpleType name="unitsType">
    <xsd:restriction base="xsd:string">
      <xsd:enumeration value="miles"/>
      <xsd:enumeration value="kilometers"/>
      <xsd:enumeration value="laps"/>
    </xsd:restriction>
  </xsd:simpleType>

</xsd:schema>
```

Admittedly, this is considerably more code than the ETML DTD that you saw in Hour 3. However, you have to consider the fact that XSDs provide a more exacting approach to data modeling by incorporating rich data types. A quick study of the XSD code for ETML reveals that this schema does a much better job of modeling ETML data than its DTD counterpart. This is primarily due to the data typing features of XSD. Additionally, because XSD is an XML-based language, the code should be a little more familiar to you than the more cryptic code used in DTDs.

The `trainlog` element is described first in the XSD as containing a sequence of `session` elements (lines 4–11). The `sessionType` data type is created to represent `session` elements (line 13) and contains child elements that store the duration, distance, location, and comments for a training session (lines 15–18). The `sessionType` data type also includes several attributes that store the date, type, and heart rate for the training session (lines 21–23). The remaining `distanceType` (line 26), `typeType` (line 34), and `unitsType` (line 42) data types model the remaining content in ETML documents.

Of course, no schema would be complete without an example XML document that puts it through its paces. Listing 7.2 contains the training log document, modified slightly to accommodate the needs of the XSD schema.

LISTING 7.2 **The Training Log Example ETML Document**

```
 1: <?xml version="1.0"?>
 2:
 3: <trainlog
 4:   xmlns:xsi="http://www.w3.org/2001/XMLSchema-instance"
 5:   xsi:noNamespaceSchemaLocation="etml.xsd">
 6:   <session date="2005-11-19" type="running" heartrate="158">
 7:     <duration>PT45M</duration>
 8:     <distance units="miles">5.5</distance>
 9:     <location>Warner Park</location>
10:     <comments>Mid-morning run, a little winded throughout.</comments>
11:   </session>
12:
13:   <session date="2005-11-21" type="cycling" heartrate="153">
14:     <duration>PT2H30M</duration>
15:     <distance units="miles">37.0</distance>
16:     <location>Natchez Trace Parkway</location>
17:     <comments>Hilly ride, felt strong as an ox.</comments>
18:   </session>
19:
20:   <session date="2005-11-24" type="running" heartrate="156">
21:     <duration>PT1H30M</duration>
22:     <distance units="miles">8.5</distance>
23:     <location>Warner Park</location>
24:     <comments>Afternoon run, felt reasonably strong.</comments>
25:   </session>
26: </trainlog>
```

Other than including the standard `noNamespaceSchemaLocation` attribute to identify the XSD schema document (line 5), the changes to the training log document have to do with the stricter data typing features of XSDs. For example, the `date` attributes and `duration` elements conform to the `xsd:date` and `xsd:duration` simple types (lines 6, 7, 14, 15, 21, and 22). Beyond those changes, the document is the same as the one you saw in Hour 3 with the DTD version of the ETML schema. This version of the document, however, is considered valid with respect to the ETML XSD, whereas the previous version is considered valid with respect to the ETML DTD.

RELAX NG and the Future of XML Schema

This hour has painstakingly led you down the path of crafting schemas as XSDs as opposed to using the older DTD technology. Yet another schema technology has emerged that is worth addressing before sending you on your way with XML Schema. I'm referring to RELAX NG (pronounced "relaxing"), which is a schema technology with many of the benefits of XML Schema minus the verbose coding required of XSDs. You can think of RELAX NG as somewhat of a hybrid schema technology that falls somewhere between DTDs and XSDs. RELAX NG schemas represent a dramatic improvement over DTDs in terms of power and flexibility, yet they can be expressed in a compact format that requires less coding complexity than XML Schema. As an example of the difference between RELAX NG and XML Schema, the RELAX NG language consists of 28 elements, whereas XML Schema consists of 42 elements.

So have you wasted an hour of your life learning about an overly complex XML schema technology? The answer is a resounding no. XML Schema is still the reigning successor to DTDs, and enjoys considerably more widespread support than RELAX NG. However, given the shorter learning curve and simpler syntax, I would be remiss if I didn't at least mention that RELAX NG is another viable option in terms of developing your own schemas. In fact, RELAX NG allows you to do a few things that aren't even possible in XML Schema. But like I said, RELAX NG is a relatively new technology that has yet to establish itself as an industry-wide XML schema technology. Although I certainly encourage you to learn more about RELAX NG, it's important for you to know how to create schemas as XSDs for the immediate future.

It's tough to speculate about the future of XML Schema and whether or not RELAX NG stands a realistic chance of upending it as the de facto standard for expressing XML schemas. For now, your best bet is to become fluent in XML Schema while possibly starting to get acquainted with RELAX NG if you have a desire to look forward and explore other schema options. The good news is that you've now learned about two different schema technologies, so if RELAX NG ever catches on in a big way you shouldn't have too much trouble learning a third technology. To find out more about

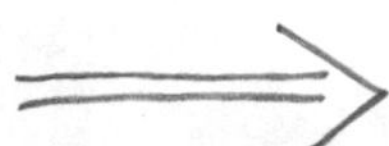

RELAX NG, visit the RELAX NG web site at http://www.relaxng.org/.

Summary

Although DTDs certainly represent a technology that is sufficient for modeling XML document data, XML Schema provides a much more advanced alternative that is rapidly replacing DTDs for defining XML schemas. XSD schemas are constructed using the XSD markup language, which includes elements and attributes for describing the structure of custom XML-based markup languages. This means that you create XSD schema documents in the same manner as you create any other XML document, which makes XSD schemas immediately more accessible to XML developers than DTDs.

This hour explored the inner workings of XSD schemas and taught you the fundamental skills necessary to design and create them. After explaining the different types of XSD data and how to use each of them, the hour showed you a complete example schema created in XSD. Admittedly, XSD is a fairly complex topic that is a bit tough to absorb all at once. Much of the complexity can be eliminated if you rely on a schema tool such as those mentioned in this lesson.

Q&A

Q. ***Are there any simple types other than the ones mentioned in this hour?***

A. Yes. In addition to the simple types you learned about in this hour, there are a few other types such as binary and uriReference that I didn't mention. These types were left out of the lesson primarily for the sake of brevity, as it is difficult to cover the entirety of the XSD language in a single hour. Besides, the aim of this hour is not to make you an XSD expert but to give you the essential knowledge required to design and create XSD schemas.

Q. ***How do I find out more about regular expressions and how they are used to create patterned types?***

A. You can learn an immense amount about regular expressions from the book *Sams Teach Yourself Regular Expressions in 10 Minutes*, by Ben Forta. Or check out Stephen Ramsay's online regular expression tutorial, which is located at http://etext.lib.virginia.edu/services/helpsheets/unix/regex.html. This tutorial is hosted by the University of Virginia's Electronic Text Center.

Q. ***I still don't quite understand the distinction between local and global components in an XSD schema. What gives?***

A. Elements and attributes are considered global if they are declared directly below the `xsd:schema` element. If they are declared anywhere else, they are considered local. Global elements and attributes are used differently in that they must be referenced in order to factor into a schema. Contrast this with local elements and attributes, which are automatically referenced simply by virtue of being local.

Workshop

The Workshop is designed to help you anticipate possible questions, review what you've learned, and begin learning how to put your knowledge into practice.

Quiz

1. What file extension is used to identify XSD schema documents?
2. What two primary attributes are used with the `xsd:element` element to describe an element in an XSD schema?
3. What simple type would you use to represent a recurring monthly bill in an XSD schema?
4. How do you control how many times an element may appear within an XSD schema?

Quiz Answers

1. XSD schema documents are stored with a file extension of `.xsd`.
2. The two primary attributes used with the `xsd:element` element to describe an element in an XSD schema are `name` and `type`.
3. Both the `xsd:recurringDate` and `xsd:recurringDay` types are sufficient to store the date of a recurring monthly bill. The `xsd:recurringDate` type would be better if you cared about knowing the month of the bill, whereas the `xsd:recurringDay` type would work fine if you were interested only in the day of the month.
4. The `xsd:minOccurs` and `xsd:maxOccurs` attributes allow you to control how many times an element appears within an XSD schema.

Exercises

1. Using the `pets.xml` document from Hour 1, create a `pets.xsd` schema document that uses XSD to describe a virtual pet markup language.
2. Modify the `pets.xml` document so that it can be validated against the new `pets.xsd` schema document.

HOUR 8
Validating XML Documents

> In the future, airplanes will be flown by a dog and a pilot. And the dog's job will be to make sure that if the pilot tries to touch any of the buttons, the dog bites him.
>
> —Scott Adams

In the quote, the job of Scott Adams's dog is to prevent human error in piloting an airplane. The idea is that computers will have things enough under control that human pilots will only get in the way. Although the complete removal of human pilots is not too probable in the near future, the prospect of computer-flown airplanes highlights the need for rock solid software systems that are 100% error free. Whether or not you look forward to flying on an airplane piloted entirely by computers (I, for one, do not!), as an XML developer you should make it a huge priority to develop XML documents that are 100% error free. Fortunately, schemas (DTDs and XSDs) make it possible to assess the validity of XML documents. This hour shows you how to use various tools to validate documents against a DTD or XSD.

In this hour, you'll learn

- The ins and outs of document validation
- The basics of validation tools and how to use them
- How to assess and repair invalid XML documents

Document Validation Revisited

As you know by now, the goal of most XML documents is to be valid. Document validity is extremely important because it guarantees that the data within a document conforms to a standard set of guidelines as laid out in a schema (DTD, XSD, or RELAX NG schema). Not all documents have to be valid, which is why I used the word "most" a moment ago. For example, many XML applications use XML to code small chunks of data that really don't require the thorough validation options made possible by a schema. Even in this case, however, all XML documents must be well formed. A well-formed document, as you may recall, is a document that adheres to the fundamental structure of the XML language. Rules for well-formed documents include matching start tags with end tags and setting values for all attributes used, among others.

An XML application can certainly determine if a document is well formed without any other information, but it requires a schema in order to assess document validity. This schema typically comes in the form of a DTD (Document Type Definition) or XSD (XML Schema Definition), which you learned about in Hour 3, "Defining Data with DTD Schemas," and Hour 7, "Using XML Schema." To recap, schemas allow you to establish the following ground rules that XML documents must adhere to in order to be considered valid:

- Establish the elements that can appear in an XML document, along with the attributes that can be used with each
- Determine whether an element is empty or contains content (text and/or child elements)
- Determine the number and sequence of child elements within an element
- Set the default value for attributes

It's probably safe to say that you have a good grasp on the usefulness of schemas, but you might be wondering about the details of how an XML document is actually validated with a schema. This task begins with the XML processor, which is typically a part of an XML application. The job of an XML processor is to process XML documents and somehow make the results available for further processing or display within an application. A modern web browser, such as Internet Explorer, Firefox, Safari, or Opera, includes an XML processor that is capable of processing an XML document and displaying it using a style sheet. The XML processor knows nothing about the style sheet—it just hands over the processed XML content for the browser to render.

The actual processing of an XML document is carried out by a special piece of software known as an *XML parser*. An XML parser is responsible for the nitty-gritty details of reading the characters in an XML document and resolving them into meaningful tags and relevant data. There are two types of parsers capable of being used during the processing of an XML document:

- Standard (non-validating) parser
- Validating parser

A standard XML parser, or non-valid parser, reads and analyzes a document to ensure that it is well formed. A standard parser checks to make sure that you've followed the basic language and syntax rules of XML. Standard XML parsers do not check to see if a document is valid—that's the job of a validating parser. A validating parser picks up where a standard parser leaves off by comparing a document with its schema and making sure it adheres to the rules laid out in the schema. Because a document must be well-formed as part of being valid, a standard parser is still used when a document is being validated. In other words, a standard parser first checks to see if a document is well-formed, and then a validating parser checks to see if it is valid.

By the Way

> In actuality, a validating parser includes a standard parser so that there is technically only one parser that can operate in two different modes.

When you begin looking for a means to validate your documents, make sure you find an XML application that includes a validating parser. Without a validating parser, there is no way to validate your documents. You can still see if they are well formed by using a standard parser only, which is certainly important, but it's generally a good idea to go ahead and carry out a full validation.

Validation Tools

It's good to develop an eye for clean XML code, which makes it possible to develop XML documents with a minimal amount of errors. However, it's difficult for any human to perform such a technical task flawlessly, which is where XML validation tools come into play. XML validation tools are used to analyze the contents of XML documents to make sure they conform to a schema. There are two main types of validation tools available:

- Web-based tools
- Standalone tools

Web-based tools are web pages that allow you to enter the path (URI) of an XML document to have it validated. The upside to web-based tools is that they can be used without installing special software—just open the web page in a web browser and go for it! The downside to web-based validation tools is that they sometimes don't work well when you aren't dealing with files that are publicly available on the Internet. For example, if you're working on an XML document on your local hard drive, it can be tough getting a web-based validation tool to work properly if the schema is also stored locally. Typically it's a matter of getting the tool to recognize the schema; if the schema is located on the Internet there usually isn't a problem, but if it's located on your local hard drive, it can be tough getting things to work properly.

If you're planning to do a lot of XML development work on your local hard drive, you might want to consider using a standalone validation tool. Standalone validation tools are tools that you must install on your computer in order to use. These kinds of tools range from full-blown XML editors such as XML Spy to command-line XML validators such as the W3C's XSV validator. Standalone validation tools have the benefit of allowing you to validate local files with ease. The drawback to these tools is that some of them aren't cheap, and they must be installed on your computer. However, if you don't mind spending a little money, a standalone tool can come in extremely handy.

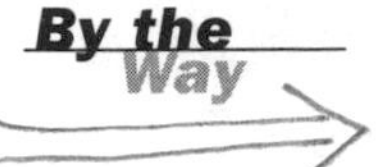

For the record, not all standalone tools cost money. For example, the W3C's XSV validator is available for free download at http://www.ltg.ed.ac.uk/~ht/xsv-status.html. XMLStarlet is another good option. It is an open source command-line XML tool that is freely available to download at http://xmlstar.sourceforge.net/.

Regardless of what type of validation tool you decide to use, there is a big distinction between validating documents against DTDs and validating them against XSDs. Although some tools support both types of schemas, many tools do not. You should therefore consider what type of schema you plan on using when assessing the different tools out there.

DTD Validation

DTDs have been around much longer than XSDs, so you'll find that there are many more validation tools available for DTDs. One of the best tools I've found is made available by Brown University's Scholarly Technology Group, or STG. STG's tool comes in the form of a web page known as the XML Validation web page, which is accessible online

at http://www.stg.brown.edu/service/xmlvalid/. Of course, this validation tool falls into the category of web-based tools. Figure 8.1 shows the STG XML Validation web page.

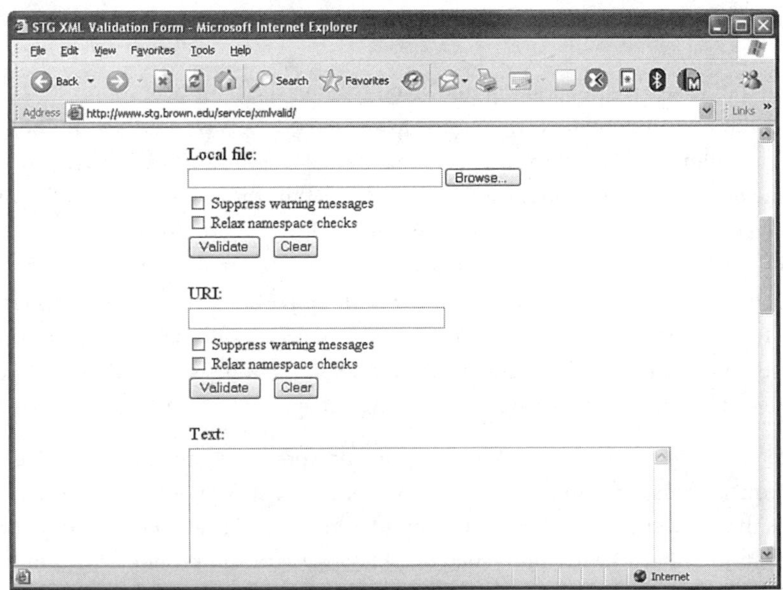

FIGURE 8.1 Brown University's Scholarly Technology Group has an XML Validation web page that can be used to validate DTDs.

Similar to most web-based validation tools, there are two approaches available for validating documents with the XML Validation web page:

- Access the document on the Internet
- Access the document locally

Depending on your circumstances, the latter option is probably the simplest because you will likely be developing XML documents locally. As I mentioned earlier, sometimes validators have problems with local schemas, so the easier route in terms of having the validator run smoothly is to stick your document(s) and schema on a computer that is accessible on the Internet via a URI. That way you are guaranteeing that the validator can find the document and its schema, both of which are required for validation.

By the Way

> If you're able to post your schema to the Web so that it is available online, you can still use the XML Validation web page to validate local XML documents.

After specifying the document to the XML Validation web page and clicking the Validate button, any errors found during validation will be displayed in your web browser (see Figure 8.2).

The figure reveals errors that were introduced when I deliberately removed the final closing </comments> tag, which invalidates the document. Fortunately, the XML Validation web page caught the problem and alerted me. After repairing the problem and initiating the validation process again, everything turns out fine (see Figure 8.3).

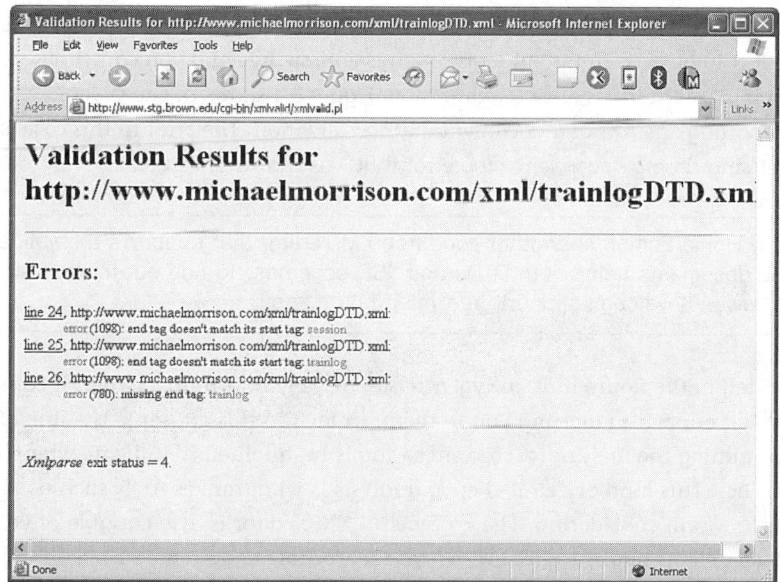

FIGURE 8.2
The STG XML Validation web page reveals errors in an XML document during validation.

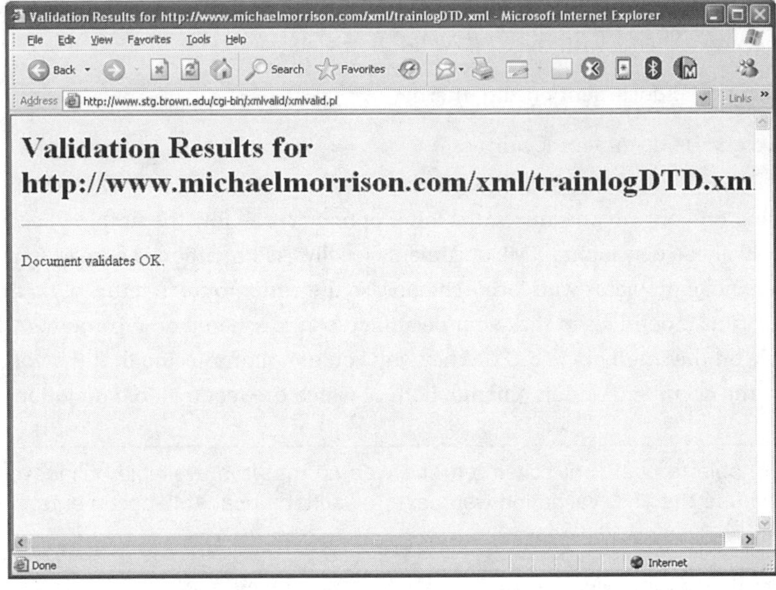

FIGURE 8.3 The STG XML Validation web page reports that a document is indeed valid.

By the Way

The online STG Validation web page only validates documents against DTDs, so you won't be able to use it to validate against XSDs.

If you want a quick (and affordable) way to validate local documents against a DTD, then I highly recommend the <oXygen/> XML Editor by SyncRO Soft, which you first learned about in Hour 2, "Creating XML Documents." You can download the <oXygen/> XML Editor for free at http://www.oxygenxml.com/. You'll have to register the product in order to run it but registration is entirely free and you can choose not to receive email solicitations during registration. Figure 8.4 shows the <oXygen/> XML Editor reporting an error in a document during validation. The error in this case is the same missing closing `</comment>` tag error that was shown in Figure 8.2.

By the Way

XMLSpy Home Edition is another good free XML editor that supports the validation of XML documents using both DTDs and XSD schemas. To find out more, visit http://www.altova.com/support_freexmlspyhome.asp.

You can tell in the figure that <oXygen/> is extremely informative when it comes to detecting errors and alerting you to them. In fact, in this example the line of code containing the missing `</comments>` tag is highlighted to indicate where the problem lies. This kind of detailed error analysis is what makes tools such as <oXygen/> worth considering. The <oXygen/> XML Editor is also capable of validating documents against XSDs, which you learn how to do next.

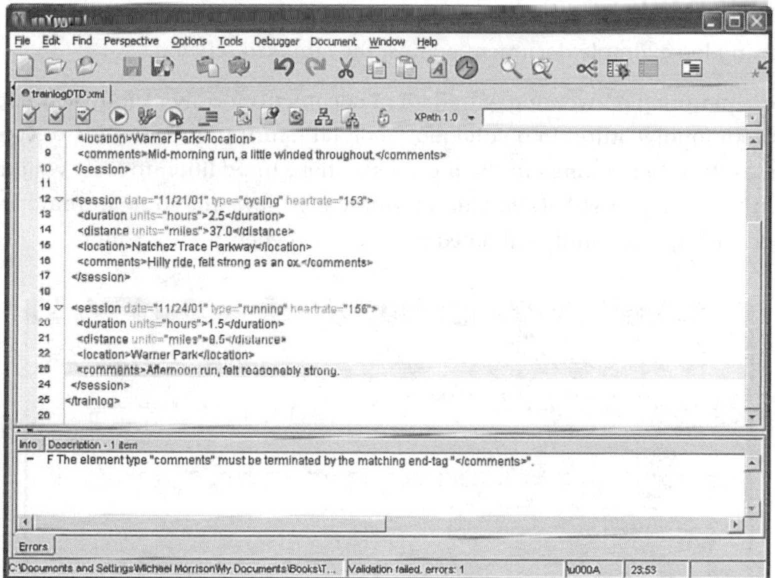

FIGURE 8.4
The <oXygen/> XML Editor is a good tool for performing DTD document validation on local XML documents.

XSD Validation

You'll be glad to know that validating XML documents against an XSD is not much different than validating them against DTDs. It's still important to have the XSD properly associated with the documents, as you learned how to do in the previous lesson. Once that's done, it's basically a matter of feeding the document to a validation tool that is capable of handling XSD schemas. The W3C offers an online XSD validation tool called the W3C Validator for XML Schema, which is located at http://www.w3.org/2001/03/webdata/xsv/. This web-based validator works similarly to the web-based DTD validator you learned about in the previous section. You specify the URI of a document and the validator does all the work. Although the W3C Validator for XML Schema can certainly get the job done, it has a limitation in that you must have the schema file hosted online in order to validate documents.

> The underlying XML processor used in the W3C Validator for XML Schema web page is called XSV and is also available from the W3C as a standalone validator. You can download this standalone command-line validator for free from the W3C at http://www.ltg.ed.ac.uk/~ht/xsv-status.html.

An even better online validation tool for use with local files is the online XML Schema Validator, which is very easy to use. This validator is accessible online at http://apps.gotdotnet.com/xmltools/xsdvalidator/. What makes this online validator particularly useful is that it allows you to specify both the XML document and its XSD schema as local files, which means the schema file doesn't have to be publicly accessible online. Figure 8.5 shows the XML Schema Validator successfully validating the training log example document against the etml.xsd schema.

If you are planning on working with a lot of documents locally or maybe are looking for additional features in a validation tool, I'd return to the familiar <oXygen/> XML Editor that I mentioned in the previous section. In addition to DTD validation, <oXygen/> also supports XSD validation. Figure 8.6 shows the same training log document being successfully validated using the <oXygen/> XML Editor.

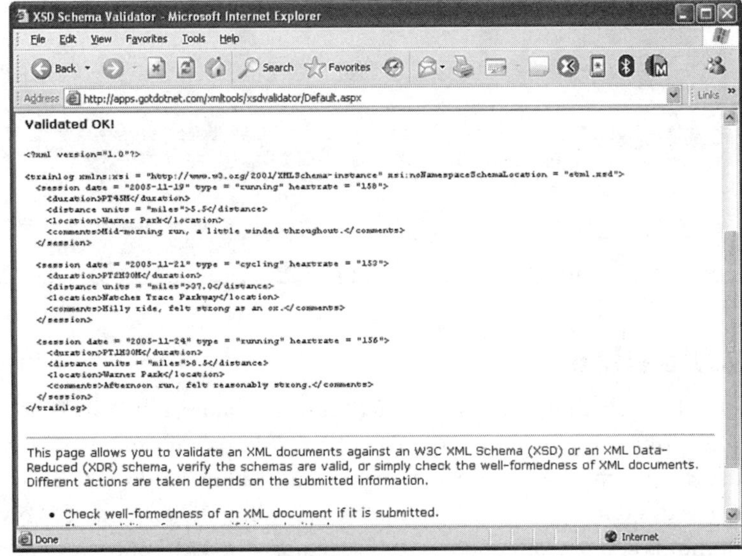

FIGURE 8.5
The online XML Schema Validator serves as an excellent tool for validating an XML document against an XSD schema.

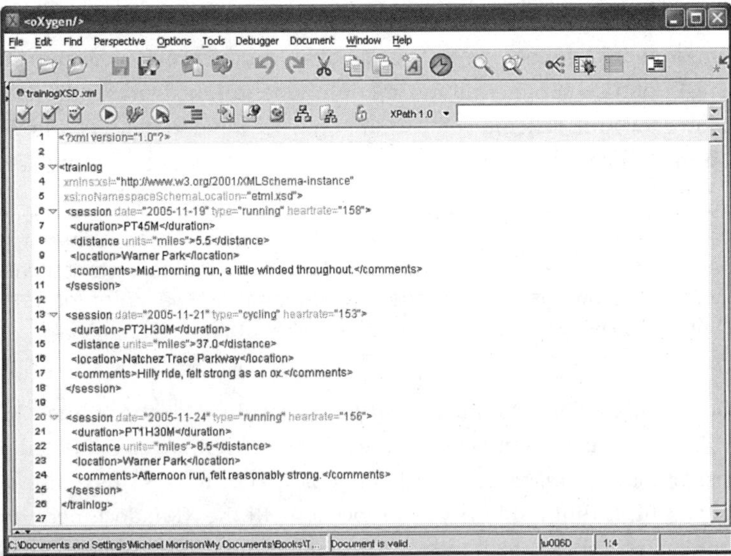

FIGURE 8.6
The <oXygen/> XML Editor is also useful for validating XML documents against XSDs.

Validate Document

The <oXygen/> XML Editor is an excellent and freely available local tool for use in validating XML documents with either DTD or XSD schemas.

Repairing Invalid Documents

If you have any programming experience, the term "debugging" is no doubt familiar to you. If not, get ready because debugging is often the most difficult part of any software development project. Debugging refers to the process of finding and fixing errors in a software application. Depending on the complexity of the code in an application, debugging can get quite messy. The process of repairing invalid XML documents is in many ways similar to debugging software. However, XML isn't a programming language and XML documents aren't programs, which makes things considerably easier for XML developers. That's the good news.

The other good news is that validation tools give you a huge boost when it comes to making your XML documents free of errors. Not only do most validation tools alert you to the existence of errors in a document, but also most of them will give you a pretty good idea about where the errors are in the document. This is no small benefit. Even an experienced XML developer can overlook the most obvious errors after staring at code for long periods of time. Not only that, but XML is an extremely picky language, which leaves the door wide open for you to make mistakes. Errors are, unfortunately, a natural part of the development process, be it software, XML documents, or typing skills that you are developing.

So, knowing that your XML documents are bound to have a few mistakes, how do you go about finding and eliminating the errors? The first step is to run the document through a standard XML parser to check that the document is well formed. Remember that any validation tool will check if a document is well formed if you don't associate the document with a schema. As an example, the <oXygen/> XML Editor includes a toolbar button for simply checking that a document is well formed, as opposed to carrying out a full document validation (see Figure 8.7).

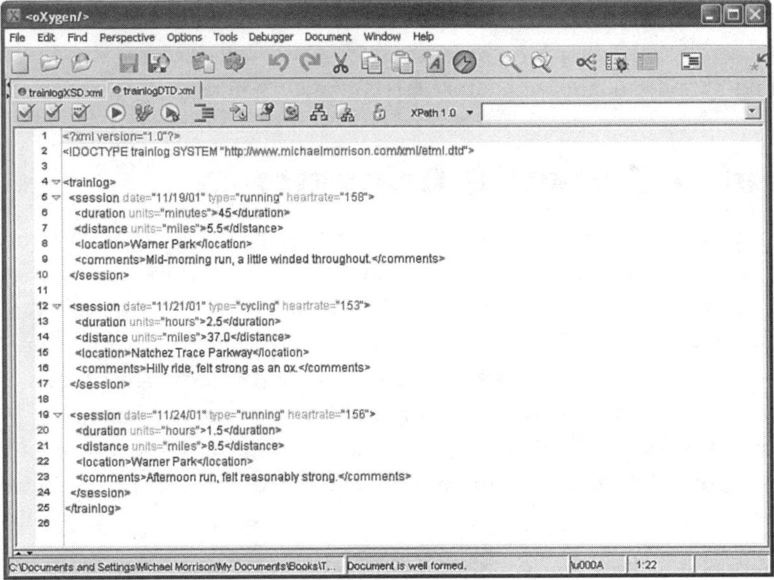

FIGURE 8.7 It is often helpful to test an XML document for well formedness before taking things to the next level and performing a full validation against a schema.

Check That Document is Well Formed

The first time you create a document, consider taking it for a spin through a validation tool without associating it with a schema. At this stage the tool will report only errors in the document that have to do with it being well formed. In other words, no validity checks will be made, which is fine for now.

Errors occurring during the well-formed check include typos in element and attribute names, unmatched tag pairs, and unquoted attribute values, to name a few. These errors should be relatively easy to find, and at some point you should get pretty good at creating documents that are close to being well formed on the first try. In other words, it isn't too terribly difficult to avoid the errors that keep a document from being well formed.

After you've determined that your document is well formed, you can wire it back to a schema and take a shot at checking it for validity. Don't be too disappointed if several errors are reported the first time around. Keep in mind that you are working with a very demanding technology in XML that insists on things being absolutely 100% accurate. You must use elements and attributes in the exact manner as they are laid out in a schema; anything else will lead to validity errors.

Perhaps the trickiest validity error is that of invalid nesting. If you accidentally close an element in the wrong place with a misplaced end tag, it can really confuse a validation tool and give you some strange results. Following is a simple example of what I'm talking about:

```
<session date="2001-11-19" type="running" heartrate="158">
  <duration>PT45M</duration>
  <distance units="miles">5.5</distance>
  <location>Warner Park</location>
  <comments>Mid-morning run, a little winded throughout.
</session>
</comments>
```

In this code the closing `</comments>` tag appears after the closing `</session>` tag, which is an overlap error because the entire `comments` element should be inside of the `session` element. The problem with this kind of error is that it often confuses the validation tool. There is no doubting that you'll get an error report, but it may not isolate the error as accurately as you had hoped. It's even possible for the validation tool to get confused to the extent that a domino effect results, where the single misplaced tag causes many other errors. So, if you get a slew of errors that don't seem to make much sense, study your document carefully and make sure all of your start and end tags match up properly.

Beyond the misplaced end tag problem, most validity errors are relatively easy to track down with the help of a good validation tool. Just pay close attention to the output of the tool, and tackle each error one at a time. With a little diligence, you can have valid documents without much work.

Summary

In previous hours you learned how to create XML documents and schemas that could be used to validate those documents for technical accuracy. What you didn't learn how to do, however, was actually carry out the validation of XML documents. Document validation isn't something you can carry out yourself with a pencil and piece of paper, or even a calculator—validation is an automated process carried out by a special software application known as a validation tool, or validator. Validation tools are a critical part of the XML development process because they allow you to determine the correctness of your documents.

In this hour you learned how document validation is carried out by XML applications. More specifically, you learned about standard and validating parsers and how they fit into the validation equation. You then learned how to use some of the different validation tools available for use in validating XML documents, including both online and local tools. And finally, you found out how to track down and repair errors in XML documents.

Q&A

Q. ***Is it possible to validate HTML web pages?***

A. Strictly speaking, it isn't possible to validate HTML-based documents because HTML isn't actually an XML language and therefore doesn't conform to the rules of XML. However, you can code web pages in XHTML, which is a markup language that can be validated. XHTML is an XML-based language that is very similar to HTML but with the improved structure of XML. You learn all about XHTML in Hour 21, "Adding Structure to the Web with XHTML," including how to validate XHTML web pages.

Q. ***Do I have to check a document for well formedness before moving on to checking it for validity?***

A. No. I recommend the two-stage check on a document only because it helps to clarify the different types of errors commonly found in XML documents. Your goal should be to develop enough XML coding skills to avoid most well-formedness errors, which frees you up to spend most of your time tackling the peskier validity errors. Knowing this, at some point you may decide to jump straight into the validity check for documents as you gain experience.

Workshop

The Workshop is designed to help you anticipate possible questions, review what you've learned, and begin learning how to put your knowledge into practice.

Quiz

1. What is an XML processor?
2. What's the difference between a standard parser and a validating parser?
3. What is the main limitation of some web-based XML validation tools?

Quiz Answers

1. An XML processor is usually part of a larger XML application, and its job is to process XML documents and somehow make the results available for further processing or display within the application.
2. A standard parser first checks to see if a document is well formed, whereas a validating parser further checks to see if it is valid.

3. Some web-based XML validation tools can be difficult to use when the documents to be validated (and their associated schemas) are stored on a local hard drive. The XML Schema Validator mentioned in this lesson is one notable online tool that doesn't suffer from this problem.

Exercises

1. Modify one of the training log example documents so that the code intentionally violates the ETML schema. Run the file through a validation tool and take note of the error(s) reported.

2. Repair the error code in the training log document and make sure that it validates properly in a validation tool.

PART III

Formatting and Displaying XML Documents

HOUR 9
XML Formatting Strategies

> XML is like a VW Jetta: environmentally sensitive, slow, dependable, and terminally uncool. Lasts a lifetime.
>
> —Nat Torkington

As terminally uncool as XML may be perceived by some, one aspect of XML that certainly isn't uncool is XML formatting. The reason is because you can dress up XML quite a bit by formatting it properly. There are two fundamentally different approaches to formatting XML documents, both of which you learn about in this hour and in the remainder of this part of the book. I'm referring to Cascading Style Sheets (CSS) and eXtensible Style Language (XSL). CSS is already in use around the Web as a means of formatting HTML web pages above and beyond the limited formatting capabilities of HTML. XSL, on the other hand, is purely designed for use with XML and is ultimately much more powerful and flexible than CSS. Even so, these technologies aren't really in competition with each other. As you learn in this hour, they offer unique solutions to different problems, so you will likely find a use for each of them in different scenarios.

In this hour, you'll learn

- The basics of style sheets and XML formatting
- When and why to use CSS and XSL on the Web
- The practical differences between CSS and XSL style sheets
- How to format a basic XML document using CSS and XSLT style sheets

Style Sheets and XML Formatting

Very few XML-based markup languages are designed to accommodate the formatting of content described with them. This is actually by design—the whole premise of XML is to provide a way of associating meaning to information while separating the appearance of the information. The appearance of information is very much a secondary issue in XML. Of course, there are situations where it can be very important to view XML content in a more understandable context than raw XML code (elements and attributes), in which case it becomes necessary to format the content for display. Formatting XML content for display primarily involves determining the layout and positioning of the content, along with the fonts and colors used to render the content and any related graphics that accompany the content. XML content is typically formatted for specific display purposes, such as within a web browser.

Similar to HTML, XML documents are formatted using special formatting instructions known as styles. A style can be something as simple as a font size or as powerful as a transformation of an XML element into an HTML element or an element in some other XML-based language. The general mechanism used to apply formatting to XML documents is known as a style sheet. I say "general" because there are two different approaches to styling XML documents with style sheets: CSS (Cascading Style Sheets) and XSL (eXtensible Style Language). Although I'd love to jump into a detailed discussion of CSS and XSL, I think a quick history lesson is in order so that you understand the relevance of style sheets. The next couple of sections provide you with some background on style sheets as they relate to HTML, along with how they enter the picture with XML. I'll make it as brief as possible so that you can get down to the business of seeing style sheets in action with XML.

The Need for Style Sheets

If it wasn't for the success of HTML, it's unlikely that XML would have ever been created. The concept of using a markup language to code information is nothing new, but the idea of doing it with a simple, compact language is relatively new. HTML is the first markup language that made it possible to code information in a compact format that could be displayed without too much complexity. However, HTML wasn't intended to be a presentation language. Generally speaking, markup languages are designed to add structure and context to information, which usually has nothing to do with how the information is displayed. The idea is that you use markup code to describe the content of documents and then apply styles to the content to render it for display purposes. The problem with this approach is that it has only recently been adopted by HTML. This has to do with the fact that HTML evolved so rapidly that presentation elements were added to the language without any concern over how it might complicate things.

In its original form, HTML stuck to the notion of being a purely content-based markup language. More specifically, HTML was designed as a markup language that allowed physicists to share technical notes. Early web browsers allowed you to view HTML documents, but the browsers, not the HTML markup, determined the layout of the documents. For example, paragraphs marked up with the <p> tag might have been displayed in a 12-point Arial font in a certain browser. A different browser might have used a 14-point Helvetica font. The point is that the browsers made the presentation decisions, not the documents themselves, which is in keeping with the general concept of a markup language.

As you probably know, things changed quickly for HTML when the popularity of the Web necessitated improvements in the appearance of web pages. In fact, HTML quickly turned into something it was never meant to be—a jumbled mess of content and presentation markup. At the time it made sense to hack on presentation elements to HTML because it allowed for better-looking web pages. Another factor that complicated HTML was the "browser wars," which pitted web browser vendors against one another in a game of feature one-upmanship that resulted in all kinds of new HTML presentation tags. These tags proved extremely problematic for web developers because they were usually supported on only one browser or another.

To summarize my HTML soapbox speech, we all got a little carried away and tried to turn HTML into something it was never intended to be. No one really thought about what would happen after a few years of tacking on tag after presentation tag to HTML. Fortunately, the web development community took some time to assess the future of the Web and went back to the ideal of separating content from presentation. Style sheets provide the mechanism that makes it possible to separate content from presentation and bring some order to HTML. Whereas style sheets are a good idea for HTML documents, they are a necessity for displaying XML documents—more on this in a moment. A style sheet addresses the presentation needs of HTML documents by defining layout and formatting rules that tell a browser how to display the different parts of a document.

Unlike HTML, XML doesn't include any standard elements that can be used to describe the appearance of XML documents. For example, there is no standard `<b>` tag in XML for adding bold formatting to text in XML. For this reason, style sheets are an absolute necessity when it comes to displaying XML documents.

By the Way

Technically, you could create your own XML-based markup language and include any presentation-specific tags you wanted, such as `<bold>`, `<big>`, `<small>`, `<blurry>`, and so on. However, web browsers are designed specifically to understand HTML and HTML only and therefore wouldn't inherently understand your presentation tags. This is why style sheets are so important to XML.

Getting to Know CSS and XSL

Style sheets aren't really anything new to web developers, but they were initially slow to take off primarily due to the fact that browser support for them was sketchy for quite some time. *Cascading Style Sheets*, or *CSS*, represent the HTML approach to style sheets because they were designed specifically to solve the presentation problems inherent in HTML. Because CSS originally targeted HTML, it has been around the longest and has garnered the most support among web developers. Even so, only recently has

CSS finally gained reasonably consistent support in major web browsers; all major web browsers now more or less offer full support for the latest CSS standard, CSS 2.

eXtensible Style Language, or *XSL*, is a much newer technology than CSS and represents the pure XML approach to styling XML documents. XSL has had somewhat of a hurdle to clear in terms of browser acceptance but the latest releases of most major web browsers provide solid support for a subset of XSL known as XSLT (XSL Transformation), which allows you to translate XML documents into HTML. XSLT doesn't tackle the same layout and formatting issues as CSS and therefore isn't really a competing technology. The layout and formatting portion of XSL is known as *XSL Formatting Objects*, or *XSL-FO*, and is unfortunately not as fully supported as XSLT. For the time being, XSL-FO is primarily being used to format XML data for printing. In fact, XSL-FO is commonly used to generate printer-friendly Adobe Acrobat PDF documents from XML documents.

Generally speaking, you can think of XSL's relationship to XML as being similar to CSS's relationship to HTML. This comparison isn't entirely accurate since XSL effectively defines a superset of the styling functionality in CSS thanks to XSL-FO, whereas XSLT offers a transformation feature that has no equivalent in CSS. But in very broad terms, you can think of XSL as the pure XML equivalent of CSS. The next couple of sections explain CSS and XSL in more detail.

Cascading Style Sheets (CSS)

As you've learned, CSS is a style sheet language designed to style HTML documents, thereby allowing web developers to separate content from presentation. Prior to CSS, the only options for styling HTML documents beyond the presentation tags built into HTML were scripting languages and hybrid solutions such as Dynamic HTML (DHTML). CSS is much simpler to learn and use than these approaches, which makes it ideal for styling HTML documents, and it doesn't impose any of the security risks associated with scripts. Although CSS was designed for use with HTML, there is nothing stopping you from using it with XML. In fact, it is quite useful for styling XML documents.

When a CSS style sheet is applied to an XML document, it uses the structure of the document as the basis for applying style rules. More specifically, the hierarchical "tree" of document data is used to apply style rules. Although this works great in some scenarios, it's sometimes necessary to alter the structure of an XML document before applying style rules. For example, you might want to sort the contents of a document alphabetically before displaying it. CSS is very useful for styling XML data, but it has no way of allowing you to collate, sort, or otherwise rearrange document data. This type of task is best suited to a transformation technology such as XSLT. The bottom line is that CSS is better suited to the simple styling of XML documents for display purposes. Of course, you can always transform a document using XSLT and then style it with CSS, which is in some ways the best of both worlds, at least in terms of XML and traditional style sheets.

> On behalf of die-hard CSS advocates, I'd like to point out that you can transform an XML document using a scripting language and the Document Object Model (DOM) prior to applying CSS style sheets, which achieves roughly the same effect as using XSLT to transform the document. Although the DOM certainly presents an option for transforming XML documents, there are those of us who would rather use a structured transformation language instead of having to rely on custom scripts. You learn how to use scripts and the DOM with XML in Part IV, "Processing and Managing XML Data."

Extensible Style Language (XSL)

Earlier in the hour I mentioned that XSL consists of two primary components that address the styling of XML documents: XSLT and XSL-FO. XSLT stands for XSL Transformation and is the component of XSL that allows you to transform an XML document from one language to another. For example, with XSLT you could translate one of your custom ETML training log documents into HTML that is capable of being displayed in a web browser. The other part of XSL is XSL-FO, which stands for XSL Formatting Objects. XSL-FO is somewhat of a supercharged CSS designed specifically for XML. Both XSLT and XSL-FO are implemented as XML-based markup languages. Using these two languages, web developers theoretically have complete control over both the transformation of XML document content and its subsequent display. I say "theoretically" because XSL-FO has yet to catch on as a browser rendering style sheet language, and thus far has been relegated to assisting in formatting XML documents for printing.

Because both components of XSL are implemented as XML languages, style sheets created from them are XML documents. This allows you to create XSL style sheets using familiar XML syntax, not to mention being able to use XML development tools. You might see a familiar connection between XSL and another XML technology, XML Schema. As you may recall from the previous hour, XML Schema is implemented as an XML language (XSD) that replaces a pre-XML approach (DTD) for describing the structure of XML documents. XSL is similar in that it, too, employs XML languages to eventually replace a pre-XML approach (CSS) to styling XML documents.

Rendering XML with Style Sheets

Although the general premise of style sheets is to provide a means of displaying XML content, it's important to understand that style sheets don't necessarily have complete control over how XML content appears. For example, text that is styled with emphasis in a style sheet might be displayed in italics in a traditional browser, but it could be spoken with emphasis in a browser for the visually impaired. This distinction doesn't necessarily impact the creation of style sheets, but it is worth keeping in mind, especially as new types of web-enabled devices are created. Some of these new devices will render documents in different ways than we're currently accustomed to. On the other hand, it is possible to create style sheets that are very exacting when it comes to how XML data is displayed. For example, using XSL-FO you can specify the exact dimensions of a printed page, including margin sizes and the specific location of XML content on the page. The degree to which you have control over the appearance of styled XML content largely has to do with whether the content is being rendered in a web browser or in some other medium, such as print.

The concept of different devices rendering XML documents in different ways has been referred to as *cross-medium rendering* due to the fact that the devices typically represent different mediums. Historically, HTML has had to contend with *cross-browser rendering*, which was caused by different browsers supporting different presentation tags. Even though style sheets alleviate the cross-browser problem, they don't always deal with the cross-medium problem. To understand what I mean by this, consider CSS style sheets, which provide a means of applying layout rules to XML so that it can be displayed. The relatively simplistic styling approach taken by CSS isn't powerful enough to deal with the cross-medium issue because it can't transform an XML document into a different format, which is often required to successfully render a document in a different medium.

XSLT addresses the need for transforming XML documents according to a set of highly structured patterns. For display purposes, you can use XSLT to translate an XML document into an HTML document. This is the primary way XML developers are currently using XSL because it doesn't require anything more on the part of browsers than support for XSLT; they don't have to be able to render a document directly from XML. CSS doesn't involve any transformation; it simply provides a means of describing how different parts of a document should be displayed.

> Some people incorrectly perceive XSL and CSS as competing technologies, but they really aren't. In fact, it can be very advantageous to use XSLT and CSS together. Competition primarily enters the picture with XSL-FO, which indeed does everything that CSS can do, and much more. Even so, the popularity of CSS as a style sheet technology for web pages will likely prevent XSL-FO from seriously encroaching on it in the near term. For now, we'll likely see CSS continue to be used as the dominant style sheet technology for web-based XML formatting, while XSL-FO will continue to rise in importance for print-based XML formatting.

Leveraging CSS, XSLT, and XSL-FO

You've already spent some time learning about the differences between CSS and XSL, but it's worth going through a more detailed comparison so that you have a solid understanding of your style sheet options. More importantly, I want to point out some of the issues for choosing one style sheet technology over the other, especially when working with documents in a web environment. The technologies are just similar enough that it can be difficult determining when to use which one. You may find that the best approach to styling XML documents is a hybrid approach involving both XSL and CSS.

There are several key differences between CSS, XSLT, and XSL-FO, which I've alluded to earlier in the hour:

- CSS allows you to style HTML documents (XSLT cannot, and XSL-FO cannot unless the documents are valid XHTML documents)
- XSL-FO allows you to style XML documents via an XML syntax (CSS and XSLT cannot), although web support is lacking
- XSLT allows you to transform XML documents (CSS and XSL-FO cannot)

You're here to learn about XML, not HTML, so the first difference between CSS and XSLT/XSL-FO might not seem to matter much. However, when you consider the fact that many XML applications currently involve HTML documents to some degree, this may be an issue when assessing the appropriate style sheet technology for a given project. And more importantly, you have to consider the fact that XSL-FO has yet to garner browser support, which means that it isn't a viable option for formatting data to be displayed on the Web.

The third difference is critical in that CSS provides no direct means of transforming XML documents. You can use a scripting language with the DOM to transform XML documents, but that's another issue that requires considerable knowledge of XML scripting, which you gain in Part IV. Unlike scripting languages, CSS was explicitly designed for use by nonprogrammers, which explains why it is so easy to learn and use. CSS simply attaches style properties to elements in an XML/HTML document. The simplicity of CSS comes with limitations, some of which follow:

- CSS cannot reuse document data
- CSS cannot conditionally select document data (other than hiding specific types of elements)
- CSS cannot calculate quantities or store values in variables
- CSS cannot generate dynamic text, such as page numbers

These limitations of CSS are important because they are noticeably missing in XSLT. In other words, XSLT is capable of carrying out these tasks and therefore doesn't suffer from the same weaknesses. If you don't mind a steeper learning curve, the XSLT capabilities for searching and rearranging document content are far superior to both CSS and XSL-FO. Of course, XSLT doesn't directly support formatting styles in the way that CSS and XSL-FO do, so you may find that using XSLT by itself still falls short in some regards. This may lead you to consider pairing XSLT with CSS or XSL-FO for the ultimate flexibility in styling XML documents. Following are a couple of ways that XSLT and CSS/XSL-FO can be used together to provide a hybrid XML style sheet solution:

1. Use XSLT to transform XML documents into HTML documents that are styled with CSS style sheets.
2. Use XSLT to transform XML documents into XML documents that are styled with CSS or XSL-FO style sheets.

The first approach represents the most straightforward combination of XSLT and CSS because its results are in HTML form, which is more easily understood by web browsers. In fact, a web browser doesn't even know that XML is involved when using this approach; all that the browser sees is a regular HTML document that is the result of an XSLT transformation on the server. The second approach is interesting because it involves styling XML code directly in browsers. This means that it isn't necessary to first transform XML documents into HTML/XHTML documents; the only transformation that takes place in this case is the transformation from one XML document into another XML document that is better suited for presentation.

The emphasis for now needs to be on styling XML documents for the Web using CSS as opposed to XSL-FO because CSS is much more widely supported in browsers. However, this may change as web developers continue to inject more XML into their web sites, which could lead browser vendors to eventually offer better support for XSL-FO.

Style Sheets in Action

Every style sheet regardless of its type is a text file. CSS style sheets adhere to their own text format, whereas XSLT and XSL-FO style sheets are considered XML documents. CSS style sheets are always given a file extension of `.css`. XSLT and XSL-FO style sheets are a little different in that they can use one of several file extensions. First of all, it's completely legal to use the general `.xml` file extension for both XSLT and XSL-FO style sheets. However, if you want to get more specific you can use the

`.xsl` file extension for either type of style sheet. Or if you want to take things a step further, you can use the `.xslt` file extension for XSLT style sheets and `.fo` file extension for XSL-FO style sheets. The bottom line is that the type of the file is determined only when the content is processed, so the file extension is more for your purposes in quickly identifying the types of files.

By the Way

> The XSLT example later in this lesson uses the `.xsl` file extension to reference an XSLT style sheet.

The next few hours spend plenty of time exploring the inner workings of CSS and XSL, but I hate for you to leave this hour without seeing a practical example of the technologies in action. Earlier in the book I used an XML document (`talltales.xml`) that contained questions and answers for a trivia game called Tall Tales as an example. I'd like to revisit that document, as it presents a perfect opportunity to demonstrate the basic usage of CSS and XSLT style sheets. Listing 9.1 is the Tall Tales trivia document.

By the Way

> If you're wondering why I don't provide an example of an XSL-FO style sheet here, it's because I want you to be able to immediately see the results in a web browser. As you learn in Hour 14, "Formatting XML with XSL-FO," XSL-FO requires the assistance of a special processor application known as a FOP (XSL-FO Processor).

LISTING 9.1 The Tall Tales Example XML Document

```
<?xml version="1.0"?>

<talltales>
  <tt answer="a">
    <question>
      In 1994, a man had an accident while robbing a pizza restaurant in
      Akron, Ohio, that resulted in his arrest. What happened to him?
    </question>
    <a>He slipped on a patch of grease on the floor and knocked himself
    out.</a>
    <b>He backed into a police car while attempting to drive off.</b>
    <c>He choked on a breadstick that he had grabbed as he was running
    out.</c>
  </tt>

  <tt answer="c">
    <question>
      In 1993, a man was charged with burglary in Martinsville, Indiana,
      after the homeowners discovered his presence. How were the homeowners
      alerted to his presence?
    </question>
    <a>He had rung the doorbell before entering.</a>
    <b>He had rattled some pots and pans while making himself a waffle in
    their kitchen.</b>
    <c>He was playing their piano.</c>
```

LISTING 9.1 Continued

```
  </tt>

  <tt answer="a">
    <question>
      In 1994, the Nestle UK food company was fined for injuries suffered
      by a 36 year-old employee at a plant in York, England. What happened
      to the man?
    </question>
    <a>He fell in a giant mixing bowl and was whipped for over a minute.</a>
    <b>He developed an ulcer while working as a candy bar tester.</b>
    <c>He was hit in the head with a large piece of flying chocolate.</c>
  </tt>
</talltales>
```

Nothing is too tricky here; it's just XML code for questions and answers in a quirky trivia game. Notice that each question/answer set is enclosed within a tt element—this will be important in a moment when you see the CSS and XSLT style sheets used to transform the document.

It's worth pointing out that there are slightly different versions of the XML document required for each style sheet. This is because an XML document must reference the appropriate style sheet that is used to format its content.

The CSS Solution

The CSS solution to styling any XML document is simply to provide style rules for the different elements in the document. These style rules are applied to all of the elements in a document in order to provide a visualization of the document. In the case of the Tall Tales document, there are really only five elements of interest: tt, question, a, b, and c. Listing 9.2 is the CSS style sheet (talltales.css) that defines style rules for these elements.

LISTING 9.2 The talltales.css CSS Style Sheet for Formatting the Tall Tales XML Document

```
talltales {
  background-image: url(background.gif);
  background-repeat: repeat;
}

tt {
  display: block;
  width: 700px;
  padding: 10px;
  margin: 10px;
  border: 5px groove #353A54;
  background-color: #353A54;
}
```

```

question {
  display: block;
  color: #F4EECA;
  font-family: Verdana, Arial;
  font-size: 13pt;
  text-align: left;
}

a, b, c {
  display: block;
  color: #6388A0;
  font-family: Verdana, Arial;
  font-size: 12pt;
  text-indent: 14px;
  text-align: left;
}
```

Before we go any further, understand that I don't expect you to understand the inner workings of this CSS code. You don't formally learn about CSS style rules until the next hour—right now I just wanted to hit you with a practical example so you could at least see what a CSS style sheet looks like. If you already have experience with CSS by way of HTML, this style sheet should be pretty easy to understand. If not, you can hopefully study it and at least take in the high points. For example, it's not too hard to figure out that colors and fonts are being set for each of the elements. Figure 9.1 shows the result of using this style sheet to display the Tall Tales XML document in Firefox.

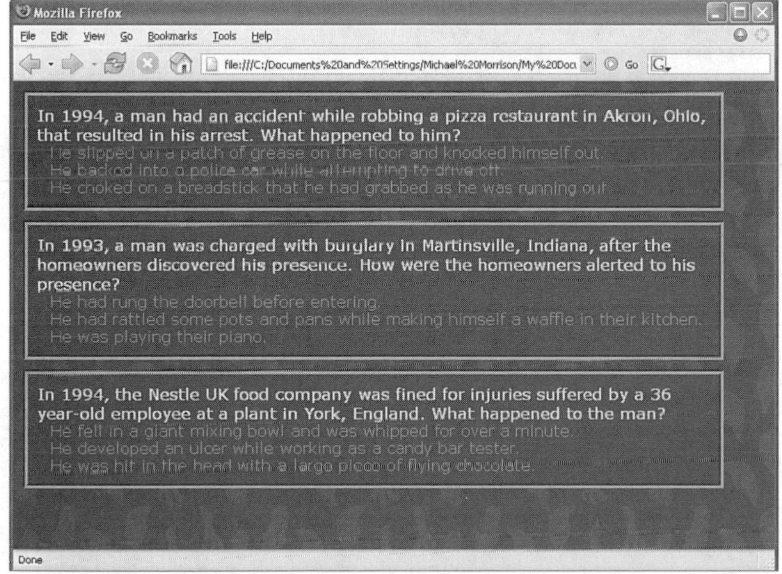

FIGURE 9.1 The Tall Tales example document is displayed in Firefox using a CSS style sheet.

By the Way

> As with all the examples throughout the book, the complete code for the Tall Tales example is available from my web site at http://www.michaelmorrison.com/. The version of the Tall Tales XML document that is styled via CSS is titled `talltales_css.xml`.

Although you can't quite make out the colors in this figure, it's apparent from the style sheet code that colors are being used to display the elements. Now it's time to take a look at how XSLT can be used to arrive at the same visual result.

The XSLT Solution

The XSLT approach to the Tall Tales document involves translating the document into HTML. Although it's possible to simply translate the document into HTML and let HTML do the job of determining how the data is displayed, a better idea is to use inline CSS styles to format the data directly within the HTML code. Keep in mind that when you translate an XML document into HTML using XSLT, you can include anything that you would otherwise include in an HTML document, including inline CSS styles. Listing 9.3 shows the XSLT style sheet (`talltales.xslt`) for use with the Tall Tales document.

LISTING 9.3 The `talltales.xsl` XSLT Style Sheet for Transforming the Tall Tales XML Document into HTML

```
<?xml version="1.0"?>
<xsl:stylesheet version="1.0"
  xmlns:xsl="http://www.w3.org/1999/XSL/Transform"
  xmlns="http://www.w3.org/1999/xhtml">
  <xsl:template match="/">
    <html xmlns="http://www.w3.org/1999/xhtml">
      <head>
      </head>
      <body style="background-image: url(background.gif); background-repeat:
      repeat">
        <xsl:for-each select="talltales/tt">
          <div style="width:700px; padding:10px; margin: 10px;
            border:5px groove #353A54; background-color:#353A54">
            <xsl:apply-templates select="question"/>
            <xsl:apply-templates select="a"/>
            <xsl:apply-templates select="b"/>
            <xsl:apply-templates select="c"/>
          </div>
        </xsl:for-each>
      </body>
    </html>
  </xsl:template>

  <xsl:template match="question">
    <div style="color:#F4EECA; font-family:Verdana,Arial; font-size:13pt">
      <xsl:value-of select="."/>
    </div>
```

```
  </xsl:template>

  <xsl:template match="a|b|c">
    <div style="color:#6388A0; font-family:Verdana,Arial; font-size:12pt;
    text-indent:14px">
      <xsl:value-of select="."/>
    </div>
  </xsl:template>
</xsl:stylesheet>
```

Notice that this style sheet is considerably more complex than its CSS counterpart. This has to do with the fact that this style sheet is actually constructing an HTML document on the fly. In other words, the XSLT code is describing how to build an HTML document out of XML data, complete with inline CSS styles. Again, you could accomplish a similar feat without the CSS styles, but you wouldn't be able to make the resulting page look exactly like the result of the CSS style sheet. This is because XSLT isn't in the business of controlling font sizes and colors; XSLT is all about transforming data. Figure 9.2 shows the result of viewing the Tall Tales document in Internet Explorer using the XSLT style sheet.

The version of the Tall Tales XML document that is styled via XSLT is titled talltales_xslt.xml, and is available for download as part of the complete example code for this book at my web site (http://www.michaelmorrison.com/).

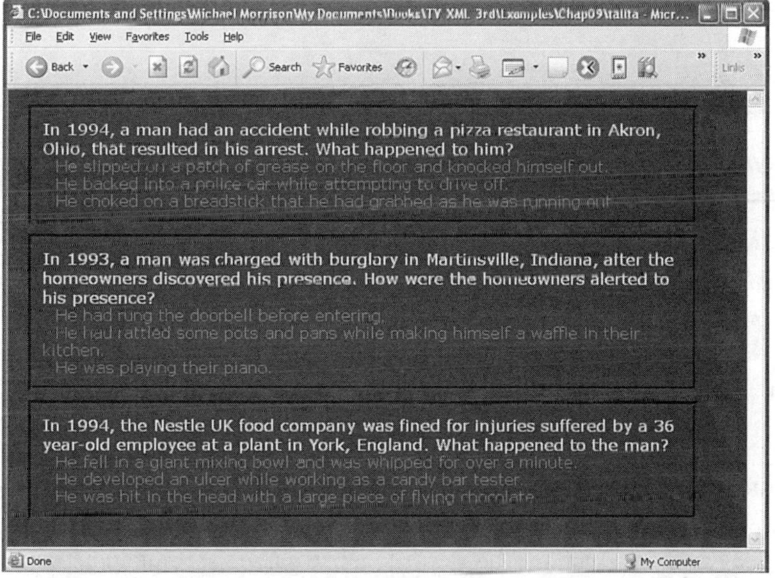

FIGURE 9.2
The Tall Tales example document is displayed in Internet Explorer using an XSLT style sheet.

If you look back to Figure 9.1, you'll be hard pressed to tell the difference between it and this figure. In fact, the only noticeable difference is the file name of the document in the title bar of the web browser. This reveals how it is often possible to accomplish similar tasks using either CSS or XSLT. Obviously, CSS is superior for styling simple XML documents due to the simplicity of CSS style sheets. However, any time you need to massage the data in an XML document before displaying it, you'll have to go with XSLT.

Summary

Style sheets represent an important technological innovation with respect to the Web because they make it possible to exert exacting control over the appearance of content in both HTML and XML documents. Style sheets allow markup languages such as HTML and other custom XML-based languages to focus on their primary job—structuring data according to its meaning. With a clean separation between content and presentation, documents coded in HTML and XML are better organized and more easily managed.

This hour introduced you to the basics of style sheets, including the three main style sheet technologies that are applicable to XML: CSS, XSLT, and XSL-FO. Although these technologies all solve similar problems, they are very different technologies with unique pros and cons. Although you learned the fundamentals of how and when to use each type of style sheet, the remaining hours in this part of the book paint a much clearer picture of what can be done in the way of styling XML data with CSS, XSLT, and XSL-FO style sheets.

Q&A

Q. ***Why is it so important to separate the presentation of a document from its content?***

A. It's been proven time and again that mixing data with its presentation severely hampers the structure and organization of the data because it becomes very difficult to draw a line between what is content and what is presentation. For example, it is currently difficult for search engines to extract meaningful information about web pages because most HTML documents are concerned solely with how information is to be displayed. If those documents were coded according to meaning, as opposed to worrying so much about presentation, the Web and its search engines would be much smarter. Of course, we all care about how information looks, especially on the Web, so no one ever said to do away with presentation. The idea is to make a clean separation between content and presentation so that both of them can be more easily managed.

A good example of how this concept is being applied to a very practical web service is Yahoo!'s Flickr online photo service (http://www.flickr.com/), which allows you to associate keywords with photographs that you post online. As more and more people add context to their photographs via keywords, it will be increasingly possible to search the Web for the content of photographs, which is something previously impossible. With photographs, the content is inherently linked with the presentation but keywords allow you to tack on additional information about the content.

Q. *What does it mean to state that XSL-FO is a superset of CSS?*

A. When I say that XSL-FO is a superset of CSS, I mean that XSL-FO encompasses the functionality of CSS and also goes far beyond CSS. In other words, XSL-FO is designed to support the features of CSS along with many new features of its own. The idea behind this approach is to provide a smooth migration path between CSS and XSL-FO because XSL-FO inherently supports CSS features.

Workshop

The Workshop is designed to help you anticipate possible questions, review what you've learned, and begin learning how to put your knowledge into practice.

Quiz

1. What is the significance of style sheets for HTML documents?
2. What kinds of standard elements does XML include for describing the appearance of XML documents?
3. What are the two major parts of XSL?
4. In the Tall Tales trivia example, how did the `talltales.xsl` style sheet make use of CSS to format the `talltales_xslt.xml` document?

Quiz Answers

1. A style sheet addresses the presentation needs of HTML documents by defining layout and formatting rules that tell a browser how to display the different parts of a document.
2. XML doesn't include any kind of standard elements for describing the appearance of XML documents, which is why style sheets are so important for displaying XML documents.

3. The two major parts of XSL are XSLT (XSL Transformation) and XSL-FO (XSL Formatting Objects). XSLT allows you to translate XML documents into other languages, but it doesn't tackle the same layout and formatting issues as CSS. XSL-FO addresses the layout and formatting of XML documents, and is considered a superset of CSS.

4. The `talltales.xsl` style sheet made use of inline CSS styles to format the `talltales_xslt.xml` document, which means that style rules were applied directly within HTML tags.

Exercises

1. Modify the `talltales.css` style sheet so that the fonts and colors are different. Open the `talltales_css.xml` document in a web browser to view the results.

2. Try to match the changes you just made to the `talltales.css` style sheet in the `talltales.xsl` style sheet. Open the `talltales_xslt.xml` document in a web browser to view the results.

HOUR 10

Styling XML Content with CSS

It's not an optical illusion; it just looks like one.

—Phil White

Fortunately, due to its relative simplicity, there are no optical illusions associated with CSS (Cascading Style Sheets); all of the visual "trickery" in CSS is made possible with clear and concise style properties. CSS allows you to attach formatting styles to individual elements within an XML document. These styles are then used to determine how the elements in the document are rendered for display within a web browser. Even though the XML language doesn't inherently include any mechanism for defining how a document looks, CSS makes it possible to add a view to XML documents. This hour explores CSS inside and out, including how to create style sheets for XML documents with CSS. You find out that CSS style properties, although simple to use, provide a considerable degree of flexibility over the positioning and formatting of XML content. You also learn how to control the flow of text on a page, not to mention how to use fonts, colors, background images, and letter spacing.

In this hour, you'll learn

- The basic structure and syntax of CSS
- How to create a basic CSS style sheet for an existing XML document
- How to control the layering of elements with CSS
- How to use margins and padding to control the spacing around and within elements
- How to format text using several different CSS style properties

Getting to Know CSS

You learned in the previous hour that CSS allows you to format XML content so that it can be displayed in web browsers. CSS first came about as a means of improving the presentation of HTML content, but it turns out that it also works quite well with XML content. CSS is itself a language that defines style constructs such as fonts, colors, and positioning, which are used to describe how data is displayed. CSS styles are stored in style sheets, which contain style rules that apply styles to elements of a given type. Style sheet rules are usually placed in external style sheet documents with the filename extension `.css`.

The "cascading" part of CSS refers to the manner in which style sheet rules are applied to elements in an XML (or HTML) document. More specifically, styles in CSS form a hierarchy where more specific styles override more general styles. It is the responsibility of CSS to determine the precedence of style rules according to this hierarchy, which gives the rules a cascading effect. In some ways, you can think of the cascading mechanism in CSS as being similar to genetic inheritance, where general traits are passed on from a parent, but more specific traits are entirely unique to an individual; base style rules are applied throughout a style sheet but can be overridden by more specific style rules.

By the Way

> Like many web-related technologies, CSS has undergone revisions since its original release. The original version of CSS was known as CSS1 and included basic support for formatting web page content. CSS2 built on the feature set of CSS1 by adding powerful new features, such as the absolute positioning of content. There is a CSS3 in the works, but popular web browsers only support CSS1 and CSS2. All of the CSS example code in this book is compliant with CSS1 and CSS2, which means you should have no problem using it with popular web browsers.

The application of CSS style rules is determined by *selectors*, which are CSS constructs that identify portions of an XML document. A selector establishes the link between a document and a style or set of styles. There are three kinds of selectors used in CSS:

- *Element type*—Selects an element of a given type
- *Attribute class*—Selects an element of a certain class that is identified by a special attribute
- *Attribute ID*—Selects an element with an ID that is identified by a special attribute

An *element type selector* selects an element of a given type and applies a style or set of styles to it. This is the simplest approach to using CSS because there is a simple one-to-one mapping between element types and styles. As an example, you could use an element type selector to define a set of styles dictating the margins and font for an element named `message` in an XML document. Any messages marked up with this element would be displayed according to the styles defined in the style rule with the `message` element type selector. Following is an example of such a style rule:

```
message {
  display:block;
  margin-bottom:5px;
  font-family:Courier;
  font-size:14pt;
}
```

This example uses an element type selector to select the message element and apply a series of styles to it. The end result is that all elements of type message appearing in a document will have a 5-pixel margin and will be rendered in a 14-point Courier font. Following is an example of how you might mark up a message in an XML document:

```
<message>
It's very lonely here — I really miss you.
</message>
```

By the Way

> As you know, there is no standard message element in XML; in fact, there are no standard elements of any kind in XML. This example simply demonstrates how you would apply a style to an element that stores a text message. Notice that the XML code says nothing about how the element is to be displayed—this is relegated to the CSS style rule.

An attribute class selector is a little more specific than the element type selector in that it allows you to apply styles to elements based upon an attribute. In addition to applying styles based upon a type of element, CSS uses attribute selectors to look for specific elements containing a special attribute with a certain value. This attribute is named class and is capable of having virtually any value you desire. The premise of the class attribute is that you use it to define classes of styles within a given element type. Following is an example of how you might define a special class of messages that are urgent:

```
message.urgent {
  display:block;
  margin-bottom:5px;
  font-family:Courier;
  font-size:14pt;
  font-style:italic;
  color:red;
}
```

The class name in this example is urgent, which is identified by separating it from the element type with a period (.). Following is an example of how you would mark up a paragraph corresponding to this style rule:

```
<message class="urgent">
The sky is falling!
</message>
```

As you can see, the urgent class name is provided as the value of the class attribute of the <message> tag. This is the standard approach to using CSS attribute class selectors in XML documents. However, there is one other option when it comes to using CSS selectors: attribute ID selectors.

For the utmost in styling flexibility, you can use an *attribute ID selector*, which establishes a style rule that can be applied to any element regardless of its type. Like attribute class selectors, attribute ID selectors rely on a special attribute. However, in this case the attribute is named `id`, and it isn't associated with any particular element type. Following is an example of creating a style rule using an attribute ID selector:

```
#groovy {
  color:green;
  font-family:Times;
  font-style:italic;
  font-weight:bold;
}
```

This example creates a style rule with an attribute ID selector named `groovy`; the pound sign (#) is used to indicate that this is an attribute ID selector. To use this style, you simply reference it as a value of the `id` attribute in any element type. Following is an example of how you might use the style with a `message` element:

```
<message id="groovy">
I'm feeling pretty groovy!
</message>
```

Unlike the `urgent` attribute class selector, which is specific to the `message` element, the `groovy` attribute ID selector can be used with any element, in which case the element will be displayed with the `groovy` styles. For example, following is an example of how the `groovy` selector can be used with an element named `note`:

```
<note id="groovy">
Pick up leisure suit from laundry.
</note>
```

Although selectors play an important role in determining how styles are applied to documents, they are only a part of the CSS equation. The other major part of style sheet syntax is the *style declaration*, which is used to specify a style property and its associated value. You've already seen style declarations in the preceding selector examples, but now it's time to learn how they work. Style declarations in CSS are similar in some ways to XML attributes in that they assign a value to a property. CSS supports a wide range of style properties that can be set to establish the style of a given style rule. Together with selectors, style declarations comprise the syntax of a CSS style rule, which follows:

```
Selector {
  Property1:Value1;
  Property2:Value2;
  ...
}
```

Following is the message style rule that you saw earlier, which helps to reveal the structure of style declarations:

```
message {
  display:block;
  margin-bottom:5px;
  font-family:Courier;
  font-size:14pt;
}
```

The message example style rule includes four style properties: display, margin-bottom, font-family, and font-size. Each of these properties has a value associated with it that together comprise the style rule of the message element. Notice that each style property and value is separated by a colon (:), whereas the property/value pairs are separated by semicolons (;).

By the Way

> Although semicolons are used to separate styles, not terminate them, it's generally a good practice to terminate the last property/value pair in a style rule with a semicolon so that if you ever decide to add additional styles you will already have a separator in place.

The message example showed how to create a style rule for a single element. It is also possible to create a style rule for multiple elements, in which case the style rule applies to all of the elements. To establish a style rule for multiple elements, you create the style declaration and separate the element types with commas (,) in a single style rule:

```
ssnum, phonenum, email {
  display:none;
}
```

In this example, the value none is set in the display style property for the ssnum, phonenum, and email elements. The idea behind this example is that these elements contain sensitive information that you wouldn't want displayed; setting the display property to none results in the elements not being displayed.

A CSS Style Primer

You now have a basic knowledge of CSS style sheets and how they are based upon style rules that describe the appearance of elements in XML documents. It's now worth taking time to get you acquainted with some of the more commonly used style properties in CSS. CSS includes a variety of style properties that are used to control fonts, colors, alignment, and margins, to name just a few facets of XML content styling. The style properties in CSS can be broadly grouped into two major categories:

- Layout properties
- Formatting properties

Layout properties consist of properties that impact the positioning of XML content. For example, layout properties allow you to control the width, height margin, padding, and alignment of content and even go so far as to allow you to place content at exact positions on a page.

Layout Properties

One of the most important layout properties is the `display` property, which describes how an element is displayed with respect to other elements. There are four possible values for the `display` property:

- `block`—The element is displayed on a new line, as in a new paragraph
- `list-item`—The element is displayed on a new line with a list-item mark (bullet) next to it
- `inline`—The element is displayed inline with the current paragraph
- `none`—The element is not displayed

It's easier to understand the `display` property if you visualize each element in an XML document occupying a rectangular area when displayed. The `display` property controls the manner in which this rectangular area is displayed. For example, the `block` value results in the element being placed on a new line by itself, whereas the `inline` value places the element next to the content immediately preceding it. The `display` property is one of the few style properties that you will define for most style rules. Following is an example of how to set the display property:

```
display:block;
```

> The `display` property relies on a concept known as *relative positioning*, which means that elements are positioned relative to the location of other elements on a page. CSS also supports *absolute positioning*, which allows you to place an element at an exact location on a page, independent of other elements. You learn more about both of these types of positioning later in the hour.

You control the size of the rectangular area for an element with the `width` and `height` attributes. Like many size-related CSS properties, `width` and `height` property values can be specified in several different units of measurement:

- `in`—Inches
- `cm`—Centimeters
- `mm`—Millimeters

- px—Pixels
- pt—Points

These unit types are used immediately after the value of a measurement in a style sheet. You can mix and match units however you choose within a style sheet, but it's generally a good idea to be consistent across a set of similar style properties. For example, you might want to stick with points for font properties or pixels for dimensions. Following is an example of setting the width of an element using pixel units:

```
width:200px;
```

Formatting Properties

CSS formatting properties are used to control the appearance of XML content, as opposed to controlling the physical position of the content. One of the most commonly used formatting properties is the `border` property, which is used to establish a visible boundary around an element with a box or partial box. The following border properties provide a means of describing the borders of an element:

- `border-width`—The width of the border edge
- `border-color`—The color of the border edge
- `border-style`—The style of the border edge
- `border-left`—The left side of the border
- `border-right`—The right side of the border
- `border-top`—The top of the border
- `border-bottom`—The bottom of the border
- `border`—All the border sides

The `border-width` property is used to establish the width of the border edge and is often expressed in pixels, as the following code demonstrates:

```
border-width:5px;
```

The `border-color` and `border-style` properties are used to set the border color and style, respectively. Following is an example of how these two properties are set:

```
border-color:blue;
border-style:dotted;
```

The `border-style` property can be set to any of the following values:

- `solid`—A single-line border
- `double`—A double-line border
- `dashed`—A dashed border
- `dotted`—A dotted border
- `groove`—A border with a groove appearance
- `ridge`—A border with a ridge appearance
- `inset`—A border with an inset appearance
- `outset`—A border with an outset appearance
- `none`—No border

The `border-style` property values are fairly self-explanatory; the `solid` and `double` styles are the most common. The default value of the `border-style` property is `none`, which is why elements don't have a border unless you set the `border` property to a different style.

The `border-left`, `border-right`, `border-top`, and `border-bottom` properties allow you to set the border for each side of an element individually. If you want a border to appear the same on all four sides, you can use the single `border` property and express the border styles more concisely. Following is an example of using the `border` property to set a border that consists of two red lines that are a total of 10 pixels in width:

```
border:10px double red;
```

The color of an element's border can be set with the `border-color` property, and the color of the inner region of an element can be set using the `color` and `background-color` properties. The `color` property sets the color of text in an element, and the `background-color` property sets the color of the background behind the text. Following is an example of setting both color properties to predefined colors:

```
color:black;
background-color:orange;
```

You can also assign custom colors to these properties by specifying the colors as hexadecimal RGB (Red Green Blue) values. Following is an example of such assignments:

```
background-color:#999999;
color:rgb(0,0,255);
```

In addition to setting the color of XML content and its associated background, you can also control the alignment and indentation associated with the content. This is accomplished with the `text-align` and `text-indent` properties, as the following code demonstrates:

```
text-align:center;
text-indent:12px;
```

After you have an element properly aligned and indented, you might be interested in setting its font. The following CSS font properties are used to set the various parameters associated with fonts:

- `font-family`—The family of the font
- `font-size`—The size of the font
- `font-style`—The style of the font (`normal` or `italic`)
- `font-weight`—The weight of the font (`light`, `medium`, `bold`, and so on)

The `font-family` property specifies a prioritized list of font family names. A prioritized list is used instead of a single value to provide alternatives in case a font isn't available on a given system. The `font-size` property specifies the size of the font using a unit of measurement, usually points. Finally, the `font-style` property sets the style of the font, whereas the `font-weight` property sets the weight of the font. Following is an example of setting these font properties:

```
font-family: Arial, sans-serif;
font-size: 36pt;
font-style: italic;
font-weight: medium;
```

Style rules wouldn't be of much use if you didn't have a means of wiring them to an XML document in order to style the document's content. Let's move on and find out how this is done.

Wiring a Style Sheet to an XML Document

CSS style sheets used with XML documents are usually referred to as external style sheets because they are stored in separate text files with a `.css` extension. The `.css` file is then referenced by XML documents that use the style sheet to determine how their content is displayed. The `xml-stylesheet` processing instruction is used to associate an external style sheet with an XML document. This processing instruction includes a couple of attributes that determine the type and location of the style sheet:

- `type`—The type of the style sheet (`text/css`, for example)
- `href`—The location of the style sheet

These two attributes are both required in order to wire a style sheet to an XML document. Following is an example of how to use the `xml-stylesheet` processing instruction with the `type` and `href` attributes:

```
<?xml-stylesheet type="text/css" href="talltales.css"?>
```

In this example, the `type` attribute is used to specify that the type of the style sheet is `text/css`, which means that the style sheet is a CSS style sheet. The style sheet file is then referenced in the `href` attribute, which in this case points to the file `talltales.css`.

By the Way

> It is necessary to specify the type of a style sheet in the xml-stylesheet processing instruction because there are other types of style sheets, such as XSLT and XSL-FO style sheets, which you learn about in upcoming lessons.

External style sheets represent the only way to use CSS directly with XML documents without the assistance of any other technology. I say this because it is possible to incorporate style sheets into the formatting of XML documents a little differently when you are also using XSLT. More specifically, with XSLT you are actually translating an XML document into an HTML document for display purposes. Knowing this, it is possible to use inline styles directly with HTML elements in order to apply styles to XML content indirectly. You can also use external style sheets with HTML documents that are translated from XML. You learn how to carry out both of these style approaches in Hour 11, "Getting Started with XSL."

Your First CSS Style Sheet

None of this style sheet stuff would make much sense if you didn't get to see it in the context of a complete example. Listing 10.1 contains the code for an XML document that stores a couple of contacts. This document is an example of how you might use XML to store a contact list for personal or business contacts.

LISTING 10.1 The Contacts Example XML Document

```
<?xml version="1.0"?>
<?xml-stylesheet type="text/css" href="contacts.css"?>
<!DOCTYPE contacts SYSTEM "contacts.dtd">

<contacts>
  <!— This is my good friend Frank. —>
  <contact>
    <name>Frank Rizzo</name>
    <address>1212 W 304th Street</address>
    <city>New York</city>
    <state>New York</state>
    <zip>10011</zip>
    <phone>
```

```
14:       <voice>212-555-1212</voice>
15:       <fax>212-555-1342</fax>
16:       <mobile>212-555-1115</mobile>
17:     </phone>
18:     <email>frank.rizzo@franksratchetco.com</email>
19:     <company>Frank&apos;s Ratchet Service</company>
20:     <notes>I owe Frank 50 dollars.</notes>
21:   </contact>
22:
23:   <!— This is my old college roommate Sol. —>
24:   <contact>
25:     <name>Sol Rosenberg</name>
26:     <address>1162 E 412th Street</address>
27:     <city>New York</city>
28:     <state>New York</state>
29:     <zip>10011</zip>
30:     <phone>
31:       <voice>212-555-1818</voice>
32:       <fax>212-555-1828</fax>
33:       <mobile>212-555-1521</mobile>
34:     </phone>
35:     <email>srosenberg@rosenbergshoesglasses.com</email>
36:     <company>Rosenberg&apos;s Shoes &amp; Glasses</company>
37:     <notes>Sol collects Civil War artifacts.</notes>
38:   </contact>
39: </contacts>
```

Notice in the code for the Contacts document that an external style sheet (`contacts.css`) is associated with the document through the `xml-stylesheet` processing instruction (line 2). Beyond that, there is nothing specific to style sheets in the XML code. However, it's important to understand the role of a style sheet in this example, which is to display the mailing address for each contact. Knowing this, it is necessary to hide the phone number and company name when formatting the content for display. This is accomplished in the `contacts.css` style sheet, which is shown in Listing 10.2.

LISTING 10.2 **The `contacts.css` Style Sheet Used to Format the Contacts XML Document**

```
contact {
  display:block;
  width:350px;
  padding:5px;
  margin-bottom:10px;
  border:5px double black;
  color:black;
  background-color:white;
  text-align:left;
}

name {
  display:block;
  font-family:Verdana, Arial;
  font-size:18pt;
```

LISTING 10.2 Continued

```
16:   font-weight:bold;
17: }
18:
19: address {
20:   display:block;
21:   font-family:Verdana, Arial;
22:   font-size:14pt;
23: }
24:
25: city, state, zip {
26:   display:inline;
27:   font-family:Verdana, Arial;
28:   font-size:14pt;
29: }
30:
31: phone, email, company, notes {
32:   display:none;
33: }
```

This style sheet relies on familiar style properties that you learned about in this hour. Each relevant element in the Contacts document (`contact`, `name`, `address`, `city`, `state`, `zip`, `phone`, `email`, `company`, and `notes`) is styled in the style sheet so that its display parameters are clearly stated. A border is established around the `contact` element (line 6), which contains the remaining elements. The other important code to notice is the code that hides the `phone`, `email`, `company`, and `notes` elements so that they aren't displayed (lines 31–33). This style sheet results in the contacts being displayed as a list of mailing addresses that easily could be printed out as address labels (see Figure 10.1).

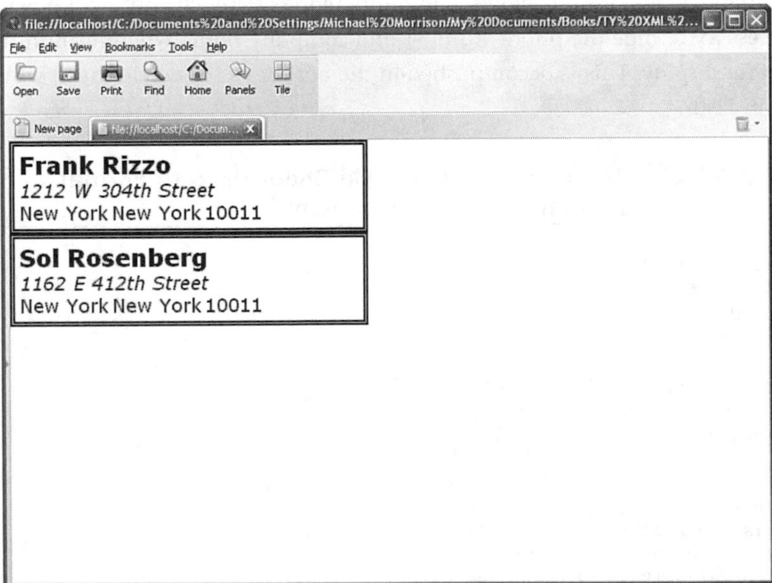

FIGURE 10.1 The Contacts example document is displayed in Opera using the `contacts.css` style sheet.

Although the `contacts.css` style sheet is relatively simple in structure, it is nonetheless a good example of how CSS can be used to format and position XML content on a page for viewing.

Inside CSS Positioning

Earlier in the lesson you learned how to position XML content using the default approach to CSS positioning, which is known as relative positioning. In *relative positioning*, content is displayed according to the flow of a page, where each element physically appears after the element preceding it in an XML document. The content for an XML element still appears within a rectangular area, but the area itself is positioned relative to other elements that are being displayed. You can think of relative positioning as being akin to laying out checkers on a checkerboard; the checkers are arranged from left to right, and when you get to the edge of the board you move on to the next row. Elements that are styled with the `block` value for the `display` property are automatically placed on a new row, whereas `inline` elements are placed on the same row immediately next to the element preceding them.

Although relative positioning might sound somewhat limiting, you have to keep in mind that child elements are always positioned relative to their parents. So, the hierarchy of elements in an XML document can dramatically affect how the elements appear when styled with CSS. As an example, take a look back at the code for the `contacts.css` style sheet in Listing 10.2 in the previous section. You'll notice that the `contact` and `name` elements appear to be completely independent from a CSS perspective, but when used in XML code the `name` element is a child of the `contact` element. Therefore, when using relative positioning, the `name` element is displayed with respect to the `contact` element. In other words, the `name` element appears within the rectangular area set aside for the `contact` element, which in this case is 350 pixels wide.

By the Way

> Relative positioning is the default positioning approach used by CSS, so if you don't specify the positioning of a style rule, it will default to relative positioning.

The other type of positioning supported by CSS is known as *absolute positioning* because it allows you to set the exact position of XML content on a page. Although absolute positioning gives you the freedom to spell out exactly where an element is to appear, this position is still relative to any parent elements that appear on the page. Even so, absolute positioning allows you to specify the exact location of an element's rectangular area with respect to its parent's area, which is very different from relative positioning.

By the Way

> There is a potential problem associated with the freedom of placing elements anywhere you want on a page via absolute positioning. I'm referring to overlap, which is when an element takes up space used by another element. In this case, CSS relies on the z-index of each element to determine which element is on the top and which is on the bottom. You learn more about the z-index of elements in the next section. For now, let's take a look at exactly how you control whether or not a style rule uses relative or absolute positioning.

The type of positioning (relative or absolute) used by a particular style rule is determined by the `position` property, which is capable of having one of the following two values: `relative` or `absolute`. After specifying the type of positioning, you then specify the position of a style rule using the following properties:

- `left`—The left position offset
- `right`—The right position offset
- `top`—The top position offset
- `bottom`—The bottom position offset

These position properties are interpreted differently depending on the type of positioning used. Under relative positioning, the position of an element is specified as an offset relative to the original position of the element. So, if you set the `left` property of an element to `25px`, the left side of the element will be shifted over 25 pixels from its original (relative) position. Because the original position of the element is relative to other elements, the final position is still considered a relative position. An absolute position, on the other hand, is specified relative to the parent of the element to which the style is applied. So, if you set the `left` property of an element to `25px` under absolute positioning, the left side of the element will appear 25 pixels to the right of the parent element's left edge.

To better understand the difference between absolute and relative positioning, check out the following XML code:

```
<squares>
  <square class="one">
  Square One
  </square>
  <square class="two">
  Square Two
  </square>
  <square class="three">
```

```
  Square Three
  </square>
  <square class="four">
  Square Four
  </square>
</squares>
```

Admittedly, this XML code doesn't mean much, but it's a good way to demonstrate the difference between relative and absolute positioning. Notice in the code that there are several `square` elements, each with a different class and therefore a different style rule. Listing 10.3 contains a style sheet for this code that uses relative positioning to arrange the squares.

LISTING 10.3 The `squares_rel.css` Style Sheet That Uses Relative Positioning to Style the Squares XML Document

```
 1: square {
 2:   display:block;
 3:   position:relative;
 4:   width:100px;
 5:   height:75px;
 6:   border:10px single black;
 7:   color:black;
 8:   text-align:center;
 9: }
10:
11: square.one {
12:   background-color:red;
13: }
14:
15: square.two {
16:   background-color:green;
17: }
18:
19: square.three {
20:   background-color:blue;
21: }
22:
23: square.four {
24:   background-color:yellow;
25: }
```

This code sets the `position` style property to `relative` (line 3), which explicitly causes the `square` style rule to use relative positioning. Because the remaining style rules are inherited from the `square` style rule, they also inherit its relative positioning. In fact, the only difference between the other style rules is that they have different background colors. Figure 10.2 shows the Squares document as it is displayed in Internet Explorer using the style sheet with relative positioning.

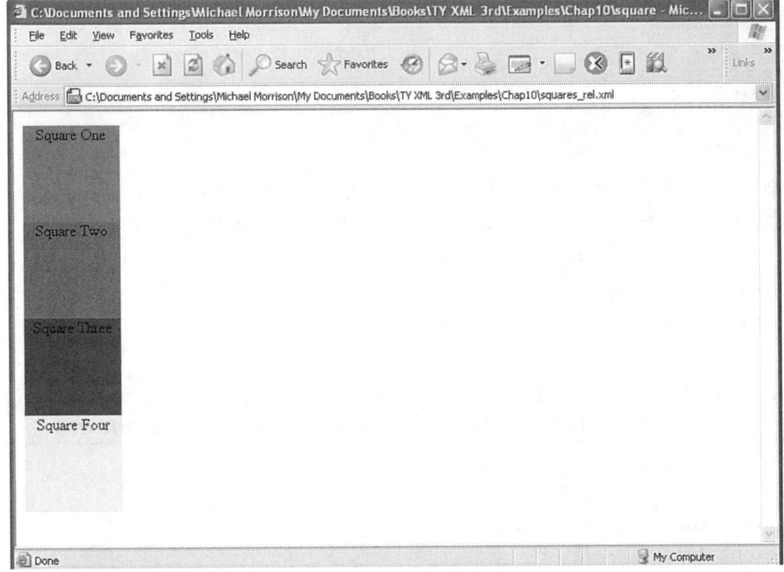

FIGURE 10.2 The Squares example document is displayed in Internet Explorer using a style sheet with relative positioning.

Notice in the figure that the `square` elements are displayed one after the next, which is what you would expect from relative positioning. To make things more interesting, you can change the positioning to absolute and explicitly specify the placement of the squares. Listing 10.4 contains a modified style sheet for the Squares document that uses absolute positioning to arrange the squares.

LISTING 10.4 The `squares_abs.css` Style Sheet That Uses Absolute Positioning to Style the Squares XML Document

```
square {
  display:block;
  position:absolute;
  width:100px;
  height:75px;
  border:10px single black;
  color:black;
  text-align:center;
}

square.one {
  background-color:red;
  left:0px;
  top:0px;
}

square.two {
  background-color:green;
```

```
19:   left:75px;
20:   top:25px;
21: }
22:
23: square.three {
24:   background-color:blue;
25:   left:150px;
26:   top:50px;
27: }
28:
29: square.four {
30:   background-color:yellow;
31:   left:225px;
32:   top:75px;
33: }
```

This style sheet sets the `position` property to `absolute`, which is necessary in order for the style sheet to use absolute positioning (line 3). Additionally, the `left` and `top` properties are set for each of the inherited square style rules. However, the position of each of these rules is set so that the elements will be displayed overlapping each other, as shown in Figure 10.3.

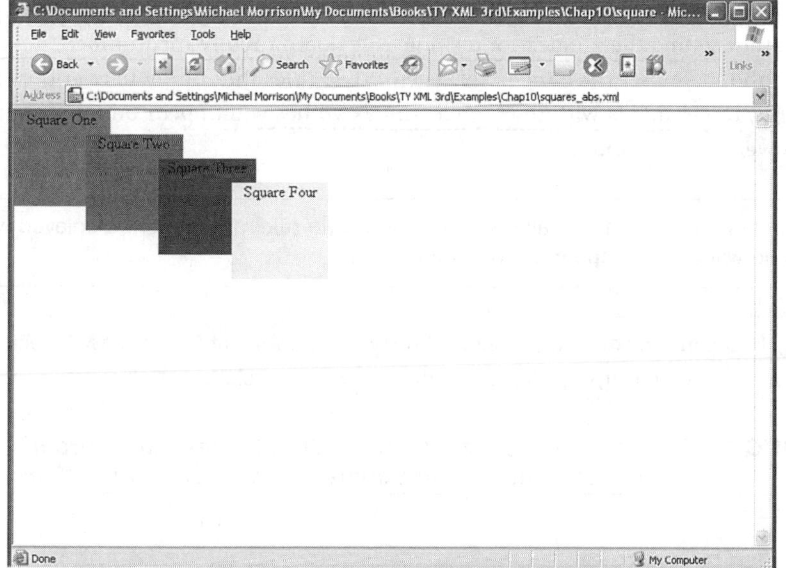

FIGURE 10.3 The Squares example document is displayed in Internet Explorer using a style sheet with absolute positioning.

This figure shows how absolute positioning allows you to place elements exactly where you want them. It also reveals how easy it is to arrange elements so that they overlap each other. You might be curious as to how a web browser knows which elements to draw on top when they overlap. Fortunately, CSS includes a style property that gives you complete control over the appearance of overlapped elements.

Tinkering with the z-Index

You just saw how it doesn't take much trouble to position elements on a page so that they overlap each other. There are no doubt situations where you'd like to be able to carefully control the manner in which elements overlap each other. For this reason, CSS includes the `z-index` property, which allows you to set the order of elements with respect to how they stack on top of each other. Although the name z-index might sound a little strange, it refers to the notion of a third dimension (Z) that projects into the computer screen, in addition to the two dimensions (X and Y) that go across and down the screen. Another way to think of the z-index is the relative position of a magazine within a stack of magazines. A magazine nearer the top of the stack has a higher z-index than a magazine lower in the stack. Similarly, an overlapped element with a higher z-index is displayed on top of an element with a lower z-index.

The z-index of a style rule is specified using the `z-index` property, which is set to a numeric value that indicates the relative z-index of the rule. The number assigned to a z-index has meaning only with respect to other style rules in a style sheet, which means that setting the z-index for a single rule doesn't really mean much. On the other hand, if you set the z-index for several style rules that apply to overlapped elements, the elements with the higher z-index values will appear on top of elements with lower z-index values.

Regardless of the z-index value you set for a style rule, an element displayed with the rule will always appear on top of its parent.

Listing 10.5 contains another version of a style sheet for the Squares XML document that has z-index settings to alter the natural overlap of elements.

LISTING 10.5 The `squares_z.css` Style Sheet Alters the z-order of Elements in the Squares XML Document

```
square {
  display:block;
  position:absolute;
  width:100px;
  height:75px;
  border:10px single black;
  color:black;
  text-align:center;
}

square.one {
  background-color:red;
  z-index:0;
```

```
14:   left:0px;
15:   top:0px;
16: }
17:
18: square.two {
19:   background-color:green;
20:   z-index:3;
21:   left:75px;
22:   top:25px;
23: }
24:
25: square.three {
26:   background-color:blue;
27:   z-index:2;
28:   left:150px;
29:   top:50px;
30: }
31:
32: square.four {
33:   background-color:yellow;
34:   z-index:1;
35:   left:225px;
36:   top:75px;
37: }
```

The only change in this code from what you saw in Listing 10.4 is the addition of the z-index settings in each of the derived square style rules. Notice that the first square has a setting of 0 (line 13), which should make it the lowest element in terms of the z-index, whereas the second square has the highest z-index (line 20). Figure 10.4 shows the Squares document as displayed with this style sheet, which clearly shows how the z-index impacts the displayed content.

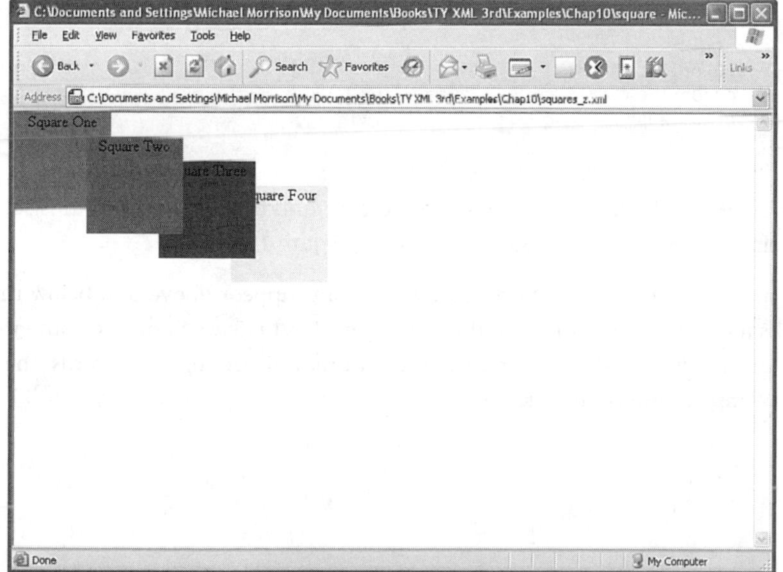

FIGURE 10.4
The Squares example document is displayed in Internet Explorer using a style sheet that alters the z-order of the squares.

The figure reveals how the `z-index` style property makes it possible to carefully control the overlap of elements.

Creating Margins

CSS supports margins that allow you to add empty space around the outside of the rectangular area for an element. Following are the style properties that you use to set the margins for style rules:

- `margin-top`—Sets the top margin
- `margin-right`—Sets the right margin
- `margin-bottom`—Sets the bottom margin
- `margin-left`—Sets the left margin
- `margin`—Sets the top, right, bottom, and left margins as a single property

You can specify margins using any of the individual margin properties or with the single `margin` property. Regardless of how you set the margins for a style rule, it's important to note that you can specify the size of a margin using either units or a percentage. If you decide to set a margin as a percentage, keep in mind that the percentage is calculated based upon the size of the entire page, not the size of the element. So, if you set the `margin-left` property to `25%`, the left margin of the element will end up being 25% of the width of the entire page. The following code shows how to set the top and bottom margins for one of the squares in the Squares XML document that you've been working with throughout this hour:

```
square.two {
  background-color:green;
  margin-top:5px;
  margin-bottom:20px;
}
```

In this example, the top margin is set to 5 pixels, and the bottom margin is set to 20 pixels. The results of this code are shown in Figure 10.5.

This figure shows how the top and bottom margins appear above and below the second square. Keep in mind that these margins don't encroach on the content area of any of the squares—they all maintain their original size. In other words, the margins appear around the elements.

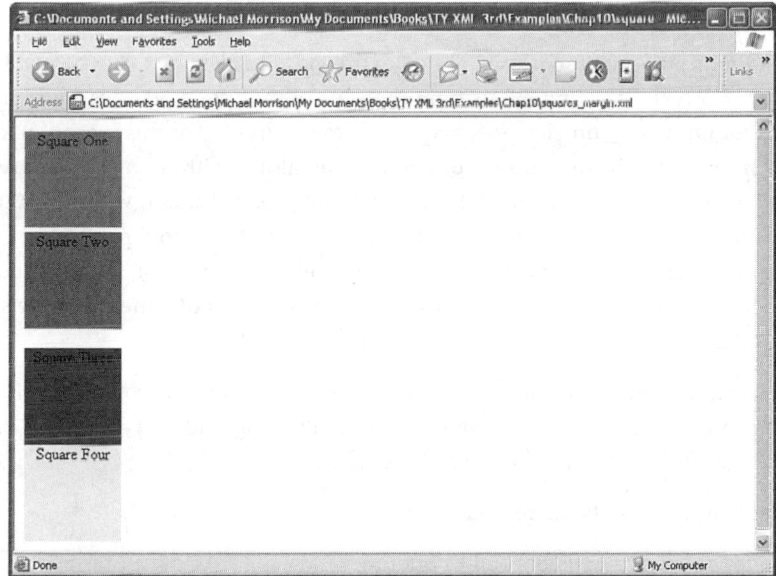

FIGURE 10.5
The Squares example document is displayed in Internet Explorer using a style sheet that sets top and bottom margins for one of the squares.

If you want to set all the margins for a style rule, you'll probably want to simplify the code and use the `margin` property. This property is somewhat flexible in that it offers three different approaches to specifying the margins for a style rule. These different approaches vary based upon how many values you use when setting the `margin` property:

- One value—The size of all the margins
- Two values—The size of the top/bottom margins and the left/right margins (in that order)

- Four values—The size of the top, right, bottom, and left margins (in that order)

As you can see, the `margin` property allows you to provide one, two, or four values when you set it. Following is an example of how you would set the vertical margins (top/bottom) to 5 pixels and the horizontal margins (left/right) to 10% for a style rule:

```
margin:5px 10%;
```

In this code, the top and bottom margins are both set to 5 pixels, whereas the left and right margins are both set to 10%. Of course, if you wanted to be a little clearer you could achieve the same effect with the following setting:

```
margin:5px 10% 5px 10%;
```

A Little Padding for Safety

Similar to margins, padding is used to add extra space to elements via CSS style properties. However, padding differs from margins in that padding adds space inside the rectangular area of an element, as opposed to around it. For this reason, padding actually imposes on the amount of content area available within an element. As an example, if you create a style rule for an element that establishes a width of 50 pixels and a height of 30 pixels and then sets the padding of the rule to 5 pixels, the remaining content area will be 40 pixels by 20 pixels. Also, because the padding of an element appears within the element's content area, it will assume the same style as the content of the element, such as the background color.

You specify the padding of a style rule using one of the padding properties, which work very much like the margin properties. The following padding properties are available for use in setting the padding of style rules:

- `padding-top`—Sets the top padding
- `padding-right`—Sets the right padding
- `padding-bottom`—Sets the bottom padding
- `padding-left`—Sets the left padding
- `padding`—Sets the top, right, bottom, and left padding as a single property

Similar to margins, you can set the padding of style rules using individual padding properties or the single `padding` property. Padding can also be expressed using either a unit of measurement or a percentage. Following is an example of how you might set the left and right padding for a style rule so that there are 10 pixels of padding on each side of an element's content:

```
padding-left:10px;
padding0-right:10px;
```

Also similar to margins, you can set all of the padding for a style rule with a single property, the `padding` property. You can use the same three approaches available for the `margin` property to set the `padding` property. Following is an example of how you would set the vertical padding (top/bottom) to 12 pixels and the horizontal padding (left/right) to 8 pixels for a style rule:

```
padding:12px 8px;
```

Following is more explicit code that performs the same task by specifying all of the padding values:

```
padding:12px 8px 12px 8px;
```

Keeping Things Aligned

There are a couple of style properties that allow you to control the alignment of XML content: `text-align` and `vertical-align`. The `text-align` property aligns XML content horizontally within its bounding area and can be set to `left`, `right`, or `center`. Following is an example of using the `text-align` property to center a contact in the `contacts.css` style sheet that you saw earlier in the lesson:

```
contact {
  display:block;
  width:350px;
  margin-bottom:10px;
  border:5px double black;
  color:black;
  background-color:white;
  text-align:center;
}
```

The last style property defined in this style rule sets the `text-align` style to `center`, which results in the text inside of the `contact` element being centered within the element's borders.

The `vertical-align` property is similar to `text-align` except that it is used to align elements vertically. The `vertical-align` property specifies how an element is aligned with its parent or in some cases the current line of elements on the page. When I say "current line," I'm really referring to the vertical placement of elements that appear within the same parent element. In other words, I'm talking about inline elements. If several inline elements appear on the same line, you can set their vertical alignments the same to align them vertically. Following are the acceptable values for use with the `vertical-align` property:

- `top`—Aligns the top of an element with the current line
- `middle`—Aligns the middle of an element with the middle of its parent
- `bottom`—Aligns the bottom of an element with the current line
- `text-top`—Aligns the top of an element with the top of its parent
- `baseline`—Aligns the baseline of an element with the baseline of its parent
- `text-bottom`—Aligns the bottom of an element with the bottom of its parent
- `sub`—Aligns an element as a subscript of its parent
- `super`—Aligns an element as a superscript of its parent

These property values are self-explanatory for the most part. The only tricky issue relates to whether a value aligns an element with the current line or its parent.

When aligning an element with its parent, the baseline of the parent is the bottom of any text appearing in the parent, excluding letters that reach down below others, such as the letters g and y. Following is an example of how the `vertical-align` property is used to center text vertically:

```
contact {
  display:block;
  width:275px;
  margin-bottom:10px;
  border:5px double black;
  color:black;
  background-color:white;
  text-align:center;
  vertical-align:middle;
}
```

This code shows how simple it is to modify a style rule so that the XML content is aligned vertically.

The Ins and Outs of Text Formatting

CSS allows you to position and format a wide range of content, including HTML content, but when it comes to XML content you are primarily dealing with text. Knowing this, it's important to have a solid understanding of how CSS is used to format text content. The next few sections tackle the following aspects of text formatting with CSS:

- Fonts
- Colors and image backgrounds
- Text spacing

Working with Fonts

When it comes to text formatting, nothing really impacts the overall appearance of text more so than the font used to display the text. You learned earlier in the lesson that CSS includes several styles for setting the font for text content. However, I now want to take a closer look at these font properties and also show you a more concise way to specify the font for a style rule. Following are the CSS font style properties that you can use to alter the font of text content:

- `font-style`—Sets the style of a font
- `font-weight`—Sets the thickness of a font
- `font-size`—Sets the size of a font

- `font-family`—Sets the family of a font
- `font`—Sets the style, thickness, size, and family of a font within a single property

If you recall from earlier, the `font-style` property allows you to set the style of a font and can be set to `normal` or `italic`; the default value is `normal`. The `font-weight` property sets the weight, or thickness, of a font and can be set to any of the following values: `extra-light`, `light`, `demi-light`, `medium`, `demi-bold`, `bold`, or `extra-bold`. The default value of the `font-weight` property is medium, which is an average font weight. The `font-size` property sets the size of a font using a unit of measure such as points (`pt`). The `I` property sets the family, or face, of a font, which is the name used to describe the font. Following is an example of how you use these four style properties together to establish a font style rule:

```
title {
  display:block;
  font-style:italic;
  font-weight:bold;
  font-size:18pt;
  font-family:Courier, serif;
}
```

Notice in this code that the `font-family` style rule actually consists of two family names: `Courier` and `serif`. The reason for this is because there is no guarantee that a particular font will be available on a given system. To solve this problem, you can list alternate font families that will be used in the event that the primary family isn't available. In the `title` example, the `Courier` font family is specified as the primary family, but the secondary serif family will be used if the `Courier` family isn't available. If none of the font families are available, it is the responsibility of a web browser to find a suitable match within the font families that are available.

Although the previous `title` example shows a perfectly reasonable approach to setting the font styles for a style rule, there is a better approach if you plan on setting several font styles. I'm referring to the `font` style property, which combines the other four font styles into a single property. To use the `font` property, you simply list the style, weight, size, and family of the font separated by spaces. Following is an example of how the `font` property makes the `title` style rule much more concise:

```
title {
  display:block;
  font:italic bold 18pt Courier, serif;
}
```

As this code reveals, the `font` property provides a good way to simplify the code for font styles. However, the `font` property is really only a convenience property and doesn't actually add any features of its own.

Jazzing Up Text with Colors and Image Backgrounds

If changing the font of text doesn't provide you with enough flexibility, you can go a step further and spice up text by altering its color and background appearance. Using CSS, it is possible to set the color of text, the background color shown behind text, and even a background image that appears behind text. Following are the properties that make this kind of visual trickery happen:

- `color`—Sets the foreground color of text
- `background-color`—Sets the background color of text
- `background-image`—Sets the background image of text
- `background-repeat`—Determines how the background image of text appears
- `background`—Sets the background color, image, and repeat of text within a single property

The color property sets the color of text and can be set to any of the following standard colors: `aqua`, `black`, `blue`, `fuchsia`, `gray`, `green`, `lime`, `maroon`, `navy`, `olive`, `purple`, `red`, `silver`, `teal`, `white`, and `yellow`. Following is an example of how you might set the color in a style rule using the color property:

```
title {
  display:block;
  font:italic bold 18pt Courier, serif;
  color:green;
}
```

In this example, the text color of the `title` element is set to `green`, which results in the text content for the element being displayed in green. If you'd like to specify a color other than one of the standard colors, you can create a custom color and assign it to the `color` property. To do so, you must create the custom color as a combination of the primary colors red, green, and blue. The combination of red, green, and blue color components is known as RGB and is the color system used to specify custom colors in CSS. The red, green, and blue color components are expressed as hexadecimal numbers that are stuck together to form a complete custom color value, such as `#00FF00`, which is the color green.

> If you've never worked with hexadecimal numbers they will no doubt look strange to you at first. This is because hexadecimal numbers use a combination of letters and numeric digits, as opposed to just numeric digits. Instead of consisting of numbers from 0 to 10, the hexadecimal system consists of numbers from 0 to F, where the letters A through F continue on from 9. In other words, A is 10, B is 11, and so on. The lowest two-digit hexadecimal number is 00, whereas the highest is FF.

A custom color consists of six digits, which are actually three two-digit pairs, preceded by a number symbol (#). Each one of the two-digit pairs represents one of the three primary color components (red, green, and blue). Perhaps the best way to understand how custom numbers are encoded in hexadecimal is to look at the hexadecimal values for several of the standard colors:

- `aqua—#00FFFF`
- `black—#000000`
- `blue—#0000FF`
- `fuchsia—#FF00FF`
- `gray—#808080`
- `green—#00FF00`

These few examples should give you an idea as to how custom colors are described by hexadecimal values. Following is an example of how you would set the color property to the color blue using a hexadecimal value:

```
color:#0000FF;
```

Now that you have a better understanding of how color works in CSS, let's return to the discussion of formatting text with color. Similar to the `color` property, the `background-color` property accepts a color, but in this case the color represents the background color of a style rule, not the text color. Following is an example of the background-color property in action:

```
title {
  display:block;
  font:italic bold 18pt Courier, serif;
  color:green;
  background-color:#808080;
}
```

In this example, green text is drawn over a gray background thanks to the `color` and `background-color` properties. If a background color isn't quite fancy enough for you, you can specify a background image that is displayed behind the text content of an element. The `background-image` property accomplishes this task, as the following example reveals:

```
title {
  display:block;
  font:italic bold 18pt Courier, serif;
  color:green;
  background-image:url(jungle.gif);
}
```

In this example, the background image named `jungle.gif` is specified for the `title` style rule. Notice that the image URL is enclosed in parentheses that follow the word `url`; this is how image URLs must be specified when using the `background-image` property.

It is possible to specify both a background color and a background image, in which case the background color will show through any transparent areas of the image.

When you set a background image for a style rule, the image is automatically tiled to fill the entire rectangular area of the element that is displayed. If you want to control the manner in which a background image is tiled, you can do so with the `background-repeat` property, which accepts the following values: `repeat`, `repeat-x`, `repeat-y`, and `no-repeat`. The default value is `repeat`. The `no-repeat` value displays the background image once, whereas the `repeat-x` and `repeat-y` values tile the image repeatedly in the X and Y directions, respectively. Following is an example of setting the `background-repeat` property to have a background image appear only once:

```
title {
  display:block;
  font:italic bold 18pt Courier, serif;
  color:green;
  background-image:url(monkey.gif);
  background-repeat:no-repeat;
}
```

If you'd like to specify several background properties without entering as much code, you can use the `background` property, which sets the background color, image, and repeat properties in a single style. Following is an example of setting the `background` property for the `title` style rule:

```
title {
  display:block;
  font:italic bold 18pt Courier, serif;
  color:green;
  background:green url(jungle.gif) no-repeat;
}
```

In this example, the `background` property is used to set a background color, to set a background image, and also to specify that the image be displayed only once.

Tweaking the Spacing of Text

You can achieve some interesting text effects by playing around with the spacing between characters. There are two CSS style properties that allow you to control the indentation and character spacing of text: `text-indent` and `letter-spacing`.

These two properties both can be specified in units that you are hopefully familiar with by now: points (`pt`), inches (`in`), centimeters (`cm`), or pixels (`px`). Following is an example of how to set the indentation of a paragraph of text using the `text-indent` property:

```
message {
  display:block;
  text-indent:1.5in;
}
```

This code sets the indentation of the `message` element to one-and-a-half inches, which means the first line of the text in the element is displayed an inch-and-a-half over from the left edge of the element's rectangular area.

Although the `letter-spacing` property impacts text much differently than the `text-indent` property, it is specified similarly. Following is an example of how to alter the character spacing of the `message` element:

```
message {
  display:block;
  text-indent:1.5in;
  letter-spacing:5pt;
}
```

In this example, the letter spacing of the `message` style rule is set to 5 points, which means the individual characters in the message are separated by an additional 5 points when displayed. An interesting facet of the `letter-spacing` property is that it can also be used to move letters closer together by specifying a negative value.

Your Second Complete Style Sheet

It's time to take a turn for the practical and put together another complete CSS style sheet example. This example involves an XML document called `news.xml` that contains a news story marked up with XML code. Listing 10.6 contains the code for the News example document, which could feasibly be used by a newspaper or newsletter website to encode stories.

LISTING 10.6 The News Example XML Document

```
<?xml version="1.0"?>
<?xml-stylesheet type="text/css" href="news.css"?>

<news>
  <header>
    <headline>
    Local Author Creates Free Online Music Game
    </headline>
    <byline>
```

LISTING 10.6 Continued

```
    By Brent Andrews
    </byline>
    <dateline>
      <location>Nashville, Tennessee</location>
      <date>Monday October 17 2005 12:08 CST</date>
    </dateline>
  </header>

  <story>
    <p>Local nerd author Michael Morrison is involved in yet another unusual
    project. Following up on the success of his quirky trivia game Tall
    Tales, Morrison has gone back to his technical roots with his latest
    project, Guess That Groove. Guess That Groove acts as somewhat of an
    online version of the popular television game show Name That Tune. What
    makes Guess That Groove so unique is how it relies on actual digitized
    music recordings to present popular songs from the last seventy years of
    music.</p>
    <p>Located online at <url>www.guessthatgroove.com</url>, the service is
    entirely free. Morrison explained that the business model is based upon
    commission fees from linked sites such as Amazon.com and iTunes, which
    offer game players an option to purchase CDs and individual music tracks
    that they encounter throughout the game. It's too early to tell whether
    Morrison has hit on another social phenomonon along the lines of Tall
    Tales. Regarding the potential success of the online game, Morrison
    replied, <quote>It was a lot of fun to create and I enjoy playing it
    myself, so in some ways I already consider it a success</quote>.</p>
  </story>
</news>
```

Admittedly, the news story in this case may not qualify as front-page material, but it does reveal how the XML markup is used to add context to the content in the story. The goal of this example is to create a style sheet that displays the news story in a format similar to how you are accustomed to seeing printed stories in a newspaper. In other words, the title should appear in a large font followed by a much smaller byline and dateline and then the body of the story. The elements that factor into the style sheet are `headline`, `byline`, `dateline`, `p`, `url`, and `quote`. You could easily use absolute positioning to carefully lay out each of the elements in this example document, but it is not necessary. Rather than go into the details of absolute positioning, it is simpler in this case to carefully align the elements with the `text-align` property so that they appear where you want them. Listing 10.7 contains the code for the `news.css` style sheet, which is used to style the News XML document for display.

LISTING 10.7 The `news.css` Style Sheet Used to Format the News XML Document

```
headline {
  display:block;
  width:450px;
  border-bottom:5px double black;
  text-align:left;
  color:black;
```

```
 7:   font-family:Verdana, Arial;
 8:   font-size:26pt;
 9: }
10:
11: byline {
12:   display:inline;
13:   width:200px;
14:   text-align:left;
15:   color:black;
16:   font-family:Verdana, Arial;
17:   font-size:12pt;
18: }
19:
20: dateline {
21:   display:inline;
22:   width:250px;
23:   text-align:right;
24:   color:gray;
25:   font-family:Verdana, Arial;
26:   font-size:10pt;
27: }
28:
29: p {
30:   display:block;
31:   width:450px;
32:   margin-bottom:8px;
33:   color:black;
34:   font-family:Verdana, Arial;
35:   font-size:10pt;
36: }
37:
38: url {
39:   display:inline;
40:   font-weight:bold;
41: }
42:
43: quote {
44:   display:inline;
45:   font-style:italic;
46: }
```

Although this style sheet is a bit larger than the Contacts style sheet you saw earlier in the lesson, it is actually very straightforward if you study each of the style rules carefully. For example, the `headline` style rule has a width, bottom border, text color, and font, and it has its text aligned left (lines 1–9). The `byline` style rule is defined as an inline rule (line 21) and aligns text to the right (line 23). The `p` style rule sets a bottom margin in order to provide exact spacing between paragraphs (line 32). All of the style rules use different sized fonts except for `url` and `quote`, which inherit the font size of their parent style rule, which in this case is `p`. The resulting view of the News document using the `news.css` style sheet is shown in Figure 10.6.

Notice in the figure how the style sheet takes the XML data and formats it into a layout resembling a story printed in a newspaper. Additionally, the URL and quote in the story are further styled so that they are called out in the text.

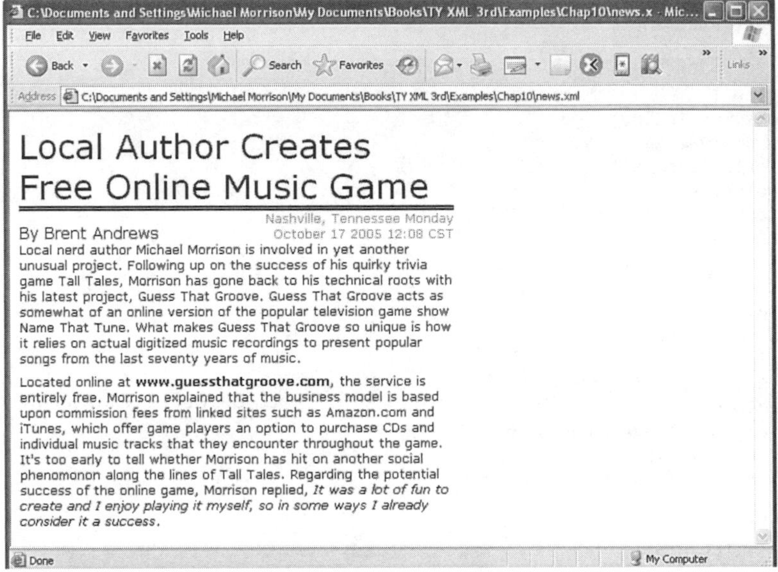

FIGURE 10.6
The News example document is displayed in Internet Explorer using the `news.css` style sheet.

Summary

Cascading Style Sheets (CSS) were originally created for use with HTML, but they also work quite well with XML. CSS focuses purely on the positioning and formatting of XML content and doesn't involve itself with processing or otherwise translating XML code. However, when it comes to positioning and formatting XML content for display within web pages, CSS proves to be a powerful and easy-to-use technology. CSS gives you the ability to carefully control the positioning of XML content on a page and align it as desired. Once you've positioned XML content on a page, you have the option of formatting the text using a variety of different CSS style properties. Through these style properties, you can control the font, color, background, and spacing of text, which gives you considerable flexibility in determining the appearance of text.

This hour introduced you to CSS and how it is used to style XML documents. You got started by learning the basics of CSS, including the fundamental layout and formatting styles that are used to style XML content. You then learned how to associate an external style sheet with an XML document, which is a necessity if you plan on seeing the fruits of your CSS labors. You also found out the difference between relative and absolute positioning and how each are used to position elements. You learned about several other CSS positioning features such as z-index, margins, padding, content alignment, fonts, colors, backgrounds, and text spacing. And finally, you wrapped up the hour by exploring a complete CSS example that pulled together most of what you learned throughout the lesson.

Q&A

Q. ***Why can't I just place style rules directly in XML code?***

A. XML code must adhere to XML syntax, which consists of elements and attributes. CSS is not an XML-based markup language, which immediately excludes its usage within XML documents using familiar XML elements and attributes. Technically, it could be possible to use inline CSS styles with XML content by way of a special attribute, such as `style`, which is supported in HTML. However, even this special attribute would need to be supported by the particular XML-based markup language being used in the document. Because there is no such standard XML language, the `style` attribute isn't recognized in XML documents for viewing in web browsers. In other words, you must use external style sheets if you plan on using CSS alone to style your XML documents.

Q. ***How do you know when to use relative versus absolute positioning?***

A. Although there are no set guidelines regarding the usage of relative versus absolute positioning, the general idea is that absolute positioning is required only when you want to exert a fine degree of control over how content is positioned. This has to do with the fact that absolute positioning allows you to position content down to the exact pixel, whereas relative positioning is less exacting in terms of how it positions content. This isn't to say that relative positioning can't do a good job of positioning XML content; it just means that absolute positioning is more explicit.

Q. ***If you don't specify the z-index of two elements that overlap each other, how do you know which element will appear on top?***

A. If the `z-index` property isn't set for overlapping elements, the element appearing later in the XML content will appear on top. The easy way to remember this is to think of a web browser drawing each element on a page as it reads it from the XML document; elements read later in the document are drawn on top of those read earlier.

Q. ***Is there a way to know if a font is installed on a system when specifying it in a style sheet?***

A. No. Different users may have different fonts installed, and there is no way to predict which fonts will be available. The best solution to this problem is to use popular fonts or system fonts and always provide a secondary font that is ideally a system font.

Workshop

The Workshop is designed to help you anticipate possible questions, review what you've learned, and begin learning how to put your knowledge into practice.

Quiz

1. What is the purpose of an element type selector?
2. How does the `block` value differ from the `inline` value in the `display` property?
3. How do you associate an external CSS style sheet with an XML document?
4. How would you specify that a style rule is supposed to indent the first line of a paragraph by 6 centimeters?

Quiz Answers

1. An element type selector selects an element of a given type and applies a style or set of styles to it. This represents the simplest approach to using CSS because there is a one-to-one mapping between element types and styles.
2. When used with the `display` property, the `block` value results in an element being placed on a new line by itself, whereas the `inline` value places the element next to the content immediately preceding it.
3. The `xml-stylesheet` processing instruction is used to associate an external CSS style sheet with an XML document.
4. To specify that a style rule is supposed to indent the first line of a paragraph by 6 centimeters, you would use the style setting `text-indent:6cm`.

Exercises

1. Modify the `news.css` style sheet so that the story text is displayed with a gray background. Hint: This requires you to modify the style rule for the `p` element.
2. Modify the `news.css` style sheet so that the letter spacing of the headline is wider than normal.

HOUR 11

Getting Started with XSL

> Someone told me that each equation I included in the book would halve the sales.
>
> —Stephen Hawking (on his book *A Brief History of Time*)

Unlike Mr. Hawking, I'm not afraid of a little extra complexity hurting the sales of this book. In fact, it's necessary because XSL is a more complex style sheet technology than CSS, so there is no way to thoroughly cover style sheets without things getting a little messy. Fortunately, as you learn in this hour, XSL is a technology that has considerably more to offer than CSS. XSL is designed to do a whole lot more than just format XML content for display purposes; it gives you the ability to completely transform XML documents. You learn in this hour how to transform XML documents into HTML documents that can be viewed in web browsers. Additionally, you should realize that the extra complexity in XSL is quite worth the learning curve because of its immense power and flexibility.

In this hour, you'll learn

- The basics of XSL and the technologies that comprise it
- The building blocks of the XSL Transformation (XSLT) language
- How to wire an XSL style sheet to an XML document
- How to develop an XSLT style sheet

XSL Basics

As you've learned in previous hours, style sheets are special documents or pieces of code that are used to format XML content for display purposes. This definition of a style sheet is perfectly accurate for CSS, which is a style sheet technology that originated as a means of adding tighter control of HTML content formatting. XSL is also a style sheet technology, but it reaches beyond the simple formatting of content by also allowing you to completely transform content. Unlike CSS, XSL was solely designed as a style sheet technology for XML. In many ways, XSL accomplishes the same things that can be accomplished using CSS. However, XSL goes much further than CSS in its support for manipulating the structure of XML documents.

As you might expect, XSL is implemented using XML, which means that you code XSL style sheets using XML code. Even so, you may find it necessary to still use CSS in conjunction with XSL, at least in the near future. The reason for this has to do with the current state of XSL support in web browsers. The component of XSL currently supported in web browsers is XSLT, which allows you to transform XML documents via style sheet code. XSLT doesn't directly support the formatting of XML content for display purposes. The formatting component of XSL is XSL Formatting Objects, or XSL-FO, which consists of special style objects that can be applied to XML content to format it for display. Support for XSL-FO is currently weak in major web browsers, which doesn't make XSL-FO a viable alternative for the Web at the moment. In the meantime, XSLT is quite useful when paired with CSS; XSLT allows you to transform any XML document into HTML that can be styled and displayed with CSS in a web browser.

> Although XSL-FO isn't currently a good option for styling XML documents for web browsers, it is quite effective at styling XML documents for printing. For example, you can use XSL-FO to convert an XML document into an Adobe Acrobat PDF document that has a very exacting layout. You learn how to carry out this exact task in Hour 14, "Formatting XML with XSL-FO."

It is important to understand how an XSL style sheet is processed and applied to an XML document. This task begins with an XML processor, which is responsible for reading an XML document and processing it into meaningful pieces of information known as *nodes*. More specifically, you learned earlier in the book that XML documents are processed into a hierarchical tree containing nodes for each piece of information in a document. For example, every element and attribute in a document represents a node in the tree representation of a document. Thinking of an XML document as a tree is extremely important when it comes to understanding XSL. After a document has been processed into a tree, a special processor known as an XSL processor begins applying the rules of an XSL style sheet to the document tree.

The XSL processor starts with the root node (root element) in the tree and uses it as the basis for performing pattern matching in the style sheet. *Pattern matching* is the process of using patterns to identify nodes in the tree that are to be processed according to XSL styles. These patterns are stored within constructs known as *templates* in XSL style sheets. The XSL processor analyzes templates and the patterns associated with them to process different parts of the document tree. When a match is made, the portion of the tree matching the given pattern is processed by the appropriate style sheet template. At this point, the rules of the template are applied to the content to generate a result tree. The *result tree* is itself a tree of data, but the data in this case has somehow been transformed by the style sheet. To put it another way, the XSL processor takes a document tree as input and generates another tree, a result tree, as output. Figure 11.1 illustrates the process of using a pattern to match a portion of a document tree and then applying a pattern to it to generate a result tree.

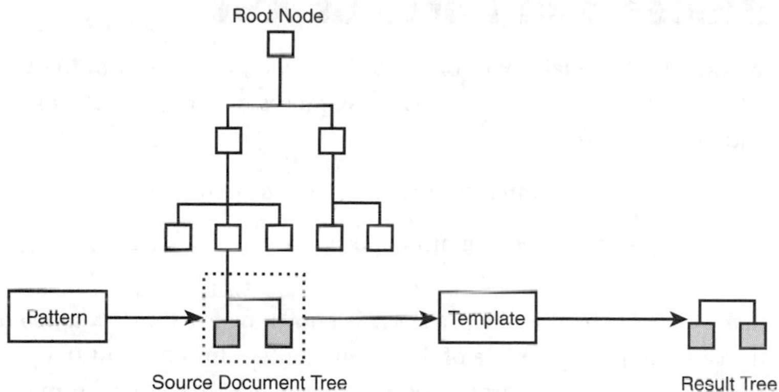

FIGURE 11.1 A pattern is used to match a portion of a document, which is then transformed into a result tree using a template.

By the Way

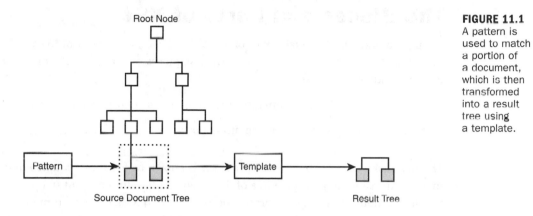

When I refer to a "tree" of data, I'm really talking about the logical structure of the data. To better understand what I mean, think in terms of your family tree, where each relationship forms a branch and each person forms a leaf, or node, on the tree. The same logical relationships apply to XML trees, except the nodes are elements and attributes as opposed to people.

The result tree may contain XML code, HTML code, or special objects known as XSL formatting objects. In the case of XML code, the result tree represents a transformation from one form of XML to another. In the case of HTML code, the result tree represents a transformation from XML code into HTML code that can be viewed in a web browser. Technically speaking, you can't use traditional HTML code as the basis for an XSL result tree because traditional HTML isn't considered an XML-based language. However, if the HTML code adheres to XHTML standards, which is a stricter version of HTML formulated as an XML language, everything will work fine. You learn more about XHTML in Hour 21, "Adding Structure to the Web with XHTML." You also learn how to transform XML code into HTML (XHTML) later in this hour in the section titled, "Your First XSLT Style Sheet."

In order to finish creating the result tree, the XSL processor continues processing each node in the document tree, applying all the templates defined in the style sheet. When all the nodes have been processed and all the style sheet templates applied, the XSL processor returns the completed result tree, which is often in a format suitable for display. I say "often" because it is possible to use XSL to transform a from one XML language to another instead of to XHTML, in which case the resulting document may or may not be used for display purposes.

The Pieces and Parts of XSL

In order to understand the relevance of XSL technologies, it's important to examine the role of the XSL processor once more. The XSL processor is responsible for performing two fundamental tasks:

- Construct a result tree from a transformation of a source document tree
- Interpret the result tree for formatting purposes

The first task addressed by the XSL processor is known as *tree transformation* and involves transforming a source tree of document content into a result tree. Tree transformation is basically the process of transforming XML content from one XML language into another and involves the use of XSLT. The second task performed by the XSL processor involves examining the result tree for formatting information and formatting the content for each node accordingly. This task requires the use of XSL-FO and is currently not supported very well in web browsers. Even so, it is a critical part of XSL that will likely play a significant role in the future of XML.

Although it certainly seems convenient to break up XSL processing into two tasks, there is a much more important reason for doing so than mere convenience. One way to understand this significance is to consider CSS, which supports only the formatting of XML content. The limitations of CSS are obvious when you consider that a source document can't really be modified in any way for display purposes. On the other hand, with XSL you have complete freedom to massage the source document at will during the transformation part of the document processing. The one-two punch of transformation followed by formatting provides an incredible degree of flexibility for rendering XML documents for display.

The two fundamental tasks taken on by the XML processor directly correspond to two XSL technologies: XSLT and XSL-FO. Additionally, there is a third XSL technology, XPath, which factors heavily into XSLT. XSLT and XSL-FO are both implemented as XML languages, which makes their syntax familiar. This also means that style sheets created from them are XML documents. The interesting thing about these two components of XSL is that they can be used together or separately. You can use XSLT to transform documents without any concern over how the documents are formatted. Similarly, you can use XSL Formatting Objects to format XML documents without necessarily performing any transformation on them.

> **By the Way**
>
> Keep in mind that while web browsers have been slow to adopt XSL-FO, there are plenty of tools available for formatting XML code using XSL-FO. Later in the book in Hour 14 you find out how to use one of these tools to convert an XML document into a PDF document via XSL-FO.

The important thing to keep in mind regarding the structure of XSL is the fact that XSL is really three languages, not one. XSLT is the XSL transformation language that is used to transform XML documents from one vocabulary to another. XSL-FO is the XSL formatting language that is used to apply formatting styles to XML documents for presentation purposes. And finally, XPath is a special non-XML expression language used to address parts of an XML document.

> **By the Way**
>
> Although you learn the basics of XPath in this hour and the next, you aren't formally introduced to it until Hour 22, "Addressing and Linking XML Documents." In that hour you learn the details of how to address portions of an XML document using XPath.

XSL Transformation

XSL Transformation (*XSLT*) is the transformation component of the XSL style sheet technology. XSLT consists of an XML-based markup language that is used to create style sheets for transforming XML documents. These style sheets operate on parsed XML data in a tree form, which is then output as a result tree consisting of the transformed data. XSLT uses a powerful pattern-matching mechanism to select portions of an XML document for transformation. When a pattern is matched for a portion of a tree, a template is used to determine how that portion of the tree is transformed. You learn more about how templates and patterns are used to transform XML documents a little later in this lesson.

An integral part of XSLT is a technology known as XPath, which is used to select nodes for processing and generating text. The next section examines XPath in more detail. The remainder of this hour and the next tackles XSLT in greater detail.

XPath

XPath is a non-XML expression language that is used to address parts of an XML document. XPath is different from its other XSL counterparts (XSLT and XSL-FO) in that it isn't implemented as an XML language. This is due to the fact that XPath expressions are used in situations where XML markup isn't really applicable, such as within attribute values. As you know, attribute values are simple text and therefore can't contain additional XML markup. So, although XPath expressions are used within XML markup, they don't directly use familiar XML tags and attributes themselves.

The central function of XPath is to provide an abstract means of addressing XML document parts—for this reason, XPath forms the basis for document addressing in XSLT. The syntax used by XPath is designed for use in URIs and XML attribute values, which requires it to be extremely concise. The name XPath is based on the notion of using a path notation to address XML documents, much as you might use a path in a file system to describe the location of a file. Similar to XSLT, XPath operates under the assumption that a document has been parsed into a tree of nodes. XPath defines different node types that are used to describe the nodes that appear within a tree. There is always a single root node that serves as the root of an XPath tree, and that appears as the first node in the tree. Every element in a document has a corresponding element node that appears in the tree under the root node. Within an element node there are other types of nodes that correspond to the element's content. Element nodes may have a unique identifier associated with them, which is used to reference the node with XPath.

Following is an example of a simple XPath expression, which demonstrates how XPath expressions are used in attribute values:

```
<xsl:for-each select="contacts/contact">
```

This code shows how an XPath expression is used within an XSLT element (`xsl:for-each`) to reference elements named `contact` that are children of an element named `contacts`. Although it isn't important for you to understand the implications of this code in an XSLT style sheet, it is important to realize that XPath is used to address certain nodes (elements) within a document.

When an XPath expression is used in an XSLT style sheet, the evaluation of the expression results in a data object of a specific type, such as a Boolean (true/false) or a number. The manner in which an XPath expression is evaluated is entirely dependent upon the context of the expression, which isn't determined by XPath. The context of an XPath expression is determined by XSLT, which in turn determines how expressions are evaluated. This is the abstract nature of XPath that allows it to be used as a helper technology alongside XSLT to address parts of documents.

> XPath's role in XSL doesn't end with XSLT—XPath is also used with XLink and XPointer, which you learn about in Hour 22.

XSL Formatting Objects

XSL Formatting Objects (*XSL-FO*) represents the formatting component of the XSL style sheet technology and is designed to be a functional superset of CSS. This means that XSL-FO contains all of the functionality of CSS, even though it uses its own XML based syntax. Similar to XSLT, XSL-FO is implemented as an XML language, which is beneficial for both minimizing the learning curve for XML developers and easing its integration into existing XML tools. Also like XSLT, XSL-FO operates on a tree of XML data, which can either be parsed directly from a document or transformed from a document using XSLT. For formatting purposes, XSL-FO treats every node in the tree as a *formatting object*, with each node supporting a wide range of presentation styles. You can apply styles by setting attributes on a given element (node) in the tree.

There are formatting objects that correspond to different aspects of document formatting such as layout, pagination, and content styling. Every formatting object has properties that are used to somehow describe the object. Some properties directly specify a formatted result, such as a color or font, whereas other properties establish constraints on a set of possible formatted results. Following is perhaps the simplest possible example of XSL-FO, which sets the font family and font size for a block of text:

```
<fo:block font-family="Arial" font-size="16pt">
  This text has been styled with XSL-FO!
</fo:block>
```

As you can see, this code performs a similar function to CSS in establishing the font family and font size of a block of text. XSL-FO actually goes further than CSS in allowing you to control the formatting of XML content in extreme detail. The layout model employed by XSL-FO is described in terms of rectangular areas and spaces, which isn't too surprising considering that this approach is employed by most desktop publishing applications. Rectangular areas in XSL-FO are not objects themselves, however; it is up to formatting objects to establish rectangular areas and the relationships between them. This is somewhat similar to rectangular areas in CSS, where you establish the size of an area (box) by setting the width and height of a paragraph of text. XSL-FO also offers a very high degree of control over print-specific page attributes such as page margins.

The XSL processor is heavily involved in carrying out the functionality in XSL-FO style sheets. When the XSL processor processes a formatting object within a style sheet, the object is mapped into a rectangular area on the display surface. The properties of the object determine how it is formatted, along with the parameters of the area into which it is mapped.

By the Way

> The immediate downside to XSL-FO is that there is little support for it in major web browsers. For this reason, coverage of XSL-FO in this book focuses solely on formatting XML data for print purposes (Hour 14).

An XSLT Primer

Seeing as how XSL-FO is extremely limited in current major web browsers, the practical usage of XSL with respect to the Web must focus on XSLT for the time being. This isn't entirely a bad thing when you consider the learning curve for XSL in general. It may be that by staggering the adoption of the two technologies, the W3C may be inadvertently giving developers time to get up to speed with XSLT before tackling XSL-FO. The remainder of this hour focuses on XSLT and how you can use it to transform XML documents.

As you now know, the purpose of an XSLT style sheet is to process the nodes of an XML document and apply a pattern-matching mechanism to determine which nodes are to be transformed. Both the pattern-matching mechanism and the details of each transformation are spelled out in an XSLT style sheet. More specifically, an XSLT style sheet consists of one or more templates that describe patterns and expressions, which are used to match XML content for transformation purposes. The three fundamental constructs in an XSL style sheet are as follows:

- Templates
- Patterns
- Expressions

Before getting into these constructs, however, you need to learn about the `xsl:stylesheet` element and learn how the XSLT namespace is used in XSLT style sheets. The `stylesheet` element is the document (root) element for XSL style sheets and is part of the XSLT namespace. You are required to declare the XSLT namespace in order to use XSLT elements and attributes. Following is an example of declaring the XSLT namespace inside of the `stylesheet` element:

```
<xsl:stylesheet version="1.0" xmlns:xsl="http://www.w3.org/1999/XSL/Transform">
```

This example namespace declaration sets the prefix for the XSLT namespace to `xsl`, which is the standard prefix used in XSL style sheets. You must precede all XSLT elements and attributes with this prefix. Notice in the code that the XSLT namespace is http://www.w3.org/1999/XSL/Transform. Another important aspect of this code is the `version` attribute, which sets the version of XSL used in the style sheet. Currently the only version of XSL is 1.0, so you should set the `version` attribute to `1.0` in your style sheets.

By the Way

> The XSLT namespace is specific to XSLT and does not apply to all of XSL. If you plan on developing style sheets that use XSL-FO, you'll also need to declare the XSL-FO namespace, which is http://www.w3.org/1999/XSL/Format and typically has the prefix `fo`. Furthermore, if you plan on using XSLT to transform web pages, it's a good idea to declare the XHTML namespace: http://www.w3.org/1999/xhtml.

Templates

A *template* is an XSL construct that describes output to be generated based upon certain pattern-matching criteria. The idea behind a template is to define a transformation mechanism that applies to a certain portion of an XML document, which is a node or group of nodes. Although it is possible to create style sheets consisting of a single template, you will more than likely create multiple templates to transform different portions of the XML document tree.

Templates are defined in XSL style sheets using the `xsl:template` element, which is primarily a container element for patterns, expressions, and transformation logic. The `xsl:template` element uses an optional attribute named `match` to match patterns and expressions in an XSLT style sheet. You can think of the `match` attribute as specifying a portion of the XML tree for a document. The widest possible match for a document is to set the `match` attribute to `/`, which indicates that the root of the tree is to be matched. This results in the entire tree being selected for transformation by the template, as the following code demonstrates:

```
<xsl:template match="/">
...
</xsl:template>
```

If you have any experience with databases, you might recognize the `match` attribute as being somewhat similar to a query in a database language. To understand what I mean by this, consider the following example, which uses the `match` attribute to match only elements named `state`:

```
<xsl:template match="state">
...
</xsl:template>
```

This template would come in useful for XML documents that have elements named state. For example, the template would match the `state` element in the following XML code:

```
<contact>
  <name>Frank Rizzo</name>
  <address>1212 W 304th Street</address>
  <city>New York</city>
  <state>New York</state>
  <zip>10011</zip>
</contact>
```

Matching a portion of an XML document wouldn't mean much if the template didn't carry out any kind of transformation. Transformation logic is created using several template constructs that are used to control the application of templates in XSL style sheets. These template constructs are actually elements defined in the XSLT namespace. Following are some of the more commonly used XSLT elements:

- `xsl:value-of`—Inserts the value of an element or attribute
- `xsl:if`—Performs a conditional selection (this or that)
- `xsl:for-each`—Loops through the elements in a document
- `xsl:apply-templates`—Applies a template in a style sheet

A crucial part of XSLT document transformation is the insertion of document content into the result tree, which is carried out with the `xsl:value-of` element. The `xsl:value-of` element provides the mechanism for transforming XML documents because it allows you to output XML data in virtually any context, such as within HTML markup. The `xsl:value-of` element requires an attribute named `select` that identifies the specific content to be inserted. Following is an example of a simple template that uses the `xsl:value-of` element and the `select` attribute to output the value of an element named `title`:

```
<xsl:template match="title">
  <xsl:value-of select="."/>
</xsl:template>
```

In this example, the `select` attribute is set to `.`, which indicates that the current node is to be inserted into the result tree. The value of the `select` attribute works very much like the path of a file on a hard drive. For example, a file on a hard drive might be specified as `\docs\letters\lovenote.txt`. This path indicates the folder hierarchy of the file `lovenote.txt`. In a similar way, the `select` attribute specifies the location of the node to be inserted in the result tree. A dot (`.`) indicates a node in the current context, as determined by the `match` attribute. An element or attribute name indicates a node beneath the current node, whereas two dots (`..`) indicate the parent of the current node. This approach to specifying node paths using a special expression language is covered in much greater detail in Hour 22.

To get an idea as to how the previous example template (matching `title` elements) can be used to transform XML code, take a look at the following code excerpt:

```
<book>
  <title>All The King's Men</title>
  <author>Robert Penn Warren</author>
</book>
<book>
  <title>Atlas Shrugged</title>
```

```
  <author>Ayn Rand</author>
</book>
<book>
  <title>Ain't Nobody's Business If You Do</title>
  <author>Peter McWilliams</author>
</book>
```

Applying the previous template to this code would result in the following results:

```
All The King's Men
Atlas Shrugged
Ain't Nobody's Business If You Do
```

As you can see, the titles of the books are plucked out of the code because the template matched `title` elements and then inserted their contents into the resulting document.

In addition to inserting XML content using the `xsl:value-of` element in a style sheet, it is also possible to conditionally carry out portions of the logic in a style sheet. More specifically, the `xsl:if` element is used to perform conditional matches in templates. This element uses the same `match` attribute as the `xsl:template` element to establish conditional branching in templates. Following is an example of how the `xsl:if` element is used to test if the name of a `state` attribute is equal to `TN`:

```
<xsl:if match="@state=TN">
  <xsl:apply-templates select="location"/>
</xsl:if>
```

This code might be used as part of an online mapping application. Notice in the code that the `state` attribute is preceded by an "at" symbol (@); this symbol is used in XPath to identify an attribute, as opposed to an element. Another important aspect of this code is the manner in which the `location` template is applied only if the `state` attribute is equal to `TN`. The end result is that only the `location` elements whose `state` attribute is set to `TN` are processed for transformation.

If you have any programming experience, you are no doubt familiar with loops, which allow you to repeatedly perform an operation on a number of items. If you don't have programming experience, understand that a loop is a way of performing an action over and over. In the case of XSLT, loops are created with the `xsl:for-each` element, which is used to loop through elements in a document. The `xsl:for-each` element requires a `select` attribute that determines which elements are selected as part of the loop's iteration. Following is an example of using the `xsl:for-each` element to iterate through a list of locations:

```
<xsl:for-each select="locations/location">
  <h1><xsl:value-of select="@city"/>, <xsl:value-of select="@state"/></h1>
  <h2><xsl:value-of select="description"/></h2>
</xsl:for-each>
```

In this example, the xsl:for-each element is used to loop through location elements that are stored within the parent locations element. Within the loop, the city and state attributes are inserted into the result tree, along with the description element. This template is interesting in that it uses carefully placed HTML elements to transform the XML code into HTML code that can be viewed in a web browser. Following is some example code to which you might apply this template:

```
</locations>
  <location city="Washington" state="DC">
    <description>The United States Capital</description>
  </location>
  <location city="Nashville" state="TN">
    <description>Music City USA</description>
  </location>
  <location city="Chicago" state="IL">
    <description>The Windy City</description>
  </location>
</locations>
```

Applying the previous template to this code yields the following results:

```
<h1>Washington, DC</h1>
<h2>The United States Capital</h2>
<h1>Nashville, TN</h1>
<h2>Music City USA</h2>
<h1>Chicago, IL</h1>
<h2>The Windy City</h2>
```

As you can see, the template successfully transforms the XML code into XHTML code that is capable of being viewed in a web browser. Notice that the cities and states are combined within large heading elements (h1), followed by the descriptions, which are coded in smaller heading elements (h2).

In order for a template to be applied to XML content, you must explicitly apply the template with the xsl:apply-templates element. The xsl:apply-templates element supports the familiar select attribute, which performs a similar role to the one it does in the xsl:for-each element. When the XSL processor encounters an xsl:apply-templates element in a style sheet, the template corresponding to the pattern or expression in the select attribute is applied, which means that relevant document data is fed into the template and transformed. Following is an example of applying a template using the xsl:apply-templates element:

```
<xsl:apply-templates select="location"/>
```

The exception to the rule of having to use the xsl:apply-templates element to apply templates in an XSLT style sheet is the root element, whose template is automatically applied if one exists.

This code results in the template for the `location` element being invoked in the current context.

Patterns and Expressions

Patterns and expressions are used in XSLT templates to perform matches and are ultimately responsible for determining what portions of an XML document are passed through a particular template for transformation. A *pattern* describes a branch of an XML tree, which in turn consists of a set of hierarchical nodes. Patterns are used throughout XSL to describe portions of a document tree for applying templates. Patterns can be constructed to perform relatively complex pattern-matching tasks. When you think of patterns in this light, they form somewhat of a mini-query language that can be used to provide exacting controls over the portions of an XML document that are selected for transformation in templates.

As you learned earlier, the syntax used by XSL patterns is somewhat similar to that used when specifying paths to files on a disk drive. For example, the `contacts/contact/phone` pattern selects phone elements that are children of a `contact` element, which itself is a child of a `contacts` element. It is possible, and often useful, to select the entire document tree in a pattern, which is carried out with a single forward slash (/). This pattern is also known as the *root pattern* and is assumed in other patterns if you leave it off. For example, the `contacts/contact/phone` pattern is assumed to begin at the root of the document, which means that `contacts` is the root element for the document.

Expressions are similar to patterns in that they also impact which nodes are selected for transformation. However, expressions are capable of carrying out processing of their own, such as mathematical calculations, text processing, and conditional tests. XSL includes numerous built-in functions that are used to construct expressions within style sheets. Following is a simple example of an expression:

```
<xsl:value-of select="sum(@price)"/>
```

This code demonstrates how to use the standard `sum()` function to calculate the sum of the `price` attributes within a particular set of elements. This could be useful in a shopping cart application that needs to calculate a subtotal of the items located in the cart.

Admittedly, this discussion isn't the last word on XSL patterns and expressions. Fortunately, you learn a great deal more about patterns and expressions in Hour 22. In the meantime, this introduction will get you started creating XSL style sheets.

Wiring an XSL Style Sheet to an XML Document

In Hour 10, "Styling XML Content with CSS," you learned how to create and connect CSS style sheets to XML documents. These types of style sheets are known as external style sheets because they are stored in separate, external files. XSL style sheets are also typically stored in external files, in which case you must wire them to XML documents in order for them to be applied. XSL style sheets are typically stored in files with a `.xsl` filename extension and are wired to XML documents using the `xml-stylesheet` processing instruction. The `xml-stylesheet` processing instruction includes a couple of attributes that determine the type and location of the style sheet:

By the Way

> You can also use the general file extension .xml or the more specific extension .xslt for your XSLT style sheets. The extension really doesn't matter so long as you reference the style sheet properly from the XML document to which it applies.

- `type`—The type of the style sheet (`text/xsl`, for example)
- `href`—The location of the style sheet

By the Way

> You may notice that this discussion focuses on XSL style sheets in general, as opposed to XSLT style sheets. That's because XSLT style sheets are really just a specific kind of XSL style sheet, and from the perspective of an XML document there is no difference between the two. So, when it comes to associating an XSLT style sheet with an XML document, you simply reference it as an XSL style sheet.

These two attributes should be somewhat familiar to you from the discussion of CSS because they are also used to wire CSS to XML documents. The difference in their usage with XSL is revealed in their values—the `type` attribute must be set to `text/xsl` for XSL style sheets, whereas the `href` attribute must be set to the name of the XSL style sheet. These two attributes are both required in order to wire an XSL style sheet to an XML document. Following is an example of how to use the `xml-stylesheet` processing instruction with an XSL style sheet:

```
<?xml-stylesheet type="text/xsl" href="contacts.xsl"?>
```

In this example, the `type` attribute is used to specify that the type of the style sheet is `text/xsl`, which means that the style sheet is an XSL style sheet. The style sheet file is then referenced in the `href` attribute, which in this case points to the file `contacts.xsl`.

Your First XSLT Style Sheet

With just enough XSLT knowledge to get you in trouble, why not go ahead and tackle a complete example style sheet? Don't worry, this example shouldn't be too hard to grasp because it is focuses on familiar territory. I'm referring to the Contacts example XML document from Hour 10. If you recall, in that hour you created a CSS style sheet to display the content from an XML document containing a list of contacts. Now it's time to take a look at how similar functionality is carried out using an XSLT style sheet. In fact, you take things a bit further in the XSLT version of the Contacts style sheet. To refresh your memory, the Contacts XML document is shown in Listing 11.1.

LISTING 11.1 The Familiar Contacts Example XML Document

```
<?xml version="1.0"?>
<?xml-stylesheet type="text/xsl" href="contacts.xsl"?>
<!DOCTYPE contacts SYSTEM "contacts.dtd">

<contacts>
  <!-- This is my good friend Frank. -->
  <contact>
    <name>Frank Rizzo</name>
    <address>1212 W 304th Street</address>
    <city>New York</city>
    <state>New York</state>
    <zip>10011</zip>
    <phone>
      <voice>212-555-1212</voice>
      <fax>212-555-1342</fax>
      <mobile>212-555-1115</mobile>
    </phone>
    <email>frank.rizzo@franksratchetco.com</email>
    <company>Frank&apos;s Ratchet Service</company>
    <notes>I owe Frank 50 dollars.</notes>
  </contact>

  <!-- This is my old college roommate Sol. -->
  <contact>
    <name>Sol Rosenberg</name>
    <address>1162 E 412th Street</address>
    <city>New York</city>
    <state>New York</state>
    <zip>10011</zip>
    <phone>
      <voice>212-555-1818</voice>
      <fax>212-555-1828</fax>
      <mobile>212-555-1521</mobile>
    </phone>
    <email>srosenberg@rosenbergshoesglasses.com</email>
    <company>Rosenberg&apos;s Shoes &amp; Glasses</company>
    <notes>Sol collects Civil War artifacts.</notes>
  </contact>
</contacts>
```

The only noticeable change in this version of the Contacts document is the `xml-stylesheet` declaration (line 2), which now references the style sheet file `contacts.xsl`. Beyond this change, the document is exactly as it appeared in Hour 10. In Hour 10, the role of the XSLT style sheet was to display the contacts in a format somewhat like a mailing list, where the phone numbers, email address, company name, and notes are hidden. This time around the style sheet is going to provide more of a contact manager view of the contacts and only hide the fax number, company name, and notes. In other words, you're going to see a more complete view of each contact.

Before getting into the XSLT code, it's worth reminding you that XSLT isn't directly capable of formatting the document content for display; don't forget that XSLT is used only to transform XML code. Knowing this, it becomes apparent that CSS must still enter the picture with this example. However, in this case CSS is used purely for display formatting, whereas XSLT takes care of determining which portions of the document are displayed.

In order to use CSS with XSLT, it is necessary to transform an XML document into HTML, or more specifically, XHTML. If you recall, XHTML is the more structured version of HTML that conforms to the rules of XML. The idea is to transform relevant XML content into an XHTML web page that uses CSS styles for specific display formatting. The resulting XHTML document can then be displayed in a web browser. Listing 11.2 contains the XSLT style sheet (`contacts.xsl`) that carries out this functionality.

LISTING 11.2 The `contacts.xsl` Style Sheet Used to Transform and Format the Contacts XML Document

```
<?xml version="1.0"?>
<xsl:stylesheet version="1.0"
  xmlns:xsl="http://www.w3.org/1999/XSL/Transform"
  xmlns="http://www.w3.org/1999/xhtml">
  <xsl:template match="/">
    <html xmlns="http://www.w3.org/1999/xhtml">
      <head><title>Contact List</title></head>
      <body style="background-color:silver">
        <xsl:for-each select="contacts/contact">
          <div style="width:450px; padding:5px; margin-bottom:10px;
          border:5px double black; color:black; background-color:white;
          text-align:left">
            <xsl:apply-templates select="name"/>
            <xsl:apply-templates select="address"/>
            <xsl:apply-templates select="city"/>
            <xsl:apply-templates select="state"/>
            <xsl:apply-templates select="zip"/>
            <hr />
            <xsl:apply-templates select="phone/voice"/>
```

```
            <xsl:apply-templates select="phone/mobile"/>
            <hr />
            <xsl:apply-templates select="email"/>
          </div>
        </xsl:for-each>
      </body>
    </html>
  </xsl:template>

  <xsl:template match="name">
    <div style="font-family:Verdana, Arial; font-size:18pt; font-weight:bold">
      <xsl:value-of select="."/>
    </div>
  </xsl:template>

  <xsl:template match="address">
    <div style="font-family:Verdana, Arial; font-size:14pt">
      <xsl:value-of select="."/>
    </div>
  </xsl:template>

  <xsl:template match="city">
    <span style="font-family:Verdana, Arial; font-size:14pt">
      <xsl:value-of select="."/>,&#32;
    </span>
  </xsl:template>

  <xsl:template match="state">
    <span style="font-family:Verdana, Arial; font-size:14pt">
      <xsl:value-of select="."/>&#32;
    </span>
  </xsl:template>

  <xsl:template match="zip">
    <span style="font-family:Verdana, Arial; font-size:14pt">
      <xsl:value-of select="."/>
    </span>
  </xsl:template>

  <xsl:template match="phone/voice">
    <div style="font-family:Verdana, Arial; font-size:14pt">
      <img src="phone.gif" alt="Voice Phone" />&#32;
      <xsl:value-of select="."/>
    </div>
  </xsl:template>

  <xsl:template match="phone/mobile">
    <div style="font-family:Verdana, Arial; font-size:14pt">
      <img src="mobilephone.gif" alt="Mobile Phone" />&#32;
      <xsl:value-of select="."/>
    </div>
  </xsl:template>
```

LISTING 11.2 Continued

```
73:   <xsl:template match="email">
74:     <div style="font-family:Verdana, Arial; font-size:12pt">
75:       <img src="email.gif" alt="Email" />&#32;
76:       <xsl:value-of select="."/>
77:     </div>
78:   </xsl:template>
79: </xsl:stylesheet>
```

I know, there is quite a bit of code in this style sheet. Even so, the functionality of the code is relatively straightforward. The style sheet begins by declaring the XSLT and XHSTML namespaces (lines 3–4). With that bit of standard bookkeeping out of the way, the style sheet creates a template used to match the root element of the document (line 5); this is indicated by the `match` attribute being set to `/`. Notice that within this template there is XHTML code that is used to construct an XHTML web page. Inside the body of the newly constructed web page is where the interesting things take place with the style sheet (lines 9–24).

An `xsl:for-each` element is used to loop through the `contact` elements in the document (line 9); each of the contacts is displayed inside of a `div` element. The specific content associated with a contact is inserted into the `div` element using the `xsl:apply-templates` element to apply a template to each piece of information. More specifically, templates are applied to the `name`, `address`, `city`, `state`, `zip`, `phone/voice`, `phone/mobile`, and `email` child elements of the `contact` element (lines 13–22), along with a couple of horizontal rules in between the templates to provide some visual organization. Of course, in order to apply these templates, the templates themselves must exist.

The first child template matches the `name` element (lines 29–33) and uses CSS to format the content in the `name` element for display. Notice that the `xsl:value-of` element is used to insert the content of the `name` element into the transformed XHTML code. The dot (`.`) specified in the `select` attribute indicates that the value applies to the current node, which is the `name` element. Similar templates are defined for the remaining child elements, which are transformed and formatted in a similar fashion.

The end result of this style sheet is a transformed XHTML document that can be viewed as a web page in a web browser. Figure 11.2 shows the resulting web page generated by this XSLT style sheet.

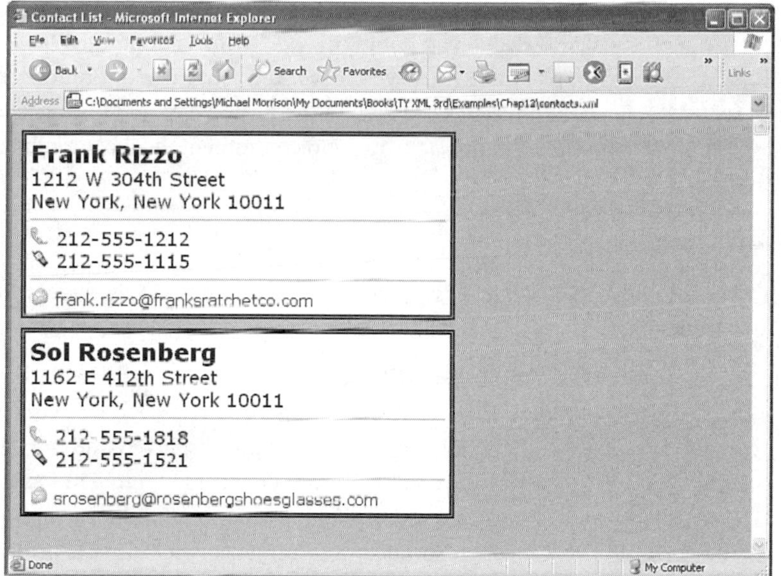

FIGURE 11.2 The Contacts example document is displayed in Internet Explorer using the `contacts.xsl` style sheet.

The figure reveals how the `contacts.xsl` style sheet carries out similar functionality as its CSS counterpart from Hour 10, but with noticeably more flair. The flexibility of being able to transform XML code into any XHTML code you want is what allows the XSLT version of the Contacts style sheet to look a bit flashier. Again, this is because the XSLT style sheet is literally transforming XML content into XHTML content, applying CSS styles to the XHTML, and ultimately making the end result available for display in a web browser. Although this style sheet certainly demonstrates the basic functionality of XSLT, it doesn't touch the powerful transformation features at your disposal with XSLT. I'll leave that for the next hour.

Summary

XSL (Extensible Style Language) is an extremely powerful style sheet technology that is aimed at providing a purely XML-based solution for the transformation and formatting of XML documents. XSL consists of three fundamental technologies: XSL Transformation (XSLT), XPath, and XSL Formatting Objects (XSL-FO). XSLT tackles the transformation aspect of XSL and is capable of transforming an XML document in a particular language into a completely different XML-based language. XPath is used within XSLT to identify portions of an XML document for transformation. XSL-FO addresses the need for a high-powered XML-based formatting language. XSL-FO has limited support in current web browsers, but XSLT and XPath are more than ready to deliver for web-based applications.

This hour introduced you to the different technologies that comprise XSL. Perhaps more important is the practical knowledge you gained of XSLT, which culminated in a complete XSLT style sheet example. Just in case you're worried that this hour hit only the high points of XSLT, the next hour digs deeper into the technology and uncovers topics such as sorting nodes and using expressions to perform mathematical computations.

Q&A

Q. ***Why bother with XSLT when I can just use CSS to create style sheets for XML documents?***

A. If all you need to do is simply display the content in an XML document, CSS may in fact be your best option. However, XSLT allows you to process XML content and gives you a fine degree of control over what content is displayed and the order in which it appears. So, even though XSLT doesn't directly play a role in formatting documents for display, it provides a considerable amount of indirect control when it comes to isolating data, sorting data (numerically or alphabetically, for example), and performing calculations on data within XML documents.

Q. ***How can there be separate namespaces for XSLT and XSL-FO if they are both part of XSL?***

A. XSLT and XSL-FO have different namespaces because they are different languages. Keep in mind that each of these technologies is implemented as an XML-based markup language. Because it is possible to use the two technologies independently of one another, they occupy separate namespaces. You can certainly use both XSLT and XSL-FO in the same XSL style sheet, in which case you would declare both namespaces with their own prefixes. For the time being, however, you will likely create XSL style sheets using only XSLT, in which case you can refer to the style sheet as an XSLT style sheet.

Workshop

The Workshop is designed to help you anticipate possible questions, review what you've learned, and begin learning how to put your knowledge into practice.

Quiz

1. In regard to an XSL processor, what is pattern matching?
2. Which two XSL technologies would you rely on if you only needed to transform an XML document?

3. How do you define templates in XSLT style sheets?

4. What is the difference between patterns and expressions?

Quiz Answers

1. Pattern matching is the process of using patterns to identify nodes in the source document tree that are to be processed according to XSL styles and transformed into a result tree.

2. XSLT and XPath are the two XSL technologies that you would rely on if you only needed to transform an XML document. XSL-FO enters the picture only if you planned on formatting a document using XSL.

3. Templates are defined in XSL style sheets using the `xsl:template` element, which is primarily a container element for patterns, expressions, and transformation logic.

4. A pattern identifies a branch of an XML tree for transformation purposes. Expressions are similar to patterns in that they also impact which nodes are selected for transformation. However, unlike patterns, expressions are capable of carrying out processing of their own, such as mathematical calculations, text processing, and conditional tests.

Exercises

1. Add a new element named `im` to the Contacts XML document that you saw in this chapter. The `im` element is used to store the instant messaging address of the contact. Because there are several different instant messaging services available, you should provide an attribute to the `im` element called `service` that identifies the instant messaging service (that is, Yahoo, AIM, MSN, and so on).

2. Modify the Contacts DTD so that it supports the new `im` element and its `service` attribute.

3. Modify the `contacts.xsl` style sheet to create a template for transforming the new `im` element. If you really want to make it fancy, include a conditional statement in the template to display a different image for the appropriate instant messaging service. Make sure to also modify the style sheet so that the `im` template is applied along with the other contact templates.

HOUR 12

Transforming XML with XSLT

I don't have any solution but I certainly admire the problem.

—Ashleigh Brilliant

When it comes to transforming XML, it's safe to admire both the problem and the solution, which just so happens to be XSLT. But you already knew that because in the previous hour you learned the basics of XSLT and were quickly introduced to the XSLT language and the way to use it to create basic XSLT style sheets. This hour picks up where the previous one left off by examining the XSLT language in more detail and showing you some interesting ways in which XSLT can be used to transform XML content. More specifically, you learn how to sort and process nodes, as well as how to perform conditional tests and computational operations with expressions. This hour arms you with the XSLT knowledge necessary to create practical XSLT style sheets that you can use in your own XML projects.

In this hour, you'll learn

- More details about the XSLT style sheet language
- How to process and sort nodes in an XSLT style sheet
- How to use patterns and expressions in XSLT
- How to apply XSLT style sheets to more challenging document transformation tasks

A Closer Look at XSLT

As you know, XSLT is an XML-based markup language that includes its own set of elements and attributes that are used to create XSLT style sheets. These style sheets are used with XML documents to transform XML content in some manner. This transformation can be something as simple as sorting the content according to a certain piece of information, such as sorting products by price, or it can be as powerful as transforming content into a completely different XML language. Regardless of how you use XSLT style sheets, it's important to have a solid understanding of the XSLT language and what it has to offer.

An XSLT style sheet is broken down into two types of information: instructions and literals. *Instructions* are the XSLT elements and attributes that describe exactly how XML content is to be transformed. *Literals*, on the other hand, are static pieces of information that are placed directly in the resulting document and therefore aren't processed in any way. You can think of the relationship between instructions and literals as the relationship between text and blanks in a traditional paper form that you might fill out, such as an IRS tax form. (I apologize for the scary IRS reference but when people think of forms, many of them think of taxes.) Anyway, the comparison to paper forms has to do with the fact that text on a form is static and doesn't change, whereas the blanks are subject to being filled in by whomever is using the form. In the case of XSLT, the blanks are "filled in" by XSLT instructions that determine the XML content to be placed in the blanks. The resulting output document is the combination of transformed XML content and the literals located throughout a style sheet.

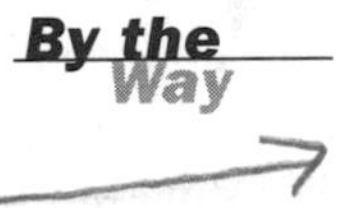

Literals play a significant role in XSLT whenever you transform an XML document into an XHTML document for display in a web browser. In order to successfully generate an XHTML document using XSLT, you must place XHTML code throughout the style sheet as literals. XSL instructions are then used to transform XML content and place it within the XHTML code.

XML content is merged with literals in a style sheet by way of the `xsl:value-of` element, which inserts the value of an element or attribute in the output document. To get a better understanding of how this works, consider the following example:

```
<p>Hello, my name is <xsl:value-of select="name"/></p>
```

This code shows how the `xsl:value-of` element is used to insert the value of a `name` element into an XHTML paragraph. In this example, the `xsl:value-of` element is the instruction, and the remaining XHTML code is the literal. Now that you understand the difference between instructions and literals, let's move on to more important business.

Creating and Applying Templates

You learned in the previous hour that templates are used in XSLT style sheets to transform a particular portion of an XML document for output to a result tree. Templates are created using the `xsl:template` element, which requires an attribute named `match` that determines which nodes of the source document tree are processed by the template. The value assigned to the `match` attribute is a pattern or expression that resolves to a set of nodes. An example of a commonly used value for the `match` attribute is a forward slash (/), which identifies the root node of a document:

```
<xsl:template match="/">
...
</xsl:template>
```

This root template is significant because it serves as the first template applied to a document. Technically, it isn't necessary to include a root template in your style sheets because the XSL processor will automatically start applying other templates with the root element if no root template exists. However, if you want to control the manner in which other templates are applied, you'll want to create a root template. Keep in mind that you can also refer to a root element directly by name, as the following example shows:

```
<xsl:template match="news">
...
</xsl:template>
```

Because the news value assigned to the `match` attribute in this example is the root element of the News document from Hour 10, "Styling XML Content with CSS," it has the same effect as using the forward slash to identify the root element. Although the root element gets things started in an XSLT style sheet, most of the action takes place in other templates. Templates in an XSLT style sheet are used to transform specific portions of an XML document, which are identified using the `match` attribute, as the following example demonstrates:

```
<xsl:template match="headline">
...
</xsl:template>
```

In this example, the `headline` element is matched by the template, which means the template is used to transform all content in the News document that is contained within a `headline` element. This template is usually applied from the parent template of the `headline` element, which in this case is the `news` element. In other words, the `headline` template would be applied from within the `news` template. Following is a portion of XML code for a news document to which this template could be applied:

```
<header>
  <headline>
  Local Author Creates Free Online Music Game
  </headline>
  <byline>
  By Brent Andrews
  </byline>
  <dateline>
    <location>Nashville, Tennessee</location>
    <date>Monday October 17 2005 12:08 CST</date>
  </dateline>
</header>
```

There are trickier approaches to specifying nodes using the `match` attribute. These approaches require knowledge of XPath, which you learn about in Hour 22, "Addressing and Linking XML Documents."

In this code, the headline element matches up with the previous example template. It then becomes important to apply the template and somehow transform the headline element. What do I mean by "applying" a template? Applying a template means that you are invoking the template so that it actually carries out the transformation logic defined in it. It isn't always necessary to explicitly apply every template that you create because the XSL processor will automatically attempt to figure out which templates to apply to certain parts of a document using the match attributes of the templates. However, you will usually apply at least one template to get the ball rolling; templates are applied using the xsl:apply-templates element. The xsl:apply-templates element supports an attribute named select that identifies the nodes to which the template is applied. If you don't specify a value for the select attribute, the template will be applied to all of the child nodes of the current node. So, the select attribute serves to limit the nodes to which a template is applied.

By the Way

Similar to the match attribute of the xsl:template element, the select attribute of the xsl:apply-templates element allows you to use XPath to carry out more advanced node selections. You learn a little more about how this is accomplished later in this hour in the section titled "Pattern Essentials." You get the whole scoop on XPath in Hour 22.

If you want to apply the root template to a document, you can simply place an empty xsl:apply-templates element directly in the root template:

```
<xsl:template match="/">
  <xsl:apply-templates/>
</xsl:template>
```

In this example, the default template is automatically applied to the root node of the document, after which the xsl:apply-templates element makes sure the remaining templates are applied to children of the root element. This may sound a little confusing, so let's take a second to understand exactly what is happening. This code defines a template that handles the default node of the document, as indicated by the forward slash (/) value of the match attribute. When the XSL processor encounters the root node of the document, it automatically matches it up with this template and invokes the template to process the node. The xsl:apply-templates element within the template doesn't include a select attribute, which means that templates matching any children of the root node should be applied (illustrated in Figure 12.1).

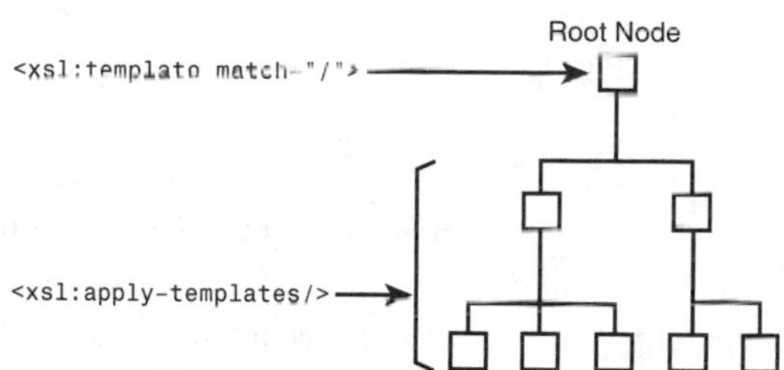

FIGURE 12.1 The `xsl:apply-templates` element is applied to the child elements of an XML document.

If you wanted to target a specific set of nodes, you could identify it using the `select` attribute of the `xsl:apply-templates` element:

```
<xsl:template match="/">
  <xsl:apply-templates select="//headline"/>
</xsl:template>
```

In this example, the `headline` child node is identified in the `select` attribute, which means only templates matching `headline` nodes are applied. This demonstrates how the `select` attribute limits the set of nodes to which templates are applied. Incidentally, the two forward slashes (`//`) before the `headline` element name indicate that the selected `headline` elements are children of the current node (`news`).

Processing Nodes

There are several elements defined in XSLT that are used to process nodes. These node-processing elements perform a range of operations and ultimately provide you with somewhat of a programming approach to creating templates. The first of these elements is `xsl:for-each`, which allows you to process a set of nodes individually according to a certain transformation. The `xsl:for-each` element is particularly useful for database transformations where you have a set of data that must be formatted into a list or table. The `xsl:for-each` element accepts a `select` attribute that works similarly to the `select` attribute in the `xsl:apply-templates` element. Following is an excerpt of code from the `contacts.xsl` style sheet that you saw in the previous hour, which demonstrates the usefulness of the `xsl:for-each` element:

```
<xsl:for-each select="contacts/contact">
  <div style="width:450px; padding:5px; margin-bottom:10px; border:5px double black;
    color:black; background-color:white; text-align:left">
    <xsl:apply-templates select="name"/>
    <xsl:apply-templates select="address"/>
    <xsl:apply-templates select="city"/>
    <xsl:apply-templates select="state"/>
    <xsl:apply-templates select="zip"/>
    <hr />
    <xsl:apply-templates select="phone/voice"/>
    <xsl:apply-templates select="phone/mobile"/>
```

```
    <hr />
    <xsl:apply-templates select="email"/>
  </div>
</xsl:for-each>
```

In this example, the `xsl:for-each` element is used to loop through the `contact` elements in a document. For each `contact` element in the document, the transformation code within the loop is applied. More specifically, an XHTML `div` element is created with the appropriate styles, and several templates are applied for every child `contact` element. This usage of the `xsl:for-each` element allows you to effectively display a formatted list of contacts.

Another interesting XSLT node-processing element is the `xsl:if` element, which allows you to include conditional processing within a template. Transformation code within an `xsl:if` element is conditionally carried out based upon the result of the conditional expression for the element. This expression is specified in the `test` attribute of the `xsl:if` element. You learn a great deal more about expressions in Hour 22, but a quick example might help to reveal how easy they are to use with the `xsl:if` element:

```
<xsl:template match="name">
  <div style="font-family:Times, serif; font-size:15pt; font-weight:bold">
    <xsl:value-of select="."/>
    <xsl:if test=". = 'Michael Morrison'">
      <span> (that's me!)</span>
    </xsl:if>
  </div>
</xsl:template>
```

This code shows how you can conditionally add a literal to the output document based upon the value of the `name` element. The `test` attribute of the `xsl:if` element checks to see if the content of the `name` element is equal to `'Michael Morrison'`. If the conditional expression is true, the literal text (`that's me!`) is inserted into the output document just after the value of the `name` element. If not, the value of the `name` element is inserted like normal.

If you find that you need to conditionally choose between more than one possible value, you can use the `xsl:choose` element in conjunction with the `xsl:when` and `xsl:otherwise` elements. The `xsl:choose` element works a lot like the `xsl:if` element except that it supports multiple conditional sections, which are identified by `xsl:when` elements. Following is the general form of the `xsl:choose` element:

```
<xsl:choose>
<xsl:when test="">
</xsl:when>

<xsl:when test="">
</xsl:when>
```

```
<xsl:otherwise>
</xsl:otherwise>
</xsl:choose>
```

This code shows two different conditional sections of transformation code, which is evident by the two `xsl:when` elements. The final `xsl:otherwise` element identifies transformation code that is carried out if none of the previous `xsl:when` conditionals apply. Following is an example that should help show how to use these elements to create multiple conditionals:

```
<xsl:template match="name">
  <div style="font-family:Times, serif; font-size:15pt; font-weight:bold">
    <xsl:value-of select="."/>
    <xsl:choose>
      <xsl:when test=". = 'Michael Morrison'">
        <span> (that's me!)</span>
      </xsl:when>

      <xsl:when test=". = 'Steve Morrison'">
        <span> (brother)</span>
      </xsl:when>

      <xsl:when test=". = 'Milton James'">
        <span> (friend)</span>
      </xsl:when>

      <xsl:otherwise">
        <span> (don't know this guy!)</span>
      </xsl:otherwise>
    </xsl:choose>
  </div>
</xsl:template>
```

This example uses an `xsl:choose` element and three `xsl:when` elements to provide three conditional transformations that add unique text next to `name` elements whose content matches the conditionals. An `xsl:choose` element is also specified to handle any `name` elements that don't match the conditionals.

Sorting Nodes

I've mentioned several times that one of the enormous benefits of using XSLT to transform XML documents is that you can carefully organize document content before formatting it for display with CSS or XSL-FO. One of the most common operations performed on databases is sorting, in which items are organized according to the value of a particular type of information such as date, quantity, or price. XSLT supports sorting through the `xsl:sort` element. This element allows you to sort the nodes in a node set according to specified criteria. The criteria for an XSLT sort operation are determined by the `select`, `order`, and `data-type` attributes of the `xsl:sort` element.

A set of nodes is sorted based upon a key, which is a pattern or expression that identifies a piece of information in the set. For example, if you wanted to sort a set of nodes on an attribute named price, the sorting key would be set to @price. This value is assigned to the select attribute of the xsl:sort element. Another important attribute in the xsl:sort element is order, which is set to either ascending (the default) or descending. The final attribute of interest with the xsl:sort element is data-type, which allows you to specify the type of data being sorted; this attribute is important because it impacts the manner in which the sorting is carried out. The data-type attribute can be set to one of the following values: text or number. Following is an example of an xsl:sort element that is used to sort a list of names alphabetically in descending order:

```
<xsl:sort select="name" order="descending" data-type="text"/>
```

This example uses the name element as the key and then sorts nodes within the node set in descending order. The data type is set to text to indicate that the sorting routine is text-based. Following is an example of how you might use this code in the context of a real style sheet:

```
<xsl:for-each select="contacts/contact">
  <xsl:sort select="name" order="descending"/>
  <div style="width:450px; padding:5px; margin-bottom:10px; border:5px double black;
    color:black; background-color:white; text-align:left">
    <xsl:apply-templates select="name"/>
    <xsl:apply-templates select="address"/>
    <xsl:apply-templates select="city"/>
    <xsl:apply-templates select="state"/>
    <xsl:apply-templates select="zip"/>
    <hr />
    <xsl:apply-templates select="phone/voice"/>
    <xsl:apply-templates select="phone/mobile"/>
    <hr />
    <xsl:apply-templates select="email"/>
  </div>
</xsl:for-each>
```

You probably recognize this XSLT code from the familiar contacts.xsl style sheet. In this example the xsl:sort element is used to sort the contacts prior to displaying each of them.

Pattern Essentials

Patterns have crept into the XSLT discussion several times throughout this hour and the previous hour. I'd like to mention one more time that you explore patterns more thoroughly in Hour 22. However, XSLT uses patterns enough that I think it would be helpful to cheat a little and give you a quick primer on how to use them. This section isn't intended to make you a pattern expert, but it will hopefully give you some insight into how patterns fit into XSLT.

As you know by now, patterns are used to address parts of XML documents much as paths in file systems are used to address folders and files. Patterns can be used to isolate specific nodes or groups of nodes and can be specified as absolute or relative. An absolute pattern spells out the exact location of a node or node set, whereas a relative pattern identifies a node or node set relative to a certain context. In the previous `contacts.xsl` example, the pattern `contacts/contact` is an absolute pattern, whereas the pattern `name` is a relative pattern. The `name` pattern is relative because it makes an assumption about the current context.

Patterns are used in several situations throughout XSLT, but the majority of the time you'll use them to set the `select` and `match` attributes of standard XSLT elements. The simplest pattern is the pattern that references the current node, which is a simple period (`.`). Following is an example of how to use this pattern:

```
<xsl:value-of select="."/>
```

The current node pattern is obviously highly dependent upon the context of the document. A pattern that isn't dependent upon context is the root pattern, which is identified with a single forward slash (/). The root pattern identifies the location of a document's root element no matter where it appears. To create an absolute pattern, you must begin with the root element and specify the exact hierarchy of nodes leading to a node or node set.

Other patterns are used to reference nodes that are above or below the current node. For example, a child node pattern is created by simply specifying the name of the node. A parent node, on the other hand, is created using two periods (`..`). Following is an example of using a pattern to access a parent node:

```
<xsl:value-of select=".."/>
```

You can put patterns together to get more interesting results. For example, to address a sibling node, you must first go to the parent and then reference the sibling as a child. In other words, you use the parent pattern (`..`) followed by a forward slash (/) followed by the sibling node name, as in the following example:

```
<xsl:value-of select="../brother"/>
```

If you want to select all of the child nodes of a given node, you can use the double slash (//) pattern, as in the following example:

```
<xsl:value-of select="//"/>
```

Lest you think patterns are limited to elements, you can easily address attributes by specifying the attribute name preceded by an at symbol (@), as in the following example:

```
<xsl:value-of select="info/@ssnum"/>
```

This code assumes that the current node contains a child element named info that has an attribute named ssnum.

Putting Expressions to Work

Similar to patterns, expressions play an important role in determining how XSLT style sheets transform XML content. However, expressions differ from patterns in that expressions are capable of carrying out programmatic operations such as comparisons and calculations. Expressions are created using patterns and additional XSLT constructs such as comparison operators and functions. The next couple of sections explain how to use these constructs to create XSLT expressions.

Working with Operators

Earlier in the hour you learned how to use the xsl:if and xsl:when elements to add conditional logic to XSLT style sheets. What you didn't learn, however, was how powerful the actual conditional test of these elements can be. Both of these elements rely on an attribute named test to specify a conditional expression that essentially results in a value of true or false; if the resulting value is true, the associated XSLT code is carried out. The specific expression used by the test attribute is quite flexible and can involve several different comparison operators. Following are some of the most commonly used comparison operators that can appear within the test attribute:

- =—Checks to see if two pieces of data are equal
- !=—Checks to see if two pieces of data are unequal
- <—Checks to see if one piece of data is less than another
- <=—Checks to see if one piece of data is less than or equal to another

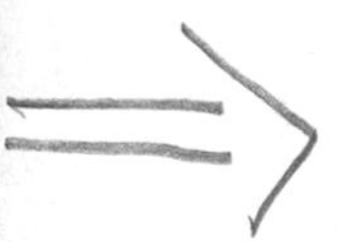

- >—Checks to see if one piece of data is greater than another
- >=—Checks to see if one piece of data is greater than or equal to another
- and—Checks to see if two conditional expressions are both true
- or—Checks to see if at least one of two conditional expressions is true

> Although the less-than and greater-than operators look strange at first, upon closer inspection you can see that they are actually just entities. If you recall, an entity is identified by sandwiching its name between an ampersand (&) and a semicolon (;). So, the greater-than-or-equal-to operator, which is specified as >=, is ultimately resolved into >=.

To use these operators, you simply combine them with patterns and literal values to create expressions. For example, the following code shows how to create an xsl:if element that invokes a section of code only if the content of the child element named countdown is less than or equal to zero:

```
<xsl:if test="countdown &lt;= 0">
  Lift off!
</xsl:if>
```

The and and or operators carry out a logical comparison between two other expressions that must evaluate to a true or false value. As an example, if you wanted to expand the countdown example so that you could count in either direction, the following code would do the trick:

```
<xsl:if test="countdown &lt;= 0 or countdown &gt; 10">
  Lift off!
</xsl:if>
```

The or operator used in this example causes "lift-off" to occur if the value of countdown is either less than or equal to zero, or greater than 10. This example demonstrates how multiple comparison operators can be used together to create more powerful conditional expressions.

In addition to comparison operators, there are also a few familiar math operators that you may find useful:

- *—Multiplies two numeric values
- div—Divides two numeric values and returns the integer result
- mod—Divides two numeric values and returns the integer remainder

- +—Adds two numeric values
- -—Subtracts two numeric values

These operators can be used in expressions to perform math operations on XML data. Following is an example of how you might multiply the contents of two child elements (quantity and unitprice) in order to calculate a shopping cart total that is displayed in an XHTML document:

```
<div>
  Total price = <xsl:value-of select="quantity * unitprice"/>
</div>
```

This code reveals the flexibility of the select attribute and how a math operator can be used within it to carry out simple calculations. The values stored in the quantity and unitprice child elements are multiplied using the multiplication operator (*).

The result of the multiplication is inserted into the output document as the content of an XHTML `div` element.

Using Standard Functions

If you thought operators were neat, you will be really impressed with the standard functions built into XSLT. These functions are much more interesting than operators because they carry out calculations that would otherwise be quite tedious using simple math operators alone. Following are some of the more commonly used standard functions supported in XSLT:

- `ceiling()`—Round up a decimal value to the nearest integer
- `floor()`—Round down a decimal value to the nearest integer
- `round()`—Round a decimal value to the nearest integer
- `sum()`—Add a set of numeric values
- `count()`—Determine the quantity of values in a set

Although these functions are somewhat self-explanatory in terms of what kinds of calculations they carry out, it doesn't hurt to see a few of them at work in the context of a style sheet. Following is an example of how you might add up the values of a set of nodes to calculate a total with the `sum()` function:

```
<div>
  Total amount = $<xsl:value-of select="sum(cart/item/@price)"/>
</div>
```

This example would work well for a shopping cart XML document that includes a `cart` element that holds several `item` elements representing each item in the shopping cart. Notice that the `price` attribute of each `item` element is used as the basis for the sum calculation. Following is an example of the kind of XML code that could be transformed using this XSLT example:

```
<cart>
  <item price="199.99">
  DVD Player
  </item>
  <item price="699.99">
  32-Inch Television
  </item>
  <item price="249.99">
  Surround-Sound Speaker System
  </item>
</cart>
```

When applied to this code, the previous XSLT example adds together the prices of the three items to arrive at a total of 1149.97. This shopping cart example could also benefit from knowing how many items are in the shopping cart, which is accomplished with the following code:

```
<div>
  Number of items = <xsl:value-of select="count(cart/item)"/>
</div>
```

The `count()` function is used in this example to count the number of `item` elements contained within the `cart` element. As this example demonstrates, the standard functions built into XSLT allow you to perform very useful computations with little effort.

A Complete XSLT Example

As you've seen in the past few hours, I like to reinforce style sheet knowledge with complete example style sheets. At this point I'd like to revisit the News XML document that you saw back in Hour 10. If you recall, this document contained content for a news story complete with XML code to identify the relevant portions of the story such as the headline, byline, and body text. Listing 12.1 shows the code for the News XML document, just in case your memory is a little fuzzy.

LISTING 12.1 The News Example XML Document

```
<?xml version="1.0"?>
<?xml-stylesheet type="text/xsl" href="news.xsl"?>

<news>
  <header>
    <headline>
    Local Author Creates Free Online Music Game
    </headline>
    <byline>
    By Brent Andrews
    </byline>
    <dateline>
      <location>Nashville, Tennessee</location>
      <date>Monday October 17 2005 12:08 CST</date>
    </dateline>
  </header>

  <story>
    <p>Local nerd author Michael Morrison is involved in yet another unusual
    project. Following up on the success of his quirky trivia game Tall
    Tales, Morrison has gone back to his technical roots with his latest
    project, Guess That Groove. Guess That Groove acts as somewhat of an
    online version of the popular television game show Name That Tune. What
    makes Guess That Groove so unique is how it relies on actual digitized
    music recordings to present popular songs from the last seventy years of
    music.</p>
    <p>Located online at <url>www.guessthatgroove.com</url>, the service is
```

LISTING 12.1 Continued

```
28:     entirely free. Morrison explained that the business model is based upon
29:     commission fees from linked sites such as Amazon.com and iTunes, which
30:     offer game players an option to purchase CDs and individual music tracks
31:     that they encounter throughout the game. It's too early to tell whether
32:     Morrison has hit on another social phenomonon along the lines of Tall
33:     Tales. Regarding the potential success of the online game, Morrison
34:     replied, <quote>It was a lot of fun to create and I enjoy playing it
35:     myself, so in some ways I already consider it a success</quote>.</p>
36:   </story>
37: </news>
```

If you're very observant, you might notice that this News XML code is actually a little different than the code you saw in Hour 10. The only change in this code occurs in line 2 where an XSL style sheet (`news.xsl`) is referenced, as opposed to a CSS style sheet. Otherwise, the document is identical to the original. In Hour 10 you created a CSS to format the document so that it could be viewed in a web browser. Given your newfound knowledge of XSLT, can you think about how an XSLT style sheet might be structured to transform this document so that it can be viewed in a web browser?

Obviously, XSLT alone won't be enough to prep the document for display because XSLT isn't capable of carrying out content formatting directly. The approach you saw in the previous hour involves transforming the XML code into XHTML code that is understood by web browsers, as well as applying CSS styles. You're going to use the same approach here in the XSLT style sheet for the News document. In order to transform each portion of the document, it is necessary to create a template that matches each major element found in the document. With those templates in place, you simply create a root template that establishes the XHTML document structure and invokes the other templates. Listing 12.2 contains the complete source code for the `news.xsl` style sheet, which uses this exact strategy to transform the News XML document for display within a web browser.

LISTING 12.2 The `news.xsl` Style Sheet Used to Transform and Format the News XML Document

```
<?xml version="1.0"?>
<xsl:stylesheet version="1.0" xmlns:xsl="http://www.w3.org/1999/XSL/Transform">
  <xsl:template match="/">
    <html><head><title>Contact List</title></head>
      <body style="text-align: center; background-image: url(newspaper.jpg);
      background-repeat: repeat">
        <xsl:apply-templates/>
      </body>
    </html>
  </xsl:template>

  <xsl:template match="headline">
    <div style="width:450px; border-bottom:5px double black; text-align:left;
```

```
13:         color:black; font-family:Verdana, Arial; font-size:26pt">
14:         <xsl:value-of select="."/>
15:       </div>
16:     </xsl:template>
17:
18:     <xsl:template match="byline">
19:       <span style="width:200px; text-align:left; color:black; font-family:Verdana,
20:       Arial; font-size:12pt">
21:         <xsl:value-of select="."/>
22:       </span>
23:     </xsl:template>
24:
25:     <xsl:template match="dateline">
26:       <span style="width:250px; text-align:right; color:gray; font-family:Verdana,
27:       Arial; font-size:10pt; font-style:italic">
28:         <xsl:value-of select="."/>
29:       </span>
30:     </xsl:template>
31:
32:     <xsl:template match="p">
33:       <div style="width:450px; text-align: left; margin-bottom:8px; color:black;
34:         font-family:Verdana, Arial; font-size:10pt">
35:         <xsl:apply-templates/>
36:       </div>
37:     </xsl:template>
38:
39:     <xsl:template match="url">
40:       <span style="font-weight:bold">
41:         <xsl:value-of select="."/>
42:       </span>
43:     </xsl:template>
44:
45:     <xsl:template match="quote">
46:       <span style="font-style:italic">
47:         <xsl:value-of select="."/>
48:       </span>
49:     </xsl:template>
50: </xsl:stylesheet>
```

The general structure of this style sheet should be somewhat familiar to you from the Contacts example in the previous hour. Similar to the `contacts.xsl` style sheet, this style sheet uses an empty `apply-templates` element within its root template to indirectly invoke all of the other templates in the style sheet (line 6). Notice that the root template includes XHTML code that establishes the resulting web page (lines 4–8). From there, the `headline` template formats the headline of the News document using a `div` element and CSS styles (lines 11–16). The remaining templates continue with a similar process of placing XML content into the framework of an XHTML document and carefully applying CSS styles to get the desired formatting. Figure 12.2 shows the resulting XHTML document as viewed in Internet Explorer.

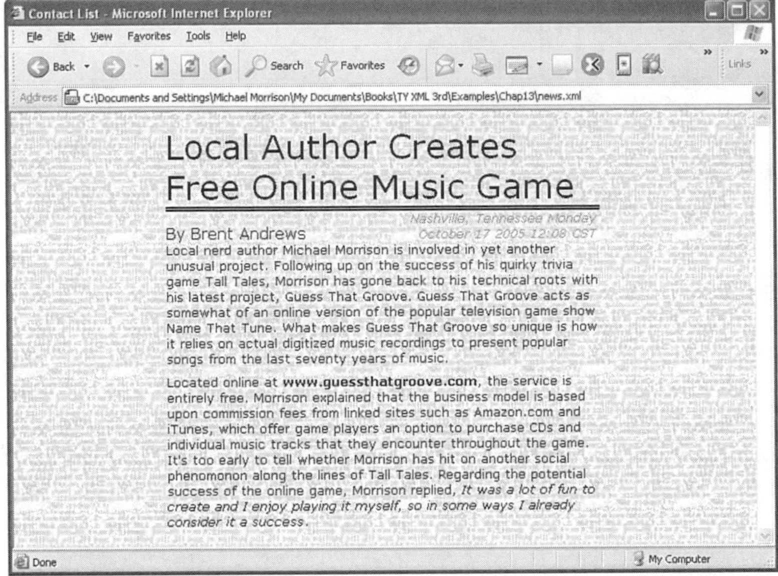

FIGURE 12.2 The News example document is displayed in Internet Explorer using the `news.xsl` style sheet.

This figure shows how an XSLT style sheet is used to transform XML content so that it appears highly formatted in a web browser. Of course, the formatting aspect of the style sheet is actually carried out with CSS, but XSLT is still at the heart of the transformation. Other than the new tiled background image, the resulting styled page looks very much like the News page styled with CSS back in Hour 10.

Yet Another XSLT Example

I'm a little concerned about the fact that you've only seen how to create an XSLT style sheet that mimics the functionality of an existing CSS style sheet. The reason for the concern is because you might be wondering why you wouldn't just create the style sheet in CSS since the CSS version is obviously simpler to code. The answer is that you probably would be smarter to use CSS for the example style sheets that you've seen thus far because they really do nothing more than format XML content for display. The real power of XSLT is revealed when you must go a step further and actually manipulate and extract information from XML content. In this section you create an XSLT style sheet that conditionally displays content according to its value and that also performs an interesting calculation on information in a document.

The example document for this style sheet is a document that stores a list of vehicles for sale. If you've ever shopped for cars on the Internet, you are probably familiar with the process of searching through lists of cars according to certain criteria. In this example you learn how to use an XSLT style sheet to format vehicle information intelligently. The Vehicles example document is coded in a custom XML language that would be suitable for an online car shopping web site. Listing 12.3 contains the code for the vehicles.xml document.

LISTING 12.3 The Vehicles Example XML Document

```
<?xml version="1.0"?>
<?xml-stylesheet type="text/xsl" href="vehicles.xsl"?>

<vehicles>
  <vehicle year="2004" make="Acura" model="3.2TL">
    <mileage>13495</mileage>
    <color>green</color>
    <price>33900</price>
    <carfax buyback="no" />
  </vehicle>

  <vehicle year="2005" make="Acura" model="3.2TL">
    <mileage>07541</mileage>
    <color>white</color>
    <price>33900</price>
    <carfax buyback="yes" />
  </vehicle>

  <vehicle year="2004" make="Acura" model="3.2TL">
    <mileage>18753</mileage>
    <color>white</color>
    <price>32900</price>
    <carfax buyback="yes" />
  </vehicle>

  <vehicle year="2004" make="Acura" model="3.2TL">
    <mileage>28434</mileage>
    <color>black</color>
    <price>31995</price>
    <carfax buyback="yes" />
  </vehicle>

  <vehicle year="2004" make="Acura" model="3.2TL">
    <mileage>22422</mileage>
    <color>silver</color>
    <price>31995</price>
    <carfax buyback="no" />
  </vehicle>

  <vehicle year="2004" make="Acura" model="3.2TL">
    <mileage>18350</mileage>
    <color>silver</color>
    <price>32995</price>
    <carfax buyback="no" />
  </vehicle>

  <vehicle year="2004" make="Acura" model="3.2TL">
    <mileage>12163</mileage>
    <color>gold</color>
    <price>31995</price>
```

LISTING 12.3 Continued

```
    <carfax buyback="yes" />
  </vehicle>

  <vehicle year="2004" make="Acura" model="3.2TL">
    <mileage>23182</mileage>
    <color>silver</color>
    <price>31995</price>
    <carfax buyback="no" />
  </vehicle>

  <vehicle year="2003" make="Acura" model="3.2TL">
    <mileage>37775</mileage>
    <color>grey</color>
    <price>22995</price>
    <carfax buyback="yes" />
  </vehicle>

  <vehicle year="2003" make="Acura" model="3.2TL">
    <mileage>34503</mileage>
    <color>black</color>
    <price>22995</price>
    <carfax buyback="yes" />
  </vehicle>
  <vehicle year="2003" make="Acura" model="3.2TL">
    <mileage>42670</mileage>
    <color>black</color>
    <price>23995</price>
    <carfax buyback="no" />
  </vehicle>

  <vehicle year="2003" make="Acura" model="3.2TL">
    <mileage>48405</mileage>
    <color>gold</color>
    <price>22995</price>
    <carfax buyback="yes" />
  </vehicle>
</vehicles>
```

This example document represents XML data that you might receive as part of a search result for a specific type of car, in this case an Acura TL. The XML code shows how the Vehicles document relies on a relatively simple markup language consisting of only a few elements: `vehicles`, `vehicle`, `mileage`, `color`, `price`, and `carfax`. Each vehicle in the document is coded as a `vehicle` element within the parent `vehicles` element. In addition to the mileage, color, and price of each vehicle, which are coded as child elements, the year, make, and model of each vehicle are coded as attributes of the `vehicle` element. There is an additional child element called `carfax` that is used to code whether or not a vehicle is covered under the CARFAX Buyback Guarantee. This element includes an attribute named `buyback` that can be set to either `yes` or `no`.

The online automotive service CARFAX offers a search that you can perform to find out the history of vehicles. The CARFAX Buyback Guarantee helps to ensure that the information about a vehicle on CARFAX is accurate. If not, CARFAX will buy the car back from you. To learn more about CARFAX, visit them online at http://www.carfax.com.

So what exactly should an XSLT style sheet do with this document? For the purposes of this example, I'd first like to see the style sheet sort the vehicles according to a certain criterion, such as price. Following is a template that carries out this kind of sorting process using the `xsl:sort` element and its `order` attribute:

```
<xsl:template match="vehicles">
  <xsl:apply-templates select="vehicle">
    <xsl:sort select="@price" order="ascending"/>
  </xsl:apply-templates>
</xsl:template>
```

This template sorts vehicles according to price and in ascending order (cheapest to most expensive). Although price is certainly an important factor, not all buyers are driven solely by price. In fact, you may be determined to buy a car with low miles, and it could very well be that the CARFAX guarantee is important to you. Knowing this, I thought it might be interesting to highlight vehicles that are under a certain mileage (20k miles) and that have the CARFAX guarantee. This task can be carried out using `xsl:when` and `xsl:otherwise` elements, which allow you to conditionally transform XML content, in addition to sorting vehicles by price.

One final piece of information that would be interesting to know is the average price of the vehicles in the document; lucky for us, XSLT is quite capable of performing this calculation without much work. Following is an example of how this calculation could be carried out in a template:

```
<xsl:value-of select="round(sum(vehicles/vehicle/price) div
  count(vehicles/vehicle))"/>
```

This code makes use of the `round()`, `sum()`, and `count()` functions to carry out the average price calculation.

The complete XSLT style sheet for the Vehicles document is similar to the other XSLT style sheets you've seen—it must transform the XML content into XHTML so that it can be viewed in a web browser. Unlike those style sheets, however, this one must be structured a little differently. First off, the root template has much more responsibility because there is a fair amount of formatting involved in listing the vehicles, because they need to be listed in a tabular format. Additionally, the template for the main `vehicles` element is kind of interesting because it must sort its child vehicle elements according to the price of each vehicle.

I think you knowenough about the required functionality of the Vehicles style sheet to take a look at the complete code for it, which is shown in Listing 12.4.

LISTING 12.4 The `vehicles.xsl` Style Sheet Used to Transform and Format the Vehicles XML Document

```
<?xml version="1.0"?>
<xsl:stylesheet version="1.0" xmlns:xsl="http://www.w3.org/1999/XSL/Transform">
  <xsl:template match="/">
    <html>
      <head>
        <title>Used Vehicles</title>
      </head>

      <body background="money.jpg">
        <h1 style="background-color:#446600;
          color:#FFFFFF; font-size:20pt; text-align:center;
          letter-spacing: 12pt">Used Vehicles</h1>
        <table align="center" border="2px">
          <tr>
            <th>Year</th>
            <th>Make</th>
            <th>Model</th>
            <th>Mileage</th>
            <th>Color</th>
            <th>Price</th>
            <th>CARFAX</th>
          </tr>
          <xsl:apply-templates/>
          <tr style="font-weight:bold">
            <td colspan="3"></td>
            <td colspan="2">Average price:</td>
            <td>
              $<xsl:value-of select="round(sum(vehicles/vehicle/price) div
              count(vehicles/vehicle))"/>
            </td>
          </tr>
        </table>
      </body>
    </html>
  </xsl:template>

  <xsl:template match="vehicles">
      <xsl:apply-templates select="vehicle">
        <xsl:sort select="price" order="ascending"/>
      </xsl:apply-templates>
  </xsl:template>

  <xsl:template match="vehicle">
    <xsl:choose>
      <xsl:when test="mileage &lt; 20000 and carfax/@buyback = 'yes'">
        <tr style="color:#446600; font-weight:bold">
          <td><xsl:value-of select="@year"/></td>
          <td><xsl:value-of select="@make"/></td>
          <td><xsl:value-of select="@model"/></td>
          <td><xsl:value-of select="mileage"/></td>
          <xsl:apply-templates select="color" />
          <td>$<xsl:value-of select="price"/></td>
```

```
          <xsl:apply-templates select="carfax" />
        </tr>
      </xsl:when>
      <xsl:otherwise>
        <tr>
          <td><xsl:value-of select="@year"/></td>
          <td><xsl:value-of select="@make"/></td>
          <td><xsl:value-of select="@model"/></td>
          <td><xsl:value-of select="mileage"/></td>
          <xsl:apply-templates select="color" />
          <td>$<xsl:value-of select="price"/></td>
          <xsl:apply-templates select="carfax" />
        </tr>
      </xsl:otherwise>
    </xsl:choose>
  </xsl:template>

  <xsl:template match="color">
    <xsl:choose>
      <xsl:when test=". = 'black'">
        <td style="background: #000000"></td>
      </xsl:when>
      <xsl:when test=". = 'red'">
        <td style="background: #880000"></td>
      </xsl:when>
      <xsl:when test=". = 'green'">
        <td style="background: #008800"></td>
      </xsl:when>
      <xsl:when test=". = 'blue'">
        <td style="background: #000088"></td>
      </xsl:when>
      <xsl:when test=". = 'silver'">
        <td style="background: #CCCCCC"></td>
      </xsl:when>
      <xsl:when test=". = 'gray' or . = 'grey'">
        <td style="background: #666666"></td>
      </xsl:when>
      <xsl:when test=". = 'gold'">
        <td style="background: #CC9933"></td>
      </xsl:when>
      <xsl:otherwise>
        <td style="background: #FFFFFF"></td>
      </xsl:otherwise>
    </xsl:choose>
  </xsl:template>

  <xsl:template match="carfax">
    <xsl:choose>
      <xsl:when test="@buyback = 'yes'">
        <td style="text-align: center"><img src="checkmark.gif"
          alt="CARFAX Buyback Guarantee" /></td>
      </xsl:when>
      <xsl:otherwise>
        <td></td>
      </xsl:otherwise>
    </xsl:choose>
  </xsl:template>
</xsl:stylesheet>
```

Although the code is a little long compared to the other style sheets you've seen, it does some pretty neat things with the vehicle data. First of all, the XHTML web page is set up and a table is created with a caption for the vehicle list; this all takes place in the first part of the root template (lines 4–22). On line 23 the `xsl:apply-templates` element is used to invoke the other templates in the style sheet, which results in the vehicle data getting transformed and formatted into XHTML table data. The root template then continues by calculating and displaying the average price of the vehicles on the last row of the table (lines 24–31). Notice that the `round()`, `sum()`, and `count()` functions are all used in this calculation, along with the `div` operator.

There are four other templates defined in this style sheet: `vehicles`, `vehicle`, `color`, and `carfax`. The `vehicles` template invokes the `vehicle` template and also sorts the `vehicle` elements using the `xsl:sort` element (line 39). The sort is an ascending sort according to the `price` attribute of the `vehicle` elements.

The `vehicle` template is intriguing in that it uses the `xsl:choose`, `xsl:when`, and `xsl:otherwise` elements to set up two branches of code that are conditionally carried out based upon the values of the `mileage` element and the `buyback` attribute of the `carfax` element within each `vehicle` element. More specifically, vehicles with mileage less than 20,000 miles that have the CARFAX guarantee are highlighted (line 45). Notice on this line (45) that a fairly interesting expression is used to check for vehicles matching the mileage and CARFAX requirements. If there is a match with this expression, the details of the vehicle are displayed in a green, bold font (lines 46–54); if there is no match, the vehicle details are displayed in a normal font, as indicated in the `xsl:otherwise` element (lines 57–65).

The last two templates focus on the color and CARFAX information for each vehicle. Instead of just displaying the name of the color as text, a colored rectangle is drawn on the screen to help provide a better visual interface to the data. In other words, you see the actual color of the vehicle instead of the name of the color. The `color` template (lines 70–97) is what makes this functionality possible.

The `carfax` template appears last, and is responsible for displaying an image of a checkmark that identifies whether a vehicle is covered by the CARFAX BuyBack Guarantee. The value of the `buyback` attribute is used in the conditional, and if its value is set to `yes` the image `checkmark.gif` is displayed.

You now have a pretty good idea regarding what the resulting web page should look like given the code in the `vehicles.xsl` style sheet. Figure 12.3 shows the `vehicles.xml` document as viewed in Internet Explorer using this style sheet.

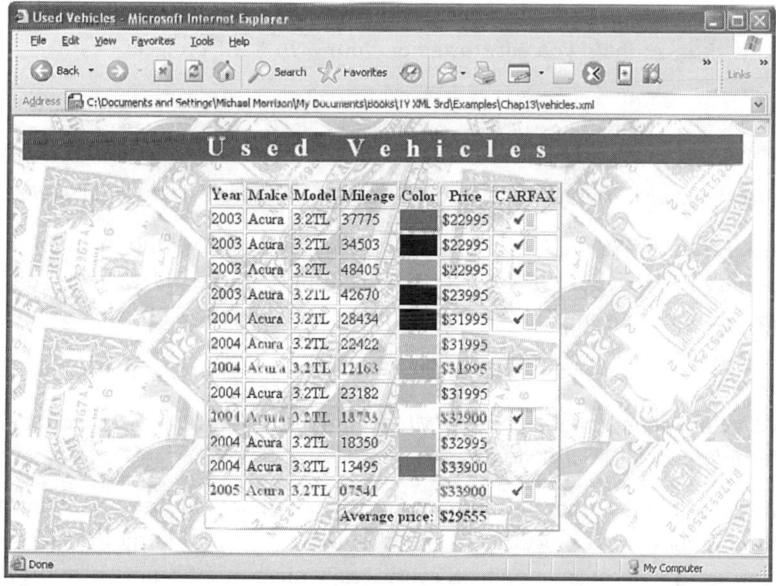

FIGURE 12.3
The Vehicles example document is displayed in Internet Explorer using the `vehicles.xsl` style sheet.

The figure reveals how the XSLT style sheet manipulates the Vehicles XML document in several ways. First off, the vehicles are sorted according to increasing price, which allows you to quickly determine their different price points. Secondly, all the vehicles with less than 20,000 miles that have a CARFAX BuyBack Guarantee are highlighted with a bold font in a different color to make them stand out. Finally, the average price of the vehicles is calculated and displayed as the last item in the table, which would be useful information for a buyer trying to gauge how much vehicles cost.

Summary

Although XSLT style sheets can be used in conjunction with CSS to perform basic XML document formatting, the real power of XSLT is revealed when you actually manipulate the content of a document in order to facilitate a more meaningful presentation. Fortunately, XSLT includes rich features for carrying out a variety of different transformation tasks. Some of the XSLT features that make it so flexible are patterns and expressions, along with the ability to use them to process and sort nodes. Of course, at the core of every XSLT style sheet is a set of templates that are used to transform different parts of XML documents.

This hour taught you a great deal about templates and how they are created and applied in XSLT style sheets. You also learned how to process and sort nodes, not to mention how to use patterns and expressions. The hour culminated in a couple of complete XSLT example style sheets, which hopefully gave you some practical knowledge that can help you get started on your own XSLT projects.

Q&A

Q. ***Are there any limitations regarding the use of literals in an XSLT style sheet?***

A. Yes. Because XSLT style sheets are coded in XML, everything in them must adhere to the syntax rules of XML. This applies to literals as well, which means that tags must be nested properly, start tags must have end tags, and so on.

Q. ***What happens to nodes in an XML document that aren't matched by a template in an XSLT style sheet?***

A. If nodes in a document aren't matched by a template in an XSLT style sheet, those nodes aren't processed or transformed. Keep in mind that it isn't necessary for a style sheet to address every single piece of information in an XML document; it's perfectly acceptable to pick out highly specific information from a document if so desired. The degree to which document content is processed is entirely dependent on each specific application of XSLT.

Q. ***Are there any other functions I can use with XSLT beyond the standard functions mentioned in this hour?***

A. Yes. There are several other standard XSLT functions that weren't covered in this hour; you can learn more about them by visiting the XSLT page at the W3C web site, which is located at http://www.w3.org/TR/xslt. Additionally, XSLT supports the inclusion of extended functions in different implementations of XSLT. For example, a web browser vendor could add browser-specific functions to their implementation of XSLT. You'll have to check with the specific browser you are targeting to see if extended XSLT functions are supported.

Q. ***In regard to an XSLT style sheet, what happens if a document doesn't validate against a DTD/XSD schema?***

A. If a document doesn't validate against a provided schema, a web browser will still apply the style sheet and display the document. However, if the document isn't well formed, the style sheet is never processed and the document isn't displayed.

Workshop

The Workshop is designed to help you anticipate possible questions, review what you've learned, and begin learning how to put your knowledge into practice.

Quiz

1. What is the difference between instructions and literals in XSLT style sheets?
2. What is the significance of a forward slash (/) when used by itself in the match attribute of an XSLT element such as xsl:template?
3. If you use the xsl:choose, xsl:when, and xsl:otherwise elements to create a conditional section of a style sheet, when does the code within the xsl:otherwise element get carried out?
4. How do you reference the current node in the select attribute of an XSLT element such as xsl:value-of?

Quiz Answers

1. Instructions are the XSLT elements and attributes that describe how XML content is to be transformed, whereas literals are static pieces of information that are placed directly in the output document without being processed.
2. A forward slash (/) identifies the root node of a document when specified in the match attribute of an XSLT element such as xsl:template.
3. The code in an xsl:otherwise element gets carried out when none of the xsl:when conditionals apply.
4. A period (.) is used to reference the current node in the select attribute of an XSLT element such as xsl:value-of.

Exercises

1. Modify the vehicles.xml document so that it includes several more vehicles of varying model years and prices. Open the document in a web browser to see how the vehicles.xsl style sheet automatically sorts the vehicles, identifies the vehicles with low mileage and CARFAX guarantees, and calculates an average price.
2. Modify the vehicles.xsl style sheet so that only vehicles with model years greater than or equal to 2005 are highlighted. Hint: You must use the >= comparison operator to determine if each vehicle's year attribute is greater than or equal to 2005.

HOUR 13

Access Your iTunes Music Library via XML

> XML is easy. It is the problems people are trying to address with XML that are hard.
>
> — Jonathan Borden

One problem being addressed with XML is not very hard at all, and is actually quite fun. I'm referring to Apple's iTunes digital music service, which you probably didn't realize had anything to do with XML. It turns out that Apple chose XML as the storage format for the library of songs in the iTunes desktop application. The songs themselves are still stored in Apple's proprietary AAC media format but iTunes keeps track of the songs and pertinent information about them through an XML file. It is this XML file that you focus on in this lesson. More specifically, you learn how to transform your iTunes library so that you can make your song list available on the Web. You even find out how to potentially spin your iTunes song list into a money-making opportunity by providing links to the songs where other people can buy them and earn you a commission from Apple.

In this hour, you'll learn

- How XML fits into Apple's iTunes digital music service
- About the inner workings of an iTunes music library
- How to link to tracks in the iTunes music store
- How to transform your iTunes music library into an HTML web page that you can publish on the Web

The Role of XML in iTunes

Just in case you aren't familiar with it, iTunes is Apple's wildly successful online music service, where you can download individual songs in a digital format for around a dollar each. Music downloaded through iTunes is compatible with Apple's line of iPod music players. If you aren't familiar with iPod music players, I may not be able to help you! They've become quite the cultural phenomenon in terms of bringing digital music to the masses. To learn more about the iTunes service and iPod players, visit http://www.apple.com/itunes/.

> Digital songs on the iTunes music service are stored in Apple's AAC (Advanced Audio Codec) format, which is roughly similar to Microsoft's WMA (Windows Media Audio) format. Both formats are essentially takeoffs on the immensely popular MP3 format that started it all. Apple and Microsoft both added security features to their formats to help prevent piracy.

So what does iTunes have to do with XML? XML enters the picture with iTunes in a couple of different ways. First and foremost, the iTunes desktop application uses XML code as the basis for storing the list of songs, or tracks, in your personal iTunes music library. This XML library code goes beyond just listing the names of the tracks in your library. In fact, it includes information such as the artist, album, genre, and track number on the album (CD) of each track, along with numerous other data fields related to the digitized song file. For example, the XML code includes the bit rate and sample rate of each track, which directly relates to the quality of the music.

Because the iTunes library track listing is stored in XML, you can access it and manipulate it just as you would any other XML document. One neat thing you can do is to transform the XML song list into HTML so that it can be displayed in a web browser. This is exactly what you learn how to do in this hour.

Before you get started accessing your iTunes library, it's worth mentioning another facet of iTunes that is heavily connected to XML. I'm referring to *podcasts*, which are digital audio files that typically contain talk shows or other prerecorded themed speech or music. You can think of a podcast as a radio show stored in a file that you can carry with you and listen to whenever you want. Anyone can create his own podcasts and share them with the world via iTunes. After recording and formatting the actual podcast media file, the key to sharing it involves creating an XML document based upon the RSS (Really Simple Syndication) language. You learn how to create news feeds using RSS in Hour 24, "Syndicating the Web with RSS News Feeds." For now, take a look at what's available in terms of podcasts by browsing to the Podcasts genre in iTunes. Figure 13.1 shows a podcast highlighted in iTunes.

Unlike normal music tracks that you purchase and download in iTunes, you subscribe to podcasts because they are typically regularly updated with new content. Also, the vast majority of podcasts that you'll find on iTunes are free. In the figure, the podcast The Dumpster Diving Geek is highlighted—this is a free podcast related to scavenging for high-tech gadgets.

FIGURE 13.1
Podcasts in iTunes are broken down into lots of different categories.

Although podcasting is certainly an interesting subject, it isn't the primary focus of this lesson. This hour primarily addresses the song library in iTunes, and how to use the fact that it is encoded in XML to share it with the world via the Web.

Digging Into the iTunes Library File

I've already mentioned several times that the iTunes library file is stored in an XML format but I haven't given you any clues regarding how to find or access the file. The file is stored in a different location depending on whether you're using a Windows or Macintosh computer. Either way, the file is named iTunes Music Library.xml. Following are the locations where you can find the file on each type of computer:

- Windows—`My Documents/My Music/iTunes/iTunes Music Library.xml`
- Mac—`Music/iTunes/iTunes Music Library.xml`

If, for some reason, you have trouble finding the iTunes XML library file or if you're just too lazy to drill down into the folders to find it, there is a simpler alternative—just export the file directly from within iTunes. Click File on the main iTunes menu, followed by Export Library. You'll be given an opportunity to specify the location and filename of the exported XML library file. When you have the library file handy, you can begin studying it and figuring out how to manipulate the XML code for your own needs.

Listing 13.1 contains an excerpt from an iTunes library file. Keep in mind that there is a lot more information in the library file that I've left out. The emphasis for this lesson is on extracting XML data pertaining to the tracks referenced in the library, so the listing only shows the XML code for a single track.

LISTING 13.1 The XML Code for a Single Track Within an iTunes Library File

```
 1: <dict>
 2:   <key>Track ID</key><integer>35</integer>
 3:   <key>Name</key><string>Landslide</string>
 4:   <key>Artist</key><string>Fleetwood Mac</string>
 5:   <key>Album</key><string>The Dance</string>
 6:   <key>Genre</key><string>Rock</string>
 7:   <key>Kind</key><string>Protected AAC audio file</string>
 8:   <key>Size</key><integer>4285488</integer>
 9:   <key>Total Time</key><integer>268283</integer>
10:   <key>Disc Number</key><integer>1</integer>
11:   <key>Disc Count</key><integer>1</integer>
12:   <key>Track Number</key><integer>9</integer>
13:   <key>Track Count</key><integer>17</integer>
14:   <key>Year</key><integer>1997</integer>
15:   <key>Bit Rate</key><integer>128</integer>
16:   <key>Sample Rate</key><integer>44100</integer>
17: </dict>s
```

Based upon what you've learned throughout the book thus far, you've probably already realized that this isn't your average run-of-the-mill XML code. In fact, Apple deviated considerably from traditional XML design sense by structuring the iTunes library file as pairs of key values instead of more meaningful XML tags. In other words, just about everything in an iTunes library is stored as a key with a corresponding value. As an example, the artist for the track is coded using a `<key>` tag with `Artist` as its content (line 4). Immediately following this `<key>` tag is a corresponding `<string>` tag that holds the name of the artist associated with the key; in this case, `Fleetwood Mac`.

You can continue examining the code in the listing to see how other information about the track is coded using key values. The key-value pairings always consist of a `<key>` tag followed by a tag that indicates the type of the data stored, such as `<string>` or `<integer>`. An example of an integer key-value is the track number, which is the number of the track on the actual album or CD (line 12). In this example, the song "Landslide" is track number 9 on the CD *The Dance* by Fleetwood Mac.

By the Way

> There is a DTD available from Apple for validating iTunes music library files. You can access the DTD online at http://www.apple.com/DTDs/PropertyList-1.0.dtd.

Taking a step back for a moment, it's worth noting that the key-value information for a track occurs within a `dict` element. `dict` stands for dictionary, which simply refers to a data structure consisting of keys and values. A complete library file consists of multiple nested `dict` elements that are used to store various pieces of information related to the library, such as the list of tracks in the library along with any playlists. Because you're only concerned at the moment with extracting and viewing the library of songs, it isn't necessary to deal with playlist data.

You now have some idea regarding the structure of the iTunes library file but there is another topic worth addressing before you start ripping through the XML code to generate a view of it that is browser friendly. I'm referring to the creation of links to the iTunes music store.

Linking to Tracks in the iTunes Store

Although it would certainly still be an interesting example if I just showed you how to transform the iTunes music library into a format that can be shared and viewed on the Web, that doesn't serve enough of a practical purpose. It doesn't do you much good to share your music library with others unless they have a means of accessing tracks within the library and playing or purchasing the tracks themselves. For this reason, it's important to include links back to the iTunes music store for all of the tracks in your music library. And if you sign up to become an iTunes affiliate, you can even earn commissions on other people buying songs from your music list.

The trick to tying your music library to the iTunes music store involves being able to generate links to individual tracks within the store. These links vary a little based upon whether or not you are an iTunes affiliate attempting to earn commissions or if you just want to provide a link without any financial angle. I'm going to assume the latter because becoming an iTunes affiliate is somewhat of another topic.

> **By the Way**
>
> To learn more about becoming an iTunes affiliate, visit the iTunes Affiliates web site at http://www.apple.com/itunes/affiliates/.

There are essentially three different kinds of links you're going to focus on in regard to the iTunes music store and your music library:

- Link to a track (song)
- Link to an album (CD)
- Link to an artist

As you can see, these types of links are increasingly more general as you go from track to album to artist. The idea is that you can give visitors to your music library page the option of looking up a specific song on iTunes or browsing more generally based upon the album or the artist.

Every link to the iTunes music store begins with a common base search URL:

```
itms://phobos.apple.com/WebObjects/MZSearch.woa/wa/advancedSearchResults?
```

When entered by itself as you see it here, this link will simply launch iTunes and lead you to the main iTunes search page, as shown in Figure 13.2.

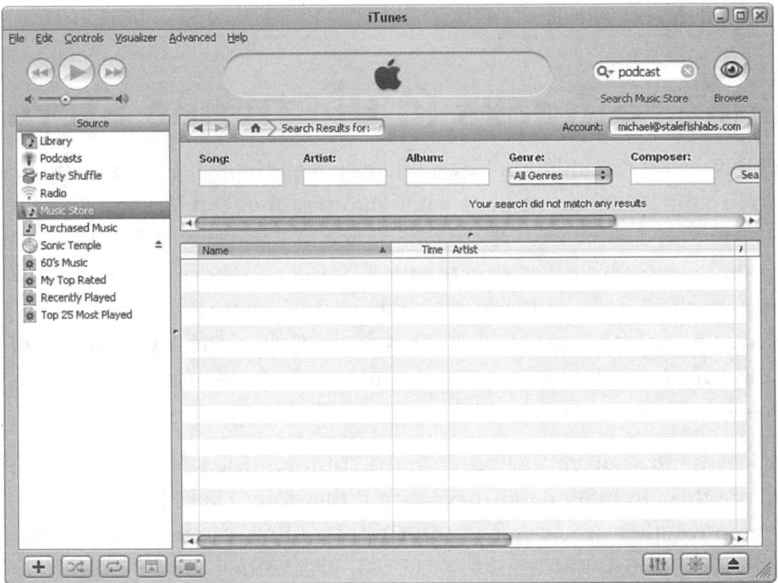

FIGURE 13.2 The base search URL for iTunes leads you to the main iTunes search page.

The figure should give you a clue as to how you're going to build links into the iTunes music store. By appending search fields onto the base URL, you are effectively initiating an iTunes search via a URL. There are three main search parameters you're interested in when it comes to initiating such a search:

- `songTerm`—Search for a song (track)
- `albumTerm`—Search for an album (CD)
- `artistTerm`—Search for an artist

You can use any combination of these search parameters to come up with a specific search URL that hones in on matching iTunes music. For example, to search for a specific song by a specific artist that appears on a specific album, you'll want to specify all three parameters. Following is an example of such a URL:

```
itms://phobos.apple.com/WebObjects/MZSearch.woa/wa/advancedSearchResults?songTerm=
Hoist That Rag&albumTerm=Real Gone&artistTerm=Tom Waits
```

By the Way

Keep in mind that in XML code you must convert ampersand (&) characters to the `&` character entity.

In this example, the song "Hoist That Rag" on the album *Real Gone* by Tom Waits is searched on iTunes. The resulting song as found in iTunes appears in Figure 13.3.

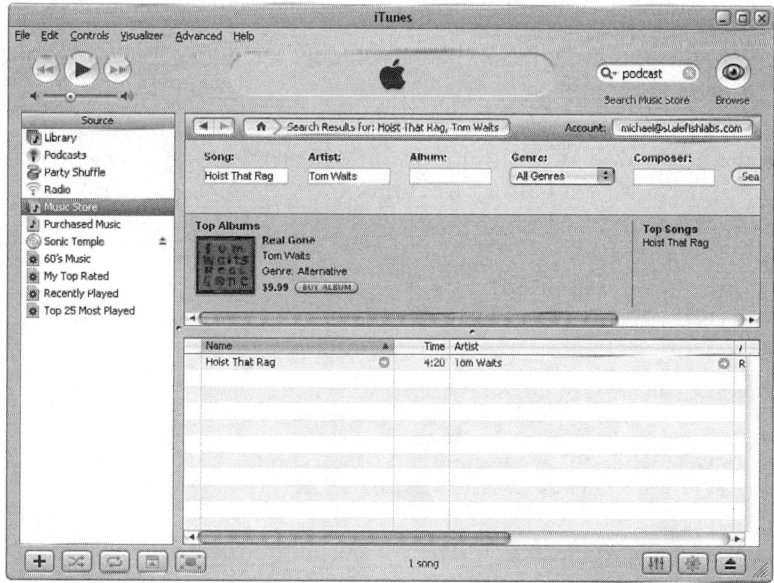

FIGURE 13.3
An iTunes search URL for a specific song results in the song being selected in iTunes.

Of course, you can be more general if you want a search to focus on an individual album or artist, as opposed to a specific song. Following is a URL that searches for the artist Trashcan Sinatras.

```
itms://phobos.apple.com/WebObjects/MZSearch.woa/wa/advancedSearchResults?
artistTerm=Trashcan Sinatras
```

Just in case you've been following along without actually trying any of the examples, please feel free to enter some of these URLs into a real web browser to try them out. Also make sure to try altering the URLs to search for some music of your own. Of course, you'll need to have iTunes installed in order for any of the search URLs to work.

Building an iTunes Web Viewer

You now have some basic knowledge of the iTunes XML library file along with how to build links to tracks, albums, and artists within the iTunes music store. You're ready to pull everything together into a practical example that allows you to publish your iTunes music library online, complete with links that allow people to listen to samples, buy the tracks, and browse the albums and artists.

Revisiting the iTunes XML Music Library

You're going to create an XSLT stylesheet that transforms your iTunes XML library document into an HTML document that is suitable for viewing in a web browser. But before you get into the code for the stylesheet, let's take one more look at the XML code for a library file. Listing 13.2 contains partial code for an iTunes library file where the code for a music track is visible.

LISTING 13.2 A Partial Listing of an iTunes Music Library.xml Music Library Document

```
<?xml version="1.0" encoding="UTF-8"?>
<!DOCTYPE plist PUBLIC "-//Apple Computer//DTD PLIST 1.0//EN"
"http://www.apple.com/DTDs/
  PropertyList-: 1.0.dtd">
<?xml-stylesheet href="itunesview.xsl" type="text/xsl"?>
<plist version="1.0">
<dict>
  <key>Major Version</key><integer>1</integer>
  <key>Minor Version</key><integer>1</integer>
  <key>Application Version</key><string>4.9</string>
  <key>Music Folder</key><string>file://localhost/C:/Documents%20and%20Settings/
  Michael%20Morrison/My%20Documents/My%20Music/iTunes/iTunes%20Music/
  </string>
  <key>Library Persistent ID</key><string>45B7F87C7466C64A</string>
  <key>Tracks</key>
  <dict>
    ...
    <key>37</key>
    <dict>
      <key>Track ID</key><integer>37</integer>
      <key>Name</key><string>Thinking Of You</string>
      <key>Artist</key><string>Lenny Kravitz</string>
      <key>Composer</key><string>Lenny Kravitz/Lysa Trenier</string>
      <key>Album</key><string>5</string>
      <key>Genre</key><string>Pop/Funk</string>
      <key>Kind</key><string>MPEG audio file</string>
      <key>Size</key><integer>6141310</integer>
      <key>Total Time</key><integer>383764</integer>
      <key>Track Number</key><integer>32</integer>
      <key>Year</key><integer>1998</integer>
      <key>Date Modified</key><date>2005-06-08T20:04:06Z</date>
      <key>Date Added</key><date>2004-05-06T04:29:57Z</date>
```

```
32:         <key>Bit Rate</key><integer>128</integer>
33:         <key>Sample Rate</key><integer>44100</integer>
34:         <key>Comments</key><string>By ScazzT</string>
35:         <key>Play Count</key><integer>6</integer>
36:         <key>Play Date</key><integer>-1088231274</integer>
37:         <key>Play Date UTC</key><date>2005-08-13T05:00:22Z</date>
38:         <key>Track Type</key><string>File</string>
39:         <key>Location</key><string>file://localhost/C:/
40:         Documents%20and%20Settings/Michael%20Morrison/My%20Documents/
41:         My%20Music/Masheed/Lenny%20Kravitz%20-%20Thinking%20Of%20You.mp3/
42:         </string>
43:         <key>File Folder Count</key><integer>-1</integer>
44:         <key>Library Folder Count</key><integer>-1</integer>
45:       </dict>
46:       ...
47: </dict>
48: </plist>
```

This XML-coded iTunes music track contains all the information you need to crank out an XSLT stylesheet that rips out the important information and transforms it into something pretty that can be viewed in a web browser. Just in case you aren't seeing it right off, lines 18 through 45 contain the key-value pairings for the song "Thinking Of You" by Lenny Kravitz.

Because stylesheets aren't magically associated with XML documents automatically, you must make a small addition to your XML music library document in order to wire it to the XSLT stylesheet that you're about to see. This line of code is already present in the XML library document shown in Listing 13.2. Just check out line 4 to see how the familiar `xml-stylesheet` directive is used to link the stylesheet to the XML document. Make sure to add this line of code to your own XML library document or the stylesheet will have no effect.

Inside the iTunes Viewer XSLT Stylesheet

The stylesheet that transforms the iTunes music library document is really only interested in three pieces of information in the document: the track name, artist, and album. This information is relatively easy to find within the document because the `<key>` tag contains the text `Name`, `Artist`, and `Album` for each piece of information, respectively. Therefore, the job of the stylesheet is to look through the XML code for tags whose content is equal to `Name`, `Artist`, or `Album`, and then grab the contents of the adjacent "value" tag (`<string>` in this case).

Listing 13.3 contains the complete code for the `itunesview.xsl` XSLT stylesheet, which transforms the tracks in an iTunes music library document into a nicely formatted list complete with links back to the iTunes music store.

LISTING 13.3 The `itunesview.xsl` XSLT Stylesheet Transforms an iTunes Music Library into a Cleanly Formatted HTML Web Page

```
<?xml version="1.0"?>
<xsl:stylesheet version="1.0" xmlns:xsl="http://www.w3.org/1999/XSL/Transform">
  <xsl:template match="/">
    <html><head><title>My iTunes Songs</title></head>
    <style>
      <xsl:comment>
      h1 {
        text-align:center;
        font-family:arial;
        font-size:18pt;
        color:#669966;
      }
      table {
        border-style:none;
        padding:0px;
        margin:0px;
        text-align:left;
      }
      th {
        font-family:arial;
        font-size:14pt;
        background-color:#669966;
        color:#FFFFFF;
      }
      td {
        font-family:arial;
        font-size:11pt;
        color:#669966;
      }
      a:link {
        text-decoration:none;
        color:#669966;
      }
      a:hover {
        font-weight:bold;
        text-decoration:none;
        color:#66BB66;
      }
      a:visited {
        text-decoration:none;
        color:#333333;
      }
      </xsl:comment>
    </style>
    <body>
      <h1>My iTunes Songs</h1>
      <table style="width:100%">
        <tr style="font-weight:bold">
```

```
        <th style="width:40%">Name</th>
        <th style="width:20%">Artist</th>
        <th style="width:40%">Album</th>
      </tr>
      <xsl:call-template name="main" />
    </table>
  </body>
  </html>
</xsl:template>

<xsl:template name="main">
  <xsl:for-each select="/*/*/dict[1]/dict">
    <xsl:element name="tr">
      <xsl:call-template name="song" />
    </xsl:element>
  </xsl:for-each>
</xsl:template>

<xsl:template name="song">
  <tr>
    <xsl:if test="position() mod 2 != 1">
      <xsl:attribute name="style">background-color:#EEEEEE
      </xsl:attribute>
    </xsl:if>

    <td style="height=20px">
      <xsl:element name="a">
        <xsl:attribute name="href">
          itms://phobos.apple.com/WebObjects/MZSearch.woa/wa/
          advancedSearchResults?songTerm=<xsl:value-of select=
          "child::*[preceding-sibling::* = 'Name']" />&amp;artistTerm=
          <xsl:value-of select="child::*[preceding-sibling::* =
          'Artist']" />&amp;albumTerm=<xsl:value-of select=
          "child::*[preceding-sibling::* = 'Album']" />
        </xsl:attribute>
        <img src="itunes.gif" alt="iTunes" style="border:none" />
        <xsl:text> </xsl:text><xsl:value-of select=
        "child::*[preceding-sibling::* = 'Name']" />
      </xsl:element>
    </td>

    <td>
      <xsl:element name="a">
        <xsl:attribute name="href">
          itms://phobos.apple.com/WebObjects/MZSearch.woa/wa/
          advancedSearchResults?artistTerm=<xsl:value-of select=
          "child::*[preceding-sibling::* = 'Artist']" />
        </xsl:attribute>
        <xsl:value-of select="child::*[preceding-sibling::* =
        'Artist']" />
      </xsl:element>
    </td>

    <td>
      <xsl:element name="a">
        <xsl:attribute name="href">
          itms://phobos.apple.com/WebObjects/MZSearch.woa/wa/
```

LISTING 13.3 Continued

```
111:             advancedSearchResults?artistTerm=<xsl:value-of select=
112:             "child::*[preceding-sibling::* = 'Artist']" />&amp;albumTerm=
113:             <xsl:value-of select="child::*[preceding-sibling::* =
114:             'Album']" />
115:           </xsl:attribute>
116:           <xsl:value-of select="child::*[preceding-sibling::* =
117:           'Album']" />
118:         </xsl:element>
119:       </td>
120:     </tr>
121:   </xsl:template>
122: </xsl:stylesheet>
```

I realize this is a pretty hefty listing but don't let it intimidate you. If you take a closer look at the code, you'll realize that almost the first half of it is an internal CSS stylesheet aimed at making the resulting HTML document more visually appealing. In other words, there is nothing critical in lines 5 through 48 that would prevent the XSLT stylesheet from working if you deleted those lines. However, the internal CSS stylesheet is still useful in that it formats and styles the output so that it is easier to view.

The real meat of the XSLT stylesheet begins on line 72 where the song template begins. This template is initiated from line 67 within the main template upon finding nested `<dict>` tags. If you refer back to Listing 13.2 (lines 15 through 18), you'll notice that songs in the music library are coded within `<dict>` tags (one for each song) that are nested within a higher level `<dict>` tag. The main template in the stylesheet uses this relationship as the basis for determining if it has encountered song data. If so, the song template is called to further process the song data.

The song template comprises the remainder of the stylesheet. It starts off by performing a sneaky little trick to draw an alternating background color for each song (lines 74 to 77). This gives the resulting page a horizontally striped appearance that helps you distinguish each song from the next. To alternate the background color for each song, the `position()` function is called to determine the position of the current node. The specific value that this function returns isn't really important so long as it serves as a counter as you progress through the songs. The `mod` operator that is applied to the return value of the `position()` function results in a different background color being applied for evenly numbered rows of song data.

After the background color trick, the song template moves on to laying out the cell data for the three table cells (song, artist, and album) that represent a song row in the HTML table. The first cell is the song cell, and it consists of the song name coded as an anchor link that links to the song in the iTunes music store. Lines 80 through 92 reveal how the `<a>` tag is coded for the song link, including the dynamically assembled `href` attribute (lines 81 through 88), an iTunes logo image (line 89), and the actual song name itself (lines 90 and 91). The remaining code in the song template carries out a similar task for the artist and album cells within the table.

Viewing the End Result in a Browser

You're finally ready to see the end result of all your hard work. Just open your music library XML document in a web browser to view it transformed as an HTML web page. Figure 13.4 shows a sample iTunes library as viewed in Internet Explorer.

By the Way

> If for some reason your iTunes music library isn't styled when you open it in a web browser, check to make sure that you've added the line of code that links the `itunesview.xsl` stylesheet to the XML document (see line 4 of Listing 13.2).

FIGURE 13.4
This iTunes music library has been successfully transformed thanks to the `itunesview.xsl` XSLT stylesheet.

As the figure reveals, all of the tracks in the iTunes XML library document are transformed into a cleanly formatted web page that is easy to read. Perhaps even more interesting is how the songs, artists, and albums all serve as links to relevant areas of the iTunes music store. By clicking any of these links you are led directly to the song, artist, or album in the music store. Figure 13.5 shows the iTunes application after clicking the song Sissyneck in Figure 13.4.

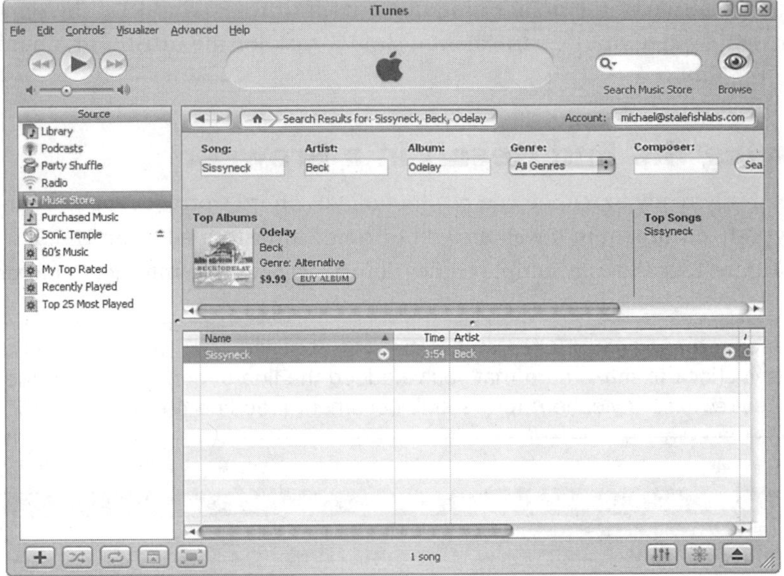

FIGURE 13.5 Clicking a song on the transformed web page takes you to the song in the iTunes music store.

As promised, clicking the song in the music library web page leads straight to the song in the music library within the iTunes application. So, if this page is published on the Web, anyone who visits it and clicks a link will be led to the appropriate search result within her own iTunes desktop application, which is where the music store is located.

Summary

This lesson took a dramatic turn toward the practical and the entertaining by showing you how XML is used in an extremely popular real-world application. More specifically, you learned how an iTunes music library is coded as an XML document that can be manipulated without too much difficulty. You worked through the specific XML format used by iTunes as well how to create an XSLT stylesheet that drills into that format and extracts information about individual tracks. This hour even showed you how to construct hyperlinks to the iTunes music store so that you can provide links between your music library and iTunes for people to buy the songs listed in your library. All of this learning culminated in a complete example that allows you to make your iTunes music library available on the Web for other people to view and use as a basis for shopping for iTunes music.

Q&A

Q. *Can I use any version of iTunes to access the music library as XML?*

A. No. Early versions of iTunes stored the music library as specially formatted text without XML tags. Your best bet is to download the latest version of iTunes from Apple at http://www.apple.com/itunes/download/.

Q. *Can I use what I learned in this hour about iTunes and XML to create podcasts?*

A. Not exactly. Although iTunes podcasts do rely on XML in order to be published properly, they use a different XML format that is based on RSS (Really Simple Syndication). So, there is really no correlation between the XML code used to store an iTunes music library and the XML code used to syndicate a podcast. RSS is discussed in detail in Hour 24.

Q. *How do I keep my music library current if I want to publish it on the Web?*

A. Because the `itunesview.xsl` stylesheet is entirely external, all you must do to update your music library online is to grab (copy or export) the latest XML music library file from iTunes and paste in the line of code that links the stylesheet to it. Publish this file over the previous version and your library is updated and ready to roll!

Workshop

The Workshop is designed to help you anticipate possible questions, review what you've learned, and begin learning how to put your knowledge into practice.

Quiz

1. What XML markup language does iTunes use to store its music library?
2. What is the purpose of the `<key>` tag in an iTunes music library?
3. What three search parameters are used to build link URLs into the iTunes music store?

Quiz Answers

1. Okay, this was a bit of a trick question. The iTunes music library XML format isn't based on any specific XML markup language. Instead, it uses somewhat

of a generic dictionary format that maps keys to values. The DTD for the format is available online at http://www.apple.com/DTDs/PropertyList-1.0.dtd.

2. The iTunes music library format is based on key-value pairs of data where a key identifies the name of the data and a subsequent type tag contains the data itself. The `<key>` tag marks up the name of the data in this pairing.

3. The three search parameters used to build link URLs into the iTunes music store are `songTerm`, `albumTerm`, and `artistTerm`.

Exercises

1. Add the line of code to link the iTunes viewer stylesheet to your own iTunes music library XML document. Open the document in a browser and experiment with the links.

2. Visit http://www.apple.com/itunes/affiliates/ and consider becoming an iTunes affiliate so that you can publish your music library online and maybe earn some commissions off of your excellent taste in music. Make sure to change the link code in the stylesheet to include your affiliate ID so that you'll actually get commission credit when someone buys a song after following a link from your music library.

HOUR 14

Formatting XML with XSL-FO

> You got it buddy: the large print giveth and the small print taketh away.
>
> —Tom Waits

As Tom Waits points out in the quote, the size of the print determines a whole lot about what you're getting into, at least when it comes to marketing. This chapter isn't about marketing but it does address print size. It's about XSL-FO, an XML stylesheet technology that is in some ways akin to a supercharged CSS. XSL-FO is the other half of the XML stylesheet equation, with XSLT being the original half that you learned about in Hour 11, "Getting Started with XSL," and Hour 12, "Transforming XML with XSLT." XSL-FO is a very high-powered style language that is particularly well suited to print. It allows you to take exacting control over every little detail of the printed page, including margins, headers, footers, and so on. XSL-FO could also be applied to the Web as a high-end replacement for CSS but browsers have yet to adopt it as a page formatting and layout standard. So, for now you have to consider XSL-FO as a technology primarily useful for print. Fortunately, there is a need for such a technology. This hour introduces you to the XSL-FO language, and how it is used to render highly formatted printed pages based upon XML code.

In this hour, you'll learn

- What XSL-FO is and how it came to be
- About the nuts and bolts of the XSL-FO language
- How to validate XSL-FO documents
- How to convert an XSL-FO document to a PDF document that can be viewed in Adobe Acrobat Reader

What Is XSL-FO?

Back in Hour 11 you learned about the various technologies that enter into the picture with respect to XML stylesheets. You found out that XSL-FO, which stands for XSL Formatting Objects, is the formatting component of the XSL stylesheet technology and is designed to be a functional superset of CSS. This means that XSL-FO contains all of the functionality of CSS, even though it uses its own XML-based syntax. Like its transformation counterpart, XSLT, XSL-FO is implemented as an XML language, which is beneficial for both minimizing the learning curve for XML developers and easing its integration into existing XML tools. Also like XSLT, XSL-FO operates on a tree of XML data, which can either be parsed directly from a document or transformed from a document using XSLT.

XSL-FO began back in the late 1990s when the W3C set out to create a page description language that could be used to format and display XML data. The idea behind this page description language is that it would allow XML developers to completely separate XML content from the details of how that content is rendered on a page for display. To facilitate the translation of raw XML data into a styled format, the W3C also began creating a transformation language. This transformation language became XSLT, while the descriptive formatting language became XSL-FO. However, XSLT caught on much quicker, and ultimately became the standard stylesheet mechanism for XML document processing and transformation. Many web developers now regularly use XSLT in combination with CSS to transform and style XML documents.

This scenario has fallen short of the W3C's initial goal of having XSLT and XSL-FO be the one-two transformation/style punch. The reality is that CSS was already widely supported and understood, so it only made sense for it to represent the first wave of style XML documents. XSL-FO offers everything CSS has to offer and much more, so we may eventually see XSL-FO begin to make its way into web pages at some point in the future. For now, however, XSL-FO is relegated to more of a specialized role in helping to layout and format very specific types of print documents.

By the Way

> Comparisons are often made between XSL-FO and CSS, and for the most part they are valid. One critical distinction between the two technologies is that CSS styles are always attached to an existing document tree, whereas XSL-FO establishes its own document structure. In other words, you apply CSS styles to XML data, whereas XSL-FO represents a complete merger of data and styles. In practice, XML data is typically still maintained separately from its XSLT stylesheet, which is then used to combine the data and XSL-FO styles into a complete XSL-FO document.

The good news is that aside from web browsers, there is actually a great deal of support for XSL-FO in back-end XML development tools. You learn about one such tool later in this lesson when you find out how to convert XSL-FO documents to PDF documents.

Working with the XSL-FO Language

The XSL-FO language is an XML-based language that serves as a functional superset of CSS. This means that XSL-FO can do everything CSS can do, and much more. It doesn't mean, however, that XSL-FO uses the same syntax as CSS—it does not. Because XSL-FO code is XML code, it should be immediately familiar to you, at least in its general structure and syntax.

Before you actually get into the guts of XSL-FO code, you might be curious as to how you go about manipulating and using XSL-FO. Because web browsers aren't really a viable option just yet, you have to look to other tools for XSL-FO document processing. One popular XSL-FO tool is called FOP, which stands for Formatting Objects Processor. FOP is a freely available open source tool that you can download from the Apache XML Graphics Project at http://xmlgraphics.apache.org/fop/. A good commercial option for XSL-FO processing is XEP, which is available for purchase from the RenderX web site at http://www.renderx.com/. You learn more about both of these tools, especially FOP, later in the hour.

By the Way

> Stylus Studio is another popular commercial tool that supports XSL-FO. Check it out at http://www.stylusstudio.com/xsl_fo_processing.html.

The remainder of this section introduces you to the tags and attributes that make up the XSL-FO language, and ultimately give you the power to format and style XML content to your heart's desire.

The Core XSL-FO Document Structure

Strangely enough, the W3C hasn't made available an official DTD for XSL-FO, so I can't just show you a DTD in order to explain the language. And in fact, even if such an official DTD existed, it would be far too complicated to make out the language in one sitting, or 10 sittings for that matter! It turns out that XSL-FO is a very "deep" language, supporting numerous objects and options. All of the inner workings of the XSL-FO language could easily fill an entire book. Because our goal here is to knock out XSL-FO in an hour, I'll focus instead on the core language components that allow you to perform basic XML document formatting.

By the Way

> An "experimental" DTD for XSL-FO does exist, although it wasn't created by the W3C. It was created by RenderX, the makers of the XEP XSL-FO processor. Later in the lesson you learn how to use the RenderX XSL-FO DTD to validate XSL-FO documents.

So without further ado, Listing 14.1 contains the code for a skeletal XSL-FO document.

LISTING 14.1 A Skeletal XSL-FO Document

```
1: <?xml version="1.0" encoding="utf-8"?>
2:
3: <fo:root xmlns:fo="http://www.w3.org/1999/XSL/Format">
4:   <fo:layout-master-set>
5:     <fo:simple-page-master master-name="skeleton">
6:       <fo:region-body margin="1in"/>
7:     </fo:simple-page-master>
8:   </fo:layout-master-set>
9:
10:   <fo:page-sequence master-reference="skeleton">
11:     <fo:flow flow-name="xsl-region-body">
12:       <fo:block>Howdy, world!</fo:block>
13:     </fo:flow>
14:   </fo:page-sequence>
15: </fo:root>
```

Perhaps the first thing to notice in this code is the XSL-FO namespace, which is assigned the prefix `fo` (line 3). The namespace itself is located at http://www.w3.org/1999/XSL/Format. Throughout the remainder of the document, the `fo` prefix is used in front of every XSL-FO tag; this is typically how XSL-FO documents are coded. You may also notice that the root element of the skeletal document is `fo:root`—this is the standard root element for all XSL-FO documents.

The next element is where things get interesting. I'm referring to `fo:layout-master-set`, which encloses one or more page masters (line 5). Although it may sound imposing, a page master is just a description of a formatted page. For example, a page master describes the size and orientation of a page, along with its margins and other pertinent layout details. Every XSL-FO document must contain at least one page master that is coded as a child of the `fo:layout-master-set` element. Each page master is coded using the `fo:simple-page-master` element or the `fo:page-sequence` element, the latter of which is used to code a sequence of page masters as opposed to a single page master. An example of where you might want to have multiple page masters is a report where there is a cover page that is formatted differently than the internal pages; the cover page would have its own page master, while the internal pages would use a different page master.

> An XSL-FO document can only have one `fo:layout-master-set` element, which houses all of the page masters and page master sequences for the document.

In the skeleton sample document, a single page master is created that simply sets the margin of the page to one inch (lines 5 to 7). The `fo:simple-page-master` element is used to declare the page master (line 5), and within it the `fo:region-body` element is used to define the primary content region on the page. You'll notice that the `fo:simple-page-master` element is given an attribute named `master-name`, which in this case is assigned the value `skeleton` (line 5). This attribute serves as a unique ID for the master page, which is used later in the document to associate content with the page.

Getting back to the `fo:region-body` element, its purpose is to define the main content region of the master page. This element has other parameters that you can use to carefully control how it is laid out on the page but in this example its margins are collectively set to one inch (line 6).

At this point you now have an XSL-FO document with a master page arranged as shown in Figure 14.1.

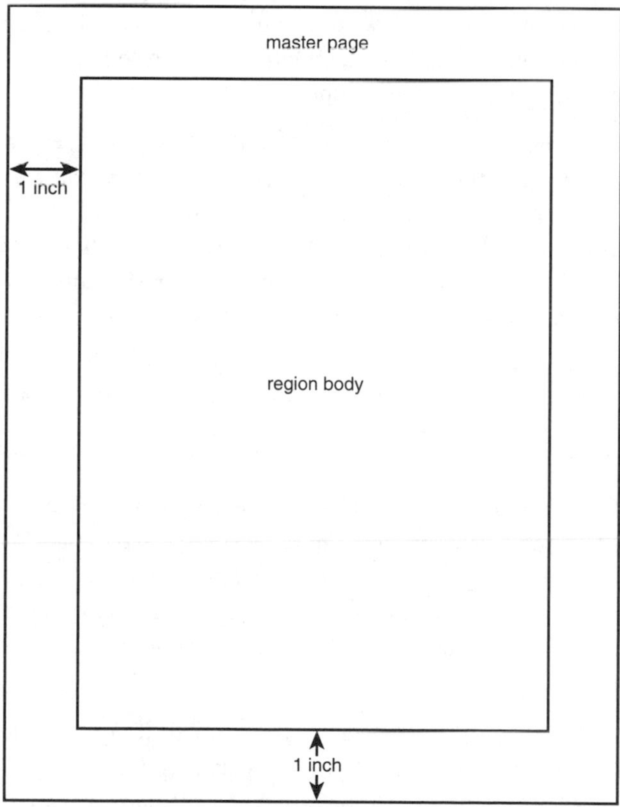

FIGURE 14.1 The skeletal XSL-FO document's master page consists of a content region with one-inch margins.

By the Way

> Although the page in the figure is accurate, it doesn't tell the entire story in terms of margins. The region body margins specified in the skeleton document only apply to the region body content area, which is typically inset on the page. To control the margins at the edges of the page, you will typically set margins for the master page itself. Because no master page margins were set in the example, the region body margins effectively serve as general page margins.

But you're not finished with the code in the skeleton document just yet. The last block of code in the document describes a page sequence, which is where formatted content actually enters the picture. The `fo:page-sequence` element is used to house content in an XSL-FO document, and can be thought of as roughly similar to the `body` element in an HTML document. The key thing to note about the `fo:page-sequence` element is how it is associated with a master page via its `master-reference` attribute (line 10). This is very important because a page sequence must be associated with a master page in order to be laid out. In this way, you can think of a master page as somewhat of a layout template, while the content that gets placed in the template is contained within a page sequence.

Continuing along, the `fo:flow` element within the `fo:page-sequence` element is used to flow content onto the page. Just as HTML content flows onto the page in the order it is specified in an HTML document, so does content in an XSL-FO document. The term "flow" is used with this element because content is allowed to flow across multiple pages. Contrast this with static content, which resides on a single page. The specific elements within a flow determine exactly how the flow commences.

By the Way

> When content in a flow is too large to fit on one page, it automatically flows onto another page.

In the skeleton example, the `fo:block` element is used to flow a block of text onto the page. The `fo:block` element is conceptually similar to `div` in HTML in that it represents a rectangular region of text. So if you string along a sequence of `fo:block` elements within a flow, they will be laid out one below the next. The opposite of the `fo:block` element is the `fo:inline` element, which is comparable to `span` in HTML.

The only piece of code in the skeleton XSL-FO document that you haven't learned about is the `flow-name` attribute of the `fo:flow` element (line 11). This attribute determines where the content of the flow will go on the page. Each page is actually divided into several standard regions, one of which is the region body (`xsl-region-body`), which is the main content area. Other possible values for the `flow-name` attribute include `xsl-region-before`, `xsl-region-after`, `xsl-region-start`, and `xsl-region-end`, to name a few. The *region-before* area is typically used to set header information for a page, whereas *region-after* similarly applies to footer information. Figure 14.2 shows how these different regions factor into the content area of a page.

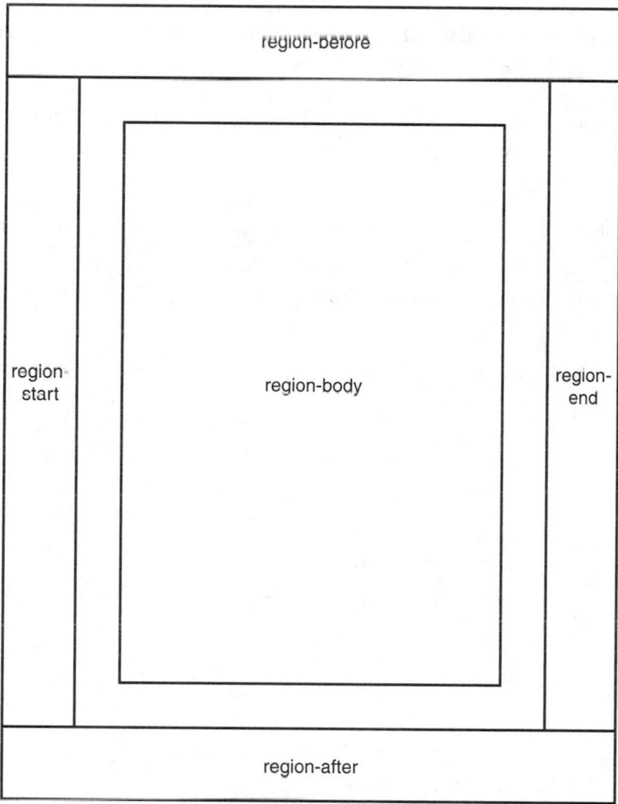

FIGURE 14.2
The content area of a page in XSL-FO is divided into multiple regions that can be targeted with individual flows.

In the skeleton sample document, only the region-body area of the page is used to place content, which means the other areas just collapse to nothing.

I realize I've thrown a lot of XSL-FO information at you quickly, so allow me to quickly summarize the skeleton document in terms of the tags that it uses:

- `<fo:root>`—The root of the document, responsible for declaring the XSL-FO namespace
- `<fo:layout-master-set>`—Stores one or more page master layouts
- `<fo:simple-page-master>`—Represents a simple page master, which serves as a template for a specific type of page

- <fo:region-body>—The main content area within a master page layout
- <fo:page-sequence>—A container for content that gets laid out on a page
- <fo:flow>—A more specific container for content that is allowed to flow from one page to another as necessary
- <fo:block>—A rectangular content region that resides on its own line on the page; similar to <div> in HTML
- <fo:inline>—A rectangular content region that appears inline with other content; similar to <span> in HTML

Although XSL-FO is admittedly a little tricky to get the grasp of initially, you now understand the basics of a minimal XSL-FO document. Let's push forward and learn a few more specifics about how to use the XSL-FO language.

Styling Text in XSL-FO

Finally, it's time to see where XSL-FO has some similarity with other technologies that you may be more familiar with. I'm talking about CSS, in which case XSL-FO's text styling properties are very similar to those used in CSS. In XSL-FO, you set the font specifics for text using attributes on the <fo:block> and <fo:inline> tags. More specifically, the `font-size`, `font-family`, and `font-weight` attributes can all be used to set the font for a block or inline content. These attributes are set just like their CSS counterparts.

Following is an example of setting the font size and font family for a block in XSL-FO:

```
<fo:block text-align="end" font-size="10pt" font-family="serif"
background-color="black" color="white">
  Great Sporting Events
</fo:block>
```

In this example, the text content `Great Sporting Events` is styled using a 10-point, serif font. Furthermore, the alignment of the text is set to `end` via the `text-align` attribute, which is equivalent to right-alignment in CSS. There is no concept of left or right in XSL-FO—instead, you use `start` and `end` when referring to the alignment of content that you might otherwise think of as being left-aligned or right-aligned. Of course, `center` is still perfectly legit in XSL-FO when it comes to alignment.

The `background-color` and `color` attributes in this code are direct carry-overs from CSS. You can use them just as you would the similarly named CSS styles.

Controlling Spacing and Borders

There are a few spacing and border properties that you can set when it comes to XSL-FO content. In fact, there are many more than I have the space to cover, so I'm only going to focus on a couple of them. The `space-before` and `space-after` attributes are used to control the spacing before and after a block. Because we're talking about blocks, the spacing applies vertically to the top (`space-before`) and bottom (`space-after`) of the block. In this way, the `space-before` and `space-after` attributes work sort of like top and bottom margins, except they apply outside of the margins.

Following is an example of setting the space after a block so that the next content is spaced a little further down the page:

```
<fo:block font-size="18pt" font-family="sans-serif" space-after="5pt"
background-color="black" color="white" text-align="center" padding-top="0pt">
  Great Sporting Events
</fo:block>
```

Also notice in this code that the padding-top attribute is set, which controls the padding along the top of the block. All of the standard CSS margin and padding styles are available for you in XSL-FO as attributes of the `<fo:block>` tag. These attributes include `margin`, `margin-left`, `margin-right`, `margin-top`, `margin-bottom`, `padding`, `padding-left`, `padding-right`, `padding-top`, and `padding-bottom`. There are also several familiar border attributes that you can use with blocks: `border`, `border-left`, `border-right`, `border-top`, and `border-bottom`.

Just to make sure you understand how all these spacing and border properties affect XSL-FO block content, take a look at Figure 14.3.

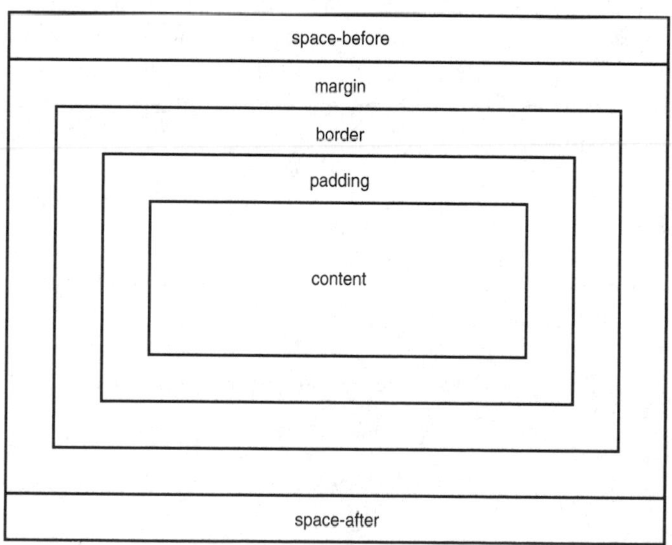

FIGURE 14.3 The various spacing and border attributes allow you to carefully control the area around XSL-FO block content.

Keep in mind that you will rarely if ever use all of these attributes at once, which means that the others will collapse and not actually affect the spacing of the content.

Managing Pages

Earlier when I explained page masters, I mentioned that the size of a page is controlled by a page master but I didn't actually show you how. The size of a page is set using the `page-width` and `page-height` attributes of the `fo:simple-page-master` element. As with most measurements in XSL-FO, you can use a variety of different units when specifying the page size, such as inches (`in`), centimeters (`cm`), and points (`pt`). The page size refers to the physical size of the printed page in most cases, which you will likely set to either 8.5×11 (inches) or 11×17 (inches), to note a few popular page sizes. Following is an example of specifying an 8.5×11 page size:

```
<fo:simple-page-master master-name="main" page-width="8.5in"
page-height="11in" margin-left="1in" margin-right="1in"
margin-top="0.5in" margin-bottom="0.5in">
  <fo:region-body margin-top="0.25in" margin-bottom="0.25in"/>
</fo:simple-page-master>
```

This code also shows how to establish margins for both the master page and the region body within the content area of the page.

Managing pages in an XSL-FO document isn't just about setting their size. It's also important to keep up with page numbers and ensure that they are displayed appropriately, if so desired. The `<fo:page-number>` tag is used to insert the page number into the content of a page. This page number is automatically calculated, meaning that you don't have to do any more than insert the tag to get automatic page numbering. Of course, you will likely want the page number to be displayed in the header or footer for the page, which means you'll need to allocate some space via the `extent` attribute. Following is an example of how to establish a quarter-inch footer to house the page number:

```
<fo:region-after extent="0.25in" />
```

This code should be placed in the page master so that the footer gets established. The next step is then to use the `<fo:page-number>` tag to place the page number in content that results in the displaying of the page number:

```
<fo:static-content flow-name="xsl-region-before">
  <fo:block text-align="end" font-size="10pt" font-family="serif"
  line-height="14pt" >
    Great Sporting Events - p. <fo:page-number/>
  </fo:block>
</fo:static-content>
```

Earlier in the lesson I talked about static content but I didn't show you an example. Here is a perfect example of static content, which means content that doesn't flow down the page. Static content isn't static in a sense that it can certainly change, as with the page number, but its position and spacing on the page are static.

This code contains one other new wrinkle that you haven't learned about yet: the `line-height` attribute. This attribute is used to establish the minimum height of a block. You can use this attribute to ensure that a block is a certain minimum height regardless of the content contained within it.

Validating an XSL-FO Document

As with any XML documents that you create, it's important to be able to validate XSL-FO documents to ensure that they are coded properly according to the XSL-FO language. The W3C doesn't offer an official XSL-FO DTD, which is necessary in order to validate XSL-FO documents. However, RenderX, the makers of the XEP XSL-FO processor, offer an experimental DTD that works fine for validating XSL-FO documents. Relying on RenderX's DTD, you can still use the standard W3C online validation tool to validate your XSL-FO documents. But first you need to wire the RenderX DTD to your XSL-FO documents.

The RenderX XSL-FO DTD is located online at http://xep.xattic.com/xep/resources/validators/dtd/fo.dtd. You wire this DTD into your XSL-FO documents via the following line of code just after the XML processor directive near the top of a document:

```
<!DOCTYPE fo:root SYSTEM
"http://xep.xattic.com/xep/resources/validators/dtd/fo.dtd">
```

With this code in place, you can now pass your XSL-FO documents into the standard W3C Markup Validation Service at http://validator.w3.org/.

Converting an XSL-FO Document to PDF

The point of all this effort in learning about the XSL-FO language is to do something useful, such as generate a highly formatted PDF document suitable for viewing in Adobe's popular Acrobat Reader application. As I mentioned earlier in the lesson, a handy tool for carrying out the XSL-FO to PDF translation is FOP, which is a free command-line tool made available by the Apache XML Graphics Project at http://xmlgraphics.apache.org/fop/.

After downloading and installing FOP, you need to tweak a setting in a FOP batch file before attempting to run the application. This file is called `fop.bat`, and it contains a variable called `LOCAL_FOP_HOME` that you must set to the actual FOP installation folder. As an example, if you install FOP to the folder `\fop-0.20.5`, you'll need to change the line of code for the `LOCAL_FOP_HOME` variable in `fop.bat` to the following:

```
set LOCAL_FOP_HOME=c:\fop-0.20.5
```

By the Way

> The `fop.bat` batch file is used in Windows versions of FOP. The UNIX/Linux equivalent is `fop.sh`, which is the shell script for running FOP.

With the FOP batch file configured properly, you're ready to take FOP for a spin. The quickest way to use it is to just copy the `.fo` file that you want to process to the main FOP folder. Then open a command-line prompt, navigate to the main fop folder, and issue the following command:

```
fop fofile.fo pdffile.pdf
```

The first argument to FOP, `fofile.fo`, is the name of the XSL-FO file that you want to process, whereas the second argument is the name of the resulting PDF file. Following is how you would process the `skeleton.fo` document using FOP:

```
fop skeleton.fo skeleton.pdf
```

Figure 14.4 shows the resulting skeleton PDF document as viewed in Adobe Acrobat Reader.

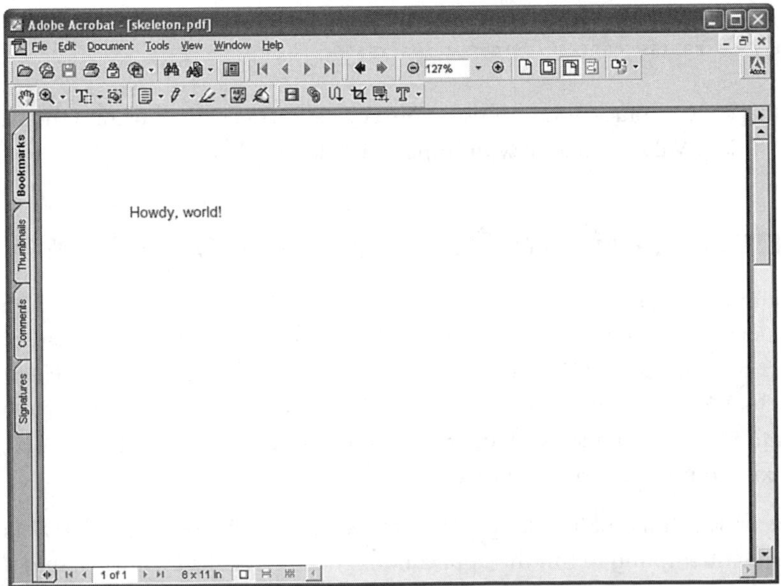

FIGURE 14.4
The Skeleton PDF document as viewed in Adobe Acrobat Reader.

I realize the skeleton PDF document isn't much to get excited about but it is a full-blown PDF document that was generated straight from an XSL-FO document, which is no small feat. The remainder of the lesson guides you through a more complete XSL-FO example that results in the generation of a much more interesting PDF document.

A More Complete XSL-FO Example

You really can't appreciate the power of XSL-FO without applying it to a substantial amount of content, consisting of at least a few pages of text. I thought a good example might be an excerpt from a book that my brother is writing about his crazy life. Without getting off on too much of a tangent, I'll just say that my brother has experienced quite a lot of extraordinary situations in his life, mostly self-induced. The excerpt I'm using as an example here includes a funny childhood story of my brother along with a clever football ticket caper that he pulled while in high school. Anyway, back to XSL-FO!

By the Way

> You'll need to download the source code for this example to view it in its entirety. Just visit my web site at http://www.michaelmorrison.com/ to download the complete source code for the book.

Listing 14.2 contains the partial code for the Great Sporting Events sample XSL-FO document, which contains plenty of text to flow across several pages.

LISTING 14.2 The Great Sporting Events XSL-FO Document

```
<?xml version="1.0" encoding="utf-8"?>
<!DOCTYPE fo:root SYSTEM
"http://xep.xattic.com/xep/resources/validators/dtd/fo.dtd">

<fo:root xmlns:fo="http://www.w3.org/1999/XSL/Format">
  <fo:layout-master-set>
    <fo:simple-page-master master-name="main" page-width="8.5in"
    page-height="11in" margin-left="1in" margin-right="1in"
    margin-top="0.5in" margin-bottom="0.5in">
      <fo:region-body margin-top="0.25in" margin-bottom="0.25in"/>
      <fo:region-before extent="0.25in"/>
      <fo:region-after extent="0.25in"/>
    </fo:simple-page-master>
  </fo:layout-master-set>

  <fo:page-sequence master-reference="main" initial-page-number="1">
    <fo:static-content flow-name="xsl-region-before">
      <fo:block text-align="end" font-size="10pt" font-family="serif"
      line-height="14pt" >
        Great Sporting Events - p. <fo:page-number/>
      </fo:block>
```

LISTING 14.2 Continued

```
    </fo:static-content>

    <fo:flow flow-name="xsl-region-body">
      <fo:block font-size="18pt" font-family="sans-serif" line-height="26pt"
      space-after="5pt" background-color="black" color="white"
      text-align="center" padding-top="0pt">
        Great Sporting Events
      </fo:block>

      <fo:block font-size="16pt"  font-family="sans-serif"  line-
      height="20pt"
      space-before="10pt" space-after="10pt"
      text-align="center" padding-top="0pt">
        by Steve Morrison
      </fo:block>

      <fo:block font-size="12pt" font-family="sans-serif" line-height="15pt"
      space-after="3pt" text-align="start">
        Sports have always seemed to be a large part of my life either as an
        athlete participating or as a fan. I was raised in a very sports-
        oriented environment. My father was still a young man when I was
        born.
        He was very athletic and as a child, I went with him as he played
        fast-pitch softball, softball, basketball and sometimes was allowed
        to go to the golf course with him. As I recall, all of these
        activities were held at public parks and recreation centers. I think
        my brother and I got our competitiveness directly from our dad. None
        of us are sore losers, but we love to win and hate to lose.
      </fo:block>

      <fo:block font-size="16pt" font-family="sans-serif" line-height="20pt"
      space-before="10pt" space-after="7.5pt"
      text-align="start" padding-top="0pt">
        Missing Gym Rat
      </fo:block>

      <fo:block font-size="12pt" font-family="sans-serif" line-height="15pt"
      space-after="3pt" text-align="start">
        I remember one occasion at the local recreation center where my dad
        and his buddies played softball and basketball regularly. On this
        particular night, they were playing some hotly contested pick-up
        basketball games and I ran all over the rec. center as the night
        wore on. I was probably 5 years old and my mom had stayed home that
        night.
        This obviously allowed me quite a bit of freedom as my dad played
        ball. Near the end of the night, my dad and another player got into
        a little scrap. A little fighting was not all that dangerous back in
        1970. This was not uncommon and would usually end up with the two
        combatants shaking hands and later having a beer together. I
        remember being worried as I watched the scuffle. Afterwards,
        everyone started playing again so I wandered on off to play in the
        center. After what seemed like a long time, I entered the gym and to
```

```
70:          my amazement, it was completely empty. I ran to the lobby of the
71:          center and the doors were locked and I saw no cars in the parking
72:          lot. It wasn't very long before the man that worked at the center
73:          unlocked the front doors and my dad was with him.
74:        </fo:block>
75:
76:        …
77:
78:        <fo:block font-size="12pt" font-family="sans-serif" line-height="15pt"
79:        space-after="3pt" text-align="start">
80:          We returned to the golf course in time to watch the opening kick-off
81:          on T.V. and soon returned all of our &quot;borrowed&quot; items. The
82:          failure of that plan still pains me today.
83:        </fo:block>
84:      </fo:flow>
85:    </fo:page-sequence>
86: </fo:root>
```

Similar to the skeleton example earlier in the lesson, this document contains a single master page that applies to all of the pages in the document. However, that's pretty much where the similarities between the two examples end. The Great Sporting Events document establishes a header and footer, along with a document body region (lines 9 through 11). The page number is displayed in the header along with the name of the document, as is evident in lines 16 through 21 where a static block is created. Notice that the initial page number is established in the `fo:page-sequence` element via the `initial-page-number` attribute (line 15).

With the header nailed down, the flowed content then begins with the title of the document, which is created as a block with large white centered text against a black background (lines 24 to 28). The author of the document, Steve Morrison, is then displayed in the next block in smaller centered text (lines 30 to 34). From there, the bulk of document content begins with block after block of story text.

There are two subheadings worth pointing out, one of which isn't visible in the listing. The subheading that is visible appears as a block on lines 49 through 53, and simply breaks up the text into a sub-story with the heading `Missing Gym Rat`. One other thing to note is how standard XML conventions are used in terms of referencing quotes as entities (`"`), as is visible on line 81.

I encourage you to study the Great Sporting Events XSL-FO code to make sure that you understand fully how it works. When you're satisfied that you follow what's going on, you're ready to run the document through FOP to generate a PDF file via the following command:

```
fop sportsstory.fo sportsstory.pdf
```

The resulting PDF document is shown in Figure 14.5 as viewed in Adobe Acrobat Reader.

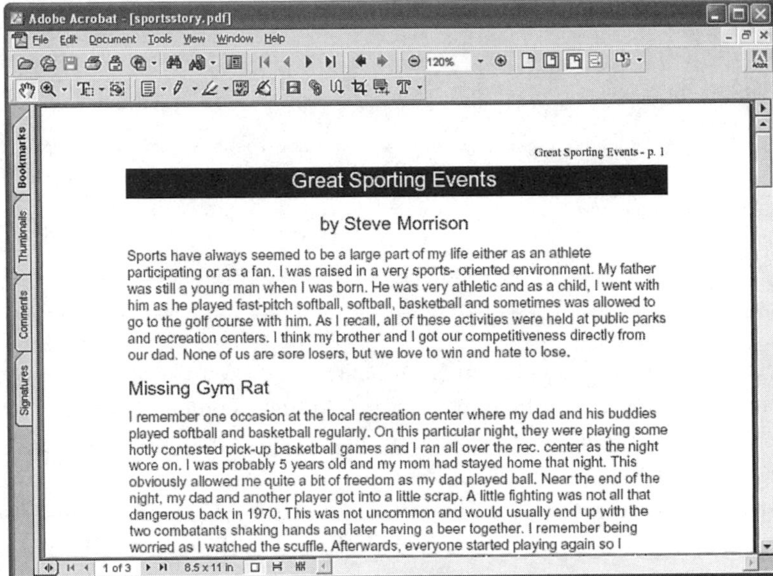

Great Sporting Events - p. 1

Great Sporting Events

by Steve Morrison

Sports have always seemed to be a large part of my life either as an athlete participating or as a fan. I was raised in a very sports- oriented environment. My father was still a young man when I was born. He was very athletic and as a child, I went with him as he played fast-pitch softball, softball, basketball and sometimes was allowed to go to the golf course with him. As I recall, all of these activities were held at public parks and recreation centers. I think my brother and I got our competitiveness directly from our dad. None of us are sore losers, but we love to win and hate to lose.

Missing Gym Rat

I remember one occasion at the local recreation center where my dad and his buddies played softball and basketball regularly. On this particular night, they were playing some hotly contested pick-up basketball games and I ran all over the rec. center as the night wore on. I was probably 5 years old and my mom had stayed home that night. This obviously allowed me quite a bit of freedom as my dad played ball. Near the end of the night, my dad and another player got into a little scrap. A little fighting was not all that dangerous back in 1970. This was not uncommon and would usually end up with the two combatants shaking hands and later having a beer together. I remember being worried as I watched the scuffle. Afterwards, everyone started playing again so I

FIGURE 14.5 The Great Sporting Events PDF document as viewed in Adobe Acrobat Reader.

The XSL-FO styles that you carefully analyzed in Listing 14.2 are realized in the PDF document shown in the figure. The resulting PDF document is actually three pages, which means you can use Acrobat Reader's forward and back page navigation features to view each page in the document.

Summary

Although I'd love to tell you that this hour provided a comprehensive introduction to XSL-FO, the truth is that this lesson really only served as a bare bones introduction to XSL-FO. This is because XSL-FO is one of the most detailed XML technologies you are likely to encounter, and therefore requires much more than an hour of your time to truly get to know well. Having said that, this lesson did provide a serviceable introduction to XSL-FO, including the basics of coding XSL-FO documents and converting them to PDF using a handy little tool called FOP. You didn't see the specifics of how to transform a raw XML document to XSL-FO using XSLT but you have the skills to carry out such a transformation based on earlier lessons in the book. If you find yourself intrigued by the possibilities of using XSL-FO to carefully format XML data for print, I encourage you to further explore XSL-FO on your own. A good place to start is the Wikipedia entry for XSL-FO, which includes several useful links to other XSL-FO resources: http://en.wikipedia.org/wiki/XSL-FO.

Q&A

Q. ***Are XSL-FO documents usually coded by hand?***

A. No. In fact, XSL-FO is intended to be generated automatically using a transformation language such as XSLT. In a real-world scenario, you would likely use XSLT to automatically transform an XML document into an XSL-FO document, and then use an XSL-FO processor to generate a PDF document automatically. All these steps would take place behind the scenes without any manual involvement. In this lesson I showed you the "brute force" method to creating an XSL-FO document by hand and converting it to PDF so that you could better understand how the XSL-FO language works.

Q. ***Should I consider switching from CSS to XSL-FO to style my XML documents?***

A. It depends entirely upon your specific circumstances. If you're talking about styling XML documents for the web, the answer is currently a resounding no. There just isn't enough XSL-FO browser support to consider it a viable web technology at the moment. However, if you're talking about styling XML content for print, XSL-FO may very well be a good option as a high-powered replacement for CSS.

Workshop

The Workshop is designed to help you anticipate possible questions, review what you've learned, and begin learning how to put your knowledge into practice.

Quiz

1. How does XSL-FO relate to CSS?
2. What are the XSL-FO equivalents of the `<div>` and `<span>` tags in HTML?
3. How do you validate an XSL-FO document?

Quiz Answers

1. XSL-FO is a functional superset of CSS but an entirely separate technology. Unlike CSS, XSL-FO is used to code entire documents including both content and formatting, whereas CSS is designed purely for applying formatting styles to existing documents. Also unlike CSS, XSL-FO is an XML-based language, whereas CSS relies on its own unique syntax.
2. The XSL-FO equivalents of the `<div>` and `<span>` tags in HTML are `<fo:block>` and `<fo:inline>`, respectively.
3. To validate an XSL-FO document, you currently must reference the RenderX experimental XSL-FO DTD in the document, and then pass the document through the standard W3C Markup Validation Service (http://validator.w3.org/).

Exercises

1. Develop an XSLT stylesheet to transform an existing XML document into an XSL-FO document.
2. Feed the newly generated XSL-FO document into FOP to generate a PDF of the resulting formatted XSL-FO document.

HOUR 15

Using XML to Hack Google Maps

> I have an existential map. It has "You are here" written all over it.
>
> —Steven Wright

Unlike Steven Wright's existential map, Google Maps is an online mapping tool that is without a doubt one of the coolest online resources I've ever used. Online map services aren't really new but Google Maps is so unique in its map interface that it is truly a groundbreaking application. Google Maps provides both a traditional vector map view along with a satellite photography view and even a hybrid view that overlays vector street information onto the photographic satellite map. One of the features that makes Google Maps so interesting is the fact that it is customizable via a programming interface that Google has made available to web developers. And as you might be guessing, XML factors heavily into Google Maps and how you go about customizing it. This hour introduces you to the inner workings of Google Maps and guides you through a complete XML-based map customization example.

In this hour, you'll learn

- What Google Maps is and why it is so interesting
- The basics of the Google Maps API and how to obtain an API key to access it
- How to convert a physical address into geocoordinates for mapping purposes
- How to create a complete XML-based custom Google Maps application

Getting to Know Google Maps

If you've never heard of it, Google Maps is a free online mapping service made available by Google that is truly revolutionary in nature. What makes Google Maps so interesting is how it allows you to drag and zoom maps in real time, along with a seamless merger of vector map graphics and real satellite imagery. While all of these features are certainly impressive, the killer feature of Google Maps that has impressed most hardcore web users is its speed. If you've done much web development, you'll likely be amazed at how responsive Google Maps is to user input such as dragging and zooming maps. I know I was the first time I ever used it. The newness has admittedly worn off of Google Maps by now but the fun has really only just begun. In June of 2005, Google made available to the public an API (Application Programming Interface) for Google Maps that allows web developers to build custom mapping applications. Later in this hour you will build a custom mapping application. Before you get into that, however, it's important to get familiar with Google Maps and what all it has to offer.

You can visit Google Maps online at http://maps.google.com/. If you've never used Google Maps, I encourage you to follow that link now and start exploring the service.

When Google Maps first starts up, there is nothing particularly surprising about it since all you see is a map of the United States. But keep in mind that this is Google we're talking about, the masters of the search engine. Try entering a search in Google Maps to watch it come to life. For example, enter "pizza near Nashville" in the main search box and click the Search button (feel free to insert your hometown here). Figure 15.1 shows the resulting map after searching for pizza restaurants near Nashville, TN.

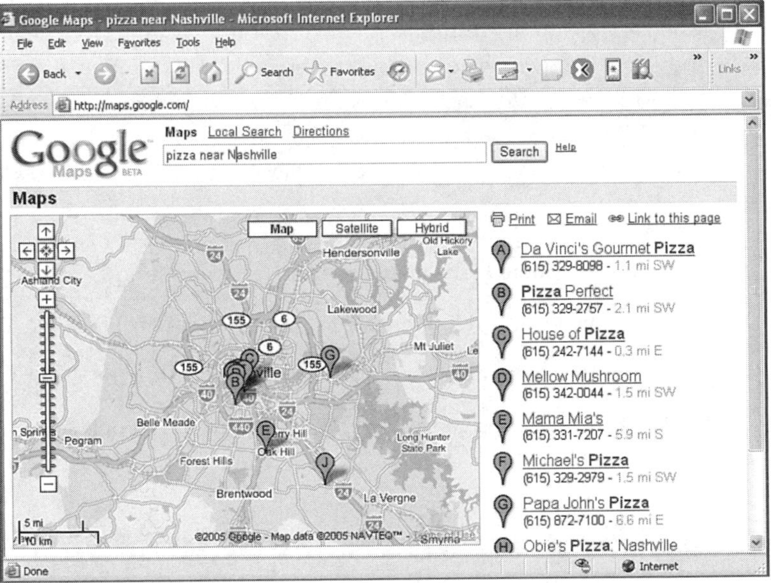

FIGURE 15.1 The search feature in Google Maps is surprisingly effective at finding places of interest.

Ah, now you're starting to see some of the power of Google Maps. Take things a step further by clicking one of the markers on the screen that represents the location of a pizza joint. Figure 15.2 shows how an information window appears that identifies the name of the location along with its address and a link to the restaurant on CitySearch.com.

By the way, if you're ever in Nashville, I highly recommend Pizza Perfect!

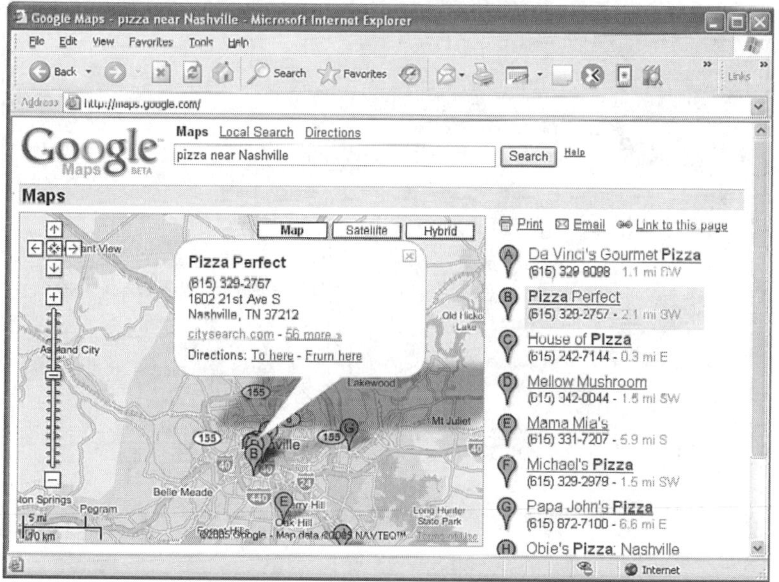

FIGURE 15.2
Clicking a marker in Google Maps brings up an information window with details about the location.

Keep in mind that at any point while using Google Maps you can click and drag the map or click on the zoom control in the upper-left corner of the map. Or maybe you want to see an actual satellite photo image of the map instead of vector map graphics. Just click the Satellite button in the upper-right corner of the map. More than likely you'll find the Hybrid view to be more useful than the Satellite view. The Hybrid view displays a satellite image with streets and street names overlaid, which makes most maps much easier to discern.

You can use the plus (+) and minus (-) keys on your keyboard as a shortcut for zooming in and out of a map, respectively.

Local search is another very handy feature of Google Maps that you won't want to overlook. While viewing any map on the screen, you can click Local Search and then perform a search on any piece of information. As an example, let's say you're planning on visiting Franklin, TN on business and you're interested in doing a little cycling on the Natchez Trace Parkway while you're in town. You've already been exploring the area in Google Maps but you don't know anything about area bicycle shops. Just enter "bicycle rental" as a local search and let Google Maps do the rest.

Figure 15.3 shows how a local search turns up numerous bicycle shops within a reasonable proximity to the original map location.

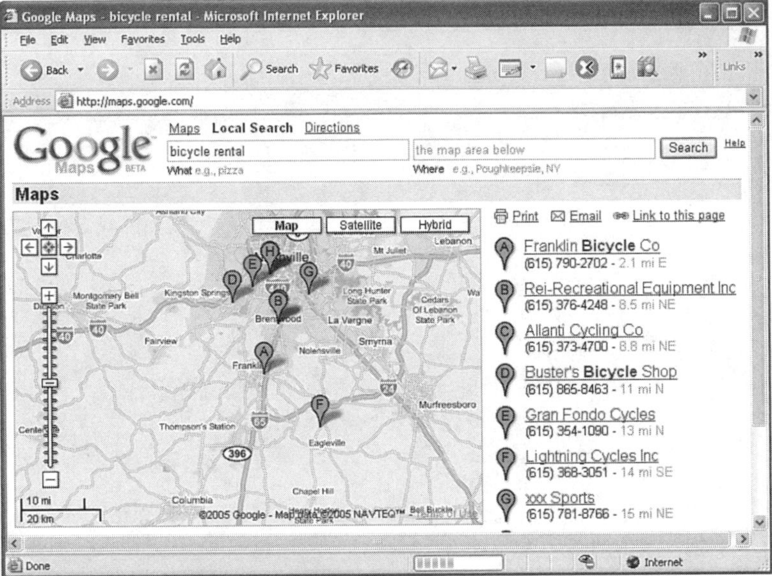

FIGURE 15.3 Performing a local search on Google Maps allows you to search for locations within the current map area in view.

Another interesting application Google has in the works is RideFinder, which is a real-time GPS-based system for tracking taxicabs using Google Maps. Using RideFinder, you can check for the nearest cab to your location and find yourself a ride home. RideFinder uses GPS transmitters that are placed in cabs to determine the locations of the cabs as they make their rounds. RideFinder is currently available for several major cities in the U.S. and is expected to continue expanding into new cities. To learn more about RideFinder, visit it on the Web at http://labs.google.com/ridefinder.

There are lots of other interesting features that Google Maps has to offer but at some point I have to bring my Google Maps love fest to a halt and get to the point of this lesson, which is how to use XML to customize Google Maps. However, I'd like to leave you with a few Google Maps–related links to explore as you learn more about the service and what all it can do:

- Google Moon—The Moon as viewed through Google Maps; make sure you zoom all the way in (http://moon.google.com/)
- GeoBloggers—Photographs that rely on Google Maps to show you where they were taken (http://www.geobloggers.com/)
- Chicago Crime—Locations of crimes committed in the Chicago metropolitan area (http://www.chicagocrime.org/)

- Cheap Gas—Locations of gas stations selling the cheapest gas (http://www.ahding.com/cheapgas/)
- New York City Subway—Locations of New York City subway stations (http://monkeyhomes.com/map/nycsubway.php)
- GeoWorldNews—World news with the location of each story marked (http://www.parsec.it/geoworldnews/)
- Recent Earthquakes—Locations of recent earthquakes (http://chimi.org/quake/index.html)
- Urinal Dot Net—Locations of public urinals around the United States (http://urinal.net/google_map.html)
- Google Maps Directory—Directory of Google Maps applications (http://www.gmdir.com/)

By the Way

In addition to some of the interesting Google applications that have been created, there are also some interesting finds that people have made while using Google Maps. For example, one astute Google Maps user spotted a building suspiciously shaped like a swastika (http://maps.google.com/maps?q = san + diego&ll = 32.676505, -117.157559&spn = 0.004739, 0.009917&t = k&hl = en) and therefore deemed it a potential hideout for Adolf Hitler. Another person spotted a pattern on a Peruvian sand dune that some say resembles the face of Jesus... or Charles Manson (http://maps.google.com/maps?ll = -16.337013, -71.959763&spn = 0.110893, 0.158186&t = k&hl = en). I'm not making this stuff up!

In this list, I've provided plenty of interesting sites to keep you busy for the remainder of this hour but if you can tear yourself away from Google Maps for just a moment, it's time to dig into the details of what it takes to customize Google Maps to create your own mapping application.

Google Maps Customization Basics

Customizing Google Maps to create your own mapping application is fairly straightforward but it does require a couple of preliminary steps before you can even start thinking about XML code or web pages. First off, although Google exposes the Google Maps API for anyone to use, they do require you to obtain a special API key in order to use the API in your own web pages. Secondly, you need to understand some basics about the Google Maps API and how it is used to create and customize maps via JavaScript code. And finally, locations in Google Maps are specified via geocoordinates, which you probably don't have readily available for the locations you're interested in mapping. For this reason, you need to learn how to obtain the latitude and longitude of a location based upon its physical (mailing) address. The next few sections explore each of these topics in more detail.

Getting Your Own API Key

The easiest part of the map creation process is obtaining your own Google Maps API key. This virtual key is literally your key to being able to view, test, and share your map creations with others. A Google Maps API key is completely free of charge, and is presumably required so that Google can keep close tabs on how its technology is being used. Keep in mind that Google Maps is technically still a beta product, which means that it is still under development. So in many ways you are playing the role of tester when using Google Maps.

Anyway, getting back to the API key, you can sign up and obtain your key by visiting http://www.google.com/apis/maps/signup.html. This page requires you to enter the URL of the web site to which you plan on publishing your maps. A single API key gives you the ability to publish maps to one folder on one web server. As an example, if I register an API key for http://www.michaelmorrison.com/maps, I can only publish maps to the maps folder on my web server and nowhere else. Well, technically I can publish them wherever I want on my web server but they'll only work if I place them in the maps folder. Make sure you actually publish your maps to the URL you specify when obtaining your API key.

The API key is provided to you as a long text code that you will cut and paste into your mapping code later. For now, copy and paste the code into a text file and save it for later.

Touring the Google Maps API

The Google Maps API consists of a set of JavaScript functions that you call in order to create and manipulate a map within an HTML web page. Every map must have a standard `<script>` tag in the head of the HTML document that references the Google Maps API and specifies your API key. Following is an example of how this `<script>` tag is coded:

```
<script src="http://maps.google.com/maps?file=api&v=1&key=
ABQIAAAASyb3gcwJHvHRgYeL6xQGZRScAy-
eqpGBgb_U5UIf4tD_qtSUMBQD201ZWuwo7NWFLUKzESpdimx61w"
type="text/javascript"></script>
```

The API key is too long to fit on one line of printed text in this book, which is why you see it broken across multiple lines. In your HTML code, don't add any spaces or line breaks in the API key or it won't work. After placing the `<script>` tag in the head of a web page, you can begin calling API functions to create the map itself.

The `GMap()` function is called to create a new map. This function expects as its only argument the element on the page that is to contain the map:

```
var map = new GMap(document.getElementById("map"));
```

The map container element is typically a `div` element, as in the following sample code:

```
<div id="map" style="width:700px; height:450px"></div>
```

Notice that the ID of the `div` element is `map`, which corresponds to the ID of the element passed into the `GMap()` function. This is how the map gets connected to a container element on the web page.

By the Way

> If all this talk of functions and arguments is flying right over your head, don't worry. It really isn't critical that you understand the JavaScript code in this example in order to use XML to customize it. However, in case you do have some JavaScript knowledge, I want to at least lay down the basics of how the Google Maps API works. If you'd like to learn more about JavaScript, I recommend *Teach Yourself JavaScript in 21 Days* and *JavaScript Bible*.

The Google Maps API offers several different user interface controls that you can use. The standard control that consists of full-sized pan/zoom buttons is represented by the `GLargeMapControl` object. There is also a smaller control called `GSmallMapControl`, as well as a control with no pan features at all called `GSmallZoomControl`. To set the control for a map, you call the `addControl()` method on the newly created map, like this:

```
map.addControl(new GLargeMapControl());
```

There is also a control that determines whether or not you can switch between the different map views (Map, Satellite, and Hybrid). To enable this control, add the `GMapTypeControl` object to the map with the following piece of code:

```
map.addControl(new GMapTypeControl());
```

With the map and controls in place, you're ready to set the default area for the map, which is based upon a geocoordinate as well as a zoom level. You learn how to find a geocoordinate for a location in the next section. For now, just understand that it consists of two numbers that represent the latitude and longitude of a location. Furthermore, the zoom level of the map is set to an integer number that you will likely need to experiment with in order to find a zoom level that suits your specific map. Following is the code that centers and zooms a map at a specific geocoordinate and zoom level:

```
var point = new GPoint(-86.853171, 36.071689);
map.centerAndZoom(point, 6);
```

The last step in creating a custom map is creating the markers on the map, which can also involve using custom icon images if you so choose. Custom icons in Google Maps actually consist of two images: the icon image and a shadow for the icon. You learn more about these images a bit later in the hour. For now, take a look at the following code, which shows how to create a marker with a custom icon, as well as how to set a listener function that opens an information window when the marker is clicked.

```
var icon = new GIcon();
icon.iconSize = new GSize(48, 40);
icon.shadowSize = new GSize(75, 32);
icon.iconAnchor = new GPoint(24, 38);
icon.infoWindowAnchor = new GPoint(24, 20);
icon.image = "mapicon.png";
icon.shadow = "mapicon_sh.png";
var marker = new GMarker(point, icon);
GEvent.addListener(marker, "click", function() { marker.openInfoWindowXslt(
  description, "styles.xsl"); });
```

The main things to note in this code are how the various icon sizes are specified, including the relative offset of the icon anchor and the information window anchor. These offsets determine how the marker icon image is positioned relative to the location on the map, as well as the offset of the information window with respect to the marker. The last two lines of code look messier than they truly are—all they do is open an information window and display an XML element in it, while making sure that the element is coded using the `styles.xsl` stylesheet. The job of this stylesheet is to transform the XML description of a location on the map into HTML code that can be displayed in a browser.

I realize I hit you pretty fast with the Google Maps API and code that puts it to work. Not to worry because you see all of this code again in the context of a real custom Google Maps web page. For now, I just wanted to lay the groundwork and start getting you comfortable with the script code required to get a custom map up and running.

Obtaining the Geocoordinates of a Location

Although Google Maps is typically queried based upon the mailing address of a location, when you deal directly with the Google Maps API you are required to deal with more accurate location data. More specifically, you must specify the latitude and longitude of a location, also known as its geocoordinates, when specifying its position to the Google Maps API. Because you probably haven't committed to memory the latitude and longitude of your favorite hangouts, you'll likely need to use a tool to find out the coordinates of any address that you want to include on a map. Fortunately, exactly such a tool exists in the form of the geocoder.us web site, located at http://geocoder.us/.

This web site allows you to enter an address much as you would enter it in Google Maps. Assuming the address is successfully found, geocoder displays the latitude and longitude of the address, which you can then use in Google Maps to specify the exact position of the location. Figure 15.4 shows the geocoder online tool displaying the latitude and longitude of a well-known address.

If you happen to have a GPS receiver, you can also determine the latitude and longitude of any location using the receiver. Of course, you'll have to physically travel to the location so that its latitude and longitude are registered on your GPS device.

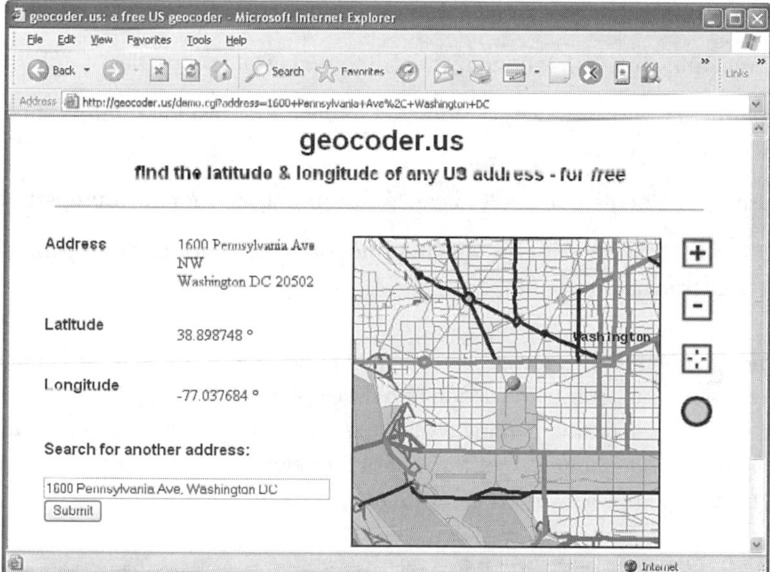

FIGURE 15.4
The geocoder.us web site is extremely handy for converting physical addresses to geocoordinates (latitude and longitude).

The figure reveals the geocoordinates for the White House, which is located at 1600 Pennsylvania Avenue in Washington, DC. You can use the geocoder.us web site to look up any address that you want, keeping in mind that you can always cheat and use a nearby address if for some reason the address you're looking for isn't found. Later in this hour you'll use the latitude and longitude values displayed on the geocoder.us web site to fill in details regarding the locations of real estate projects in XML code.

Brainstorming a Custom Mapping Application

There are all kinds of interesting prospects out there when it comes to dreaming up your own custom Google Maps application. The sample application that you work through in the remainder of this lesson is based upon an application that I desperately needed to develop for a real-world project. I was hired to revamp the web site of a local construction company that wanted an interactive map of its projects, among other things. Although I could've certainly used image maps, JavaScript, and other traditional web trickery to put together somewhat of an interactive project map, it occurred to me that Google Maps might make an ideal environment for this task. So I ended up developing a custom Google Maps application that displays the builder's projects around town. I even took things a step further by using custom markers to provide visual cues as to whether a project is active (still has properties for sale) or completed (sold out).

In this example, the custom mapping application involved several facets:

- Developing an XML language for coding real estate properties
- Interacting with the Google Maps API to open and display a map centered on a certain location
- Using the Google Maps API to create custom markers for each property
- Using XSLT to present a unique information window for each property when it is clicked in Google Maps

The remainder of this hour focuses on a slightly pared down version of this application. However, before you get into the design and development of the application, you may want to try out the real thing online. Visit http://www.haurysmith.com/condomap.htm to see the real-world example application that I developed for the construction company. This web page is shown in Figure 15.5.

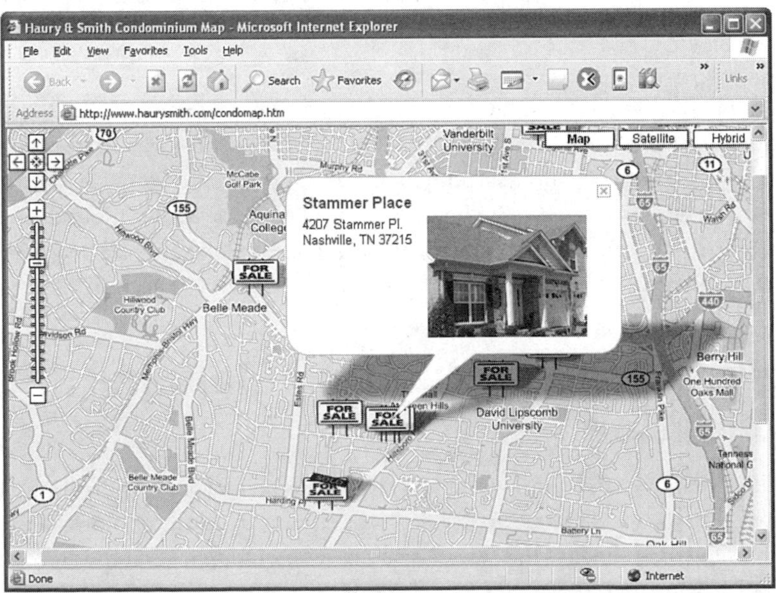

FIGURE 15.5
The Haury & Smith sample mapping application demonstrates how Google Maps can be used in a practical commercial context.

Again, you spend the rest of this lesson developing a Google Maps application very similar to the one shown in the figure. With this knowledge, you'll be ready to develop your own mapping applications with relatively little effort.

By the Way

> Real estate isn't the only custom Google Maps application I've tackled. I'm in the process of developing the world's first interactive skatepark map where you'll eventually be able to find the location of every skateboard (extreme sports) park in the world using Google Maps. Check out http://www.skateparkmap.com/ to find out more.

Developing a Custom Map Document

Developing a custom Google Maps application first involves deciding on a format for the data that you plan on feeding into Google Maps. This is where XML enters the picture in regard to Google Maps. Because the sample application you're working through in this lesson involves real estate developments, it's worth considering what pieces of information you might want to code in an XML document in order to map a piece of real estate property:

- Property name
- Physical address (mailing address)
- Thumbnail image for a Google Maps information window
- Geocoordinates (latitude and longitude)
- Status (active or completed)

By the Way

> In the actual Haury & Smith custom mapping application that I developed, a URL is also specified for each real estate property to link from the map back to an information page on the main web site. Because there is no web site associated with the example in this lesson, I left out the URL.

These pieces of information are sufficient to describe any real estate property for the purposes of displaying information about the property in Google Maps. The trick is then determining the best way to effectively represent this information in the context of an XML document. Listing 15.1 contains the partial code for a document that solves this problem with ease.

LISTING 15.1 **The** `condos.xml` **Document Containing Condominium Map Data**

```
1: <?xml version="1.0"?>
2:
3: <projects>
4:   <proj status="active">
5:     <location lat="36.122238" long="-86.845028" />
6:     <description>
7:       <name>Woodmont Close</name>
8:       <address>131 Woodmont Blvd.</address>
9:       <address2>Nashville, TN 37205</address2>
10:      <img>condowc.jpg</img>
11:    </description>
12:  </proj>
13:  <proj status="active">
14:    <location lat="36.101232" long="-86.820759" />
15:    <description>
16:      <name>Village Hall</name>
17:      <address>2140 Hobbs Rd.</address>
18:      <address2>Nashville, TN 37215</address2>
19:      <img>condovh.jpg</img>
20:    </description>
21:  </proj>
22:  ...
23:  <proj status="completed">
24:    <location lat="36.091559" long="-86.832686" />
25:    <description>
26:      <name>Harding Hall</name>
27:      <address>2120 Harding Pl.</address>
28:      <address2>Nashville, TN 37215</address2>
29:      <img>condohh.jpg</img>
30:    </description>
31:  </proj>
32: </projects>
```

The listing contains the complete code for the `condos.xml` sample document that houses XML data for the real estate sample mapping application. As its name implies, the real estate properties coded in the document are condominium developments. However, all Google Maps will ultimately care about is the data stored in the `<location>` tag for each piece of property. The `<location>` tag is where the latitude and longitude for each condominium development is specified. More specifically, this information is provided via the `lat` and `long` attributes (lines 5, 14, and 24). Everything else in the document is just supplementary data to provide additional information when the user clicks one of the markers on the map. Even so, this information plays an important role in overall application.

The document is laid out as a series of `<proj>` tags that each represents an individual real estate project. These tags appear within the root `<projects>` tag (line 3). Each `<proj>` tag includes a `status` attribute that can be set to either `active` or `completed` based upon the status of the real estate project (whether it still has units available or it is sold out). The value of the `status` attribute determines what kind of visual marker is displayed on the map for a given project. Inside of the `<proj>` tag is a `<description>` tag that describes more details about a real estate project. The `<name>`, `<address>`, `<address2>`, and `<img>` tags all combine to provide information that will appear in the information window in Google Maps when the user clicks on a marker.

It's important to point out that the project images in this sample document are specified without any path information, which means that they are expected to reside in the same folder as the XML document.

You now have a solid enough grasp on the underlying data for the mapping application example to push on further and learn how to assemble the code and stylesheet that actually make it work.

Hacking Together a Custom Google Map

Developing a customized map for Google Maps is really a three-step process. The first step is putting together a suitable XML document to house your map data. The second step is creating an HTML web page that creates the map and handles the majority of the work in running the application. And the third step is creating an XSLT stylesheet that is responsible for formatting content to be displayed in an information window when a marker is clicked on the map. You've already completed the first step, and now it's time to knock out the second two.

Displaying the Custom Map

Earlier in the lesson I let you in on the fact that interacting with the Google Maps API requires a decent understanding of the JavaScript programming language. Knowing this, it shouldn't come as too much of a surprise that the HTML document that actually displays a custom Google Map contains a fair amount of JavaScript code. Fortunately, even if you don't know much about JavaScript I've already primed you with the how and why that a typical mapping application uses the Google Maps API. With that in mind, take a look at Listing 15.2, which contains the complete code for the `condomap.html` web page.

LISTING 15.2 **The HTML Document that Houses the Customized Google Map**

```
<!DOCTYPE html PUBLIC "-//W3C//DTD XHTML 1.0 Strict//EN"
  "http://www.w3.org/TR/xhtml1/DTD/xhtml1-strict.dtd">
<html xmlns="http://www.w3.org/1999/xhtml">
  <head>
```

LISTING 15.2 Continued

```
    <title>Condominium Map</title>
    <script src="http://maps.google.com/maps?file=api&v=1&key=
    ABQIAAAASyb3gcwJHvHRgYeL6xQGZRScAy-eqpGBgb_U5UIf4tD_
    qtSUMBQD201ZWuwo7NWFLUKzESpdimx61w" type="text/javascript"></script>
  </head>
  <body style="text-align:center">
   <p style="font:bold 14pt arial; color:maroon">Condominium Map</p>
   <div id="map" style="width:700px; height:450px"></div>
   <script type="text/javascript">
   //<![CDATA[
   // Initialize the map and icon variables
   var map = new GMap(document.getElementById("map"));
   map.addControl(new GLargeMapControl());
   map.addControl(new GMapTypeControl());
   var point = new GPoint(-86.853171, 36.071689);
   map.centerAndZoom(point, 6);
   var baseIcon = new GIcon();
   baseIcon.iconSize = new GSize(48, 40);
   baseIcon.shadowSize = new GSize(75, 32);
   baseIcon.iconAnchor = new GPoint(24, 38);
   baseIcon.infoWindowAnchor = new GPoint(24, 20);

   function createMarker(proj, point, description) {
    // Create the custom icon
    var icon = new GIcon(baseIcon);
    if (proj.getAttribute("status") == "active") {
     icon.image = "mapicon_forsale.png";
     icon.shadow = "mapicon_forsale_sh.png";
    }
    else {
     icon.image = "mapicon_sold.png";
     icon.shadow = "mapicon_sold_sh.png";
    }

    // Create the marker and register the info window listener function
    var marker = new GMarker(point, icon);
    GEvent.addListener(marker, "click", function() {
     marker.openInfoWindowXslt(description, "projects.xsl"); });
    return marker;
   }

   // Open and process the condo XML document
   var request = GXmlHttp.create();
   request.open("GET", "condos.xml", true);
   request.onreadystatechange = function() {
    if (request.readyState == 4) {
     // Get the nodes
     var xmlDoc = request.responseXML;
     var projs = xmlDoc.documentElement.getElementsByTagName("proj");
     var locations = xmlDoc.documentElement.getElementsByTagName(
      "location");
     var descriptions = xmlDoc.documentElement.getElementsByTagName(
      "description");

     // Iterate through the nodes, creating a marker for each
     for (var i = 0; i < projs.length; i++) {
      var point = new GPoint(parseFloat(locations[i].getAttribute(
```

```
62:            "long")), parseFloat(locations[i].getAttribute("lat")));
63:          var marker = createMarker(projs[i], point, descriptions[i]);
64:          map.addOverlay(marker);
65:        }
66:      }
67:    }
68:    request.send(null);
69:    //]]>
70:    </script>
71:  </body>
72: </html>
```

Roughly the first part of this web page should be somewhat familiar to you thanks to the earlier primer on the Google Maps API. Most of this code follows the general template you saw earlier regarding how a map is created (line 16), controls are added (lines 17 and 18), a default view is established (lines 19 and 20), and so on. Even the code that creates a custom icon is somewhat similar to the icon code you saw earlier in the hour except in this case the `status` attribute (of the `<proj>` tag) in the XML document is checked to determine which icon to use (lines 30 through 37). This is the code that results in a different marker being displayed on the map based upon the status (active or completed) of each real estate project. You'll notice that two marker images are set for each status condition: one for the marker icon and one for its shadow. Figure 15.6 shows the four marker icons used in this sample application.

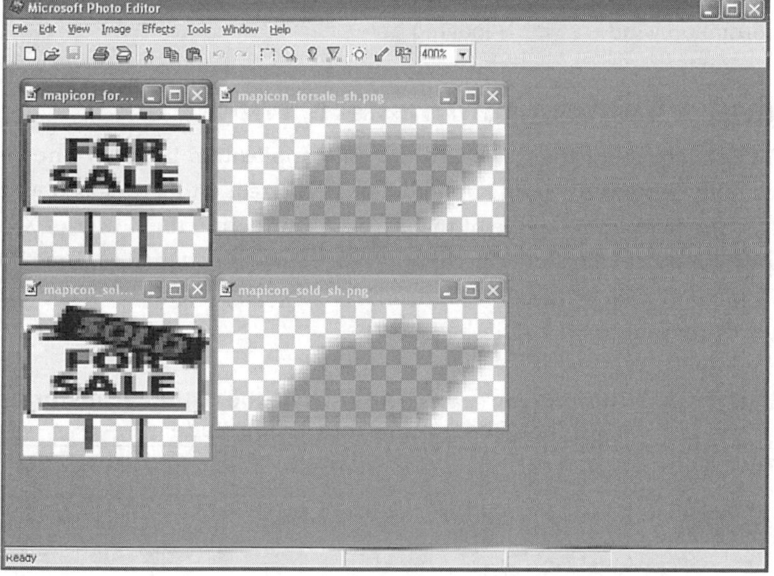

FIGURE 15.6
The condominium map sample mapping application relies on four custom marker icon images.

The figure shows how a marker that appears on a Google Maps map actually consists of two icons: the marker image and a shadow image with transparency. When combined, these two icons provide a clever visual trick that makes the markers appear to rise off of the map in 3D.

Getting back to the code for the mapping HTML document, each custom icon is used to create a custom marker in the `createMarker()` function that also establishes the information window and links it to the `projects.xsl` stylesheet (lines 40 to 43). This code is a little tricky in that a special listener function is created to automatically display an information window in response to the user clicking a marker. It isn't terribly important for you to understand every nuance in this code—the main thing to note is that this is where the `projects.xsl` stylesheet is getting connected to the information window.

The last big chunk of code in the HTML document is where the XML document is opened, read, and processed. The XML file is opened on line 48, and then its relevant nodes (`proj`, `location`, and `description`) are grabbed on lines 53 through 57. A loop is then entered that cycles through the projects, creating a marker on the map for each one via calls to the previously mentioned `createMarker()` function (lines 60 through 65).

The HTML document has now created the custom map in Google Maps, complete with unique markers and information windows ready to spring into action when the markers are clicked. The last thing to address is the XSLT stylesheet that makes the information windows worth looking at.

Styling a Custom Information Window

The XSLT stylesheet for the condominium map application has only one responsibility: format the name and address of the real estate project and display it next to the thumbnail image of the project. Considering the power of XSLT, this is a fairly simple responsibility because it only requires performing some basic transforming of XML content into styled HTML content. Listing 15.3 contains the code for the `projects.xsl` stylesheet.

LISTING 15.3 The `projects.xsl` XSLT Stylesheet that Transforms a Project Description into HTML Code

```
<?xml version="1.0"?>

<xsl:stylesheet version="1.0" xmlns:xsl="http://www.w3.org/1999/XSL/
Transform">
  <xsl:template match="/">
    <xsl:apply-templates select="description" />
  </xsl:template>

```

```
 9:   <xsl:template match="description">
10:     <table style="width:320px; height:140px; text-align:left">
11:       <tr>
12:         <td colspan="2" style="font-family:arial; font-weight:bold;
13:         color:maroon">
14:           <xsl:value-of select="name" />
15:         </td>
16:       </tr>
17:       <tr style="vertical-align:top">
18:         <td style="font-family:arial">
19:           <div style="font-size:10pt">
20:             <xsl:value-of select="address" /><br />
21:             <xsl:value-of select="address2" />
22:           </div>
23:         </td>
24:         <td>
25:         <div>
26:           <xsl:apply-templates select="img" />
27:         </div>
28:         </td>
29:       </tr>
30:     </table>
31:   </xsl:template>
32:
33:   <xsl:template match="img">
34:     <img>
35:       <xsl:attribute name="width">166px</xsl:attribute>
36:       <xsl:attribute name="height">125px</xsl:attribute>
37:       <xsl:attribute name="src"><xsl:value-of select="." /></xsl:attribute>
38:     </img>
39:   </xsl:template>
40: </xsl:stylesheet>
```

The stylesheet begins by immediately matching up the <description> tag and applying the description template (lines 5 to 7). The <description> tag serves as the container for the more specific project description tags (<name>, <address>, <address2>, and <img>), so it makes sense to start out by processing it first. Within the description template, the project name is first transformed into HTML so that it appears as a row in a table in a bold maroon font (lines 11 through 16). The table cell for the name is given a column span (colspan) of 2 to indicate that it spans both of the cells in the next row. This is necessary so that the name remains aligned to the left edge of the information window.

The second row in the table consists of two cells; the first cell contains the address of the project while the second cell contains the thumbnail image. The address of the project is transformed so that it appears aligned to the top of the cell (lines 18 to 23). The thumbnail image is placed in the next cell with no special formatting (lines 24 to 28), although the <img> tag does use its own template to get the job done (lines 33 through 39). The main point of this template is to specify the width and height of the image, which is consistent for all of the project thumbnails, along with specifying the actual source file for the image.

This wraps up the XSLT stylesheet for the condominium map example. You're finally ready to try out everything in a web browser and see how the finished product works.

Testing Out the Finished Map

This sample application represents one of the most complete examples you see in this book. It's admittedly somewhat of a challenge to merge several different technologies into a single example without it getting overly complex but this example remained reasonably manageable while combining XML, JavaScript, and XSLT in a single application. Hopefully you'll find the end result to be worth the effort. Figure 15.7 shows the condominium map example upon first being loaded as viewed in Internet Explorer.

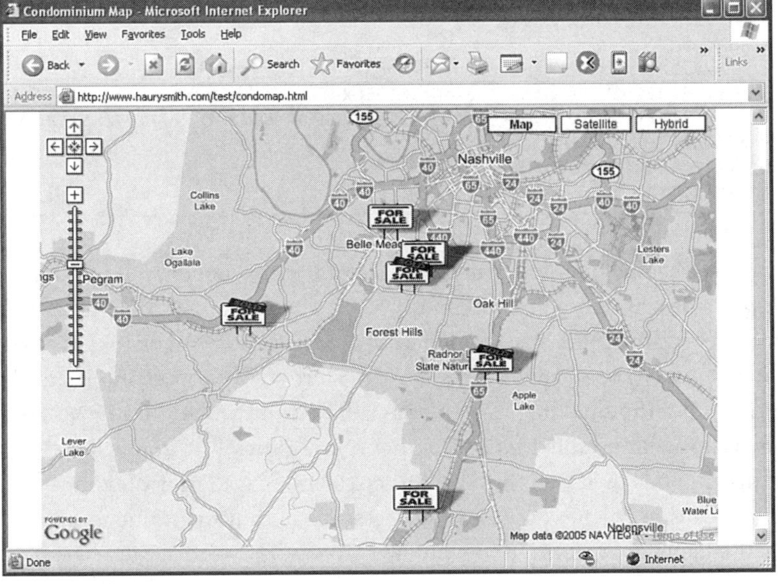

FIGURE 15.7 The condominium map sample application starts out with all of the project markers in view.

Not surprisingly, the application starts out with all the project markers in view on the map. This is no accident, by the way—I carefully selected the initial viewing area and zoom level of the map (line 20 in Listing 15.2) so that you could see all of the projects. Don't forget that what makes your custom Google Maps application so cool is that you can still use all of the familiar navigational features built into Google Maps. You can drag the map around to view other areas, as well as zoom in and out on the projects and their surroundings. You can also switch back and forth between Map, Satellite, and Hybrid views. Perhaps most importantly, you can click any of the project markers to get information about each specific project. Figure 15.8 shows the condominium map zoomed in very tight with one of the project information windows open.

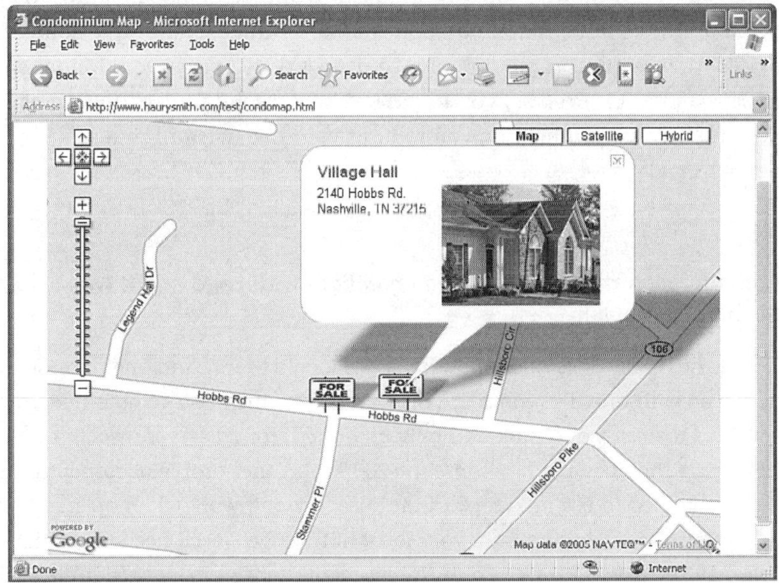

FIGURE 15.8 Clicking on a marker in the example opens up an information window containing the project name, address, and thumbnail image.

This map reveals how close two of the projects are located to each other. Hopefully it also reveals how valuable this tool could be to potential customers who are searching for real estate in a certain neighborhood or area of a city. It's important to keep in mind the practical implications of a custom mapping application, and what value it brings to other people who might end up using it.

Summary

This hour took you on a journey through one of the most interesting and compelling tools in the online world, Google Maps. I realize at times I probably sounded like a cheerleader for Google Maps but the reality is that I've personally found it to be incredibly handy for all kinds of different things. Yes, I've used it for common mapping tasks such as helping with driving directions and finding landmarks when traveling, but I've also used it to gain a unique perspective on the world around me. Who would've thought a few years ago that the Web would make it possible to view up-to-date crime statistics on a map of where they occurred? Or what about tracking taxicabs live as they drive through major cities? These are the tip of the iceberg in terms of how an application such as Google Maps can improve our interactions with the world. And thanks to Google opening up its API to developers, you can be a part of it all.

This hour not only taught you how Google Maps works from a programming perspective but it also showed you how to take advantage of Google Maps to construct your own unique mapping applications. Granted, creating a Google Maps application requires a mixture of several web development disciplines such as JavaScript and XSLT. Even so, you found out how a solid understanding of XML can go a long way toward helping you roll out your own custom maps.

Q&A

Q. ***I tried to open the example condomap.html web page and it won't work. What's the problem?***

A. Google has strict rules about how you use Google Maps, and one of these rules has to do with only hosting maps on servers for which you've obtained an API key. This means that a page can only be hosted from a server associated with the API key in the document. Because the API key in the sample document is one that I obtained to use on a server that I use, it won't work when opened from anywhere else, including from your local hard drive. You'll need to obtain your own API key from Google at http://www.google.com/apis/maps/signup.html, and then host the example map on your own server. I know that's a pain but it's the way Google has it set up.

Q. ***Can I use another online mapping service such as MapQuest to create custom maps?***

A. Yes, but MapQuest appears to only make its programming interface available to businesses that are interested in partnering with MapQuest. At least for now, Google Maps is much friendlier to the hobbyist and small-time web developer who want to experiment with creating custom mapping applications. For this reason alone Google Maps is a better option than MapQuest for creating XML-based mapping applications. That Google Maps is a more interesting technology outside of custom maps is just icing on the cake.

Q. ***Can I use Google Maps to beat a speeding ticket in court?***

A. Absolutely! I recently read a story about a guy who was pulled over for running a red light. In court, the policeman explained how the driver ran the red light while turning onto a one-way street. The driver countered by explaining that the only reason he ran the light was because of a rapidly approaching oncoming vehicle that he had to wait on before continuing through the intersection. The judge challenged the driver's assertion that the street was a two-way street. Thanks to a notebook computer and a sketchy Wi-Fi connection, the driver quickly launched Google Maps in the courtroom and zoomed in on the intersection in question. Indeed, Google Maps revealed a two-way street, confirming the driver's assertion. Google Maps 1, Police 0.

Q. ***Is the moon really made of cheese?***

A. Visit http://moon.google.com/ and find out for yourself—make sure you zoom in on the map.

Workshop

The Workshop is designed to help you anticipate possible questions, review what you've learned, and begin learning how to put your knowledge into practice.

Quiz

1. What's the difference between the Satellite and Hybrid views in Google Maps?
2. What must you obtain from Google before publishing your own custom Google Maps applications?
3. What on Earth is a geocoordinate?

Quiz Answers

1. The Satellite view in Google Maps shows a satellite image of the current map area, whereas the Hybrid view shows the satellite image along with overlaid streets and street names.
2. In order to view your own custom Google Maps applications, you must obtain an API key from Google and place it in the web page that creates the map. This web page must then be published to the exact URL location that you specified when obtaining the API key.
3. A geocoordinate is a fancy way of referring to the latitude and longitude of a location. Although there is a temptation to say that geocoordinates only apply to planet Earth, Google Moon is an example of how geocoordinates could be applied to locations on any celestial body.

Exercises

1. Add some additional projects to the `condos.xml` data document. Make sure you provide an accurate latitude and longitude for the projects so that they appear in the proper locations on the map.
2. Try your hand at creating different custom icon images for the markers in the condominium map example. Copy these images over the existing images in the example to see how they look on the map.

PART IV

Processing and Managing XML Data

HOUR 16

Parsing XML with the DOM

> The DOM very rarely makes sense, especially when it comes to namespaces. If you want to retain your sanity, avoid it.
>
> —Michael Kay

It simply isn't possible to write a book about XML while avoiding the DOM, or Document Object Model. The truth is that the DOM won't lead you down the path to insanity, although I can certainly respect Mr. Kay's opinion since I've struggled with the DOM myself from time to time. For this reason, you shouldn't think of the DOM as the end-all tool to XML processing for the Web. It's just one of many tools that you should have in your XML development arsenal, ready to engage when needed. This hour explores the DOM and the basics of how it is used. In doing so, you learn how it provides a set of interfaces that can be used to represent an entire XML document programmatically. This hour discusses

- What the Document Object Model is
- The interfaces that make up the DOM
- How to build programs that traverse the DOM
- How to access specific data inside an XML document using the DOM
- How to modify an XML document using the DOM

What Is the DOM?

If you're a seasoned HTML or JavaScript expert, you might already be familiar with the Document Object Model, or DOM. When you're creating dynamic web pages, it's common to access elements on a web page from JavaScript using the DOM. The principles involved are basically the same for accessing XML documents using the DOM.

The DOM is a standard method for exposing the elements in a document as a data structure in your programming language of choice. In other words, the DOM provides access to all the pieces and parts of a web page or XML document. A program, called a DOM parser, reads through the XML code in a file (or from some other source of input), and provides a data structure that you can access from your application. In the XML world, the DOM parser can also write its data structure out as XML so that you can save any changes that you make to the data structure.

Like XML itself, the DOM is a standard developed by the World Wide Web Consortium (W3C). Most of the details of how the DOM works are left up to the specific implementations. It's important to understand that there are multiple levels of the DOM. DOM level 1 is concerned with basic XML and HTML. DOM level 2 adds specifications for XML namespaces, Cascading Style Sheets (CSS), events, and various traversal schemes. DOM level 3, which is currently still in the works, will round out its XML coverage, include support for more user interface events, and support XPath (see Hours 11, "Getting Started with XSL," and 12, "Transforming XML with XSLT," for more on XPath). This hour focuses on how to use level 1 of the DOM since it is the most widely implemented. You can find the DOM specifications online at http://www.w3.org/DOM/.

By the Way

> All of the DOMs prior to the W3C's creation of the Level 1 DOM are loosely referred to as the Level 0 DOM. However, this isn't truly a single DOM but it instead a grouping of all the vendor-specific DOMs that ran rampant in the early days of the dynamic web.

How the DOM Works

The DOM is really a collection of programming interfaces (you learn about each interface in the DOM a bit later), all of which extend a basic interface called `Node`. The DOM represents an XML document as a tree structure, where each "thing" in the document is a node on the tree. Each node is associated with an interface that is more specific than the generic `Node` interface. Some nodes are elements, others are attributes, and still others are comments. Each interface has its own properties and methods.

For example, the top-level node in the DOM model is a `Document` object. It can have exactly one Element object as a child (the root element of the document), one `DocumentType` object, and one `DOMImplementation` object. When you're dealing with XML, the various interfaces supplied correspond to the structural entities in XML documents. If you're dealing with XHTML (or HTML), then interfaces associated with them are also included in the DOM hierarchy.

Let's look at a simple XML document and then look at how that document is represented by the DOM. An excerpt from the document is provided in Listing 16.1, and the DOM representation appears in Figure 16.1.

LISTING 16.1 A Simple XML Document

```
<?xml version="1.0"?>

<vehicles>
  <vehicle year="2004" make="Acura" model="3.2TL">
    <mileage>13495</mileage>
    <color>green</color>
    <price>33900</price>
    <carfax buyback="no" />
  </vehicle>

  <vehicle year="2005" make="Acura" model="3.2TL">
    <mileage>07541</mileage>
    <color>white</color>
    <price>33900</price>
    <carfax buyback="yes" />
  </vehicle>

  ...
</vehicles>
```

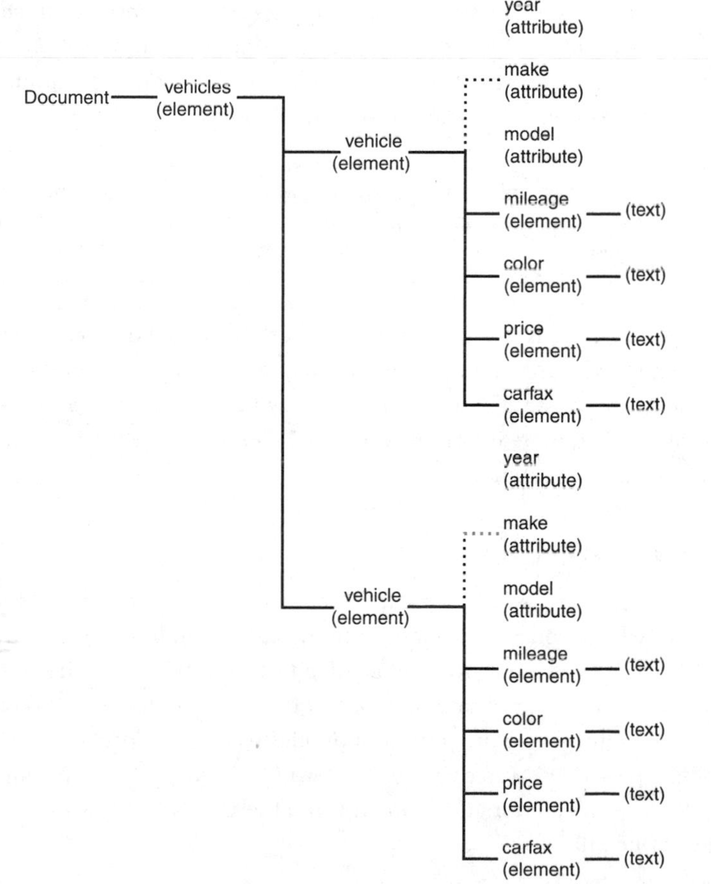

FIGURE 16.1 The DOM representation of an XML document.

As you can see, the DOM representation of the document mirrors the structure of the XML document. Figure 16.1 contains a subset of the interfaces available in the DOM. For example, the dealership node expresses the element interface (`Element`), and the vehicle attribute nodes express the attribute interface (`Attribute`).

Language Bindings

The implementation of the DOM in a particular language is referred to as a language binding. The *language binding* is the set of objects native to the language in question that implements each of the interfaces in the DOM specification. When a DOM parser parses an XML document, it copies the document's data and structure into a data structure implemented using the language mapping associated with the parser.

The DOM specification includes bindings for Java and ECMAScript. ECMAScript is the standardized version of JavaScript managed by Ecma International (http://www.ecma-international.org/). Developers can create language bindings from the DOM to their language simply by following the IDL (*Interface Definition Language*) in the DOM specification. Beyond Java and JavaScript (ECMAScript), other DOM data bindings readily exist such as bindings for the Python programming language that has grown in popularity for web development.

By the Way

> Ecma International was originally known as ECMA, which stood for European Computer Manufacturers Association. The name change came about to reflect the fact that the organization had expanded to a more international focus.

The language mapping is the most important part of the DOM specification. It is not concerned with the actual act of parsing the document. As long as a valid DOM tree is generated by the parser, it can work in any way that the developer of the parser chooses. You can find more information about DOM language bindings at http://www.w3.org/DOM/Bindings.

Using the DOM Tree

After the parser has created the DOM tree, you can begin using the DOM to access the document within your application. In many cases, you'll use other libraries that accept the DOM tree as input. You will be able to obtain the object that represents the DOM tree from the parser and then pass it along to whatever method uses it. For example, you might have a program that applies styles to a document using XSLT that accepts a parsed DOM tree as input. Alternatively, you can write your own programs that access the data in a document using the DOM. That's what the examples later in this hour will do.

DOM Interfaces

As I've already mentioned, in order to comply with the DOM, an implementation must include the interfaces required by the DOM specification. Each of the interfaces is associated with a particular type of node found in a DOM tree. Rather than listing and describing all of these interfaces, I'm going to focus on the interfaces that you will use most frequently in the course of writing applications that use the DOM. Later in the lesson you'll work through a sample application that uses several of these interfaces.

The `Node` Interface

The `Node` interface is the interface from which all other interfaces are derived. Regardless of whatever else a particular entity in a DOM tree is, it's still a node. The `Node` interface exposes some attributes and methods that are shared by everything that's in a DOM tree. These attributes and methods are largely associated with keeping track of the parents, siblings, and children of the node. Nodes also have attributes that contain their names, values, and a pointer to the document with which they are associated.

The `Document` Interface

The `Document` interface is the root node of a DOM tree. There's one important thing to point out here: the document node in a DOM tree is not the root element of the XML document—it's one level above that. Every document has one child element node that contains the root element of the XML document. Document nodes have other attributes that are associated with the document itself, rather than with the root element. That's why a DOM tree has one more level in its hierarchy than an XML document.

In addition to the root level element of the document, the document node also contains a pointer to a `DocumentType` node and a `DOMImplementation` node. Neither of these nodes are commonly referenced on programs which use the DOM, so I'm not going to discuss them individually. For more information, check out the DOM specification at http://www.w3.org/DOM/DOMTR.

The `Element` Interface

The `Element` interface represents an element in an XML (or HTML) document. The only attribute specific to an element node is the tag name (of course, it inherits all of the attributes of a standard node as well). It includes methods that enable you to retrieve, add, and remove attributes from the element. It also enables you to retrieve child elements that have a specific name. (You can already fetch all of the children of an element using the methods it inherits from the Node interface.)

The Attr Interface

The Attr interface represents an attribute of an element. Despite the fact that they inherit the Node interface, they are not actually nodes on the DOM tree because they are not children of an element. Rather, they are part of the element itself. What this means in practical terms is that any methods inherited from the Node interface that deal with traversing the DOM tree return null (nothing). You can't fetch the parents, siblings, or children of an attribute, because in terms of the DOM, they don't have any of those things.

Attributes have three properties—a name, a value, and a Boolean flag indicating whether or not the attribute was explicitly included in the document that was parsed. They have no methods specific to themselves.

The NodeList Interface

The NodeList interface is different from the other interfaces I've discussed so far. It's not a pointer to an entity in a DOM tree; rather, it's an abstract data structure that enables DOM implementations to handle collections of nodes. For example, if you call the method of the Element interface that returns all the children of an element with a particular name, the collection of child elements is returned as a node list (NodeList). You can then iterate over the node list and extract all of the element nodes from it. The only interface it must implement is one that returns items by index. Its only attribute is the size of the collection. Using the size and the method, which returns items, you can iterate over the members of the collection.

Binding XML Data to a Web Page

Before you get into the specifics of how to use the DOM to access XML data, it's worth taking a quick look at how you can access an XML document from within a web page without any programming at all. More specifically, I'll be taking advantage of some features specific to Microsoft Internet Explorer (versions 5 and above). Internet Explorer has some XML-related features that make it uniquely suited for certain XML tasks. Thanks to a feature called XML data binding, you can include an XML document within your HTML document or provide a link to an external XML document, and then bind its data to visual HTML elements on the web page. Internet Explorer will automatically parse that XML document and insert its contents into the appropriate HTML elements. Listing 16.2 contains a web page that demonstrates XML data binding.

> Mozilla Firefox supports a similar form of XML data binding through a technology called XBL (eXtensible Binding Language). Data bindings in FireFox work similarly to those in Internet Explorer, except that Firefox relies on XBL to handle the binding specifics.

LISTING 16.2 An HTML Page That Binds XML Data to Table Cells

```
 1: <html>
 2:   <head>
 3:     <title>Vehicles</title>
 4:   </head>
 5:
 6:   <body>
 7:     <xml id="vehicles" src="vehicles.xml"></xml>
 8:
 9:     <h1 style="background-color:#000000;
10:       color:#FFFFFF; font-size:20pt; text-align:center;
11:       letter-spacing: 12pt">Used Vehicles</h1>
12:     <table align="center" border="2px" datasrc="#vehicles">
13:       <tr>
14:         <td><span datafld="year"></span></td>
15:         <td><span datafld="make"></span></td>
16:         <td><span datafld="model"></span></td>
17:         <td><span datafld="mileage"></span></td>
18:         <td><span datafld="color"></span></td>
19:         <td><span datafld="price"></span></td>
20:       </tr>
21:     </table>
22:   </body>
23: </html>
```

The code for this web page is quite short when you consider that it is extracting XML data from an external file and displaying it in table cells. The key to the code is the `<xml>` tag (line 7), which is part of an XML feature called data islands. Data islands allow you to link to or embed XML data directly within an HTML document. In this case, the file `vehicles.xml` is linked into the HTML document. You can then use data binding to wire the XML data to HTML elements. The primary binding occurs on line 12 when the `datasrc` attribute is matched up with the `id` of the `<xml>` tag from line 7. From there, all you have to do is associate each XML element with an HTML `<span>` tag within the table. This takes place on lines 14 through 19 via the `datafld` attribute, which references each specific XML element (see Listing 16.1 for a recap of the elements in the `vehicles.xml` document).

The end result of this code is the XML data being arranged in a table within the web page, as shown in Figure 16.2.

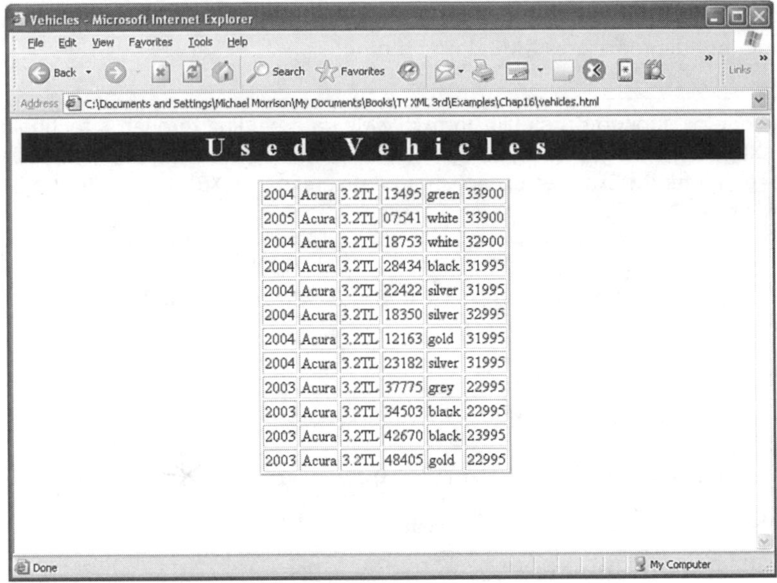

2004	Acura	3.2TL	13495	green	33900
2005	Acura	3.2TL	07541	white	33900
2004	Acura	3.2TL	18753	white	32900
2004	Acura	3.2TL	28434	black	31995
2004	Acura	3.2TL	22422	silver	31995
2004	Acura	3.2TL	18350	silver	32995
2004	Acura	3.2TL	12163	gold	31995
2004	Acura	3.2TL	23182	silver	31995
2003	Acura	3.2TL	37775	grey	22995
2003	Acura	3.2TL	34503	black	22995
2003	Acura	3.2TL	42670	black	23995
2003	Acura	3.2TL	48405	gold	22995

FIGURE 16.2 The `vehicles.xml` is binded to a table in this sample web page.

Although data binding essentially results in a straight "data dump" into HTML elements, it is nonetheless a very quick and easy way to access XML data from within an HTML web page. However, you'll likely want to get dirty with a little programming and the DOM to really get the most out of web-based XML documents.

Using the DOM to Access XML Data

For the sake of simplicity, the remaining examples in this hour are written in JavaScript. One of the huge advantages of the DOM is that the interfaces that make up the DOM are basically the same regardless of whether you write your program in Java, C++, Visual Basic, JavaScript, Perl, or any other language with a DOM implementation. JavaScript programs that are run within the context of a web browser are interpreted (so they don't have to be compiled) and don't have a lot of overhead or structure that require a lot of knowledge beforehand in order to be understood. In other words, you can hit the ground running with JavaScript and the DOM pretty quickly.

Loading an XML Document

It turns out that perhaps the trickiest part of DOM programming with JavaScript is initially loading the document into memory so that you can access it programmatically. No one has settled on a standard approach for initially loading an XML document, so we're unfortunately left dealing with different approaches for different browsers. Following is the code to load an XML document into Internet Explorer:

```
var xmlDoc;
xmlDoc = new ActiveXObject("Microsoft.XMLDOM");
xmlDoc.load("condos.xml");
```

As this code reveals, you must first create an ActiveX object (`Microsoft.XML.DOM`) and then call the `load()` method on the object to load a specific XML document. Okay, that technique is pretty straightforward, right? Problem is, it won't work in Firefox. Following is the equivalent code for loading an XML document in Firefox:

```
xmlDoc = document.implementation.createDocument("", "", null);
xmlDoc.load("condos.xml");
```

This code is obviously different from the Internet Explorer version, or at least the creation of the `xmlDoc` object is different. If you want your pages to work on both major browsers, and I'm sure you do, you'll need to include code to conditionally load the XML document differently based on the browser. Here's the code to pull off this feat:

```
if (window.ActiveXObject) {
  xmlDoc = new ActiveXObject("Microsoft.XMLDOM");
  xmlDoc.load("condos.xml");
}
else {
  xmlDoc = document.implementation.createDocument("", "", null);
  xmlDoc.load("condos.xml");
}
```

This code takes advantage of the fact that Firefox doesn't have an `ActiveXObject` in the `window` object that represents the browser. You can therefore use the presence of this object as the basis for using the Internet Explorer approach to loading an XML document. If the object isn't there, the Firefox approach is used.

When the XML document is loaded, you can move on to processing the XML data. However, there is one more browser inconsistency to deal with. The inconsistency has to do with how the two major browsers load XML documents. You will typically create a JavaScript function that processes XML data, and you'll likely want this function to get called right after loading the documents. Following is the code to handle calling a function named `printRootNode()` upon loading the XML document `condos.xml`:

```
if (window.ActiveXObject) {
  xmlDoc = new ActiveXObject("Microsoft.XMLDOM");
  xmlDoc.load("condos.xml");
  printRootNode();
}
else {
  xmlDoc = document.implementation.createDocument("", "", null);
  xmlDoc.load("condos.xml");
  xmlDoc.onload = printRootNode;
}
```

This is basically the same code you just saw with a couple of extra lines that call the `printRootNode()` function a bit differently for each browser. You now have the framework for an HTML page that can load an XML document and call a JavaScript function to get busy processing the document data.

Traversing the DOM Tree

When you have the `xmlDoc` variable set with the newly loaded XML document, you'll likely want to call a function to start processing the document. In the previous code a function named `printRootNode()` is called presumably to print the root node of the document. This function is actually just the starting point for printing all of the nodes in the document. Let's look at a script that prints out the names of all of the nodes in the document tree. Listing 16.3 contains the code for a complete web page containing such a script.

LISTING 16.3 An HTML Page That Prints All of the Nodes in an XML Document

```
<html>
  <head>
    <title>Condominium List</title>
    <script type="text/javascript">
      var xmlDoc;
      function loadXMLDoc() {
        // XML loader for IE
        if (window.ActiveXObject) {
          xmlDoc = new ActiveXObject("Microsoft.XMLDOM");
          xmlDoc.load("condos.xml");
          printRootNode();
        }
        // XML loader for other browsers
        else {
          xmlDoc = document.implementation.createDocument("", "", null);
          xmlDoc.load("condos.xml");
          xmlDoc.onload = printRootNode;
        }
      }

      function printRootNode() {
        printNode(xmlDoc);
      }

      function printNode(node) {
        document.write("<span style='font-weight:bold'>Node name: " +
          node.nodeName + "</span><br />\n");
        if (node.nodeValue != null)
          document.write("Node value: " + node.nodeValue + "<br />\n");

        for (var i = 0; i < node.childNodes.length; i++)
          printNode(node.childNodes[i]);
      }
    </script>
```

```
35:    </head>
36:
37:    <body onload="loadXMLDoc()">
38:    </body>
39: </html>
```

Let's look at this script in detail. First off, notice that virtually all of the script code is located in functions in the head of the document, which means that it doesn't automatically get executed. However, the `loadXMLDoc()` function gets called in the <body> tag thanks to the `onload` attribute (line 37). This is all it takes to get the code started processing the XML document.

By the Way

> When you include JavaScript code on a page, any code that's not inside a function will be executed as soon as the browser interprets it. Code placed in a function is only executed when the function is called.

The `loadXMLDoc()` handles the XML document loading task you learned about earlier and then calls the `printRootNode()` function to start printing the nodes (lines 11 and 17). The `printRootNode()` function is really just a helper function used to start printing the nodes (lines 21 through 23). It is necessary because the real function that prints the nodes, `printNode()`, requires an attribute but there is no good way to pass along an attribute in the Firefox version of the load routine (line 17). So, you have to print the root node using the `printRootNode()` function, and from there on the `printNode()` function takes over.

By the Way

> Most scripts that interact with an entire XML document tree start at the root node and work their way down the tree, as shown in this example.

The rest of the code inside the script tag is inside the `printNode()` function, and is executed when the `printNode()` function is called by `printRootNode()`. As you know, a document node provides all of the methods of the `Node` interface as well as those specific to the document interface. The `printNode()`function will work with any node, including a document node; it is called and passed the `xmlDoc` variable as its argument to print the root node.

You may be wondering exactly how the `printNode()` can print an entire document tree when it is only called and passed the root node. The answer has to do with a common programming technique called *recursion*. Recursion is to tree-like data structures what loops are to list data structures. When you want to process a number of similar things that are in a list, you simply process them one at a time until you've processed all of the items in that list. Recursion is a bit more complex. When you're dealing with tree-like data structures, you have to work your way down each branch in the tree until you reach the end.

Let's look at an example not associated with the DOM first. When you want to find a file on your computer's hard drive manually, and you have no idea where it is located, the fastest way to find it is to recursively search all of the directories on the hard drive. The process goes something like this (starting at the root directory):

1. Is the file in this directory? If so, we're finished.
2. If not, does this directory contain any subdirectories? If not, skip to step 4.
3. If there are subdirectories, move to the first subdirectory and go back to step 1.
4. Move up one directory. Move to the next subdirectory in this directory, and skip to step 1. If there are no additional subdirectories in this directory, repeat this step.

That's one recursive algorithm. The most important thing to understand about recursion is that all of the items being processed recursively must be similar enough to be processed in the same way.

This helps to explain why all of the interfaces in the DOM are extensions of the basic `Node` interface. You can write one recursive function that will process all of the nodes in a DOM tree using the methods that they have in common. `printNode()` is one such function

First, let's examine the function declaration. You've already seen a few functions, but let's back up and clarify how functions work in JavaScript. In JavaScript, you indicate that you're creating a function by using the `function` keyword. The name of the function is supplied next, followed by the list of arguments accepted by the function. The name of this function is `printNode()`, and it accepts one argument, which is given the name `node`. This argument is intended to be a node that's part of a DOM tree. Within the function, you can use the `name` argument to refer to the node that is passed into the function.

In the body of the function, the first thing that happens is the `nodeName` property of the node currently being processed is printed (lines 26 and 27). If a node value exists, it is printed next (lines 28 and 29). Then, the function loops over the children of the node currently being processed and calls the `printNode()` function on each of the children (lines 31 and 32). This is where the recursion comes in. The same function, `printNode()`, is called repeatedly to process every node in the tree. Figure 16.3 contains this page, as viewed in Internet Explorer.

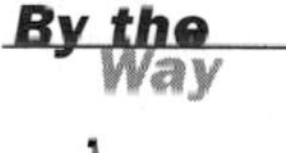

It's worth mentioning that recursion is both a powerful and dangerous programming technique. It's not difficult at all to accidentally create a recursive function that calls itself repeatedly and never stops. You should exercise great care when writing recursive functions. Having said that, recursive functions can be very valuable when processing tree-like structures such as XML documents.

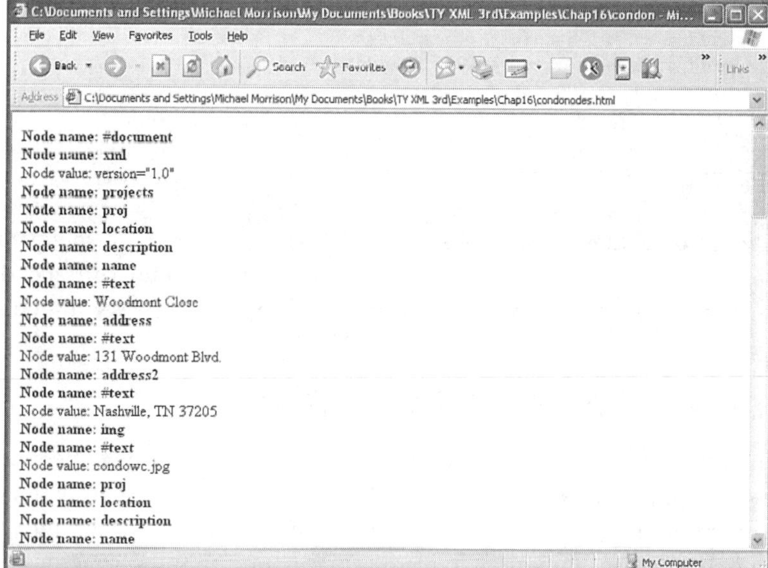

FIGURE 16.3
The output of a function that prints the names and values of all of the nodes in a DOM tree.

This example is based on the condos.xml document from the previous hour, which is partially shown in Listing 16.4.

LISTING 16.4 The condos.xml Example XML Document

```
<?xml version="1.0"?>

<projects>
  <proj status="active">
    <location lat="36.122238" long="-86.845028" />
    <description>
      <name>Woodmont Close</name>
      <address>131 Woodmont Blvd.</address>
      <address2>Nashville, TN 37205</address2>
      <img>condowc.jpg</img>
    </description>
  </proj>
  <proj status="active">
    <location lat="36.101232" long="-86.820759" />
    <description>
      <name>Village Hall</name>
```

LISTING 16.4 Continued

```
17:       <address>2140 Hobbs Rd.</address>
18:       <address2>Nashville, TN 37215</address2>
19:       <img>condovh.jpg</img>
20:     </description>
21:   </proj>
22:   ...
23:   <proj status="completed">
24:     <location lat="36.091559" long="-86.832686" />
25:     <description>
26:       <name>Harding Hall</name>
27:       <address>2120 Harding Pl.</address>
28:       <address2>Nashville, TN 37215</address2>
29:       <img>condohh.jpg</img>
30:     </description>
31:   </proj>
32: </projects>
```

Hopefully this code allows you to make sense of the output shown in Figure 16.3. For example, the printed XML data that is partially visible in the figure corresponds to the first project in the `condos.xml` document, which appears in lines 4 through 12.

A Complete DOM Example

Printing all of the nitty-gritty details of an XML document is certainly interesting but it isn't exactly practical. What is more practical is printing the contents of an XML document but in such a way that it is more accessible to the person viewing the resulting web page. If you recall from the previous hour, you saw a cool sample page that showed how to map condominium projects on a custom map in Google Maps. The condominium data is the same data you just saw in Listing 16.4. You can use JavaScript and the DOM to print a formatted listing of this data that could potentially be used to provide a directory of condominium projects. This is an example of how the exact same XML data can be manipulated through different technologies to provide surprisingly different views.

The code that prints the condominium listing is structured roughly similar to the example you saw in the previous section that printed all of the nodes of a document. However, in this case there is no recursion because you aren't "walking" the document tree. Instead, you pluck out nodes of a particular type and then print them. For example, you know that all nodes corresponding to the `<name>` tag contain project names. So, to print the name of a project just grab the array of `<name>` tags and print each of them out. This technique is used to print the name, address (two lines), and image for each condominium project.

Listing 16.5 contains the complete code for the condominium list example web page.

LISTING 16.5 An HTML Page That Prints the Condominium Document as a Formatted List

```
1: <html>
2:   <head>
3:     <title>Condominium List</title>
4:     <script type="text/javascript">
5:       var xmlDoc;
6:       function loadXMLDoc() {
7:         // XML loader for IE
8:         if (window.ActiveXObject) {
9:           xmlDoc = new ActiveXObject("Microsoft.XMLDOM");
10:          xmlDoc.load("condos.xml");
11:          printCondos();
12:        }
13:        // XML loader for other browsers
14:        else {
15:          xmlDoc = document.implementation.createDocument("", "", null);
16:          xmlDoc.load("condos.xml");
17:          xmlDoc.onload = printCondos;
18:        }
19:      }
20:
21:      function printCondos() {
22:        var nameNodes = xmlDoc.getElementsByTagName("name");
23:        var addrNodes = xmlDoc.getElementsByTagName("address");
24:        var addr2Nodes = xmlDoc.getElementsByTagName("address2");
25:        var imgNodes = xmlDoc.getElementsByTagName("img");
26:        for (var i = 0; i < nameNodes.length; i++) {
27:          document.write("<div style='font-family:arial; font-weight:bold;
28:            color:maroon'>" + nameNodes[i].firstChild.nodeValue +
29:            "</div>");
30:          document.write("<div style='font-family:arial'>" +
31:            addrNodes[i].firstChild.nodeValue + "<br />");
32:          document.write(addr2Nodes[i].firstChild.nodeValue + "</div>");
33:          document.write("<img src='" + imgNodes[i].firstChild.nodeValue +
34:            "' alt='" + nameNodes[i].firstChild.nodeValue + "' /><hr />");
35:        }
36:      }
37:    </script>
38:  </head>
39:
40:  <body onload="loadXMLDoc()">
41:  </body>
42: </html>
```

This code starts out familiar in that it relies on the `loadXMLDoc()` function to load the condos.xml document (lines 9, 10, 15, and 16), as well as calling the `printCondos()` function to print the relevant document content (lines 11 and 17). The `printCondos()` function is where all the action takes place.

The `printCondos()` function starts off by extracting four arrays of nodes from the XML document (lines 22 to 25). Each of these arrays corresponds to a certain tag in the document. For example, the project names that are coded using the `<name>` tag in the XML document are grabbed as an array of nodes by calling the DOM's `getElementsByTagName()` function (line 22). The name of the tag is passed into the function, and the result is an array containing elements that match that tag name.

After the four arrays of elements are extracted, a loop is created that iterates through each element and prints it to the page (lines 26 through 35). Even the image associated with each condo is printed, and its resulting HTML `<img>` tag is coded to include the project name in the required `alt` attribute so that when you hover the mouse over the image in a web browser the name of the project will appear. Speaking of viewing the page in a web browser, Figure 16.4 shows the results of this script in Mozilla Firefox.

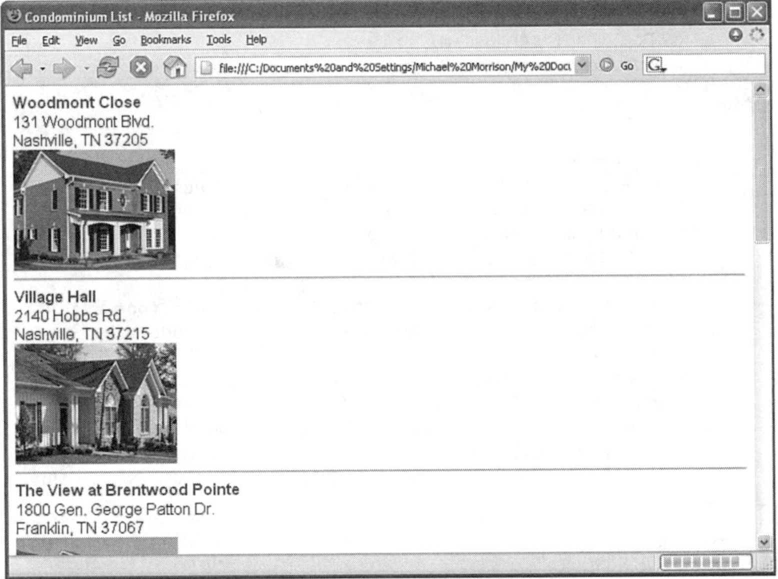

FIGURE 16.4 All of the condominiums in the `condos.xml` document are printed as a formatted list.

The figure reveals how the condominium list is formatted on an HTML page as a vertical sequence. You could just as easily modify the script so that the condos are arranged in a table or in some other layout that suits your particular needs. The point is that the DOM allows you to access the XML data and render it to an HTML web page any way you want.

Updating the DOM Tree

Not only does the DOM enable you to access an XML data structure in a number of ways, but it also enables you to alter an XML data structure. Rather than providing you with another lengthy program example that explains how to alter the DOM tree, I'll just show you some specific examples that demonstrate how such tasks are performed. Note that if you were using a language other than JavaScript, you could store the updated DOM tree on disk once the tree has been updated. However, JavaScript runs within the context of a web browser and has no access to the file system, so any changes you make to a DOM tree in a JavaScript program will be lost as soon as you leave that page.

First, let's look at how you can access a specific node in a tree. In the earlier examples in this hour, you saw how to iterate over all of the children of a particular node. You will probably want to be more specific when you're updating the tree. The key method in taking more exacting control of the document tree is the `item()` method of the `NodeList` interface. When you call the `item()` method and supply it with an index, it returns the node associated with that index. Let's say you have the document node of a DOM tree assigned to the variable xmlDoc. To access the root level element of the document, you can use the following code:

```
xmlDoc.childNodes.item(0);
```

Or, if you prefer, simply

```
xmlDoc.childNodes.firstChild;
```

In order to be valid XML, you can have only one element at the top level of your tree, so when you want to add a node, you need to add it to the root element. You can assign the root element to a variable like this:

```
var root = xmlDoc.childNodes.firstChild;
```

After you've done that, you can add an element as its child. However, first you'll need an element node. You can create one using the document object, like this:

```
var newElement = xmlDoc.createElement("automobile");
```

Then, you can add it to your tree, like this:

```
root.appendChild(newElement);
```

If you want, you can then add an attribute to the node you just inserted into the tree:

```
var attr = doc.createAttribute("make");
attr.text = "Suburu";
root.childNodes.lastChild.setAttributeNode(attr);
```

First, you create an attribute just like you created the element before. Then you set its value, and finally you add it to the element you just added to the tree. Note that the `lastChild()` method is used to access the node you just added. Because you just appended the node to the tree, you know that it's the last child of the root element.

It's just as easy to update and remove items in the DOM. To update the attribute you just added, you just need to access it in the DOM tree and change its value, like so:

```
root.childNodes.lastChild.setAttribute("make", "BMW");
```

As you can see, there's a method specifically used to update a named attribute. To remove that attribute, just call the following method:

```
root.childNodes.lastChild.removeAttribute("make");
```

Now let's look at updating and removing elements themselves. There are two ways to do so—you can replace child nodes or remove them. First, let's look at replacing them. In order to replace an element, you'll need to create a new element to put in place of the old one, and then call the method that swaps them:

```
var replacementElem = xmlDoc.createElement("customer");
var oldNode = root.replaceChild(replacementElem, root.childNodes.lastChild);
```

As you can see, to replace a child of a node, you just have to pass in the new node and a reference to the node that will be replaced. The node that was replaced is assigned to the variable `oldNode`—if you want to do something else with it. Removing a node is even easier:

```
var anotherOldNode = root.removeChild(root.childNodes.lastChild);
```

The node that was removed is assigned to the variable `anotherOldNode`.

Hopefully this brief introduction to document tree manipulation has given you some ideas about how to go about using the DOM to tinker with your own XML documents.

Summary

The DOM is a W3C standard that describes how the structure of XML and HTML documents can be expressed as a native data structure within various programming languages. The DOM standard is language neutral, and implementations exist for a number of languages, including JavaScript, Java, C++, Perl, and Visual Basic. In this hour, you learned about the various interfaces that make up the DOM and how you can access data stored within the DOM structure from JavaScript. Even though the syntax of the language you use with the DOM might differ significantly from the syntax used in these JavaScript examples, the means of accessing the DOM will be basically the same. On the other hand, you may be quite content to stick with JavaScript as your language of choice for interacting with the DOM.

Q&A

Q. ***Why don't some of the example programs in this hour work in Mozilla Firefox and Opera?***

A. Unfortunately, some advanced XML features such as XML data islands and data binding vary from browser to browser, and aren't even supported in some browsers. This hour focuses on the Internet Explorer version of data islands and data binding. Mozilla Firefox has similar features although they are coded a little differently, while Opera has no support for either feature.

Q. ***Can large documents create performance issues when I use the DOM?***

A. Yes. As you know, DOM parsers create a data structure that contains all of the data in an XML document, which means that all of the data is loaded into memory at once. If your XML document is really large (in comparison to the amount of RAM in the computer that your application runs on), performance issues can arise. In those cases, it may make more sense to use a SAX parser because it does not deal with the document as a whole. SAX is covered in the next hour, "SAX: The Simple API for XML."

Workshop

The Workshop is designed to help you anticipate possible questions, review what you've learned, and begin learning how to put your knowledge into practice.

Quiz

1. From which interface in the DOM are all the others derived?
2. The DOM is specific to which programming language?
3. How do the `NodeList` and `NamedNodeList` interfaces differ?
4. Which interfaces support attributes?

Quiz Answers

1. All of the interfaces in the DOM are derived from the `Node` interface, with the exception of the `NodeList` interface.
2. Sorry, this is a trick question! The DOM is not specific to any programming language.

3. The `NamedNodeList` interface is an extension of the `NodeList` interface—it adds support for retrieval of members using the node name.

4. The `Element` and `Entity` interfaces support attributes.

Exercises

1. Write a script that converts all of the attributes in an XML document into child elements of the elements that they were associated with.

2. Write a program that shows the names of only those elements that have attributes and no children.

HOUR 17

SAX: The Simple API for XML

Which painting in the National Gallery would I save if there was a fire? The one nearest the door of course.

—George Bernard Shaw

If you share Mr. Shaw's propensity for practicality, you will probably find this lesson quite interesting. Through most of this book, the discussion on XML has focused on its use as a structured document format. However, XML is also often used as a format for data storage. Unlike proprietary file formats, XML documents follow consistent structural rules and can be tested not only for well-formedness but also for compliance with specific str... rules. There are a variety of tools out there that allow you to interact with the struc... documents. The previous hour focused on one of these technologies, the W... Object Model (DOM). This hour tackles another such technology, known ... (Simple API for XML) is an API that can be used to analyze and extract ... XML document.

In this hour, you'll learn

- What SAX is and how it works
- How to get a SAX parser for your favorite programming l...
- How to write a Java program that uses a SAX parser to ...

What Is SAX?

SAX is a programming interface for event-based parsi... means that SAX takes a very different approach to p... the DOM. If you recall from previous hours, XML ... The parser reads the XML document; verifies that ... parser, validates it against a schema or DTD. What happ... you're using. In some cases, it might copy the data into a data ... the programming language you're using. In other cases, it might trans... into a presentation format or apply styles to it. The SAX parser doesn't do anythi... data other than trigger certain events. It's up to the user of the SAX parser to determine what happens when those events occur.

What I mean when I say that SAX is a programming interface is that it isn't a program, it's a document—a standard—that describes how a SAX parser should be written. It explains which events must be supported in a compliant SAX parser and leaves it up to the implementers to make sure that the parsers they write comply.

By the Way

> An interface is basically a contract offered by someone who writes a program or specifies how a program should work. It says that as long as you implement all of the features specified in the interface, any programs written to use that interface will work as expected. When someone writes a parser that implements the SAX interface, it means that any program that supports all of the events specified in the SAX interface can use that parser.

A Really Brief History of SAX

Most of the time when you're dealing with XML, one standards body or another developed the various technologies. With SAX, that isn't the case. SAX was developed by members of the `xml-dev` mailing list in order to provide XML developers with a way to deal with XML documents in a simple and straightforward manner. One of the lead developers in this mailing list was Dave Megginson, whose name often comes up in discussions related to SAX, and who has resumed maintaining SAX after a hiatus. You can find out more about SAX at http://www.saxproject.org/.

The original version of SAX, 1.0, was released in May 1998. The most recent version is SAX 2.0.2, which was released in April 2004. Earlier versions of the SAX API were implemented initially as Java interfaces. However, you can write a SAX parser in any language, and indeed, there are SAX parsers available for most popular programming languages. However, I'm going to talk about the features that were made available in the Java version—you can assume they'll also be available under whatever implementation you choose to use. Let's look at the specifics of these two releases.

By the Way

> SAX 2.0.2 is a fairly minor enhancement of the original SAX 2.0 release that came out back in May 2000. Throughout the remainder of this lesson I generally refer to the latest release of SAX as version 2.0.

SAX 1.0

SAX 1.0 provides support for triggering events on all of the standard content in an XML document. Rather than telling you everything it does support, it's easier to tell you that SAX 1.0 does not support namespaces. A program that uses a SAX 1.0 parser must support the following methods, which are automatically invoked when events occur during the parsing of a document:

- `characters()`—Returns the characters found inside an element
- `endDocument()`—Triggered when parsing of the document is complete
- `endElement()`—Triggered when the closing tag for any element is encountered
- `ignorableWhitespace()`—Triggered when whitespace is encountered between elements
- `processingInstruction()`—Triggered when a processing instruction is encountered in the document
- `startElement()`—Triggered when the opening tag for an element is encountered

By the Way

> If you don't have a programming background, allow me to clarify that a method is a sequence of programming code that performs a certain task. Methods are very similar to functions in programming languages other than Java.

SAX 1.0 also handles attributes of elements by providing them through its interface when the `startElement()` method of the document handler is called. SAX 1.0 has been deprecated now that SAX 2.0 has been implemented. In the Java world, most SAX 2.0 libraries (such as Xerces) still support SAX 1.0 so that they'll work with legacy SAX 1.0 applications. But if you're writing a new application that uses SAX, you should use SAX 2.0.

SAX 2.0

SAX 2.0 is an extension of SAX 1.0 that provides support for namespaces. As such, programs that communicate with a SAX 2.0 parser must support the following methods:

- `startPrefixMapping()`—Triggered when a prefix mapping (mapping a namespace to an entity prefix) is encountered
- `endPrefixMapping()`—Triggered when a prefix mapping is closed
- `skippedEntity()`—Triggered whenever an entity is skipped for any number of reasons

Writing Programs That Use SAX Parsers

Unless you really develop an interest in XML parsing, chances are you won't be writing a SAX parser. Rather, you'll be writing a program that interacts with a SAX parser. Writing a program that works with a SAX parser is in some ways similar to writing a program with a graphical user interface (GUI), such as a traditional application for Windows or Macintosh. When you write a GUI program, the GUI library turns actions that the user takes into events that are returned to you by the library. Your job as a programmer is then to write event handlers that respond to incoming events. For example, with JavaScript, certain elements on a web page can generate events that can be handled by JavaScript. Links generate `onClick` and `onMouseOver` events. There are also documentwide events in JavaScript, such as `onLoad`.

In regard to event handling, SAX works the same way conceptually as JavaScript. When a SAX parser parses the data in an XML document, it fires events based on the data that it is currently parsing. All of the methods listed previously that are associated with SAX are called by the parser when the associated event occurs. It's up to the application programmer to decide what action to take when those events are caught.

For example, you might want to print out just the contents of all of the `title` elements in a document, or you might want to construct a complex data structure based on all of the information you find in the document. The SAX parser doesn't care; it just provides you with all of the data in the document in a linear manner so that you can do whatever you like with it.

You might be asking yourself at this point why you would ever care to parse an XML document at such a low level. In other words, why would you ever want to print out just the contents of the `title` elements in a document? The main answer to this question has to do with data maintenance and integrity. As you continue to build and maintain larger and larger XML documents, you may find that you need to extract and study portions of the documents to find editorial errors or any other inconsistencies that are difficult to find when viewing raw XML code. A custom application built around a SAX parser can be used to drill down into an XML document and spit out any subset of the data that you want.

Obtaining a SAX Parser

If you want to write an application that uses SAX, the first thing you have to do is obtain a SAX parser. There are several SAX parsers available, and it's ultimately up to your own specific development needs as to which parser you should use. Furthermore, you'll need to look at the documentation for the parser that you choose in order to figure out how to integrate the parser with your applications. Following are several of the more popular SAX parsers you might want to consider using.

- Xerces
- `libxml`
- Python SAX API

The next few sections provide more information about these SAX parsers, along with how to download and install them.

Xerces

Xerces is the XML parser from the Apache Software Foundation. It's used as part of several other Apache XML and Java-related projects and can be used by itself as well. In addition to supporting SAX, it also supports DOM Level 2, which you learned about in the previous hour, as well as XML Schema validation.

You can obtain Xerces, along with lots of other open source XML-related software, at http://xml.apache.org/. Xerces is completely free as it is open source software released under the Apache Software License.

The Xerces library is available in both `.tar.gz` and `.zip` formats—download the one that's appropriate for your platform. Included in the package are `xercesImpl.jar` and `xml-apis.jar`, which contain the compiled class files for the Xerces library itself, and `xercesSamples.jar`, compiled versions of the sample programs that come with Xerces. The package also includes documentation, source code for the sample programs, and some sample data files.

By the Way

> A `.JAR` file is a lot like a `.ZIP` file except that it is typically used to package compressed Java programs for distribution; JAR stands for Java ARchive.

In order to use the Xerces library, you just need to include the two aforementioned `.JAR` files (`xercesImpl.jar` and `xml-apis.jar`) in your class path when compiling and running programs that use it.

libxml

`libxml` is a package of Perl modules that contains a number of XML processing libraries. One of these is `XML::Parser::PerlSAX`. The easiest way to install it is to download it from CPAN (http://www.cpan.org/) and follow the instructions to install it on your local system. The methods provided by the `PerlSAX` module are basically identical to those in the Java version of SAX—they both implement the same interface in ways appropriate to Perl and Java, respectively.

Python

If you're a Python programmer, things are particularly easy for you. Recent versions of Python (from 2.0 on) provide built-in support for SAX without any additional software. To use the SAX library in your programs, you just need to include the line

```
from xml.sax import saxutils
```

Using SAX with Java

The sample program in this chapter is written in Java and uses the Xerces SAX parser, which I mentioned earlier. If you're a Java programmer, I'm sure you're perfectly happy with this state of affairs. If you have no interest in Java, much of the remainder of this lesson probably won't be to your liking. However, the purpose of this chapter is to explain how SAX works, and while there are SAX parsers available for many languages, it started out in the Java world. And even if you have no interest in digesting the upcoming Java code, you can still experiment with the sample Java program, running it on your XML documents and analyzing the results. The syntax for this program is relatively simple, and I've commented the code to make it as clear as possible.

Even if you don't care about Java programming, you may still want to see the output of the sample program on your own computer. To run the program, you'll need Sun's Java Development Kit (JDK) and the Xerces library mentioned previously. I already explained how to download and install Xerces; to get the JDK, just go to http://java.sun.com/j2se/.

You'll need to download the J2SE (Java 2 Standard Edition) SDK and install it. Once it's installed, you can run the sample program. Just put the sample program's `.java` source code file in the directory where you put `xercesImpl.jar` and `xml-apis.jar` (you can put it anywhere you like, but this route is probably easiest), open a command prompt in that directory, and type the following:

```
javac -classpath xercesImpl.jar;xml-apis.jar;. DocumentPrinter.java
```

> Alternatively, you can copy the `xercesImpl.jar` and `xml-apis.jar` files to the same location as the sample program and then compile and run the program from there. The main point is that the program needs to be able to access the `.JAR` files.

If your copy of the code for `DocumentPrinter.java` is correct and `xercesImpl.jar` and `xml-apis.jar` are really in the current folder, the `DocumentPrinter` class will be compiled and a file called `DocumentPrinter.class` will result. To run the program, use the following command:

```
java -classpath xercesImpl.jar;xml-apis.jar;. DocumentPrinter file.xml
```

You should replace `file.xml` with the name of the XML file that you want to process. As an example, here's how you would initiate the Document Printer sample program using the vehicles XML file from Hour 12, "Transforming XML with XSLT":

```
java -classpath xercesImpl.jar;xml-apis.jar;. DocumentPrinter vehicles.xml
```

Listing 17.1 contains a partial listing of the resulting output of running the DocumentPrinter SAX sample program on the `vehicles.xml` document.

LISTING 17.1 **The Document Printer Sample Program Uses a SAX Parser to Display Detailed Information About the `vehicles.xml` Document**

```
Start document.
Received processing instruction:
Target: xml-stylesheet
Data: href="vehicles.xsl" type="text/xsl"
Start element: vehicles
Start element: vehicle
Start element: mileage
Received characters: 13495
End of element: mileage
Start element: color
Received characters: green
End of element: color
Start element: price
Received characters: 33900
End of element: price
End of element: vehicle
...
Start element: vehicle
Start element: mileage
Received characters: 48405
End of element: mileage
Start element: color
Received characters: gold
End of element: color
Start element: price
Received characters: 22995
End of element: price
End of element: vehicle
End of element: vehicles
End of document reached.
```

Just to refresh your memory, following is a brief code excerpt from the `vehicles.xml` document:

```
<vehicle year="2004" make="Acura" model="3.2TL">
  <mileage>13495</mileage>
  <color>green</color>
  <price>33900</price>
</vehicle>
```

In fact, this piece of code is for the first vehicle in the document, which matches up with the code on lines 6 through 16 in Listing 17.1. If you carefully compare the XML code with the listing, you'll notice how the program parsed and output information about every element in the document. This is the kind of detailed control you have at your disposal when using a tool such as a SAX parser.

Inside the SAX Sample Program

Let's look at how the program you just saw uses a SAX parser to parse an XML document. The program just prints out messages that explain what it's doing at each step while parsing, along with the associated data from the XML document. You could easily replace this code with code that performs more useful tasks, such as performing a calculation or otherwise transforming the data, but because the purpose of this program is just to illustrate how the SAX parser works, the diagnostic messages are fine.

Because you already know the scoop on SAX, Java, and the Xerces SAX parser for Java, let's go ahead and jump right into the program code. Here are the first 12 lines of Java code:

```
import org.xml.sax.Attributes;
import org.xml.sax.ContentHandler;
import org.xml.sax.ErrorHandler;
import org.xml.sax.Locator;
import org.xml.sax.SAXParseException;
import org.xml.sax.XMLReader;

public class DocumentPrinter implements ContentHandler, ErrorHandler {
  // A constant containing the name of the SAX parser to use.
  private static final String PARSER_NAME
    = "org.apache.xerces.parsers.SAXParser";
```

This code imports classes that will be used later on and declares the class (program) that you're currently writing. The `import` statements indicate which classes will be used by this program. In this case, all of the classes that will be used are from the `org.xml.sax` package and are included in the `xercesImpl.jar` and `xml-apis.jar` archives.

This class, called `DocumentPrinter`, implements two interfaces—`ContentHandler` and `ErrorHandler`. These two interfaces are part of the standard SAX 2.0 package and are included in the `import` list. A program that implements `ContentHandler` is set up to handle events passed back in the normal course of parsing an XML document, and a program that implements `ErrorHandler` can handle any error events generated during SAX parsing.

In the Java world, an interface is a framework that specifies a list of methods that must be defined in a class. An interface is useful because it guarantees that any class that implements it meets the requirements of that interface. If you fail to include all of the methods required by the interface, your program will not compile. Because this program implements `ContentHandler` and `ErrorHandler`, the parser can be certain that it is capable of handling all of the events it triggers as it parses a document.

After the class has been declared, a single member variable is created for the class, `PARSER_NAME`. This variable is a constant that contains the name of the class that you're going to use as the SAX parser. As you learned earlier, there is any number of SAX parsers available. The Xerces parser just so happens to be one of the better Java SAX parsers out there, which explains the parser name of `org.apache.xerces.parsers.SAXParser`.

By the Way

> Although SAX is certainly a popular Java-based XML parser given its relatively long history, it has some serious competition from Sun, the makers of Java. The latest version of Java (J2SE 5.0) now includes an XML API called JAXP that serves as a built-in XML parser for Java. To learn more about JAXP, visit http://java.sun.com/xml/jaxp/.

The `main()` Method

Every command-line Java application begins its life with the `main()` method. In the Java world, the `main` method indicates that a class is a standalone program, as opposed to one that just provides functionality used by other classes. Perhaps more importantly, it's the method that gets run when you start the program. The purpose of this method is to set up the parser and get the name of the document to be parsed from the arguments passed in to the program. Here's the code:

```
public static void main(String[] args) {
  if (args.length == 0) {
    System.out.println("No XML document path specified.");
    System.exit(1);
  }

  DocumentPrinter dp = new DocumentPrinter();
  XMLReader parser;
```

```
    try {
      parser = (XMLReader)Class.forName(PARSER_NAME).newInstance();
      parser.setContentHandler(dp);
      parser.setErrorHandler(dp);
      parser.parse(args[0]);
    }
    // Normally it's a bad idea to catch generic exceptions like this.
    catch (Exception ex) {
      System.out.println(ex.getMessage());
      ex.printStackTrace();
    }
  }
```

This program expects that the user will specify the path to an XML document as its only command-line argument. If no such argument is submitted, the program will exit and instruct the user to supply that argument when running the program.

Next, the program creates an instance of the `DocumentPrinter` object and assigns it to the variable `dp`. You'll need this object later when you tell the parser which `ContentHandler` and `ErrorHandler` to use. After instantiating `dp`, a `try...catch` block is opened to house the parsing code. This is necessary because some of the methods called to carry out the parsing can throw exceptions that must be caught within the program. All of the real work in the program takes place inside the `try` block.

By the Way

> The `try...catch` block is the standard way in which Java handles errors that crop up during the execution of a program. It enables the program to compensate and work around those errors if the user chooses to do so. In this case, you simply print out information about the error and allow the program to exit gracefully.

Within the `try...catch` block, the first order of business is creating a parser object. This object is actually an instance of the class named in the variable `PARSER_NAME`. The fact that you're using it through the `XMLReader` interface means that you can call only those methods included in that interface. For this application, that's fine. The class specified in the `PARSER_NAME` variable is then loaded and assigned to the variable `parser`. Because SAX 2.0 parsers must implement `XMLReader`, you can refer to the interface as an object of that type rather than referring to the class by its own name—`SAXParser`.

After the parser has been created, you can start setting its properties. Before actually parsing the document, however, you have to specify the content and error handlers that the parser will use. Because the `DocumentPrinter` class can play both of those roles, you simply set both of those properties to `dp` (the `DocumentPrinter` object you just created). At this point, all you have to do is call the `parse()` method on the URI passed in on the command line, which is exactly what the code does.

Implementing the `ContentHandler` Interface

The skeleton for the program is now in place. The rest of the program consists of methods that fulfill the requirements of the `ContentHandler` and `ErrorHandler` interfaces. More specifically, these methods respond to events that are triggered during the parsing of an XML document. In this program, the methods just print out the content that they receive.

The first of these methods is the `characters()` method, which is called whenever content is parsed in a document. Following is the code for this method:

```
public void characters(char[] ch, int start, int length) {
  String chars = "";
  for (int i = start; i < start + length; i++)
    chars = chars + ch[i];

    if ((chars.trim()).length() > 0)
      System.out.println("Received characters: " + chars);
}
```

The `characters()` method receives content found within elements. It accepts three arguments: an array of characters, the position in the array where the content starts, and the amount of content received. In this method, a `for` loop is used to extract the content from the array, starting at the position in the array where the content starts, and iterating over each element until the position of the last element is reached. When all of the characters are gathered, the code checks to make sure they aren't just empty spaces, and then prints the results if not.

By the Way

> It's important not to just process all of the characters in the array of characters passed in unless that truly is your intent. The array can contain lots of padding on both sides of the relevant content, and including it all will result in a lot of extra characters along with the content that you actually want. On the other hand, if you know that the code contains parsed character data (PCDATA) that you want to read verbatim, then by all means process all of the characters.

The next two methods, `startDocument()` and `endDocument()`, are called when the beginning and end of the document are encountered, respectively. They accept no arguments and are called only once each during document parsing, for obvious reasons. Here's the code for these methods:

```
public void startDocument() {
  System.out.println("Start document.");
}
```

```
public void endDocument() {
  System.out.println("End of document reached.");
}
```

Next let's look at the `startElement()` and `endElement()` methods, which accept the most complex set of arguments of any of the methods that make up a `ContentHandler`:

```
public void startElement(String namespaceURI, String localName,
  String qName, Attributes atts) {
  System.out.println("Start element: " + localName);
}

public void endElement(String namespaceURI, String localName,
  String qName) {
  System.out.println("End of element: " + localName);
}
```

The `startElement()` method accepts four arguments from the parser. The first is the namespace URI, which you'll see elsewhere as well. The namespace URI is the URI for the namespace associated with the element. If a namespace is used in the document, the URI for the namespace is provided in a namespace declaration. The local name is the name of the element without the namespace prefix. The qualified name is the name of the element including the namespace prefix if there is one. Finally, the attributes are provided as an instance of the `Attributes` object. The `endElement()` method accepts the same first three arguments but not the final attributes argument.

By the Way

SAX parsers must have namespace processing turned on in order to populate all of these attributes. If that option is deactivated, any of the arguments (other than the attributes) may be populated with empty strings. The method for turning on namespace processing varies depending on which parser you use.

Let's look at attribute processing specifically. Attributes are supplied to the `startElement()` method as an instance of the `Attributes` object. In the sample code, you use three methods of the `Attributes` object: `getLength()`, `getLocalName()`, and `getValue()`. The `getLength()` method is used to iterate over the attributes supplied to the method call, while `getLocalName()` and `getValue()` accept the index of the attribute being retrieved as arguments. The code retrieves each attribute and prints out its name and value. In case you're curious, the full list of methods for the `Attributes` object appears in Table 17.1.

TABLE 17.1 Methods of the `Attributes` Object

Method	Purpose
`getIndex(String qName)`	Retrieves an attribute's index using its qualified name
`getIndex(String uri, String localPart)`	Retrieves an attribute's index using its namespace URI and the local portion of its name
`getLength()`	Returns the number of attributes in the element
`getLocalName(int index)`	Returns the local name of the attribute associated with the index
`getQName(int index)`	Returns the qualified name of the attribute associated with the index
`getType(int index)`	Returns the type of the attribute with the supplied index
`getType(String uri, String localName)`	Looks up the type of the attribute with the namespace URI and name specified
`getURI(int index)`	Looks up the namespace URI of the attribute with the index specified
`getValue(int index)`	Looks up the value of the attribute using the index
`getValue(String qName)`	Looks up the value of the attribute using the qualified name
`getValue(String uri, String localName)`	Looks up the value of the attribute using the namespace URI and local name

Getting back to the `endElement()` method, its operation is basically the same as that of `startElement()` except that it doesn't accept the attributes of the element as an argument.

The next two methods, `startPrefixMapping()` and `endPrefixMapping()`, have to do with prefix mappings for namespaces:

```
public void startPrefixMapping(String prefix, String uri) {
  System.out.println("Prefix mapping: " + prefix);
  System.out.println("URI: " + uri);
}

public void endPrefixMapping(String prefix) {
  System.out.println("End of prefix mapping: " + prefix);
}
```

These methods are used to report the beginning and end of namespace prefix mappings when they are encountered in a document.

The next method, `ignorableWhitespace()`, is similar to `characters()`, except that it returns whitespace from element content that can be ignored.

```
public void ignorableWhitespace(char[] ch, int start, int length) {
  System.out.println("Received whitespace.");
}
```

Next on the method agenda is `processingInstruction()`, which reports processing instructions to the content handler. For example, a stylesheet can be associated with an XML document using the following processing instruction:

```
<?xml-stylesheet href="mystyle.css" type="text/css"?>
```

The method that handles such instructions is

```
public void processingInstruction(String target, String data) {
  System.out.println("Received processing instruction:");
  System.out.println("Target: " + target);
  System.out.println("Data: " + data);
}
```

The last method you need to be concerned with is `setDocumentLocator()`, which is called when each and every event is processed. Nothing is output by this method in this program, but I'll explain what its purpose is anyway. Whenever an entity in a document is processed, the parser calls `setDocumentLocator()` with a `Locator` object. The `Locator` object contains information about where in the document the entity currently being processed is located. Here's the "do nothing" source code for the method:

```
public void setDocumentLocator(Locator locator) { }
```

The methods of a `Locator` object are described in Table 17.2.

TABLE 17.2 The Methods of a `Locator` Object

Method	Purpose
`getColumnNumber()`	Returns the column number of the current position in the document being parsed
`getLineNumber()`	Returns the line number of the current position in the document being parsed
`getPublicId()`	Returns the public identifier of the current document event
`getSystemId()`	Returns the system identifier of the current document event

Because the sample program doesn't concern itself with the specifics of locators, none of these methods are actually used. However, it's good for you to know about them in case you need to develop a program that somehow is interested in locators.

Implementing the `ErrorHandler` Interface

I mentioned earlier that the `DocumentPrinter` class implements two interfaces, `ContentHandler` and `ErrorHandler`. Let's look at the methods that are used to implement the `ErrorHandler` interface. There are three types of errors that a SAX parser can generate—errors, fatal errors, and warnings. Classes that implement the `ErrorHandler` interface must provide methods to handle all three types of errors. Here's the source code for the three methods:

```
public void error(SAXParseException exception) { }

public void fatalError(SAXParseException exception) { }

public void warning(SAXParseException exception) { }
```

As you can see, each of the three methods accepts the same argument—a `SAXParseException` object. The only difference between them is that they are called under different circumstances. To keep things simple, the sample program doesn't output any error notifications. For the sake of completeness, the full list of methods supported by `SAXParseException` appears in Table 17.3.

TABLE 17.3 Methods of the `SAXParseException` Interface

Method	Purpose
`getColumnNumber()`	Returns the column number of the current position in the document being parsed
`getLineNumber()`	Returns the line number of the current position in the document being parsed
`getPublicId()`	Returns the public identifier of the current document event
`getSystemId()`	Returns the system identifier of the current document event

Similar to the `Locator` methods, these methods aren't used in the Document Printer sample program, so you don't have to worry about the ins and outs of how they work.

Testing the Document Printer Program

Now that you understand how the code works in the Document Printer sample program, let's take it for a test drive one more time. This time around, you're running the program to parse the condos.xml sample document from the previous hour. Here's an excerpt from that document in case it's already gotten a bit fuzzy in your memory:

```
<proj status="active">
  <location lat="36.122238" long="-86.845028" />
  <description>
    <name>Woodmont Close</name>
    <address>131 Woodmont Blvd.</address>
    <address2>Nashville, TN 37205</address2>
    <img>condowc.jpg</img>
  </description>
</proj>
```

And here's the command required to run this document through the Document Printer program:

```
java -classpath xercesImpl.jar;xml-apis.jar;. DocumentPrinter condos.xml
```

Finally, Listing 17.2 contains the output of the Document Printer program after feeding it the condominium map data stored in the condos.xml document.

LISTING 17.2 The Output of the Document Printer Example Program After Processing the condos.xml Document

```
Start document.
Start element: projects
Start element: proj
Start element: location
End of element: location
Start element: description
Start element: name
Received characters: Woodmont Close
End of element: name
Start element: address
Received characters: 131 Woodmont Blvd.
End of element: address
Start element: address2
Received characters: Nashville, TN 37205
End of element: address2
Start element: img
Received characters: condowc.jpg
End of element: img
End of element: description
End of element: proj
...
Start element: proj
Start element: location
End of element: location
Start element: description
```

```
26: Start element: name
27: Received characters: Harding Hall
28: End of element: name
29: Start element: address
30: Received characters: 2120 Harding Pl.
31: End of element: address
32: Start element: address2
33: Received characters: Nashville, TN 37215
34: End of element: address2
35: Start element: img
36: Received characters: condohh.jpg
37: End of element: img
38: End of element: description
39: End of element: proj
40: End of element: projects
41: End of document reached.
```

The excerpt from the `condos.xml` document that you saw a moment ago corresponds to the first `proj` element in the XML document. Lines 3 through 20 show how the Document Printer program parses and displays detailed information for this element and all of its content.

Summary

In this hour, you learned about one of the two popular APIs for parsing XML files SAX. You already covered the DOM in the previous lesson, so this lesson wrapped up some loose ends in terms of giving you a more rounded understanding of XML parsing. SAX (Simple API for XML) is an event-driven parser that is usually combined with a custom program designed to process the events generated by the parser. You worked through an example of such an application in this hour that demonstrated how to use the Xerces SAX parser to iterate through the entities in an XML document and print out detailed information about them.

Q&A

Q. ***I didn't get any of that Java stuff; how am I supposed to use SAX?***

A. If you found the Java code confusing, you may be better off looking at the documentation for the SAX implementation for a programming language that you're more comfortable using. You may want to do some online investigating to find a SAX parser that's appropriate for you. Keep in mind that the Xerces SAX parser (http://xml.apache.org/) that you used in this lesson is also available for the C++ and Perl languages. Also, if you prefer using JavaScript or Visual Basic you may want to consider using the DOM for XML processing, which you explored in Hour 16, "Parsing XML with the DOM."

Q. *How do I access the data structure created by SAX?*

A. The catch with SAX is that it doesn't create its own data structure; it's up to the programmer who writes the event handlers to generate a data structure, print the XML, or do whatever it is they want to do with the data as it's processed by the SAX parser.

Workshop

The Workshop is designed to help you anticipate possible questions, review what you've learned, and begin learning how to put your knowledge into practice.

Quiz

1. What is an event-driven parser?
2. What standards body was responsible for the creation of SAX?
3. Which important feature was added when SAX was upgraded from version 1.0 to 2.0?

Quiz Answers

1. An event-driven parser iterates through an XML document and calls specific methods in another program as it processes entities in the document being parsed.
2. I admit it, this was a trick question; a standards body did not create SAX. Rather, members of the `xml-dev` mailing list created it through a grassroots effort.
3. SAX 2.0 added support for namespaces.

Exercises

1. Modify the sample program in this hour so that it reproduces the XML document that is supplied as input.
2. Reproduce the sample program in the language that you do your development in (if it's not Java).

HOUR 18

Querying XML Data with XQuery

> For those not familiar with XQuery—it is like XPath + XSLT + Methamphetamines.
>
> —Brian McCallister

I bet this is the first chapter in a computer book to open with a line about methamphetamines. And for good reason, I might add! The idea behind that quote is that XQuery is like a jacked up version of XPath with a little XSLT sprinkled in for good measure. In other words, XQuery is a technology that packs some punch when it comes to drilling deep into XML data and extracting exactly the data in which you're interested. This hour introduces you to *XQuery* and shows you some practical ways to put the language to use with your own XML code.

In this hour, you'll learn the following:

- What XQuery is
- How to write queries using XQuery
- What the Saxon XQuery processor has to offer
- How to execute your own queries using XQuery

What Is XQuery?

In order to explain what XQuery is, I'll first talk about the problem it's designed to solve. As you already know all too well, XML documents have a treelike structure. Let's say you wanted to find all of the elements in a document named `color`. Given what you've learned so far, you'd probably use the DOM to read the document into your application and then iterate over the entire tree in order to extract all the elements called `color`. Sounds easy enough, right? Let's say you wanted to find only the `color` elements that are inside elements called `automobile` or you want to return only those `color` elements that have the value `blue`. I think you can see where I'm going.

When you use XML for data storage, these sorts of problems are very common, so XQuery was created to simplify handling them. If you have an application that supports XQuery, you can write simple queries to perform all the tasks I mentioned in the previous paragraph and many, many more.

XQuery has been around for quite a while but has been slow to catch on. Part of this probably has to do with the fact that XML has yet to replace relational databases as the data storage medium of choice for modern applications, and it may never do so. However, XML has proven itself useful in just about every role outside of efficient data storage and retrieval, and could therefore benefit from an XML-specific query language. Enter XQuery.

By the Way

> For the latest information on XQuery, check out the W3C's XQuery page at http://www.w3.org/TR/xquery/.

XQuery aims to provide XML developers with the data querying power that SQL (Structured Query Language) provides to database developers. Unlike relational databases, which typically have SQL querying features built into their database management systems, you have to use a special tool in order to execute XQuery queries on XML data. This is primarily because there is no concept of a management system for XML data because the data is simply text. Later in the hour you learn how to use a tool to perform XML queries using XQuery.

By the Way

> For a look at how to use SQL to perform queries on a relational database and generate XML results, check out Hour 19, "Using XML with Databases."

XML Data Querying 101

XQuery is one of those technologies that is best understood by jumping in and experimenting with it. So, let's hit the ground running and look at how XQuery is used to query an XML document. The sample XML document, a trimmed down version of a document included in earlier chapters, shown in Listing 18.1, is used in the examples that follow.

LISTING 18.1 A Sample XML Document Containing Vehicle Data

```
<?xml version="1.0"?>

<vehicles>
  <vehicle year="2004" make="Acura" model="3.2TL">
    <mileage>13495</mileage>
    <color>green</color>
    <price>33900</price>
```

```
    <options>
      <option>navigation system</option>
      <option>heated seats</option>
    </options>
  </vehicle>

  <vehicle year="2005" make="Acura" model="3.2TL">
    <mileage>07541</mileage>
    <color>white</color>
    <price>33900</price>
    <options>
      <option>spoiler</option>
      <option>ground effects</option>
    </options>
  </vehicle>

  <vehicle year="2004" make="Acura" model="3.2TL">
    <mileage>18753</mileage>
    <color>white</color>
    <price>32900</price>
    <options />
  </vehicle>
</vehicles>
```

Now let's take a look at some simple XQuery queries that can be used to retrieve data from that document. The syntax for XQuery is very lean, and in fact borrows heavily from a related technology called XPath; you learn a great deal more about XPath in Hour 22, "Addressing and Linking XML Documents." As an example, the query that retrieves all of the `color` elements from the document is:

```
for $c in //color
return $c
```

This query returns the following:

```
<?xml version="1.0" encoding="UTF-8"?>
<color>green</color>
<color>white</color>
<color>white</color>
```

By the Way

> The queries are intended to be typed into an application that supports XQuery, or to be used within XQuery queries that are passed into an XQuery processor. The results of the query are displayed afterward, to show what would be returned.

This query asks to return all of the child elements named `color` in the document. The `//` operator is used to return elements anywhere below another element, which in this case indicates that all `color` elements in the document should be returned. You could have just as easily coded this example as:

```
for $c in vehicles/vehicle/color
return $c
```

The $c in these examples serves as a variable, or placeholder, that holds the results of the query. You can think of the query results as a loop where each matching element is grabbed one after the next. In this case, all you're doing is returning the results for further processing or for writing to an XML document.

If you're familiar with the `for` loop in a programming language such as BASIC, Java, or C++, the `for` construct in XQuery won't be entirely foreign, even if it doesn't involve setting up a counter as in traditional `for` loops.

As the previous code reveals, a/ at the beginning of a query string indicates the root level of the document structure or a relative folder level separation. For example, the query that follows wouldn't return anything because `color` is not the root level element of the document.

```
/color
```

All of this node addressing syntax is technically part of XPath, which makes up a considerable part of the XQuery technology. You learn a great deal more about the ins and outs of XPath in Hour 22. As you can see, aside from a few wrinkles, requesting elements from an XML document using XQuery/XPath isn't all that different from locating files in a file system using a command shell.

In XQuery/XPath, expressions within square brackets ([]) are subqueries. Those expressions are not used to retrieve elements themselves but to qualify the elements that are retrieved. For example, a query such as

```
//vehicle/color
```

retrieves `color` elements that are children of `vehicle` elements. On the other hand, this query

```
//vehicle[color]
```

retrieves `vehicle` elements that have a `color` element as a child. Subqueries are particularly useful when you use them with filters to write very specific queries.

Querying with Wildcards

Continuing along with the vehicle code example, let's say you want to find all of the `option` elements that are grandchildren of the `vehicle` element. To get them all from the sample document, you could just use the query `vehicles/vehicle/options/option`. However, let's say that you didn't know that the intervening element was `options` or that there were other elements that could intervene between `vehicle` and `option`. In that case, you could use the following query:

```
for $o in vehicles/vehicle/*/option
return $o
```

Following are the results of this query:

```
<?xml version="1.0" encoding="UTF-8"?>
<option>navigation system</option>
<option>heated seats</option>
<option>spoiler</option>
<option>ground effects</option>
```

The wildcard (*) matches any element. You can also use it at the end of a query to match all the children of a particular element.

Using Filters to Search for Specific Information

After you've mastered the extraction of specific elements from XML files, you can move on to searching for elements that contain information you specify. Let's say you want to find higher-level elements containing a particular value in a child element. The `[]` operator indicates that the expression within the square braces should be searched but that the element listed to the left of the square braces should be returned. For example, the following expression would read "return any `vehicle` elements that contain a `color` element with a value of `green`:

```
for $v in //vehicle[color='green']
return $v
```

Here are the results:

```
<?xml version="1.0" encoding="UTF-8"?>
<vehicle year="2004" make="Acura" model="3.2TL">
  <mileage>13495</mileage>
  <color>green</color>
  <price>33900</price>
  <options>
    <option>navigation system</option>
    <option>heated seats</option>
  </options>
</vehicle>
```

The full `vehicle` element is returned because it appears to the left of the search expression enclosed in the square braces. You can also use Boolean operators such as and and `or` to string multiple search expressions together. For example, to find all of the vehicles with a `color` of `green` or a `price less than 34000`, you would use the following query:

```
for $v in //vehicle[color='green' or price<'34000']
return $v
```

This query results in the following:

```
<?xml version="1.0" encoding="UTF-8"?>
<vehicle year="2004" make="Acura" model="3.2TL">
  <mileage>13495</mileage>
  <color>green</color>
  <price>33900</price>
  <options>
    <option>navigation system</option>
    <option>heated seats</option>
  </options>
</vehicle>
<vehicle year="2004" make="Acura" model="3.2TL">
  <mileage>18753</mileage>
  <color>white</color>
  <price>32900</price>
  <options/>
</vehicle>
```

The `!=` operator is also available when you want to write expressions to test for inequality. Additionally, there are actually three common Boolean operators: `and`, `or`, and `not`. For example, you can combine these operators to write complex queries, such as this:

```
for $v in //vehicle[not(color='blue' or color='green') and @year='2004']
return $v
```

This example is a little more interesting in that it looks for vehicles that aren't blue or green but that are in the model year 2004. Following are the results:

```
<?xml version="1.0" encoding="UTF-8"?>
<vehicle year="2004" make="Acura" model="3.2TL">
    <mileage>18753</mileage>
    <color>white</color>
    <price>32900</price>
    <options/>
</vehicle>
```

You might be wondering about the at symbol (`@`) in front of the `year` in the query. If you recall from the vehicles sample document (Listing 18.1), `year` is an attribute, not a child element—`@` is used to reference attributes in XQuery. More on attributes in a moment.

Just to make sure you understand subqueries, what if you wanted to retrieve just the options for any white cars in the document? Here's the query:

```
//vehicle[color='white']/options
```

And here's the result:

```
<?xml version="1.0" encoding="UTF-8"?>
<options>
  <option>spoiler</option>
```

```
  <option>ground effects</option>
</options>
<options/>
```

Let's break down that query. Remember that `//` means "anywhere in the hierarchy." The `//vehicle` part indicates that you're looking for elements inside a `vehicle` element. The `[color='white']` part indicates that you're interested only in `vehicle` elements containing `color` elements with a value of `white`. The part you haven't yet seen is `/options`. This indicates that the results should be any `options` elements under `vehicle` elements that contain a `color` element matching `white`.

Referencing Attributes

The next thing to look at is attributes. When you want to refer to an attribute, place an `@` sign before its name. So, to find all the `year` attributes of `vehicle` elements, use the following query:

```
//vehicle/@year
```

You can write a slightly different query that returns all of the `vehicle` elements that have `year` attributes as well:

```
//vehicle[@year]
```

This naturally leads up to writing a query that returns all the `vehicle` elements that have a `year` attribute with a certain value, say `2005`. That complete query is

```
for $v in //vehicle[@year="2005"]
return $v
```

Processing XQuery Results

Thus far I've focused solely on tweaking queries and returning the raw result, which is a collection of nodes. Realistically, you will often want to further process the results of a query to extract information from the nodes and transform it for display purposes or to pass along to another application or service. It's very straightforward to further process query results and package them within other surrounding XML code to effectively create transformed data. You can even transform query results into HTML code that can be viewed as a web page.

The key to incorporating query results into surrounding code is curly braces (`{}`), which you use to surround query data. Before you can do that, however, you need to know how to access the content within a node. You do this by calling the XQuery `data()` function and supplying it with the node in question. Following is an example of formatting a query result:

```
for $c in //color
return <p>Vehicle color: {data($c)}</p>
```

When executed on the vehicle sample document, this code results in the following:

```
<?xml version="1.0" encoding="UTF-8"?>
<p>Vehicle color: green</p>
<p>Vehicle color: white</p>
<p>Vehicle color: white</p>
```

As you can see, the value of each `color` element is extracted and included in a <p> tag that would be suitable for inclusion within an HTML document.

You can also process attributes directly from a query string to get more interesting results, as in the following query:

```
xquery version "1.0";
<p>
Following are all of the white vehicles:<br />
{ for $v in //vehicle[color='white']
return <div>{data($v/@year)} - {data($v/@make)} - {data($v/@model)}</div>
}
</p>
```

This code demonstrates how a query can be placed within other XML (XHTML) code by enclosing it in `{}`. The resulting XHTML code is then readily viewed within a web browser:

```
<?xml version="1.0" encoding="UTF-8"?>
<p>
Following are all of the white vehicles:<br/>
   <div>2005 - Acura - 3.2TL</div>
   <div>2004 - Acura - 3.2TL</div>
</p>
```

One last trick for formatting queries involves the XQuery `order by` statement, which allows you to set the order of query results. Following is the same query you just saw, except this time the query results are ordered by price:

```
xquery version "1.0";
<p>
Following are all of the white vehicles:<br />
{ for $v in //vehicle[color='white']
order by $v/price
return <div>{data($v/@year)} - {data($v/@make)} - {data($v/@model)}</div>
}
</p>
```

Because the price isn't shown in the output, this ordering isn't quite so meaningful in this particular example, but it will be as you explore more interesting examples a little later in the hour.

Getting to Know Saxon

None of this XQuery stuff would mean much if you didn't have a tool that can process and return query results. One such tool that I've found to be particularly useful is Saxon, which was developed by Michael Kay. Saxon comes in two versions, a commercial version and a free open source version. You'll find that the free open source version of Saxon will probably serve your needs just fine, at least for now as you learn the ropes of XQuery. If you have some grand plans for XQuery in the works, by all means check into the full commercial version of XQuery as well. You can find both versions online at http://www.saxonica.com/.

Saxon is a command-line tool that you use to execute XQuery queries. Saxon is built as a Java application, so you'll need to have the Java runtime installed in order to run Saxon. You can download the Java runtime (J2SE) from http://java.sun.com/j2se/1.4.2/download.html. After downloading and installing both Java and Saxon, it's important to set the Java `CLASSPATH` environment variable before attempting to run Saxon. The purpose of this variable is to let Java know where all of the executable class files are located when it tries to run an application. In the case of Saxon, you're interested in letting Java know about the file `saxon8.jar`, which is located in the main Saxon folder, usually `\saxon`.

To set the `CLASSPATH` variable for Saxon, just issue this command at the command line:

```
set classpath=%classpath%;\saxon\saxon8.jar
```

By the Way

> You may want to double-check the Saxon documentation for your specific version to make sure the `.JAR` file has the same name as I've mentioned here (`saxon8.jar`). If not, just change the code to match the file you have.

You're now ready to run Saxon but you need to know how to run it. However, before you get to that you need to understand how queries are stored for XQuery. XQuery documents are stored in files with a `.XQ` file extension. In addition to the query code, all XQuery documents are required to start with the following line of code:

```
xquery version "1.0";
```

The query code then follows after this line. So you have an XQuery document with a `.XQ` file extension and an XML file with probably a `.XML` file extension, and you're ready to run the query on the XML document. Just issue the following command at the command line:

```
java net.sf.saxon.Query -s xmldoc.xml querydoc.xq > outdoc.xml
```

In this sample command, xmldoc.xml is the XML source document, querydoc.xq is the XQuery document, and outdoc.xml is the output document that the query results are written to. There are numerous other options you can use with Saxon but this basic command is all you need to get going running your own queries.

Practical XML Querying with XQuery and Saxon

I promised earlier that I would pull together everything you've learned about XQuery and show you a couple of practical examples. The remainder of the lesson focuses on a couple of sample queries that operate on the same XML data. This data is stored in the familiar training log XML document that you've seen in earlier lessons. A partial listing of this document is shown in Listing 18.2.

LISTING 18.2 A Partial Listing of the Training Log XML Document

```
<?xml version="1.0"?>
<!DOCTYPE trainlog SYSTEM "etml.dtd">

<trainlog>
  <!— This session was part of the marathon training group run. —>
  <session date="11/19/05" type="running" heartrate="158">
    <duration units="minutes">45</duration>
    <distance units="miles">5.5</distance>
    <location>Warner Park</location>
    <comments>Mid-morning run, a little winded throughout.</comments>
  </session>

  <session date="11/21/05" type="cycling" heartrate="153">
    <duration units="hours">2.5</duration>
    <distance units="miles">37.0</distance>
    <location>Natchez Trace Parkway</location>
    <comments>Hilly ride, felt strong as an ox.</comments>
  </session>

  ...
</trainlog>
```

The first sample query I want to show you involves plucking out a certain type of training session and then transforming it into a different XML format. This might be useful in a situation where you are interfacing two applications that don't share the same data format. Listing 18.3 contains the code for the query, which is stored in the file trainlog1.xq.

LISTING 18.3 A Query to Retrieve and Transform Running Sessions

```
xquery version "1.0";

<runsessions>
```

```
  { for $s in //trainlog/session[@type="running"]
    order by $s/date
    return <location>{$s/@date} {data($s/location)} ({data($s/distance)}
{data($s/distance/@units)})</location>
  }
</runsessions>
```

To issue this query against the `trainlog.xml` document using Saxon, just issue the following command from within the main Saxon folder:

```
java net.sf.saxon.Query -s trainlog.xml trainlog1.xq >output1.xml
```

By the Way

> If you run the sample query from within the main Saxon folder as I've suggested, make sure to copy the sample files into that folder so that Saxon can access them. Otherwise, you can add the main Saxon folder to your path and run it from anywhere.

This command executes the query and writes the results to the file `output1.xml`, which is shown in Listing 18.4.

LISTING 18.4 The XQuery Results of the Running Query

```
<?xml version="1.0" encoding="UTF-8"?>
<runsessions>
  <location date="11/19/05">Warner Park (5.5miles)</location>
  <location date="11/24/05">Warner Park (8.5miles)</location>
  <location date="11/26/05">Metro Center (7.5miles)</location>
  <location date="11/29/05">Warner Park (10.0miles)</location>
  <location date="11/31/05">Warner Park (12.5miles)</location>
  <location date="12/04/05">Warner Park (13.5miles)</location>
</runsessions>
```

As the listing reveals, only the running training sessions are returned, and they are formatted into a new XML structure that is somewhat different than the original training log. The `<location>` tag may look familiar but it now contains the `date` attribute, which was previously a part of the `<session>` tag. The new code also combines the location, distance, and distance units into the content of the `<location>` tag. And finally, the individual `location` elements are packaged within a new root element named `runsessions`.

Although the previous example is certainly interesting in terms of how it transforms XML data, it doesn't give you anything remarkable to look at. What would be even better is to see the results of a query in a web browser. Of course, this requires transforming query results into HTML code. Listing 18.5 contains a query that grabs every training log session and transforms it into an HTML document with carefully formatted table rows for each row of query data.

LISTING 18.5 A Query to Format Training Sessions into an HTML Document

```
 1: xquery version "1.0";
 2:
 3: <html>
 4:   <head>
 5:     <title>Training Sessions</title>
 6:   </head>
 7:
 8:   <body style="text-align:center">
 9:     <h1>Training Sessions</h1>
10:     <table border="1px">
11:       <tr>
12:         <th>Date</th>
13:         <th>Type</th>
14:         <th>Heart Rate</th>
15:         <th>Location</th>
16:         <th>Duration</th>
17:         <th>Distance</th>
18:       </tr>
19:       { for $s in //session
20:         return <tr> <td>{data($s/@date)}</td> <td>{data($s/@type)}</td>
21:         <td>{data($s/@heartrate)}</td>
22:         <td>{data($s/location)}</td>
23:         <td>{data($s/duration)} {data($s/duration/@units)}</td>
24:         <td>{data($s/distance)} {data($s/distance/@units)}</td> </tr>
25:       }
26:     </table>
27:   </body>
28: </html>
```

This query is certainly more involved than anything you've seen thus far in this lesson but it really isn't very complicated—most of the code is just HTML wrapper code to format the query results for display. Pay particular attention to how each piece of XML data is carefully wrapped in a `<td>` element so that it is arranged within an HTML table (lines 20 through 24).

The following command is all it takes to generate an HTML document using the query in Listing 18.5:

```
java net.sf.saxon.Query -s trainlog.xml trainlog2.xq >output2.html
```

Listing 18.6 contains the transformed HTML (XHTML) document that results from this Saxon command.

LISTING 18.6 The Partial XQuery Results of the Training Session Query

```
<?xml version="1.0" encoding="UTF-8"?>
<html>
  <head>
    <title>Training Sessions</title>
  </head>
  <body style="text-align:center">
```

```
      <h1>Training Sessions</h1>
      <table border="1px">
        <tr>
          <th>Date</th>
          <th>Type</th>
          <th>Heart Rate</th>
          <th>Location</th>
          <th>Duration</th>
          <th>Distance</th>
        </tr>
        <tr>
          <td>11/19/05</td>
          <td>running</td>
          <td>158</td>
          <td>Warner Park</td>
          <td>45minutes</td>
          <td>5.5miles</td>
        </tr>
        ...
      </table>
    </body>
</html>
```

No surprises here—just a basic HTML document with a table full of training log information. I've deliberately only showed the partial results since the table data is actually fairly long due to the number of training log elements. Figure 18.1 shows this web page as viewed in Internet Explorer.

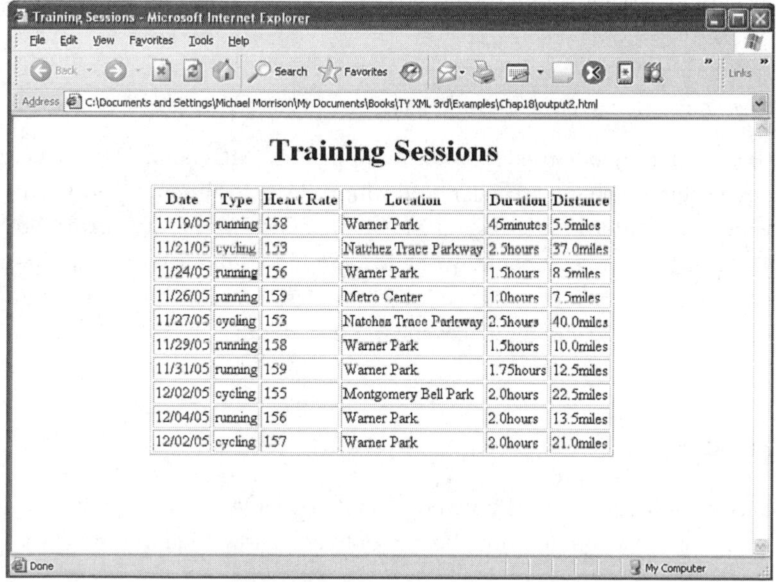

Date	Type	Heart Rate	Location	Duration	Distance
11/19/05	running	158	Warner Park	45minutes	5.5miles
11/21/05	cycling	153	Natchez Trace Parkway	2.5hours	37.0miles
11/24/05	running	156	Warner Park	1.5hours	8.5miles
11/26/05	running	159	Metro Center	1.0hours	7.5miles
11/27/05	cycling	153	Natchez Trace Parkway	2.5hours	40.0miles
11/29/05	running	158	Warner Park	1.5hours	10.0miles
11/31/05	running	159	Warner Park	1.75hours	12.5miles
12/02/05	cycling	155	Montgomery Bell Park	2.0hours	22.5miles
12/04/05	running	156	Warner Park	2.0hours	13.5miles
12/02/05	cycling	157	Warner Park	2.0hours	21.0miles

FIGURE 18.1
The training session HTML query result document as viewed in Internet Explorer.

Finally, some visible results from XQuery! XQuery is a powerful technology that makes it possible to drill down into the inner depths of XML code and extract data with a great deal of precision. This hour and the two examples you just saw truly only scratch the surface of XQuery.

Summary

This hour introduced you to XQuery, which is a query language that makes it relatively easy to extract specific elements from an XML document. XQuery is analogous to SQL in the relational database world in that it allows you to construct queries that you execute against XML documents to retrieve matching data. In this lesson, you learned how to construct a variety of different kinds of queries using XQuery. You learned that XQuery is closely linked to another XML technology, XPath. You wrapped up the hour by working your way through a couple of interesting XQuery examples, which hopefully reinforced what you learned throughout the lesson as a whole.

Q&A

Q. ***Is XQuery supported in any web browsers?***

A. Not yet. Unfortunately, none of the major browsers support XQuery just yet, although rumors abound that XQuery support is underway for upcoming releases.

Q. ***How does XQuery differ from XPath?***

A. XPath is a language used for addressing within XML documents. XQuery is a query language used to filter data within XML documents. XPath can also be used for pattern matching on XML documents and in fact serves that role within XQuery. Fundamentally, the two languages differ more in purpose than in design. XQuery solves a larger problem and incorporates XPath toward that end. Chapter 22 covers XPath in detail.

Workshop

The Workshop is designed to help you anticipate possible questions, review what you've learned, and begin learning how to put your knowledge into practice.

Quiz

1. How do the queries `//vehicle[color='red']` and `//vehicle[color='red']/color` differ?

2. How do you indicate that a query entity is an attribute rather than an element?

3. How do you embed query results within other XML code?

Quiz Answers

1. The first of the two queries returns `vehicle` elements that contain a `color` element set to `red`. The second of the two queries returns the `color` elements that are children of those same `vehicle` elements.

2. Names that begin with `@` are treated as attributes; names with no qualifier are elements.

3. Enclose the query results in `{}`.

Exercises

1. Download an implementation of XQuery, such as Saxon, and use it to write some queries against your own XML documents. You can download a free open source version of Saxon from http://www.saxonica.com/.

HOUR 19

Using XML with Databases

> Good data modeling is as important as it ever was, XML or no.
>
> —Thomas B. Passin

Although XML is certainly a great storage format for shuttling data around the Web, most web applications store their data in relational databases. Knowing this, it stands to reason that many web applications will end up accessing data from a database yet interacting with it and sharing it with other applications as XML data. This has a lot do with the fact that XML can be used not only as a document format, but also as a way to represent data in a highly structured manner. In this hour, you learn how relational databases work and how you can integrate your XML applications with relational databases. More specifically, you find out how to export database data as XML code, as well as how to make SQL queries on a database and format the results in XML. In this hour you'll learn

- The basic theory behind the relational database model
- How to use SQL, the query language for relational databases
- How to export data from a database as XML
- How to write a program that queries a database and formats the results as XML

A Quick Relational Database Primer

Before you can learn about relating XML to databases, you need to learn about databases themselves. When most people think of databases, they're thinking specifically about relational databases. All of the popular database products—Microsoft SQL Server, Oracle, IBM DB2, MySQL—use the relational model. In turn, most web and business applications use one relational database or another for data storage.

The relational database model is all about tables. All of the data is stored in a tabular format, and relationships between tables are expressed through data shared among those tables. Tables in relational databases are just like tables in HTML or tables in this book. They consist of rows and columns. Each row represents a record in the database, and each column represents one field in each of the records.

A group of tables is generally referred to as a *schema*, which conceptually isn't all that different from an XML schema. In a schema, some or all of the tables are generally related to one another. Let's look at how those relationships work. Ordinarily, every table contains a column (or group of columns) that contains data that uniquely identifies that row in the table. In most cases, this is an ID field that simply contains a number that sets that row apart from the others in the table. This value is referred to as the primary key. In relational database design, the primary key is extremely important because it is the root of relationships between tables.

Here's a simple example. Let's say you have a table called `students`. The `students` table contains, among other bits of data, a column called `id_students`. The table might also include the student's name, address, and phone number. You might also have a second table, called `majors`. This table contains the major and minor for all of the students, under the assumption that no student has more than one major or minor.

This is what is referred to as a one-to-one relationship. Each record in the `students` table can have one corresponding row in the `majors` table. There are two other types of relationships between tables—one-to-many and many-to-many. The `students` table contains a column called `id_students`, which serves as its primary key. The `majors` table should contain a column that contains student IDs. This is referred to as a foreign key, because it's a reference to a primary key in another table. The foreign key is used to implement the one-to-one relationship between the records in the two tables.

In a one-to-many relationship, a record in one table can have a reference to many records in a second table, but each record in the second table can have a reference to only one record in the first table. Here's an example: Let's say I create a table called `grades`, which contains a column for student IDs as well as columns for class names and the grades themselves. Because a student can take multiple classes, but each grade applies to only one student, the relationship between `students` and `grades` is a one-to-many relationship. In this case, `id_students` in the `grades` table is a foreign key relating to the `students` table.

An example of a many-to-many relationship is the relationship between students and classes. Each student is usually enrolled in several classes, and each class usually contains multiple students. In a relational database, such a relationship is expressed using what is sometimes referred to as a joining table—a table that exists solely to express the relationship between two pieces of data. The schema contains two tables, `students` and `classes`. You already know about the `students` table; the `classes` table contains information about the classes offered—the name of the professor, the room where the class is held, and the time at which the class is scheduled.

> **By the Way**
>
> Before you can deal with integrating databases and XML, you need to understand both databases and XML. You've been learning about XML for a while now, so consider this a crash course in database theory.

To relate `students` to `classes`, you need a third table, called `classes_students` (or a similarly descriptive name). At a bare minimum, this table must include two columns, `id_students` and `id_classes`, both of which are foreign keys pointing to the `students` and `classes` tables, respectively. These two columns are used to express the many-to-many relationship. In other words, both of the other two tables have one-to-many relationships with this table. Using this table, each student can be associated with several classes, and each class can be associated with any number of students. It may also contain properties that are specific to the relationship, rather than to either a student or a class specifically. For example, a student's grade or her attendance record for the class might be stored in this table. This table structure is illustrated in Figure 19.1.

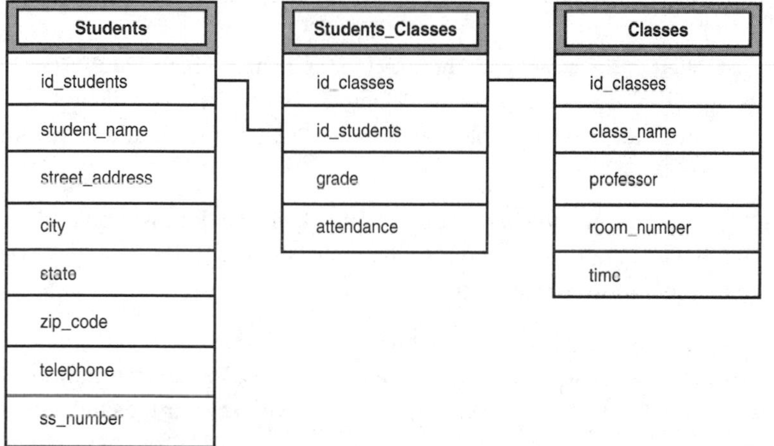

FIGURE 19.1
The tables in a many-to-many relationship.

The World's Shortest Guide to SQL

One term you can't go far into databases without encountering is SQL, which stands for Structured Query Language. SQL is the language used to retrieve, add, modify, and delete records in databases. Let's look at each of these features in turn.

> **By the Way**
>
> Incidentally, the pronunciation of SQL is somewhat of a contentious issue. The official party line is that SQL should be pronounced "es queue el." However, many people opt for the more casual and also more efficient pronunciation, "sequel." Count me in the latter camp!

Retrieving Records Using SELECT

Just about everything in SQL is carried out via a query, which is simply the act of communicating with the database according to an established set of SQL commands. The query used to retrieve data from a database is called the SELECT statement. It has several parts, not all of which are mandatory. The most basic SELECT statement is composed of two parts—the select list and the FROM clause. A very simple SELECT statement looks like this:

```
SELECT *
FROM students
```

Following are the database records returned as the results of the query:

```
+-------------+----------------+--------------------+-------+----------------+---------+
| id_students | student_name   | city               | state | classification | tuition |
+-------------+----------------+--------------------+-------+----------------+---------+
|           1 | Franklin Pierce | Hillsborough       | NH    | senior         |    5000 |
|           2 | James Polk     | Mecklenburg County | NC    | freshman       |   11000 |
|           2 | Warren Harding | Marion             | OH    | junior         |    3500 |
+-------------+----------------+--------------------+-------+----------------+---------+
```

In this case, the * is the select list. The select list indicates which database columns should be included in the query results. When a * is supplied, it indicates that all of the columns in the table or tables listed in the FROM clause should be included in the query results.

The FROM clause contains the list of tables from which the data will be retrieved. In this case, the data is retrieved from just one table, students. I'll explain how to retrieve data from multiple tables in a bit.

Let's go back to the select list. If you use a select list that isn't simply *, you include a list of column names separated by commas. You can also rename columns in the query results (useful in certain situations), using the AS keyword, as follows:

```
SELECT id_students AS id, student_name, state
FROM students
```

As the results show, only the student name and state columns are returned for the records:

```
+----+-----------------+-------+
| id | student_name    | state |
+----+-----------------+-------+
|  1 | Franklin Pierce | NH    |
|  2 | James Polk      | NC    |
|  2 | Warren Harding  | OH    |
+----+-----------------+-------+
```

The id_students column is renamed id in the query results using the reserved word 'AS'. The other keyword you'll often use in a select statement is DISTINCT. When you include DISTINCT at the beginning of a select statement, it indicates that no duplicates should be included in the query results. Here's a sample query:

```
SELECT DISTINCT city
FROM students
```

And here are the results:

```
+-------------------+
| city              |
+-------------------+
| Hillsborough      |
| Mecklenburg County |
| Marion            |
+-------------------+
```

Without DISTINCT, this query would return the city of every student in the students table. In this case, it returns only the distinct values in the table, regardless of how many of each of them there are. In this case, there are only three records in the table and each of them has a unique city, so the result set is the same as it would be if DISTINCT were left off.

The WHERE Clause

Both of the previous queries simply return all of the records in the students table. Often, you'll want to constrain the resultset so that it returns only those records you're actually interested in. The WHERE clause is used to specify which records in a table should be included in the results of a query. Here's an example:

```
SELECT student_name
FROM students
WHERE id_students = 1
```

Only the record with the matching ID is returned in the results:

```
+-----------------+
| student_name    |
+-----------------+
| Franklin Pierce |
+-----------------+
```

When you use the WHERE clause, you must include an expression that filters the query results. In this case, the expression is very simple. Given that id_students is the primary key for this table, this query is sure to return only one row. You can use other comparison operators as well, like the > or != operators. It's also possible to use

Boolean operators to create compound expressions. For example, you can retrieve all of the students who pay more than $10,000 per year in tuition and who are classified as freshmen using the following query:

```
SELECT student_name
FROM students
WHERE tuition > 10000
AND classification = 'freshman'
```

Following are the results of this query:

```
+--------+
¦ student_name ¦
+--------+
¦ James Polk   ¦
+--------+
```

There are also several other functions you can use in the `WHERE` clause that enable you to write more powerful queries. The `LIKE` function allows you to search for fields containing a particular string using a regular expression like syntax. The `BETWEEN` function allows you to search for values between the two you specify, and `IN` allows you to test whether a value is a member of a set you specify.

Because the goal in this hour is ultimately to learn how to use XML with databases, I won't go into any more detail on these query functions, but feel free to do some additional SQL learning online at http://www.w3schools.com/sql/default.asp, or pick up a book on SQL. Fortunately, you don't have to be a SQL guru to get the benefits of this lesson.

Inserting Records

The `INSERT` statement is used to insert records into a table. The syntax is simple, especially if you plan on populating every column in a table. To insert a record into `majors`, use the following statement:

```
INSERT INTO majors
VALUES (115, 50, 'Math', 'English')
```

The values in the list correspond to the `id_majors`, `id_students`, `major`, and `minor` columns respectively. If you only want to specify values for a subset of the columns in the table, you must specify the names of the columns as well, as in the following:

```
INSERT INTO students
(id_students, student_name)
VALUES (50, 'Milton James')
```

When you create tables, you can specify whether values are required in certain fields, and you can also specify default values for fields. For example, the `classification` column might default to freshman because most new student records being inserted will be for newly enrolled students, who are classified as freshmen.

Updating Records

When you want to modify one or more records in a table, the UPDATE statement is used. Here's an example:

```
UPDATE students
SET classification = 'senior'
```

The previous SQL statement will work, but I bet you can figure out what's wrong with it. Nowhere is it specified which records to update. If you don't tell it which records to update, it just assumes that you want to update all of the records in the table, thus the previous query would turn all of the students into seniors. That's probably not what you have in mind. Fortunately, the UPDATE statement supports the WHERE clause, just like the SELECT statement.

```
UPDATE students
SET classification = 'senior'
WHERE id_students = 1
```

That's more like it. This statement updates the classification of only one student. You can also update multiple columns with one query, as in the following:

```
UPDATE students
SET classification = 'freshman', tuition = 7500
WHERE id_students = 5
```

As you can see from the example, you can supply a list of fields to update with your UPDATE statement, and they will all be updated by the same query.

Deleting Records

The last SQL statement I'll discuss is the DELETE statement, which is similar to the UPDATE statement. It accepts a FROM clause, and optionally a WHERE clause. If you leave out the WHERE clause, it deletes all the records in the table. Here's an example:

```
DELETE FROM students
WHERE id_students = 1
```

You now know just enough about SQL to get into trouble! Actually, your newfound SQL knowledge will come in handy a bit later in the lesson when you develop an application that carefully extracts data from a database and encodes it in XML. But first, you find out how to export an entire database table as XML.

Databases and XML

When you integrate XML with databases, the first question that you must look at is how you're using XML in your application. There are two broad categories of XML applications—those that use XML for data storage, and those that use XML as a document format. The approach for database integration depends on which category your application falls into.

Although XML is commonly thought of as a document format, it's also very popular as a format for data storage. Many applications use XML files to store their configuration, as well as relying on remote procedure calling services like XML-RPC and SOAP to format the messages that they exchange using XML.

The fact that XML is highly structured and can be tested to ensure that it's both well-formed and valid in a standardized, programatic fashion takes a lot of the burden of reading and modifying the data file off of the application developer when he or she is writing a program.

Let's look at a couple of real world examples where XML might need to be integrated with a relational database. The structured nature of XML makes it a good choice to use as a data interchange format. Let's say that a company periodically receives inventory information from a supplier. That information might be stored in an Oracle database on a server in the supplier's system but might need to be imported into an Access database when the company receives it. XML would make a good intermediate format for the data because it's easy to write programs that import and export the data and because, by using XML, the data can be used in future applications that require it as well.

Another example might be a service that syndicates news articles. The news articles could be distributed via XML files so that they could easily be transformed for presentation on the Web, or they could be imported into a relational database and published from there.

Incidentally, there already exists an XML language for storing news articles in XML documents. You learn a great deal more about XML and how it can be used to code news articles in Hour 24, "Syndicating the Web with RSS News Feeds."

Resolving XML Data into Database Tables

The question you face when you integrate applications that use XML for data storage with relational databases is the degree to which you want to take advantage of the features of the relational database. If you simply insert entire XML documents into the database, you can't use advanced SQL features to retrieve specific bits of information from the XML documents.

Here's an XML document that is used to store information related to automobiles:

```
<dealership>
  <automobile make="Buick" model="Century" color="blue">
    <options>
      <option>cruise control</option>
      <option>CD player</option>
    </options>
  </automobile>
  <automobile make="Ford" model="Thunderbird" color="red">
    <options>
      <option>convertible</option>
      <option>leather interior</option>
      <option>heated seats</option>
    </options>
  </automobile>
</dealership>
```

Now, let's look at how you might design a database to store this information. As I mentioned earlier, the path of least resistance is just to stick the whole XML document in a field. However, that probably isn't a good idea for this file because it contains more than one automobile "record."

Instead, let's look at what a database schema for the information in the XML file would look like. A diagram of the schema appears in Figure 19.2.

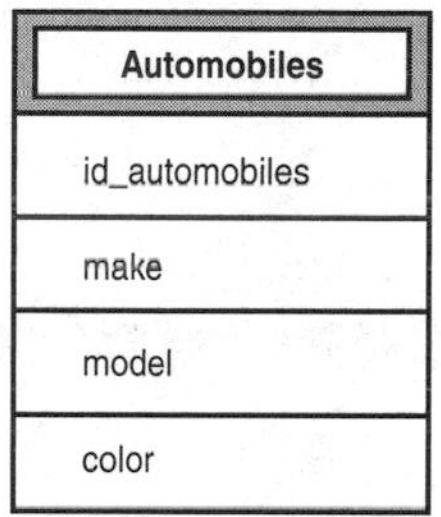

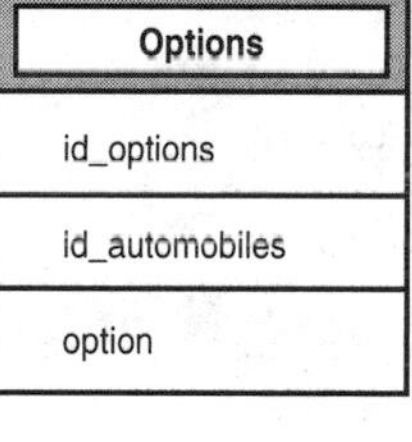

FIGURE 19.2 The schema that corresponds to the `automobiles` example XML document.

As you can see, I turned the XML document into two tables, `automobiles` and `options`. The `automobiles` table contains all the information stored in the attributes of the `automobile` tag in the XML document. Because automobiles have a one-to-many relationship to options, I created a separate table for them. In the options table, `id_automobiles` is a foreign key that relates back to a specific automobile in the automobiles table.

To make sure you understand why the automobile options were broken out into a separate database table, consider that the number of options for a single automobile can vary from one automobile to the next. This is a scenario where a single database field in the `automobiles` table can't account for a varying amount of data; hence the one-to-many relationship. Therefore, the solution is to break out the options into a separate table where each row is tied back to a specific automobile. Then you can add as many options as you want for one automobile as long as each option includes the appropriate automobile ID.

Storing XML Documents in a Database

If you're storing entire XML documents in a database, you don't need to worry about translating the XML document format into a tabular database structure. Instead, you just need to extract the information from the document that you need to use in the relational database world and create columns for that. As an example, if you store newspaper articles as XML documents, the section, headline, author, body, and perhaps more information will all be included in the XML document within their own tags. It is then possible to process the XML code to access each portion of the document.

If you store those documents in a database and plan on publishing them on the Web from that database, you may want to consider breaking up the XML data so that it can be retrieved more easily. For example, you might want separate columns for the section and writer so that you can write simple SQL statements that retrieve the documents based on those values. Either way, you would be retrieving XML code from the database, which is far different than the earlier automobile example where the database data has been translated from XML into pure database content.

Exporting an XML Document from a Database

If you need to pull data from a database for processing as XML on a one-time basis, or maybe periodically but not necessarily in real-time, you might consider just exporting the data manually. Most databases offer an "export as XML" option that converts a database table into a structured XML document with the database columns turned into XML tags. This is a very simple approach to quickly generating an XML document from a database that you might now otherwise be able to access without database tools.

I regularly use the MySQL database for online projects. MySQL is a very popular open source database that does a great job for small- to medium-scale applications. A nice front-end is available for MySQL called phpMyAdmin, which provides a web-based user interface for interacting with a MySQL database. phpMyAdmin provides a very easy-to-use export feature that will export any MySQL database as an XML document.

By the Way

If you're interested in using MySQL and phpMyAdmin, please visit http://www.mysql.com/ and http://www.phpmyadmin.net/. The details of installing and configuring a MySQL database are unfortunately beyond the scope of this lesson but you'll find plenty of information at the previously mentioned web sites.

To get started exporting an XML document from a MySQL database, open the database in phpMyAdmin, and select the table you want to export. Then click the Export tab. Within the Export options, click XML to indicate that XML is the output data format. If you want to generate an XML file that is stored on the web server, click the Save As File option. Otherwise, just click the Go button to generate the XML code and view it directly in the browser. Figure 19.3 shows how the exported XML document is shown in a web browser.

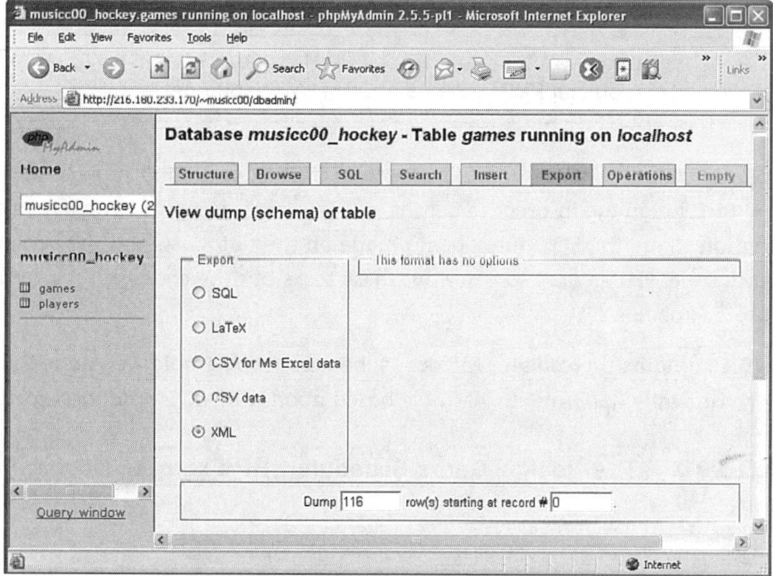

FIGURE 19.3 The newly exported XML document is immediately opened in the web browser.

Now you can choose to save the XML file locally or otherwise use the XML code for further processing and manipulation. The key point to realize is that with one button click you've converted an entire tabular database into a well-formed XML document.

Accessing Data from a Database as XML

Although manually exporting an XML document from a database can be useful, it isn't quite the same as drilling into a database via a SQL query and extracting exactly the data you need. A more realistic example would involve generating XML code on the fly based upon a SQL query. Fortunately, I have exactly such an example for you to check out.

The example you're about to see extracts data from a real database that I created to manage the statistics for my recreational hockey team, Music City Mafia. The database is a MySQL database that stores statistics for both games and players. In this example, you're only concerned with game data, which is stored in a database table called games. To access the data and initiate a SQL query, I'm using PHP, which is an open source scripting language used to create dynamic web pages. PHP has very good integration with MySQL, and is a great option for dynamic web page development that involves MySQL databases and XML.

By the Way

> PHP is a recursive acronym that stands for PHP Hypertext Processer. To learn more about PHP, visit the official PHP web site at http://www.php.net/.

Although the code you're about to see is written in PHP, you don't have to understand the PHP language in order to get the gist of what's going on. The key things to pay attention to are the SQL query being made on the database and the generation of the XML code. PHP is used to carry out these tasks but the code isn't too terribly difficult to decipher.

Listing 19.1 contains the code for the `mcm_schedule.php` sample web page that uses PHP to dynamically generate an XML file based upon a MySQL database query.

LISTING 19.1 The Hockey Game Schedule PHP Example Document

```
<?php
// Connect to the database
$mcm_db = mysql_connect("localhost", "admin", "password");
mysql_select_db("mcm_hockey", $mcm_db);

// Issue the query
$mcm_query = sprintf("SELECT date, time, opponent, location, type, outcome,
  gf, ga, overtime FROM games WHERE season=\"%s\" ORDER BY
  date", $season);
$mcm_result = mysql_query($mcm_query, $mcm_db);

// Format the query results as XML
if (mysql_num_rows($mcm_result) > 0) {
  // Assemble the XML code
```

```
15:   $xml ="<?xml version=\"1.0\" encoding=\"UTF-8\" ?>\r\n";
16:   $xml .="<games>\r\n";
17:   while (list($date, $time, $opponent, $location, $type, $outcome,
18:     $gf, $ga, $overtime) = mysql_fetch_array($mcm_result)) {
19:     $formatted_date = date("F j, Y", strtotime($date));
20:     $formatted_time = date("g:ia", strtotime($time));
21:     $xml .= sprintf("  <game date=\"%s\" time=\"%s\">\r\n",
22:       $formatted_date, $formatted_time);
23:     $xml .= sprintf("    <opponent>%s</opponent>\r\n", $opponent);
24:     $xml .= sprintf("    <location>%s</location>\r\n", $location);
25:     $xml .= sprintf("    <score outcome=\"%s\" overtime=\"%s\">
26:       %s - %s</score>\r\n", $outcome, $overtime, $gf, $ga);
27:     $xml .= "  </game>\r\n";
28:   }
29:   $xml .="</games>";
30:
31:   // Write the XML code to the file mcm_results.xml
32:   $file= fopen("mcm_results.xml", "w");
33:   fwrite($file, $xml);
34:   fclose($file);
35:
36:   echo "The XML document has been written - <a href=\"mcm_results.xml\">
37:     view the XML code.</a>";
38: } else {
39:   echo "Sorry, no matching records found.";
40: }
41: // Close the database
42: mysql_close($mcm_db);
43:?>
```

The first few lines of the page establish a database connection and open the Music City Mafia hockey database. A SQL query is then constructed based upon a parameter (`$season`) that is passed into the page via the URL. The point of this parameter is to allow you to limit the XML file to a particular season of data. For example, to generate an XML file with only the game data for the 2005 Summer hockey season, the following URL is used: http://www.musiccitymafia.com/mcm_schedule.php?season=Summer%202005.

The `%20` near the end of URL is just a separator to provide a space between the word `Summer` and the word `2005`. The result of this URL is that the mcm_schedule.php web page assigns the value `Summer 2005` to the variable `$season`, which can then be used throughout the PHP code. And, in fact, it is when the SQL query is issued in lines 7 through 9 of the listing. More specifically, the date, time, opponent, location, type, outcome, goals for, goals against, and overtime database fields are selected from the games table but only for the Summer 2005 season. The result of this query is stored in the `$mcm_result` variable (line 10).

By the Way

> In PHP programming, all variable names are preceded by a dollar sign (`$`).

The next big chunk of code goes through the results of the SQL query one record at a time, formatting the data into XML code. Notice that the XML processor directive is first generated (line 15), followed by a root tag, `<games>` (line 16). Each piece of pertinent game data is then further formatted into XML code in lines 17 through 28. The document is wrapped up with a closing `</games>` tag in line 29.

The last important step in the PHP code is writing the XML data to a file. The file is named `mcm_results.xml`, and the XML data is written to it with just a few lines of code (lines 32 to 34). A simple line of HTML code is then written to the browser so that you can access the XML file. More specifically, a link is generated that allows you to click and view the XML document (lines 36 and 37).

The remaining code in the PHP web page prints an error message if no records were found for the database query (line 39), and then closes the database (line 42).

Figure 19.4 shows the finished PHP document as viewed in Internet Explorer.

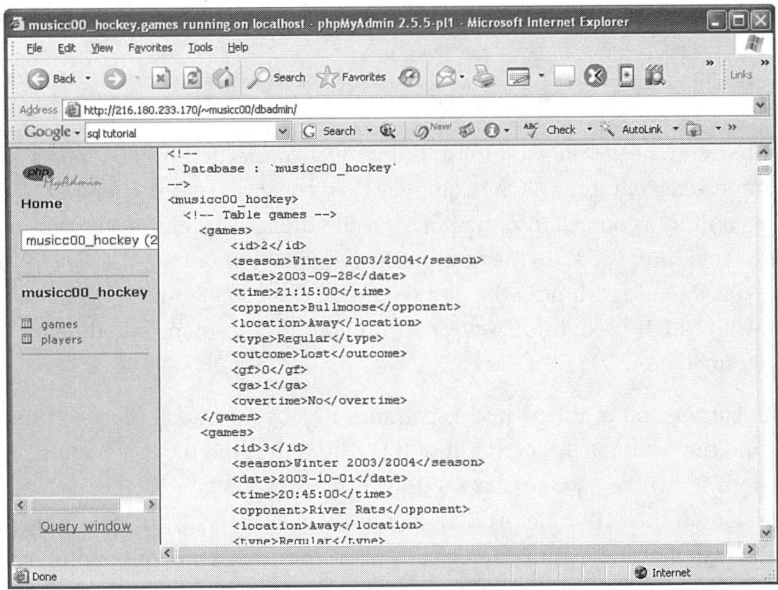

FIGURE 19.4 The hockey game schedule PHP document generates an XML file from a SQL database query, and then provides a link to the file.

Notice in the URL in the figure that the Summer 2005 season was specified, which limits the database query results to only those games in the Summer 2005 season. If you click the link on the page, the XML file is opened in the browser, as shown in Figure 19.5.

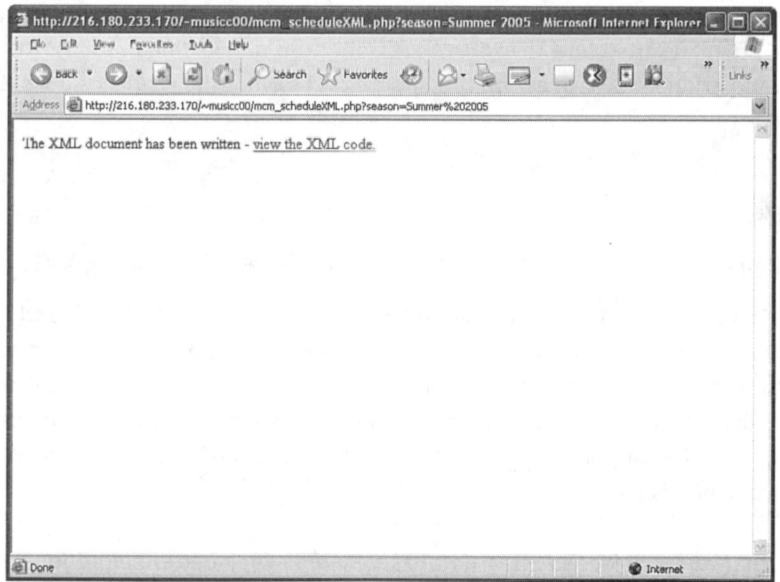

FIGURE 19.5 The resulting XML document contains cleanly formatted XML code that was dynamically generated from a database query.

This figure reveals how the dynamically generated XML document contains structured data that originated from a purely tabular database. You can now run with this XML code and manipulate it just as you would any other XML document. You can transform it using XSLT, style it using CSS or XSL-FO, or automatically process it using some kind of specialized XML tool.

By the Way

Although I've focused on the open source MySQL database throughout this lesson, many commercial databases also include support for XML. Additionally, there are native XML databases, also called NXDs, that allow you to work entirely in XML code with database queries always resulting in pure XML code. To learn more about XML database products, visit http://www.rpbourret.com/xml/XMLDatabaseProds.htm.

Summary

The purpose of this hour was to introduce the concepts behind relational databases and explain how to integrate them with your XML applications. First, I provided a brief introduction to the theory behind relational databases, which is important to understand when you're mixing them with a different sort of data structure, like the one provided by XML. I then provided a very brief overview of SQL, which is the language used to query all relational databases. I then described the issues that arise when you're integrating relational databases with XML applications, and explained how using XML for data storage and XML as a document format differ. Finally, I demonstrated how to export XML data from an existing database, as well as how to perform a SQL query on a database and format the results as an XML document.

Q&A

Q. ***Don't some databases provide features specifically for handling XML?***

A. Most major relational databases (like Oracle, Microsoft SQL Server, and IBM's DB2) support XML natively. The problem is that none of them support XML in the same way. If you use a database that provides XML support, you should look at the vendor documentation and decide whether you want to use it. The specific XML support in each of those databases is unfortunately beyond the scope of this lesson.

Q. ***What about object-oriented databases? Aren't they better suited to use with XML?***

A. Object-oriented databases are more appropriate for storing XML data than relational databases, generally speaking. They're designed explicitly to handle the treelike data structures associated with object-oriented design. Treelike is also the best way to describe most XML data structures. However, object-oriented databases have not displaced relational databases on the market and are not standardized in the same manner as relational databases.

Workshop

The Workshop is designed to help you anticipate possible questions, review what you've learned, and begin learning how to put your knowledge into practice.

Quiz

1. What SQL statement do you use to retrieve data from a database?
2. What is the drawback to exporting a database table as an XML document, such as was done in this chapter using phpMyAdmin?
3. Why is it a good idea to break down XML documents used for data storage into tables when storing the data in a relational database?

Quiz Answers

1. The SQL statement used to retrieve data from a database is the SELECT statement.

2. The drawback to exporting a database table as an XML document is that you typically have to do it manually, which isn't ideal for web applications that need to query a database for XML data dynamically. Furthermore, exporting an entire table is usually less useful than targeting data that matches a specific query.

3. When you use XML documents for data storage, it's a good idea to convert them into tables when using a relational database so that you can take advantage of SQL when you're retrieving data from the database.

Exercises

1. Set up your own MySQL database, and then modify the PHP example from this lesson to work with it.

2. Try passing in different parameters to the PHP example to alter the SQL query, and therefore the resulting XML file.

HOUR 20

Using XML to Assist Search Engines

> Google is to "the semantic web" as CompuServe was to "the web".
>
> —Joshua Allen

If you don't remember CompuServe, it was one of the earliest online communities and data service providers that offered discussion forums, news, and primitive versions of what we commonly associate with modern web portals such as Yahoo!. Although CompuServe certainly paled in comparison to the modern Web experience, it nonetheless provided a fairly interesting online community back before AOL or Yahoo! even existed. I should know—I was a CompuServe local for several years! The quote above is being a bit critical of Google by comparing its ability to perform semantic searches to CompuServe's primitive online service. Although this may be a valid argument, CompuServe was initially ahead of its time, and so is Google. Google has set the standard for searching the Web, and has numerous projects underway to help add context to Web searches and provide a more accurate means of mining the world's electronic information.

This hour explores a feature of Google's search engine called Google Sitemaps, which allows Web developers to automatically notify Google of changes in web page content so that Google can know that the pages exist, as well as indexing the pages more frequently. Of course, Google Sitemaps uses XML or I wouldn't be bothering to tell you about it. It represents a clever and efficient use of XML that serves as an important tool in any Web developer's toolkit.

In this hour, you'll learn

- The basics of web crawling and why it's important
- What Google Sitemaps is and how it can help your web site
- About the XML-based Google Sitemaps protocol, as well as how to develop Sitemap documents for your own web pages
- How to validate, submit, and automatically generate Google Sitemaps

Web Crawling Basics

You've probably heard the term web crawler before, and you may already have a pretty good idea as to what it means. Because web crawling is such an important part of this lesson, I want to give you a quick background on it before moving on to Google Sitemaps and how XML fits into it.

A *web crawler* is an automated program that browses pages on the Web according to a certain algorithm. The simplest algorithm is to simply open and follow every link on a page, and then open and follow every link on subsequent pages, and on and on. Web crawlers are typically used by search engines to index web pages for faster and more accurate searching. You can think of a web crawler as a little worker bee that is constantly out there buzzing from link to link on every web page reporting information back to a database that is part of a search engine. Pretty much all major search engines use web crawlers of one form or another.

The specific algorithms employed by web crawlers are often shrouded in secrecy, as search engine developers attempt to one-up each other in regard to accuracy and efficiency. So far Google appears to be out in front, at least when you consider how far-reaching their search results go as compared to other search engines. Even so, this is an ongoing battle that will likely be waged for a long time, so the main players could certainly change over time. In fact, Microsoft recently entered the fray with its own MSN Search service.

Getting back to web crawlers, they are important to web developers because you actually want public sites to be crawled as frequently as possible to ensure that search engines factor in your most recent web content. Up to this point, you pretty much had to cross your fingers and hope for the best when it came to a search engine's web crawler eventually getting around to crawling your site again and updating its indexes accordingly. Keep in mind that I'm not talking about your site's search ranking per se—I'm talking more about how a search engine goes about crawling your site. Of course, the content within your web pages certainly affects the site's rankings but having your site crawled more regularly doesn't necessarily have anything to do with a ranking improvement.

To understand the relationship between a web crawler and a page's ranking, consider a blog page where you discuss the inner workings of a diesel engine in detail. When this page is crawled by a search engine, it may move up the rankings for searches related to engines. Now let's say a week later your topic of choice is movies by Steven Spielberg. If the page is crawled again, the content will dictate that it isn't such a good match for engine searches, and will instead be realigned to match up with Steven Spielberg movie searches. Of course, it's also possible that both blog entries are still on the page, in which case you may dramatically move up the rankings for searches involving Steven Spielberg's first film, *Duel*, which featured a renegade 18-wheeler powered by a diesel engine.

This example is admittedly simplified, but hopefully you get the idea regarding web crawling and search engine results. The main point to be taken: increased web crawling of your web pages results in more accurate web searches but not necessarily any improvement in search rankings. Incidentally, if I had a magic XML bullet for improving search rankings, you'd be watching me on an infomercial instead of reading this book!

Getting to Know Google Sitemaps

XML enters the picture in regard to web crawling thanks to a relatively new service offered by Google called *Sitemaps*. Google Sitemaps is a beta technology that makes it possible to feed the Google search engine information about your web pages to assist Google's web crawlers. In some ways Sitemaps works similarly to RSS (Really Simple Syndication), which you learn about in Hour 24, "Syndicating the Web with RSS News Feeds." RSS is used to notify visitors to your web site about changes to the site's content. Sitemaps works in much the same way except the recipient of a Sitemap "feed" is Google, as opposed to visitors to your web site.

By the Way

Google Sitemaps is a beta technology, which means that it is still under development. This also means that the service is subject to undergoing significant changes as its designers continue to develop and refine it. So know as you're using the service that it is subject to change.

A Google Sitemap is an XML document or documents that contain a list of URLs of pages within your web site that you want to be crawled. For the utmost in accurate crawling, you should list the URL of every page on your site, which can potentially be quite a few pages. It's not uncommon for even relatively small web sites to have hundreds of pages, while larger sites can reach into the thousands or even tens of thousands of pages. Many sites also have dynamic content that is generated by specifying attributes through a URL. Examples of such pages include Microsoft Active Server (ASP) pages and PHP pages, both of which result in unique pages solely by passing in attributes to the same document via the URL of the page. You'll want to try and include every combination of attributes for these pages in order to have your site thoroughly crawled.

In addition to the URL of a page, a Sitemap also allows you to provide some cues to the crawler in regard to how frequently the page is updated. More specifically, you can include the last modification date of a page, along with how frequently the page's content changes. Google doesn't hold you to this update frequency, by the way, it's just a general estimate to help determine how frequently the page should be crawled ideally.

The last piece of information that you associate with a Sitemap is the priority ranking of the page, which is relative to other pages on your site, not other pages on the Web in general. Your inclination might be to flag all of your pages as having the highest of priority but all you would be accomplishing is giving them equal priority with respect to each other. The idea behind the page priority is to provide a mechanism for giving more important pages a higher potential for getting crawled. As an example, you might want your home page to have a higher priority than say, your "about" page. Or maybe on a storefront site you want the product catalog pages to all have a higher priority than the company history page.

Google Sitemaps is valuable beyond just causing your web pages to be crawled more regularly. You may have some pages that are effectively on islands that would otherwise never be crawled. For example, maybe you have some pages in a knowledgebase that are only accessed via search queries. Because no permanent links exist for the pages, a normal web crawler would never find them. By placing the pages in a Sitemap, you ensure that the knowledgebase is indexed and included in Google search results.

When submitting a Sitemap to Google, you're notifying Google of the specific URLs that encompass your site, basically helping it along in its job of crawling your site thoroughly and accurately. When you add a new page to your site, you should update the Sitemap and resubmit it to Google so that the page is immediately targeted for crawling. It's a way to assist Google so that your web site content is always as synchronized as possible with search engine results.

By the Way

> Google wasn't the first search engine to experiment with the concept of a submitted sitemap for the purpose of assisting its crawler. Yahoo! has a Content Acquisition Program that works roughly similar to Google Sitemaps except that you have to pay to use it. I would expect Microsoft to offer a service similar to Google Sitemaps at some point in the future seeing as how Microsoft is clearly making a run at Google with MSN Search.

After you've created a Sitemap document, you must publish it to your web site and then notify Google of its location. From there, everything else is automatic. The next section explains how to go about coding a Sitemap using XML, as well as how to submit it to Google.

Inside the Google Sitemap Protocol

Enough background information, let's look at some XML code! The language behind Google Sitemaps is an XML-based language called the *Sitemap protocol*. The Sitemap protocol is very simple, and only consists of six different tags. Following is a list of these tags and their meaning in the context of a Sitemap document:

- `<urlset>`—The root element of a Sitemap document, which serves as a container for individual `<url>` elements
- `<url>`—The storage unit for an individual URL within a Sitemap; serves as a container for the `<loc>`, `<lastmod>`, `<changefreq>`, and `<priority>` elements
- `<loc>`—The URL of a discrete page within a Sitemap; this tag is required
- `<lastmod>`—The date/time of the last change to this web page; this tag is optional
- `<changefreq>`—An estimate of how frequently the content in the web page changes; this tag is optional
- `<priority>`—The priority of the web page with respect to other pages on this site; this tag is optional

The previous section covered the information associated with a Sitemap, which these tags match up with very closely. In other words, these shouldn't come as too terribly much of a surprise given that you already knew a Sitemap is described by a URL, last modification date, change frequency, and priority ranking. However, it helps to see the tags in context to get a better feel for how a Sitemap is structured. Following is the code for a minimal Sitemap with one URL entry:

```
<?xml version="1.0" encoding="UTF-8"?>
<urlset xmlns="http://www.google.com/schemas/sitemap/0.84"
  xmlns:xsi="http://www.w3.org/2001/XMLSchema-instance"
  xsi:schemaLocation="http://www.google.com/schemas/sitemap/0.84
  http://www.google.com/schemas/sitemap/0.84/sitemap.xsd">
  <url>
    <loc>http://www.michaelmorrison.com/</loc>
    <lastmod>2005-08-23</lastmod>
    <changefreq>daily</changefreq>
    <priority>1.0</priority>
  </url>
</urlset>
```

The messiest part of this code is the `<urlset>` tag, which includes several namespace declarations, as well as a reference to a schema for the document; more on Sitemap schemas later in the section titled, "Validating Your Sitemap." As you can see, the `<urlset>` tag serves as the root of the document, and therefore contains all of the other tags in the document. The Sitemap namespace is first declared in the `<urlset>` tag, followed by the XMLSchema namespace and then the Sitemaps schema itself. All of this namespace/schema stuff is boilerplate code that will appear in every Sitemap document. Of course, if you don't feel the need to validate your Sitemap, you can leave out the schema code.

Within the `<urlset>` tag, the real work starts to take place. In this example there is only one URL, as indicated by the solitary `<url>` tag. The `<url>` tag is used to house the child tags that describe each URL in your web site. These child tags are `<loc>`, `<lastmod>`, `<changefreq>`, and `<priority>`, and together they describe a single URL for a Sitemap. Let's take a quick look at the details of each tag and how they are used.

The `<loc>` tag represents the location of a web page in the form of a URL. This URL must be a full URL complete with http:// at the start, or https:// in the case of secure pages. If your web server requires a trailing slash on domain paths, make sure to include it here, as in http://www.michaelmorrison.com/. Also keep in mind that the contents of the `<loc>` tag can't be longer than 2,048 characters. That would be a ridiculously lengthy URL, so I doubt you will encounter a problem with this upper limit on URL length. The only other thing to note about the `<loc>` tag is that it is the only required child tag of `<url>`, which means you can feasibly create a Sitemap with nothing more than the `<urlset>`, `<url>`, and `<loc>` tags. But why would you want to do that when you can use the other optional tags to give Google even more assistance in crawling your pages?

By the Way

> Each Sitemap is limited to 50,000 URLs and a 10MB compressed file size. Google Sitemaps supports compressed Sitemap files that are compressed with the gzip tool, which is freely available at http://www.gzip.org/.

The `<lastmod>` tag is used to identify the last time a page was modified, which can let the web crawler know if it needs to reindex the page based upon the modification date of the last indexed version of the page. The content in the `<lastmod>` tag must be formatted as an ISO 8601 date/time value. In practical terms, this means you can code it simply as a date with the following format: `YYYY-MM-DD`. In other words, you can omit the time if you want. If you do elect to include the time, the entire date/representation is typically expressed as `YYYY-MM-DDThh:mm:ss`. The letter `T` in the middle of the date/time is just a separator. Of course, you may already be asking yourself how the time zone factors into this format. You add the time zone onto the end of the time as a +/- offset relative to UTC (Coordinated Universal Time) in the form `hh` or `hh:mm` if you're dealing with a half-hour time zone. Following is an example of a complete date/time in the central time zone (CST), which is GMT minus five hours:

```
2005-10-31T15:43:22-05:00
```

In this example, the date is October 31, 2005, and the time is 3:43:22 p.m. CST. Notice that 24-hour time is specified in order to make the distinction between a.m. and p.m.

> **By the Way**
>
> ISO 8061 is an international date/time standard for representing a date and time as plain text. ISO 8061 supports a wider range of date/time formats than what I've explained here. Feel free to learn more about ISO 8061 online if you feel the urge to know more. http://www.w3.org/TR/NOTE-datetime.

The <changefreq> tag is used to specify how often the content on a web page changes. The change frequency of a page is obviously something that can't always be predicted and in many cases varies considerably. For this reason, you should think of the <changefreq> tag as providing a web crawler with a rough estimate of how often a page changes. Google makes no promises regarding how often it will crawl a page even if you set the change frequency to a very high value, so your best bet is to try and be realistic when determining the change frequency of your pages. Possible values for this tag include: `always`, `hourly`, `daily`, `weekly`, `monthly`, `yearly`, and `never`. The `always` value should only be used on pages that literally change every time they are viewed, while `never` is reserved for pages that are completely and permanently static (typically archived pages). The remaining values provide plenty of options for specifying how frequently a page changes.

The <priority> tag allows you to assign relative priorities to the pages on your web site. Although I mentioned it earlier, it's worth hammering home once more that this tag has nothing to do with a page's priority level as compared to other web sites, so please don't think of it as a way to boost your site as a whole. The significance of a priority ranking in this case is to help identify URLs on your web site that are more important than other URLs on your web site. In theory, this may help a web crawler isolate the most important pages on your site when targeting search results. Values for the <priority> tag range from `0.0` to `1.0`, which `1.0` being the highest priority and `0.0` being the lowest. Generally speaking, you should rank average pages as `0.5`, the most important pages as `1.0`, and the least important pages as `0.0`; this tag defaults to `0.5` if you don't specify it. Feel free to use values in between those I just suggested if you think you can assess the relative importance of pages on your site to that degree.

> **By the Way**
>
> It will do you no good to set a high priority for all of your pages, as the end result will provide Google with no basis for determine which of your pages you think are more important than others.

The restrictions on sitemap files are modest. URLs must not include embedded newlines; you must fully specify URLs because Google tries to crawl the URLs exactly as you provide them. Your sitemap files must use UTF-8 encoding. And, each sitemap file is limited to 50,000 URLs and 10MB when uncompressed.

Creating Your Own Sitemap

You've already seen the nuts and bolts of the Sitemap protocol language, along with the basic template for a Sitemap XML document. It's time to take the next step and create your very own Sitemap document, or in reality, *my* very own Sitemap document because you're going to use URLs on my web site as examples. Let's get started!

A Basic Sitemap Document

Listing 20.1 contains the code for a complete Sitemap document for my web site. By complete, I mean that it meets all of the requirements of a Sitemap document, although it doesn't actually include URLs for all of the pages on my site.

LISTING 20.1 A Complete Sitemap Document for My Web Site

```
<?xml version="1.0" encoding="UTF-8"?>
<urlset xmlns="http://www.google.com/schemas/sitemap/0.84"
  xmlns:xsi="http://www.w3.org/2001/XMLSchema-instance"
  xsi:schemaLocation="http://www.google.com/schemas/sitemap/0.84
  http://www.google.com/schemas/sitemap/0.84/sitemap.xsd">
  <url>
    <loc>http://www.michaelmorrison.com/</loc>
    <lastmod>2005-08-23</lastmod>
    <changefreq>daily</changefreq>
    <priority>1.0</priority>
  </url>
  <url>
    <loc>http://www.michaelmorrison.com/mambo/index.php?
    option=com_content&amp;task=category&amp;sectionid=2&amp;id=11&amp;
    Itemid=35</loc>
    <lastmod>2005-08-20</lastmod>
    <changefreq>weekly</changefreq>
    <priority>0.8</priority>
  </url>
  <url>
    <loc>http://www.michaelmorrison.com/mambo/index.php?
    option=com_content&amp;task=blogcategory&amp;id=16&amp;Itemid=37</loc>
    <lastmod>2005-08-23</lastmod>
    <changefreq>daily</changefreq>
    <priority>0.8</priority>
  </url>
  <url>
    <loc>http://www.michaelmorrison.com/mambo/index.php?
    option=com_simpleboard&amp;Itemid=48&amp;func=showcat&amp;catid=37</loc>
    <lastmod>2005-08-18</lastmod>
    <changefreq>daily</changefreq>
    <priority>0.6</priority>
  </url>
```

```
33:   <url>
34:     <loc>http://www.michaelmorrison.com/mambo/index.php?
35:     option=com_simpleboard&amp;Itemid=18&amp;func=showcat&amp;catid=6</loc>
36:     <lastmod>2005-08-21</lastmod>
37:     <changefreq>daily</changefreq>
38:     <priority>0.6</priority>
39:   </url>
40: </urlset>
```

This code is very similar to the Sitemap code you saw earlier in the chapter, except in this case multiple URLs are specified. Notice that I opted to use all of the optional tags in every URL—there's no good reason not to unless you just don't want to take the time to be so detailed. One thing I did skimp on a little is the `<lastmod>` tag for each URL, which I specified only as a date. However, because none of these pages are listed as having a change frequency higher than `daily`, it really isn't necessary to get more exacting with the modification date.

By the Way

> Google requires all Sitemap documents to use UTF-8 encoding (see line 1 in the example), as well as escaped entities for the following symbols: &, ', ", >, and <.

One other thing worth pointing out in this sample Sitemap is how I opted to use `0.6`, `0.8`, and `1.0` as the priority levels of the pages. Presumably, a more complete sample page would continue on down the range, finishing up at `0.0` for the least important pages.

By the Way

> A Sitemap document can only reference URLs in the same folder or a child folder of the location of the Sitemap file. In the sample in Listing 20.1, the file would need to be placed at the same level as http://www.michaelmorrison.com/ because that URL is hierarchically the highest URL in the Sitemap.

Breaking Your Mapping into Multiple Documents

If you're responsible for a really monstrous site with loads of pages, you may need to consider breaking up your Sitemap into multiple Sitemap documents, in which case you'll also need a Sitemap index document to pull them all together. A Sitemap index document is very similar to a normal Sitemap except that it uses the following tags:

- `<sitemapindex>`—The root element of a Sitemap index document, which serves as a container for individual `<sitemap>` elements
- `<sitemap>`—The storage unit for an individual Sitemap within a Sitemap index; serves as a container for the `<loc>` and `<lastmod>` elements

- <loc>—The URL of a Sitemap document; this tag is required
- <lastmod>—The date/time of the last change to the Sitemap document; this tag is optional

The first two tags work very similarly to the <urlset> and <url> tags in an individual Sitemap. However, instead of organizing URLs they organize other Sitemap documents. The remaining two tags, <loc> and <lastmod>, also work similarly to their individual Sitemap counterparts, except in this case they determine the location and last modification date of a Sitemap document, not a web page. Following is some code that demonstrates how a Sitemap index is assembled out of these tags:

```
<?xml version="1.0" encoding="UTF-8"?>
<sitemapindex xmlns="http://www.google.com/schemas/sitemap/0.84">
<sitemap>
  <loc>http://www.michaelmorrison.com/sitemap1.xml.gz</loc>
  <lastmod>2005-11-05T08:34:11-05:00</lastmod>
</sitemap>
<sitemap>
  <loc>http://www.michaelmorrison.com/sitemap2.xml.gz</loc>
  <lastmod>2005-11-19T14:18:47-05:00</lastmod>
</sitemap>
</sitemapindex>
```

This sample code shows how to include two Sitemap documents in a Sitemap index. If you pay close attention, the two Sitemap documents in this example have been compressed using the gzip tool, which explains why their file extension is .xml.gz. Also notice that the date and time of each Sitemap is different, which means that an intelligent web crawler could focus on reindexing only the URLs in the newer Sitemap.

A Sitemap index document can only reference Sitemaps that are stored on the same site as the index file.

In the Sitemap index example I didn't include schema information for validating the Sitemap index. However, there is an XSD schema available from Google that you can use to validate Sitemap indexes just as you saw earlier how an XSD schema can be referenced in an individual Sitemap. The schema for individual Sitemaps is http://www.google.com/schemas/sitemap/0.84/sitemap.xsd, while the schema for Sitemap indexes is http://www.google.com/schemas/sitemap/0.84/siteindex.xsd.

Validating Your Sitemap

Before you submit a Sitemap to Google for processing, it's a good idea to validate it using a validation tool such as the W3C Validator for XML Schema, which is located at http://www.w3.org/2001/03/webdata/xsv. This online tool allows you to either validate a Sitemap document that you've already posted to the Web or browse for a Sitemap file stored locally on your hard drive. Either way, the Sitemap should be validated against the Google Sitemap XSD Schema, which is located at http://www.google.com/schemas/sitemap/0.84/sitemap.xsd. Refer back to lines 3 and 4 in Listing 20.1 for details on how to reference the XSD schema for a Sitemap in a Sitemap document.

If you're interested in validating a Sitemap index document, make sure you use the appropriate XSD schema: http://www.google.com/schemas/sitemap/0.84/siteindex.xsd.

The W3C Validator for XML Schema allows you to choose between several different output options for the validator but in all likelihood the default option will work fine for you. All you really have to do to use the tool is specify a Sitemap file. In this case, I opted to publish my Sitemap file on the Web at the location http://www.michaelmorrison.com/sitemap.xml. After entering the URL of the file and clicking the Get Results button to initiate the validation process, Figure 20.1 shows the result of a successful validation.

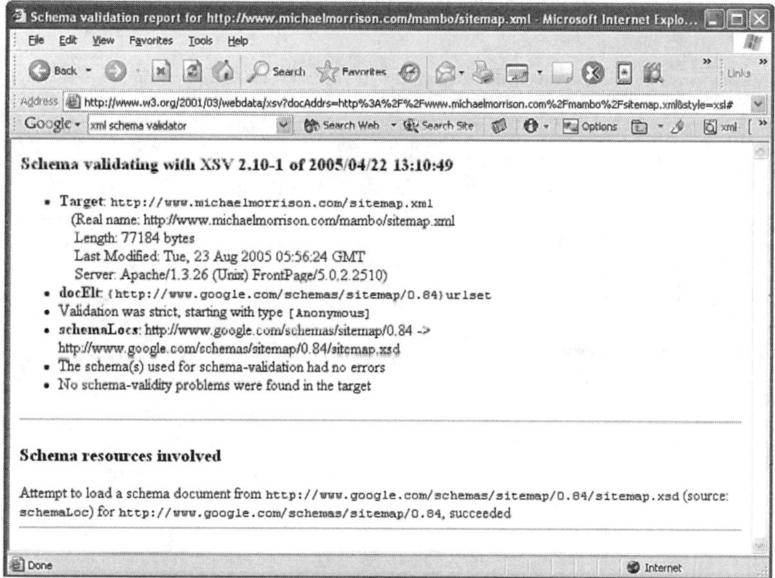

FIGURE 20.1 Successfully validating a Sitemap document means you're ready to submit it to Google.

If all goes well with the Sitemap validation, you'll see a figure similar to Figure 20.1. If not, the validator will provide you with detailed information about the kinds of errors found and where they are located. You should be able to find the errors in the document and correct them without too much trouble. Make sure you eventually arrive at a file that validates successfully before you move on to submitting the Sitemap to Google.

Validation is an important part of the Sitemap submission process because you'll only be wasting your time if you submit the Sitemap and Google can't process it. Because Google doesn't immediately process Sitemaps, you may not know that the Sitemap failed to process for several hours after submitting it. So, try and make sure to validate your Sitemap documents, especially upon first creating them.

Submitting Your Sitemap to Google

Submitting a Sitemap to Google for processing is a very simple process. First off, you need a Google account. You may have already created a Google account back in Hour 15, "Using XML to Hack Google Maps," when you found out how to create custom interactive maps for Google Maps. If so, just log in to your existing account as you did in Hour 15 via the following link: https://www.google.com/accounts/Login. After logging in, go to the main Sitemaps web page, which is located at https://www.google.com/webmasters/sitemaps/stats. This page initially doesn't show any Sitemaps for you because you've yet to submit any, as you can see in Figure 20.2.

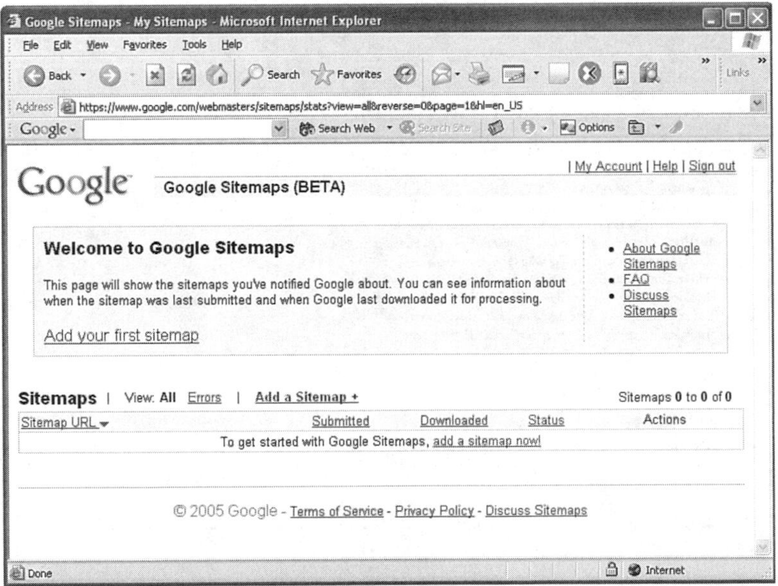

FIGURE 20.2 The Google Sitemaps web site initially shows on Sitemaps because you haven't submitted any yet.

Click the Add a Sitemap button to add a Sitemap to Google. You'll be prompted to enter the URL of the Sitemap file. At this point you should make sure that you've uploaded the Sitemap to the appropriate location on your web server. This location is typically where the home page for the site is located. Enter the complete URL for the Sitemap file into the Google Sitemaps submission page, and click the Submit URL button. Google Sitemaps will queue up the Sitemap for processing, and then provide you with information about the status of the Sitemap (see Figure 20.3).

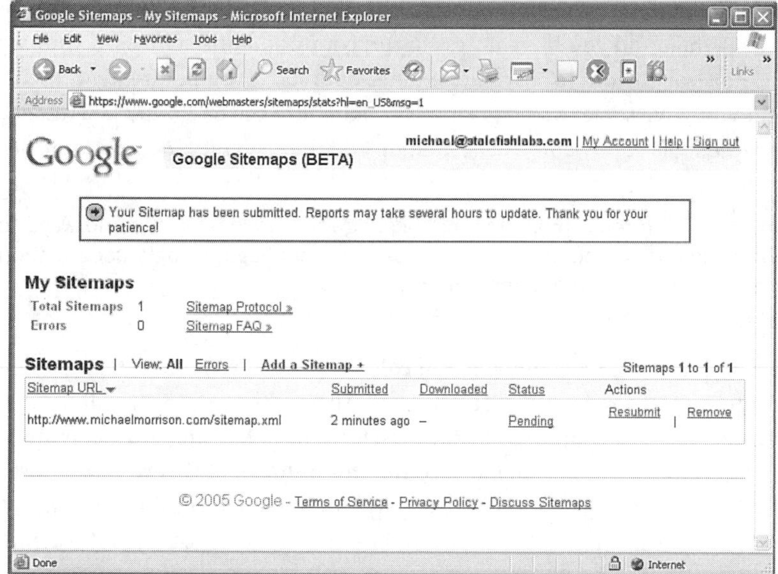

FIGURE 20.3
The status of the newly submitted Sitemap is shown on your main Google Sitemaps page.

It's important to understand that when you submit a Sitemap to Google it isn't immediately processed and crawled. In fact, it typically takes several hours for a Sitemap to be processed. You can check back to the Google Sitemaps web site to view the status of Sitemaps that you've submitted. The status of a newly submitted Sitemap will start out as `Pending`, and once it has been processed the status will change to `OK`.

That's really all it takes to make your web site more readily available to Google's web crawler. Of course, you'll want to resubmit a Sitemap whenever you add new pages to your site but otherwise the Sitemap will do the job of helping Google to crawl your pages more frequently and more accurately.

By the Way

Click the Resubmit button on the main Google Sitemaps page to inform Google that a page is being resubmitted.

Using an Automated Sitemap Tool

Although the Sitemap protocol is a fairly simple XML language to use, you're probably thinking that there has to be a better way to create Sitemaps than sitting there typing in all those URLs by hand. And in fact there is. There are actually several options available to you when it comes to automatically generating a Sitemap from your web pages. One such tool is Google's own Sitemap Generator, which is very powerful but somewhat difficult to use unless you already happen to have experience with Python and you have access to run command-line scripts on your web server. If not, you'll want to investigate other options. If you're already a Python guru and you have server access, feel free to look into the Sitemap Generator at http://www.google.com/webmasters/sitemaps/docs/en/sitemap-generator.html.

By the Way

> Python is an interpreted programming language that is similar in some ways to Perl, which is another popular web development language. Google uses Python throughout many of its tools and services.

Short of using Python, I recommend you consider using an online Sitemap generation tool to automatically generate your Sitemaps. There are many such online tools out there but one that I've found particularly useful is the XML Sitemap Generator, which is located at http://www.xml-sitemaps.com/. This online tool is very easy to use; it basically just requests a starting URL from you and then churns out a Sitemap XML document in return. What's neat is that online Sitemap generation tools such as the XML Sitemap Generator will automatically crawl your entire site figuring out the URLs of all your pages.

By the Way

> To find out about other Sitemap generation tools, visit Google's list of third-party sitemap resources at http://code.google.com/sm_thirdparty.html.

As an example, I fed the home page of my web site into the XML Sitemap Generator, and after it churned for a few minutes crawling through the pages on my site, it created a Sitemap XML file that I could download and post on my site. What I found particularly interesting is that it counted 299 pages on my site. Because my site is set up through a content management system that generates pages dynamically from a database, I never really had a good feel for how many pages were on it. The XML Sitemap Generator not only answered that question for me but it also created for me a Sitemap document ready to feed into Google to ensure that all of my pages get crawled efficiently.

Figure 20.4 shows the XML Sitemap Generator web page as it busily works away crawling my web site and figuring out URLs for the pages within.

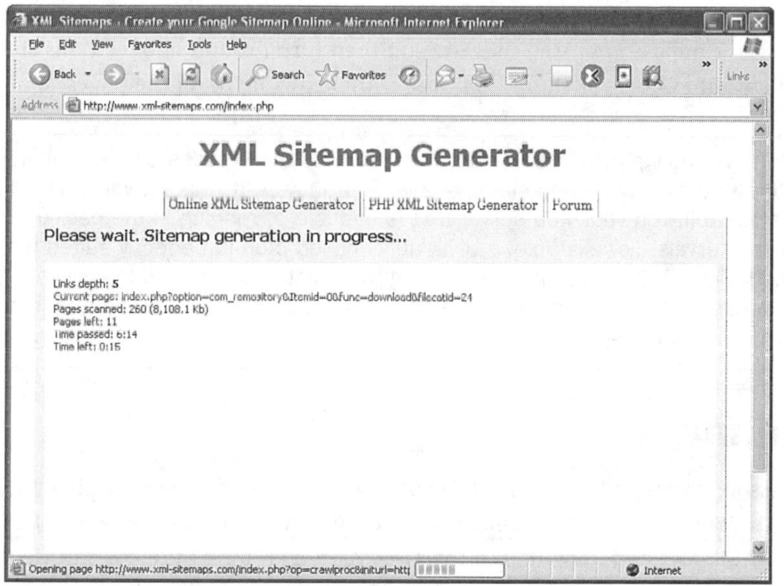

FIGURE 20.4 It's pretty interesting just watching a Sitemap generation tool crawl your site and count the number of pages, along with their sizes.

After the XML Sitemap Generator finishes, it will provide you with links to both uncompressed and compressed versions of the resulting Sitemap. Although you can submit either version to Google, you might as well go with the compressed version to speed up the transfer time unless you just want to open the uncompressed version to study the code. In that case, why not download both? Figure 20.5 shows the results of the XML Sitemap Generator tool, including the links to the newly created Sitemap files.

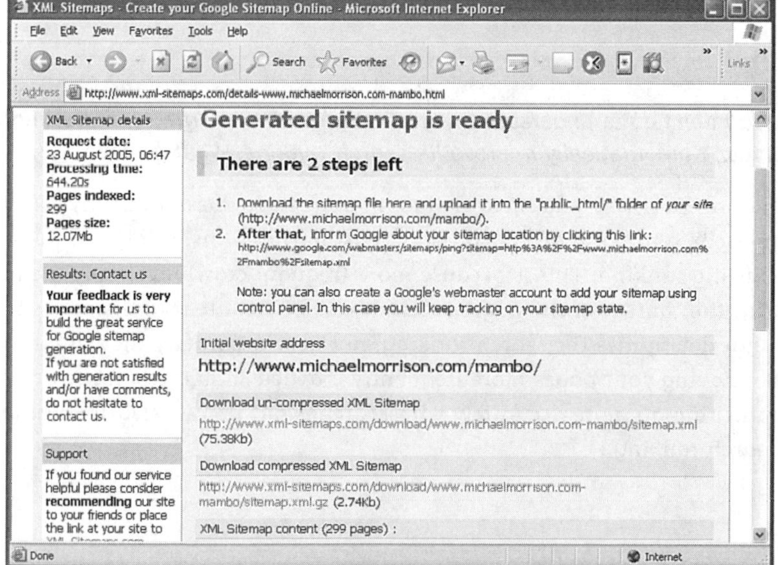

FIGURE 20.5 When the XML Sitemap Generator tool finishes, it provides you with links to download the new Sitemap in either uncompressed or compressed form.

You now have a Sitemap document that contains a thorough representation of the pages that compose your web site. You can then turn around and feed this Sitemap document into Google Sitemaps to improve the crawling of all the pages.

You may be wondering if it's possible to automate the process of resubmitting a Sitemap based upon web site changes. The answer is yes, but you'll have to use a special utility on your web server that is capable of running in the background at regular intervals. For example, a UNIX utility called cron is perfectly suited for this task. The cron utility is typically run using the crontab command. Please refer to your specific web server documentation to find out more about setting up recurring commands and/or scripts.

Summary

This lesson started out this part of the book with somewhat of an unlikely topic, the optimization of web sites with respect to search engine web crawlers. Of course, XML factored heavily into the discussion as it forms the basis of Google's Sitemaps service that allows you to seed Google's web crawler with information about the pages on your web site. You not only learned how Google Sitemaps works and how it can help you, but you also learned how the XML-based Sitemap protocol language is structured. From there, you created a Sitemap by hand and then learned how to validate it and submit it to Google for processing. After you learned how to create a Sitemap the hard way, I shared with you a much easier technique that involves generating Sitemap documents automatically using online tools. Hopefully you've left this hour with a practical web trick up your sleeve to try out on your own web sites.

Q&A

Q. ***I still don't quite understand why having a web site crawled more frequently doesn't automatically improve its search ranking. What gives?***

A. Having your web pages crawled more frequently doesn't directly affect the search ranking of the pages, at least not in terms of improving an existing ranking. This is because more frequent crawling simply means that the content of the pages is reindexed. The content of the pages is what determines the search ranking, not how accurately they are indexed. So, having your pages more frequently crawled should result in your pages matching up more accurately with searches but not necessarily a higher search ranking.

Q. *Does Google Sitemaps support any document formats other than the Sitemap protocol?*

A. Yes. Three other document formats are supported by Google Sitemaps: OAI-PMH (Open Archives Initiative Protocol for Metadata Harvesting), RSS (Really Simple Syndication)/Atom, and plain text. None of these formats are recommended over the Sitemap protocol unless you already happen to use one of them to describe or syndicate your site. And if you happen to have a text file with a list of URLs for the pages in your site, you should consider using a tool such as Google's Sitemap Generator to convert it to the Sitemap Protocol.

Q. *How do I know that Google has successfully used my Sitemap to crawl the pages on my web site?*

A. You don't. In fact, Google makes no promises in regard to how a Sitemap improves the crawling of your pages. However, there is no negative to using a Sitemap, meaning that you only stand to gain by Google potentially crawling your pages more regularly and thereby improving the accuracy of search results that are related to your web content.

Workshop

The Workshop is designed to help you anticipate possible questions, review what you've learned, and begin learning how to put your knowledge into practice.

Quiz

1. What XML encoding scheme is required of all Sitemap documents?
2. What is the purpose of the priority ranking of a URL in a Sitemap?
3. If I store a Sitemap file at the URL http://www.michaelmorrison.com/books/, can I include a URL in the sitemap for http://www.michaelmorrison.com/index.html?

Quiz Answers

1. All Sitemap documents require UTF-8 character encoding.
2. The priority ranking of a URL in a Sitemap is used to establish the relative importance of the page with respect to other pages on your web site; it has no bearing on your pages as compared to pages on other web sites. Changing all of your pages to a high priority will only have the effect of neutralizing the effectiveness of the priority ranking.

3. No. A Sitemap cannot contain URLs that are higher in the folder hierarchy than where the Sitemap file is stored. In this example, all of the Sitemap URLs would need to start at http://www.michaelmorrison.com/books/.

Exercises

1. Modify the Sitemap document example in this lesson to map the pages of your own web site. If your web site has a table of contents or an existing site map feature, you may be able to use it to help get a listing of URLs for the Sitemap document. Don't forget to post the Sitemap file to your web site and then submit the file to Google through your Google Sitemap account.

2. If you have a fairly large web site or a site that uses dynamically generated pages (ASP, PHP, and so on), try using Google's own Sitemap Generator tool or a third-party Sitemap tool. Google maintains a list of such tools at http://code.google.com/sm_thirdparty.html.

PART V

XML's Impact on HTML

HOUR 21

Adding Structure to the Web with XHTML

> I generally avoid temptation unless I can't resist it.
>
> —Mae West

One form of temptation many web developers have been unable to resist is that of hacking together web pages with poorly coded HTML. Fortunately, XML is well on its way to adding some much needed structure to the Web by ushering in a new version of HTML called XHTML, which represents a merger of XML and HTML. Considering that there is a lot of confusion surrounding the relationship between XML and HTML, XHTML often serves only to muddy the water in terms of how people perceive XML. XHTML is ultimately quite simple in that it is a version of HTML reformulated to meet the strict structural and syntax requirements of XML. XHTML makes use of the same elements and attributes as HTML, but it enforces XML rules, such as quoting all attribute values and requiring empty elements to end with `/>`. It still isn't clear if, how, or when the Web will officially transition from HTML to XHTML, but it is a likely prospect given the benefits of XML. This hour introduces you to XHTML and examines some of the consequences of migrating web pages from HTML to XHTML.

In this hour, you'll learn

- What XHTML is and why it was created
- About the differences between XHTML and HTML
- How to create and validate XHTML documents
- How to convert existing HTML documents to XHTML

XHTML: A Logical Merger

XHTML is an XML-based markup language that carries out the functionality of HTML in the spirit of XML. As you hopefully know by now, HTML is not a descendent of XML; this would be tricky considering that XML was created after HTML. HTML is actually a descendent of an older markup language technology known as *SGML (Standard*

Generalized Markup Language), which is considerably more complex than XML. XML in many ways represents a simplified reformulation of SGML, which makes XML more compact than SGML, as well as much easier to learn and process. So, XML is beneficial from the perspective of both application developers and document developers. But what exactly does this have to do with HTML? Or, to pose the question more generally, why exactly do we need XHTML?

To answer the "Why XHTML?" question, you have to first take stock of the Web and some of the problems surrounding it. Much of the Web is a jumbled mess of hacked HTML code that has very little structure. Poor coding, browser leniency, and proprietary browser extensions have all combined to create a web of HTML documents that are extremely unstructured, which is a bad thing. Don't get me wrong, things have improved since the early days of the Web but we still have a long way to go. Web browser vendors have had to create HTML processors that are capable of reading and displaying even the most horrendous HTML code so that web users never have to witness the underlying bad code in many web pages. Although this is good in terms of the web experience, it makes it very difficult to glean information from web pages in an automated manner because their structure is so inconsistent.

You know that XML documents can't suffer from bad coding because XML simply won't allow it. Knowing this, a logical answer to the HTML problem is to convert web pages to XML documents and then use stylesheets to render them. It would also be nice to have peace on earth, tasty fat-free foods, and lower taxes, but life just doesn't work that way. What I'm getting at is that HTML will likely always have a place on the Web simply because it is too deeply ingrained to replace. Besides, even though XML paired with CSS/XSLT has huge structural benefits over a purely presentational HTML web page, it involves more work and a bit more planning. There are certainly situations where it doesn't matter too much if content is separated from how it is displayed, in which case HTML represents a simpler, more efficient solution.

The point I'm trying to make is that plain HTML, in one form or another, is likely here to stay. The solution to the problem then shifts to improving HTML in some way. The most logical improvement to solve the structural problems of HTML is to express HTML as an XML language (XHTML), which allows us to reap many of the benefits of XML without turning the Web on its ear. The primary benefit of XHTML is obviously structure, which would finally force browser vendors and web developers alike to play by the rules. Browsers could strictly enforce an XHTML schema to ensure that documents are both well formed and valid. Just requiring XHTML documents to be well formed would be a significant step in the right direction; checking them for validity would be the icing on the cake.

By the Way

Although XHTML 2.0 is in the works, the latest supported version of XHTML is version 1.1. You can learn more about XHTML 1.1 by visiting the W3C web site at http://www.w3.org/MarkUp/#xhtml11.

Even as XHTML catches on and web developers migrate their HTML code to it, web browsers still have to support the old, unstructured versions of HTML for the foreseeable future. However, over time these legacy HTML documents could eventually be supplanted by valid, well-formed XHTML documents with plenty of structure. One thing that is already making the migration to XHTML smoother is the fact that a great deal of web page development is carried out with visual authoring tools that automatically generate XHTML code. This makes it virtually painless for developers to make the move to XHTML.

By the Way

You might not realize it, but another compelling reason to move the Web toward XHTML is so that new types of compact browsers with limited processing capabilities can avoid the hassles of trying to process unstructured HTML code. These browsers are becoming prevalent on devices such as mobile phones and handheld computers, and would benefit from highly structured XHTML documents to minimize processing overhead. In Hour 23, "Going Wireless with WML and XHTML Mobile," you learn about WML and XHTML Mobile, which are used to develop web pages for mobile devices.

Comparing XHTML and HTML

You probably know that the latest version of HTML is version 4.0 (4.01 to be exact), which is in wide use across the Web. XHTML is a reformulated version of HTML 4.0 that plays by the more rigid rules of XML. Fortunately, most of the differences between XHTML and HTML 4.0 are syntactic, which means that they don't dramatically impact the overall structure of HTML documents. Migrating an HTML 4.0 document to XHTML is more a matter of cleaning and tightening up the code than converting it to a new language. If you have any web pages that were developed using HTML 4.0, you'll find that they can be migrated to XHTML with relative ease. You learn how to do this later in the hour in the section titled, "Migrating HTML to XHTML."

Even though XHTML supports the same elements and attributes as HTML 4.0, there are some significant differences that are due to the fact that XHTML is an XML-based language. Given your knowledge of XML, you may already have a pretty good idea regarding some of these differences, but the following list will help you to understand exactly how XHTML documents differ from HTML documents:

- XHTML documents must be well formed.
- Element and attribute names in XHTML must be in lowercase.

- End tags in XHTML are required for nonempty elements.
- Empty elements in XHTML must consist of a start-tag/end-tag pair or an empty element.
- Attributes in XHTML cannot be used without a value.
- Attribute values in XHTML must always be quoted.
- An XHTML namespace must be declared in the root `html` element.
- The `head` and `body` elements cannot be omitted in XHTML.
- The `title` element in XHTML must be the first element in the `head` element.
- In XHTML, all script and style elements must be enclosed within `CDATA` sections.

These differences between XHTML and HTML 4.0 shouldn't come as too much of a surprise. Fortunately, none of them are too difficult to find and fix in HTML documents, which makes the move from HTML 4.0 to XHTML relatively straightforward. However, web pages developed with versions of HTML prior to 4.0 typically require more dramatic changes. This primarily has to do with the fact that HTML 4.0 does away with some previously popular formatting attributes such as `background` and instead promotes the usage of style sheets. Because XHTML doesn't support these formatting attributes, it is necessary first to convert legacy HTML (prior to 4.0) documents to HTML 4.0, which quite often involves replacing formatting attributes with CSS equivalents. Once you get a web page up to par with HTML 4.0, the move to XHTML is pretty straightforward.

Creating and Validating XHTML Documents

Because XHTML is an XML-based markup language, creating XHTML documents is very much like creating any other kind of XML document. You must first learn the XHTML language, after which you use a text editor or other XML development tool to construct a document using XHTML elements and attributes. If you've always created web pages using visual authoring tools, such as FrontPage or Dreamweaver, the concept of assembling a web page in a text editor might be new. On the other hand, if you aren't a seasoned web developer and your only experience with markup languages is XML, you'll feel right at home. The next few sections explore the basics of creating and validating XHTML documents.

Many visual web development tools support XHTML, which means that you can certainly create XHTML web pages without having to rely on a simple text editor. However, if you really want to learn how XHTML works as a language, you have to get dirty and explore XHTML code. Fortunately, many web development tools include a code view that allows you to view the underlying code for a page. If your development tool offers such a view, you can forego using a simple text editor. Such code viewers also offer editing features such as context-sensitive color highlighting and automatic tag matching, which can assist you in writing valid XHTML code.

Preparing XHTML Documents for Validation

Just as it is beneficial to validate other kinds of XML documents, it is also important to validate XHTML documents to ensure that they adhere to the XHTML language. As you know, validation is carried out through a schema, which can be either a DTD or an XSD. Both kinds of schemas are available for use with XHTML. I'll focus on the usage of an XHTML DTD to validate XHTML documents because DTDs are still more widely supported than XSDs. Before getting into the specifics of using a DTD to validate XHTML documents, it's necessary to clarify the different versions of XHTML and how they impact XHTML document validation.

The first version of XHTML was version 1.0, which focused on a direct interpretation of HTML 4.0 as an XML-based markup language. Because HTML 4.0 is a fairly large and complex markup language, the W3C decided to offer XHTML 1.0 in three different flavors, which vary in their support of HTML 4.0 features:

- Strict—No HTML presentation elements are available (`font`, `table`, and so on)
- Transitional—HTML presentation elements are available for formatting documents
- Frameset—Frames are available, as well as HTML presentation elements

These different strains of XHTML are listed in order of increasing functionality, which means that the Frameset feature set is richer and therefore more complex than the Strict feature set. These three different strains of XHTML 1.0 are realized by three different DTDs that describe the elements and attributes for each feature set. The idea is that you can use a more minimal XHTML DTD if you don't need to use certain XHTML language features, or you can use a more thorough DTD if you need additional features, such as frames.

The Strict DTD is a minimal DTD that is used to create very clean XHTML documents without any presentation markup. Documents created from this DTD require style sheets in order to be formatted for display because they don't contain any presentation markup. The Transitional DTD builds on the Strict DTD by adding support for presentation markup elements. This DTD is useful in performing a quick conversion of HTML documents to XHTML when you don't want to take the time to develop style sheets. The Frameset DTD is the broadest of the three DTDs and adds support for creating documents with frames.

The three DTDs associated with XHTML 1.0 can certainly be used to validate XHTML documents, but there is a newer version of XHTML known as XHMTL 1.1 that includes a DTD of its own. The XHTML 1.1 DTD is a reformulation of the XHTML 1.0 Strict DTD that is designed for modularity. The idea behind the XHTML 1.1 DTD is to provide a means of expanding XHTML to support other XML-based languages, such as MathML for mathematical content. Because the XHTML 1.1 DTD is based upon the Strict XHTML 1.0 DTD, it doesn't include support for presentation elements or framesets. The XHTML 1.1 DTD is therefore designed for pure XHTML documents that adhere to the XML adage of separating content from how it is formatted and displayed.

Regardless of which XHTML DTD you decide to use to validate XHTML documents, there are a few other validity requirements to which all XHTML documents must adhere:

- There must be a document type declaration (`DOCTYPE`) in the document that appears prior to the root element
- The document must validate against the DTD declared in the document type declaration; this DTD must be one of the three XHTML 1.0 DTDs or the XHTML 1.1 DTD
- The root element of the document must be `html`
- The root element of the document must designate an XHTML namespace using the `xmlns` attribute

You must declare the DTD for all XHTML documents in a document type declaration at the top of the document. A *Formal Public Identifier (FPI)* is used in the document type declaration to reference one of the standard XHTML DTDs. Following is an example of how to declare the Strict XHTML 1.0 DTD in a document type declaration:

```
<!DOCTYPE html PUBLIC "-//W3C//DTD XHTML 1.0 Strict//EN"
  "DTD/xhtml1-strict.dtd">
```

It isn't terribly important that you understand the details of the FPI in this code. The main point is that it identifies the Strict XHTML 1.0 DTD and therefore is suitable for XHTML documents that don't require formatting or frameset features. The XHTML 1.0 Transitional DTD is specified using similar code, as the following example reveals:

```
<!DOCTYPE html PUBLIC "-//W3C//DTD XHTML 1.0 Transitional//EN"
  "DTD/xhtml1-transitional.dtd">
```

The XHTML 1.0 Frameset DTD is also specified with similar code, as in the following example:

```
<!DOCTYPE html PUBLIC "-//W3C//DTD XHTML 1.0 Frameset//EN"
  "DTD/xhtml1-frameset.dtd">
```

Finally, the XHTML 1.1 DTD is specified with a document type declaration that is a little different from the others:

```
<!DOCTYPE html PUBLIC "-//W3C//DTD XHTML 1.1//EN"
  "http://www.w3.org/TR/xhtml11/DTD/xhtml11.dtd">
```

The decision regarding which XHTML DTD to use really comes down to what features your documents require. If you can get by without the presentation or frameset features, then the XHTML 1.0 Strict DTD or the XHTML 1.1 DTD are your best bet. Between the two, it's better to go with the newer XHTML 1.1 DTD because it represents the future direction of XHTML. If your documents require some presentation features, the XHTML 1.0 Transitional DTD is the one for you. And finally, if you need the whole gamut of XHTML features, including framesets, the XHTML 1.0 Frameset DTD is the way to go.

By the Way

> If you truly want to create XML documents that are geared toward the future of the Web, you should target the XHTML 1.1 DTD.

In addition to declaring an appropriate DTD in the document type declaration, a valid XHTML document must also declare the XHTML namespace in the root `html` element, and it must declare the language. Following is an example of declaring the standard XHTML namespace and the English language in the `html` element for an XHTML document:

```
<html xmlns="http://www.w3.org/1999/xhtml" xml:lang="en">
```

Putting Together an XHTML Document

XHTML documents are created in much the same way as any other XML document, or any HTML document for that matter. As long as you keep in mind the differences between XHTML and HTML, you can develop XHTML web pages just as you would create HTML web pages, assuming you don't mind creating web pages by hand. To give you a better idea as to how an XHTML document comes together, check out the code for a skeletal XHTML document in Listing 21.1.

LISTING 21.1 A Skeletal XHTML Document

```
<?xml version="1.0" encoding="UTF-8"?>
<!DOCTYPE html PUBLIC "-//W3C//DTD XHTML 1.1//EN"
  "http://www.w3.org/TR/xhtml11/DTD/xhtml11.dtd">

<html xmlns="http://www.w3.org/1999/xhtml" xml:lang="en">
  <head>
```

LISTING 21.1 Continued

```
    <title>Skeletal XHTML Document</title>
  </head>

  <body>
    <p>
      This is a skeletal XHTML document.
    </p>
  </body>
</html>
```

The `skeleton.xhtml` document admittedly doesn't do much in terms of being a useful web page, but it does demonstrate how to create a legal XHTML document. In other words, the skeletal document declares an XHTML DTD and namespace and adheres to all of the structural and syntax rules of XML. It can also be viewed directly in a web browser. The main significance of the skeletal XHTML document is that it serves as a great template for creating other XHTML documents.

Validating an XHTML Document

As with any XML document, it's very important to be able to validate XHTML documents. You've already learned about the DTDs that factor into XHTML validation, but you haven't learned exactly when XHTML documents are validated. Keep in mind that it takes processing time for any XML document to be validated, and in the case of XHTML, this could hinder the speed at which web pages are served and displayed. The ideal scenario in terms of performance is for developers to validate XHTML documents before making them publicly available, which alleviates the need for browsers to perform any validation. On the other hand, there currently is a lot of HTML code generated on the fly by scripting languages and other interactive technologies, in which case it might be necessary for a browser to sometimes validate XHTML documents.

Although there are no rules governing the appropriate time for XHTML documents to be validated, it's generally a good idea for you to take the initiative to validate your own documents before taking them live. Fortunately, the W3C provides a free online validation service known as the W3C Validator that can be used to validate XHTML documents. This validation service is available online at http://validator.w3.org/ and is shown in Figure 21.1.

You can see in the figure that the W3C Validator is used by entering the URI of an XHTML document. Of course, web pages are typically developed offline, which means you may not have published them to an accessible URI online. In this case, you can simply choose the File Upload option on the W3C Validator page, which allows you to browse your computer for an XHTML document file. If you want to exercise more control over the validation of XHTML documents that you upload, you may want to consider using the Extended File Upload Interface, which is available via a text link just below the Validate by File Upload option (see Figure 21.1).

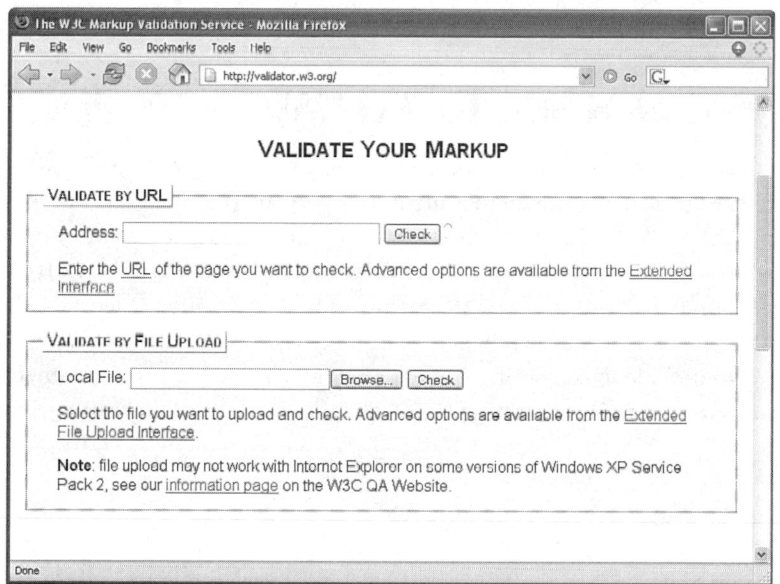

FIGURE 21.1
The W3C Validator service is capable of validating XHTML documents as well as HTML documents.

Figure 21.2 shows the results of validating the `skeleton.xhtml` document using the W3C Validator.

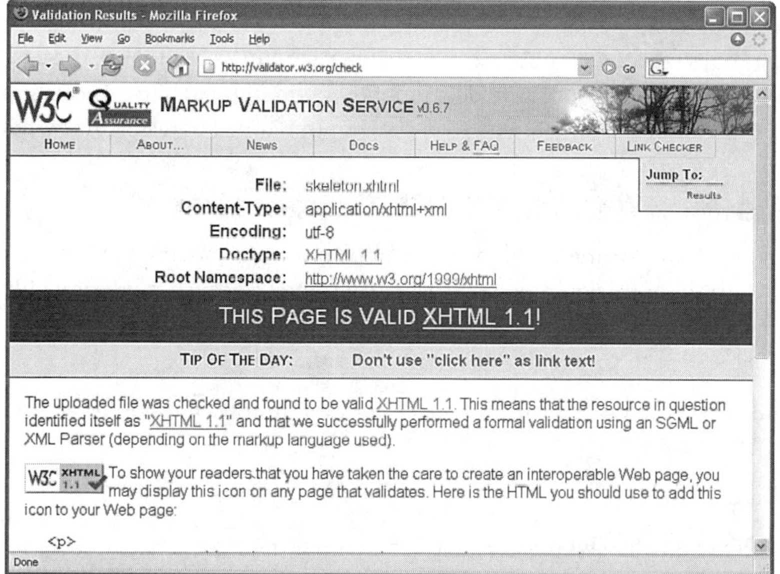

FIGURE 21.2
The results of passing the skeletal XHTML document through the W3C Validator.

As the figure reveals, the skeletal document passed the W3C Validator with flying colors, which isn't too much of a surprise. This is a handy service to have around when creating XHTML documents, especially when you consider that it is always up to date with the latest standards set forth by the W3C.

Migrating HTML to XHTML

Throughout the hour thus far I've focused on the concept of creating XHTML documents from scratch. This sounds great in theory, but the reality is that there are gazillions of HTML-based web pages in existence that could benefit from being migrated to XHTML. Fortunately, it isn't too terribly difficult to bring HTML 4.0 documents up to par with the XHTML specification. You've already learned about the ways in which XHTML documents differ from HTML 4.0 documents; these differences are your guide to converting HTML to XHTML. There are two fundamental approaches available for converting HTML documents to XHTML documents:

- Convert the documents by hand (more work, more accurate)
- Convert the documents using an automated conversion tool (less work, less accurate)

The former approach requires some serious elbow grease, but it yields the best results because you're carrying out the migration process with considerable attention to detail. On the other hand, the latter approach has the obvious benefit of automating the conversion process and saving you a lot of tedious work. However, as in any automated process, the conversion from HTML to XHTML doesn't always go perfectly smooth. That's why the first approach is the more accurate of the two, even though it requires much more effort. A middle ground hybrid approach involves first using an automated conversion tool and then making fine-tuned adjustments by hand.

Hands-on HTML to XHTML Conversion

Converting HTML documents to XHTML can be a tedious process, but if you have a strategy for the conversion process it can make things go much more smoothly. In fact, it helps to have a checklist to use as a guide while hand-coding the conversion. Follow these steps to convert HTML code to XHTML code:

1. Add (or modify) a document type declaration that declares an appropriate XHTML DTD.
2. Declare the XHTML namespace in the `html` element.
3. Convert all element and attribute names to lowercase.

4. Match every start tag with an end tag.
5. Replace > with /> at the end of all empty tags.
6. Make sure all required attributes are set.
7. Make sure all attributes have values assigned to them.
8. Enclose all attribute values in quotes (" ").
9. Make sure all elements and attributes are defined in the XHTML DTD used by the document.

If you carry out each of these steps, you should be able to arrive at a valid XHTML document without too much difficulty. A simple example will help explain the relevance of these steps a little better. Listing 21.2 contains the code for an HTML document that describes a web page chronicling the construction of a vegetable filter for a water garden. Figure 21.3 shows the veggie filter web page as viewed in Firefox.

LISTING 21.2 The Veggie Filter Sample HTML Document

```
<HTML>
  <HEAD>
    <TITLE>Constructing a Veggie Filter</TITLE>
  </HEAD>

  <BODY STYLE=background-image:url(water.jpg)>
    <H2>Constructing a Veggie Filter</H2>
    <P>
    A vegetable filter is a welcome addition to any water garden, as it
    provides a natural biofiltration mechanism above and beyond any other filter
    systems already employed. The concept behind a vegetable filter is that you
    simply pump water through the root system of aquatic plants, allowing them
    to absorb nutrients from the water and thereby assist in purifying the
    water. Below are pictures of the construction of a veggie filter that sits
    atop the pond it is helping to keep
    clean.
    <P>
    <A HREF=filter01_lg.jpg><IMG SRC=filter01.jpg STYLE=align:left BORDER=0></A>
    <A HREF=filter02_lg.jpg><IMG SRC=filter02.jpg STYLE=align:left BORDER=0></A>
    <A HREF=filter03_lg.jpg><IMG SRC=filter03.jpg STYLE=align:left BORDER=0></A>
    <A HREF=filter04_lg.jpg><IMG SRC=filter04.jpg STYLE=align:left BORDER=0></A>
    <A HREF=filter05_lg.jpg><IMG SRC=filter05.jpg STYLE=align:left BORDER=0></A>
    <A HREF=filter06_lg.jpg><IMG SRC=filter06.jpg STYLE=align:left BORDER=0></A>
    <P>
    In these photos, you see the veggie filter come together as the sand bottom
    is put into place, followed by protective felt, a leveled top, a pond liner,
    and plumbing for the pump outlets.
    <P>
    If you'd like to learn more about water gardening, contact my friends at
    Green and Hagstrom through their Web site at
    <A HREF=http://www.greenandhagstrom.com/>Green & Hagstrom Aquatic Nursery
    and Water Garden Supply</A>
  </BODY>
</HTML>
```

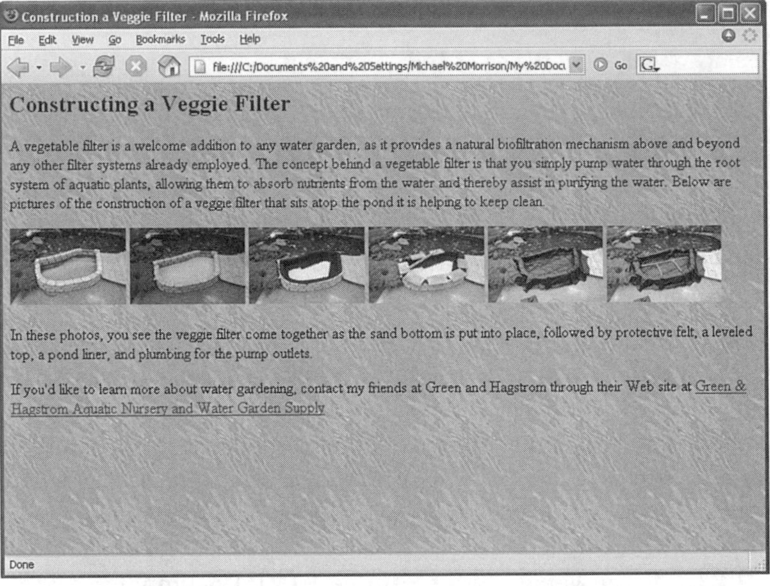

FIGURE 21.3
The veggie filter sample HTML document as viewed in Firefox.

If you study the code for the veggie filter sample HTML document, you'll notice that it doesn't meet the high standards of XHTML in terms of structure and syntax. Granted, the code is cleanly organized but it definitely doesn't qualify as a valid or even well-formed document under the rules of XHTML. Following are the major problems with this code that need to be resolved in order for the document to comply with XHTML rules:

- There is no document type declaration.
- The XHTML namespace isn't declared.
- The elements and attributes are all in uppercase.
- Not every start-tag (<P>) has an end tag (lines 8 and 17, among others).
- Empty elements (IMG) don't end with /> (lines 18 through 23).
- Some elements (IMG) are missing required attributes (ALT).
- Attribute values aren't enclosed in quotes (lines 6, 18, 19, and so on).

You might be thinking that this list of problems is uncannily similar to the list of HTML to XHTML conversion steps I mentioned earlier in the hour. This is not mere coincidence—I arrived at the list of conversion steps by addressing the most common HTML coding problems that conflict with XHTML. If you go through the document and fix all of these problems, the resulting XHTML code will look like the code shown in Listing 21.3.

LISTING 21.3 The Veggie Filter Sample XHTML Document That Was Converted by Hand

```
 1: <?xml version="1.0" encoding="UTF-8"?>
 2: <!DOCTYPE html PUBLIC "-//W3C//DTD XHTML 1.1//EN"
 3:   "http://www.w3.org/TR/xhtml11/DTD/xhtml11.dtd">
 4:
 5: <html xmlns="http://www.w3.org/1999/xhtml" xml:lang="en">
 6:   <head>
 7:     <title>Constructing a Veggie Filter</title>
 8:   </head>
 9:
10:   <body style="background-image:url(water.jpg)">
11:     <h2>Constructing a Veggie Filter</h2>
12:     <p>
13:     A vegetable filter is a welcome addition to any water garden, as it
14:     provides a natural biofiltration mechanism above and beyond any other filter
15:     systems already employed. The concept behind a vegetable filter is that you
16:     simply pump water through the root system of aquatic plants, allowing them
17:     to absorb nutrients from the water and thereby assist in purifying the
18:     water. Below are pictures of the construction of a veggie filter that sits
19:     atop the pond it is helping to keep clean.
20:     </p>
21:     <p>
22:     <a href="filter01_lg.jpg"><img src="filter01.jpg" alt="Step 1: Build the
23:       rock support walls" style="align: left; border-width: 0px"/></a>
24:     <a href="filter02_lg.jpg"><img src="filter02.jpg" alt="Step 2: Lay the
25:       sand base" style="align: left; border-width: 0px"/></a>
26:     <a href="filter03_lg.jpg"><img src="filter03.jpg" alt="Step 3: Protect the
27:       walls with felt underlayment" style="align: left; border-width: 0px"/></a>
28:     <a href="filter04_lg.jpg"><img src="filter04.jpg" alt="Step 4: Level the top
29:       edges" style="align: left; border-width: 0px"/></a>
30:     <a href="filter05_lg.jpg"><img src="filter05.jpg" alt="Step 5: Insert and
31:       trim the liner" style="align: left; border-width: 0px"/></a>
32:     <a href="filter06_lg.jpg"><img src="filter06.jpg" alt="Step 6: Assemble and
33:       place the pump plumbing" style="align: left; border-width: 0px"/></a>
34:     </p>
35:     <p>
36:     In these photos, you see the veggie filter come together as the sand bottom
37:     is put into place, followed by protective felt, a leveled top, a pond liner,
38:     and plumbing for the pump outlets.
39:     </p>
40:     <p>
41:     If you'd like to learn more about water gardening, contact my friends at
42:     Green and Hagstrom through their Web site at
43:     <a href="http://www.greenandhagstrom.com/">Green &amp; Hagstrom Aquatic
44:     Nursery and Water Garden Supply</a>
45:     </p>
46:   </body>
47: </html>
```

If you study this document carefully, you'll see that it meets all of the requirements of a valid XHTML document. For example, the <p> tags all have matching </p> closing tags (lines 12, 21, 35, and 40). If you're a skeptic and want to make sure that the document is really valid, you can run it through the W3C Validator just to make sure. Actually, I already did it for you and the document checked out fine, which means that it is a bona fide XHTML document.

Automated HTML to XHTML Conversion

If you don't like getting your hands dirty, you might consider an automated approach to converting HTML documents to XHTML. Or you might decide to go for a hybrid conversion approach that involves using an automated tool and then a little hand coding to smooth out the results. Either way, there are a few tools out there that automate the HTML to XHTML conversion process. One such tool is HTML Tidy, which was developed by Dave Raggett, an engineer at Hewlett Packard's UK Laboratories.

HTML Tidy is a command-line tool that was originally designed to clean up sloppy HTML code, but it also supports converting HTML code to XHTML code. When you think about it, converting HTML to XHTML really is nothing more than cleaning up sloppy code, which is why HTML Tidy works so well. The HTML Tidy tool is available for free download from the HTML Tidy web site at http://www.w3.org/People/Raggett/tidy/. There are also a few graphical HTML applications that serve as front ends for HTML Tidy just in case you aren't comfortable using command-line applications.

By the Way

> Dave Raggett is also the developer is HTML Slidy, which is an XHTML-based slide show tool that allows you to create PowerPoint-style slide show presentations using nothing more than XHTML code. To learn more about HTML Slidy, visit the HTML Slidy web page at http://www.w3.org/2005/03/slideshow.html.

If you run HTML Tidy without any command-line options, it will process an HTML document and clean it up. However, the resulting document won't be an XHTML document. In order for HTML Tidy to generate an XHTML document, you must specify the `-asxhtml` command-line option, which indicates that HTML Tidy is to convert the HTML document to an XHTML document. Additionally, the `-indent` option helps to clean up the formatting of the output so that the resulting XHTML code is indented and easier to understand. The output of HTML Tidy defaults to standard output, which is usually just your command-line window. Although this works if you just want to see what a converted document looks like, it doesn't help you in terms of generating a converted document file. You must specify that you want the output to be in XHTML format by using the `-output` option and specifying the output file. Following is an example command that converts the `vegfilter.html` veggie filter HTML document to XHTML using HTML Tidy:

```
tidy -asxhtml -indent -output vegfilter_t.xhtml vegfilter.html
```

This command directs the output of the HTML Tidy application to the file `vegfilter_t.xhtml`. Aside from it being a little more compressed in terms of how the content is arranged, the resulting code from HTML Tidy is very similar to the hand-coded conversion of the XHTML document. The document type is changed to XHTML 1.0 Transitional, as opposed to XHTML 1.1. Other major changes include all element and attribute types being converted to lowercase, as well as empty `img` elements fixed with a trailing `/>`. Also, all attribute values are quoted.

There is still an important aspect of the generated XHTML document that must be modified by hand. I'm referring to the `img` elements, none of which provide `alt` attributes. The `alt` attribute is a required attribute of the `img` element in HTML 4.0 and XHTML, so you must specify values for them in all images in order to make the document a valid XHTML document. Fortunately, the HTML Tidy tool caught this problem and output an error message indicating that the change needed to be made by hand (see Figure 21.4). Another required change that you'll notice in the figure is the ampersand (&) in the text `Green & Hagstrom`, which needs to be changed to the `&` entity.

```
Command Prompt
C:\Documents and Settings\Michael Morrison\My Documents\Books\TY XML 3rd\Example
s\Chap21>tidy -asxhtml vegfilter.html > vegfilter_t.xhtml
line 1 column 1 - Warning: missing <!DOCTYPE> declaration
line 30 column 52 - Warning: unescaped & which should be written as &amp;
line 17 column 29 - Warning: <img> lacks "alt" attribute
line 18 column 29 - Warning: <img> lacks "alt" attribute
line 19 column 29 - Warning: <img> lacks "alt" attribute
line 20 column 29 - Warning: <img> lacks "alt" attribute
line 21 column 29 - Warning: <img> lacks "alt" attribute
line 22 column 29 - Warning: <img> lacks "alt" attribute
Info: Document content looks like XHTML 1.0 Transitional
8 warnings, 0 errors were found!

The alt attribute should be used to give a short description
of an image; longer descriptions should be given with the
longdesc attribute which takes a URL linked to the description.
These measures are needed for people using non-graphical browsers.

For further advice on how to make your pages accessible
see http://www.w3.org/WAI/GL. You may also want to try
"http://www.cast.org/bobby/" which is a free Web-based
service for checking URLs for accessibility.

To learn more about HTML Tidy see http://tidy.sourceforge.net
Please send bug reports to html-tidy@w3.org
HTML and CSS specifications are available from http://www.w3.org/
Lobby your company to join W3C, see http://www.w3.org/Consortium

C:\Documents and Settings\Michael Morrison\My Documents\Books\TY XML 3rd\Example
s\Chap21>
```

FIGURE 21.4
HTML Tidy was able to detect conversion errors in the veggie filter sample HTML document so that you can repair them by hand.

Finalizing the conversion of the veggie filter example document involves changing the document type to XHTML 1.1 (if desired), adding `alt` attributes to the `img` elements, and adding an entity reference. Once that's done, the new XHTML document is good to go. The HTML Tidy tool significantly improves the HTML to XHTML conversion process, leaving you with relatively minor changes to make by hand.

Summary

HTML has served its purpose well by allowing people to build web pages with relative ease, but its lack of structure is limiting when it comes to intelligently processing web content. For this reason, the architects of the Web focused significant efforts on charting the future of the Web with a more structured markup language for creating web pages. This markup language is XHTML, which is a reformulated version of HTML that meets the high structural and organizational standards of XML. XHTML is still in many ways a future technology in terms of becoming a standard used by all web developers, but it is nonetheless important to XML developers and HTML developers alike.

This hour introduced you to XHTML and then explored the relationship between HTML and XHTML. You learned about the origins of both languages and why XHTML has long-term benefits that make it an ideal successor to HTML. The hour shifted gears toward the practical by showing you how to create and validate XHTML documents. You then finished up the hour by learning how to migrate legacy HTML documents to XHTML.

Q&A

Q. ***If web browsers don't know how to display XML documents, how is it that XHTML documents can be viewed in web browsers?***

A. XHTML represents the one exception to the rule about XML documents not being viewable without the aid of stylesheets. Because HTML documents are directly viewable in web browsers, even without the help of stylesheets, it only makes sense that XHTML documents should be viewable as well. However, you still must use stylesheets if you want control over the layout and formatting details of XHTML documents.

Q. ***What happens if I don't validate my XHTML documents?***

A. Nothing happens, as least for now. Web browsers currently treat XHTML documents with the same leniency that they handle HTML documents, so you can get away with creating invalid documents if you want. However, this goes against the whole premise of XHTML, which is to demand the creation of highly accurate documents. The idea is that browsers and web-based applications may at some point validate XHTML documents. So you should make an effort to police your own documents and make sure they are valid before publishing them on the Web.

Workshop

The Workshop is designed to help you anticipate possible questions, review what you've learned, and begin learning how to put your knowledge into practice.

Quiz

1. What is the relationship between HTML and XHTML?
2. How do XHTML attributes differ from typical HTML attributes?
3. What is the root element of XHTML documents?

Quiz Answers

1. XHTML is an XML-based markup language that carries out the functionality of HTML in the spirit of XML. More specifically, XHTML is a version of HTML 4.0 that plays by the more rigid rules of XML.
2. Attributes in XHTML cannot be used without a value, and all XHTML attribute values must appear within quotes.
3. The root element of XHTML documents is `html`, which is the same root element used in HTML documents.

Exercises

1. Using the `skeleton.xhtml` document as a template, create an XHTML document for a personal web page. A good example of a personal web page is an XHTML document that stores your resume. After creating the XHTML document, use the W3C Validator to validate the document.
2. Find an existing HTML document and convert it to XHTML using the list of conversion steps presented in this hour. It's up to you whether you convert the document entirely by hand or take advantage of an automated tool, such as HTML Tidy.

HOUR 22

Addressing and Linking XML Documents

> Writing for the Web without linking is like eating without digesting. It's literary bulimia.
>
> —Doc Searls

So maybe that quote is a little strong in regard to the importance of linking on the Web, but the underlying point is still very much valid. Just as XML has been leveraged to improve other facets of the Web such as the core syntax and structure of HTML, so is it being used to improve upon the very linking mechanism that forms the interconnections between pages on the Web. I'm referring to *XLink*, which is the XML linking technology that allows you to carry out advanced linking between XML documents. Coupled with another important XML technology called *XPointer*, XLink builds on the premise of HTML hyperlinks but goes several steps further in supporting advanced linking features such as two-way links. Although XML linking is still a relatively new technology, it is already having an impact on how information is connected on the Web.

Linking XML documents goes hand in hand with addressing XML documents. Yet another XML-related technology called XPath makes it possible to specify exactly where XML content is located. Just as your mailing address helps you to remember where you live, XPath provides a means of remembering where nodes are located in XML documents. Okay, you probably don't rely on your mailing address to remember where you live, but you will rely on XPath if you use technologies such as XSLT, XLink, or XPointer, which must reference parts of XML documents. XPath is the enabling technology that allows you to drill down into XML documents and reference individual pieces of information.

In this hour, you'll learn

- How to navigate through an XML document using XPath patterns
- How to build powerful expressions using XPath patterns and functions
- What technologies come together to support linking in XML
- How to reference document fragments with XPointer
- How to link XML documents with XLink

Understanding XPath

XPath is a technology that enables you to address parts of an XML document, such as a specific element or set of elements. XPath is implemented as a non-XML expression language, which makes it suitable for use in situations where XML markup isn't really applicable, such as within attribute values. As you know, attribute values are simple text and therefore can't contain additional XML markup. So, although XPath expressions are used within XML markup, they don't directly use tags and attributes themselves. This makes XPath considerably different from its XSL counterparts (XSLT and XSL-FO) in that it isn't implemented as an XML language. XPath's departure from XML syntax also makes it both flexible and compact, which are important benefits when you consider that XPath is typically used in constrained situations such as attribute values.

XPath is a very important XML technology in that it provides a flexible means of addressing XML document parts. Any time you need to reference a portion of an XML document, such as with XSLT, you ultimately must rely on XPath. The XPath language is not based upon XML, but it is somewhat familiar nonetheless because it relies on a path notation that is commonly used in computer file systems. In fact, the name XPath stems from the fact that the path notation used to address XML documents is similar to path names used in file systems to describe the locations of files. Not surprisingly, the syntax used by XPath is extremely concise because it is designed for use in URIs and XML attribute values.

Similar to other XML technologies, XPath operates under the notion that a document consists of a tree of nodes. XPath defines different types of nodes that are used to describe nodes that appear within a tree of XML content. There is always a single root node that serves as the root of an XPath tree, and that appears as the first node in the tree. Every element in a document has a corresponding element node that appears in the tree under the root node. Within an element node there are other types of nodes that correspond to the element's content. Element nodes may have a unique identifier associated with them that is used to reference the node with XPath. Figure 22.1 shows the relationship between different kinds of nodes in an XPath tree.

Nodes within an XML document can generally be broken down into element nodes, attribute nodes, and text nodes. Some nodes have names, in which case the name can consist of an optional namespace URI and a local name; a name that includes a namespace prefix is known as an expanded name. Following is an example of an expanded element name:

```
<xsl:value-of select="."/>
```

In this example, the local name is `value-of` and the namespace prefix is `xsl`. If you were to declare the XSL namespace as the default namespace for a document, you could get away with dropping the namespace prefix part of the expanded name, in which case the name becomes this:

```
<value-of select="."/>
```

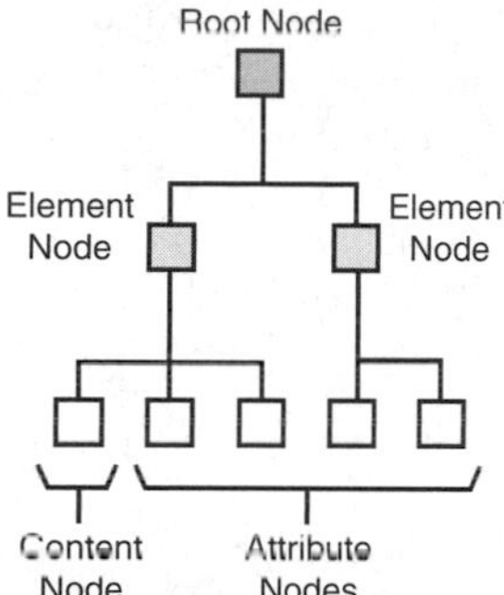

FIGURE 22.1 XPath is based upon the notion of an XML document consisting of a hierarchical tree of nodes.

If you declare more than one namespace in a document, you will have to use expanded names for at least some of the elements and attributes. It's generally a good idea to use them for all elements and attributes in this situation just to make the code clearer and eliminate the risk of name clashes.

Getting back to node types in XPath, following are the different types of nodes that can appear in an XPath tree:

- Root node
- Element nodes
- Text nodes
- Attribute nodes
- Namespace nodes
- Processing instruction nodes
- Comment nodes

You should have a pretty good feel for these node types, considering that you've learned enough about XML and have dealt with each type of node throughout the book thus far. The root node in XPath serves the same role as it does in the structure of a document: it serves as the root of an XPath tree and appears as the first node in the tree. Every element in a document has a corresponding element node that appears in the tree under the root node. Within an element node appear all of the other types of nodes that correspond to the element's content. Element nodes may have a unique identifier associated with them, which is useful when referencing the node with XPath.

The point of all this naming and referencing of nodes is to provide a means of traversing an XML document to arrive at a given node. This traversal is accomplished using expressions, which you learned a little about back in Hour 13, "Access Your iTunes Music Library via XML." You use XPath to build expressions, which are typically used in the context of some other operation, such as a document transformation. Upon being processed and evaluated, XPath expressions result in a data object of one of the following types:

- Node set—A collection of nodes
- String—A text string
- Boolean—A true/false value
- Number—A floating-point number

Similar to a database query, the data object resulting from an XPath expression can then be used as the basis for some other process, such as an XSLT transformation. For example, you might create an XPath expression that results in a node set that is transformed by an XSLT template. On the other hand, you can also use XPath with XLink, where a node result of an expression could form the basis of a linked document.

By the Way

> To learn more about the formal XPath specification, visit the XPath section of the W3C web site at http://www.w3.org/TR/xpath.

Navigating a Document with XPath Patterns

XPath expressions are usually built out of *patterns*, which describe a branch of an XML tree. A pattern therefore is used to reference one or more hierarchical nodes in a document tree. Patterns can be constructed to perform relatively complex pattern matching tasks and ultimately form somewhat of a mini-query language that is used to query documents for specific nodes. Patterns can be used to isolate specific nodes or groups of nodes and can be specified as absolute or relative. An *absolute pattern* spells out the exact location of a node or node set, whereas a *relative pattern* identifies a node or node set relative to a certain context.

The next few sections examine the ways in which patterns are used to access nodes within XML documents. To better understand how patterns are used, it's worth seeing them in the context of a real XML document. Listing 22.1 contains the code for the familiar training log sample document that you saw earlier in the book, which serves as the sample document in this hour for XPath.

LISTING 22.1 The Training Log Sample XML Document

```
01: <?xml version="1.0"?>
02: <!DOCTYPE trainlog SYSTEM "etml.dtd">
03:
04: <trainlog>
05:   <!-- This session was part of the marathon training group run. -->
06:   <session date="11/19/05" type="running" heartrate="158">
07:     <duration units="minutes">45</duration>
08:     <distance units="miles">5.5</distance>
09:     <location>Warner Park</location>
10:     <comments>Mid-morning run, a little winded throughout.</comments>
11:   </session>
12:
13:   <session date="11/21/05" type="cycling" heartrate="153">
14:     <duration units="hours">2.5</duration>
15:     <distance units="miles">37.0</distance>
16:     <location>Natchez Trace Parkway</location>
17:     <comments>Hilly ride, felt strong as an ox.</comments>
18:   </session>
19:
20:   <session date="11/24/05" type="running" heartrate="156">
21:     <duration units="hours">1.5</duration>
22:     <distance units="miles">8.5</distance>
23:     <location>Warner Park</location>
24:     <comments>Afternoon run, felt reasonably strong.</comments>
25:   </session>
26: </trainlog>
```

You may want to keep a bookmark around for this page, as several of the XPath examples throughout the next section rely on the training log sample code.

Referencing Nodes

The most basic of all XPath patterns is the pattern that references the current node, which consists of a simple period:

```
.
```

If you're traversing a document tree, a period will obtain the current node. The current node pattern is therefore a relative pattern because it makes sense only in the context of a tree of data. As a contrast to the current pattern, which is relative, consider the pattern that is used to select the root node of a document. This pattern is known as the root pattern and consists of a single forward slash:

```
/
```

If you were to use a single forward slash in an expression for the training log sample document, it would refer to the `trainlog` element (line 4) because this element is the root element of the document. Because the root pattern directly references a specific location in a document (the root node), it is considered an absolute pattern. The root pattern is extremely important to XPath because it represents the starting point of any document's node tree.

As you know, XPath relies on the hierarchical nature of XML documents to reference nodes. The relationship between nodes in this type of hierarchy is best described as a familial relationship, which means that nodes can be described as parent, child, or sibling nodes, depending upon the context of the tree. For example, the root node is the parent of all nodes. Nodes might be parents of some nodes and siblings of others. To reference child nodes using XPath, you use the name of the child node as the pattern. So, in the training log example, you can reference a `session` element (line 6, for example) as a child of the root node by simply specifying the name of the element: `session`. Of course, this assumes that the root node (line 4) is the current context for the pattern, in which case a relative child path is okay. If the root node isn't the current context, you should fully specify the child path as `/session`. Notice in this case that the root pattern is combined with a child pattern to create an absolute path.

By the Way

> I've mentioned context a few times in regard to node references. *Context* simply refers to the location within a document tree from which you are referencing a node. The context is established by the current node you are referencing. All further references are then made with respect to this node.

If there are child nodes there must also be parent nodes. To access a parent node, you must use two periods:

```
..
```

As an example, if the current context is one of the `distance` elements (line 15, for example) in the training log document, the `..` parent pattern will reference the parent of the node, which is a `session` element (line 13). You can put patterns together to get more interesting results. For example, to address a sibling node, you must first go to the parent and then reference the sibling as a child. In other words, you use the parent pattern (`..`) followed by a forward slash (`/`) followed by the sibling node name, like this:

```
../duration
```

This pattern assumes that the context is one of the child elements of the `session` element (other than `duration`). Assuming this context, the `../duration` pattern will reference the `duration` element (line 14) as a sibling node.

Thus far I've focused on referencing individual nodes. However, it's also possible to select multiple nodes. For example, you can select all of the child nodes (descendants) of a given node using the double slash pattern:

```
//
```

As an example, if the context is one of the `session` elements in the training log document (line 20, for example), you can select all of its child nodes by using double slashes. This results in the `duration` (line 21), `distance` (line 22), `location` (line 23), and `comments` (line 24) elements being selected.

Another way to select multiple nodes is to use the wildcard pattern, which is an asterisk:

```
*
```

The wildcard pattern selects all of the nodes in a given context. So, if the context was a `session` element and you used the pattern `*/distance`, all of the `distance` elements in the document would be selected. This occurs because the wildcard pattern first results in all of the sibling `session` elements being selected, after which the selection is limited to the child `distance` elements.

To summarize, following are the primary building blocks used to reference nodes in XPath:

- Current node—`.`
- Root node—`/`
- Parent node—`..`
- Child node—`Child`
- Sibling node—`/Sibling`
- All child nodes—`//`
- All nodes—`*`

These pattern building blocks form the core of XPath, but they don't tell the whole story. The next section explores attributes and subsets and how they are referenced.

Referencing Attributes and Subsets

Elements aren't the only important pieces of information in XML documents; it's also important to be able to reference attributes. Fortunately, XPath makes it quite easy to reference attributes by using the "at" symbol:

```
@
```

The at symbol is used to reference attributes by preceding an attribute name:

```
*/distance/@units
```

This code selects all of the units attributes for distance elements in the training log document, assuming that the context is one of the session elements. As you can see, attributes fit right into the path notation used by XPath and are referenced in the same manner as elements, with the addition of the at (@) symbol.

One other important feature of XPath expressions is support for the selection of subsets of nodes. You select a subset by appending square brackets ([]) to the end of a pattern and then placing an expression within the brackets that defines the subset. As an example, consider the following pattern that selects all the session elements in the training log document:

```
*/session
```

It's possible that you might want to limit the session elements to a certain type of training session, such as running. To do this, you add square brackets onto the pattern, and you create an expression that checks to see if the session type is set to running:

```
*/session[@type='running']
```

This pattern results in selecting only the session elements whose type attribute is set to running. Notice that an at symbol (@) is used in front of the attribute name (type) to indicate that it is an attribute. You can also address elements by index, as the following expression demonstrates:

```
/session[1]
```

This expression selects the first session element in the document.

Using XPath Functions

Back in Hour 13, you learned about some of the more commonly used XPath functions and how they can be used to create expressions for XSLT stylesheets. I'd like to revisit the standard XPath functions and go into a little more detail regarding their use in creating expressions. Before getting into the specifics of the XPath functions at your disposal, it's worth taking a look at their general use. The functions supported by XPath, which are available for use in creating XPath expressions, can be roughly divided along the lines of the data types on which they operate:

- Node functions
- String functions
- Boolean functions
- Number functions

The next few sections explore the functions in each of these categories in more detail. For a complete XPath function reference, please visit the XPath page at the W3C web site at http://www.w3.org/TR/xpath#corelib.

Node Functions

Node functions are XPath functions that relate to the node tree. Although all of XPath technically relates to the node tree, node functions are very direct in that they allow you to ascertain the position of nodes in a node set, as well as how many nodes are in a set. Following are the most common XPath node functions:

- `position()`—Determine the numeric position of a node
- `last()`—Determine the last node in a node set
- `count()`—Determine the number of nodes in a node set

Although these node functions might seem somewhat abstract, keep in mind that they can be used to carry out some interesting tasks when used in the context of a broader expression. For example, the following code shows how to use the `count()` function to calculate the total distance in the training log document for sessions whose distances are recorded in miles:

```
count(*/distance[@units='miles'])
```

Following is another example that shows how to reference a child node based solely upon its position within a document:

```
child::item[position()=3]
```

Assuming there are several child elements of type `item`, this code references the third child `item` element of the current context. To reference the last child item, you use the `last()` function instead of an actual number, like this:

```
child::item[position()=last()]
```

String Functions

The XPath string functions are used to manipulate strings of text. With the string functions you can concatenate strings, slice them up into substrings, and determine the length of them. Following are the most popular string functions in XPath:

- `concat()`—Concatenate two strings together
- `starts-with()`—Determine if a string begins with another string
- `contains()`—Determine if a string contains another string

- `substring-before()`—Retrieve a substring that appears before another string
- `substring-after()`—Retrieve a substring that appears after another string
- `substring()`—Retrieve a substring of a specified length starting at an index within another string
- `string-length()`—Determine the length of a string

These XPath string functions can come in quite handy when it comes to building expressions, especially when you consider that XML content is always specified as raw text. In other words, it is possible to manipulate most XML content as a string, regardless of whether the underlying value of the content is numeric or some other data type. Following is an example that demonstrates how to extract the month of a training session from a `date` attribute in the training log document:

```
substring-after(/session[1]@date, "/")
```

In this example, the `substring-after()` function is called and passed the `date` attribute. Because a forward slash (/) is passed as the second argument to the function, it is used as the basis for finding the substring. If you look back at one of the `date` attributes in the document (line 6, for example), you'll notice that the month appears just after the first forward slash. As a comparison, you could extract the year as a substring by providing the same arguments but instead using the `substring-before()` function:

```
substring-before(/session[1]@date, '/')
```

Another use of the string functions is finding nodes that contain a particular substring. For example, if you wanted to analyze your training data and look for training sessions where you felt strong, you could use the `contains()` function to select `session` elements where the `comments` child element contains the word "strong":

```
*/session[contains(comments, 'strong')]
```

In this example, the second and third `session` elements would be selected because they both contain the word "strong" in their `comments` child elements (lines 17 and 24).

Boolean Functions

Boolean functions are pretty simple in that they operate solely on Boolean (true/false) values. Following are the two primary Boolean functions that you may find useful in XPath expressions:

- `not()`—Negate a Boolean value
- `lang()`—Determine if a certain language is being used

The `not()` function is pretty straightforward in that it simply reverses a Boolean value: true becomes false and false becomes true. The `lang()` function is a little more interesting because it actually queries a node to see what language it uses. As an example, many English-language XML documents set the `xml:lang` attribute to en in the root element. Although this value typically cascades down to all elements within the document, it's possible for a document to use multiple languages. The `lang()` function allows you to check the language setting for any node. Following is an example of how to use the `not()` and `lang()` functions to determine if the English language is not being used in a document:

```
not(lang("en"))
```

Number Functions

The XPath number functions should be somewhat familiar to you since you saw them in action back in Hour 13 when you created XSLT stylesheets that relied on the number functions. Following are the most commonly used number functions in XPath:

- `ceiling()`—Round up a decimal value to the nearest integer
- `floor()`—Round down a decimal value to the nearest integer
- `round()`—Round a decimal value to the nearest integer
- `sum()`—Add a set of numeric values

Following is an example of how to use the `sum()` function to add up a bunch of attribute values:

```
sum(cart/item/@price)
```

Of course, you can make nested calls to the XPath number functions. For example, you can round the result of the `sum()` function by using the `round()` function, like this:

```
round(sum(cart/item/@price))
```

The Role of XPath

You may have noticed that I've used the word "select" a lot in this hour when explaining how an XPath expression effectively selects part of a document. However, this selection process doesn't take place within XPath alone. XPath is always used in the context of another technology such as XSLT, XPointer, or XLink. The examples of XPath that you've seen in this lesson must therefore be used in conjunction with additional code. For example, the following code shows how one of the training log expressions from earlier in the hour might be used in an XSLT stylesheet:

```
<xsl:value-of select="*/session[@type='running']" />
```

In this code, the XPath expression appears within the `select` attribute of the `xsl:value-of` element, which is responsible for inserting content from a source XML document into an output document during the transformation of the source document. Refer back to Hours 12 and 13 for more information on XSLT stylesheets and how they are used. The point I want to make here is that the XSLT `xsl:value-of` element is what makes the XPath expression useful. XPath plays a critical role in XSLT, as you probably remember from Hour 13.

Similar to its role in XSLT, XPath serves as the addressing mechanism in XPointer. XPointer is used to address parts of XML documents, and is used heavily in XLink, which you learn about in a moment. XPointer uses XPath to provide a means of navigating the tree of nodes that comprise an XML document. Sounds familiar, right? XPointer takes XPath a step further by defining a syntax for *fragment identifiers*, which are in turn used to specify parts of documents. In doing so, XPointer provides a high degree of control over the addressing of XML documents. When coupled with XLink, the control afforded by XPointer makes it possible to create interesting links between documents that simply aren't possible in HMTL, at least in theory.

HTML, XML, and Linking

Similar to HTML web pages, XML documents can also benefit greatly from links that connect them together. Knowing this, the architects of XML created a linking mechanism for XML that provides support for traditional one-way links, such as those you may be familiar with in HTML, along with more advanced links, such as two-way links. Links in XML are in fact considerably more powerful than HTML links, as you will learn in a moment when you begin exploring XLink and XPointer. Before getting into that, however, it's worth taking a moment to assess the role of links in HTML.

HTML links (*hyperlinks*) are based upon the concept of connecting one resource to another resource—a *source* is linked to a *target*. The source of an HTML link is typically displayed on a web page (via text or an image) so as to call out the fact that it links to another resource. Text links are typically displayed with an underline, and the mouse pointer usually changes when the user drags it over a link source. Traversing a link in HTML typically involves clicking the source resource, which results in the web browser navigating to the target resource. This navigation can occur in the same browser window, in which case the target resource replaces the current page, or in a new browser window.

The important thing to understand about HTML links is that although they involve two resources, they always link in one direction. In other words, one side of the link is always the source and the other side is always the target, which means you can follow a link only one way. You might think that the Back button in a web browser allows HTML links to serve as two-way links, but the Back button has nothing to do with HTML. The Back button in a web browser is a browser feature that involves keeping a running list of web pages so that the user can back through them. There is nothing inherent in HTML links that supports backing up from the target of a link to the source; the target of a link knows nothing about its source. So, HTML links are somewhat limited in that they can link only in one direction. You might be wondering how it could possibly be useful to link in two directions—we'll get to that in a moment.

By the Way

It's worth pointing out that many of the conventions we've come to expect in terms of HTML linking aren't directly related to HTML. For example, an HTML link doesn't specify anything about how it is to be displayed to the user (colored, underlined, and so forth). It is up to stylesheets, browsers, and user preferences to determine how links are presented. Although this may not seem like a big deal right now, the browser's role in displaying links may become more significant if and when browsers support XLink. This is because XLink supports links between multiple resources and in multiple directions, which makes them difficult to visualize with a simple underline or mouse pointer.

If you've spent any time coding web pages with HTML, you're no doubt familiar with the a element, also known as the anchor element, which is used to create HTML links. The anchor element identifies the target resource for an HTML link using the `href` attribute, which contains a URI. The `href` attribute can either reference a full URI or a relative URI. HTML links can link to entire documents or to a document fragment. Following is an example of an HTML link that uses a relative URI to link to a document named `fruit.html`:

```
Click <a href="fruit.html">here</a> for fruit!
```

This code assumes the document `fruit.html` is located in the same path as the document in which the code appears. If you want to link to a document located somewhere else, you'll probably take advantage of a full URI, like this:

```
Click <a href="http://www.michaelsgroceries.com/veggies.html">here</a> for veggies!
```

Document fragments are a little more interesting in terms of how they are linked in HTML. When linking to a document fragment, the `href` attribute uses a pound symbol (#) in between the URI and the fragment identifier. The following is an example of how you create an HTML link to a specific location within a document:

```
Click <a href="fruit.html#bananas">here</a> for bananas!
```

In this code, the fragment identifier bananas is used to identify a portion of the fruit.html document. You associate a fragment identifier with a portion of a document using the anchor element (a) and the id attribute in the link target. This attribute value is the name used to the right of the pound symbol (#) in the anchor element that serves as the link source. Following is an example of an HTML link that establishes a banana document fragment for a link target:

```
<a id="bananas">We have the freshest bananas for $0.99 per pound.</a>
```

This code shows how a sentence of text can be marked as a link target by setting the id attribute of the a tag with a unique fragment identifier.

> If you're already an HTML guru, I apologize for boring you with this recap of HTML links. Boring or not, it's important to have a solid grasp of HTML links because they serve as the basis for simple XML links.

HTML links are both very useful and very easy to create. Simply based on the power and usefulness of the Web, it's hard to make an argument against the strength of HTML's simplistic approach to linking documents. However, there are many ways that it can be improved, some of which you might have never thought about. For one, it would be nice if links could be bidirectional, which means that you wouldn't be dependent on a browser's implementation of a Back button in order to navigate backwards to a previous resource. Although this may seem trivial, it could be extremely useful to be able to traverse a link in either direction, thereby eliminating the need for fixed source and target resources. A bidirectional link would treat the two resources as both sources and targets depending on the context.

In addition to bidirectional links, it could be extremely beneficial to have links that reference multiple target resources. This would keep web developers from having to duplicate content for the sole purpose of providing link sources. More specifically, a link with multiple targets could present a pop-up menu with the target selections from which the user selects. An example of this type of link might be a book listing on Amazon.com. A multiple-target link for the cover image of a book could present a pop-up menu containing links to documents such as a book summary, reviews, and a sample chapter. This tightens up the user interface for the web site by reducing the content used purely for navigational purposes. It also provides a logical grouping of related links that would otherwise be coded as unrelated links using HTML anchors.

If your only exposure to document linking is HTML, you probably regard link resources as existing completely separate of one another, at least in terms of how they are displayed in a web browser. XML links shatter this notion by allowing you to use links to embed resources within other resources. In other words, the contents of a target resource can be inserted in place of the link in a source document. Granted, images are handled much like this in HTML already, but XML links offer the possibility of embedding virtually any kind of data in a document, not just an external image. Traversing embedded links in this manner ultimately results in compound documents that are built out of other resources, which has some interesting implications for the Web. For example, you could build a news web page out of paragraphs of text that are dynamically pulled from other documents around the web via links.

Speaking of link traversal, HTML links are limited in that the user must trigger their traversal. For example, the only way to invoke a link on a web page is to click the linked text or image, as shown in Figure 22.2.

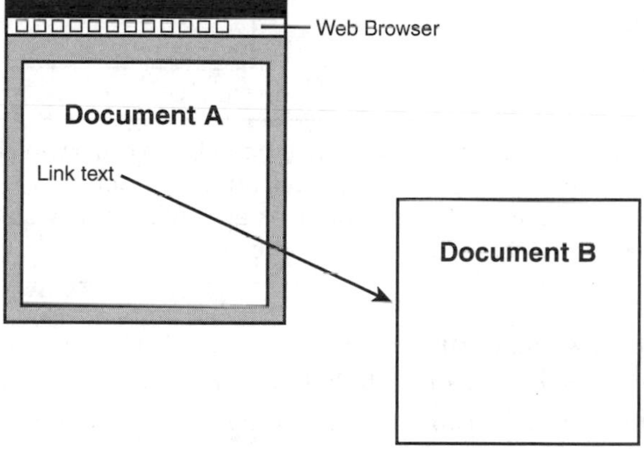

FIGURE 22.2 In order to traverse an HTML link, the user must click on linked text or a linked image, which points to another document or resource.

You may be wondering why it would be desirable to have it any other way. Well, consider the situation where a linked resource is to be embedded directly in a document to form a compound document. You might want the embedding to take place immediately upon opening the document, in which case the user would have nothing to do with the link being invoked. In this sense, the link is serving as a kind of connective tissue for components of a compound web document (see Figure 22.3), which is far beyond the role of links in HTML. Again, images already work like this in HTML via the `img` tag, but XML links open the door for many other possibilities with flexible linking.

As you're starting to see, XML links, which are made possible by the XLink technology, are much more abstract than HTML links, and therefore can be used to serve more purposes than just providing users a way of moving from one web page to the next. Admittedly, you almost have to take a few steps back and think of links in a more abstract sense to fully understand what XML links are all about. The up side to this shift in thinking is that when the significance of XLink fully sinks in, you will probably view the web quite differently.

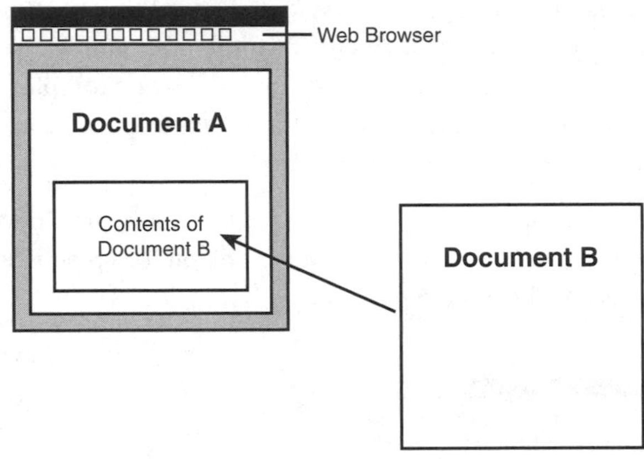

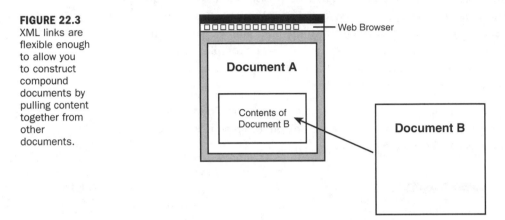

FIGURE 22.3 XML links are flexible enough to allow you to construct compound documents by pulling content together from other documents.

By the Way

> The problem at the moment is that XLink has been brutally slow to catch on, and only has limited support in Firefox and no support in Internet Explorer or any other browser. So the pie in the sky features of XLink are unfortunately still in the realm of the hypothetical, at least in terms of the Web.

Yet another facet of XLink worth pointing out is its support for creating links that reside outside of the documents they link. In other words, you can create a link in one document that connects two resources contained in other documents (see Figure 22.4). This can be particularly useful when you don't have the capability of editing the source and target documents. These kinds of links are known as out-of-line links and will probably foster the creation of link repositories. A link repository is a database of links that describe useful connections between resources on the Web.

One example of a link repository that could be built using XLink is an intricately cross-referenced legal database, where court cases are linked in such a way that a researcher in a law office could quickly find and verify precedents and track similar cases. Though it's certainly possible to create such a database and incorporate it into HTML web pages, it is cumbersome. XLink provides the exact feature set to make link repositories a practical reality.

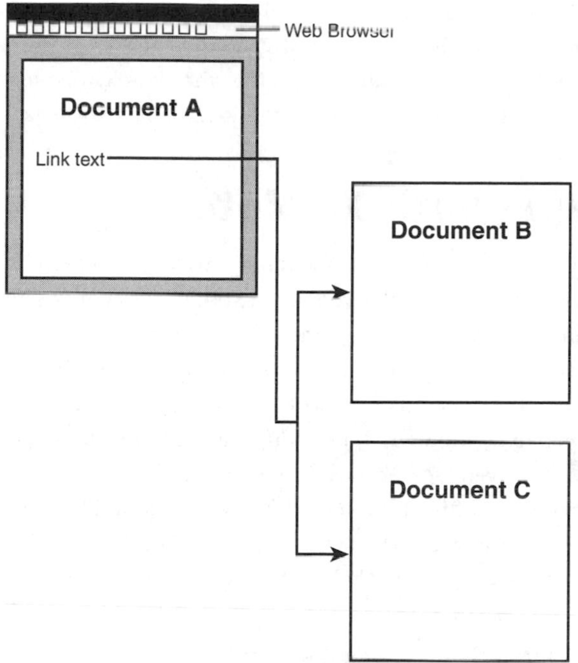

FIGURE 22.4
XML links allow you to do interesting things such as referencing multiple documents from a link within another document.

> **By the Way**
>
> One of the side benefits of out-of-line links is the fact that the links are maintained separately from the documents that they link. This separate storage of links and resources makes it possible to dramatically reduce broken links, which are otherwise difficult to track down and eliminate.

You now understand that XML linking is considerably more powerful than its HTML counterpart. Perhaps more interesting is the fact that XML links involve a concert of technologies working together. XLink is the primary technology that makes XML links possible, but it requires the help of two other technologies—XPointer and XPath. If you traced the history of XLink in the W3C, you'd learn that it originally consisted of only two components, XPointer and XLink. However, the W3C realized that XPointer wasn't the only XML technology that needed a means of addressing parts of a document. XSLT also needed a means of addressing document parts, so it was decided to separate document addressing into XPath. XPointer builds on XPath to provide support for addressing the internal structure of XML documents. XLink in turn uses XPointer to describe flexible links to specific structures within XML documents.

XLink is designed to support simple one-way links similar to those in HTML, as well as a variety of different extended links that offer interesting new ways of linking documents. XLink is implemented as an XML language, which means that it can be easily integrated into XML applications. XPointer is a non-XML language based upon XPath that is used to address internal structures in XML documents. XPointer is an important part of XLink because it specifies the syntax used to create *fragment identifiers*, which are used to reference internal document constructs.

Addressing with XPointer

XPointer allows you to walk the tree of nodes that an XML document is comprised of to address a specific node or nodes. XPointer expands the syntax set forth by XPath to provide a means of creating fragment identifiers, which are used to specify parts of documents. XPointer provides considerably more control over the referencing of XML document data than the hyperlink approach employed by HTML. For example, XPointer allows you to do things such as address an element with a given value within a list of elements of a given type. You use XPointer expressions in XML links by appending them onto the end of URIs with a pound symbol (#), as in the separation between a URI and an XPointer expression. The next few sections break down XPointer into further detail and demonstrate exactly how to create XPointer expressions.

Building XPointer Expressions

The most important component of XPointer expressions is the *location path*, which is a construct used to describe the path that must be followed to arrive at a node within an XML document tree. Location paths are the building blocks of XPointer expressions, which are evaluated to arrive at a specific location within a tree. More specifically, location paths allow you to traverse siblings, ancestors, children, and descendants of nodes, not to mention attributes. Location paths are broken down into two basic types—absolute paths and general paths.

Absolute location paths point to a specific location within an XML tree, and therefore aren't dependent on context. Following are the different absolute location paths defined in XPointer:

- `/`—Locates the root node, which is the parent node for the entire document tree
- `id(Name)`—Locates the element with an attribute ID value of `Name`
- `here()`—Locates the node containing the current XPointer expression
- `origin()`—Locates the sub-resource from which the user initiated a link (used with out-of-line links)

The most important absolute location paths are the root and `id()` paths. The root path is represented by a forward slash (`/`), and is often used at the start of an XPointer expression as the basis for absolute location paths. The `id()` location path is used to locate an element with a specific attribute value.

In addition to absolute location paths, XPointer also defines a rich set of relative location paths. Relative location paths are always relative to some node, which is known as the *context node* for the path. Following are the relative location paths available for use in XPointer expressions:

- `child`—Locates child nodes of the context node
- `descendant`—Locates nodes within the context node
- `descendant-or-self`—Same as `descendant` except the context node is also included
- `parent`—Locates nodes one level above the context node that contains the context node
- `ancestor`—Locates all nodes above the context node that contain the context node
- `ancestor-or-self`—Same as `ancestor` except the context node is also included
- `preceding-sibling`—Locates sibling nodes that precede the context node
- `following-sibling`—Locates sibling nodes that follow the context node
- `preceding`—Locates nodes that precede the context node
- `following`—Locates nodes that follow the context node
- `self`—Locates individual context nodes within a list of context nodes
- `attribute`—Locates attributes of the context node

If you're totally confused by all this context node talk, don't worry because it will all make sense in a moment. As confusing as it may seem, the relative location paths in the previous list really are quite useful and are much easier to use than you might think. The next section shows you how to use these location paths to create expressions in XPointer.

Creating XPointers

Seeing a few examples of XPointer expressions can make all the difference in understanding how XPointer is used to define document fragment identifiers. Following is an example of a simple XPointer expression:

```
child::factoid
```

This example uses the child relative location path to locate all of the children of the context node that are of element type `factoid`. Let me rephrase it in a different way: The sample expression locates element nodes of type `factoid` that are child nodes of the context node. Keep in mind that the context node is the node from which you are issuing the expression, which is a lot like the current path of a file system when you're browsing for files. Also, it's worth clarifying that the XPointer expression `child::factoid` simply describes the fragment identifier for a resource and is not a complete resource reference. When used in a complete expression, you would pair this fragment identifier with a URI that is assigned to an `href` attribute, like this:

```
href="http://www.stalefishlabs.com/factoids.xml#child::factoid"
```

In this example, a URI is specified that references the XML document named `factoids.xml`. The XPointer expression is then provided as a fragment identifier, which is separated from the URI by a pound symbol (#). This is the typical way in which XPointers are used, although expressions can certainly get more complex than this. For example, the following code shows how to use location paths to create a more elaborate expression that carries out a more intricate reference:

```
child::factoid/following-sibling::legend
```

This example first locates all child elements that are of type `factoid` and then finds the second siblings following each of those element nodes that are of type `legend`. To understand how this code works, let's break it down. You begin with the familiar `child::factoid` expression, which locates element nodes of type `factoid` that are child nodes of the context node. Adding on the `following-sibling::legend` location path causes the expression to locate sibling elements of type `legend`. Granted, this may seem like a strange use of XPointer, but keep in mind that it is designed as an all-purpose language for addressing the internal structure of XML documents. It's impossible to say how different applications might want to address document parts, which is why XPointer is so flexible.

In addition to location paths, XPointer defines several functions that perform different tasks within XPointer expressions. One class of functions is known as *node test functions*, which are used to determine the type of a node. Of course, you can use the name of an element to check if a node is of a certain element type, but the node test functions allow you to check and see if a node contains a comment, text, or processor instruction. The following is an example of how to use one of these functions:

```
/child::processing-instruction()
```

This expression results in the location of any processing instructions that are children of the root element. The reason the expression results in children of the root element is because the root element (/) is specified as the basis for the expression.

As you can see in these few examples, XPointer is a comprehensive yet flexible technology that is capable of doing some pretty interesting things. I'll readily admit that there is more to XPointer than I've touched on here; I mainly wanted to provide a solid overview and demonstrate how basic expressions are created. I encourage you to explore XPointer more on your own and experiment with creating XPointer expressions. However, before you do that you need to learn how XPointer fits into XLink.

Linking with XLink

The whole point of XPointer (no pun intended) is to provide a means of referencing portions of XML documents for the purpose of creating powerful XML links. XLink ultimately makes links possible through *linking elements*, which are elements that describe the characteristics of links. The anchor element in HTML is a good example of a linking element. Although linking elements form the basis of XLink, there are no predefined linking elements in the XLink language. Although it may seem strange at first, you won't find any standard element in the XLink language. The reason is because XML is all about the creation of custom tags (elements), which precludes the use of a fixed linking element in XLink. In other words, you are encouraged to define your own linking elements specific to a particular XML-based language, as opposed to being locked into a fixed element, such as HTML's anchor element (a).

Even though HTML's anchor element is somewhat limiting in the context of XML, there still must be some kind of mechanism in XLink that identifies links. This mechanism comes in the form of standard linking attributes that can be associated with any element. There are several of these attributes, which you learn about in the next section. For now, just understand that the presence of XLink attributes is sufficient to identify an element as a linking element.

A linking element uses a construct called a locator to connect resources involved in a link. In both HTML and XML, the `href` attribute serves as the locator for links. Although HTML and XML share this attribute, links in XML are described in much more detail than their HTML counterparts. Perhaps the most important difference is the fact that XML links completely describe the resources involved, even if a target resource is just a document fragment. In HTML, it is necessary to place an anchor element in a target fragment resource and identify it using the `id` attribute. This is not the case in XML because XLink provides the necessary ingredients to fully describe the resources involved in a link.

There are two types of linking elements supported in XLink:

- Inline links
- Out-of-line links

An *inline link* is a link whose content serves as one of the link's participating resources. Typically, an inline link has a linking element that contains content that serves as the source for the link. HTML anchor links are good examples of inline links because an anchor link contains text or an image that acts as the source for the link. Due to HTML's use of inline links, you may be curious as to how a link could work any other way. Out-of-line links extend the concept of linking in XML by allowing you to create links that are independent of the linked resources.

An *out-of-line link* is a link whose content doesn't serve as one of the link's participating resources. This means that out-of-line links are independent of their participating resources and therefore serve a very different purpose than inline links. Out-of-line links are useful for linking information in documents that you can't modify for one reason or another. For example, if you wanted to create a link between two resources that reside on other web sites, you'd use an out-of-line link. Such a link is possible because out-of-line links are geared toward opening up interesting new opportunities for how links are used to connect documents. More specifically, it would be possible to create link databases that describe relationships between information spread across the Web.

Out-of-line links partially form the concept of extended links in XML. *Extended links* are basically any links that extend the linking functionality of HTML. Out-of-line links obviously are considered extended links because HTML doesn't support any type of out-of-line linking mechanism. Extended links also support the association of more than one target resource with a given link. With extended links, you could build a table of contents for a web site that consists solely of extended links that point to the various pages in the site. If the links were gathered in a single document separate from the table of contents page itself, they would also be considered out-of-line links.

Understanding XLink Attributes

Hopefully I've sold you on the fact that XLink offers some interesting opportunities for creating XML links that are impossible in HTML. Now it's time to look at exactly how such interesting linking is made possible by XLink. Earlier I mentioned that XLink defines standard attributes that are used to establish linked elements in XML documents. Following are the XLink attributes that can be used to create linked elements:

- `type`—A string that specifies the type of link
- `href`—A locator that addresses a target resource using a URI
- `from`—A string that identifies the resource being linked from when describing an arc

- `to`—A string that identifies the resource being linked to when describing an arc
- `show`—A string that determines how a target resource is to be revealed to the user
- `actuate`—A string that determines how a link is initiated
- `role`—An application-specific string used to describe the function of a link's content
- `title`—A string that serves as a name for a link

The `type` attribute determines the type of a link and can have one of the following values: `simple`, `extended`, `locator`, `resource`, `arc`, or `group`. The `href` attribute is one with which you are already familiar, based on its use in HTML. The `from` and `to` attributes are used by *arcs*, which describe the traversal behavior of links. More specifically, an arc defines where a two-way link comes from and where it goes. Arcs could be used to establish web rings, where web pages are linked from one to the next using the `from` and `to` attributes to traverse the ring.

The `show` attribute determines how a target resource for a link is revealed to the user. There are three main values for the `show` attribute:

- `replace`—The target resource replaces the current document (default value).
- `new`—The target resource is shown in a new window.
- `embed`—The target resource is inserted into the current document in place of the link.

The functionality of the `show` attribute follows that of HTML anchor links until you get to the last possible value, `parsed`. If you set the `show` attribute to `parsed`, the link will be replaced by the target resource. This type of link allows you to divide a document into subdocuments and then link them together to form a compound document, which can help improve the organization of data.

The `actuate` attribute determines how a link is initiated and is typically set to one of the following values:

- `onRequest`—The link must be manually traversed by the user (default value).
- `onLoad`—The link is automatically traversed upon loading the source document.

Setting the `actuate` attribute to `onRequest` makes a link act like an HTML link, which means that you have to click the link in order to activate it. The `onLoad` value offers functionality not directly available in HTML by allowing a link to be traversed when a document is first loaded. The `onLoad` value is particularly useful when used in conjunction with the embed value for the show attribute; this results in a resource being automatically loaded and placed directly in a document.

The last two XLink attributes are role and title, which are used primarily for descriptive purposes. The role attribute describes the role of the content in a link, whereas title provides a human-readable title for the link that may be displayed in a browser.

Creating Links with XLink

You're now finally ready to put all of your XPointer and XLink knowledge to work and create some links that would never be possible in HTML. As an example, consider an element named employees that is used to identify a group of employees for a company. Following is an example of how you might create a simple link for the employees element:

```
<employees xmlns:xlink="http://www.w3.org/1999/xlink"
  xlink:href="employees.xml">
  Current Employees
</employees>
```

This example is the simplest possible link you can create using XLink, and it actually carries out the same functionality as an HTML anchor link, which is known as a *simple link* in XML. Notice in the code that the XLink namespace is declared and assigned to the xlink prefix, which is then used to reference the href attribute; this is the standard approach used to access all of the XLink attributes. What you may not realize is that this link takes advantage of some default attribute values. The following is another way to express the exact same link by spelling all of the pertinent XLink attribute values:

```
<employees xmlns:xlink="http://www.w3.org/1999/xlink"
  xlink:type="simple"
  xlink:href="employees.xml"
  xlink:show="replace"
  xlink:actuate="user"
  xlink:role="employees"
  xlink:title="Employee List">
  Current Employees
</employees>
```

In this code, you can more clearly see how the XLink attributes are specified in order to fully describe the link. The type attribute is set to simple, which indicates that this is a simple link. The show attribute has the value replace, which indicates that the target resource is to replace the current document when the link is traversed. The actuate attribute has the value user, which indicates that the link must be activated by the user for traversal to take place. And finally, the role and title attributes are set to indicate the meaning of the link and its name.

The previous example demonstrated how to create a link that imitates the familiar HTML anchor link. You can dramatically change a simple link just by altering the manner in which it is shown and activated. For example, take a look at the following link:

```
<resume xmlns:xlink="http://www.w3.org/1999/xlink"
  xlink:type="simple"
  xlink:href="resume_e1.xml"
  xlink:show="parsed"
  xlink:actuate="auto"
  xlink:role="employee1 resume"
  xlink:title="Employee 1 Resume"/>
```

This code shows how to effectively embed another XML document into the current document at the position where the link is located. This is accomplished by simply setting the show attribute to `parsed` and the `actuate` attribute to `auto`. When a web browser or XML application encounters this link, it will automatically load the `resume_e1.xml` document and insert it into the current document in place of the link. When you think about it, the `img` element in HTML works very much like this link except that it is geared solely toward images; the link in this example can be used with any kind of XML content.

By the Way

In case you haven't fully caught on, XPointer impacts links through the `href` attribute, which is where you specify the location of a source or target resource for a link. All of the flexibility afforded by XPointer in specifying document parts can be realized in the `href` attribute of any link.

Although simple links such as the previous example are certainly important, they barely scratch the surface in terms of what XLink is really capable of doing. Links get much more interesting when you venture into extended links. A powerful use of extended links is the *linkset*, which allows you to link to a set of target resources via a single source resource. For example, you could use an extended link to establish a link to each individual employee in a company. To create an extended link, you must create child elements of the linking element that are set to type `locator`; these elements are where you set each individual target resource via the `href` attribute. Following is an example of an extended link, which should help clarify how they work:

```
<employees xmlns:xlink="http://www.w3.org/1999/xlink"
  xlink:type="extended"
  xlink:role="employees"
  xlink:title="Employee List"
  xlink:show="replace"
  xlink:actuate="user">
```

```
  <employee xlink:type="locator" xlink:href="employee1.xml">
    Frank Rizzo
  </employee>

  <employee xlink:type="locator" xlink:href="employee2.xml">
    Sol Rosenberg
  </employee>

  <employee xlink:type="locator" xlink:href="employee3.xml">
    Jack Tors
  </employee>
</employees>
```

This example creates an extended link out of the `employees` element, but the most interesting thing about the link is that it has multiple target resources that are identified in the child `employee` elements. This is evident by the fact that each of the `employee` elements has an `href` attribute that is set to their respective target resources.

By the Way

> Keep in mind that the examples shown in this section reveal only a couple of ways to use extended links. In truth, it has yet to be revealed exactly how XLink will affect XML, and what kinds of innovative linking applications people will dream up. If web browsers eventually get on board with support for XLink, we will likely see a revolution of sorts when it comes to how links are used and perceived.

Of course, you might be wondering exactly how a link like the extended link shown here is used. In web pages, links are usually identified by colored, underlined text, and are activated simply by clicking them with the mouse. When there are multiple targets associated with a link, as in the example, it somehow becomes necessary to specify which target you want when you traverse the link. Because extended links currently aren't supported in any web browsers, it's hard to say exactly how this target resource selection will be carried out. My hunch is that you will be able to select from multiple targets that are displayed in a pop-up menu after you click a link. So, when you first click on a source resource for an extended link with multiple targets, a pop-up menu could appear with the available target links. To visit one of the links, you simply select the target from the menu. This is a reasonably intuitive way to implement the user interface portion of extended links with multiple targets, but it still isn't clear yet if browser vendors will employ this approach.

Another type of extended link is the *arc*, which is essentially a two-way link that connects two resources in such a way that the link can be traversed in either direction (forward or reverse). When you create an arc, you must first create locators for each resource involved in the link, and then you create the arc connections that connect the resources together. A web ring is a good example of how arcs work—each web page in a web ring has a Forward and Back button that allows you to view more pages in the ring. The URI of a web page in a web ring would be identified in a locator, whereas the connections between each page in the ring would be established with arcs.

A Complete XLink Example

I've mentioned a few times throughout this lesson how XLink has unfortunately yet to garner much support in major web browsers. That's the bad news. The good news is that the Firefox browser does include support for simple XLink links. You can create links in Firefox using XLink that approximate the same links supported in HTML. In other words, you can't create extended links or embedded links, which is somewhat of a bummer. Listing 22.2 contains the code for a Top Five movie list XML document that makes use of simple XLink links.

LISTING 22.2 The Top Five Sample XML Document

```
<?xml version="1.0"?>
<?xml-stylesheet type="text/css" href="topfive.css"?>

<topfive xmlns:xlink="http://www.w3.org/1999/xlink">
  <title>Top Five Movies</title>

  <intro>Following are my top five favorite movies:</intro>

  <item>
    1. <itemLink xlink:type="simple" xlink:show="replace"
    xlink:actuate="onRequest" xlink:title="Number 1"
    xlink:href="http://www.amazon.com/exec/obidos/ASIN/B00004TDTO/">
    Jaws</itemLink>
  </item>

  <item>
    2. <itemLink xlink:type="simple" xlink:show="replace"
    xlink:actuate="onRequest" xlink:title="Number 2"
    xlink:href="http://www.amazon.com/exec/obidos/ASIN/6305499128/">
    Raising Arizona</itemLink>
  </item>

  <item>
    3. <itemLink xlink:type="simple" xlink:show="replace"
    xlink:actuate="onRequest" xlink:title="Number 3"
    xlink:href="http://www.amazon.com/exec/obidos/ASIN/B00003CWTI/">
    Magnolia</itemLink>
  </item>

  <item>
    4. <itemLink xlink:type="simple" xlink:show="replace"
    xlink:actuate="onRequest" xlink:title="Number 4"
    xlink:href="http://www.amazon.com/exec/obidos/ASIN/0767821408/">
    Bottle Rocket</itemLink>
  </item>

  <item>
    5. <itemLink xlink:type="simple" xlink:show="replace"
```

LISTING 22.2 Continued

```
39:     xlink:actuate="onRequest" xlink:title="Number 5"
40:     xlink:href="http://www.amazon.com/exec/obidos/ASIN/B000286RKW/">
41:     GoodFellas</itemLink>
42:   </item>
43:
44:   <conclusion>To find out more about me, please feel free to visit
45:   <popupLink xlink:type="simple" xlink:show="new"
46:   xlink:actuate="onRequest" xlink:title="michaelmorrison.com"
47:   xlink:href="http://www.michaelmorrison.com/">
48:   my Web site</popupLink>.
49:   </conclusion>
50: </topfive>
```

This code consists of six different links: five for the top five movies and one as a contact link near the bottom of the document. The movie links all link to Amazon.com, whereas the contact link directs you to my web site. The movie links all have their `show` attributes set to `replace`, which means the linked resource is opened in the same window as (replaces) the original document. The contact link is slightly different in that its `show` attribute is set to `new` (line 45), which means the linked resource is opened in a new window. The `actuate` attribute for all of the links is set to `onRequest` (line 46), which requires the user to click the links in order for them to be navigated. Figure 22.5 shows the Top Five movie document as viewed in Firefox.

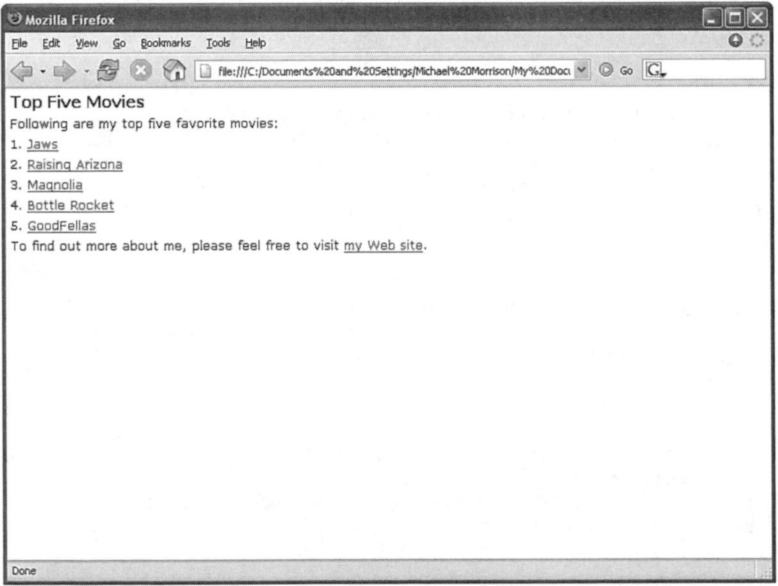

FIGURE 22.5 The Top Five sample document provides an example of how simple XLink links can be used in an XML document.

You may be wondering how the browser knows to underline the links. There isn't anything magical going on here. I just neglected to show you the CSS stylesheet that is responsible for styling the Top Five document. You can find this stylesheet along with the complete code for this book on my web site, which is located at http://www.michaelmorrison.com/.

Summary

If you think of an XML document as a hierarchical tree of data, which it is, then it's not too hard to make a comparison between XML documents and the family trees used in genealogy. This comparison is useful because it turns out that one of the best ways to interact with XML data is by thinking in terms of nodes of data that are related to each other as family members. For example, there are parent, child, and sibling nodes at most points in a document's node tree. XPath is a technology that takes advantage of this hierarchical nature of XML by allowing you to reference parts of XML documents as nodes within a node tree. Although you've heard mention of XPath earlier in the book, this hour formally introduced you to it and explored what it has to offer in terms of referencing XML documents.

XPath plays a role in two other emerging XML technologies, XLink and XPointer, which bring advanced linking support to XML, and at some point to the web. You found out about the theoretical underpinnings of XML linking and what it aims to accomplish. You then learned how to create expressions in XPointer, followed by links in XLink. Although you gained some practical knowledge of XLink and XPointer, there unfortunately is very little support for either technology in major web browsers at the moment. Even so, they are compelling enough technologies that you need to keep an eye out for them potentially making an impact in the XML landscape at some point.

Q&A

Q. ***What is the relationship between XPath and XPointer?***

A. XPath is a simple path language that uses patterns and expressions to reference portions of an XML document tree. XPointer extends XPath by offering more specific referencing capabilities within XML documents. XPointer also serves as the basis for identifying link sources and targets in XLink, which is the standard linking technology for XML.

Q. ***Why bother learning about XLink if it still isn't supported to any serious degree in major web browsers?***

A. The reason for learning about XLink has to do with the fact that it could possibly represent the future of XML document linking. The W3C spent years developing XLink with the goal of it becoming a standard technology with wide support. Admittedly, it's difficult to get excited about a technology that is somewhat intangible at the moment, but that doesn't necessarily lessen the future significance of XLink.

Q. ***Assuming XLink is eventually adopted by web browsers, how will it affect the HTML anchor link?***

A. The HTML anchor link (a) is a unique element in HTML that has special meaning to web browsers. In terms of XML, the HTML a element is just another element that happens to be interpreted as a linking element. When browsers add support for XLink, it will be very easy for them to support the a element for backward compatibility, while also supporting new XLink links. Don't forget that with XLink you can create your own anchor links with very little effort.

Workshop

The Workshop is designed to help you anticipate possible questions, review what you've learned, and begin learning how to put your knowledge into practice.

Quiz

1. How do you reference the current node in an XML document using XPath?
2. What is the difference between the / and // patterns in XPath?
3. What is a link repository?
4. What is a location path?
5. What is the difference between an inline link and an out-of-line link?

Quiz Answers

1. To reference the current node in an XML document, you use a single period (.) as the pattern.
2. The / pattern in XPath is used to reference the root node of a document, whereas the // pattern selects all the child nodes of a particular node.

3. A link repository is a database of links that describe useful connections between resources on the Web.

4. A location path is a construct used to describe the path that must be followed to arrive at a node within an XML document tree; location paths are the building blocks of XPointer expressions.

5. The content associated with an inline link serves as one of the link's participating resources, whereas the content associated with an out-of-line link does not.

Exercises

1. Now that you understand XPath a little better, modify the `vehicles` template in the `vehicles.xsl` stylesheet from Hour 13 so that only green vehicles are selected and displayed.

2. While you're at it, modify the root template in the `contacts.xsl` stylesheet from Hour 12 so that only contacts from New York City are displayed. Hint: You'll need to add a few new contacts from other places for testing purposes.

HOUR 23

Going Wireless with WML and XHTML Mobile

> HTML is dead. Web developers have to accept this and move on to XHTML.
>
> —Uttam Narsu

Those are strong words. Actually, I think they are intended more as a directive than a statement but the general idea is to push web developers toward XHTML. An important variant of XHTML is called XHTML Mobile, and its focus is on mobile devices that don't require the full XHTML feature set. You've probably experienced the challenge of trying to "browse" the web on a mobile phone. If so, you probably understand how constrained the mobile phone environment can be in terms of limited screen space, processing power, memory, and so on. Some mobile devices exist that are more flexible in this regard, but the fact remains that mobile devices have unique needs when it comes to accessing online information.

You may have heard of WML (Wireless Markup Language), which is a markup language used to code scaled down web pages for mobile devices. WML strips a transmission down to its bare essentials by providing what is basically a pared down HTML for the wireless world. Paradoxically, it offers a remarkable amount of interactivity through its action elements, navigation controls, and scripting capabilities. WML and XHTML Mobile are technically two different technologies but efforts are underway to combine them into a single technology that solidifies an XML future for mobile web browsing. This hour explores WML, XHTML Mobile, and the imminent convergence of the two.

In this hour, we'll cover

- How WML and XHTML Mobile fit into the state of the wireless web
- Decks and cards—the anatomy of a WML document
- Formatting tags for WML text
- How to provide for user entry in WML
- Blending WML with XHTML Mobile

XML and the Wireless Web

The wireless web has undergone a lot of changes, some of which affect XML's role in developing mobile content. For this reason, it's important to understand how the wireless web has evolved to where it is today, and what ramifications this evolution has for mobile XML content developers.

Back in Hour 21, "Adding Structure to the Web with XHTML," you learned how XHTML was created as a new and improved HTML that adheres to the more rigorous syntax of XML. In version 1.1 of XHTML, the features were modularized so that features could be selectively added and removed to accommodate different applications. *XHTML Basic* is one of these modularized versions of XHTML, and its focus is on supporting a limited set of features that are uniquely suited to mobile devices. For example, frames are not supported in XHTML Basic. XHTML Basic doesn't solve all of the mobile issues, however, so a profile was built on top of XHTML Basic called *XHTML Mobile*. Its job was to fill in some of the gaps in XHTML Basic. As an example, XHTML Mobile adds support for some presentation elements not found in XHTML Basic, as well as stylesheet support. XHTML Mobile is the standard markup language for WAP (Wireless Application Protocol) 2.0, which is the latest mobile industry standard for the wireless web. But let's back up for just a moment.

By the Way

> Mobile devices include any handheld or easily portable technology—cell phones, pagers, connected organizers, handheld PCs, and potentially others.

Before XHTML Mobile came along there were two primary mobile web services, WAP and iMode. iMode was created by NTTDoCoMo, and is popular in Japan and parts of Europe. WAP was created by a group of mobile industry leaders, and is the predominant standard for serving up mobile content worldwide. This version of WAP is known as WAP 1.0, and has taken a fair amount of criticism despite its success. WAP 1.0 and iMode rely on their own markup languages for coding pages served on each. More specifically, WAP 1.0 is based on WML (Wireless Markup Language) and iMode is based on cHTML (Compact HTML). These languages have both worked as basic markup languages for mobile web pages but they are lacking in many ways as we move to a more powerful XML-based wireless web.

Many of the core features in WML and cHTML converged in XHTML Mobile. A few of the WML-specific features, such as its card/deck user interface metaphor (more in this in a moment), were added to XHTML Mobile to form yet another language called WML2. WML2 represents the most complete XML-based mobile markup language for the wireless web but it isn't widely supported yet. Most current mobile browsers do support XHTML Mobile and regular WML (WML1).

For this reason, a combination of WML1 and XHTML Mobile is the best bet for mobile web development.

Let's summarize the XML-related languages that enter the picture with the wireless web:

- WML1—Widely supported, based on WAP 1.0
- cHTML—Widely supported internationally, based on iMode
- XHTML Mobile—Rapidly gaining support, based on WAP 2.0
- WML2—Very little support, considered an extension to WAP 2.0

Because I've tipped my hand that WML and XHTML Mobile represent the current approach for mobile web development, it's worth taking a closer look at those two technologies individually. As a mobile alternative to HTML, WML addresses the issues of limited bandwidth and limited screen real estate, which are common limitations of wireless devices. Wireless connections are typically slow, and the display space accommodates a relatively small number of text characters—depending on the device—and sometimes 1-bit (straight black-and-white) monochrome graphics. WML documents are extremely simple, created with a small selection of tags. WML's deck-and-card metaphor subdivides a WML document—envisioned as a "deck"—into components—"cards." This allows the document to be transmitted all at once (if desired, and space allowing), without the need for the browser to display it all at once. However, it's ultimately up to the specific browser as to how a WML document is downloaded.

Although XHTML Mobile doesn't support many of the presentation features of WML, such as the card/deck user interface, it does support the use of CSS. Technically, WAP 2.0 represents the combination of XHTML Mobile and CSS. As you've seen several times throughout the book, CSS provides a great deal of control over the formatting and display of XML content. When I refer to CSS as it applies to XHTML Mobile, I'm actually referring to a subset of CSS known as WCSS (Wireless CSS), which is somewhat of a scaled down CSS. In other words, WCSS is to XHTML Mobile what CSS is to XHTML.

The good news in regard to XHTML Mobile and WAP is that you can build pages in either language and know that they will be supported on most mobile web browsers. If backward compatibility is a huge issue, you might lean toward WML. If you want a language that more cleanly separates content from presentation, XHTML Mobile is the answer. And finally, you may find that mixing the languages across different pages provides you with the most flexibility.

When I refer to mixing WAP and XHTML Mobile, I don't mean mixing them within the same document. I mean that you can create a WAP document and link it to an XHTML Mobile document.

The remainder of the hour focuses on the WML and XHTML Mobile languages, and how to use them to build wireless web pages.

WML Essentials

WAP 1.0 and its components, like WML, are stewarded by the *WAP Forum*, an industry consortium of mobile device manufacturers and service providers. The WAP Forum is important because it serves as a single source of information on WAP-related technologies. The WAP Forum is also responsible for creating and maintaining formal specifications that result in industry standards, such as the WML language.

When I refer to WML throughout the remainder of this hour, I'm talking about any and all versions of WML1, which you may also see referred to as WML 1.x.

Nuts and Bolts

Before jumping into WML code, it's worth going over a few fundamental issues that surround any XML-based markup language. More specifically, you need to know about the WML specification, which is the last word on WML, as well as the WML DTD and MIME types associated with WML. Following is the information you need to get started with WML:

- The WML specification can be found at http://www.wapforum.org/what/technical.htm
- The WML DTD is `"-//WAPFORUM//DTD WML 1.3//EN"`, and can be found at http://www.wapforum.org/DTD/wml13.dtd
- WML MIME types, which are of interest to web servers

The WML Root Element

As any legitimate XML-based language must, WML defines a root element for conforming documents—`wml`. As such, the `wml` root element serves as the container for all other elements in WML documents. To help facilitate display and navigation in limited screen space, a WML document is conceived as a deck of cards, one of which is visible at any given time. Although the document is typically transmitted as a single unit, it is navigated piece-by-piece, or card-by-card.

The `wml` element is the parent of the `card` element, which in turn contains all other elements in the document. You can have an unlimited number of cards in each document (deck). A card is intended to, but doesn't necessarily, convey approximately one screen of information. (To scroll beyond the screen's boundaries, the user can navigate with the arrow keys.)

By the Way

> Although we speak liberally of "decks" in WML, there is no such thing as a `deck` tag. It is implied in the `wml` element. In this way, a WML document is effectively serving as a "deck" for the cards within it.

Navigation in WML

Because so little text fits on the screen of a mobile device, efficient navigation is critical in a WML document. WML provides numerous ways of getting around, from the `anchor` element, which is adopted from HTML, to the monitoring of user events. One of WML's solutions to the screen real estate crunch is its capability of mapping actions to the mobile device's *softkeys*, which are the mysterious blank buttons just below the screen. The labels (names) that appear on the screen just above them may vary from one device to another, but their intention is usually clear. For the most part, they appear only when WML code instructs them to do so.

The softkeys provide navigation controls beyond what you can fit on the screen in the content of a document. For instance, a Menu or Options key displays the equivalent of an HTML navigation bar, whereas a Reset key takes the user back to the first card in the deck. The Link button, as shown in the examples in this hour, appears when the text contains hyperlinks.

Besides anchors, WML provides a selection list tool that lets you display a series of choices as a numbered list. Thus, the user can select an option with a number key on the keypad, in addition to using the Link button.

WML offers a number of action elements (`go`, `prev`, `refresh`, and so on) that move the user from one card to another under specified contexts, such as the use of `go href="url"` in the anchor element (`a href`, and so forth, is a shorthand version of this). These elements are flexible in their implementation and can be associated with a number of parent elements in order to provide a considerable amount of mobility.

Events in WML are comparable to events in any scripting or programming language; you set up the document to wait for a specified event to happen, and when it does the program automatically carries out a designated task. Some events you can code for are `onenterforward`, `onenterbackward`, and `ontimer`, which indicate entering a card in the forward direction, entering a card backward, and the elapsed time of a timer that is associated with a card, respectively.

Content in WML

Given the nature of mobile devices, screen space is severely limited and bandwidth is precious. Thus, we can't afford to clog the airwaves with fancy formatting or layout directives, which is why WML offers only the simplest of formatting tags. WML does support tables, but they are very primitive, nothing like the sophisticated layout capabilities afforded by tables in HTML. The few text-formatting tags that do exist in WML have been adapted straight from HTML, making for a flat learning curve for traditional web developers.

Graphics support in WML is restricted to the WBMP (Wireless BitMap Picture) format, a 1-bit bitmap format whose files end in a `.wbmp` extension. One bit means on-or-off, black-or-white, which is just two colors. Besides the color depth restriction, the size is limited as well; WML images can't measure more than 64 3 64 pixels. Because you probably aren't accustomed to storing images in the WBMP format, you'll need to use a graphics converter of some sort to convert other graphics formats to WBMP. You'll find sources for such software listed in the "Inserting WBMP Images" section later in this hour.

By the Way

> It's worth pointing out that not all WAP implementations support images. It ultimately depends on the specific device being targeted as to whether or not images are an option.

Creating WML Documents

This section discusses the basics of setting up a WML document and describes several of the most common tasks involved in authoring a document for the wireless web. You'll work through an example of a mobile web site called FilmTime, which uses geographic coordinates to present a list of movies currently playing within 10 miles of the user's current position. Menus navigate the user through a series of choices about theatres, show times, and film synopses.

For the sake of simplicity, you won't worry about where FilmTime gets the user's coordinates, how it maps coordinates to a ZIP code, or how it processes database queries. You also won't worry about how the components you're authoring fit into the larger scheme of things, as the main objective is to introduce you to the elements rather than coaching you in designing a full-fledged application. In other words, this example focuses on the wireless aspects of such a web site, not on the technical details that don't directly involve WML.

By the Way

> For information and inspiration about the advanced aspects of WML (and of course, WAP), you can really take the bull by the horns and visit the formal WAP specification at http://www.wapforum.org/what/technical.htm. Or, you can go someplace more conversational, but no less exhaustive, such as `http://www.wirelessdevnet.com/`.

Though this hour does not introduce you to the full range of WML elements and their attributes, you will learn how to carry out the following tasks in WML:

- Create a deck (WML container document) and a number of cards, or sections of the document
- Enter and format text
- Navigate around other cards in the deck
- Associate events with a card element
- Set up a field for user entry
- Insert an image

The next few sections get you going with the creation of your first WML document and guide you through the fundamental tasks required to develop complete WML documents.

Before You Start—Tools of the Trade

As with just about any kind of software development, tools can ultimately determine how likely you are to succeed in completing a project. WML is no different, although its tool requirements are fairly straightforward. You will need the following items to build a wireless web site with WML:

- A text editor, such as the no-frills Windows Notepad or Simple Text, or a dedicated WML editor
- A mobile phone simulator—software that runs on your PC or online and displays content as the user sees and experiences it (on a "microbrowser"), complete with clickable buttons
- Debugging capabilities, optionally, which typically accompany the simulator

The most important tool in any WML developer's arsenal is the mobile phone simulator because it is what allows you to test WML documents in the context of a wireless device. A mobile phone simulator acts as a *microbrowser*, which is a small-scale web browser that is designed specifically for wireless devices. The wireless tool used throughout this hour is the Nokia Mobile Browser Simulator, which is available for free download from Nokia (http://www.forum.nokia.com/main/0,,034-13,00.html). The Nokia Mobile Browser Simulator is handy because it isn't very forgiving with your WML and XHTML Mobile code. It will quickly let you know if a tag or attribute is used improperly, and won't display a page until the problem is fixed.

By the Way

> If you visit the Nokia site to download the Nokia Mobile Browser Simulator, make sure you download the simulator, not the Nokia Mobile Internet Toolkit. The toolkit is an excellent set of tools but it is geared toward editing mobile content, not simulating it.

Another good alternative to the Nokia Mobile Browser Simulator is WinWAP, which actually looks more like a traditional HTML-based web browser than a WML microbrowser. WinWAP is a good test browser for WML documents because it is so simple to use. You can download a trial version of WinWAP at http://www.winwap.org/. For a more full-featured microbrowser and WML development environment, you might consider the Openwave SDK, which provides a highly useful microbrowser that resembles a virtual mobile phone. You can download the Openwave SDK for free at http://www.openwave.com/products/developer_products/.

By the Way

> You might also want to consider an online mobile phone simulator such as Wapaka. Wapaka is a Java-based microbrowser that allows you to test WML web pages on a simulated mobile phone directly in a normal web browser. Wapaka is neat in that it allows you to change devices to experiment with different screen sizes. To check out Wapaka, visit http://www.digitalairways.com/wapaka/.

Laying Down the Infrastructure

In order to transmit WML documents, you need a WML gateway and a web server in place. The cell phone transmits the user's information to a WAP gateway, which sends it on to the web server, which stores it as session information in the user profile.

Your web server needs to know how to process the MIME types of the WML documents, as mentioned in the section "Nuts and Bolts" earlier in the hour. You'll need to take a look at your web server's documentation to learn how to do that. Essentially, you need to introduce each MIME type to the server in a statement of its own. Following are the MIME types associated with WML:

- `text/vnd.wap.wmlscript`
- `image/vnd.wap.wbmp`
- `text/vnd.wap.si`

- `text/vnd.wap.sl`
- `application/vnd.wap.wbxml`
- `application/vnd.wap.wmlc`
- `application/vnd.wap.wmlscriptc`

The Basic WML Document

To view the sample WML documents, you'll need a mobile phone simulator such as the Nokia Mobile Browser Simulator, WinWAP, the Openwave SDK, or some other suitable WML tool that includes a microbrowser. Most of the major mobile phone manufacturers offer simulators that you can download and install and use to test WML pages in a microbrowser. With a microbrowser in hand, you're ready to begin creating your first WML document.

To begin creating a WML document, you must first enter the familiar XML declaration, and then reference the WML DTD. The WML root element, `wml`, is then added as a paired tag. Following is code for a skeletal WML document, which accomplishes these basic tasks:

```
<?xml version="1.0"?>
<!DOCTYPE wml PUBLIC "-//WAPFORUM//DTD WML 1.3//EN"
  "http://www.wapforum.org/DTD/wml13.dtd">

<wml>
</wml>
```

After entering this code into a text editor, you should save it with a `.wml` extension, which is standard for WML documents. Granted, some microbrowsers don't care about the file extension and will display documents okay regardless of the extension, but it's good programming practice to get it right and use the correct file extension.

> Microbrowsers for wireless content are much more proprietary than HTML browsers, which means that most major mobile device manufacturers offer their own microbrowser. Even so, the WAP standard is there to provide a high degree of consistency across different microbrowsers.

Setting Up Cards

The `card` element is the basic unit of content in WML and the parent of all lower-level elements in the document; that is to say, it is the only child of the `wml` element. So, one card and a small snippet of text is all it takes to get you to the tiny silver screen. Of course, most practical WML documents consist of multiple cards.

The p, or paragraph, element is a direct import from HTML and is a child of the card element. However, unlike its HTML counterpart, it has a number of children, discussed later in the hour. You can use it to present straight text, as shown in Listing 23.1.

LISTING 23.1 A Simple WML Document with a Single Card (hello.wml)

```
<?xml version="1.0"?>
<!DOCTYPE wml PUBLIC "-//WAPFORUM//DTD WML 1.3//EN"
  "http://www.wapforum.org/DTD/wml13.dtd">

<wml>
  <card>
    <p>Hello, Movie Lovers!</p>
  </card>
</wml>
```

Figure 23.1 shows the resulting document as viewed in a microbrowser.

FIGURE 23.1 The obligatory "Hello" document.

As you can see, it isn't too difficult to place a greeting into a WML document and make it available to the world of wireless devices.

Formatting Text

Even though wireless device screens are typically somewhat limited in terms of their graphical capabilities, it is possible to format text in WML documents to a certain extent. The good news is that if you've ever formatted text in HTML, you'll find the WML approach to be very familiar. Following are the text formatting elements used in WML:

- b—Bolds text
- big—Enlarges text relative to the browser's default text size
- em—Emphasizes text in a browser-defined fashion
- i—Italicizes text
- small—Reduces text relative to the browser's default text size
- strong—Renders text "strong," whatever that means to the given browser

Listing 23.2 shows how to put these formatting elements to use in formatting text.

LISTING 23.2 A WML Document That Shows How to Format Text (formattext.wml)

```
<?xml version="1.0"?>
<!DOCTYPE wml PUBLIC "-//WAPFORUM//DTD WML 1.3//EN"
  "http://www.wapforum.org/DTD/wml13.dtd">

<wml>
  <card>
    <p><b>FilmTime!</b></p>
    <p><big>FilmTime!</big></p>
    <p><em>FilmTime!</em></p>
    <p><i>FilmTime!</i></p>
    <p><small>FilmTime!</small></p>
    <p><strong>FilmTime!</strong></p>
  </card>
</wml>
```

The results of the code in Listing 23.2 are shown in Figure 23.2.

As you can see in the figure, WML doesn't go crazy in its support for text formatting, but it does cover the basics: bold, italic, and so on. Keep in mind that it is up to the microbrowser to determine exactly how to draw formatted text, so you may well get different results with other browsers.

A popular text layout feature of HTML is tables, which allow you to arrange text and other content in a grid-like array. Tables are supported in WML, but their role is modest as compared to tables in HTML. Think of WML tables as more like a typewriter's tabs, useful for alignment but not much else.

FIGURE 23.2
A demonstration of text formatting elements.

Four Ways to Navigate

There are many ways to structure and navigate around a document in WML, all of which have their pros and cons. Four of the more common approaches follow:

- Anchors
- The `select>option` construct
- A series of links using the OK softkey
- A separate card using other softkeys, such as the Menu key

Which navigation approach you choose may be a matter of weighing the advantages and disadvantages of the particular document you're creating, or it may be part of the style guide of the company you work for. There isn't really a right or wrong way to navigate WML documents, but generally speaking, simpler is better.

Good Old Anchors

Anchors, which form the basis of hyperlinks in HTML, have the hands-down advantage in terms of WML navigation approaches due to the familiarity from HTML. The syntax follows the HTML anchor syntax exactly:

```
<a href="url">content</a>
```

This is actually the short form of the longer anchor element. In other words, though HTML relies on the somewhat cryptic a element, WML allows you to spell it out with the anchor element, like this:

```
<anchor href="url">content</anchor>
```

The best way to get acquainted with the anchor element is to see it in the context of a sample document. The hypothetical FilmTime wireless web site presents a list of movie titles that serve as links. The user navigates the list with the up or down arrow keys and makes a selection by clicking the Link button. Alternatively, they can use the Send button (the physical one) to jump to a link. Listing 23.3 contains the code for a WML document that uses anchors to allow the user to select from a listing of movies.

LISTING 23.3 A WML Document That Presents a Movie Listing (movielist.wml)

```
<?xml version="1.0"?>
<!DOCTYPE wml PUBLIC "-//WAPFORUM//DTD WML 1.3//EN"
  "http://www.wapforum.org/DTD/wml13.dtd">

<wml>
  <card id="films">
    <p align="center"><b>***FILMTIME!***</b></p>
    <p><b>FILMS NEAR YOU</b></p>
    <p><a href="#allkingsmen">All the King's Men</a></p>
    <p><a href="#theproducers">The Producers</a></p>
    <p><a href="#kingkong">King Kong</a></p>
  </card>

  <card id="allkingsmen">
    <p><b>All the King's Men</b></p>
    <p>Remake of the classic novel, which charts the spectacular rise
      and fall of a charismatic Southern politician, &quot;Boss&quot;
      Willie Stark.</p>
  </card>

  <card id="theproducers">
    <p><b>The Producers</b></p>
    <p>Remake of a Broadway hit about two producers who set out to
      make the worst movie ever but unwittingly turn out a smash hit,
      much to their dismay.</p>
  </card>

  <card id="kingkong">
    <p><b>King Kong</b></p>
    <p>Remake of the 1933 classic, in which a giant ape is found on a
      mysterious island and brought back to New York City.</p>
  </card>
</wml>
```

As you can see, multiple card elements are used here to represent different screens of information, one for each movie. Each movie card in the document is assigned a unique ID via the id attribute (lines 14, 21, and 28). Lines 9–11 use the a element with the href attribute to link to the movie cards in the deck. The value of the href attribute is the id attribute of the card to which you're linking. The result of this code is shown in Figure 23.3. In this browser, each link is underlined, much as it would be in a traditional HTML web browser. Other browsers may render them differently, such as using square brackets around the links.

FIGURE 23.3
A list of links, HTML fashion.

The select>option Setup

The previous example showed how to allow the user to select from a list of options using anchors. You can get almost the same effect by using the select element with its child, the option element. This results in a set of radio buttons for each selection option. As with the anchor approach, the user can hit the physical Options or Send key to jump to a link.

The select element itself is a child of the p (paragraph) element, which is in turn a child of the card element. In other words, you need to place the select element within a paragraph. Listing 23.4 illustrates the select>option construction in an example that allows you to select movie theatres from a list.

LISTING 23.4 Using WML to Select a Movie Theatre (theatrelist.wml)

```
<?xml version="1.0"?>
<!DOCTYPE wml PUBLIC "-//WAPFORUM//DTD WML 1.3//EN"
  "http://www.wapforum.org/DTD/wml13.dtd">

<wml>
```

```
 6:   <card>
 7:     <p align="center"><b>***FILMTIME!***</b></p>
 8:     <p><b>KING KONG NOW PLAYING AT...</b>
 9:     <select>
10:       <option onpick="#rio">Rio</option>
11:       <option onpick="#apollo">Apollo</option>
12:       <option onpick="#crown">Crown</option>
13:     </select>
14:     </p>
15:   </card>
16:
17:   <card id="rio">
18:     <p><b>Rio Theatre</b></p>
19:     <p>455 River Street, Anytown</p>
20:     <p>111.222.3333</p>
21:     <p>3:30, 5:30, 7:30</p>
22:   </card>
23:
24:   <card id="apollo">
25:     <p><b>Apollo Theatre</b></p>
26:     <p>779 Pax Romana Drive, Chesterton</p>
27:     <p>111.222.4444</p>
28:     <p>3:45, 5:50, 7:40</p>
29:   </card>
30:
31:   <card id="crown">
32:     <p><b>Crown Theatre</b></p>
33:     <p>83 Imperial Avenue, Kingston</p>
34:     <p>111.234.5566</p>
35:     <p>2:00, 4:30, 6:45</p>
36:   </card>
37: </wml>
```

In this example, a `select` element is used (line 9) to establish a list of theatres from which the user can select. Each theatre option is represented by an `option` element accompanied by an `onpick` attribute (lines 10–12), which determines the destination of the `option` link. The link destinations correspond to card IDs that appear later in the document (lines 17, 24, and 31). The rest of the listing is similar to the anchor example in structure, and the result is shown in Figure 23.4.

Unlike the `a href` construction, `select>option's` output is a set of radio buttons, which allows the user to make the selection by navigating through the buttons.

Map to OK Button

Another approach to navigating through the cards in a WML document is to set up the choices as a sequence of cards through which the user navigates by hitting the OK softkey (accessible via Options in the Nokia microbrowser) until reaching the end of the deck. This feature is useful for presenting large chunks of narrative material. See the following section on assigning to other softkeys for a complete list of available actions.

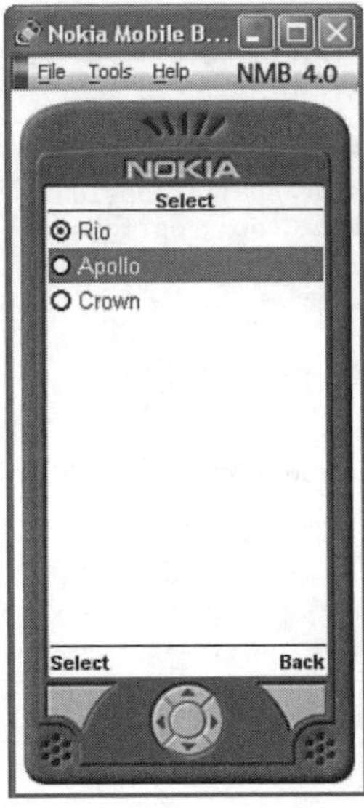

FIGURE 23.4
The `select>option` list makes it possible to easily select movies from a list.

By the Way

> If you're looking to create a document that has a presentation feel to it, you might consider combining the navigation with a timer (see "Associating an Event with a Task," next section) so that the presentation advances from one screen to the next automatically.

Listing 23.5 contains sample code for a WML document that uses the OK mapping for each card as the plot for the movie King Kong, laid out screen by screen.

LISTING 23.5 Describing a Movie Plot with WML (moviedesc_kingkong.wml)

```
<?xml version="1.0"?>
<!DOCTYPE wml PUBLIC "-//WAPFORUM//DTD WML 1.3//EN"
  "http://www.wapforum.org/DTD/wml13.dtd">

<wml>
  <card id="one">
    <do type="accept">
      <go href="#two"/>
    </do>
    <p align="center"><b>***FILMTIME!***</b></p>
    <p><i>King Kong</i> This remake of the 1933 classic follows an
      expedition to the mysterious Skull Island, where a legend of
      a giant gorilla draws explorers and filmmakers.</p>
  </card>

  <card id="two">
    <do type="accept">
      <go href="#three"/>
```

```
19:     </do>
20:     <p align="center">-2-</p>
21:     <p>The legend, however, is both real and dangerous, living in a
22:       massive jungle that has protected him and other prehistoric
23:       creatures for decades.</p>
24:   </card>
25:
26:   <card id="three">
27:     <do type="accept">
28:       <go href="#four"/>
29:     </do>
30:     <p align="center">-3-</p>
31:     <p>Kong finds solace in a beautiful woman (Naomi Watts), and is
32:       subdued enough to be captured and brought back to New York.</p>
33:   </card>
34:
35:   <card id="four">
36:     <do type="reset">
37:       <go href="#one"/>
38:     </do>
39:     <p align="center">-4-</p>
40:     <p>However, as the captors and the public will learn, it takes a
41:       lot more shackles to hold back an animal of such monstrous
42:       size.</p>
43:   </card>
44: </wml>
```

In lines 7, 17, and 27, the `accept` value of the do element's `type` attribute assigns the enclosed go action to the OK softkey. I'll admit that I'm jumping ahead here a bit, but suffice it to say that the do element, which you learn more about in a moment, is how you assign an action to the OK softkey. More specifically, the value `accept` for the `type` attribute indicates that the action applies to the OK softkey. Other possible actions are `prev` and `noop`, the last of which is designed to eliminate any default behavior in the microbrowser that might result in an unintended jump (for instance). The last card in the document, beginning on line 36, sets the Reset button.

Associating an Event with a Task

Tasks, such as moving from one card to the next, can be set so that they are triggered by actions, such as timer events. For example, you could re-create the movie plot example so that it presents the same text in the same order but uses a timer that automatically flips the display to the next card. This is accomplished with an event called `ontimer`. Events are specified using the `onevent` element, which is a child of the card element. Following is the syntax of the `onevent` element:

```
<card>
  <onevent type=type>
    action
  </onevent>
</card>
```

To create a timer, you must set the type attribute of the onevent element to ontimer and then provide a separate timer element that specifies the duration of the timer. The unit of measurement of the timer's value is a 10th of a second, which means that a value of 20 represents two seconds. Following is a code snippet that demonstrates how to set a two-second timer that flips to the second card in the movie plot document:

```
<card id="one">
  <onevent type="ontimer">
    <go href="#two"/>
  </onevent>
  <timer value="20"/>
  <p align="center"><b>***FILMTIME!***</b></p>
  <p><i>King Kong</i> This remake of the 1933 classic follows an
    expedition to the mysterious Skull Island, where a legend of
    a giant gorilla draws explorers and filmmakers.</p>
</card>
```

Better yet, there's a shortcut that allows you to include the ontimer attribute directly in the card element, eliminating the need for the onevent element and its contents:

```
<card id="two" ontimer="#three">
  <timer value="50"/>
  <p align="center">-2-</p>
  <p>The legend, however, is both real and dangerous, living in a
    massive jungle that has protected him and other prehistoric
    creatures for decades.</p>
</card>
```

Map to Menu Button

WML allows you to map cards to the Menu (or Options) and other softkeys. This is accomplished with the do element, which has an attribute named type that is set to indicate which softkeys are targeted by the mapping. The type attribute of the do element can be any of the following actions that correspond to the micro-browser's softkeys:

- accept—OK button
- delete—Delete button
- help—Help button
- options—Options or Menu button
- prev—Prev button, return to previous card
- reset—Return to first card of the deck, and/or reset variables

Listing 23.6 contains sample code for a WML document that demonstrates how to use the do element to map movie options to the Options softkey; pressing the

Options/Menu key displays a list of links to other cards. Those cards, in turn, link to cards in other WML documents.

LISTING 23.6 An Example of How to Select a Movie in WML (movieselect.html)

```
 1: <?xml version="1.0"?>
 2: <!DOCTYPE wml PUBLIC "-//WAPFORUM//DTD WML 1.3//EN"
 3:   "http://www.wapforum.org/DTD/wml13.dtd">
 4:
 5: <wml>
 6:   <card id="top">
 7:     <p>Press the Menu button for more choices:</p>
 8:     <do type="options" name="movies" label="Movies">
 9:       <go href="#movies"/>
10:     </do>
11:     <do type="options" name="synopses" label="Synopses">
12:       <go href="#synopses"/>
13:     </do>
14:     <do type="options" name="theatres" label="Theatres">
15:       <go href="#theatres"/>
16:     </do>
17:   </card>
18:
19:   <card id="movies">
20:     <p align="center"><b>***FILMTIME!***</b></p>
21:     <p><b>FILMS NEAR YOU</b></p>
22:     <p><a href="moviedesc_allkingsmen.wml">All the King's Men</a></p>
23:     <p><a href="moviedesc_theproducers.wml">The Producers</a></p>
24:     <p><a href="moviedesc_kingkong.wml">King Kong</a></p>
25:   </card>
26:
27:   <card id="synopses">
28:     <p><b>SYNOPSES</b>
29:     <select>
30:       <option onpick="movielist.wml#allkingsmen">All the King's Men</option>
31:       <option onpick="movielist.wml#theproducers">The Producers</option>
32:       <option onpick="movielist.wml#kingkong">King Kong</option>
33:     </select>
34:     </p>
35:
36:   </card>
37:
38:   <card id="theatres">
39:     <p><b>THEATRES NEAR YOU</b>
40:     <select>
41:       <option onpick="theatrelist.wml#rio">Rio</option>
42:       <option onpick="theatrelist.wml#apollo">Apollo</option>
43:       <option onpick="theatrelist.wml#crown">Crown</option>
44:     </select>
45:     </p>
46:   </card>
47: </wml>
```

This example uses several do elements to link to parts of the document within the Options softkey. For example, the first do element (line 8) links to the "movies" card because of the nested go element (line 10); the href attribute of the go element is set to #movies. This approach is also used with the two other cards ("synopses" and "theatres"). Notice that the original anchor approach to linking cards is used in the "movies" card (lines 22–24), whereas the option element is used to allow selection within the "synopses" and "theatres" cards (lines 30–32 and 41–43). Figure 23.5 shows the resulting options for this document as viewed in the Nokia Mobile Browser Simulator; keep in mind that the mapping of these options will differ when viewed on an actual wireless device because of the softkeys.

FIGURE 23.5
Menu button activated.

In this relatively simple example, not a whole lot is accomplished by putting the choices in a separate options menu rather than directly on the screen. But on a larger commercial web site with a great number of cards, it could be a very efficient design element. As an example, consider other types of corporate sites where users have become accustomed to the Menu or Options button linking to a global set of choices, such as "Company," "About," "Careers at . . . ," and so on. The point is that as a site becomes deeper in terms of content, the options approach starts to pay off versus normal anchors.

Inserting WBMP Images

As you learned earlier in the hour, it is possible to display images in WML documents. WML supports only one graphics format, WBMP, which stands for Wireless BitMap Picture. The WBMP format is a 1-bit monochrome format and, currently, the only graphics format supported by WML. Because most traditional paint applications don't support WBMP just yet, you'll have to find a converter application to convert traditional images, such as GIFs or BMPs, into the WBMP format. One such converter application is offered for free by the Waptiger WAP search engine. There is even an online version of Waptiger's WBMP Converter at http://www.waptiger.com/bmp2wbmp/ that allows you to convert 1-bit BMP bitmaps to WBMP images. This online converter allows you to browse for an image on your local computer, after which it is converted to a WBMP image that is saved on your local computer—very handy indeed!

By the Way

> WBMP images are typically limited to 150 3 150 in size, although some tools restrict them even further. For example, Waptiger's WBMP Converter only converts images that are 127 3 127 or smaller.

To display an image in WML, you must use the `img` element, which, like so many other WML elements, is a child of the `p` element. The `src`, `alt`, `height`, and `width` attributes of the `img` element come directly from HTML. Unlike traditional HTML images, however, WML limits the size of WBMP images to 643 64. Listing 23.7 contains the code for an example that demonstrates how to use the `img` element.

LISTING 23.7 Displaying an Image in a WML Document (image.wml)

```
1: <?xml version="1.0"?>
2: <!DOCTYPE wml PUBLIC "-//WAPFORUM//DTD WML 1.3//EN"
3:   "http://www.wapforum.org/DTD/wml13.dtd">
4:
5: <wml>
6:   <card>
7:     <p><img src="ftlogo.wbmp" alt="FilmTime Logo"
8:       width="64" height="39"/>
9:     </p>
10:   </card>
11: </wml>
```

This code uses the `img` element to embed the image named `ftlogo.wbmp` in the WML document (line 7). Notice that alternative text is specified for the image (line 7), as well as the width and height of the image (line 8). Figure 23.6 shows the results of viewing this document in the Nokia Mobile Browser Simulator.

The image shown in the figure is a logo for the hypothetical wireless web site FilmTime.

FIGURE 23.6
Displaying a simple WBMP image in a WML document isn't too difficult thanks to the `img` element.

Accepting User Input

Although the keyboard of a mobile device is hardly ideal for text input—sometimes the user has to press the same key three times to enter a single character—it is easy enough to support in WML documents. Keyboard support is carried out via the `input` element, which is a child of the `p` element. The user types in the current value (`input` can also be initialized to a default value) and WML assigns it, for instance, the name `email`, as in the first occurrence of the `input` element in Listing 23.8.

LISTING 23.8 Retrieving Information from the User (input.wml)

```
<?xml version="1.0"?>
<!DOCTYPE wml PUBLIC "-//WAPFORUM//DTD WML 1.3//EN"
  "http://www.wapforum.org/DTD/wml13.dtd">

<wml>
  <card id="subscribe">
    <p align="center"><b>***FILMTIME!***</b></p>
    <p>To subscribe to FILMTIME!, please enter your e-mail address:</p>
    <p><input name="email"/></p>
    <do type="accept">
      <go href="#email-ok"/>
    </do>
  </card>

  <card id="email-ok">
    <p>You entered <i>$email</i>. If this is correct, click OK.</p>
    <do type="accept">
      <go href="#username"/>
    </do>
```

```
20:   </card>
21:
22:   <card id="username">
23:     <p>Please enter your name.</p>
24:     <p><input name="username"/></p>
25:     <do type="accept">
26:       <go href="#thanks"/>
27:     </do>
28:   </card>
29:
30:   <card id="thanks">
31:     <p>Thanks, <b>$username</b>!</p>
32:     <p>Goodbye!</p>
33:   </card>
34: </wml>
```

In this example, the user is allowed to input his email address (line 9). The email address is given the name `email`, which is the name used to store the information for any further processing. When the user progresses to the next card, the email address is displayed to him by preceding its name with a dollar sign (line 16): `$email`. A similar approach is used to ask the user for his name (line 24), and then display it when telling him goodbye (lines 31 and 32).

Blending WML with XHTML Mobile

You now have a very good idea of how WML works and what is has to offer. So how does WML fit into XHTML Mobile? You learned earlier that WML is a good option if you want your mobile pages to be backwardly compatible with older phones or if you really like the "stack of cards" metaphor used to build WML pages. On the other hand, XHTML Mobile is a bit more advanced in that it allows you to use CSS styles to improve the appearance of mobile pages. You can create mobile web pages using either language but you can't use the two languages within a single document. As a hybrid solution, you might consider mixing pages that selectively use WML and XHTML Mobile whenever one makes more sense than the other. Microbrowsers that support XHTML Mobile are required to support WML, so this option should always be available to you.

By the Way

> If you recall from earlier in the lesson, XHTML Mobile actually relies on WCSS for stylesheet support. Because WCSS is simply a subset of CSS, in this lesson I refer to styles generally as CSS styles. Just know that I'm technically talking about WCSS and not full-blown CSS.

The great thing about XHTML Mobile is that it is no different than using XHTML, except that it is more limited. So, if you know XHTML you already know XHTML Mobile. At worst, you'll just have to unlearn a few things because XHTML Mobile is a bit more limited than XHTML. Generally speaking, you'll find that XHTML Mobile can do just about anything markup-wise that you will want to do on a mobile web page.

As an example of how XHTML Mobile can be used in the context of a wireless application, I've reworked the King Kong movie description document as an XHTML Mobile document. Listing 23.9 contains the code for the moviedesc_kingkong.xhtml document.

LISTING 23.9 The XHTML Mobile Version of the King Kong Movie Description Page (moviedesc_kingkong.xhtml)

```
 1: <?xml version="1.0"?>
 2: <?xml-stylesheet type="text/css" media="handheld" href="moviedesc.css"?>
 3: <!DOCTYPE html PUBLIC "-//WAPFORUM//DTD XHTML Mobile 1.0//EN"
 4:   "http://www.wapforum.org/DTD/xhtml-mobile10.dtd">
 5:
 6: <html>
 7:   <head>
 8:   </head>
 9:
10:   <body>
11:     <h1 align="center">***FILMTIME!***</h1>
12:     <p><i>King Kong</i> This remake of the 1933 classic follows an
13:       expedition to the mysterious Skull Island, where a legend of
14:       a giant gorilla draws explorers and filmmakers. The legend,
15:       however, is both real and dangerous, living in a massive
16:       jungle that has protected him and other prehistoric creatures
17:       for decades. Kong finds solace in a beautiful woman (Naomi
18:       Watts), and is subdued enough to be captured and brought back
19:       to New York. However, as the captors and the public will
20:       learn, it takes a lot more shackles to hold back an animal of
21:       such monstrous size.</p>
22:   </body>
23: </html>
```

There really aren't any surprises in the content part of this document as it consists of run-of-the-mill XHTML code with familiar `h1`, `p`, and `i` tags. The most interesting code that is unique to XHTML Mobile is the document type declaration and the stylesheet reference. The document type declaration references the XHTML Mobile 1.0 DTD (lines 3 and 4), which is publicly available at http://www.wapforum.org/DTD/xhtml-mobile10.dtd. The page imports the `moviedesc.css` stylesheet (line 2), which specifies colors and more exacting fonts for the King Kong movie content. Notice that there is an additional `media` attribute for the xml-stylesheet directive, and that it is set to `handheld`. This attribute allows you to establish the type of media that the page is targeting, which in this case consists of handheld devices.

Examples of other settings for the media attribute include `all` (the default), `print`, and `tv`. This attribute provides you with a mechanism for altering the specific formatting of content based upon how it is going to be viewed. In this case, you are formatting the content specifically for mobile handheld devices.

Listing 23.10 contains the code for the moviedesc.css stylesheet that is used to format the King Kong movie description XHTML Mobile document.

LISTING 23.10 The WCSS Stylesheet for the XHTML Mobile King Kong Movie Description Page (moviedesc.css)

```
body {
  background: #FFFFFF;
}

h1 {
  font-size: x-large;
  color: #660000;
  text-align: center;
  text-decoration: underline;
}

p {
  display: block;
  border: 1px #330000 solid;
  background: #660000;
  color: #FFFFFF;
  text-align: left;
  font-size: medium;
  padding: 4px;
}
```

Figure 23.7 shows the results of viewing the King Kong XHTML Mobile page in the Nokia Mobile Browser Simulator.

FIGURE 23.7 XHTML Mobile allows you to create mobile web pages with more interesting styles applied to them than pure WML pages.

As the figure reveals, the stylesheet dramatically affects the look of the page as compared to the earlier version that was coded in WML (refer to Figure 23.5). Although you can't quite make out the colors in this printed figure, you can easily open the page for yourself in a WAP microbrowser and get the full effect.

Summary

This hour covered everything it takes to get a complete, navigable, illustrated document onto the wireless web via WML or XHTML Mobile. You started out by learning some general information about the wireless web and the evolution of markup languages for creating wireless web pages. You then delved into the mechanics of creating a WML document, starting with the basics of working with a microbrowser simulator on your PC. You found out how to set up the deck and its component cards, design navigation routes, map tasks to the microbrowser's softkeys, and insert an image into a document. Moving up a little on the ladder, you then explored setting up the document for user input—useful for simple name or password entries. And finally, the lesson concluded by taking what you learned about WML and scaling it over to XHTML Mobile.

Q&A

Q. ***Why bother with WML if XHTML Mobile is the wave of the future?***

A. There is certainly an argument that you shouldn't bother with WML given that XHTML Mobile is likely the future of the wireless web. However, given that so many devices support WML, it's hard to move beyond it just yet. Besides, the deck of cards metaphor can be handy in that it allows you to create the effect of multiple "pages" within a single WML document. If carefully controlling the formatting of mobile pages is important to you, by all means go with XHTML Mobile. Otherwise, WML isn't a bad option due to its widespread support.

Q. ***How do I convert a normal XHTML document to XHTML Mobile?***

A. Because the syntax is identical between the two languages, the main trick is to eliminate features that aren't supported in XHTML Mobile, such as frames. Beyond that, your main challenge is in scaling down any images and simplifying styles so that pages look good on a small display that has potentially fewer colors to work with.

Workshop

The Workshop is designed to help you anticipate possible questions, review what you've learned, and begin learning how to put your knowledge into practice.

Quiz

1. WML is a component of what transmission protocol—and what does the acronym stand for?
2. What navigation technique—that is, which element and attribute—should you use if you want to present the user with a numbered list from which she can jump to other cards or documents?
3. How many bits are in a WBMP image?
4. The `select` element is a child of what WML parent element?

Quiz Answers

1. Wireless Markup Language is a component of WAP, or Wireless Access Protocol.
2. Use the `select` element with the `option` attribute.
3. Only one! That means you get a straight black-and-white image, with no shades of gray.
4. The `p` (paragraph) element.

Exercises

1. Using `do>type`, set up a Help card for the FilmTime site.
2. Design a short and simple animation sequence (suggested length 5–10 frames) played by using the `ontimer` event.

HOUR 24

Syndicating the Web with RSS News Feeds

> It's amazing that the amount of news that happens in the world every day always just exactly fits the newspaper.
>
> —Jerry Seinfeld

What is equally as amazing as Jerry Seinfeld's newspaper observation is how much news is now read online instead of from the printed page. As a professional nerd, I'm probably not the best example of your "average person" from a tech perspective, but I only read printed newspapers when I have absolutely no access to the Web. I'm actually fairly old school in terms of generally enjoying printed material from newspapers to books to magazines, but for news you can't beat the immediacy of online publishing. Which brings me to the topic of this final lesson in the book: RSS news feeds.

If you've never heard of the term RSS, don't worry because it's not as complicated as many of the acronyms you've already faced throughout this book. In fact, once you get past the messy history of RSS, you'll find that it is a fairly simple technology both to understand and to use. I won't bother telling you what the RSS acronym stands for just yet because it has a different meaning depending on which version of RSS you use. However, I will tell you that RSS has made a significant impact on the Web and how people use it. Increasing numbers of Web users are relying solely on syndicated RSS "news feeds" to find out when there is something of interest worth seeing on a web site, as opposed to actually visiting that site. A story in an RSS feed links directly to the relevant content, allowing you to bypass the main page of the site containing the content.

RSS fits into this book because it is an XML-based technology, which simply means that the language used to code news feeds is an XML markup language. There are a variety of different ways that you can use RSS. You can display RSS feeds from other web sites on your web site, you can build your own library of RSS feeds and view them regularly using special software called a news aggregator, or you can syndicate your own site using RSS so that other people can view your feeds. This hour touches on all of these uses of RSS.

In this hour, you'll learn

- The historical drama of how RSS came to be
- How to use a news aggregator to syndicate RSS news feeds
- How to create and validate your own RSS documents
- How to transform and display RSS news feeds using XSLT

A Brief History of RSS

Although the topic has lived slightly beneath the surface of the mainstream Web, few recent web technologies have caused as much excitement and feverish debate as RSS. What is seemingly a very simple technology has caused quite a bit of infighting among its creators, early adopters, and just about anyone else interested enough to weigh in on the matter. Before we get into that, let's quickly assess what RSS is. *RSS* is a technology that allows you to syndicate web content, which means that you can subscribe to web sites and easily find out about new publications to a site without actually having to visit the site. Using special software called a news aggregator, you can monitor news feeds from multiple sites and effectively keep tabs on a wide range of information without having to stop by every different site on a regular basis. You can think of RSS as providing somewhat of a "stock ticker" for web content—it allows you to keep constant tabs on when your favorite sites post something new.

Now back to the history of RSS. Before I give you my official history of RSS so that you can understand what exactly this lesson is all about, I'd like to offer up a recount of the origins of RSS as written by a good friend of mine, Stephen Tallent:

> "There was a fork in RSS land. The original RSS, version 0.91, 0.92, etc. was just simple XML. A crew didn't like it, or the persons involved with it, and splintered off and created what they called RSS 1.0, and built it using RDF style XML that bared little to no resemblance to 0.9x other than by name. That of course spawned a huge religious war and the original crew then developed RSS 2.0, having nothing to do with 1.0, and 2.0 was just an enhanced version of 0.92, still using standard XML. Then another whole crew forked off again and started ATOM, but I digress."

As Stephen points out, RSS has spawned several different versions over the past few years, all of which are still around in one form or another. It all began back in 1999 with the first incarnation of RSS, which originally stood for RDF Site Summary. This version of RSS was created by Netscape and became known as RSS 0.9. By the way, you need to pay close attention to version numbers in this discussion because they have a lot to do with the different flavors of RSS. Netscape quickly followed up on version 0.9 of RSS with version 0.91, and promptly changed the acronym to Rich Site Summary.

By the Way

> *RDF* stands for *Resource Description Framework*, which is another whole can of beans. For the purposes of this discussion, all you need to know is that RDF is a specification designed to allow web content creators to add metadata to their content.

It wasn't long at all before Netscape began to back away from RSS, and ultimately ceased development on it. Ironically, RSS was just starting to gain in popularity, so a group called RSS-DEV took up the cause and continued working on the project. This is where the first drama officially takes place in the RSS story. Back in 1997, a guy by the name of Dave Winer of Userland Software created a technology similar in some ways to RSS. Just after the creation of the RSS-DEV group, Winer entered the RSS fray by releasing his own version of RSS 0.91, which had the advantage of already being used by his company's products. The RSS-DEV group followed up with RSS 1.0 and Winer countered with RSS 0.92. Winer's branch of RSS became known as the Userland branch due to its heavy usage within his company.

In 2002, the most stable version of RSS was published by Winer in the form of RSS 2.0, with the acronym changing once more to become Really Simple Syndication. RSS 2.0 was designed to be compatible with RSS 0.92, and also includes features that allow it to be extended to support additional features such as media objects. The RSS-DEV group continued down their path and released a draft of RSS 1.1 in 2005. As of this writing, RSS 2.0 is the de facto standard version of RSS while RSS 1.1 is still somewhat of an "emerging technology."

To summarize, there are two main functional branches of RSS that you may encounter as you begin to explore syndication around the Web. Different versions of RSS within each branch are reasonably similar to each other. Following are the two branches and the versions of RSS that fit into each:

- RSS 1 Branch—RSS 0.90, 1.0, and 1.1
- RSS 2 Branch—RSS 0.91–0.94 and 2.0

So the question you have to be asking yourself is why I'm bothering to painstakingly document all of the different versions of RSS so carefully? The reason is because the underlying XML language varies quite a bit based upon the RSS language that you choose to use when syndicating your web content. Without knowing what they are and a little about how they differ, you wouldn't know which flavor of RSS to choose.

But I'll help you. Given the current state of affairs, it makes sense to focus on the latest version of RSS, which is RSS 2.0. All of the latest RSS-powered web browsers and news aggregator software supports RSS 2.0, which is really all you need to know. The remainder of this hour focuses on RSS 2.0 as you learn more about news feeds and how they are created and syndicated.

By the Way

I stopped short of mentioning Atom in this brief historical discussion of RSS. You can think of *Atom* as a third branch of RSS that competes more with RSS 2.0. There are strong voices arguing for both technologies, so all I can really tell you is that RSS 2.0 seems to have the widest industry support at the moment, which is why I've chosen to cover it exclusively in this lesson. The good news is that if you get comfortable with RSS 2.0 you won't have much trouble learning Atom if the tide should eventually turn away from RSS 2.0.

Using an RSS News Aggregator

Before you face the prospect of creating your own RSS news feeds, it's important to explore existing news feeds and learn how they work. The easiest way to do this is by installing news aggregator software and exploring feeds for yourself. One of the most popular news aggregators available now is FeedDemon, which is available in a free trial version online at http://www.feeddemon.com/. *FeedDemon* is a standalone desktop application that is completely independent of your web browser.

If you want a more integrated RSS experience, you may want to look into an aggregator that ties into Microsoft Outlook, such as NewsGator (http://www.newsgator.com/). *NewsGator* is an Outlook plug-in that integrates news feeds into Outlook by establishing a News folder under the normal Personal Folders commonly used in Outlook. NewsGator also offers a free web-based version of its news aggregator called *NewsGator Online*. This is a great way to gain an introduction to news feeds because it is free and easy to use. Interestingly enough, NewsGator recently purchased Bradbury Software, the maker of FeedDemon, so don't be surprised if FeedDemon is eventually marketed as a desktop edition of NewsGator.

By the Way

Just in case you think I'm being a bit partial to NewsGator, some other popular online news aggregators include Bloglines (http://www.bloglines.com/), NewsIsFree (http://www.newsisfree.com/), and Microsoft's experimental start.com (http://www.start.com/). Google News (http://www.newsisfree.com/) can even be considered an aggregator of sorts, although it doesn't provide as much flexibility as a true RSS feed manager. Google News is perhaps more powerful as a feed generator because you can use it to easily syndicate Google News categories and even Google searches.

One other option in regard to accessing news feeds is a browser-based feed reader such as Apple's Safari RSS browser. Safari incorporates RSS into its core, effectively making site syndication a standard component of the browser experience. Apparently other browser vendors are taking note as Microsoft has already announced RSS support in its next version of Internet Explorer. You can also install RSS plug-ins for existing browsers, such as the Sage RSS aggregator for Mozilla Firefox (http://sage.mozdev.org/).

Just so you have a good picture in your mind of how news aggregators work, let's take a quick look at a couple of examples of how to access syndicated RSS feeds. Figure 24.1 shows the NewsGator Online web-based news aggregator in action.

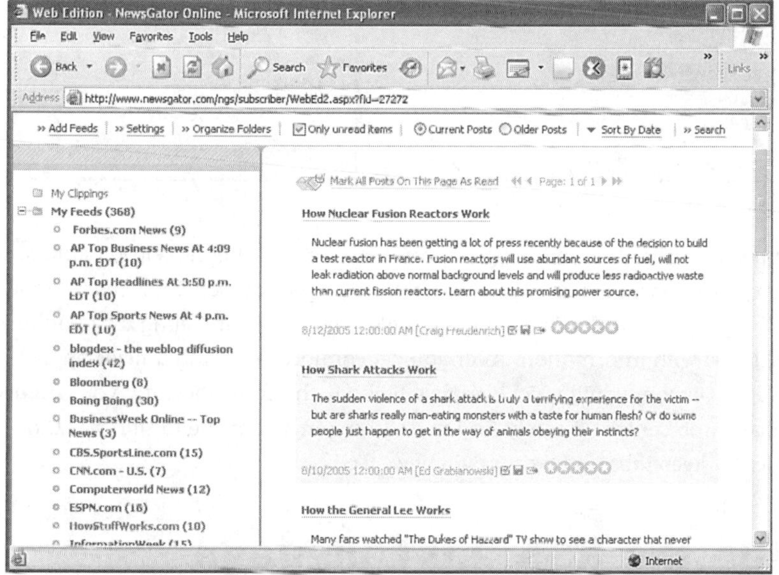

FIGURE 24.1
NewsGator Online serves as a decent news aggregator without you having to purchase or download anything.

In the figure, NewsGator Online is being used to view the HowStuffWorks.com RSS feed. This feed is regularly updated with links to articles about how things work. For example, in the figure there are articles listed ranging from how nuclear fusion reactors work to how shark attacks work to how the General Lee car (from *The Dukes of Hazzard* television show and movie) works.

If you want a more full-featured news aggregator that gives you much more control over news feeds, you may want to consider using a desktop or plug-in aggregator. Figure 24.2 shows the FeedDemon desktop aggregator as I'm viewing some very familiar content.

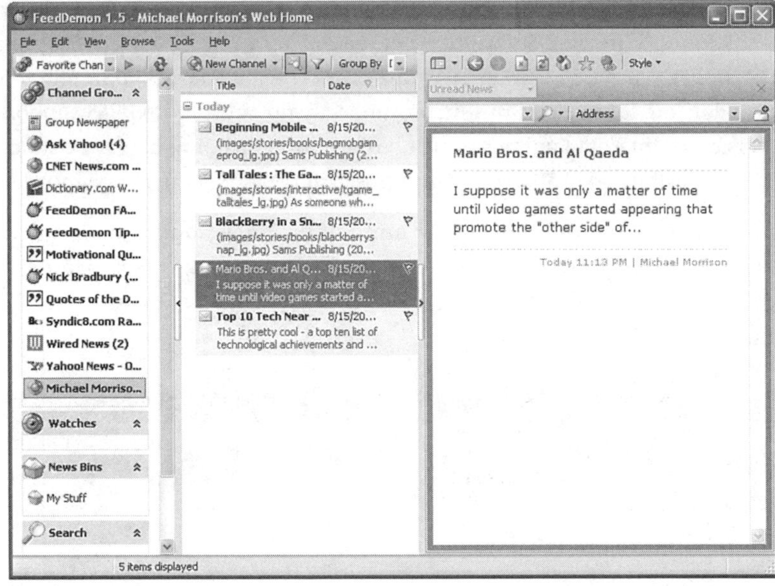

FIGURE 24.2
FeedDemon is one of the leading desktop news aggregators, and is reasonably priced.

If you pay close attention to the figure, you'll notice that the news feed being accessed is my very own news feed as syndicated from michaelmorrison.com. FeedDemon makes it possible to easily manage quite a few feeds without feeling as if you're totally overburdened with information. After you get comfortable using a news aggregator such as FeedDemon, you'll quickly realize how much more efficiently you can access and process web content. I rarely find myself hopping from site to site now that I can conveniently keep tabs on favorites via news feeds.

Inside the RSS 2.0 Language

It's time to get down to the business of sorting out exactly how XML fits into the RSS 2.0 picture. As you know by now, RSS 2.0 is an XML markup language used to syndicate web content. You may be pleasantly surprised by the relative simplicity of the RSS 2.0 language. When it comes right down to it, there isn't all that much information associated with an RSS news feed, and this simplicity translates directly over to the RSS language.

By the Way

> For the sake of brevity, from here on when I mention RSS, please assume that I'm referring to RSS 2.0.

Before getting any deeper into the RSS language, it's important to clarify a few terms. An RSS news item is a discrete piece of content that ultimately resolves to a specific link to a resource on a web site. A collection of related news items can be gathered together into a channel. As an example, if you wanted to divide your news feeds into three categories for Entertainment, Sports, and Technology, each of these categories would constitute a channel. Each piece of syndicated content (each story) within a given category constitutes a news item. An RSS document is broken down into a channel that contains news items, as shown in Figure 24.3.

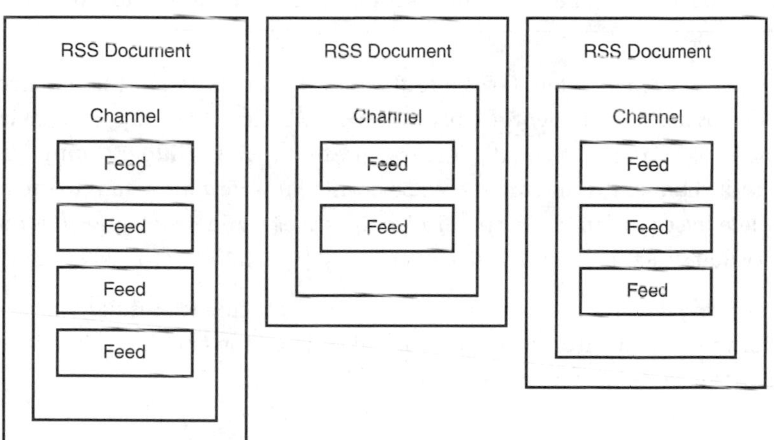

FIGURE 24.3 An RSS document consists of a single channel containing multiple items.

Notice in the figure how each document is limited to a single channel that contains multiple items. There is a lot of flexibility in terms of how many items you assign to a channel even though you can only specify one channel per document.

Getting back to the RSS language, any news item can be described using only a few pieces of information:

- Title—The title of the news item
- Description—A brief one or two sentence description of the item
- Link—The URL of the web resource associated with the item
- Publication Date—The publication date of the news item

These conceptual item descriptors translate directly to the RSS language. More specifically, a news item in RSS is coded using `<title>`, `<description>`, `<link>`, and `<pubDate>` tags. The following is an example of how these tags are used to code a real news item:

```
<title>My Car Has a Virus!</title>
<description>This is a little disturbing but I suppose it was inevitable -
wireless networking technologies are now potentially opening up automobiles to
computer viruses.</description>
```

```
<link>http://www.michaelmorrison.com/mambo/index.php?option=
com_content&amp;task=view&amp;id=229&amp;Itemid=37</link>
<pubDate>Tue, 02 Aug 2005 10:20:44 CST</pubDate>
```

The only tags absolutely required for a news item are <title> and <description>. If you leave out the <link> tag, the description of the item serves as its content. There are several other optional tags that you can use to provide further details about a news item, such as <author>, <enclosure>, and <guid> to name a few.

As you can see, the news item flows directly from the four tags I just mentioned. But these tags don't tell the entire story. All this code shows is a snippet of code for a specific news item. What you don't see is how that item fits into a channel, as well as how that channel fits into an entire RSS document. A few more tags are required to complete the equation. More specifically, the <item> and <channel> tags are used to further add structure to an RSS document.

The <item> tag represents a single news item, and in fact, encloses the four item descriptor tags you just learned about. So, you can add the enclosing <item> tag to expand the previous news item listing to look like this:

```
<item>
  <title>My Car Has a Virus!</title>
  <description>This is a little disturbing but I suppose it was inevitable -
  wireless networking technologies are now potentially opening up
  automobiles to computer viruses.</description>
  <link>http://www.michaelmorrison.com/mambo/index.php?option=
  com_content&amp;task=view&amp;id=229&amp;Itemid=37</link>
  <pubDate>Tue, 02 Aug 2005 10:20:44 CST</pubDate>
</item>
```

Nothing changed in the code other than the <title>, <description>, <link>, and <pubDate> tags being placed as children of the <item> tag. You can probably now guess that each individual news item within an RSS document takes the form of this code. But you still haven't found out how these items relate to a channel.

The <channel> tag is used to code the channel in an RSS document. The <channel> tag consists of several child tags that are used to describe the channel, followed by one or more child <item> tags that describe the individual news items. The tags used to describe a channel are actually the same as those used to describe a news item, minus the <pubDate> tag: <title>, <description>, and <link>. In this case, the tags are describing the channel itself, as opposed to a specific news item. Following is an example of a channel coded with these tags:

```
<channel>
  <title>Michael Morrison's Blog</title>
  <description>Technology, entertainment, culture, you name it...</description>
  <link>http://www.michaelmorrison.com/</link>
  ...
<channel>
```

By the Way

The only tags absolutely required for a channel are <title>, <description>, and <link>. There are several other optional tags that you can use to provide further details about the channel, such as <copyright>, <language>, and <image> to name a few.

What this example doesn't show is how the news items themselves (<items>) are contained within the <channel> tag. You see an entire RSS document come together in the next section. For now, there is one more tag to address: the <rss> tag. The <rss> tag is used to mark up the root element of RSS documents. Along with enclosing the rest of the content in the document, the <rss> tag also serves to identify the version of the RSS feed via the `version` attribute. In the case of RSS 2.0, you set this attribute to `2.0`, as this example shows:

```
<rss version="2.0">
  ...
</rss>
```

You've now seen all of the pieces and parts that go into a basic RSS document. The next section pulls together what you've learned about the RSS language and guides you through the creation of a complete RSS document that contains several news feeds.

By the Way

Back in Hour 13, "Access Your iTunes Music Library via XML," you learned about XML's role in Apple's iTunes digital music service. RSS factors heavily into iTunes when publishing podcasts to the iTunes online service. There is an entire set of iTunes-specific tags that you use to code podcast RSS feeds. <itunes:author>, <itunes:summary>, and <itunes:duration> are examples of some of the tags you must include when coding a podcast as a news feed. To learn more, visit Apple's online podcast publishing tutorial at http://phobos.apple.com/static/iTunesRSS.html.

Creating and Validating a News Feed

You're finally ready to assemble a complete RSS news feed. So without further ado, take a look at Listing 24.1, which contains the complete source code for an RSS feed that is loosely based on my own personal blog.

LISTING 24.1 The RSS Code for a Sample Blog

```
<?xml version="1.0" ?>

<rss version="2.0">
  <channel>
    <title>Michael Morrison's Blog</title>
    <description>Technology, entertainment, culture, you name it...
    </description>
    <link>http://www.michaelmorrison.com/</link>

```

LISTING 24.1 Continued

```
 9:     <item>
10:       <title>My Car Has a Virus!</title>
11:       <description>This is a little disturbing but I suppose it was inevitable -
12:       wireless networking technologies are now potentially opening up
13:       automobiles to computer viruses.</description>
14:       <link>http://www.michaelmorrison.com/mambo/index.php?option=
15:       com_content&amp;task=view&amp;id=229&amp;Itemid=37</link>
16:       <pubDate>Tue, 02 Aug 2005 10:20:44 CST</pubDate>
17:     </item>
18:
19:     <item>
20:       <title>Smart Personal Objects</title>
21:       <description>The technology is a couple of years old and it has yet to
22:       catch on in any real sense but I think it has some interesting potential.
23:       I'm referring to Microsoft's SPOT (Smart Personal Object Technology),
24:       which is currently deployed in several smart watches that are capable
25:       of receiving data over a wireless wide area radio network.</description>
26:       <link>http://www.michaelmorrison.com/mambo/index.php?option=
27:       com_content&amp;task=view&amp;id=227&amp;Itemid=37</link>
28:       <pubDate>Thu, 28 Jul 2005 00:17:07 CST</pubDate>
29:     </item>
30:
31:     <item>
32:       <title>RFID Pajamas</title>
33:       <description>Not sure how I feel about this one. A children's apparel
34:       maker in California is set to launch a line of pajamas with RFID chips
35:       sewn into them that can be used to track children.</description>
36:       <link>http://www.michaelmorrison.com/mambo/index.php?option=
37:       com_content&amp;task=view&amp;id=223&amp;Itemid=37</link>
38:       <pubDate>Mon, 18 Jul 2005 13:10:42 CST</pubDate>
39:     </item>
40:   </channel>
41: </rss>
```

This code reveals how a complete RSS document pulls together the different tags you've learned about to describe multiple news items within a single channel. The first step is to specify details about the channel, which are handled in lines 5 through 7. Once the channel is in place, you can then start listing out the news items. Each of the three news items in this example use the `<title>`, `<description>`, `<link>`, and `<pubDate>` tags to flesh out their details. Notice that the `<pubDate>` tag uses a consistent format throughout all of the items for specifying the date and time (lines 16, 28, and 38).

By the Way

> If you specify a "pubDate" that is in the future, some news aggregators may elect not to display the item until that date and time.

Hopefully you now have a pretty good feel for how an RSS document is structured. Even so, you don't have to trust my good word entirely. Instead, I encourage you to use a really handy online tool called the Feed Validator to make sure that your RSS feeds are coded properly. The Feed Validator is available online at http://www.feed-validator.org/. Its job is to read an RSS feed and make sure that it validates against the RSS specification.

By the Way

> You can name your RSS documents with a `.XML` or `.RSS` file extension—both are acceptable.

Once the mmblog.xml sample RSS document receives a clean bill of health from the Feed Validator, it's ready to be posted online where other people can syndicate it using their own news aggregator of choice. But your work isn't over. Not only is it important to know how to create RSS documents—it's just as useful knowing how to transform and display them.

Displaying a News Feed

You now know enough about the RSS language and how RSS documents are structured that you should be able to put together your own simple web-based news aggregator. To make things more interesting, it's worth designing your news reader so that it can accommodate multiple separate RSS feeds (channels), as opposed to just reading and displaying items from a single document. To make this possible, you need to create a custom XML document to describe each unique feed source.

Creating a News Feed Document

Pulling together multiple RSS feeds into a single XML document doesn't require much information. In fact, all you really need to know is the URL for each RSS document. Listing 24.2 contains the code for an XML document that describes multiple RSS feed sources.

LISTING 24.2 An XML Document (`feedtest.xml`) for Managing RSS Feeds

```
1: <?xml version="1.0" ?>
2: <?xml-stylesheet href="feeder.xsl" type="text/xsl"?>
3:
4: <feeds>
5:   <feed src="http://www.michaelmorrison.com/mmblog.xml"/>
6:   <feed src="http://www.wired.com/news/feeds/rss2/0,2610,,00.xml"/>
7:   <feed src="http://rss.cnn.com/rss/cnn_topstories.rss"/>
8: </feeds>
```

By the Way

> Notice that the first feed in the `feedtest.xml` sample document (line 5) is the familiar `mmblog.xml` document that you created in the previous section.

As you can see, this document is very straightforward in terms of using a custom `<feed>` tag with a single attribute, `src`, to represent each unique RSS feed source (lines 5 through 7). All of the feeds in the document are stored within a parent `<feeds>` tag (line 4), which serves as the root element for the document. Aside from the feeds themselves, the key to this document lies in line 2 where the stylesheet `feeder.xsl` is linked. This XSLT stylesheet provides all the functionality required to read the feeds, format the content within them, and display the results in a web browser.

Transforming the News Feed for Display

The `feedtest.xml` sample document doesn't contain much information but it's just enough to grab feed data and transform it for display purposes. The `feeder.xsl` stylesheet is responsible for reading each feed source in the sample document and processing the RSS code to display the individual news stories in each feed. Listing 24.3 contains the complete code for this XSLT stylesheet.

LISTING 24.3 The `feeder.xsl` XSLT Stylesheet for Transforming RSS Feeds into HTML Web Pages

```
<?xml version="1.0"?>
<xsl:stylesheet version="1.0"
➥xmlns:xsl="http://www.w3.org/1999/XSL/Transform">
  <xsl:template match="feeds">
    <html><head><title>Today's News</title></head>
    <style>
      <xsl:comment>
      h1 {
        width=600px;
        font-family:verdana, arial;
        font-size:12pt;
        font-weight:bold;
        color:#FFFFFF;
        background-color:#660000;
      }

      p {
        width=600px;
        font-family:verdana, arial;
        font-size:9pt;
        color:#333333;
      }

      .date {
        color:#999999;
      }

      a:link {
        font-weight:bold;
        text-decoration:none;
```

```
30:         color:#660000;
31:       }
32:
33:       a:hover {
34:         font-weight:bold;
35:         text-decoration:none;
36:         color:#990000;
37:       }
38:
39:       a:visited {
40:         font-weight:bold;
41:         text-decoration:none;
42:         color:#333333;
43:       }
44:       </xsl:comment>
45:     </style>
46:
47:     <body>
48:       <xsl:apply-templates/>
49:     </body>
50:     </html>
51:   </xsl:template>
52:
53:   <xsl:template match="feed">
54:     <xsl:apply-templates select="document(@src)"/>
55:   </xsl:template>
56:
57:   <xsl:template match="channel">
58:     <h1><xsl:value-of select="title"/></h1>
59:     <xsl:apply-templates select="item"/>
60:   </xsl:template>
61:
62:   <xsl:template match="item">
63:     <p>
64:     <xsl:element name="a">
65:       <xsl:attribute name="href">
66:         <xsl:apply-templates select="link"/>
67:       </xsl:attribute>
68:       <xsl:value-of select="title"/>
69:     </xsl:element>
70:     <br />
71:     <xsl:value-of select="description"/>
72:     <br />
73:     <span class="date">
74:     <xsl:if test="pubDate">
75:       <xsl:value-of select="pubDate"/>
76:     </xsl:if>
77:     </span>
78:     </p>
79:   </xsl:template>
80: </xsl:stylesheet>
```

Similar to other XSLT stylesheets that you've seen throughout the book, this stylesheet begins with a healthy dose of CSS code thanks to an internal CSS stylesheet (lines 5 through 45) that takes care of formatting the resulting HTML code so that it looks more appealing. This CSS code applies a maroon color scheme with neatly styled headings and story titles, not to mention graying the date of each story so that it doesn't compete as much with the description of the story. You see the visual impact of these styles in just a moment.

Of course, it's important to notice that the code that kicks off the XSLT stylesheet takes place in the feeds template, which is applied to the `<feeds>` tag in the XML document. In fact, the entire HTML document structure, including the internal CSS style sheet, is contained within the feeds template. This makes sense considering that the `<feeds>` tag serves as the root element of the feed source XML document.

A much smaller template called `feed` takes care of transforming each individual feed source. This template simply calls the XSLT `document()` function while passing in the value of the `src` attribute (line 54). The end result is that the feed source is read and pulled into the stylesheet where it can be processed as an RSS document. This single line of code is what brings the remaining XSLT templates into play: channel and item.

The channel template simply writes the title of the channel to the HTML page as an `<h1>` heading tag (line 58), and then hands off the remaining RSS news items to the item template (line 59). From there, the item template does the vast majority of work in terms of transforming RSS data into HTML data that is browser-friendly.

The item template starts by creating an anchor element that serves as a link for the news item title to the actual web resource for the item (lines 64 to 69). The description of the news item is then included as normal paragraph text (line 71), followed by the publish date (lines 73 to 77), which is styled using the CSS `date` style rule that was defined earlier in the document (lines 23 to 25). Because the `<pubDate>` tag is optional, an XSLT `if` conditional is employed to make sure that the publish date is transformed only if it actually exists.

This wraps up the XSLT stylesheet, which you can now use as your own homemade RSS aggregator. Figure 24.4 shows the `feedtext.xml` example as viewed in Internet Explorer with all of its feeds transformed and cleanly formatted.

Although I certainly recommended a more full-featured RSS news aggregator for day-to-day news viewing, there's nothing stopping you from using this example as a news aggregator. Just doctor the `feedtest.xml` document to include your own choice set of RSS feeds, and you're good to go!

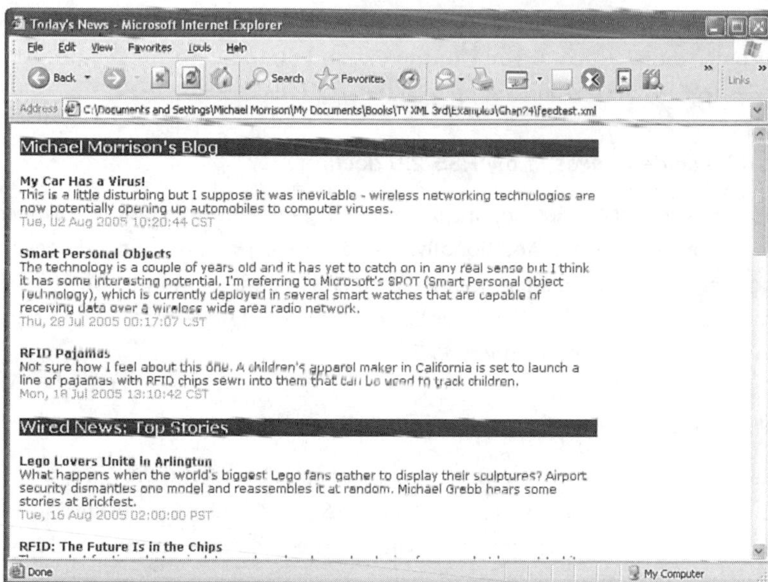

FIGURE 24.4
The sample feed viewer does a decent job of serving as a simplified news aggregator thanks to a clever XSLT stylesheet.

Summary

This hour introduced you to one of the more popular XML-based technologies in use today, RSS. Even though RSS has a somewhat confusing history, the resulting technology is relatively easy to understand and employ. Fortunately, you have lots of options when it comes to how you use RSS. If nothing else, as a web user you'll likely find RSS to be extremely useful as a means of keeping tabs on web sites that you might otherwise never take the time to visit regularly. Taking things a step further, you may elect to provide your own RSS news feeds for your own web pages. You might even get more ambitious and expand on the example in this chapter to develop a more full-featured news aggregator of your own. Regardless of how you choose to use RSS, it's an XML technology that is worth exploring and keeping tabs on.

Q&A

Q. ***Is RSS 2.0 the only version of RSS I need to concern myself with?***

A. Yes and no. RSS 2.0 is certainly the most popular version of RSS in use today, which means you should focus the vast majority of your feed-related attention to it. However, there are enough sites out there that still use other versions of RSS that you may want to consider at some point brushing up on the other versions and how they differ from version 2.0. I wouldn't make this a huge priority at the moment, however. Your knowledge of other versions of RSS becomes more critical if you want to expand on the news aggregator sample stylesheet in this lesson to support other versions of RSS.

Q. ***Can I include images in my RSS 2.0 documents?***

A. Yes. The `<channel>` tag supports a child `<image>` tag that allows you to specify an image for the channel. Additionally, the `<item>` tag supports a child `<enclosure>` tag that allows you to reference media objects including images and other media content. In fact, Apple's iTunes service relies on the `<enclosure>` tag to reference podcasts when you syndicate a podcast using RSS.

Q. ***What versions of RSS does the online Feed Validator tool support?***

A. The Feed Validator tool supports RSS versions 0.90, 0.91, 0.92, 0.93, 0.94, 1.0, and 2.0, as well as Atom. The version of RSS that it uses for validation is determined automatically by the value of the `version` attribute in the `<rss>` tag of the document being validated.

Workshop

The Workshop is designed to help you anticipate possible questions, review what you've learned, and begin learning how to put your knowledge into practice.

Quiz

1. What is an RSS channel?
2. What happens if you don't specify a `<link>` tag for an RSS news item?
3. What attribute is required of the `<rss>` tag?

Quiz Answers

1. An RSS channel is a collection of related news items. Each RSS document consists of exactly one channel.
2. If no `<link>` tag is provided for an RSS news item, the `<description>` is relied on to contain the entire content of the news item.
3. The only attribute required of the `<rss>` tag is the `version` attribute, which is very important because it establishes the version of the RSS feed.

Exercises

1. Modify the `feedtest.xml` document to include several additional news feeds. If you're having trouble finding news feeds, check out http://www.2rss.com/. Make sure to reload the page in your browser to see the new feeds displayed.

2. One topic this lesson did not cover is how to transform normal web pages into RSS news feeds so that you don't have to manually create an RSS document each time something changes on your web site. Try your hand at creating an XSLT stylesheet that automatically generates an RSS document from an existing XHTML web page.

PART VI

Appendix

APPENDIX A

XML Resources

XML is a technology that is growing by leaps and bounds. Granted, the core XML language is very established, but the many closely related technologies are evolving rapidly. For this reason, it's important to try and keep up with what's going on in the XML community. The best way to stay on top of XML is to be a committed web surfer. Fortunately, the Web is full of information on XML and is by far the best place to learn about what's new in the XML world. By regularly visiting a few web sites, you can stay abreast of the latest happenings with XML, which is important if you plan on using any XML-related technology.

This appendix is divided into several sections that target specific online XML resources. I encourage you to check out some of these resources and judge for yourself which ones you find the most useful. Keep in mind that, in addition to keeping up with changes in XML, many of the resources are also great educational outlets for sharpening your XML skills.

General XML Resources

General XML resources consist of web sites that take a wide aim at XML—these web sites provide information ranging from XML basics to heavy-duty XML application development. You'll also find some interesting articles containing general commentary on the state of XML, along with the relationship between XML technologies. Following are the general XML resources I recommend you take a look at:

- XML.com—http://www.xml.com/
- XML.org—http://www.xml.org/
- XML at About.com—http://webdesign.about.com/od/xml/
- XML Pitstop—http://www.xmlpitstop.com/
- DevX XML Zone—http://www.devx.com/xml/
- The XML Files—http://www.webdeveloper.com/xml/
- Web Monkey (XML)—http://www.hotwired.com/webmonkey/xml/

- Microsoft's XML web site—http://msdn.microsoft.com/xml/
- XML Resources—http://www.xmlresources.com/
- Wikipedia (XML)—http://en.wikipedia.org/wiki/Xml/
- W3C's XML in 10 Points—http://www.w3.org/XML/1999/XML-in-10-points

XML Tools

As with most software technologies, tools play an important role in developing applications with XML. There are a couple of different kinds of tools that enter the picture when it comes to XML development:

- Authoring tools
- Validation tools

XML authoring tools are used to create and edit XML documents. The most basic authoring tool is a simple text editor, such as Windows Notepad, which isn't XML-specific but nonetheless provides a means of creating and editing XML documents. The decision to use a more full-featured XML authoring tool has everything to do with personal preference and how much you're willing to spend. Following are some of the popular XML authoring tools that are currently available:

- <oXygen/> XML Editor—http://www.oxygenxml.com/
- XML Spy—http://www.xmlspy.com/
- XML Writer—http://www.xmlwriter.net/
- EditiX—http://www.editix.com/
- XMetaL—http://www.xmetal.com/
- Stylus Studio—http://www.stylusstudio.com/
- Adobe FrameMaker—http://www.adobe.com/products/framemaker/
- Vervet Logic Web XML Pro—http://www.vervet.com/xmlpro.php

Although most commercial XML authoring tools include support for document validation, you may need to validate documents outside of a fancy authoring tool. In this case, you will want to use a pure XML validation tool, which is actually a web site that provides services for validating XML documents. Web-based validation tools are interesting in that they don't require you to download or install anything—just point and click! Following are a few of the validation tools that support XML:

- STG XML Validation Form—http://www.stg.brown.edu/service/xmlvalid/
- W3C Validator for XML Schema—http://www.w3.org/2001/03/webdata/xsv/
- XML Schema Validator— http://apps.gotdotnet.com/xmltools/xsdvalidator/
- W3C XHTML Validation Service—http://validator.w3.org/

There are some XML tools that defy classification. Most of these "other" tools process XML documents in some way and produce results, such as transformed documents. They certainly can't be considered authoring or validation tools, so I'll just refer to them as "other" tools. Following is a list of some of these other XML tools:

- TIBCO Extensibility Platform—http://www.tibco-ext.com/
- HTML Tidy—http://www.w3.org/People/Raggett/tidy/
- XFA Script—http://www.xmlforall.com/cgi/xfa?XFAScript

The TIBCO Extensibility Platform offers a unique approach to XML schema development by providing a graphical user interface for creating schemas in a very general sense. Once a schema is constructed, you decide the format in which you want it stored, such as DTD or XSD. HTML Tidy is a command-line tool that was initially designed to clean up sloppy HTML code but also supports converting HTML code to XHTML code. XFA Script by XML For All is a scripting language implemented as an XML vocabulary. XFA Script is interesting because it uses XML syntax to implement a scripting language. XML For All also offers an XML editor called XFA Edit that is available for the Windows platform.

XML-Based Languages

As you know by now, XML is used to create markup languages geared toward representing a particular type of information. These XML-based languages represent the end-result of applying XML to solve real-world problems. Following are some of the major XML-based languages created to solve such problems:

- Wireless Markup Language (WML)—http://www.openmobilealliance.org/
- Open Financial Exchange (OFX)—http://www.ofx.net/
- eXtensible Business Reporting Language (XBRL)—http://www.xbrl.org/
- Resource Description Framework (RDF)—http://www.w3.org/RDF/

- Really Simple Syndication (RSS)—http://blogs.law.harvard.edu/tech/rss
- Mathematical Modeling Language (MathML)—http://www.w3.org/TR/REC-MathML/
- Open eBook (OeB)—http://www.openebook.org/
- OpenDocument—http://www.oasis-open.org/committees/tc_home.php?wg_abbrev=office
- Web Ontology Language (OWL)—http://www.w3.org/TR/owl-guide/
- Platform for Privacy Preferences Project (P3P)—http://www.w3.org/TR/P3P/
- Simple Object Access Protocol (SOAP)—http://www.w3.org/TR/soap/
- Scalable Vector Graphics (SVG)—http://www.w3.org/Graphics/SVG/
- Synchronized Multimedia Interchange Language (SMIL)—http://www.w3.org/TR/SMIL/
- Universal Description, Discovery, and Integration (UDDI)—http://www.uddi.org/
- Web Services Description Language (WSDL)—http://www.w3.org/TR/wsdl
- eXtensible Application Markup Language (XAML)—http://www.xaml.net/
- 3-D Modeling Language (3DML)—http://www.flatland.com/
- VoiceXML—http://www.voicexml.org/
- Chemical Markup Language (CML)—http://wwmm.ch.cam.ac.uk/moin/ChemicalMarkupLanguage
- XML News—http://www.xmlnews.org/
- Human Markup Language (HumanML)—http://www.humanmarkup.org/

XML Specifications

XML is a technology that revolves around rigid standards that are set forth by the W3C. In order for XML to be consistently used by developers, these standards must be adhered to carefully. XML standards are set forth in documents called specifications, or specs, which are easily accessible on the Web. New technology specifications typically go through several developmental stages on the way to becoming a formal *recommendation*, which is essentially a technology that is complete and ready to be adopted by the web community. A W3C specification that has yet to become a recommendation is known as a *working draft*. Following are the most important W3C specifications related to XML:

- XML—http://www.w3.org/XML/
- XML Namespaces—http://www.w3.org/TR/REC-xml-names/
- XML Schema—http://www.w3.org/XML/Schema
- XPath—http://www.w3.org/TR/xpath
- XPointer—http://www.w3.org/TR/xptr/
- XLink—http://www.w3.org/TR/xlink/
- XHTML—http://www.w3.org/TR/xhtml1/
- DOM Level 1—http://www.w3.org/DOM/
- CSS—http://www.w3.org/TR/REC-CSS2/
- XSL—http://www.w3.org/TR/xsl/
- XQuery—http://www.w3.org/TR/xquery/
- Unicode character encoding—http://www.unicode.org

Index

Numbers

A

B

D

E

F

G

H

I

M

N

O

P

S

T

X - Y - Z